ASIAN/OCEANIAN HISTORICAL DICTIONARIES
Edited by Jon Woronoff

Asia
1. *Vietnam,* by William J. Duiker. 1989
2. *Bangladesh,* 2nd ed., by Craig Baxter and Syedur Rahman. 1996
3. *Pakistan,* by Shahid Javed Burki. 1991
4. *Jordan,* by Peter Gubser. 1991
5. *Afghanistan,* by Ludwig W. Adamec. 1991
6. *Laos,* by Martin Stuart-Fox and Mary Kooyman. 1992
7. *Singapore,* by K. Mulliner and Lian The-Mulliner. 1991
8. *Israel,* by Bernard Reich. 1992
9. *Indonesia,* by Robert Cribb. 1992
10. *Hong Kong and Macau,* by Elfed Vaughan Roberts, Sum Ngai Ling, and Peter Bradshaw. 1992
11. *Korea,* by Andrew C. Nahm. 1993
12. *Taiwan,* by John F. Copper. 1993
13. *Malaysia,* by Amarjit Kaur. 1993
14. *Saudi Arabia,* by J. E. Peterson. 1993
15. *Myanmar,* by Jan Bephka. 1995
16. *Iran,* by John H. Lorentz. 1995
17. *Yemen,* by Robert D. Burrowes. 1995
18. *Thailand,* by May Kyi Win and Harold Smith. 1995
19. *Mongolia,* by Alan J. K. Sanders. 1996
20. *India,* by Surjit Mansingh. 1996
21. *Gulf Arab States,* by Malcolm C. Peck. 1996
22. *Syria,* by David Commins. 1996
23. *Palestine,* by Nafez Y. Nazzal and Laila A. Nazzal. 1997
24. *Philippines,* by Artemio R. Guillermo and May Kyi Win. 1997

Oceania
1. *Australia,* by James C. Docherty. 1992
2. *Polynesia,* by Robert D. Craig. 1993
3. *Guam and Micronesia,* by William Wuerch and Dirk Ballendorf. 1994
4. *Papua New Guinea,* by Ann Turner. 1994
5. *New Zealand,* by Keith Jackson and Alan McRobie. 1996

New Combined Series
25. *Brunei Darussalam,* by D. S. Ranjit Singh and Jatswan S. Sidhu. 1997
26. *Sri Lanka,* by S. W. R. de A. Samarasinghe and Vidyamali Samarasinghe. 1998
27. *Vietnam,* 2nd ed., by William J. Duiker. 1998
28. *People's Republic of China: 1949–1997,* by Lawrence R. Sullivan, with the assistance of Nancy Hearst. 1998
29. *Afghanistan,* 2nd ed., by Ludwig W. Adamec. 1997
30. *Lebanon,* by As'ad AbuKhalil. 1998
31. *Azerbaijan,* by Tadeusz Swietochowski and Brian C. Collins. 1999
32. *Australia,* 2nd ed., by James C. Docherty. 1999
33. *Pakistan,* 2nd ed., by Shahid Javed Burki. 1999

HISTORICAL DICTIONARY
OF PAKISTAN

Second Edition

SHAHID JAVED BURKI

Asian/Oceanian Historical Dictionaries, No. 33

The Scarecrow Press, Inc.
Lanham, Md., & London
1999

SCARECROW PRESS, INC.

Published in the United States of America
by Scarecrow Press, Inc.,
4720 Boston Way, Lanham, Maryland 20706

4 Pleydell Gardens, Folkestone
Kent CT20 2DN, England

Copyright © 1999 by Shahid Javed Burki

The first edition of this volume, by Shahid Javed Burki,
was published by Scarecrow Press in 1991.

British Library Cataloguing in Publication Information Available

Library of Congress Cataloging-in-Publication Data

Burki, Shahid Javed.
    Historical dictionary of Pakistan / Shahid Javed Burki. — 2nd ed.
        p.   cm.
    Includes bibliographical references.
    ISBN 0-8108-3634-3 (cloth : alk. paper)
    1. Pakistan—History—Dictionaries.   I. Title.
DS382.B87   1999
954.91′003—dc21   99-10725
                                                                        CIP

Printed in the United States of America

⊗™ The paper used in this publication meets the minimum requirements of
American National Standard for Information Sciences—Permanence of
Paper for Printed Library Materials, ANSI Z39.48–1984.

In memory of my parents

Salamat Ali Khan Burki (1896–1975)
Maryam Zamani Burki (1903–1998)

Contents

Editor's Foreword

S ince its creation in 1947, Pakistan has repeatedly been in the world news. It has experienced more turbulent internal events and been involved in more dramatic external ventures than most Asian countries. These include partition, wars, coups, the Afghan resistance, internal dissension, and economic successes and setbacks. Given its size and location, Pakistan still plays an important role and what happens there is very significant for the region and further afield. Despite this media coverage, Pakistan is only superficially known abroad.

These facts enhance the value of this second edition of the *Historical Dictionary of Pakistan*. Written by a Pakistani with an intimate knowledge of the country, it gives us much of the background that is missing in the day-to-day coverage. It reaches back into history to explain how and why Pakistan was founded; it sheds light on the economy and political system; it provides insight into social and cultural factors; and it tells us about the sometimes towering figures who have led the country. This is done through concise but informative entries in the dictionary, which are placed in context by a chronology and introduction. Those wishing to know more can consult the bibliography.

Shahid Javed Burki, who produced this second edition, is an expert in Pakistani affairs. He originally worked as an economist and administrator in Pakistan, holding a number of posts including those of chief economist, Government of West Pakistan and economic advisor to the Ministry of Commerce. He later joined the World Bank, where he is currently vice president of the Latin America and Caribbean Region. In 1997–98 Burki returned to Pakistan to serve as minister in charge of finance planning and economic affairs in the interim government. Shahid Javed Burki is the author of other writings on Pakistan, with several fine books to his name.

JON WORONOFF
Series Editor

Abbreviations and Acronyms

ADB	Asian Development Bank
ADBP	Agricultural Development Bank of Pakistan
ADF	Asian Development Fund
AIML	All-India Muslim League
AJP	Awami Jamoohri Party
AML	Awami Muslim League
ANP	Awami National Party
APEC	Asia Pacific Economic Cooperation
APMSO	All-Pakistan Muhajir Students Organization
APPNA	Association of Pakistani Physicians in North America
APSENA	Association of Pakistani Scientists and Engineers in North America
APWA	All-Pakistan Women's Association
BCCI	Bank of Credit and Commerce International
BCCP	Board of Cricket Control of Pakistan
BDs	Basic Democracies
BJP	Bhartiya Janata Party
BLLF	Bonded Labor Liberation Front
BSFF	Baluchistan-Sindh-Frontier Front
CCI	Council for Common Interests
CDA	Capital Development Authority
CDNS	Council for Defense and National Security
CENTO	Central Treaty Organization
CMLA	Chief Martial Law Administrator
COAS	Chief of Army Staff
COP	Combined Opposition Party
CRBC	Chasma Right Bank Canal
CSP	Civil Service of Pakistan

CTBT	Comprehensive Test Ban Treaty
DAC	Democratic Action Committee
DCMLA	Deputy Chief Martial Law Administrator
DOD	Debt Outstanding and Disbursed
DSR	Debt Service Ratio
ECC	Economic Committee of the Cabinet
EME	Electrical and Mechanical Corps
FMS	Foreign Military Sales
FPA	Family Planning Association
FSF	Federal Security Force
GDP	Gross Domestic Product
GEF	Global Environment Facility
GHQ	General Headquarters of the Army
GNP	Gross National Product
GST	General Sales Tax
HJ	Hilal-e-Jurat
IAEC	International Atomic Energy Commission
IBRD	International Bank for Reconstruction and Development
ICP	Investment Corporation of Pakistan
ICS	Indian Civil Service
IDA	International Development Association
IDB	Inter-American Development Bank
IDBP	Industrial Development Bank of Pakistan
IFC	International Finance Corporation
IJI	Islami Jamhuri Itehad
IMF	International Monetary Fund
IMFESAF	International Monetary Fund's Extended Structural Adjustment Facility
INLF	Islamic National Labor Force
ISI	Interservices Intelligence
JI	Jamaat-e-Islami
JML	Jinnah Muslim League
JUH	Jamiatul-Ulemai-Hind
JUI	Jamiatul-Ulemai-Islam
JUP	Jamiatul-Ulemai-Pakistan
KDA	Karachi Development Authority

KK	Khudai Khidmatgars
KMC	Karachi Municipal Corporation
KSE-100	Karachi Stock Exchange Index
LFO	Legal Framework Order
LIT	Lahore Improvement Trust
LUMS	Lahore University of Management Sciences
MIGA	Multilateral Investment Guarantee Association
MQM	Muhajir Qaumi Mahaz
MRD	Movement for the Restoration of Democracy
MSM	Mutahida Shariat Mahaz
NAP	National Awami Party
NCA	National Commission on Agriculture
NDC	National Defense College
NDFC	National Development Finance Corporation
NDP	National Democratic Party
NGOs	Nongovernment Organizations
NICFC	National Industrial Cooperative Finance Corporation
NIT	National Investment Trust
NLC	National Logistics Cell
NPP	National People's Party
NPT	Nuclear Nonproliferation Treaty
NU	Nadawat al Ulema
NWFP	Northwest Frontier Province
OGDC	Oil and Gas Development Corporation
OIC	Organization of the Islamic Conference
OML	Official Muslim League
OPEC	Organization of Petroleum Exporting Countries
PAI	Pakistani Awami Itehad
PBC	Pakistan Broadcasting Corporation
PDA	Pakistan Democratic Alliance
PDM	Pakistan Democratic Movement
PDP	Pakistan Democratic Party
PIA	Pakistan International Airlines
PICIC	Pakistan Industrial Credit and Investment Corporation
PIDC	Pakistan Industrial Development Corporation
PMKP	Pakistan Mazdoor Kissan Party

PML	Pakistan Muslim League
PNA	Pakistan National Alliance
PNP	Pakistan National Party
PPL	Progressive Papers Limited
PPP	Pakistan People's Party
PTC	Pakistan Television Corporation
QMA	Qaumi Mahaz-i-Azadi
QML	Qayyum Muslim League
QU	Quaid-e-Azam University
RCD	Regional Cooperation of Development
RCO	Revival of the Constitution 1973 Order
RTC	Resolution Trust Corporation
SAARC	South Asian Association for Regional Cooperation
SAP	Social Action Program
SAPTA	South Asian Preferential Trading Area
SCARP	Salinity Control and Reclamation Project
SCCP	State Cement Corporation of Pakistan
SEATO	Southeast Asia Treaty Organization
SNG	Sui Northern Gas
SNSF	Sind National Students Federation
SPAWA	Sindh Punjab Abadgar Welfare Association
SSI	Small-Scale Industry
T & T	Telephone and Telegraph Department
TFR	Total Fertility Rate
TI	Tehrik-e-Istiqlal
UBL	United Bank Limited
UF	United Front
UFLA	United Front of Leftist Alliance
UNDP	United Nations Development Program
UNEP	United Nations Environment Program
UNIDO	United Nations Industrial Development Organization
USAID	United States Agency for International Development
WAF	Women's Action Forum
WAPDA	Water and Power Development Authority
WFTU	World Federation of Trade Unions
WTO	World Trade Organization
YMCA	Young Men's Christian Association

Map

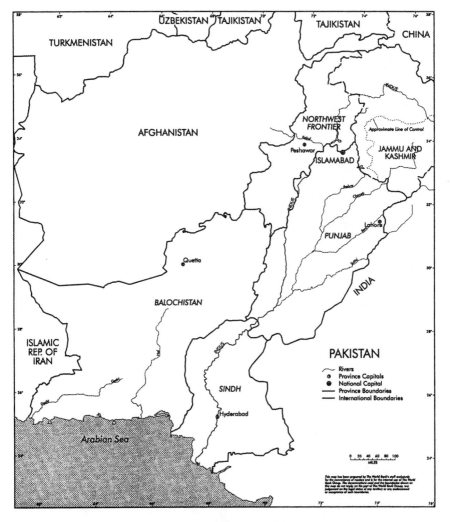

Map Pakistan and region.

Chronology

712

Muhammad Ibn Qasim, an Arab general, conquered the province of Sindh and incorporated it into the Umayyad caliphate.

977

Ibn Shayban, another general from the Arab world, was sent to add more territory to the province of Sindh. He conquered the city of Multan in the province of Punjab.

1001

Mahmud of Ghazni, an Afghan general, began to mount expeditions into northwestern India.

1026

Mahmud of Ghazni raided the temple of Somnath in Kathiawar-war, west India.

1175

Shahabuddin Muhammad of Ghauri attacked and conquered Multan.

1192

Ghauri conquered Delhi and established Muslim rule over north India.

1206

Qutubuddin Aibak established the Slave dynasty.

1290

Jalaluddin Khilji established the Khilji dynasty.

1320

The Tughluqs came to India and established their dynasty.

1414

The Tughluq dynasty was defeated by the Sayyids, who founded their dynasty.

1450

The Sayyids were defeated by the Lodis, who founded their dynasty.

1526

Babar, the Mughul invader, defeated Ibrahim Lodi, the sultan of Delhi at Panipat, a battlefield north of Delhi.

1530

Babar, the first Mughul emperor of India, died and was succeeded by his son, Humayun.

1540

Humayun was defeated by Sher Khan, a Pathan general, in the battle of Kanauj. Humayun took refuge in Afghanistan.

1555

Humayun regained his throne with the help of the Afghans by defeating Sikander Sur, the governor of Punjab, and recapturing Delhi.

1556

Humayun died in Delhi and was succeeded by Akbar, who became the third Mughul emperor of India.

1581

Akbar proclaimed a new religion, the Din Ilhai, aimed at incorporating India's two major religions, Hinduism and Islam.

1605

Akbar died and was succeeded by his son Jehangir.

1627

Jehangir died and was succeed by his son Shah Jehan as the fifth Mugul emperor of India.

1659

Shah Jehan's reign was cut short by his son, Aurangzeb, who after incarcerating his father, ascended the throne as the sixth Mughul emperor of India.

1668

Shah Jehan died in captivity.

1707

Aurangzeb, the last of the great Mughul emperors of India, died.

1757

Nawab Sirajuddaula of Bengal was defeated by the British (East India Company) at the battle of Plassey.

1774

Warren Hastings was appointed governor-general of British India.

1784

The British Parliament passed William Pitt's India Act regulating the powers of the governor-general.

1785

Lord Charles Cornwallis was appointed governor-general of India.

1793

Permanent Settlement was introduced by Lord Cornwallis, granting proprietary rights to *Zamindars* (landlords).

1798

Lord Richard Colley Wellesley was appointed governor-general of India.

1799

Tippu Sultan, the Muslim raja of Mysore, was killed before the walls of Seringapatan in an encounter with Lord Wellesley's British Indian Army.

1807

Lord Earl Minto was appointed governor-general of India.

1809

The British government in India signed the Treaty of Amritsar with Raja Ranjit Singh of Punjab, establishing the Sutlej River as the boundary between the Sikh state in the Punjab and the British Indian territories.

1848

Lord John Dalhousie was appointed governor-general of India.

1849

The province of Punjab was annexed by the British.

1857

May

10   The Sepoy Mutiny broke out in Meerut.

July

8   Delhi, the seat of the Mughul empire in India, was captured by the British from the mutineers and Emperor Bahadur Shah II was arrested and deported.

September

14   Lord Charles Canning, the governor-general of India, proclaimed the end of the mutiny and restoration of peace. The East India Company was liquidated and the monarch of Great Britain assumed sovereignty over all territories controlled by the company.

1878

The Treaty of Gandinak was signed between British India and Afghanistan.

1893

A line indicating the boundary between Afghanistan and British India was drawn. The boundary became known as the Durand Line.

1899

George Nathaniel, Lord Curzon, was appointed governor-general of India.

1901

The Punjab Alienation Act was passed by the viceroy, Lord Curzon.

1902

The Indian Army was reorganized by Lord Kitchener.

1905

The province of Bengal was partitioned on religious grounds with East Bengal becoming a predominantly Muslim province of British India.

Lord Minto was appointed viceroy of India to succeed Lord Curzon.

1906

December

30 The Muslim League was founded by Nawab Viqar ul-Mulk of Dacca.

1909

The Muslim community was granted separate representation in provincial legislatures under the Minto-Morley reforms.

1913

Muhammad Ali Jinnah joined the All-India Muslim League.

1916

The Lucknow Pact was signed between the Congress Party and the League.

December

31 An agreement was reached between the Indian National Congress and the Muslim League to work together for achieving self-government for India on the basis of separate electorates for Muslims and non-Muslims. The agreement came to be known as the Lucknow Pact.

1917

August

20 Edwin Montagu, the secretary of state for India, declared that "the policy of His Majesty's Government was that of the increasing association of Indians in every branch of administration and the gradual development of self-government institutions with a view to the progressive realization of responsible government in India as an equal part of the British Empire."

1919

The Government of India Act, 1919, was passed by the British Parliament to allow greater association of Indians in the administration of India.

April
13   Police opened fire at a public meeting in Amritsar, killing and wounding hundreds of people.

1921

The Treaty of Friendship was signed between Afghanistan and the Soviet Union, the first formal agreement between the Soviets and a foreign country.

1935

The British Parliament passed a new Government of India Act, which effected important changes in the political and administrative system in the country.

1936

Lord Linlithgow was appointed viceroy of India.

1939

Elections were held in the provinces of British India under the Government of India Act, 1935.

1940

March
23   The All-India Muslim League passed the "Pakistan Resolution" demanding the creation of an independent country for the Muslims of British India. The resolution was passed in a meeting held in Lahore with Muhammad Ali Jinnah in the chair.

1941

The Jamaat-e-Islami was founded by Maulana Maududi.

1945

The Jamiatul-Ulemai-Islam (JUI) was founded by a group of Deobandi Ulema.

1946

February
19   The British government announced the decision to send a Cabinet Mission to India to arrange for the transfer of power to the Indians.

March
24   The Cabinet Mission arrived in New Delhi.

May
16   The Cabinet Mission announced their plan to transfer power to Indians.

June
4   Indians serving in the British Indian Navy mutinied in Bombay.

6   The Cabinet Mission Plan was accepted by the All-India Muslim League.

16   The Cabinet Mission and the viceroy, Lord Wavell, announced their proposal to form an Interim Government.

August
16   The Muslim League observed "Direct Action Day." Widespread communal riots occurred in many parts of India. Hundreds of people were killed. Bengal was the most seriously affected province.

September
2   Jawaharlal Nehru was sworn in as prime minister of the Interim Government.

October
26   The All-India Muslim League joined the Interim Government, with Liaqat Ali Khan assuming the portfolio of finance.

1947

February
20   Lord Mountbatten was appointed viceroy of India.

March
2   Sirdar Khizar Hayat Tiwana resigned as the chief minister of Punjab.

8   The Indian National Congress passed a resolution demanding the partition of Punjab.

June
3   The plan to transfer power to two independent states—India and Pakistan—was announced by the viceroy, Lord Mountbatten.

August
14   The predominantly Muslim provinces of Punjab, the Northwest Frontier, Sindh in the west, and East Bengal in the east of British India were separated to form the independent state of Pakistan. Muhammad Ali Jinnah was sworn in as the first governor-general of Pakistan. Jinnah invited Liaqat Ali Khan to form a cabinet and become Pakistan's first prime minister.

October
22   Tribesmen from the northwest districts of Pakistan invaded the State of Kashmir.

26   The state of Kashmir acceded to India.

1948

September
11   Governor-General Muhammad Ali Jinnah died in Karachi.

12 Khawaja Nazimuddin was appointed the second governor-general of Pakistan.

1949

September

18 Pakistan decided not to devalue its currency with respect to the U.S. dollar, thus changing the rate of exchange with India.

October

19 Khan of Mamdot was dismissed from the chief ministership of Punjab.

1950

September

7 The Basic Principles Committee of the Constituent Assembly presented its report on the constitution.

1951

January

5 General Muhammad Ayub Khan was appointed commander-in-chief of the Pakistan Army.

February

14 Elections were held in the province of Punjab for the first time after independence.

23 A conspiracy, spearheaded by Major General Akbar Khan to oust General Ayub Khan as the army chief and overthrow the civilian government, was revealed. The event became known as the Rawalpindi Conspiracy.

October

16 Liaqat Ali Khan, Pakistan's first prime minister, was assassinated while addressing a public meeting in Company Bagh, a public park in Rawalpindi.

1952

February

21 Thirty-six students were killed in a riot protesting the rejection of Bengali as one of Pakistan's national languages.

1953

March

6 Following widespread rioting against the Ahmadiya community, the province of Punjab was put under military rule. General Azam Khan was appointed martial-law administrator.

23 Chief Minister Punjab Mumtaz Daultana resigned. He was succeeded by Feroze Khan Noon.

April

17 Khawaja Nazimuddin, Pakistan's second prime minister, was dismissed from office by Governor-General Ghulam Muhammad.

October

17 Prime Minister Muhammad Ali Bogra was elected president of the Pakistan Muslim League by 300 votes against 14 for his opponent, Qazi Muhammad Isa, former ambassador to Brazil and leader of the Muslim League in Balochistan.

November

2 The Constituent Assembly resolved that Pakistan should be made an "Islamic republic."

1954

February

25 U.S. President Eisenhower approved a military arms agreement with Pakistan.

March

5 Pakistan joined the Southeast Asia Treaty Organization (SEATO).

19 East Pakistan election results were announced. The Muslim League suffered a crushing defeat at the hands of the United Front.

26 Abdul Kasem Fazlul Haq, one of the leaders of the United Front coalition of East Pakistan, formed a new government in Dacca.

April

2 Pakistan concluded a five-year mutual defense agreement with Turkey.

May

19 Pakistan and the United States signed the Mutual Defense Assistance Agreement. Under this agreement, the United States would give material and technical military assistance to Pakistan.

30 Prime Minister Muhammad Ali Bogra dismissed East Bengal's chief minister Fazlul Haq for "treasonable activities." Iskander Mirza, federal defense secretary, was appointed to administer the province.

June

7 Prime Minister Muhammad Ali Bogra inaugurated the first flight of the government-owned Pakistan International Airlines.

16 The princely states of Kalat, Lasbela, Makran, and Kharam were merged with the province of Balochistan.

September

22 The Constituent Assembly adopted four amendments to the Government of India Act of 1935 (under which Pakistan was governed pending adoption of a constitution), sharply curtailing the powers of the governor-general.

October

24 In a nationwide broadcast, Prime Minister Muhammad Ali Bogra

announced that elections would be held as soon as possible, and that the new representatives of the people would have a fresh mandate to frame a constitution.

Governor-General Ghulam Muhammad declared a state of emergency, dissolved the Constituent Assembly and asked Prime Minister Muhammad Ali Bogra to reconstitute the Cabinet. General Ayub Khan joined the "Cabinet of Talent" as defense minister.

28 Dr. Khan Sahib, leader of the Khudai Khidmatgar (Servants of God) in the Northwest Frontier Province (NWFP), was sworn in as the ninth member of the new Cabinet, and was assigned the portfolio of Refugee Rehabilitation and Kashmir Affairs.

November

2 The Central Government took over the administration of Bahawalpur State. The state Cabinet was dismissed and the state Parliament dissolved on charges of "maladministration and inefficiency."

8 The Sindh Provincial Cabinet of Abdus Sattar Pirzada was dismissed on charges of maladministration. Pirzada said dismissal resulted from his opposition to the governor-general's projected plan of merging the whole of West Pakistan into a single unit.

9 Muhammad Ayub Khuhro was sworn in as chief minister of Sindh province.

20 The Central Government completed plans to dissolve all provincial and state governments in West Pakistan and assumed direct control of the area through the appointment of chief commissioners responsible to it.

December

20 Hussain Shaheed Suhrawardhy, leader of the Awami Muslim League, was sworn in as minister of law, and said that he would begin drafting a constitution.

1955

January

19 The Cabinet unanimously approved Pakistan's participation in the Southeast Asian Defense alliance.

March

25 The Supreme Court, in *Tamizuddin Khan vs. the Government of Pakistan,* upheld the constitutionality of the governor-general's action terminating the Constituent Assembly.

September

30 West Pakistan's four provinces were merged to form the single administrative unit of West Pakistan.

1956

March

2 Pakistan's first constitution came into effect.

September

8 Chaudhri Muhammad Ali resigned as prime minister.

10 Hussain Shaheed Suhrawardhy was sworn in as prime minister.

1957

October

14 Hussain Shaheed Suhrawardhy resigned as prime minister and was succeeded by Firoze Khan Noon, who formed a Republican party ministry.

1958

May

17 The government gave formal endorsement to the First Five Year Plan (1955–60), two years after a draft of the plan had been released.

October

7 President Iskander Mirza imposed martial law, dissolved all legislative assemblies, dismissed Prime Minister Firoze Khan Noon and appointed Commander-in-Chief Ayub Khan as chief martial-law administrator.

27 President Iskander Mirza was removed from office and General Ayub Khan assumed the presidency.

1959

January

24 Land reforms were announced by President Ayub Khan, under which no person could own or possess more than 500 acres of irrigated or 1,000 acres of unirrigated land.

1960

July

1 The Second Five Year Plan (1960–65) was launched.

September

19 The Indus Waters Treaty was signed in Karachi by Jawaharlal Nehru, prime minister of India, and Muhammad Ayub Khan, president of Pakistan.

25 Former Prime Minister Chundrigar died in London.

October

26 The Cabinet approved the master plan for Islamabad, the new capital of Pakistan.

1961
March

2   The Muslim Family Laws Ordinance was introduced.

July

13   In Washington, President Ayub Khan of Pakistan and President John F. Kennedy of the United States signed a joint communiqué, ensuring close cooperation between the two countries.

1962
March

23   A new constitution was introduced, with extensive powers given to the president. Ayub Khan was sworn in as the president under the constitution.

September

25   Leaders of the National Awami Party, Jamaat-e-Islami, Nizam-i-Islam, and a portion of the Muslim League decided to revive the defunct National Democratic Party under the leadership of former Prime Minister Hussain Shaheed Suhrawardhy.

October

18   Former Foreign Minister Manzur Qadir was sworn in as the chief justice of West Pakistan High Court.

25   Abdul Monem Khan was appointed governor of East Pakistan in place of Ghulam Farouque.

December

14   President Ayub Khan appointed Muhammad Shoaib as finance minister, Khurshid Ahmad as minister of law, and Rana Abdul Hamid as minister of health, labor, and social welfare. Muhammad Munir (law) and Abdul Qadir (finance) resigned from the Cabinet.

28   Pakistan and China announced "complete agreement in principle" on the alignment of their Himalayan border.

1963
January

23   Foreign Minister Muhammad Ali Bogra died of heart failure in Dacca.

February

16   Minister of Industries Zulfikar Ali Bhutto was appointed minister of foreign affairs.

March

2   A border agreement between Pakistan and China was signed in Peking between Zulfikar Ali Bhutto and Marshal Chen Yi, vice premier and foreign minister of China.

April
12 The Aid-to-Pakistan Consortium meeting in Paris endorsed an aid package of $500 million for the fourth year of the Second Five Year Plan.

May
22 President Ayub Khan joined the Muslim League as the party's president.

August
19 The speaker of the National Assembly, Maulvi Tamizuddin Khan, died.

September
27 The National Shipping Corporation was established under government control to build or charter ships to supplement the Pakistani fleet. The corporation was to operate on local and international routes.

October
25 The first group of government employees moved from Karachi to Islamabad, the new capital of Pakistan.

December
5 Former Prime Minister Hussain Shaheed Suhrawardy died of a heart attack in Beirut, Lebanon.

25 The National Assembly approved the Fundamental Rights Bill, which amended the 1962 Constitution, making civil rights enforceable in the courts.

1964

January
6 The government declared Jamaat-e-Islami an illegal organization and banned all its activities. Maulana Abul Ala Maududi (the party's leader) and 16 other members of the executive committee were arrested.

February
8 Prime Minister Zhou En-Lai of China arrived in Karachi for an eight-day visit to Pakistan.

April
29 The Pakistan International Airlines started service to Canton and Shanghai via Dacca.

June
26 The National Assembly approved funds for he construction of two nuclear power stations—one in Karachi and the other in Pabna, East Pakistan.

August
19 The Muslim League named Ayub Khan as its candidate for the presidential election, scheduled for January 1965.

August

29 Pakistan's first submarine, a gift from the United States, arrived in Karachi.

September

20 The Combined Opposition Party (COP) nominated Fatima Jinnah, sister of Pakistan's founder, as its candidate for the presidential election.

October

9 West Pakistan's High Court ordered the release of 44 leaders of the Jamaat-e-Islami, including Maududi and Farid Ahmad.

22 Former Governor-General and Prime Minister Khawaja Nazimuddin died in Dacca of a heart attack.

1965

January

1 The first presidential election was held under the 1962 Constitution, with Fatima Jinnah of the Combined Opposition Party (COP) opposing Field Marshal Ayub Khan of the Muslim League. Ayub Khan won a narrow victory.

4 A victory parade in Karachi, sponsored by Ayub Khan's Muslim League led by his son Gohar Ayub, was marked by violence, with a death toll of 23. The army took control of the city from the local police.

March

23 President Ayub Khan was sworn in for his second term as president.

April

23 Indian and Pakistani troops fought a major battle in the Rann of Kutch.

June

14 The government reduced the development program by 5 percent to meet defense costs in the next fiscal year.

July

1 The Third Five Year Plan was launched, with estimated expenditures of 52 billion rupees—34 billion rupees in the public and Rs.18 billion in the private sector.

13 U.S. President Lyndon B. Johnson informed President Ayub Khan of a delay in aid commitments. Ayub criticized this aid delay and defended Pakistan's ties with China and other communist countries.

August

21 Prime Minister Lal Bahadur Shastri of India charged Pakistan with sending 3,000 to 4,000 infiltrators into Kashmir and warned of an attack if "aggression" were to continue.

September

6   Pakistan declared war on India, and India attacked West Pakistan at several points, including the city of Lahore.

23 Following a resolution passed by the U.N. Security Council, India and Pakistan ceased fighting.

1966

January

10 President Ayub Khan of Pakistan and Prime Minister Lal Bahadur Shastri of Indian signed the Tashkent Declaration "affirming their obligation . . . not to have recourse to force and to settle their disputes through peaceful means."

February

12 At a Lahore meeting of opposition parties, Sheikh Mujibur Rahman presented his "six point program" for gaining autonomy for Pakistan's federating provinces.

Mujibur Rahman was arrested and charged for conspiring with Indian officials to destroy Pakistan. The event became known as the Agartala Conspiracy.

1967

November

30 The Pakistan People's Party (PPP) was formed in Lahore, with Zulfikar Ali Bhutto as its chairman. J. A. Rahim was appointed secretary-general.

1969

March

25 Field Marshal Ayub Khan resigned as the president of Pakistan and was replaced by General Agha Muhammad Yahya Khan. General Yahya Khan abrogated the Constitution of 1962, dissolved the National and Provincial Assemblies, and placed Pakistan under martial law.

1970

March

20 President Yahya Khan announced the Legal Framework Order, which prescribed the ground rules for transferring power back to civilian authorities.

April

19 Field Marshal Muhammad Ayub Khan, President of Pakistan from 1958 to 1969, died of a heart attack at his home in Islamabad.

November

12 East Pakistan's coastal districts were hit by a cyclone and tidal waves 30 feet high. More than a million people were killed.

December

7   Elections were held for the National Assembly. One hundred sixty of the 300 seats in the assembly were captured by the Awami League, whereas 81 seats were won by the Pakistan People's Party.

1971

March

21   Mujibur Rahman was arrested by the army in Dacca. Military operations were started against the Awami League followers.

November

4   Indian Prime Minister Indira Gandhi assured U.S. President Richard Nixon in a meeting in Washington that "India has never wished the destruction of Pakistan or its permanent crippling."

16   Indian troops moved into East Pakistan and began to advance toward Dacca.

December

16   The Pakistani Army surrendered to Lieutenant General Jagjit Singh Aurora of the Indian Army in a ceremony held at Dacca.

20   Zulfikar Ali Bhutto was sworn in as the president of Pakistan.

1972

January

3   In a mammoth public meeting held in Karachi, Bhutto sought and received the people's approval to release Sheikh Mujibur Rahman from jail.

March

3   Lieutenant General Gul Hassan, chief of staff of the army, and Air Marshal Rahim Khan, commander of the air force, were replaced by General Tikka Khan and Air Marshal Zafar Choudhery, respectively.

April

4   The National Assembly was convened in Islamabad to frame a new constitution for Pakistan.

July

3   A peace agreement was signed at Simla (India) by Indira Gandhi and Zulfikar Ali Bhutto, the prime minister and president of India and Pakistan, respectively.

October

11   The Federal Security Force (FSF) was established as a parliamentary organization to help the police in the task of maintaining law and order.

20   A constitutional accord was signed in Islamabad by the leaders of various political parties.

1973

April

12 The constitution was authenticated by President Zulfikar Ali Bhutto.

August

14 Pakistan's third constitution came into effect.

1974

February

22 A conference for heads of government and state of 37 Muslim countries began in Lahore and was hosted by Prime Minister Zulfikar Ali Bhutto.

Pakistan recognized Bangladesh.

May

5 India exploded a nuclear device, thereby joining the United States, the Soviet Union, Great Britain, France, and China as a member of the nuclear club.

September

11 The National Assembly declared the Ahmadiya sect to be a non-Muslim community.

December

13 Dr. Mubashir Hasan replaced J. A. Rahim as secretary-general of the Pakistan People's Party.

1975

January

10 The Pakistan People's Party was reorganized, and work on an election manifesto was started.

February

8 Hayat Muhammad Khan Sherpao, chief minister of the Northwest Frontier Province, was assassinated while addressing a public meeting in Peshawar.

12 The United States lifted the arms embargo on Pakistan, which was imposed during the 1965 Pakistan war with India.

15 The National Awami Party led by Abdul Wali Khan was declared illegal and banned.

1976

March

11 President Muhammad Daud of Afghanistan visited Islamabad to hold discussions with Prime Minister Zulfikar Ali Bhutto.

17 Prime Minister Bhutto visited President Muhammad Daud of Afghanistan in Kabul.

May

22 Muhammad Zia ul-Haq, the Pakistan Army's most junior lieutenant general, was chosen by Zulfikar Ali Bhutto to be chief of the Army Staff.

December

25 Pakistan celebrated the 100th anniversary of Muhammad Ali Jinnah's birth. He was the country's founder and its first governor-general.

1977

January

7 In a speech in the National Assembly, Prime Minister Bhutto announced March 7 as the date for the next general elections.

11 The Pakistan National Alliance (PNA) was formed by nine political parties to face Zulfikar Ali Bhutto's' Pakistan People's Party in the national and provincial elections.

March

7 General elections were held to elect 200 members of the National Assembly.

10 Elections were held for the four provincial assemblies.

July

5 General Zia ul-Haq, the chief of the Army Staff, removed Prime Minister Zulfikar Ali Bhutto from office, declared martial law, and appointed himself the chief martial-law administrator.

20 Martial Law Order No. 12 was promulgated, giving General Zia ul-Haq, the chief martial-law administrator, sweeping powers to detain people suspected of acting against the interest of the state.

September

3 Zulfikar Ali Bhutto was charged with conspiracy to murder.

4 Martial Law Regulation No. 21 was issued, requiring all politicians to submit declarations of the assets they held in 1970 and 1977.

18 Zulfikar Ali Bhutto was arrested in Larkana. His cousin Mumtaz Ali Bhutto was also imprisoned.

November

10 The Supreme Court issued its judgment on *Begum Nusrat Bhutto vs. Chief of Army Staff and Federation of Pakistan,* validating the imposition of martial law.

30 A presidential ordinance was issued, repealing the Federal Security Force Act of 1973 and disbanding the FSF.

1978

January

1 The Hyderabad Special Tribunal, which had been trying the cases of a number of political leaders including Wali Khan, was disbanded. More than 11,000 persons, imprisoned for political reasons by the government of Zulfikar Ali Bhutto, were released.

March

14 President Muhammad Daud of Afghanistan visited Islamabad.

18 In a unanimous opinion of the Lahore High Court, the charges against Zulfikar Ali Bhutto were found to have been "proved to the hilt." The deposed prime minister and co-defendants were sentenced to death.

April

30 President Muhammad Daud of Afghanistan was assassinated, and his government was overthrown by elements of the Afghan Army.

July

25 The martial law administration published a "white paper," reporting the results of its inquiry into the conduct of the Bhutto government during the 1977 election.

September

12 General Zia ul-Haq visited Noor Muhammad Tarraki, the Marxist leader of Afghanistan, in Kabul.

16 General Zia ul-Haq, the chief martial-law administrator (CMLA), was sworn in as Pakistan's sixth president, replacing Fazal Elahi Chaudhry.

December

5 Afghanistan and the Soviet Union signed a 20-year Treaty of Friendship and Cooperation. According to Article 4 of the treaty, both countries "will hold consultations and, with the agreement of both parties, take appropriate measures with a view to ensuring the security and territorial integrity of the two countries."

1979

February

10 *Shariat* benches, made up of three Muslim judges (*Qazis*), were established in the high courts.

March

12 Pakistan announced its decision to withdraw from the Central Treaty Organization (CENTO), the last of its remaining alliances with the Western world.

April

4 Zulfikar Ali Bhutto was executed in Rawalpindi's central prison and buried in the Bhutto family graveyard near Larkana.

August
23 President Zia ul-Haq announced his government's decision to hold elections for local bodies on a nonparty basis.

October
16 A number of Islamization measures were announced by President Zia ul-Haq.

President Zia ul-Haq announced the decision to indefinitely postpone the elections set for November 17. Anticipating adverse reactions from most political parties, the government toughened martial law regulation against political activity.

November
17 Maulana Abul Ala Maududi, the former *amir* (president) of Jamaat-e-Islami, died in Lahore.

20 Fanatic followers of a Sunni Moslem extremist group occupied the Grand Mosque in Mecca, Saudi Arabia.

21 The United States Embassy in Islamabad was sacked and burned by a mob. Two U.S. marines died in the fire.

December
27 The Soviet Army invaded Afghanistan. President Hafizullah Amin was executed and Babrak Kamal was installed as the new head of state.

1980
March
17 The Islamic University was founded in Islamabad.

June
20 The Zakat and Ushr Ordinance (No. XVII of 1980) was promulgated.

1981
April
27 The Ministry of Finance issued a notification exempting Shias from the levy of *zakat.*

1983
January
25 The government established an ombudsman's office, the *Wafaqi Mohtasib.*

1984
January
10 Benazir Bhutto left Karachi for London after having been allowed to leave Pakistan for medical treatment.

19 The countries belonging to the Organization of the Islamic Conference met for their fourth summit at Casablanca. President Zia ul-Haq played a prominent role in getting Egypt readmitted to the organization.

1985

January
1 Non-Islamic banking was abolished.
12 The election schedule was announced by President Zia ul-Haq.

February
25 General elections were held for the 200-member National Assembly.

March
23 Muhammad Khan Junejo was invited by General Zia ul-Haq to form a civilian Cabinet.

July
1 The economy was declared to be in conformity with Islam.

December
30 Martial law was lifted.

1986

January
18 Prime Minister Muhammad Khan Junejo was elected chairman of the Pakistan Muslim League.

April
10 Benazir Bhutto returned to Pakistan and addressed a mammoth public meeting in Lahore.

July
23 The National People's Party (NPP) was formed under the chairmanship of Ghulam Mustafa Jatoi.

August
8 The seventh round of "proximity talks" between Afghanistan and Pakistan on the Afghanistan issue were suspended in Geneva.
14 The Movement for the Restoration of Democracy (MRD) launched a campaign against the government, demanding new general elections.
16 Benazir Bhutto was arrested in Karachi.

September
6 Benazir Bhutto was released from prison.

November
20 Army troops were called out to assist police in quelling riots in Karachi.

December
13 The Pakistani government launched an operation to remove 20,000 Afghan refugees from Sohrab Goth in Karachi.

22 A new federal Cabinet was sworn into office by President Zia ul-Haq, with Muhammad Khan Junejo as prime minister.

1987

February

25 Eighth round of "proximity talks" between the governments of Pakistan and Afghanistan began in Geneva under the auspices of the United States with Diego Cordovez, undersecretary for political affairs, providing the link between the two delegations.

November

30 Local body elections were held in the four provinces of Pakistan.

December

18 Benazir Bhutto was married to Asif Ali Zardari in Karachi.

1988

April

10 An explosion in the ammunition depot in Ojheri, an army camp near Rawalpindi and Islamabad, killed 100 people while injuring another 1,000.

May

15 Prime Minister Muhammad Khan Junejo expanded the federal government to 33 members by taking in five new ministers and three new ministers of state.

29 President Zia ul-Haq dismissed the government of Prime Minster Junejo, dissolved the National Assembly, and ordered new elections to be held within 90 days.

31 President Zia ul-Haq dissolved all provincial assemblies.

August

17 President Zia ul-Haq was killed in a plane crash near the city of Bahawalpur in south Punjab. Also lost in the crash was a number of senior officers of the Pakistan army, including the chairman of the Joint Chiefs of Staff, General Akhtar Abdur Rahman. Arnold Raphael, U.S. ambassador to Pakistan, also died. Ghulam Ishaq Khan, chairman of the Senate, was sworn in as acting president. General Mirza Aslam Beg was appointed chief of the Army Staff.

November

17 Elections were held for the National Assembly; the Pakistan People's Party won 92 out of the 207 seats contested.

December

2 Benazir Bhutto was sworn in as prime minister.

8 The government submitted a revised budget to the National Assembly.

12 Ghulam Ishaq Khan was elected president of Pakistan.

15 Balochistan Governor Muhammad Musa dissolved the Provincial Assembly on the grounds that no party had won a majority and therefore could not form a stable government.

31 During a meeting of the South Asian Association for Regional Cooperation (SAARC) in Islamabad, Prime Minister Benazir Bhutto and Indian Prime Minister Rajiv Gandhi held private talks and signed agreements on cultural relations, taxation, and safeguarding the two countries' nuclear installations.

1989

January

23 The Balochistan High Court declared the December dissolution of the Provincial Assembly unconstitutional and ordered the body's reconstitution.

28 The Election Commission announced the results of the January 23 by-elections for 13 National Assembly seats and 7 Provincial Assembly seats. Islami Jamhuri Itehad (IJI) won 7 seats, PPP 4 seats, Awami National Party 1 seat, and Muhajir Qaumi Mahaz 1 seat. In Punjab, IJI won 3 seats, PPP 1 seat, and the 5th seat was taken by an independent candidate. The 2 Northwest Frontier Province seats were won by the PPP.

February

5 Nawab Muhammad Akbar Khan Bugti of the Balochistan National Alliance was sworn in as chief minister of Balochistan.

15 The Soviet Union completed the withdrawal of its troops from Afghanistan.

March

10 The Supreme Court ruled that the May 29, 1988 dissolution of the National Assembly was unconstitutional.

13 In the Punjab assembly, Chief Minister Nawaz Sharif won a vote of confidence in a session demanded by the PPP.

April

30 Labor Minister Malik Mukhtar Ahmad Awan announced the lifting of a ban on trade-union activities.

May

22 The government approved a 20-year plan for developing nuclear power generation. The program was to rely heavily on co-manufacturing with foreign firms.

June

3   The budget for the 1989–90 fiscal year was presented to the National Assembly by Minister of State Ihsanul Haq Piracha.

4   Ghulam Mustafa Jatoi was elected to lead a 94-member opposition coalition in the National Assembly.

July

20   The Afghan mujahideen began their assault on Khost, a town close to the Pakistan border.

21   Officials in New Delhi, India said that Pakistan was violating the informal understanding reached between the two countries on the Siachen Glacier.

September

3   The *New York Times* carried a story according to which the United States and Pakistan had changed their policy with respect to the provision of arms and supplies to the mujahideen. Under the new policy, assistance was to be provided directly to the fighters in Afghanistan and not through the seven political groups operating out of Pakistan, as had been done previously.

8   The government denied a report published in the *Financial Times* that a number of army officers had been arrested following a failed coup attempt against Benazir Bhutto.

13   General Aslam Beg, chief of the Army Staff, said that the purpose of the armed-forces exercise planned for later in the year was to test their readiness for effective defense. The exercise was named *Zarbe Momin.*

15   The U.S. Senate approved a $460 million aid package for Pakistan for 1989–90 while voicing concern over the direction of the country's nuclear-development policy. Half of the amount fell in the category of foreign military sales (FMS).

20   Prime Minister Bhutto reshuffled her Cabinet.

October

1   Pakistan rejoined the Commonwealth.

31   Prime Minister Bhutto survived a vote of no-confidence by a narrow margin of 12 votes.

November

11   Prime Minister Bhutto included three members from IJI, the opposition party, in her Cabinet.

13   Prime Minister Li Peng of China arrived in Pakistan for his first visit to the country.

December

26 Hyderabad was put under 24-hour curfew following riots that claimed scores of lives in four days.

1990

January

29 The Federal Cabinet, meeting under the chairmanship of Senior Minister Nusrat Bhutto, took stock of the situation created by continuing troubles in Kashmir. There were reports of massing of troops by India and Pakistan along their common border.

February

2 Prime Minister V. P. Singh of India warned Pakistan to stay out of Kashmir and to stop assisting the forces of opposition in the Indian state. He promised Pakistan "a fitting reply" if it continued its activist policy in Kashmir.

18 President François Mitterrand of France arrived in Pakistan on a first-ever visit to the country by the French head of state.

26 Aftab Shahban Mirani was sworn in as chief minister of Sindh province.

28 The Board of Investment, meeting under the chairmanship of Prime Minister Benazir Bhutto, approved 13 projects at a cost of 5.7 billion rupees.

March

1 The Soviet Union suggested that the solution to the Kashmir problem should be sought within the framework of the 1972 Simla Accord between India and Pakistan.

April

1 Vaseem Jaffrey, the prime minister's advisor for finance, defended the government's decision to raise petroleum and fertilizer prices.

24 The U.S. State Department expressed the hope that talks between India and Pakistan would avert another war on the unresolved Kashmir dispute.

25 Talks were held in New York between Foreign Ministers Yaqub Khan and Kumar Gujral of Pakistan and India, respectively, on the situation in Kashmir.

May

3 Prime Minister Toshiki Kaifu of Japan met with Prime Minister Benazir Bhutto in Islamabad. After the talks, Bhutto offered to meet with V. P. Singh, her Indian counterpart, in order to avert a war between the two countries.

14 A strike by businessmen shut down all commercial areas of Karachi.

The strike was to protest the government's inability to stop crimes and kidnappings against the business community.

20 Prime Minister Benazir Bhutto arrived in Cairo to explain Pakistan's position to Egyptian President Hosni Mubarak.

30 Ethnic violence in Karachi spread to a number of areas in the city, bringing the death toll to 103 in four days of fighting.

June

2 Ethnic troubles continued in Karachi, bringing the number of dead to 200.

7 Minister of State for Finance Ihsanul Haq Piracha presented the budget for the 1990–91 fiscal year.

26 The government announced the trade policy for 1990–91.

July

10 Prime Minister Benazir Bhutto arrived in Baghdad, Iraq at the start of her second mission to the Middle East to solicit support for Pakistan on the issue of Kashmir.

20 Indian Foreign Secretary Muchkund Dubey said in Islamabad that his country did not want war with Pakistan on the issue of Kashmir.

August

6 President Ghulam Ishaq Khan dismissed Prime Minister Benazir Bhutto and her Cabinet, dissolved the National Assembly, and ordered national elections for October 24, 1990. Ghulam Mustafa Jatoi, the leader of the opposition in the National Assembly, was sworn in as caretaker prime minister. Senators Sartaj Aziz and Sahibzada Yaqub Khan were appointed finance and foreign ministers, respectively.

20 Pakistan announced its intention to contribute its forces to the coalition army being assembled in the Middle East under the leadership of the United States in response to Iraq's invasion of Kuwait.

22 Twenty-seven people were killed, including two women and four children, in Karachi when gunmen raided various camps and offices of Muhajir Qaumi Mahaz.

31 Caretaker Prime Minister Ghulam Mustafa Jatoi asked India to pull back its troops from the border with Pakistan.

September

4 President Ghulam Ishaq Khan filed "references" against three former federal ministers for alleged misdeeds and corruption. The references were made to special tribunals set up to investigate the conduct in office of elected officials during the administration of Benazir Bhutto.

12 The special tribunal comprising Justice Munir A. Sheikh returned the

"reference" to President Ghulam Ishaq Khan that had been filed by the president against former minister Jehangir Badr for want of sufficient evidence to warrant further proceedings.

20 President Ghulam Ishaq Khan met with President Yang Shangkun of China in Beijing.

30 Benazir Bhutto appeared in Karachi before Justice Wajihuddin Ahmad in response to a "reference" filed against her by President Ishaq Khan.

October

24 Elections were held all over Pakistan. Bhutto's PPP lost in all the provinces to IJI, an alliance of rightist parties.

November

10 An 18-member federal government was sworn in by President Ghulam Ishaq Khan. Nawaz Sharif became prime minister, while Sartaj Aziz and Sahibzada Yaqub Khan stayed on as finance and foreign ministers, respectively.

21 The fifth summit of the South Asian Association for Regional Cooperation was held in Male, Maldives. Prime Minister Nawaz Sharif met with Chandra Shekhar, his Indian counterpart.

December

9 While on a visit to Sindh, Prime Minister Nawaz Sharif announced a special Rs.12 billion program for the development and reconstruction of the provincial economy.

15 The Cabinet meeting under the chairmanship of Prime Minister Nawaz Sharif decided to allow the establishment of passenger and cargo airlines in the private sector.

1991

January

5 The government announced plans to distribute 350,000 acres of land to the *haris* (landless peasants) in Sind.

10 The government coalition, IJI, won the majority of the seats in the national and provincial by-elections.

18 Demonstrations were held all over Pakistan to protest the bombing of Iraq by the United States and other coalition forces.

25 Prime Minister Nawaz Sharif met in Amman with King Hussein of Jordan to find a solution to the crisis in the Gulf.

February

1 A devastating earthquake hit the northern areas of Pakistan. The death toll was estimated at more than a thousand.

25 Prime Minister Nawaz Sharif went on a visit to China.

26 Foreign Minister Sahibzada Yaqub Khan resigned from the Cabinet.

March

14 Elections were held for the Senate. The government coalition, IJI, maintained its control of the upper house.

July

20 Azad Kashmir President Abdul Qayyum Khan resigned.

September

9 The Sindh High Court acquitted Asif Ali Zardari, Benazir Bhutto's husband, of charges of fraud and corruption.

Unidentified gunmen assassinated Fazle Haq, former governor of the Northwest Frontier Province.

December

19 Opposition members walked out of the National Assembly when President Ghulam Ishaq Khan rose to deliver his annual address.

1992

January

1 China revealed that it had agreed to build a nuclear power station at Chasma on the Indus River.

February

6 In a meeting with the *Washington Post*, Foreign Secretary Shahrayar Khan admitted that Pakistan had acquired the technology to build nuclear weapons.

May

5 Jamaat-e-Islami announced the decision to leave the ruling coalition formed by Islami Jamhuri Itehad.

July

14 Sunni gunmen killed several Shiite Muslims while they were observing the death anniversary of Imam Hussain.

August

18 Indian and Pakistani officials met to hold talks on Kashmir.

October

10 Asif Ali Zardari was acquitted of some more charges of corruption and fraud by the Sindh High Court.

1993

February

5 Pakistan observed a strike against India's presence in Kashmir.

March

27 Pakistan Muslim League leaders nominated Nawaz Sharif to succeed Muhammad Khan Junejo as the party's president.

April

17 In a nationally televised speech, Prime Minister Nawaz Sharif accused President Ishaq Khan of "unscrupulous and dirty politics."

18 President Ghulam Ishaq Khan dismissed Prime Minister Nawaz Sharif and dissolved the National Assembly. A caretaker administration was appointed under Prime Minister Balkh Sher Mazari.

May

20 The Supreme Court held the prime minister's dismissal unconstitutional. Sharif was reinstated.

July

18 President Ghulam Ishaq Khan dissolved the National Assembly for the second time in three months and then resigned. Prime Minister Nawaz Sharif also resigned. Moeen Qureshi was appointed caretaker prime minister.

August

19 The prime minister announced a program of structural reforms.

October

6 The Pakistan People's Party won the most seats in the National Assembly but did not obtain a majority.

17 Benazir Bhutto was sworn in as prime minister. She saw off caretaker Prime Minister Moeen Qureshi at the Islamabad airport.

December

4 Farooq Ahmad Khan Leghari of the Pakistan People's Party was elected president.

1994

January

26 Bhutto brought new ministers—Anwar Saifullah Khan, Khalid Ahmad Kharal, Makhdum Fahim Amin, Mustafa Khar, Ahmad Mukhtar—into the Cabinet.

February

26 Western governments announced pledges amounting to $2.5 billion to support the development plan.

May

26 President Farooq Leghari visited Washington and held talks with senior U.S. officials.

June

5   Murtaza Bhutto, the brother of Prime Minister Benazir Bhutto, was released from jail.

6   The Bhutto government announced the budget for the 1994–95 financial year.

26   The Federation of Pakistan Chambers of Commerce and Industry went on strike to protest government budget proposals.

August

25   The government announced plans to expel one million immigrants of Afghan, Burmese, Bangladesh, Indian, and Iranian origin who had settled in Karachi.

September

1   Bhutto decided against visiting Gaza without permission from Israel.

11   Opposition launched "oust Bhutto" campaign with a train march from Karachi to Peshawar.

21   A strike call by opposition leader Nawaz Sharif resulted in widespread violence and disruption of economic activity.

30   Sixty persons were reported killed in Karachi in MQM-related violence.

October

10   Some 1,100 opponents of Benazir Bhutto were arrested by the government.

18   The army was called out in Karachi after 13 persons were killed in sectarian violence involving the Sunni and Shia communities.

31   Eighty-four persons were reported to have been killed during the month in MQM-associated violence.

November

12   Suffering a major diplomatic defeat, Pakistan was forced to withdraw a resolution on Kashmir tabled at the U.N. General Assembly.

13   Mian Muhammad Sharif, Nawaz Sharif's father, was arrested.

30   One-hundred-four persons were reported killed during the month in MQM-related violence.

December

4   Muhammad Salahuddin, editor of the Urdu newspaper *Takbeer,* was shot dead outside his office in Karachi.

31   One hundred sixty-eight persons were reported killed during the month in MQM-related violence.

1995

January

10–12 U.S. Defense Secretary William Perry visited Pakistan.

12 Khalid Latif, chairman of Allied Bank, Pakistan's second largest private-sector bank, was arrested by the government.

16 India rejected preconditions set by Pakistan for the resumption of bilateral talks on Kashmir.

31 Ninety-two persons were reported to have been killed during the month in MQM-related violence.

February

12 Ramzi Youssef, the main suspect in the terrorist bombing of the World Trade Center in New York, was arrested in Islamabad and immediately deported to the United States.

18 Opposition leader Ijaz ul-Haq—member of the National Assembly and the son of the late Zia ul-Haq—was arrested.

28 One-hundred-seventy persons were reported to have been killed during the month in MQM-related violence.

October

29 The government devalued the rupee by 7 percent and increased fuel prices and import duties.

November

13 Prime Minister Benazir Bhutto ordered the arrest of Mian Muhammad Sharif, the father of Nawaz Sharif, on charges of tax evasion.

December

21 President Leghari appointed General Jehangir Karamat chief of the Army Staff.

1996

January

1 Pakistan and India exchanged a list of nuclear installations.

13 General Jehangir Karamat assumed the position of chief of the Army Staff.

28 A banking tribunal directed two Iteffaq Group concerns owned by Nawaz Sharif and his family to deposit Rs.1,770 million against bad debts claimed by two banks.

31 One-hundred-five people were reported killed in Karachi violence during January.

February

5 The United States accused China of supplying nuclear-weapons technology to Pakistan in 1995.

6 The *Pakistan Times,* a Press Trust paper, was sold to a private group.

8 The Privatization Commission approved the sale of 26 percent of the shares of United Bank Limited to a Saudi businessman.

29 Fifty-six persons were reported killed in violence in Karachi during February.

March

6 Pakistan completed construction on its first multipurpose nuclear reactor.

12 Prominent female journalist, Razia Bhatti, editor of *Newsline,* a Karachi monthly, died.

20 The Supreme Court ruled that the government did not have the executive power to appoint judges to the superior courts. Such appointments had to have the consent of the chief justices of high courts or the chief justice of the Supreme Court.

31 Twenty-four persons were reported killed in violence in Karachi during March.

April

6 Javed Ashraf, a leader of the Pakistan Muslim League, was assassinated in Lahore.

14 Seven people died in a bomb attack on the Shaukat Khanum Memorial Hospital, which was established by Imran Khan.

23 The Aid to Pakistan Consortium approved Pakistan's request for $2.3 billion in assistance for the 1996–97 fiscal year.

May

4 The government announced that wheat output for the 1995–96 growing year was a record 18 million tons.

6 The government canceled the sale of the United Bank Limited to a Saudi businessman.

10 The United States decided not to impose sanctions on China for the alleged transfer of nuclear technology to Pakistan.

27 The Supreme Court declared that the president had the final authority to appoint the chief justice.

June

13 A Rs.500 billion budget for the 1996–97 was presented to the National Assembly. Defense expenditure was raised 14 percent to Rs.131 billion, debt servicing to Rs.186 billion, and development expenditure to Rs. 104 billion.

20 The business community organized a protest against the taxation proposals in the budget.

26   The Supreme Court restored local bodies in Punjab.

July

20   Leaders of the Jamaat-e-Islami began a 1,000-km whistle-stop tour of the country to oust the "corrupt and incompetent" government headed by Benazir Bhutto.

31   Prime Minister Bhutto brought seven new ministers into her Cabinet including her husband, Asif Ali Zardari, who was assigned the portfolio of Investment.

August

18   Firing by gunmen during a Shia funeral left 18 dead and 100 injured.

20   India vetoed the draft Comprehensive Treaty to Ban Tests (CTBT). Pakistan regretted the Indian decision.

26   The first consignment of U.S. arms released under the Brown amendment arrived in Karachi.

September

13   Sectarian tensions mounted in Kurram Agency as the death toll rose to 200.

20   Mir Murtaza Bhutto and six of his followers were killed in an ambush in Karachi.

24   Gunmen killed 21 worshippers at a Sunni mosque in Multan, Punjab.

October

2   Prime Minister Bhutto met with James Wolfenshon, President of the World Bank, and senior officials of the International Monetary Fund to discuss Pakistan's economic situation.

27   The Jamaat-e-Islami organized strikes in Lahore, Rawalpindi, and Islamabad. More than 150 persons were arrested in Lahore.

28   Naveed Qamar was appointed finance minister.

30   Four army officers accused of a coup attempt were sentenced to various terms of imprisonment.

November

5   President Farooq Leghari dismissed Prime Minister Bhutto, dissolved the National Assembly, and appointed a caretaker administration with Meraj Khalid as prime minister. Shahid Hamid and Umar Afridi were appointed ministers of defense and interior, respectively. The Punjab assembly was also dismissed and Tariq Rahim was appointed governor. Asif Ali Zardari was arrested.

7   The Sindh assembly was dissolved and Mumtaz Bhutto was appointed chief minister.

8   Shahid Javed Burki took leave of absence from the World Bank and joined the Cabinet. He was put in charge of finance, planning, and economic affairs. The Balochistan Assembly was dissolved.

12   The NWFP Assembly was dissolved.

18   President Leghari instituted the Ehetasab Ordinance to address the problem of corruption.

December

1   Chinese president Jiang Zemin arrived in Pakistan.

15   President Farooq Leghari filed a document with the Supreme Court to defend his action against the Bhutto government.

16   The Supreme Court dismissed the petition to postpone elections. The chief election commissioner approved the election schedule.

23   Nine thousand five-hundred-forty persons filed nomination papers for elections.

1997

January

4   Shahid Javed Burki traveled to Beijing to enlist Chinese support for resolving the balance-of-payments crisis.

6   President Leghari established the Council for Defense and National Security, consisting of military leaders and members of the caretaker administration, to advise the government.

29   The Supreme Court upheld the dismissal of the administration of Benazir Bhutto by the president, accepting President Leghari's contention that the dismissed government had been corrupt and was also responsible for hundreds of "extrajudicial" killings in Karachi.

February

3   Nawaz Sharif's Muslim League scored a massive electoral victory, whereas Benazir Bhutto's Pakistan People's Party performed very poorly.

17   Nawaz Sharif was sworn in as prime minister; Sartaj Aziz was appointed minister of finance. Shahbaz Sharif became the chief minister of Punjab.

23   Prime Minister Sharif appealed to the Pakistanis living abroad to donate generously to a fund set up to reduce the country's external debt.

March

1   The United States placed Pakistan on the decertification list for drug-producing and -transit countries. Pakistan was granted a waiver on attendant sanctions, however.

9   Benazir Bhutto was elected chairperson for life of the Pakistan People's Party.

12 The Pakistan Muslim League won 23 seats in the Senate out of the 46 contested. This gave the PML two-thirds majority in both houses of Parliament, sufficient to amend the constitution.

21 Waseem Sajjad was elected chairman of the Senate.

April

1 Both houses of Parliament unanimously adopted the thirteenth amendment to the constitution, taking away the power of the president to dissolve the National Assembly and dismiss the prime minister.

9 The Pakistani and Indian foreign ministers met in New Delhi, the highest level meeting between the two countries in seven years.

15 Scarcity of wheat flour led to riots in Lahore.

December

2 President Farooq Leghari resigned.

31 Muhammad Rafiq Tarar was elected president.

1998

February

1 The U.S. State Department issued a harsh criticism concerning human-rights treatment in Pakistan.

March

7–17 A population census was conducted with the help of the armed forces. Because of local opposition the count could not be carried out in Quetta, the capital of Balochistan.

April

1 Corruption case against Asif Ali Zardari began to be heard by a magistrate in London.

2 A magistrate in London rejected the plea by Benazir Bhutto and Asif Zardari to stop the government of Pakistan's investigation against them.

10 Pakistan test fired the Ghauri, a medium-range missile.

12 Pakistan refuted reports that foreign assistance was received by the country in the production of the Ghauri missile.

14 Mahmud Akbar Khan, a Pakistan Muslim League member of the National, was killed by gunmen in Sheikhupura, Punjab.

May

10 A spokesman for Pakistan People's Party announced that a court had issued warrants for the arrest of Benazir Bhutto.

11 India announced the successful testing of three nuclear devices in a desert testing ground near the border with Pakistan. The announcement of the test by the prime minister was followed soon after by condemna-

tion from most of the important world capitals. The United States threatened to impose economic sanctions, while Pakistan suggested that it may also be forced to act.

13 India carried out two more tests of nuclear devices. U.S. President Bill Clinton called the tests a "terrible mistake" and announced economic sanctions against India.

28 Pakistan conducted five tests of nuclear devices at a site in Balochistan.

30 Pakistan followed up with one more test of a nuclear device. The United States and Japan imposed sanctions on Pakistan.

June

2 Israel denied Pakistan's allegation that it was preparing an attack on its nuclear facilities.

3 Prime Minister Sharif set up a National Self-Reliance Fund and appealed to all Pakistanis for donations to help the country face the situation created by the imposition of sanctions.

16 Prime Minister Sharif ordered stern action against 25 top bank-loan defaulters, including seven persons belonging to the Pakistan Muslim League.

July

2 The federal government appointed a six-man committee to oversee the law-and-order situation in Karachi.

3 The Supreme Court ordered the Lahore High Court to decide the government's case against Hub Power Company, one of the dozen private companies that had invested in power generation during the time Benazir Bhutto was prime minister.

14 The Karachi Stock Exchange Index (KSE-100) closed at 755, an all-time low.

August

7 Terrorists bombed United States' embassies in Kenya and Tanzania, killing more than 200 people, including 12 Americans. Pakistan arrested Muhammad Siddique Odeh, a Palestinian man at the Karachi airport who confessed to having worked with a group that bombed the embassies.

18 Pakistan arrested two additional suspects in the embassy bombings.

19 A judge in Switzerland indicted Benazir Bhutto on charges of money-laundering tied to contracts with two Geneva-based companies.

20 The United States fired cruise missiles at Khost, Afghanistan to attack the camps maintained by Osama bin Laden. The U.S. action came in

response to the terrorist's attacks on its embassies in East Africa. Some missiles landed in Pakistan, killing several people.

21 Pakistanis protested against the U.S. missile attack.

23 Pakistan lodged a formal complaint with the United Nations that the United States violated its air space in the missile attacks on Afghanistan.

October

7 General Jehangir Karamat, chief of the Army Staff, resigned after giving a speech at the Naval Staff College in Lahore. The speech was highly critical of the way the Prime Minister Nawaz Sharif was handling the economy. Lieutenant General Pervez Musharaf was promoted and appointed chief of the Army Staff.

8 The National Assembly passed the Fifteenth amendment to the Constitution by a vote of 151 in favor, 16 against, and 40 abstaining. The amendment adopted the *sharia*—the Islamic law—as the law of the land. It was sent to the senate for ratification.

12 The government initiated action against Hubco, a power-generation company owned in part by National Power of the United Kingdom. The company was accused of having bribed senior officials in the government of Benazir Bhutto in order to receive favorable terms.

17 Hakim Muhammad Said, former Governor of Sindh and a prominent social worker, was shot dead by unknown assailants.

November

6 Hafiz Pasha, Advisor to the Prime Minister for Finance, resigned. He was replaced by Ishaq Dar as Finance Minister.

7 The army was brought in to manage the affairs of the Water and Power Development Authority.

December

2–4 Prime Minister Nawaz Sharif visited Washington and held meetings with President Bill Clinton and other senior U.S. officials.

18 Three army personnel were ambushed and killed in Karachi.

24 Military courts were set up in Karachi to try people accused of terrorism.

1999

February

20 Prime Minister Atal Bihari Vajpayee traveled by bus to Lahore to inaugurate a bus service between India and Pakistan.

21 India and Pakistani prime ministers issued a statement—the Lahore Declaration—promising to work towards an improvement in relations between the two countries.

April

10 India test-fired the Agni II missile (with a range of 2,000 kilometers).

14 Pakistan launched the Ghanri II missile (with range of 2,500 kilometers).

15 Former Prime Minister Benazir Bhutto and her husband Asif Zardari were convicted of corruption and sentenced to five years in prison. The court also issued orders for the confiscation of their property.

21–22 Prime Minister Nawaz Sharif visited Moscow for discussions with President Boris Yeltsin. Russia and Pakistan issued a joint statement pledging for the establishment of durable peace and security in the region.

Introduction

At what point should one begin a history of Pakistan? Should one start with August 14, 1947, when Lord Louis Mountbatten administered the oath of office to Muhammad Ali Jinnah, Pakistan's first governor-general? That was the day Pakistan was born, a day before its twin, India. The earlier date was fixed so that Lord Mountbatten, after swearing in Jinnah, could travel back to Delhi to be sworn in himself as the first governor-general of independent India. But by starting in 1947 it is not possible to tell the entire story of Pakistan.

One should perhaps go back another seven years, to March 23, 1940, when Muhammad Ali Jinnah sat on the dais in Lahore at the annual meeting of the Muslim League while A. K. Fazlul Haq, a prominent Bengali leader, moved a resolution demanding the creation of separate *states* for the Muslims of British India. This resolution was later to be named the Pakistan resolution once it was decided that the Muslims did not want states but only one country to be called Pakistan. The demand for Pakistan was made after a great deal of thought. Some historians have suggested recently that Jinnah really did not wish to partition India but asked for the creation of Pakistan only to secure a better deal for the Muslims within a united India.[1] The accepted historical wisdom, however, holds that Jinnah, upset with the leadership of the Indian National Congress for not accommodating Muslims in the provincial governments formed after the elections of 1937, was persuaded that the only way out for his community was to leave the fold of India and work for the creation of a separate homeland once the British left their domain in South Asia. Abul Kalam Azad, one of the few prominent Muslim leaders to remain with the Congress Party while most leaders joined the rival Muslim League, believed that had the Congress—in particular its leader, Jawaharlal Nehru—been more generous toward the Muslims after the elections of 1937, the Muslim community would not have parted company with the Hindus.[2] If Azad's version of history is correct, one should begin Pakistan's story in 1937, ten years before the country was born, three years before the Muslims formally asked for the country's creation.

1

One could go back even earlier to 1857, when the Muslim community fought its last battle against the British advance into India. This struggle took the form of a mass mutiny of mostly Muslim soldiers serving in the army of the East Asia Company. This episode was to be remembered as the Great Indian Mutiny or the First War of Indian Independence depending on who was writing the history. There is no doubt that 1857 was the turning point for one segment of the Muslim community in India. It certainly prepared the ground for the creation of Pakistan 90 years later.

To really understand the circumstances that resulted in the birth of Pakistan, however, one has to go far back into history, to the eighth century when Islam first arrived in South Asia. Another reason we should journey that far back is that much of modern Pakistan's history—the conflict between Sindh and Punjab, for instance—can be traced back to the way Islam entered India.

The Arrival of Islam in India

Pakistan's history really begins with the arrival of Islam in India in the eighth century. In 712, Muhammad Ibn Qasim conquered and incorporated Sindh province in the Umayyad caliphate, headquartered in Baghdad, Iraq. Under the Abbasids, the successors of the Umayyads, Sindh was culturally integrated in the Dar al Islam, the nation of Islam. The Arab control of Sindh was consolidated in the eighth and ninth centuries; in 977 Ibn Shayban was sent by the Fatimid caliphs, by now the rulers of Dar al Islam, to conquer the adjacent province of Punjab. Multan, a city in the south of Punjab, was conquered and annexed to the Arab domain.

In the eleventh century Islam began to encroach on India from another direction. Mahmud of Ghazni, a general operating from a southwestern province of Afghanistan, began to mount expeditions into northwest India. His purpose was to plunder rather than to conquer. His first incursion came in 1001 when he defeated Jaipai, a Hindu ruler, in a battle fought near Peshawar. His most famous foray into India was in 1026, when he destroyed the famed temple of Somnath, in Kathiawar, and took the accumulated wealth within the temple back to Ghazni. His last Indian expedition was made in 1027 against Multan, which was by then a Muslim city, under the control of the Arab viceroys of Sindh.

This entrance of Islam into the Indus Valley from two different directions—from the Arabian Sea in the southwest by the Arabs and through the Khyber and other passes in the northwest by the Afghans—profoundly affected the social, cultural, and political life of the area that was to become Pakistan. The Arab Islam commingled with the native cultures and religions and laid the ground for the founding of several Sufi orders in Sindh. The saints of Sindh were the direct descendants of these orders and they were to have a significant influence on the economy and political structure of the lower Indus valley. The Islam that came to the northwestern parts of the Indus valley through Afghanistan was much more spartan in character; it was also much less accommodating of indigenous cultures and faiths. Its descendants settled in the Northwestern Frontier Province and in the northern districts of Punjab. These two Islamic traditions found it difficult to coexist, even when the Indus valley gained independence in the shape of Pakistan.

Shabuddin Muhammad of Ghauri followed Mahmud of Ghazni into India, but his objective was to conquer rather than plunder. It was also from Ghazni that Ghauri started on his Indian campaign, beginning with an attack on Multan in 1175, and culminating with his victory over Prithvi Raj of Delhi in 1192. This victory led to the establishment of Muslim rule over northern India. Delhi became the capital of the Muslim rulers.

Ghauri's sway over northern India was cut short by his death in 1206. A succession of Muslim sultanates followed Ghauri and ruled India from 1206 to 1526. The Slave dynasty (1206–1290) was founded by Qutubuddin Aibak, who was originally a slave in the service of Ghauri. In 1290, the Slave dynasty was overthrown by Jalaluddin Khilji, who established the Khilji dynasty (1290–1320), which was replaced in 1320 by the Tughluqs. The Tughluq dynasty (1320–1388) was succeeded by the Sayyid dynasty (1414–1450), which in turn was followed by the Lodi dynasty (1450–1526). Ibrahim Lodi was defeated by Babar in the battle of Panipat in 1526; Babar went on to Delhi, proclaimed himself the emperor of India and established the Mughul empire, which lasted until 1857.

Although the first five Mughul emperors of India, from Babar (1526–1530) to Shahjahan (1627–1658), were Muslims, they showed considerable tolerance toward other religions, in particular Hinduism, the dominant faith of the region. Most of them brought Hindu women into their harems and allowed Hindus to hold senior court and military appointments. One of them—Akbar the Great (1556–1605)—went so far as to proclaim his own religion, Dine-Ilhai, as a synthesis of the common faiths of India. Aurangzeb (1658–1707), the last of the great Mughul emperors, adopted a different stance, however. He was not prepared to accommodate other religions and was also not tolerant of the independent states on the borders of Mughul India. Attempting to bring all of South Asia under his control and to spread Islam among his subjects, Aurangzeb exhausted his own energies as well as those of the Mughul state.

It was the turmoil created by Aurangzeb's forays into South India that provided the British East India Company the opportunity to establish its trading outposts in Bengal. As the Mughul power declined, that of the company increased. The traders became generals able to use their immense profits to hire native soldiers and build an army. The East India Company army was better equipped and disciplined than the militias commanded by local warlords, who took over the periphery of the shrinking Mughul empire. The Mughul empire in India had all the attributes of a large continental state: strong at the center and weak around its periphery. It was the periphery that the British successfully penetrated.

The British advance toward the center took about a century; the only major challenge to it came in 1857 when the soldiers, or "sepoys," paid by the Company, rebelled against their employers. The Great Indian Mutiny of 1857 was the result; the leaderless sepoys inflicted a great deal of damage on the British, but they were finally defeated and brought under the control of the Company's forces. The mutiny produced important political consequences for Muslim India: the East India Company was dissolved; Bahadur Shah, the last Mughul emperor, was deported from India; and India was made a part of the British empire. The capital was moved from Muslim-dominated Delhi to Calcutta, a new city the British had founded and in which the Hindu merchants flourished. After more than 1,000 years of uninterrupted rule in some part or another of India, the Muslims were now without a territory they could call their own.

It took the Muslims 90 years, from 1857 to 1947, to reestablish a state of their own in the Indian subcontinent. But the passage from subjugation to independence was not an easy one: It produced what the British administrators in India began to describe as the "Muslim problem."

British India's Three Muslim Communities

In the 1940s when the demand for Pakistan gained momentum, there were some 100 million Muslims in British India, slightly more than one-fourth of the total population. Religion was the only thing these people shared; there were some vast differences of language, culture, social, and economic backgrounds between, for example, the Muslims of the Punjab and those of Bengal. Within this one Muslim nation there existed at least three separate communities: one in the northwest (the provinces of Punjab, Sindh, and Northwest Frontier, the princely states of Bahawalpur, Kalat, and Khaipur); the second in the northeast (the provinces of Bengal and Assam); and the third in the north-central part of British India (United and Central provinces, provinces of Bihar, Orissa, and Bombay, the capital city of Delhi, and numerous princely states scattered all over this part of the country). The first two communities constituted clear majorities in their areas: of the total population of 60 million in the northwest, 60 percent professed Islam to be their religion; of 90 million in the northeast, some 55 percent were Muslims. It was only in the north-central provinces that Muslims were a small minority, comprising no more than 20 percent of the total population. Muslims who belonged to this community were more educated, urbanized, and modernized than those in the other two. Although agriculture was the principal source of income for the Muslims in the northwest and northeast, those in the north-central provinces depended mostly on government, law, medicine, commerce, and industry for their livelihood.

In many ways the Muslims of the northwest had benefited from the British raj. There was some threat of economic competition from the non-Muslims once the British lifted the protection they had provided, but for them this threat constituted only a minor worry. The Muslim landed aristocracy was powerful in the countryside, the religious leaders had a great deal of support in villages as well as towns, and even the small urban community of Muslims had been reasonably well accommodated in the professions and in public services. The Muslims in the northeast constituted a totally different socioeconomic class. Unlike the northwestern Muslims, they owned little land, did not have much education, and had not found a comfortable place for themselves in the modern administrative and economic institutions the British had brought to India. Those in the northwest constituted the aristocracy of the Indian Muslim society; those in the northeast made up its peasantry.

In between these two social and economic polar extremes were the Muslims of Delhi, the United and Central provinces, Bihar, Orissa, and Bombay. They were the descendants of the Mughul raj: sons, grandsons, great-grandsons of the families that had, for over two centuries, served the Mughul administration in various capacities. This was the elite the British conquest of India had hurt the most; they were deprived not only of their traditional jobs, but also of their social and cultural status. In 1857 this community made one disorganized but bloody attempt to regain the power it had lost to the British. The community called it the War of Independence; the British labeled it the Great Indian Mutiny. The British, with great force and much brutality, put down the mutiny. Once the situation had returned to normal, the Muslims found that their position had become even more precarious, in part because the languages they used were downgraded.[3] Up to 1857 the East India Company that governed the British territories had continued to use Persian and Urdu as quasi-official languages. After 1857 the responsibility of administering these territories passed to the officials appointed directly by the government in Great Britain.

One important consequence of this change was the adoption of English as the medium of official communication; because the Muslims had shown considerable disdain for all things English, including the language, they suddenly found themselves functionally illiterate and unemployed. The places they vacated were quickly occupied by the Hindus. "The pliant and adaptable Hindu was not agitated by the scruples which had tormented the

Muslims," wrote W. W. Hunter, a contemporary British administrator. The Muslims stayed away—or, some believed, were deliberately kept away—from the British raj. "A hundred and seventy years ago," Hunter went on to say, "it was impossible for a well-born Mussulman to become poor; at present it is almost impossible for him to continue to be rich. . . . There is no Government office in which a Muslim could hope for any post above the rank of porter, messenger, filler of inkpots and a mender of pens."[4]

Bringing this community out of this state of self-imposed exile, therefore, became a major preoccupation with a number of Muslim reformers. The most successful of these was Sir Sayyid Ahmad Khan who, having started his professional career as a minor government functionary, discovered that his people would not be able to make much headway without modern education. For Pakistan (its creation as well as its political and social development), Sir Sayyid's educational program had two important consequences. First, those who accepted his outlook and his philosophy were able to find their way back into the economic and social life of modern India. The university that he founded in the town of Aligarh soon began to produce graduates who could easily move into the upper ranks of the British Indian Army and also into the upper echelons of the rapidly expanding administrative system of the British raj. They could enter as well the modern professions—law, medicine, banking, commerce, industry, teaching—that had helped the Hindus advance rapidly in British India. It was this Aligarh generation that not only provided the Pakistan Movement with its leadership but was to provide later the new country of Pakistan with its first ruling elite.

The second important consequence of Sir Sayyid's efforts was that they helped at least one segment of the Indian Muslim community to modernize by changing its identity. Aligarh made it possible for a large number of Muslims to finally leave behind the "Mughul" society of the early-nineteenth century, in which Muslims identified primarily with family and lineage, and through these with the Mughul political system. At Aligarh University young Muslims discovered a new political identity. The Aligarh generation began to seek for themselves and for the members of their community a political future in which they could practice their religion in comfort and in which they could preserve their culture from being overrun by the more numerous Hindus. In many ways Aligarh prepared the ground in which Muhammad Ali Jinnah could plant the seed of Pakistan—a separate homeland for the Muslims of British India. For this seed to sprout and grow, however, the political waters of the other two communities of Muslim India were needed.

The other Muslim communities, those in the northwest and northeast, by and large remained untouched by the reform movement that affected the Muslims in the central provinces and by the growing sentiment that the Muslims of British India must aggressively seek a separate identity for themselves. This was the case in particular for the Muslim community of India's northwestern provinces—Punjab, Sindh, and the Frontier—where, as already noted, the Muslims were comfortable with their present situation as well as with their future prospects. If Aligarh touched this community, it was only slightly. Some prominent families from the northwestern provinces sent their sons to Aligarh; but these sons, after graduation, seldom returned to their families. Aided by modern education and in full command of English, they usually found their way into either government service—into the various branches of the civil administration or the army—or into one of the many modern professions. Many of the Aligarh graduates from the northwest were to play very significant political roles in Pakistan. In these roles they were torn between the teachings of Aligarh—the virtues of parliamentary democracy and laissez-faire economics—and the values of the society to which they belonged, which favored paternalism and statism.

Towards the Demand for Pakistan

Although the leadership of the Pakistan movement came essentially from among the Muslim minority provinces of British India—Muhammad Ali Jinnah was from Bombay; Liaqat Ali Khan, his principal lieutenant, was from a small Punjab city on the border of the United Provinces; Chaudhry Khaliquzzman was from the United Provinces; the Nawab of Bhopal and the Raja of Mahmudabad were from two of the several princely states in and around the Central Provinces; I. I. Chundrigar was from Bombay—the Pakistan movement would not have developed the force it did without winning the support of the Muslim-dominated provinces in the northwestern and northeastern parts of the country. Initially, the idea of Pakistan was slow to take hold. Once it caught on in Bengal, parts of Assam, Punjab, Sindh, Balochistan, and the Northwest Frontier Province, the emergence of Pakistan became inevitable. But it was a different dynamic that brought about the conversion of these three Muslim communities to the idea of Pakistan. It was political frustration that persuaded the Muslims of the north-central provinces to opt for the idea of Pakistan; religion played an important role in winning over the northwestern Muslims; and social and economic deprivation were the main reasons for the support eventually given by the northeastern Muslims to the demand for Pakistan. Each of these three dynamics deserves a further word of explanation.

Muslims of Central India and the Demand for Pakistan

The collapse of the Mughul empire was eventually to take the Muslims of the central provinces of British India toward partial secularization and modernization. But there was a long period of agonized soul searching in between, a period during which a number of Islamic revivalist groups fought, at times bitterly, with the modernists for the control of the minds of this community. Success ultimately came to Sir Sayyid; his efforts brought the Muslims back from self-imposed exile.

During the first three decades of the twentieth century, the Muslim University at Aligarh had an extraordinary impact on the Muslim community; thousands of its young graduates went into the field of government, law, medicine, finance, industry, and commerce. These were new areas for the Muslims of India; without some form of presence within them, it would not have been possible for the Muslims to set up a modern political apparatus. Previous to the emergence of the Muslim League, political organizations among Muslims had taken the form of religious parties aiming at the revival of Islam. None of these parties had sought to play a secular political role. The Muslim League, under the leadership of Jinnah, provided a potent political weapon to the Muslims of India. There is, of course, no reason why the establishment of a modern political party should have led the Muslims of India toward the partition of India. For more than three decades the Muslim League had fought for the protection of Muslim rights within one Indian polity. It was only when the Muslims perceived that they could not gain these rights without establishing a state of their own that many of them—especially those in the north-central provinces—were attracted to the idea of Pakistan.

Whether the British administration in New Delhi or the provincial administrations set up by the Hindu-dominated Indian National Congress after the elections of 1937 discriminated against the Muslims is a question that has attracted a great deal of debate. It is not necessary to settle the debate one way or the other; what is important is to emphasize that, in politics, perceptions are often much more important than reality, and in the early years of the twentieth century many Indian Muslims came to feel this tension.

By the mid-1940s a very large number of Indian Muslims had convinced themselves that their community would be at a very serious disadvantage in a state under the political and economic control of non-Muslims. Reference has already been made to the modes of life and attitudes of mind that separated the Indian Muslim from the non-Muslim, especially the Hindu. Two events, one in 1937 and the other in 1946, were to lend political color to this feeling of separation.

In 1935, after failing to get various Indian groups—the Hindus, the Muslims, the Princes—to agree to a political solution to the "Indian Problem," the British promulgated the Government of India Act of 1935. The act was described by the British themselves as "their last and, in the event, most portentous essay in balancing and ruling India." The core of the act was the establishment of autonomy with a representative parliamentary system of government for 11 provinces of British India. These provinces—and also the princely states, it was hoped—were expected to join an all-India federation. The federation itself was to have a representative parliamentary system. But the act failed to produce a political balance; when provincial elections were held in 1937 under the provisions of the act, the Hindu-dominated Indian National Congress formed governments in 8 out of the 11 provinces. The Muslim League captured only 104 out of 489 seats reserved for Muslims, most of them in the north-central provinces. In the Muslim-majority provinces it performed very poorly; in Punjab it won only one of 86 Muslim seats, in Bengal, 37 out of 119 seats.

Even this poor showing would not have sent the Muslim League on a separatist route if the Congress had managed to assuage the fear of the Muslims in the minority provinces. It was expected that the Congress would include the representatives of the League in the administration of those provinces in which the latter had showed considerable electoral success. These were the north-central provinces. This the Congress failed to do: The administration in the United Provinces included two Muslims, one from the Congress, the other a renegade Muslim Leaguer; in the Central Province, a deserting League member joined the administration; in Bombay the Congress turned to an "independent" Muslim. "In the light of these consequences, the Congress policy, though politically understandable, was a blunder of the first order. It is often attributed to Pandit Nehru," said a contemporary historian.[5]

On March 23, 1940, at a crowded open meeting held in Lahore, a number of prominent leaders of the Muslim League moved a resolution demanding the separation of the Muslim majority areas into independent states in which the Muslims of British India would be permitted to lead their lives according to their political, social, and religious culture. Jinnah—who came to be called Quaid-e-Azam (the Great Leader) by his large and devout following—was now convinced that India was not inhabited by one community of Indians, but by two nations, one Hindu and the other Muslim. But the idea of Pakistan did not originate with him: Muhammad Iqbal, the "poet philosopher," had suggested it earlier as an objective that the Indian Muslim community should begin to work toward. Having campaigned for Hindu–Muslim unity for more than two decades, Jinnah reached the same conclusion reluctantly, and much later than Iqbal. Once he reached it he was prepared to employ all his formidable political skills and expertise into bringing about the partition of British India.

That a nation should be split in two by a religious conflict was not new in the contemporary world. But the conflict between Hindus and Muslims ran very deep. It was not only religion that separated these two groups of people, but whole modes of life and attitudes of mind. Each was a permanent hereditary group, without intermarriage (save most exceptionally at the highest and lower social extremes) or internal absorption. It is, therefore, not only for the sake of completing the historical record that the story of modern-day Pakistan should begin long before the independence day on August 14, 1947. A historian must go back a number of years and discover the ways in which and the reasons for which the Indian Muslims accepted the idea of Pakistan. The explanation for a number of developments—economic, political, and social—that were to occur later are to be found in the politics of their conversion to the Pakistan idea.

Jawaharlal Nehru was also responsible for the other important political event that confirmed to the Muslims of India that the creation of a separate homeland was the best possible outcome for them. This happened in 1946. Before concluding that it was not possible to leave to the Indians a united India, the British made one more attempt to find a solution for the Indian problem. The government of Prime Minister Clement Attlee in London sent a three-man Cabinet Mission to explore with the leaders of India some way for keeping the provinces together. Their exploration led to the formulation of the "Cabinet Mission Plan," which suggested an Indian confederation of three units, with the rather pedestrian nomenclature of A, B, and C groupings. Two of these groups of provinces were to be formed from the Muslim majority states and provinces in the northwest and northeastern parts of the country; the rest of India made up the third group. What probably won the support of the Muslim League for this plan was the provision that after a decent interval of time—the duration of which was left undefined by the Cabinet Mission, but was generally believed to be 15 years—any of these three groups could opt out of the federation.

The Congress called the plan "the plan to get Pakistan by the back door"; however, after the Muslim League had accepted the plan, the Congress also gave it its approval. According to Maulana Abdul Kalam Azad, "the acceptance of the Cabinet Mission Plan . . . was a glorious event in the history of the freedom movement in India. . . . We rejoiced but we did not then know that our joy was premature and bitter disappointment awaited us."[6] Jawaharlal Nehru, by declaring in public within one month of the Congress acceptance of the plan that his party reserved the right to block the secession of any of the groups from the Indian union, killed Maulana Azad's joy and also the prospect of keeping India united. In retrospect, it has been argued by many historians that the plan was unworkable; that Nehru was justified in withdrawing his support; that, had the plan been implemented, the provision that allowed federating units the right to secede would have eventually divided India into at least three states.

In retrospect, it can also be argued that the outcome the opponents of the plan feared did come about; that, 25 years after the announcement of the plan, British India did split into three states; that, had the plan been accepted by Nehru and his colleagues, the emergence of Pakistan and Bangladesh would probably have been achieved with less bloodshed and less trauma; that, having spent 15 years together within the framework of one federation, India, Pakistan, and Bangladesh, even as independent states, might have been able to work together in greater harmony.

The rapidly unfolding events of the summer of 1946—first the acceptance of the Cabinet Mission Plan by both the League and the Congress, then the unilateral rejection of some of its features by Nehru, then the League's total withdrawal from negotiations—left the Muslim leadership of the central provinces convinced that they had to work for the establishment of Pakistan. Jawaharlal Nehru's clumsy handling of the discussions with the Cabinet Mission confirmed the fears of these Muslims that their political, economic, and social rights would not be protected in a Hindu India.

The summer of 1946 was an important milestone on the way to Pakistan; but for an independent Muslim state to be created, support had to be obtained from the provinces—especially the populous provinces of Punjab and Bengal—for the idea of Pakistan. Right up to this time these provinces had withheld this support; now they quickly climbed on the Pakistan bandwagon. The circumstances that converted Punjab and Bengal to the idea of Pakistan were very different from those that had persuaded the Muslims of north-central India. In these reasons lie the seeds for much that was to happen later in the history of the areas of British India that now form the states of Pakistan and Bangladesh.

Punjab, Sindh, and the Northwest Frontier Province and the Idea of Pakistan

Islam does not separate religion from state. In the strict meaning of the term—at least in the sense that has come to be understood after Ayatollah Khomeini's revolution in Iran—Mughul India was not a Muslim state. Nevertheless, the Mughuls did not always keep the affairs of the mosque separate from those of the state. Whenever and wherever religion was strong— in particular, whenever the institutions of religion were stronger than those of the state—the Mughuls were happy to bring about a fusion between the two. Such a fusion occurred in the rural areas of Punjab and other northwestern provinces of Mughul India. In the Punjab the *khanqas*—local shrines generally run by hereditary leaders called *sajjada nashins*—thus came to be integrated into the complex system of administrative and political controls that the Mughul Court operated from Delhi. "By the end of the Mughul period, therefore, the religious influence of many of the sajjada nashins as custodians of the local outposts of Islam had become closely associated with their political influence as local outposts of the Muslim state."[7]

The British did not disturb this arrangement; they continued to rely on the support of the landlords and sajjada nashins for controlling the countryside. It proved to be a wise policy. When the Muslims of the north-central provinces mutinied against the British raj, their co-religionists in the northwest not only remained loyal but also helped to put down the rebellion. But the northwestern provinces could not have remained impervious to the ferment that was taking place in the areas to their south—in Delhi and in the old Mughul province of Oudh. There were two aspects to this ferment: one, religious, which urged the Muslims to return to the ways of Islam now that they had lost the umbrella of the Mughuls; the other urged the Muslims to recognize the changes that had occurred in their environment and to adapt to them.

Given the fact that the Muslim communities of Delhi and Oudh were urban communities with a high level of literacy, albeit in Persian and Urdu, it is not surprising that the modernists under Sir Sayyid triumphed over those who sought the revival of Islam. Having failed in the north-central provinces, the revivalists turned to Punjab and Sindh where the Chisti Muslim order founded a number of khanqas in the countryside. If the British had dismantled the arrangement that the Mughuls had used to bring their rule to the northwestern provinces, there can be no doubt that the revivalists would have caused a great deal of trouble for the raj. But the British retained the system and the new khanqas were obliged not to work against the interest of the established order. Consequently, Muslim politics in the northwestern provinces remained dormant for more than a century after the incorporation of Sindh, Punjab, and the Northwest Frontier Province in British India.

Jinnah and the Muslim League initially misread this situation; being urban, modern, and relatively secular, they showed considerable distaste for the established order in the northwestern provinces. Whatever support they won was from the small community of urban Muslims of this area; as this part of British India was much less urbanized than the parts to which Jinnah and many of his more important colleagues belonged, it is not surprising that their performance in the elections of 1937 was so poor that the League, as discussed previously, was able to win only one of the 87 seats reserved for Muslims in the Punjab legislature.

Jinnah's failure to obtain constitutional concessions from the Congress —his failure, especially, in getting Muslim Leaguers included in the provincial administrations formed by the Congress after the election of 1937, and Jawaharlal Nehru's about-face on the proposals submitted by the Cabinet Mission—seemed to have convinced the Muslim leadership that the only alternative left to it was to campaign for the establishment of Pakistan, that such a campaign could succeed only if the Muslims in the Muslim majority areas gave it their support, and that this support could be gained only on the grounds of religion. One direct consequence of the failure of the Cabinet

Mission Plan was, therefore, to change the political language of the Muslim League; a religious idiom now came to be used. It was no longer the protection of the economic, social, and political rights of the Muslims of India that was at issue: What was at issue was the provision of a safe haven for the followers of Islam.

With the use of this idiom, the Muslim revivalists were able to provide Jinnah and his Muslim League with an altogether new image. Even the non-religious leadership took up the new slogan. Shaukat Hayat Khan, the son of Sir Sikander Hayat Khan, who as the chief minister of Punjab had kept Jinnah and the Muslim League at bay, found himself declaring that Pakistan would have a "government of the Quran." The conversion of Punjab, and with it of other provinces of the northwest, was complete. Consequently, the League won a comfortable electoral victory in 1946: This victory, along with the turn of events in Bengal, assured the Muslims the establishment of the state of Pakistan. "The most vital religious support for Pakistan came from the sajjada nashins of the revival shrines, who had long sought an outlet for expressing their religious concern in the political arena."[8] In the election of 1946 the Muslim League won 54 seats in the Punjab, 65 percent of the total allotted to the Muslim population of the province. This was indeed a great triumph; nine years earlier, in the election of 1937, the League had gained only one seat.

Bengal and the Idea of Pakistan

Social considerations brought the Muslims of the north-central provinces to demand the establishment of Pakistan, a separate homeland for the Muslims of India; religion, especially in a revivalist form, persuaded the Muslims of the northwestern provinces to embrace this idea a few years later; a growing feeling of social deprivation was finally to win over the Muslims of the northeastern provinces to this idea. The economic situation of the Bengali and Assami Muslims was considerably weaker than those of the Muslims from other communities and was to become the main reason for their conversion to the idea of Muslim separatism. Now wise to the ways of Muslim politics in India, Jinnah was prepared to tailor his approach to the different circumstances of his co-religionists in different parts of the country. The large Bengali and Assami Muslim peasantry wanted protection from the predatory practices of the Hindu landlords. Jinnah's Muslim League was prepared to promise such protection.

This it did by bringing into its fold A. K. Fazlul Haq, Sher-e-Bengal (the tiger of Bengal). He was, as noted previously, one of the cosponsors of the Lahore resolution that demanded the setting up of a separate homeland for the Muslims of India. But advocating "partition" as a way of protecting the rights of a minority community or the rights of a majority community if it was economically underprivileged—as were the Muslims in Bengal—was not something new for Fazlul Haq. He was one of the several politicians who had earlier convinced the British that the partition of Bengal into two provinces—the east dominated by the Muslims and the west dominated by the Hindus—was the only way of improving the economic circumstances of this Muslim community. A movement was launched to get the British to annul the partition; it was called *swadeshi* or "own country" agitation because it encouraged not only the boycotting of British goods but also the production and use of Indian-made products. The swadeshi movement succeeded in its objective and the British administration reunited the two parts of Bengal. Fazlul Haq was unhappy:

> I can assure the [British] officials that the Muslim community of Bengal can well survive the effects of even the most unsympathetic administrative measures and they will also survive the injustice done to them by the annulment of Partition. . . . I refer to the annulment, because I wish to protest against the manner in which the feelings of an entire community had been trampled under foot in utter indifference to the principles which have all along guided British rule in their country.[9]

The annulment was a bitter blow to the aspiration of the Muslims of Bengal. They had to wait another six decades before they were able to obtain what they maintained to be their legitimate right. The emergence of Bangladesh as an independent state in December 1971 gave the Bengalis what they had long aspired for: a political entity that allowed full expression of Bengali Muslim nationalism. But before this could happen, India had to be partitioned first on religious grounds. It was only with the creation of Pakistan in 1947 that Bangladesh was to become possible in 1971.

The annulment of partition provided the Bengali Muslim community with a political cause that lay dormant for nearly three decades. It was only in the late 1930s that the Bengali Muslims once again began to think in terms of partition and separation—this time not only for themselves but for all Muslims of British India. Fazlul Haq joined Jinnah in drafting and sponsoring the Lahore resolution. In presenting the resolution to the 1940 Lahore meeting, he reminded his audience of the long tradition of Muslim nationalism among the people of Bengal:

> Though I am leading a coalition government in Bengal, I am Muslim first and Bengalee afterwards. . . . It was in Bengal in the year 1906 that the flag of [the] Muslim League was first unfurled and now it is my privilege as the leader of Bengal to move the resolution for homeland of the Muslims from the selfsame platform of the Muslim League.[10]

The passage of this resolution on March 23, 1940, was the first step toward the partition of British India and toward the emergence of Pakistan as an independent Muslim state. The state of Pakistan, therefore, was the product of a number of different aspirations expressed quite unambiguously by three rather different Muslim communities of British India. It was because of the extraordinary political genius of Muhammad Ali Jinnah that these aspirations could be accommodated within one movement; that Bengalis, Punjabis, and Muslims of United Provinces could work together resolutely toward one political objective: the attainment of Pakistan. For seven years—from the passage of the Lahore Resolution in 1940 to independence in 1947—all differences were brushed aside as Jinnah led his Muslim League to electoral victories in all the provinces that were important for the future state of Pakistan.

But what kind of country did the Muslims create for themselves in the territory of British India, where they constituted a majority? It was meant to achieve different things for different people: emancipation from the Hindu landlords for the peasantry of Bengal and Assam; the creation of new economic and political opportunities for the frustrated urban Muslim classes of Delhi, Bombay, and the United and Central Provinces; establishment of an Islamic state for the *pirs* and *sajjada nashins* of Sindh, Punjab, and the Northwest Frontier.

Certainly the task was not easy; to this day it remains unfinished. Bangladesh, the eastern wing of a two-winged country, left in 1971 after a bitter conflict and a civil war; and the western wing, the modern-day Pakistan, once again began the arduous task of nation building that remains unfinished to this day.

Six Periods in Pakistan's History

The remaining part of this introduction will deal only with the new Pakistan—the country that emerged after the secession of East Pakistan as Bangladesh in December 1971. As suggested, it is important to include a discussion of Bengali Muslim nationalism in order to understand the dynamism of the extraordinary political movement that culminated in the creation of Pakistan. To appreciate the history of modern Bangladesh, even when it formed the eastern wing of the country, is less relevant.

Pakistan's evolution is best understood if its 50-year history is divided into six periods. The first period lasted for 11 years, from 1947, the year of Pakistan's birth, to 1958 when the Pakistani military first intervened in politics. The second period covers 13 years of the first long military rule, from October 1958 to December 1971. The third period, from December 1971 to July 1977, witnessed the emergence of the first strong political government led by a civilian politician. The fourth period lasted for 11 years from 1977 to 1988 when Pakistan was under the rule of the military. The fifth period saw the reappearance of democracy. This period lasted for nearly 9 years and ended with the induction of the second strong political government led by a civilian politician and commenced the start of the sixth period in the country's history.

A Struggling Democracy (1947–1958)

For two reasons Pakistan found it difficult to overcome the trauma of partition. It took the country more than 11 years to create the environment within which the lingering pangs of birth could be dealt with. To begin with, although the sister state of India could continue with the institutions established by the British, Pakistan had to start with a completely new state. A new government, with new ministries and departments, moved to a new capital, Karachi. A new diplomatic corps had to be organized and a new military force had to be created. A new currency had to be printed; for several months, Pakistan used the Indian rupee with the word "Pakistan" stamped on it as its legal tender. A new central bank had to be established. A new court system had to be set up. All of these were daunting tasks.

All this was made even more difficult in light of the second problem partition brought to the new country. Within a few months of Pakistan's creation, it received eight million Muslim refugees from India, while six million Hindus and Sikhs left in the opposite direction. Nobody had expected a transfer of population of this magnitude. When the first population census was taken in February 1951, 30 months after the country's birth, West Pakistan, the western wing of the country, had been thoroughly cleansed ethnically. The proportion of Muslims living in this area had increased by 15 percentage points, going from 79 percent to 94 percent of the total. It also had a large number of foreign-born citizens; one out of every four West Pakistanis was a refugee. Resettling eight million refugees, a very large number of whom were economically destitute, occupied most of the energies of the new government. The exchange of population also had a profound social and political impact, the full implication of which has still not been totally grasped.

The refugees came in two streams. One stream originated in the north-central provinces of British India and went to Karachi and other cities of Sindh. The people in this stream quickly assumed control of most of the modern institutions created after independence. They staffed the civil administration; set up businesses; and went into such modern professions as banking, law, medicine, and teaching. Because their political base was narrow, they were not in a great hurry to establish modern political institutions they, because of their small number, could not dominate. The other stream of refugees came from the eastern districts of Punjab, which were now part of India. The people from this stream settled mostly in Pakistan's Punjab and took over the land and agricultural businesses vacated by the departing Hindus and Sikhs. The armed forces also offered employment opportunities to which a large number of the new settlers were attracted. The great migration from India, therefore, transformed the social scene of what was now West Pakistan. The refugees who went to Sindh took over the modern sectors of the economy and dominated most institutions of government. The refugees who settled in Punjab carved a niche for themselves in agriculture and entered the armed forces in large numbers.

The fact that most established leadership groups in what was now West Pakistan had not been warm to the idea of Pakistan created political space for the new arrivals at the top of the political structure. Operating from the top, the refugees sought to broaden their base but because this was a time-consuming task, Pakistan's political development proceeded very slowly. However, neither of these two streams of migrants had formed clear views on what kind of political structure it wanted the country they helped create to adopt. The host population, comfortable with the institutions the British had created—or adapted from the systems operated by the Sikh and Mughul rulers—would have preferred a strong executive capable of delivering the services they wanted. Enthusiasm for the Islamic revivalist sentiment that had grown during the campaign for the establishment of Pakistan had created the expectation that the new country would Islamize some of the established systems. Some elements within the host population, therefore, wished to introduce some Islamic features into the mode of governance. The presence of East Bengal added the fourth variable to this complicated political equation. The result was a political impasse that lasted for nearly nine years, at the end of which sprang Pakistan's first constitution.

The institutions the Constitution of 1958 sought to establish, however—a parliamentary form of government, a federation of states with a fair degree of decentralization, an independent judiciary, and the separation of the mosque from the institutions of state—had few strong supporters in West Pakistan. It reflected more the wishes of the eastern wing of the country. Accordingly, the Constitution was not seriously mourned when it was abrogated 31 months after its adoption.

The structure of Pakistani society as it evolved after the country was born also had a profound impact on the way its economy developed during this period. With the refugees from north-central India in control of most institutions of government and with the National Assembly not powerful enough to influence economic decision-making, the policy-makers were able to deflect the government's resources away from the sectors dominated by the host population. Agriculture was starved of resources, while the new sectors of manufacturing, large-scale commerce, and construction were lavished with funds. India's decision to terminate all trade with Pakistan in 1949 further helped the pace of industrialization. The first period in Pakistan's history witnessed only a modest increase in the rate of growth of the gross domestic product, a sharp increase in industrial production, and stagnation of agricultural output. Although its western provinces had been known as the granary of India, by 1954 Pakistan had become a net importer of food grains.

First Military Period, 1958–1971

When General Ayub Khan, the first Pakistani to command the army, began to plan the military takeover, he was convinced that his move would have popular support. There were many reasons for his confidence. The political chaos of the previous 11 years, economic dislocations caused by the trade war with India, and the resentment of the host population over loss of power to the refugee community were some of the factors that had created a deep crisis of governance in the country. Pakistan was ready for a dramatic change and it came in October 1958 in the form of military rule. Ayub Khan and his associates moved with caution. The first step was to persuade General Iskander Mirza to issue a proclamation putting the country under martial law. This was done on October 8 and Ayub Khan was appointed chief martial-law administrator. The second step was taken on October 27 when President Mirza was persuaded to resign and Ayub Khan took over as president.[11]

It took Ayub Khan four years to decide on the political structure he needed to govern. He wished to accomplish two things: First, he wanted to bring the indigenous population back into the political fold. He chose an ingenious device for accomplishing this objective. A system of local government—the Basic Democracies—was put in place that gave significant powers to local communities and also brought them closer to the instruments of the state. In the constitution promulgated in 1962, 80,000 Basic Democrats, 40,000 from each wing of the country, and directly elected by the people became, in turn, the electoral college for choosing the president and the members of the National and Provincial Assemblies. Second, the new constitution provided a strong executive at the center, thus bringing back the figure of great political authority with which West Pakistan's indigenous population had become so familiar while the Mughuls, Sikhs, and British ruled these areas. The Constitution of 1962 was thus able to "indigenize"[12] the politics of West Pakistan that had been so disturbed by the arrival of millions of refugees from India.

By relocating the capital from Karachi to Islamabad, a new city built near Rawalpindi, the headquarters of the Pakistan army, Ayub Khan helped to further erode the political power and the control of the refugee community on public institutions. The landed aristocracy, discredited earlier by its failure to enthusiastically support the Pakistan movement, walked into the political space the refugee community was forced to vacate. This was, of course, deeply resented by the refugees, who many years later proclaimed themselves a separate nationality—separate from the Balochis, Pathans, Punjabis, and Sindhis and organized themselves under the banner of a new political entity called the Muhajir Qaumi Mahaz. On the other hand, the landlords were pleased to be back on the center stage of politics. No man better personified this development than Nawab Amir Muhammad Khan Kalabagh, who as governor of West Pakistan wielded the kind of power and influence possessed by the governors of the days of the British raj. Pakistan's political culture returned to the values held in the first half of the twentieth century.

Ayub Khan's social and political engineering brought stability and laid the ground for the remarkable economic progress made during the "decade of development." During the 1958–69 period, the gross domestic product (GDP) increased at the annual rate of 6.7 percent. Consequently, when Ayub Khan was forced to leave office, Pakistan's GDP was twice the size of the 1958 GDP. Agriculture led this recovery; in the late 1960s Pakistan witnessed what came to be called the "green revolution"—a sharp increase in agricultural productivity fueled by the adoption of high-yielding wheat and rice varieties. With small- and medium-sized farmers at the vanguard of this revolution, there was a palpable improvement in income distribution in the countryside. The effect of the revolution was also felt in the small towns that provided services and markets for the rapidly modernizing agricultural sector.

While the countryside was in the throes of the green revolution, large-scale industries continued to expand, moving into new product lines and into new areas of the country. Under Ayub Khan, Punjab and the Northwest Frontier also began to industrialize. Had the political sector been more accommodating, the economic progress achieved during the Ayub Khan period might have been sustained. The virtual exclusion of large segments of the population—in particular the muhajir community of Karachi and the urban professionals—created considerable resentment against the regime, the extent of which surprised the ruling elite. The active opposition Ayub Khan faced in the presidential elections of 1965 was the first manifestation of this growing sentiment. It was contained briefly by the September 1965 war with India, but resurfaced with even greater force following the end of the war and the signing of the Tashkent agreement with India in 1966. Zulfikar Ali Bhutto, Ayub Khan's foreign minister, left the government, accusing the president of surrendering at Tashkent what he believed had been achieved on the battlefield. In March 1969 Ayub Khan was forced out by the military, which now considered him a liability rather than an asset.

General Yahya Khan, Pakistan's second military president, saw the country's breakup. His handling of the political agitation that resulted in Ayub Khan's removal from office unleashed political forces he was not able to contain. East Pakistan, unable to take advantage of the massive electoral victory in the general elections of 1970—the first to be held on the basis of adult franchise—rebelled against the domination of West Pakistan. After a brief but bitter civil war, East Pakistan emerged as the independent country of Bangladesh in December 1971. Yahya Khan, presiding over a demoralized country, surrendered the presidency to Zulfikar Ali Bhutto, whose Pakistan People's Party (PPP) had won a remarkable victory in the 1970 elections at the expense of the Muslim League.

A Populist Interlude, 1971–1977

The third period in Pakistan's history also began with a social revolution that was as profound as the one caused by the arrival of eight million refugees from India or the one produced by Ayub Khan's politics of indigenization at the start of the second period. Social transformation at the beginning of the third period resulted from the practice of naive socialism. Bhutto's rhetoric and the policies followed by his administration once he took office bestowed a considerable amount of political and economic power on a number of groups that had been largely excluded from the political and economic system. The socioeconomic groups that benefited during Bhutto's short tenure included the urban poor, workers in large-scale organized industries, and urban professionals.

The policies adopted by the Bhutto government to reach this new constituency were spelt out in considerable detail in the "Foundation Papers" of the PPP issued soon after the formation of the organization in 1968. The approach to be adopted was a simple one. Because the founding fathers of the PPP believed that the private sector as it was organized in Pakistan would neither benefit the poor nor bring about an improvement in income distribution, the state had to intervene directly in managing industrial, commercial, and financial assets. This approach was implemented aggressively once the PPP was in power. In a series of acts of nationalization executed in 1972–74, the state assumed control over large segments of industry and commerce operated by private entrepreneurs. It also took over all commercial banks and insurance companies. It went so far as to nationalize educational institutions that were operating in the private sector.

Bhutto believed that in order to run an economic system dominated by the state he had to concentrate political power in his hands and in the hands of his close associates. He began to subvert the constitution he had himself drafted the moment it was promulgated. The subversion was meant to take away all power from the instruments of government that he did not fully control. The powers of the National Assembly were curtailed and fundamental rights granted by the constitution were suspended. A paramilitary force—the

Federal Security Force (FSF)—was created, ostensibly to help police maintain law and order. In fact, it was used to openly intimidate and harass the regime's opponents. Even Bhutto's close associates were not spared if they dared disagree with him. There were rumors that the FSF had been ordered to kill some of Bhutto's more intransigent opponents. Later, it was one of these murders that resulted in Bhutto's receiving the death sentence and his subsequent execution.

Bhutto's social and economic policies and the way he conducted himself in office produced a number of predictable results. Of special concern for many people was the loss of political liberty. There was an expectation of a return to democracy following the end of the long military rule. Instead, Bhutto established a form of "civilian dictatorship" that was much more vicious than the military rule of Presidents Ayub Khan and Yahya Khan. Economic difficulties further aggravated the situation. There is now good understanding among economists on how this type of approach—called here *naive socialism*—can do a great deal of damage to the economy. This happens for three reasons: First, countries with a highly intrusive state of the type developed by Bhutto tend to have a higher share of the unofficial economy in total GDP. This occurs as private entrepreneurs escape government's controls and regulations and move "underground." Second, a large underground economy usually feeds corruption as the owners of assets in this part of the economy have either to bribe officials to remain hidden or have to buy services, such as protection of property and enforcement of contracts. Third, as more and more people escape underground, the government is unable to collect taxes. With the tax base narrowing, the government can longer provide the services expected of it.[13] This in turn weakens the government and affects its legitimacy. All of this occurred during the Bhutto period and ultimately contributed to his downfall.

Although some of the consequences of Bhutto's economic policies took time to materialize, the damage being done to the economy became palpable quickly. For instance, the increase in GDP slowed down to a rate only slightly higher than the rate of population growth. The result was a rise in the number of people living in poverty and deterioration in income distribution. Rigidities introduced in the labor market by policies that made it difficult for owners of firms to fire workers reduced the rate of growth of employment and, consequently, increased the number of people unemployed. Although it was not immediately apparent, Bhutto's socialism impoverished the very people he was hoping to help.

People's reactions to these developments came following the elections of 1977 in which the opposition had expected to do much better than indicated by official results. The results announced by the Election Commission indicated a massive victory for Bhutto's Pakistan People's Party. The opposition, convinced that the regime had rigged the elections, took to the streets and brought down the government. On July 5, 1977 the army, under the command of General Zia ul-Haq, intervened for the third time in Pakistan's political history. Bhutto's removal from office began the second long interval of army rule and the fourth period in Pakistan's history.

Second Long Military Rule, 1977–1988

Unlike the first three periods in Pakistan's history, the fourth did not begin with a major social change. But like the three periods before it, this period also ultimately witnessed a significant transformation of the society. This change occurred gradually but left a deep and lasting impression. By the time Zia ul-Haq left the scene—he was killed in an airplane crash that also claimed the lives of several senior officers of the army—Pakistan had been thoroughly "Islamized." It had lost much of its Western orientation and was considerably closer to the Muslim countries of West Asia.

In all probability, Zia did not assume control of the country intending to keep it under martial law for a long time and to remain in power himself for an extended period. He became involved largely because of a fear that the failure to act on his part could bring about a serious rift within the ranks of the armed forces. The ferocity with which the opposition had fought Bhutto after the elections of 1977 not only surprised the prime minister. It was also unanticipated by the army intelligence. Called to the aid of civil authority, the army had to use great force against street agitators. With casualties mounting among the agitators, middle-ranking officers in the army began to question why they were being called on to kill innocent people to protect an unpopular regime. Zia listened and decided to move against Bhutto in order to prevent the army from being politicized. Once Pakistan was placed under martial law, Zia took one thing at a time. Unlike Ayub Khan, he did not have a clear strategy for the future.

Zia belonged to the social group—urban, middle-class professionals—that had high expectations for Bhutto when he took over the reins of government. Greatly disappointed with the way Bhutto had behaved in office, this class was at the forefront of the agitation that brought down the prime minister. Zia believed that Bhutto's term in office had created a serious divide between the rulers and the middle classes. Ordinary citizens of Pakistan expected some decency from the people in power. They had seen little of that from Bhutto and his close associates. One way of closing the gap was to tell the people that the rulers were not much different from them, that they shared the same set of values. Zia believed that this message could be communicated clearly if he explicitly followed what was expected from a Muslim leader. He would bring comfort to those who had been disillusioned by Bhutto by spearheading a movement to bring Islamic values to the country. After all, Pakistan had been created for the Muslims of British India. It was now necessary to turn this Muslim country into an Islamic state. Zia's program of Islamization moved on three fronts—social, political, and economic. He was a practicing Muslim himself and set a personal example of piety and modesty that he expected his associates to follow. Zia's beliefs were the beliefs of the lower and middle classes of Pakistan. He observed the basic tenets of Islam in a very public way. Official meetings were interrupted to allow time for prayers. Prayer times were announced on public radio and television. Government working hours were adjusted to make it easier for people to fast during the month of Ramadan. Zia encouraged government officials to go to *haj* and *umrah*; he performed the pilgrimage to Mecca himself a number of times. He expected that women would stay at home and not enter the workplace.

Zia sought to bring Islam into politics in several overt ways. Although he had decided not to abrogate the Constitution of 1973 and thus had not followed the example set by Ayub Khan and Yahya Khan, he brought changes in the political structure that were supposed to make it Islamic. He nominated a *majlis-e-shura* (an assembly) to take the place of the National Assembly, which had been dissolved following the imposition of martial law. The people nominated to the assembly were supposed to be good Muslims. New clauses were inserted in the constitution to recognize in an explicit way that Pakistan was not just a country with the majority of its citizens belonging to the Islamic religion but was an Islamic state. Among the changes incorporated was the creation of the Shariat Court to ensure that all laws enacted by the legislature were Islamic. If the citizens were troubled by some legislation on the grounds that it went against the teachings of Islam, they were encouraged to go to the Shariat Court.

Efforts were also made to Islamize the economy. The most significant changes introduced by the Zia regime in its Islamization efforts related to the banking and fiscal systems. Commercial and investment banks were no longer permitted to charge interest on the loans made by them or to pay interest on the deposits kept with them. All depositors were treated as shareholders earning a return on their equity. By loaning money the banks became partners in the business for which funds were provided. The government introduced *zakat*, an Islamic tax on wealth, the proceeds from which were used to assist the "deserving." Zakat funds were managed by zakat committees that were responsible for identifying the "*mustahiqeen*," the deserving. Zakat funds were also allocated to *madrasas* (religious schools). The curriculum taught in these schools had to have the approval of boards of education set up for this purpose. Although Islam encourages private enterprise, the Zia administration made few efforts to reduce the size of the state inherited from Bhutto. A few small-scale enterprises that had been taken over by the Bhutto government were privatized but the role of the state remained large and intrusive. The tendencies detailed previously—the growth of the underground economy, increase in the levels of corruption, and the inability of the state to provide basic services to the people—continued during the Zia period.

Apart from Islamization, the Zia government left one more enduring legacy. When, in December 1979, the Soviet Union sent its troops into Afghanistan to protect the communist regime established a few years earlier, Zia enthusiastically recruited Pakistan to the cause of ridding its neighbor of communism. In this it had the support of the United States and Saudi Arabia. Pakistan became the conduit for arms that began to flow from the West to the Afghan *mujahideen* (freedom fighters); its intelligence services, in particular the Interservices Intelligence (ISI), provided active support to the Afghans and the freedom fighters were allowed to operate bases in Pakistani territory. The mujahideen won; the Soviet troops withdrew from Afghanistan in 1989 and two years later the weight of the military endeavor in Afghanistan contributed to the collapse of the Soviet Union. These successes notwithstanding, Pakistan paid a heavy price for its involvement in this conflict. For years to come it had to suffer the consequences of its support to the mujahideen, which included the flow of arms into the country and the development of a drug trade. Zia's emphasis on Islamization and his support for the war against the Soviet occupation of Afghanistan brought an exceptionally militant Islam to Pakistan. "Sectarianism"—a violent confrontation between different sects of Islam—which arrived in Pakistan in the middle of the 1990s was the direct consequence of the policies of President Zia ul-Haq.

Competitive Democracy, 1988–1997

The fifth period in Pakistan's history began with an unforeseen development: President Zia ul-Haq's death in an air crash near the city of Bahawalpur on August 17, 1988. Had Zia not died, there were indications that he would have tried to perpetuate his rule by changing the constitution. The "Islamabad establishment"—the name given by Benazir Bhutto to the coalition of groups that wielded an enormous amount of political power in Pakistan's capital and included the senior army and civil officials and the representatives of large-scale industry and commerce—was not prepared to accept this move. The group briefly toyed with the idea of putting the country back under martial law but decided in favor of accepting the constitutional provision that in case of the death of the president, he would be succeeded by the chairman of the Senate, the upper house of the national legislature. The fact that Ghulam Ishaq Khan, a veteran civil servant turned politician, occupied this position contributed to this decision. Khan was a prominent member of the Islamabad establishment.

The caretaker regime headed by the acting president decided to hold elections in October 1988 and when Benazir Bhutto's PPP won the most seats in the National Assembly, the establishment then decided to offer her the prime ministership provided that she accepted some conditions. These included the formation of an informal governing council made up of the president, the prime minister, and the chief of the army staff. This arrangement came to be known as the "troika" and was responsible for making all important decisions. When Bhutto tried to free herself of this constraint she was dismissed under Article 58.2(b) of the constitution, which had been inserted by President Zia ul-Haq. Another general election in October 1990 brought Mian Nawaz Sharif, a Zia protégé, to power. He too felt constrained by the "troika" arrangement and his efforts to gain independence met with the same fate—dismissal by President Ghulam Ishaq Khan under Article 58.2(b).

Sharif appealed his dismissal to the Supreme Court and won his case. He was reinstalled as prime minister but the president refused to cooperate. A constitutional crisis was the result of these maneuvers. The crisis was resolved by the army, which worked behind the scenes, forcing both the president and the prime minister out of office. Yet another election was held in October 1993 and resulted in Benazir Bhutto coming back to Islamabad as prime minister. The main lesson Bhutto learned from her previous occupation of this office was to get one of her loyal lieutenants to be elected president. Farooq Ahmad Khan Leghari became president in December 1993 and served under Bhutto's shadow for nearly three years. He surprised her in November 1996 by using Article 58.2(b) to send her out of office. The people of Pakistan went back to the polls again in February 1997 and presented an overwhelming mandate to Nawaz Sharif, the leader of the opposition and the president of the Muslim League.

The fact that Pakistan held four elections, had three administrations, and saw its prime ministers being dismissed three times by its presidents suggests extreme political instability during this period. The reason for this was simple. The country had failed to bridge the great divide that separated the structure of the society from the structure of the political system. The society had evolved rapidly since independence. A number of new socioeconomic groups had emerged that wanted to carve out a place for themselves in the political structure. This was not provided, because the political system remained dominated by one socioeconomic group: the landed aristocracy. This group, although powerful, was insecure about the future. It realized that if the political system was allowed to evolve as envisaged in the constitution, it would lose a great deal of power to the new groups. The Constitution of 1973 had provided for the reapportionment of seats in the National

Assembly on the basis of population distribution. The distribution of population was to be determined by censuses held every 10 years. This was not done; the landed interests were able to prevent a census from being held for 17 years. With the political system thus atrophied, the groups not fully represented had no choice but to resort to extraconstitutional means. Their pressure contributed to the periodic dismissals of prime ministers.

This political instability also had an effect on the economic situation. During this period the consequences of the policies adopted during the Bhutto and Zia periods continued to take their toll. The three effects of these policies already identified—the growth of the underground economy, government's inability to raise enough resources to provide basic services to the people, and increasing corruption—became even more pronounced. The leaders increasingly allowed themselves to be influenced by the group of people that recent economic literature has begun to identify as "gate-keepers." The gate-keepers were usually the relatives, friends, and political associates of those in power who were able to lay claim to large amounts of public resources by avoiding any kind of scrutiny. By the time Prime Minister Benazir Bhutto was dismissed for the second time in six years, Pakistan was perceived to be the second most-corrupt country in the world. This ranking was awarded by Transparency International, a Berlin-based, nongovernmental organization that specializes in anticorruption work.

Dealing with Postponed Structural Problems, 1997–

The elections of February 1997 brought new administrations to power not only in Islamabad, the federal capital, but also in Lahore, the capital of Punjab, the largest province. The federal and Punjab provincial governments were formed by the Muslim League, the party in opposition during Benazir Bhutto's term in office. The League governments took office with very comfortable majorities in the National and Provincial Assemblies. The party received a clear mandate from the people to set the country back on track; in particular, to provide good governance and restore health to the battered economy. The question is whether the conduct of the new leadership in its first few months in office suggests that the long-postponed structural problems are finally beginning to be addressed.

The country faces serious political, social, and economic problems. In the field of politics the main problem has been the unrepresentative nature of the system—the fact that a small number of landlords were able to exert so much influence in spite of the decline of the proportion of people living in the countryside and in spite of the reduced share of agriculture in national income. The decision by the Nawaz Sharif government to hold a population census in March 1998 set the stage for the long-delayed reapportionment of seats in the national and provincial legislatures. The second political structural problem relates to the confusion created by the informal "troika" system in which the responsibility for major decisions—and therefore the accountability for them—was divided among three individuals: the president, the prime minister, and the chief of the Army Staff. Nawaz Sharif dealt with this issue by using his comfortable position in the National Assembly to rush through some major changes in the constitution. The prime minister was able to easily introduce two amendments to the constitution, something that could not have been done by any administration during the period 1988–96, because the constitution, in order to be amended, required a two-thirds majority in both houses of the Parliament. The thirteenth amendment removed Article 58.2(b), which had been used with great frequency by presidents to dismiss prime ministers. The fourteenth amendment took away the right of the members of the Assemblies to cross party lines, a practice that had introduced a great deal of corruption into the political system. Both amendments further strengthened the prime minister. The prime minister's confrontation with the judiciary in the fall of 1997 on the issue of "contempt of court"—Nawaz Sharif had spoken of the justices of the Supreme Court in unflattering terms and the judges had responded by instituting proceedings of contempt of court against the prime minister—was only resolved with the resignation of President Farooq Leghari and the removal of Chief Justice Sajjad Ali Shah. Muhammad Rafiq Tarar, the new president, was a close friend of the Sharif family, and the Supreme Court, under a new chief justice, was content to tread with caution.

Within a year of assuming office, Nawaz Sharif, therefore, had accumulated enough power in his hands to parallel that wielded by Muhammad Ali Jinnah and Muhammad Ayub Khan during their own times. The concentration of so much power in one pair of hands had swung the pendulum to the other extreme, however. Political power was no longer dispersed among three officials, but was concentrated in one office, that of the prime minister. The question as to whether this power would be used to bring responsible governance or whether it would be deployed for personal gain as had happened in the past would be answered only in time. The first test for the new power structure came in May 1998 when India exploded five nuclear devices in an area close to its border with Pakistan, and Pakistan responded with tests of its own two weeks later. The nuclear tests and the Western response to them plunged Pakistan into a deep economic crisis, which the country was ill-equipped to handle.

The major social structural problem faced by Pakistan concerns the serious erosion of values that had occurred as a result of the policies adopted by a number of regimes over a period of four decades. As Pakistan entered the second half century of its existence, it was challenged by a serious loss of institutions that could bring good governance to the country. Increasingly, the people were forced to rely on their own devices to meet their needs. This in turn made the government dysfunctional. It is clear that the rulers must create new institutions or rebuild those that have been weakened over time in order for people to work for social betterment rather than personal gain or the gain of the families and small communities to which they belong. This institutional engineering will have to cover a number of areas: the judicial and legal systems, law enforcement, municipal and local government, educational and health systems, and so forth.

Finally, health has to be restored to the economy, which lost the dynamism of its earlier years. For four decades following independence, Pakistan was able to achieve rates of growth in its national economy—on the order of 6 percent a year—which helped it to address the problem of poverty and laid the foundation for the modernization of the economy. Foreign flows of capital played an important role in sustaining this level of growth over a period of four decades. With the geopolitical changes that have occurred following the collapse of the Soviet Union and a sharp increase in private flows of capital, countries such as Pakistan will have to rely on their own resources for financing investment and generating high rates of economic growth.

If foreign capital is to be invited into the country, Pakistan will have to demonstrate a high level of credit worthiness. This was seriously impaired by the response of the industrial world to Pakistan's nuclear tests and the way the Sharif government handled the economic crisis that resulted from the imposition of economic sanctions that followed the tests. For Pakistan to reduce its dependence on external capital, it will have to marshal domestic resources for development. Such an effort will require a deep social and economic structural change that will have to involve all segments of society. The tax system will have to be overhauled, banks will have to be restructured and privatized, public-sector corporations will have to be reformed and placed in the hands of private entrepreneurs, people will have to pay for the services they have been receiving free from the government. All these changes will require a broad consensus among different political and social groups. If this does not happen, the rate of economic growth will decline to 3 to 4 percent a year, only a little more than the rate of increase in population. With the GDP increasing at this rate, mass poverty will return to Pakistan and the country will have to face serious social and political instability as a consequence.

Notes

1. Ayesha Jalal, *The Sole Spokesman: Jinnah the Muslim League and the Demand for Pakistan* (Lahore: Sang-e-Mal Publications, 1992).
2. Abul Kalam Azad, *India Wins Freedom* (Calcutta: Longmans, 1958).
3. One of the better accounts of the Indian mutiny is to be found in Christopher Hibbert, *The Great Indian Mutiny, India 1857* (New York: Viking, 1978).
4. W. W. Hunter, *The Indian Mussulmans* (London: Tubner, 1871), 179–80.
5. A. A. Rauoof, *Meet Mr. Jinnah* (Lahore: Muhammad Ashraf, 1947), 23.
6. Azad, *India Wins Freedom,* op. cit., 58.
7. David Gilmartin, "Religious Leadership and the Pakistan Movement in the Punjab," *Modern Asian Studies* 13, No. 3 (July 1979): 498.
8. Ibid., 502.
9. A. K. Zainul Abedin, *Memorable Speeches of Sher-e-Bengal* (Barisal: Al Helal Publishing, 1978), 31.
10. Ibid., 35.
11. For information on the way he assumed power, see Muhammad Ayub Khan, *Friends Not Masters: A Political Autobiography* (London: Oxford University Press, 1967).
12. This term was first used by me in my book, *Pakistan Under Bhutto, 1971–77* (London: Macmillan, 1980), to describe the return to politics of the traditional power elite of West Pakistan.
13. There is a growing literature that examines the dynamics implied in this analysis. See, for instance, Simon Johnson, Daniel Kaufman, and Andrei Schleifer, "The Unofficial Economy in Transition," *Brookings Papers on Economic Activity,* Fall 1997, Washington, DC.

The Dictionary

⊷ **A** ⊷

ABDALI, AHMAD SHAH (1722–1773). Ahmad Khan, also known as Ahmad Shah Durrani and Baba-i-Afghan (father of the Afghan nation), ruled Afghanistan and surrounding areas for 26 years, from 1746 to 1773. He swept across the mountains into India eight times. His expedition in 1752 led to the annexation of Lahore (q.v.) and Multan thereby extending his sway over the whole of what is today Punjab (q.v.) province in Pakistan. His invasions of India had a number of major consequences for the subcontinent. They resulted in the sharp decline of the Mughul Empire (q.v.), the rise of the Marathas in India's southwest, the rise of the Sikhs in Punjab, and the emergence of Britain's East India Company (q.v.) as a political power in India. According to some Pathan politicians, the use of the name Pukhtunkhawa (q.v.) to describe the Pathan areas is not new. It can be found in the poetry of Ahmad Shah Abdali.

ABEDI, AGHA HASAN (1922–1985). Agha Hasan Abedi was born in Lucknow, the capital city of the province the British called United Provinces. His father was a tax collector for the estate of Raja of Muhammadabad, one of the many Muslim princes who retained a measure of autonomy within British India. The partition of British India in 1947 brought Abedi and his parents to Karachi (q.v.) along with millions of other Muslims who left India to come to Pakistan.

In Pakistan, Abedi joined the Habib Bank as a teller but left it in 1959 to found another bank, the United Bank Limited (UBL) (q.v.), with start-up capital provided by the Saigol family. Under Abedi's management, the UBL grew quickly and established branches in all parts of Pakistan. The members of the extended Saigol family also benefited from a close association with the bank, as they were able to draw on its assets to fund their rapidly expanding industrial empire. It was the close association of industry and finance of this type that contributed to the nationalization of both by the administration of Zulfikar Ali Bhutto (q.v.) in January 1972. With the UBL in government hands, Abedi was without a job. He was not

31

unemployed very long, however; the Bank of Credit and Commerce International (BCCI) was established in September 1972 with capital put up by the ruler of Abu Dhabi. Within a year of its creation the BCCI had established offices in London, Luxembourg, Beirut, and the Gulf States, and by 1975 it had grown into a financial institution with assets of $2.2 billion and $113 million in capital.

The BCCI continued to expand rapidly; it established operations in all parts of the world, including representative offices in the United States. There was not a single developing country of any significance in which the bank did not have an active presence. The BCCI prospered in the financial "go-go" days of the late 1980s. This period was marked by the availability of large amounts of liquidity produced by the sharp increase in the price of oil exported by the OPEC countries. The United Arab Emirates, an OPEC member, was a major supplier of capital for the new bank. The BCCI adopted an aggressive posture aimed at increasing its market share in the industrial countries. This caused it to adopt unconventional ways of attracting new customers and eventually contributed to its demise in 1991.

Two of the BCCI's operations drew the attention of bank regulators in the industrial world: heavy losses sustained in commodity dealings in the late 1980s and the impression that its managers encouraged its officers to obtain deposits without regard to their origin. That the bank had accepted deposits of money linked with drug traffic in North and South America was confirmed when it pleaded guilty to drug-laundering charges filed against it in a court in Florida in the fall of 1988. In the meantime, the bank suffered another setback. Abedi became ill, suffered a series of heart attacks, and had to receive a heart transplant. On July 5, 1991, a concerted operation organized by the Bank of England resulted in the closure of BCCI in all industrial and most developing countries. At that time the bank's assets were said to be approximately $20 billion.

ACQUIRED IMMUNODEFICIENCY SYNDROME (AIDS). Acquired Immunodeficiency Syndrome was identified as a disease in 1981. Since then AIDS is reckoned to have destroyed the immune systems of some seven million people across the world. The continent of Africa was the first victim of the disease but, by the late 1980s and the early 1990s, Asia had overtaken Africa as the area most affected by the scourge. Pakistan reported far fewer cases of AIDS than neighboring India. In India, largely as a result of millions of people living on the streets where prostitutes worked actively, AIDS became a major killer by the mid-1990s. Social taboos against prostitution and better urban conditions contained the situation in Pakistan. Social taboos also worked against the maintenance of better statistics in the country and the adoption of programs to cultivate "safe sex" habits among the people. The real incidence of the disease in Pakistan is much higher than the 40,000 reported by the government in late 1990s.

ADIL, ENVER. In 1962 the administration of President Ayub Khan (q.v.) launched an ambitious plan of action aimed at bringing a significant decline in the rate of fertility. The president called on Enver Adil, a member of the powerful Civil Service of Pakistan, to head the Family Planning Program. Adil, well known in bureaucratic circles for his exceptional dynamism and dedication, succeeded in breathing life into the program by convincing not only the government but also a number of foreign donors to provide him with generous support. He also focused on getting the message out to the people that small families were advantageous. Khushal Gharana (happy family) posters began to appear in all the major newspapers of the country and were also displayed prominently in all the major cities. Some political observers believe that Adil's highly visible campaign may have created some of the political problems— including the alienation of the powerful conservative elements in the society—to which President Ayub Khan finally succumbed in March 1969. No Pakistani administration since has focused so much attention on family planning.

AFAQ AHMED (1954–). Born in Karachi, Afaq Ahmed came under the spell of Altaf Hussain, a muhajir (refugee from India) student leader who went on to establish the Muhajir Qaumi Mahaz (MQM) (q.v.). For a number years, Afaq Ahmed was a close associate of Altaf Hussain. In 1992, however, he split with the MQM and formed his own faction and called it MQM (Haqiqi) (q.v.). It was widely believed that Afaq Ahmed's move was motivated by the armed forces, which at that point were conducting a campaign against the MQM. Afaq Ahmed and his associates, of course, denied any such association with the officialdom. After battling both the mainstream MQM and the police for two years, Afaq Ahmed announced a new political program in April 1996. He demanded the establishment of another province in Pakistan in which the muhajir community would be in a majority.

AFGHANI, ABDUS SATTAR (1952–). Abdus Sattar Afghani, a Pathan settler in Karachi (q.v.) and prominent leader of the Jamaat-e-Islami (q.v.), was the mayor of Karachi before the Karachi Municipal Corporation (KMC) was dissolved by the Sindh provincial government in 1987. The mayor's dismissal and the dissolution of the municipal corporation came after the ethnic riots in the winter of 1986–87, in which hundreds of lives were lost. In January 1988, the KMC elected Farooq Sattar (q.v.) of the Muhajir Qaumi Mahaz (q.v.) as the city's mayor, signifying a dramatic shift in the center of gravity of ethnic policies in the city, from recent migrants such as the Pathans and the Punjabis who had settled in the city in the 1950s and 1960s, to the muhajirs who came in from India in 1947.

AFGHANISTAN–PAKISTAN RELATIONS. Pakistan's relations with Afghanistan reach far back in history, to the time the area that now comprises Pakistan began to be invaded and peopled by those from the country called Afghanistan. In the eleventh century, Afghan kings installed themselves in Delhi and founded what came to be called the Delhi Sultanate. The Sultanate gave way to another invader who came into India through the Afghanistan passes. He was Babar (q.v.), the first of the great Mughuls, whose Mughul empire (q.v.) lasted until the establishment of the British colony in India. When a segment of the Indian Muslim community challenged the British in 1857 in what the British called the Great Indian Mutiny (q.v.), a large group of Muslims left India and settled in Afghanistan.

However, the collapse of the British empire in India created an expectation in Afghanistan that it could bring about an adjustment in its southern border. After all, the Afghans had never accepted the Durand line drawn by the British to demarcate the border between Afghanistan and India. Upon the departure of the British from India, the Afghans saw an opportunity. It was for this reason that they decided to withhold recognition of Pakistan after the latter gained independence in 1947. Afghanistan was also the only country to vote against the admission of Pakistan to the United Nations.

After such an inauspicious beginning it was not surprising that the relations between Pakistan and Afghanistan never became warm. Having failed to win an adjustment in the Durand line, Afghanistan chose to force a decision on Pakistan by giving its support to the "Pukhtunistan movement" in Pakistan's Northwest Frontier Province (NWFP) (q.v.). The Afghan leaders never defined the precise boundaries of Pukhtunistan, keeping vague as to the disposition of the Pukhtun areas in their own country. In 1947, Prime Minister Hashim Khan of Afghanistan said that "if an independent Pukhtunistan cannot be set up, the Frontier Province could join Afghanistan." The Afghan-inspired Pukhtunistan movement reached its climax in 1950 when, during the Jashan-i-Kabul (the Kabul festival), Pukhtunistan flags were hoisted in the city.

The Pukhtunistan campaign by the Afghan leaders soured the relations between the two countries for over a quarter century. On two occasions it led to the rupture of diplomatic relations: in 1955, when Kabul objected to the merger of the NWFP into the "One Unit" of West Pakistan (q.v.) and in 1961 when Afghanistan actively supported tribal insurgency in the northern areas of Pakistan. During the administration of Zulfikar Ali Bhutto (q.v.), there was some improvement in the relations between the countries, as the Afghan President Muhammad Daud made an attempt to pull his country out of the Soviet sphere of influence. This move by Daud may have led to his assassination and the eventual invasion of Afghanistan by the Soviet Union.

The Soviet troops entered Kabul in December 1979 and brought about a dramatic change. This event not only affected Pakistan's relations with Afghanistan, but also completely altered for a time Pakistan's geopolitical situation. As millions of Afghan refugees began to pour into Pakistan and thousands of these refugees took up arms against the invading troops from the Soviet Union, Pakistan acquired the status of a "front-line state"; it formed the front line against the expansion of the Soviet power toward the non-Communist countries of the Middle East and South Asia. The United States began to rearm Pakistan and to supply military training and material to Afghan mujahideen pursuing war against the Soviet from camps and sanctuaries in Pakistan. A number of other countries also began to assist the mujahideen war effort. These included Saudi Arabia and China. The mujahideen succeeded beyond the expectation of their friends. Not only did they stall the Soviet advance in Afghanistan, restricting its presence and therefore its influence on the country's major cities, they also inflicted a heavy economic loss on the Soviet Union, which it was unable to sustain for long. This economic loss eventually led to the collapse of the Soviet empire. After lengthy negotiations conducted in a series of meetings held in Geneva under the auspices of the United Nations (UN), Afghanistan, Pakistan, the United States, and the Soviet Union signed an accord in the spring of 1988 that permitted the Soviets to pull out their troops from Afghanistan.

The Soviet withdrawal was completed within the schedule agreed at Geneva—the last Soviet soldier was gone by December 1988—but this did not bring peace to Afghanistan. The two warring sides, President Najibullah's government and the mujahideen, continued to receive arms and equipment from their supporters. The collapse of the Soviet Union created a new situation not only for Kabul, however, but also for a number of countries in the region, including the Muslim republics of the former Soviet Union. These republics became independent in late 1991 and began to exert pressure on Pakistan and the Najibullah government in Kabul to work toward durable peace. In January 1992, Pakistan announced a fundamental change in its position with respect to Afghanistan: it accepted the UN's formula for ending the Afghan conflict. It agreed to the establishment of an interim government in Kabul with participation allowed to President Najibullah's political group, a position that was originally unacceptable to the Pakistan-based mujahideen groups but to which they eventually agreed under pressure from Pakistan and presumably the United States. But this arrangement did not last for very long. The mujahideen marched into Kabul and President Najibullah took refuge in the UN compound. Following a number of peace initiatives brokered by the UN, Pakistan, and Saudi Arabia, a government of sorts emerged in Kabul under the leadership of President Burhanuddin Rabbani.

But peace did not come to the country. In 1995, a new force emerged in the country as a group of Taliban (q.v.) (students) marched into the country from Pakistan and quickly conquered one-third of the country. Although the Taliban were able to bring the Pathan areas of Afghanistan under their control, they had great difficulty in extending their influence over the areas peopled by such other ethnic groups as the Uzbeks and Tajiks. This complication remains unresolved and almost two decades after the Soviet troops entered Afghanistan, the country remains at war. There are no signs that the ethnic groups fighting to control the areas not under the command of the Taliban will come to terms with the Taliban. In some quarters, Pakistan has been blamed for prolonging the war in Afghanistan. It is alleged to have supported the conquest of Afghanistan by the Taliban.

AFRIDI, SHAHID (1980–). Shahid Afridi entered cricket history on October 4, 1996, in a one-day match played in Nairobi between Pakistan and Sri Lanka. Afridi, playing for the first time for Pakistan, scored 100 runs off 37 balls, surpassing the previous record held by Sanath Jayasruiya of Sri Lanka who had scored 100 runs off 48 balls in April 1996 in a match played against Pakistan in Singapore. Afridi hit 11 sixes and six fours in his record-breaking performance.

AGARTALA CONSPIRACY. *See* MUJIBUR RAHMAN, SHEIKH; QADIR, SHEIKH MANZUR

AGRICULTURE. As a result of the very significant changes in Pakistan's economy since the country's birth in 1947, agriculture has lost its preeminent position. Its share in national output was much larger in 1947, the year Pakistan was born. Since then its contribution has declined as other sectors of the economy have grown in size. In 1947, agriculture accounted for 53 percent of the Gross Domestic Product; by 1998, its share had declined to less than 25 percent. That notwithstanding, as a result of the two "green revolutions" (q.v.)—one in the late 1960s and early 1970s, the other in the late 1980s and early 1990s—the agricultural sector has progressed from the state of subsistence to that of commercialization. This transformation has had a profound impact on reducing the incidence of rural poverty.

In the late 1940s—the years immediately following partition and the birth of Pakistan—less than one-fifth of Pakistan's total land area was cultivated. Fifty years later, in the late 1990s, this proportion had increased to more than one-quarter. During this period more than six million hectares of additional land was brought under cultivation, almost entirely because of an increase in irrigation. In the late 1940s, 62 percent of the cultivated land was classified as irrigated; in the late 1990s, the proportion had increased to 76 percent.

The output of all major crops increased by significant amounts in the period since independence. The largest percentage of increase occurred for cotton and the least for wheat (qq.v.). These increases were the result of both additional land devoted to these crops as well as increase in productivity. The sharp growth in the output of Pakistan's main crops helped to alleviate rural poverty, particularly in the 1960s, the period of President of Ayub Khan (q.v.). In 1960–70, for instance, food-grain output increased at the yearly rate of 5 percent and per capita food availability increased at the rate of 2.3 percent a year. There was a dramatic change in the situation in the 1970s, however, the period dominated by the socialist government of Zulfikar Ali Bhutto (q.v.). In 1970–79, food-grain output increased by 3 percent a year but per capita food availability grew by only 0.32 percent per annum. During the Ayub period, therefore, Pakistan nearly achieved food self-sufficiency. During the 1970s, however, the country once again became dependent on large amounts of food imports.

In the late 1980s, Pakistan witnessed the "second green revolution," which saw an enormous increase in both the productivity and output of cotton, the mainstay of the country's economy. The agricultural sector came under stress in the 1990s, however. Pressure on the national budget reduced public-sector expenditure on the maintenance of the vast irrigation network with the result that the availability of water per unit of irrigated land declined. The agricultural sector also had to deal with pest attacks, in particular on cotton. Consequently, in the 1990s agricultural output failed to keep pace with growth in population and increase in domestic demand.

AGRICULTURE TAX. In Pakistan, agricultural incomes have been, by and large, exempt from tax. Under the constitution of 1973 the national legislature does not have the authority to tax agricultural incomes; that power was bestowed by the constitution on the provincial assemblies in which landed interests have had a greater presence than in the national assembly.

The only serious attempt to tax agriculture was made by the administration of caretaker Prime Minister Moeen Qureshi (q.v.) in the summer of 1993. Qureshi's government used the "producer index unit" (PIU) concept to estimate agricultural incomes. This concept had been developed to implement the land reforms of 1959 (q.v.), introduced by the government of President Ayub Khan (q.v.). A PIU is calculated on the basis of national productivity of land; the value of the unit of rain-fed land, therefore, is much lower than that of canal-irrigated land. Qureshi fixed the value of one PIU at Rs.250 ($7 at the rate of exchange in January 1996). Owners with farmland worth less than Rs.1 million ($29,000) were exempt from the tax; a "wealth tax" ranging between 0.5 percent and 2.5 percent of the value of land as calculated in terms of PIUs was levied on larger farms.

Prime Minister Qureshi did not have to secure legislative approval to levy this tax because all assemblies, national as well as provincial, stood dissolved while he was in office. The wealth tax was instituted through a presidential ordinance and its levy was regarded as one of the major accomplishments of the caretaker administration.

Under the constitution, all presidential ordinances have to be subsequently approved by the National Assembly; once the National Assembly was back in business and Prime Minister Benazir Bhutto (q.v.) had replaced Moeen Qureshi, the agricultural wealth tax ran into predictable political trouble. It was ultimately endorsed by the national legislature but in a considerably watered-down version. Accordingly, the amounts collected were embarrassingly low; for instance, in the 1994–95 fiscal year only Rs.2.5 million ($71,000) was collected.

An awareness of the very low ratio of tax to gross domestic product in Pakistan and an even lower rate of taxation on agricultural incomes allowed Pakistan to be persuaded by the International Monetary Fund (IMF), as a part of the program the two sides negotiated in late 1995, to raise the value of the PIU by 60 percent, from Rs.250 to Rs.600 as a part of the budget of 1996–97. In 1996, the World Bank (q.v.) added the imposition of an agriculture tax as a condition for moving forward with its program to assist Pakistan in the modernization of the agriculture sector. It is unlikely that the pressure that was being exerted by the IMF and the World Bank would have resulted in bringing incomes from agriculture into the tax structure had Prime Minister Benazir Bhutto remained in power. Her dismissal in November 1996 provided the caretaker government that held office for three months the opportunity to move in this area. Its program—although modest in scope—succeeded in extending the fiscal system to agriculture. The program was endorsed by the government of Prime Minister Mian Nawaz Sharif (q.v.), which came into office in February 1997.

AHMAD, MIRZA GHULAM (1835–1908). Mirza Ghulam Ahmad was born into a prominent landowning family of Qadian, a small town in the Gurdaspur district of Punjab (q.v.). He is said to have received a series of divine revelations, the most prominent and controversial being the call to prophethood within the fold of Islam. Ghulam Ahmad also claimed that the prophesies revealed that he represented the second coming of Jesus Christ, who, in fact, had not been crucified but had migrated to Kashmir and had been buried there. Ghulam Ahmad founded the Jamaat-e-Ahmadiyas in 1889 and in 1901 he persuaded the British administration of India to list his disciples, Ahmadiyas (q.v.), as a separate sect of Islam.

AHMADIYAS, THE. The Ahmadiya community (Jamaat-e-Ahmadiyas) was founded in 1889 by Mirza Ghulam Ahmad (q.v.) at Qadian, a small town in the Gurdaspur district of Punjab (q.v.). Ghulam Ahmad claimed that he was in direct communion with God and was receiving revelations. One of these revelations—Ghulam Ahmad's claim to prophethood—met with intense opposition, and some ridicule from Muslim theologians. This claim ran counter to the Muslim doctrine of Khatam-e-Nubuwat (end of prophethood), which holds that Muhammad, the prophet of Islam, was the last prophet. Ghulam Ahmad's disciples called themselves Ahmadiyas; his detractors called his followers Qadianis, after the place of his birth.

The proselytizing zeal of the community, its success in bringing in new converts, its ability to run a tight organization that emphasized pursuit of common objectives by the members of the community, the success achieved by some of its members in business and Pakistan's civil bureaucracy, brought the Ahmadiyas into direct conflict with a number of religious parties and organizations in Pakistan. Jamaat-e-Islami (q.v.), the most important religious party in Pakistan, pursued anti-Ahmadiyaism with great passion. The Jamaat-e-Islami's near obsession with the Ahmadiya community was to profoundly effect not only the Ahmadiyas but the political development of Pakistan.

In 1953, the Jamaat-e-Islami, working in consort with a number of other religious organizations, launched a campaign against the Ahmadiyas. The campaign was organized under the banner raised by the Khatam-e-Nubuwat movement, which sought to draw the attention of the Muslim citizens of Pakistan to the fact that the Ahmadiyas had presented a serious challenge to one of the basic assumptions of Islam: that

Muhammad was the last prophet. The campaign turned violent, especially after equivocation by an exceptionally weak government at the center. Prime Minister Khawaja Nazimuddin (q.v.)—a Bengali politician operating in a political world basically hostile to the Bengalis—hesitated to move against the agitators. Thus encouraged, the agitators became more confident and began to seek much more than their initial demands. Their original objective was to convince the government to declare the Ahmadiyas a non-Muslim community. Now they wanted the members of the community to be dismissed from government and the assets of those who had succeeded in business and industry to be confiscated by the government. Once it was clear that the movement was out of control of the civilian authorities in Punjab—2,000 people had already been killed in the strife associated with the campaign—the federal government in Karachi (q.v.) enlisted the help of the armed forces to bring peace and order in the troubled areas of the province. A limited martial law was declared and the army, under the command of Lt. General Azam Khan (q.v.), was able to restore order quickly. The army's success in Lahore (q.v.) and other troubled cities of Punjab emboldened it and laid the ground for the coup d'etat of 1958.

The anti-Ahmadiya movement resurfaced again in 1974 and began to pressure the government of Prime Minister Zulfikar Ali Bhutto (q.v.) to move against the followers of Ghulam Ahmad. Bhutto, by this time confronting a united opposition that had also been gaining strength, decided to split the forces arrayed against him. He opted to oblige the ulemas of Islam who were spearheading the growing movement against him. The National Assembly passed a bill declaring the Ahmadiyas to be non-Muslims; subsequently, the government prohibited the Ahmadiyas to call their places of worship mosques or to decorate them with verses from the Koran, to use the *azan* (call to prayer) to summon their members for prayers, and to issue translations of the Koran. These moves by the government further encouraged intolerance toward the members of the Ahmadiya community. In 1984, 10 years after the decision to declare the Ahmadiyas to be non-Muslims, the community's head moved to London and called the annual assembly of his followers to be held in that city. That was the first time in nearly a hundred years that the Ahmadiyas had met outside India and Pakistan.

In January 1998 Pakistan elected Muhammad Rafiq Tarar (q.v.) as its ninth president. Before turning to politics, Tarar had served in several capacities in the judicial branch of the government. On several occasions he had openly expressed his contempt for the Ahmadiya community. The Ahmadiya community saw Tarar's election as one more reason for not expecting fair treatment from official circles in Pakistan.

Five million Ahmadiyas are estimated to be still living in Pakistan, whereas another million live outside the country. Those living outside are either converts from other religions or have migrated from Pakistan.

AHSEN, VICE-ADMIRAL S. M. (1920–1990). Vice-Admiral S. M. Ahsen was the commander-in-chief of the Pakistan navy—a position to which he was appointed in 1966—at the time Pakistan was placed under martial law for the second time in its history. It is not clear whether General Agha Muhammad Yahya Khan (q.v.), commander in chief of the army, consulted with Ahsen when he decided to move against President Muhammad Ayub Khan (q.v) in March 1969. Having proclaimed martial law, however, Yahya Khan asked Vice-Admiral Ahsen and Air Marshal Nur Khan (q.v.), commander in chief of the Air Force, to join him in governing Pakistan. Vice-Admiral Ahsen and Air Marshal Nur Khan were appointed deputy martial-law administrators and were also invited to join the five-member Administration Council that functioned for a few months as the supreme governing body in the country. In August 1969 Ahsen was appointed governor of East Pakistan, whereas Nur Khan was appointed governor of West Pakistan.

Once in Dacca, Ahsen came to the conclusion that the use of force was not a viable option for solving the problem of East Pakistan. He advocated political accommodation but Yahya and his colleagues were determined to keep Bengal within the fold of Pakistan, if need be by the use of military force. Whatever the reasons for his differences with Yahya, they resulted in Ahsen's resignation in 1971. Vice-Admiral Ahsen returned to Karachi (q.v.) and A. M. Malik, a veteran Bengali politician, was appointed to succeed him. Ahsen died in Karachi in 1990.

AID TO PAKISTAN CONSORTIUM. The Aid to Pakistan Consortium was formed in 1960 to lend coherence to the policies being pursued and programs and projects being financed by the donor community. The group is expected to meet in Paris every spring to discuss Pakistan's economic plans for the following financial year. It also reviews important development issues on the basis of the documentation prepared by the World Bank (q.v.) and the government of Pakistan. The outcome of the consortium meeting is issued in the form of a communiqué that expresses the collective impression of its members about the economic performance of Pakistan, the country's mid-term development objectives, and the amount of foreign flows the country requires in order to close the "foreign exchange gap." The communiqué usually announces an amount the consortium members are willing to pledge to Pakistan for the following year.

The Consortium meeting is chaired by the World Bank Vice President in charge of the region that includes Pakistan. The donor countries that normally attend the Paris meetings include all bilateral and multilateral donors active in Pakistan. The number of delegations attending the meetings has increased over time but the volume of assistance provided peaked in the late 1980s. In the 1980s, the war in Afghanistan bestowed the status of a "front-line state" on Pakistan and the Western donors were willing to provide generous amounts of financial assistance to the country to encourage it to resist the Soviet expansion into South Asia. The end of the war against the Soviet occupation of Afghanistan and the subsequent collapse of the Soviet Union reduced Pakistan's geopolitical importance and with it the generosity of the donor community. Over the years the bilateral donors attending the Paris meetings have included: Australia, Belgium, Canada, France, Germany, Italy, Japan, the Netherlands, Norway, Sweden, Switzerland, the United Kingdom, and the United States of America. In addition to the World Bank, the Consortium also has a number of multilateral donors including: the Asian Development Bank, the International Monetary Fund, Islamic Development Bank, United Nations Development Program, International Fund for Agricultural Development, International Finance Corporation, Organization for Economic Cooperation and Development, Saudi Fund for Development, United Nations High Commissioner for Refugees, and World Food Program.

In recent years the members of the Consortium have begun to put pressure on Pakistan to invest more in social development and to reduce its budget deficit. Some members of the group have also begun to take note of Pakistan's high defense expenditure, arguing that by committing large amount of resources to the military, Pakistan was starving a number of sectors of vital investments.

AJMAL KHATTAK (1924–). Ajmal Khattak was born in the Northwest Frontier Province (NWFP) (q.v.) and was active in Pathan politics for nearly four decades. He was a strong and open proponent for a loose federal arrangement in Pakistan; he was convinced that only within such a political structure would the country be able to accommodate the wishes and aspirations of the smaller provinces.

Ajmal Khattak was an active member of the National Awami Party (NAP) (q.v.). While Khan Abdul Wali Khan (q.v.) was the party's chairman, Khattak functioned as the secretary-general. In 1973 the government of Prime Minister Zulfikar Ali Bhutto (q.v.) moved against the NAP; the party was declared to be an illegal organization, allegedly working against the integrity of the state of Pakistan. Fearing arrest, Khattak escaped to neighboring Afghanistan, where he lived for 15 years in what he described as "self-exile." After the establishment of a communist regime in Kabul, Pathans on both sides of the Pakistan–Afghanistan border lost interest in creating an autonomous Pathan state. They were more interested in ridding Afghanistan of the occupying Soviet forces. That notwithstanding, Khattak continued to work for the establishment of an autonomous Pathan state straddling Pakistan and Afghanistan. This campaign, for obvious reasons, did not win Khattak many friends in Islamabad (q.v.), Pakistan's capital, especially when the government of Zia ul-Haq (q.v.) was investing so much effort in dislodging the communists from Kabul. Khattak's stance was also not popular among the Afghan mujahideen who were battling the Soviet troops in Afghanistan. He had, therefore, to wait until the departure of the Soviets from Afghanistan and Zia's death before he felt it was safe to return to Pakistan. Khattak came back to Peshawar in 1989 and once again became active in the politics of the Northwest Frontier Province. In 1996 Khattak became secretary general of the Awami National Party (q.v.).

Ajmal Khattak was also a poet; he published a dozen books of poems, one in Urdu and the rest in Pushto, his mother tongue. *See also* Afghanistan–Pakistan Relations.

AKBAR KHAN, MAJOR GENERAL (1920–1994). Major General Akbar Khan was one of the many military officers who were to perform actively on Pakistan's political stage. He first gained public attention as the senior commander in the first Indo–Pakistan war (q.v.) under the pseudonym of "General Tariq" (after the Muslim leader who crossed the Straits of Gibraltar into Spain at the beginning of the eighth century). Pakistan deployed Akbar Khan's troops in 1948 to assist the Pathan tribesmen in Kashmir (q.v.). The invasion of Kashmir by the Pathan warriors was encouraged by Pakistan once it became clear that the state's maharaja (ruler) was not anxious to accede to Pakistan. But Pakistan was not as yet prepared to get directly involved by sending its troops into Kashmir. The Pakistan commander in chief, a British officer who had stayed behind to serve the new country while Pakistan was in the process of grooming its own people to take charge, was not willing to lead Pakistan into open conflict with India. Accordingly, the Pakistani army gave the Pathans support in logistics but watched them operate from a safe distance. Akbar Khan was not happy with this passive approach.

Akbar Khan came to the attention of the public again in 1951 when he was accused of masterminding an attempt to overthrow the government of Prime Minister Liaqat Ali Khan (q.v.). The conspiracy was hatched in Rawalpindi (q.v.), the city that housed the army's general headquarters.

The case of the Rawalpindi Conspiracy (q.v.) was the first indication of the unhappiness within the ranks of the army with the way Pakistan was being run and managed by the politicians. The Rawalpindi conspirators were arrested, tried by a military court, and sentenced to serve long prison terms. Akbar Khan was awarded a life sentence by the special court.

After staying in the political wilderness for more than two decades, Akbar Khan reappeared briefly in the early 1970s as Zulfikar Ali Bhutto's (q.v.) minister of state for defense. He played a marginal role in the Bhutto Cabinet.

AKBAR, SAID (c.1925–1951). Said Akbar was an unemployed youth from the Northwest Frontier Province (NWFP) (q.v.) who assassinated Prime Minister Liaqat Ali Khan (q.v.) in Rawalpindi (q.v.) on October 16, 1951. The assassination took place in the Company Bagh—now called Liaqat Bagh—just as the prime minister had begun to address a large public meeting. Said Akbar had positioned himself close to the speaker's dais and was thus able to fire his weapon, a pistol, from close range. He was himself caught and shot dead by the police moments after he killed Liaqat Ali Khan. Said Akbar left no clues as to his motives for assassinating the prime minister. He had arrived in Rawalpindi a day before and had spent the night in a local hotel. A commission was set up to investigate the assassination but could not come to any definitive conclusion. There was a strong suspicion that the prime minister's assassination may have been ordered by a group of Punjabi politicians who wanted to capture power at the center.

AKHTAR ABDUR RAHMAN KHAN, GENERAL (1926–1988). Akhtar Abdur Rahman Khan was born in a village near Jullundhur and joined the Pakistan army soon after Pakistan achieved independence. He rose rapidly, especially under President Zia ul-Haq (q.v.) who appointed him to the critical position of Director General the Interservices Intelligence (ISI) (q.v.). Rahman's ISI functioned as the conduit of arms and funds that flowed to the Afghanistan (q.v.) mujahideen (q.v.) from the United States and Saudi Arabia. This assistance was provided to support the mujahideen effort against the occupying forces of the Soviet Union. In March 1987 Rahman was promoted to the rank of full general and appointed by the president to be chairman of the Joint Chiefs of Staff. Rahman was killed in an aircrash on August 17, 1988, which also took the life of President Zia ul-Haq.

Rahman was survived by four sons, Akbar, Humayun, Haroon, and Ghazi, all of whom lived and worked in the United States while their father was in charge of ISI and was the chairman of the Joint Chiefs of

Staff. After their father's death they returned to Pakistan and Humayun went into politics. He was elected to the National Assembly in the elections of 1990 and 1993 as a Muslim League (q.v.) candidate. The Muslim League did not give him a ticket for the elections of 1997, however. There were reports of major differences between the Rahman and Sharif families. These differences, having been resolved, Prime Minister Nawaz Sharif (q.v.) appointed Humayun Akhtar Khan to head the Board of Investment with the status of minister of state. By this time the brothers had amassed a vast fortune and had set up a number of industries.

AKHTAR HUSSAIN (1914–1986). Akhtar Hussain was one of Pakistan's many civil servants who were to perform important political roles. He was a member of the elitist Indian Civil Service (ICS) and chose to transfer to Pakistan after the country gained independence in 1947. In 1957, Akhtar Hussain succeeded Mushtaq Ahmad Gurmani as governor of West Pakistan and stayed in that position even after the country was placed under martial law by General Ayub Khan (q.v.) in October 1959. In 1959, he was appointed to chair the Land Reform Commission set up by the military government to bring about a more equitable distribution of land in the country. In 1960, Nawab Amir Muhammad Khan of Kalabagh was appointed to succeed Akhtar Hussain as governor of West Pakistan. *See also* Land Reforms of 1959.

AKHTAR MALIK, LIEUTENANT GENERAL (RETIRED). *See* MUSA, GENERAL (RETIRED) MUHAMMAD.

AL-FARAN. Al-Faran, a little-known militant group operating in the Indian part of the state of Kashmir (q.v.), gained considerable international attention in the summer of 1995 with the kidnapping of Western tourists, including an American. The group sought the release of a number of Kashmiri activists who were held in Indian jails. The Indian response was clear: They were not prepared to give in to the demands of "terrorist" groups operating in Kashmir. With the Indians holding their ground, the group attempted to increase its pressure on the government by killing one of its captives, a Norwegian tourist. The Indian position did not change and Al-Faran, after months of negotiations with the authorities, continued to hold the tourists as hostages. The group faded away from prominence as the situation in Kashmir stabilized.

AL-HUDA INSTITUTE OF ISLAMIC EDUCATION FOR WOMEN. The Al-Huda Institute of Islamic Education for Women was started in 1994 in Islamabad by Farhat Hashmi. The institute offers a number of programs that concentrate teachings of selected *surahs* of the Koran, *tajweed, seerah* of the *sahaba* (teachings of the companions of Prophet Muhammad), and *fiqh* (Islamic jurisprudence). The Institute began with only 50 students but its success led to its expansion into the other areas. The Al-Huda Model School for Girls was set up in 1996. It concentrates on teaching the Koran including *hifz* (memorizing the entire text of the holy book). Another program, the Al-Huda School of Islamic Studies, was also added the same year. In 1997, the government provided the institute with a plot of land to build a new campus. Expansion plans include starting similar institutions in other major cities of the country, including Lahore and Karachi (qq.v.).

ALI, BABAR (1927–). Babar Ali belongs to a family with deep roots in Lahore (q.v.), Pakistan's second largest city. The family also has ties to the countryside. The family has been active for many years in agriculture as well as industry. After receiving an education in the United States, Babar Ali set up Packages, one of the most successful modern enterprises in the country. Using Packages as the base, Babar Ali moved into the food-processing business. In 1974, he was tapped by Prime Minister Zulfikar Ali Bhutto (q.v.) to manage the Fertilizer Corporation of Pakistan, one of the several public-sector enterprises established by the government to manage nationalized industries. In 1993, Babar Ali returned to public life briefly as minister of finance in the caretaker administration headed by Moeen Qureshi (q.v.).

Babar Ali's most important contribution was the establishment of the Lahore University of Management Sciences (LUMS) (q.v.), a business school modeled after the Harvard Business School. The success of LUMS opened the sector of education to private initiative, an important development, as Pakistan was doing poorly in providing quality education.

ALLIED BANK LIMITED. Allied Bank Limited was one of the five state-owned domestic commercial banks to emerge from the nationalization of 1972. It was the second bank to be privatized by the government of Prime Minister Nawaz Sharif (q.v.). The privatization of the first nationalized commercial bank, Muslim Commercial Bank, had led to a court battle between two interested parties. This dispute earned a measure of skepticism for the entire privatization effort of the administration. An impression was created that the Privatization Commission, headed by Lt. Gen. (retired) Saeed Qadir (q.v.), was not able or prepared to resist the government's pressure to transfer publicly owned assets to the friends and associates of the prime minister. In handling the privatization of Allied Bank, therefore, the Commission adopted a different approach. It accepted the offer of the bank's employees to purchase it. The employees had campaigned hard to convince the government that their offer, made under the Employee Stock Ownership Plan (ESOP), would help to win back public confidence in the government's privatization scheme. The government took this advice and handed over the Allied Bank to its employees. The bank's privatization was completed in the fall of 1991 but the government continued to hold a sizable share of the institution's capital. In the 1992–93 financial year, the bank reported an impressive turnaround from the time it was under the control of the government in terms of the return on assets and the cost of doing business. Its performance under the management of Khalid Latif (q.v.) was cited as an example of the benefits that accrued to the economy from the privatization of publicly owned financial institutions.

The change of government in October 1993, which saw Benazir Bhutto (q.v.) return to power in Islamabad (q.v.) as prime minister, proved difficult for Khalid Latif, the bank's president and the person who had negotiated the privatization deal with the Privatization Commission. The government used its leverage as a large shareholder to remove Latif from office and to appoint a president it could influence and work with. Latif was sent to prison, accused of conspiring to defraud the government. He was denied bail by the courts and had to spend five months in jail before he was able to win his release.

ALL-INDIA MUSLIM LEAGUE (AIML). *See* MUSLIM LEAGUE, THE; PAKISTAN MUSLIM LEAGUE (PML), THE.

ALL-PAKISTAN MUHAJIR STUDENTS ORGANIZATION (APM-SO). The All-Pakistan Muhajir Students Organization was formed by Altaf Hussain (q.v.), a muhajir (refugee from India), of Karachi University in 1978. The APMSO's aim was to protect the interests of the muhajir students of Karachi University and other educational institutions in the city. It took a couple of years before the new organization gained acceptance among the muhajir students. Although the muhajirs constituted a majority on the campus of Karachi University, the APMSO candidates secured only 95 out of the 10,000 votes cast in the student elections of 1979. The Organization's performance improved dramatically in the elections of 1980 when it obtained 900 votes, putting it in second place after Jamiat-e-Tuleba, the student organization affiliated with the Jamaat-e-Islami (q.v.). It surpassed the Jamiat-e-Tuleba by a wide margin in subsequent elections. The APMSO's success in the muhajir student community encouraged Altaf Hussain to launch the Muhajir Qaumi Mahaz (q.v.).

ALL-PAKISTAN WOMEN'S ASSOCIATION (APWA). The All-Pakistan Women's Association was formed soon after the establishment of Pakistan. Its objective was to promote and protect the social and economic rights of women in a country where the conservative elements in the society interpreted dictates of Islam in ways that were highly detrimental to women. Mrs. Raana Liaqat, the wife of Liaqat Ali Khan (q.v.), Pakistan's first prime minister, took an active interest in women's affairs and became the first president of the APWA.

The APWA set up branches in all provinces of the country, staffed mostly by the spouses of senior government officials. As such, the organization was often not in a position to work actively for women's advancement when the government in power adopted policies that were not supportive of giving women social, economic, and political rights equal to those of men. The most important critical test for the APWA came during the presidency of Zia ul-Haq (q.v.). His administration (1977–88) introduced Islamic laws into the country that discriminated against women. The APWA proved unequal to the challenge posed by the Zia regime and several new organizations, such as the Women's Action Forum (q.v.), had to be established by women to protest and fight this encroachment on their rights.

Although the APWA was unable to help the women of Pakistan in dealing with the challenge posed by Islamists in the country, it helped hundreds of thousands of women improve their economic situation. In this mission, which included setting up training centers for women to acquire some basic skills and the establishment of retail stores that sell products made by the women in these centers, the APWA's close association with the officialdom served it very well.

ALTAF HUSSAIN (1951–). Altaf Hussain is the founder/president of the Muhajir Qaumi Mahaz (MQM) (q.v.). He was born into a lower-middle-class family that had migrated to Pakistan after British India's partition in 1947. The family was originally from the city of Agra in the Indian state of Uttar Pradesh. In Karachi (q.v.), the family lived first in government housing in Abyssinia Lines and then moved to Jehangir Road.

Altaf Hussain's first move into politics was made in 1978 when he organized the All-Pakistan Muhajir Students Organization (APMSO) (q.v.). The APMSO had to initially compete, sometimes violently, with Jamiat-e-Tuleba, the student organization affiliated with Jamaat-e-Islami (q.v.). Recurrent violence on the campus of Karachi University, sometimes at the instigation of the APMSO but more often in response to provocation by the Jamiat, resulted in the arrest and imprisonment of Altaf Hussain on August 14, 1979. This was the first of many incarcerations he was to suffer at the hands of the military authorities. His first confinement in prison lasted nine months; on his release, Altaf Hussain decided to expand his political activities beyond the campus of Karachi University. The ground for such a move had already been prepared—the APMSO had done a great deal of social work in the predominantly muhajir colonies of Golimar, Korangi, Malir, Nazimabad, and New Karachi.

The MQM was officially launched on March 18, 1984, as a movement to protect the interests and aspirations of Karachi's muhajir community. After the ethnic riots in the winter of 1986–87 involving the three largest ethnic communities of Karachi—the muhajirs, the Pathans, and the Punjabis—the leadership of the MQM decided to convert the movement into a political party and to extend its reach beyond Karachi to other cities of Sindh province, where the muhajir community had a large presence.

The National Assembly elections of November 1988 presented the MQM with the first opportunity to demonstrate its strength; it did so by capturing an impressive 11 out of 13 Karachi seats. A few days after the 1988 election results were announced, Altaf Hussain strengthened the hand of Benazir Bhutto (q.v.) by declaring his support for her, indicating, however, that even if she succeeded in forming a government, the MQM members would not join her Cabinet. In 1989, within a year of Bhutto's return to political power, relations between Hussain and the prime minister deteriorated to such an extent that he formally withdrew his support for her government.

Soon after the rupture between Bhutto and Altaf Hussain, the government decided to allow the army authorities in Karachi a free hand in launching a vigorous campaign against the MQM. The reason for the army's move against the MQM was the belief that much of the violence in Karachi could be laid at the door of Altaf Hussain and his followers. To support this view, the army authorities announced the discovery of "torture chambers" in the areas MQM considered to be its strongholds. It was claimed that these chambers were used to discipline errant MQM members. The army authorities also encouraged a split in the ranks of the MQM; a splinter group, called the MQM (Haqiqi) (q.v.) was formed. The split in the ranks of the MQM led to further worsening of the law-and-order situation in Karachi, as the members of the two groups fought pitched battles in Karachi's streets.

The problem in Karachi contributed to the decision by President Ghulam Ishaq Khan (q.v.) in August 1990 to dismiss the government of Prime Minister Benazir Bhutto, dissolve the National and Provincial Assemblies, and ask the electorate to go back to the polls for the third time in five years. The elections of 1990 (q.v.) reconfirmed the hold of Altaf Hussain on the muhajir community of Karachi and southern Sindh (q.v.). The MQM once again won 11 out of Karachi's 13 seats. It was invited to join the Cabinet of Mian Nawaz Sharif (q.v.) whose coalition, the Islami Jamhuri Itehad (IJI) (q.v.), had won a comfortable majority in the election. The MQM accepted the offer and sent its representatives to Islamabad (q.v.) while Altaf Hussain stayed in Karachi to manage the affairs of his party. The understanding with the new prime minister also proved to be short lived, however, and the MQM withdrew its support from the IJI administration. Violence returned to Karachi as the army was once again called in to deal with Altaf Hussain and his followers. For the second time in two years, the situation in Karachi resulted in the demise of the government in Islamabad. President Ghulam Ishaq Khan dismissed the prime minister and called the voters to return to the polling booths.

In the elections of October 1993 (q.v.), the MQM once again demonstrated that it had not lost any of its political appeal. While it boycotted the National Assembly elections, it participated in the elections to the Sindh Provincial Assembly in which it won almost all of the seats in Karachi and several in Hyderabad. In October 1993, Benazir Bhutto was back in power as prime minister but showed little interest in reaching an accommodation with Altaf Hussain. In late 1994, the army was withdrawn from Karachi, which resulted in a sharp escalation in violence in the city, most of it the consequence of MQM activists who battled with law-enforcement agencies. In 1995, 1,800 persons were killed in Karachi while Altaf Hussain slipped out of Pakistan and took up residence in London as an exile.

From his exile in London Altaf Hussain continued to guide the MQM, including authorizing his representatives to begin formal discussions with the administration of Benazir Bhutto to find a solution to the problem of Karachi. Numerous rounds of discussions were held but the two sides failed to bridge their differences and Karachi remained in the grip of violence for all of 1995. Benazir Bhutto's dismissal in November 1996 and the elections of February 1997 brought the MQM into the mainstream of Pakistani politics. Mian Nawaz Sharif, who took office as prime minister after the 1997 elections, invited the MQM to join the federal Cabinet. The invitation was accepted but Altaf Hussain continued to live in exile in London. However, in 1998 the MQM members resigned from the federal and provincial governments.

AL-ZULFIKAR. Al-Zulfikar was formed by Murtaza Bhutto and Shahnawaz Bhutto (qq.v.) in 1979. Named after their father, Zulfikar Ali Bhutto (q.v.), the organization's main aim was to avenge their father's execution on April 4, 1979, by the government of President Zia ul-Haq (q.v.). Al-Zulfikar initially operated out of Kabul, Afghanistan in the late 1970s and early 1980s. It moved its operations to Damascus, Syria after Afghanistan was invaded by the Soviet Union.

The organization's most spectacular act was committed in 1981 when its functionaries hijacked a Pakistan International Airlines plane on a flight from Karachi to Peshawar (qq.v.). The plane was first taken to Kabul where the hijackers killed one passenger and threw his body on the tarmac. It was then flown to Damascus. It was only after President Zia ul-Haq agreed to release more than 50 political prisoners that Al-Zulfikar released the plane and its passengers. The plane remained under the control of Al-Zulfikar for 11 days.

Al-Zulfikar was also said to have been behind the campaign launched by the Movement for the Restoration of Democracy (MRD) (q.v.) in 1983. A series of cases were filed by the Zia government against Murtaza Bhutto, which made it difficult for him to return to the country even after his sister, Benazir Bhutto (q.v.), became prime minister in 1988. He came back in 1995 and was promptly dispatched to jail where he stayed for several months.

President Zia ul-Haq's death in 1988 and the return of democracy eliminated the need for the existence of Al-Zulfikar and it disappeared from the political scene. Most of its members joined the Murtaza Bhutto wing of the Pakistan People's Party (PPP) (q.v.) after Bhutto was released from prison and formally entered politics. Murtaza Bhutto's death in September 1996 dealt another blow to Al-Zulfikar, in particular to its original membership.

AMENDMENT TO THE CONSTITUTION OF 1973, THE EIGHTH. *See* ARTICLE 58.2(b) OF THE CONSTITUTION OF 1973.

AMENDMENT TO THE CONSTITUTION OF 1973, THE THIR-TEENTH. The thirteenth amendment to the constitution was passed by the two houses of the Majlis-e-Shoora—the National Assembly and the Senate—at midnight on April 2, 1997. It was signed by the president on April 3 and published in the official gazette on April 4. The thirteenth amendment took away most of the powers that had been given to the president by the eighth amendment, including the power to dismiss the prime minister and dissolve the National Assembly. This power, given to the president by Article 58.2(b) of the Constitution (q.v.) was used four times by the president: in May 1988 by President Zia ul-Haq (q.v.) against Prime Minister Muhammad Khan Junejo (q.v.), in August 1990 by President Ghulam Ishaq Khan (q.v.) to dismiss Prime Minister Benazir Bhutto (q.v.), in April 1993 by President Ghulam Ishaq Khan against Prime Minister Nawaz Sharif (q.v.), and, finally, by President Farooq Ahmad Khan Leghari (q.v.) to dismiss Prime Minister Benazir Bhutto in November 1996. Nawaz Sharif, back as prime minister with a large majority, was anxious to take away these powers from the president.

Sharif moved secretly and with dispatch. The Senate and the National Assembly suspended the rules of business under which each operates in order to move the amendment quickly through the two houses. After the bill was passed—it had the full backing of the opposition—Prime Minister Sharif flew to Choti, the ancestral village of Farooq Leghari, to inform the president of the action taken. The president did not object to the move and agreed to sign the bill as soon as it was presented to him.

The constitutionality of the thirteenth and fourteenth amendments was challenged in the Supreme Court and on December 1, 1997 Chief Justice Sajjad Ali Shah (q.v.) ordered the suspension of the thirteenth amendment. For a few hours—and at a time when the conflict between the president and the prime minister had reached the point at which it was clear that there could be no resolution if the two feuding leaders stayed in their positions—the president had the authority to dismiss the prime minister. He chose not to use the restored power and announced his own resignation. Following the president's resignation, ten judges of the Supreme Court removed Chief Justice Sajjad Ali Shah from office. *See also* Article 58.2(b) of the Constitution of 1973.

ANTI-TERRORISM ACT OF 1997. Troubled by the growing incidence of violence in the country, some of it related to conflict among different religious, ethnic, and social groups, the government of Prime Minister Nawaz Sharif (q.v.) decided to take some extraordinary measures to deal with the situation. The Anti-Terrorism Act of 1997 was one consequence of these moves. The government's concern—if not the precise initiatives taken by it—was shared by most segments of the population. It was troubling for many people, however, that the government chose to rush the legislation through the National Assembly in a great hurry without much debate. The passage of the act was seen as one more indication of the consolidation of power in the hands of the executive that had occurred since the assumption of power by Prime Minister Nawaz Sharif.

The legislation empowered the government to prosecute people accused of terrorist acts by bypassing normal judicial channels. Special tribunals could be established that could move expeditiously by side stepping the cumbersome procedures that had to be followed by courts. The act's passage was challenged by its opponents—especially human rights activists—on the ground that it was not constitutional. In March 1998, the Lahore High Court gave the government 90 days within which to bring the provisions into line with the constitution. *See also* Terrorism.

ANWAR, KHURSHID (1912–1984). Khurshid Anwar was one of the best-known popular musicians of Pakistan. His main contribution was to popularize classical music. He was born in Lahore (q.v.) and studied philosophy before turning to music. He chose Tawakkul Hussain Khan of the Gawaliar Gharana (a music school) as his *ustaad* (teacher). His first big break came when he was invited to Bombay by A.R. Kardar, a well-known producer of Indian musicals, to write the score for *Kurmai*, a Punjabi production. The score was a great success and Khurshid Anwar stayed with the film industry for the rest of his life. He moved to Lahore after the birth of Pakistan and wrote the scores of such popular films as *Intizar, Zehr-e-Ishq, Jhoomar, Koel, Ghoongat,* and *Heer Ranja.* His last composition was for *Mirza Jat,* a Punjabi film.

ANWARUL HAQ, CHIEF JUSTICE SHEIKH (1925–1995). Pakistan's judiciary played an active role in the country's political development. It chose on several occasions to uphold the decisions of the executive on all those matters that profoundly affected politics. The "doctrine of necessity" (q.v.) was invoked to justify even the seemingly unconstitutional acts of governor generals, presidents, and prime ministers in order not to create political havoc. Chief Justice Anwarul Haq continued with this tradition when he presided over the Supreme Court for more than three years, from 1977 to March 1981.

Born in Jullundhur, East Punjab, to a prominent Muslim family, Anwarul Haq joined the prestigious Indian Civil Service (ICS). Instead of remaining with the executive branch, however, he chose to join the judicial branch of the ICS. After serving as a judge of the Lahore High Court for a number of years, he was appointed to the Supreme Court in 1975. He was appointed chief justice of the Supreme Court in 1977. During his tenure as chief justice, the Supreme Court delivered several controversial decisions including the decision to uphold the death sentence imposed on Zulfikar Ali Bhutto (q.v.) by the Lahore High Court. In confirming the death sentence, the seven-member court split four to three with Chief Justice Anwarul Haq siding with the majority.

Chief Justice Anwarul Haq also presided over the Supreme Court bench that awarded legitimacy to Zia ul-Haq's (q.v.) coup d'etat against the government of Prime Minister Zulfikar Ali Bhutto. In *Nusrat Bhutto vs. Government of Pakistan,* the Supreme Court once again invoked the doctrine of necessity to keep in place an established political order no matter how that order had come into being.

In March 1981, Anwarul Haq chose to retire from the Supreme Court rather than take the oath of office under the Provisional Constitutional Order promulgated by the administration of Zia ul-Haq. *See also* Judiciary, The.

ARIF, GENERAL (RETIRED) KHALID MAHMUD (1930–). General Khalid Mahmud Arif served President Zia ul-Haq (q.v.) from 1977, when the military took over political control of Pakistan, to 1987, when he retired from the military. He was Zia ul-Haq's principal advisor during this period. The most momentous decision of the Zia period came in 1978–79. In 1978 Zulfikar Ali Bhutto (q.v.) was tried for murder and sentenced to death by the Lahore High Court. In early 1979, the death sentence was upheld by the Supreme Court, and Bhutto was executed in Rawalpindi (q.v.) on April 4 of that year. General Arif was by Zia's side as he made these decisions. It was also during this period that General Zia promised several times to hold general elections but each time failed to keep his word. Once again he turned to Arif for advice and council as he prolonged his stay in power. In 1983, the opposition launched its most serious challenge to the military regime in the form of the Movement for the Restoration of Democracy (q.v.). Both Zia and Arif, turning to history for a lesson, decided to deal firmly with the opposition. They did not want to commit the mistakes made in 1969 by President Ayub Khan (q.v.) and in 1977 by Zulfikar Ali Bhutto when both sought to accommodate the opposition.

General Arif was important to Zia ul-Haq not only because of the loyalty he showed to his friend. General Arif was also President Zia's main link with the armed forces and as such played a critical role in ensuring that the president continued to receive the support of the senior officers. As Zia got more involved with the affairs of state, he left military matters mostly to General Arif. In March 1984, K. M. Arif was promoted to the rank of full (four-star) general and appointed vice chief of army staff (VCOAS). As the VCOAS, General Arif was the effective head of the army. He was perhaps the only person Zia could have trusted to lead the armed forces at that time. General Arif retired in March 1987, after completing his three-year term and was replaced by General Aslam Beg (q.v.).

Unlike some of his other colleagues—Generals Hameed Gul (q.v.) and Aslam Beg among them—General Arif did not seek a political career for himself after retiring from the army. He chose instead to influence public opinion on important matters by contributing columns to *Dawn*, Pakistan's largest-circulating English-language newspaper.

ARTICLE 58.2(B) OF THE CONSTITUTION OF 1973. Article 58.2(b) was inserted into the constitution of 1973 (q.v.) by the eighth amendment. The eighth amendment to the constitution was the price exacted by President Zia ul-Haq (q.v.) for bringing back democracy to Pakistan. The amendment was passed by the National Assembly without much debate in November 1985. Once the constitution was amended, President Zia lifted martial law and democracy began its slow return.

Article 58.2(b) read as follows: "Notwithstanding anything contained in clause (2) of Article 48, the President may also dissolve the National Assembly in his discretion where in his opinion, a situation has arisen in which the Government of the Federation cannot be carried out in accordance with the provisions of the Constitution and appeal to the electorate is necessary." Zia used Article 58.2(b) to dismiss Prime Minister Muhammad Khan Junejo (q.v.) on May 29, 1988, on grounds of incompetence and inefficiency. Zia's action was challenged by Junejo but was declared by the Supreme Court to be within Zia's constitutional rights. The article was used again two years later by President Ghulam Ishaq Khan when he dismissed Prime Minister Benazir Bhutto (qq.v.). This happened on August 6, 1990, and Ghulam Ishaq Khan used a long list of accusations to justify the constitutionality of his action. Once again the Supreme Court went along with the president.

The article was used for the third time on April 18, 1993, by President Ghulam Ishaq Khan to send home the administration of Prime Minister Nawaz Sharif (q.v.) and the National Assembly that supported him. The charge sheet prepared by the president was similar to the one that had caused the dismissal of Benazir Bhutto. This time the Supreme Court was not persuaded, however. It passed a landmark judgment setting aside the president's order and restoring both the government of Nawaz Sharif as well as the National Assembly. By the decision in the Nawaz Sharif case, the Supreme Court gave a considerably more restricted meaning to the article than did the interpretation used by the two preceding presidents.

The fourth use of the article was by President Farooq Leghari (q.v.) when he dismissed the administration of Benazir Bhutto on November 5, 1996. As required by the constitution, new elections were held on February 3, 1997, in which Mian Nawaz Sharif's Pakistan Muslim League (q.v.) won an overwhelming victory. Sharif did not lose much time in using his massive presence in the national legislature to pass the thirteenth amendment to the constitution, the main provision of which was to repeal Article 58.2 (b). This happened in March 1997 and President Farooq Leghari gave his assent to the amendment, thereby losing the power that he had used to set the stage for the return of Nawaz Sharif as prime minister. *See also* Amendment to the Constitution of 1973, the Thirteenth.

ASGHAR KHAN, AIR MARSHAL (RETIRED) (1928–). Asghar Khan entered politics after two successful careers in government: as the first commander in chief of the Pakistan air force and then as chairman of Pakistan International Airlines. He left the air force soon after

Pakistan's 1965 war with India convinced him that Ayub Khan (q.v.) had failed the country and that Pakistan needed a new type of leader.

Asghar Khan began his political career by joining the Justice Party in 1969 but then decided to form his own political organization, the Tehrik-e-Istiqlal (q.v.). He played an active role in the agitation that led to the resignation of President Ayub Khan in March 1969 and the demise of the political system founded by the discredited president. The political agitation against the government of Ayub Khan proved to be the high point of Asghar Khan's political career. During the peak of the campaign in the early part of 1969, Asghar Khan shared the limelight with Zulfikar Ali Bhutto (q.v.). This fact was recognized by the Ayub regime as both Asghar Khan and Bhutto had to spend several months in prison.

Asghar Khan ran for a seat in the National Assembly in the general elections of 1970 (q.v.), the first election to be held in Pakistan since independence. He chose Rawalpindi (q.v.) as his constituency in the belief that the city, with a large voting population associated in one way or the other with the armed forces, would appreciate the contributions that could be made by a retired air marshal. He lost the election to Khurshid Hasan Mir, however, a close associate of Zulfikar Ali Bhutto and a prominent member of the Pakistan People's Party (PPP) (q.v.). The success of Bhutto's PPP in the 1970 elections and Bhutto's quick ascent to power after that diminished the political stature of Asghar Khan. He remained in opposition during the Bhutto years, ignored by both the government and the middle-class constituency that he sought to cultivate.

Asghar Khan took part in the elections of 1977, the first to be held after the breakup of Pakistan and the first to be conducted under the constitution of 1973 (q.v.). He was instrumental in organizing the Pakistan National Alliance (PNA) (q.v.), a coalition of political parties opposed to Bhutto. The results of the elections as announced by the government, surprised Asghar Khan and other leaders of the PNA. The opposition had expected to perform much better than indicated by official results. Asghar Khan and several other important members of the opposition failed to win seats in the National Assembly. They refused to accept the outcome of the elections and launched a movement against the government of Zulfikar Ali Bhutto. As had happened in 1969, Asghar Khan did not reap the fruits of his endeavors. The agitation against the regime of Zulfikar Ali Bhutto brought the army back to power, this time under General Zia ul-Haq (q.v.).

Asghar Khan spent the early years of Zia ul-Haq's martial law under house arrest. Although the military government was prepared to work with a number of political parties that had come together under the umbrella of the PNA, it ignored Asghar Khan's Tehrik-e-Istiqlal. The Tehrik joined the Movement for the Restoration of Democracy (MRD) (q.v.) in 1981, participated in the agitation launched by the MRD in 1983 against the government of Zia ul-Haq, but left the movement in 1986. The confrontation between Nawaz Sharif and Benazir Bhutto (qq.v.) that was to dominate Pakistan's politics so completely after the death of President Zia ul-Haq in August 1988 left little space for any other politician not aligned with the two main parties. Asghar Khan saw the handwriting on the wall and finally retired from politics in early 1996.

ASHRAF, JAVED (1951–1996). Ashraf Javed, a young activist of the Pakistan Muslim League (PML) (Nawaz Group) (q.v.), was generally regarded as s rising star in the party's leadership. He was secretary-general of the Lahore chapter of the PML and also worked as political secretary to Mian Shahbaz Sharif, brother of Nawaz Sharif (qq.v.) and the leader of the opposition in the Punjab Provincial Assembly. While Shahbaz Sharif was in jail, waiting to be tried on charges of corruption, Javed Ashraf looked after the affairs of the party in the provincial legislature.

Ashraf's political career was cut short when he was killed in Lahore in an encounter with the police on April 3, 1996. His death added another chapter, a bloody one, to the feud between Prime Minister Benazir Bhutto (q.v.) and Nawaz Sharif, the leader of the opposition in the National Assembly.

ASIAN DEVELOPMENT BANK (ADB). The Asian Development Bank was established in 1968 as a part of the regional development banking system under the aegis of the United Nations. The ADB has its headquarters in Manila, the Philippines, and has over 50 members including the Central Asian states of the former Soviet Union. Japan and the United States are the largest contributors of funds to the ADB, each with a share of 16 percent of the prescribed capital of $23 billion.

Pakistan is one of the principal recipients of assistance from the ADB. It has received loans worth $1.75 billion since 1968, making it the second largest beneficiary of the bank's operations. About 55 percent of the loans made by the ADB came from the Asian Development Fund (ADF), the soft arm of the bank. Credits from the ADF are free of interest charges; only a small service charge is received from the beneficiaries. The ADB has provided assistance for a number of important projects including the Swabi Salinity Control and Reclamation Project ($118 million). In 1995, the ADB joined the World Bank and a number of other donors to finance the Ghazi Borotha Hydroelectric project.

ASIA PACIFIC ECONOMIC COOPERATION (APEC). On June 24, 1992, during a three-day meeting held in Bangkok attended by 14 countries, the decision to convert the Asia Pacific Economic Cooperation into a permanent institution was taken. A small secretariat was set up to guide the APEC toward its new role. The APEC, created in 1989, had made little progress; its main achievement during the first three years of its existence was to hold annual conferences and to devise 10 programs of economic cooperation in fields ranging from fisheries to lowering trade barriers. The Bangkok meeting chose to push the 14 members of the organization—Australia, Brunei, Canada, China, Hong Kong, Indonesia, Japan, Korea, Malaysia, New Zealand, the Philippines, Singapore, Thailand, and the United States—toward greater economic and trade cooperation in order to protect the region against the possible collapse of the Uruguay round of trade negotiations and the consequent deglobalization of world trading.

Whether the APEC develops into a major trading block would depend in part on the success of the European Union to move toward greater economic integration, the speed with which the United States, Canada, and Mexico are able to develop the North American Free Trade Area, and the degree to which the Association of South East Asian Nations (ASEAN) countries are prepared to allow such large trading countries as China, Japan, and the United States to gain preferential entry into their territories. If these difficulties are overcome, the APEC has the potential of becoming one of the largest trading blocs in the world. If that were to happen, the consequences for countries such as Pakistan could be serious as these countries would be excluded from all major regional trading arrangements.

ASIF NAWAZ, GENERAL (1937–1993). Born on January 3, 1937 in his ancestral village of Chakri Rajghan (Jhelum District), Asif Nawaz belonged to a military family of the Janjua Rajput clan from the Salt Range area of the Punjab (q.v.), which is well known for producing soldiers. Educated at the Roman Catholic missionary Convent of Jesus and Mary in Srinagar in prepartition India and then at St. Mary's School in Rawalpindi (q.v.), he joined the Pakistan army training program for officer cadets at the age of 16 and, after an introductory course in Kohat, was selected for the Royal Military Academy at Sandhurst, England, where he received his commission in 1957.

Asif Nawaz managed to escape martial law duties for most of the period during which General Zia ul-Haq (q.v.) ruled Pakistan. But he was promoted to major general and given command of the 7th Infantry Division in Peshawar (q.v.) in 1982. He took over as commandant of the Pakistan Military Academy in Kakul in 1985. On 23 May 1988, he was promoted to lieutenant general, among the last batch of promotions approved by the civilian Prime Minister Muhammad Khan Junejo (q.v.), and posted as corps commander of V Corps in Karachi (q.v.). Asif Nawaz was brought from Karachi to Rawalpindi (q.v.) as chief of General Staff under General Mirza Aslam Beg (q.v.) in April 1991 and nominated a month later by President Ghulam Ishaq Khan (q.v.) as the chief of Army Staff-designate to succeed General Beg on August 17, 1991. Asif Nawaz was the tenth army chief of Pakistan and the eighth Pakistani in that job. He died in Rawalpindi following a massive heart attack that occurred while exercising on a treadmill at Army House in Rawalpindi; he was buried in his native village.

ASMA JAHANGIR. Asma Jahangir—also known by her maiden name, Asma Jilani—has played a significant role in promoting human rights in Pakistan. She has concentrated in particular on the rights of women and minorities, thereby inviting the wrath of conservative and religious forces in the country. In 1986 she founded a nongovernmental organization, the Human Rights Commission, for documenting, and thus making people aware of "the rampant mistreatment and exploitation of women, children, minorities, and laborers by religious zealots." She became the Commission's first secretary-general.

In 1995 Asma Jahangir came to the attention of the international human rights community for taking up the cause of two Pakistani Christians who had been sentenced to death under the "blasphemy laws." Although her role in this case drew a great deal of hostile criticism from religious elements, including death threats, it brought her international fame and recognition. In July she was chosen to receive the Ramon Magsaysay award for public service. She was cited for "challenging Pakistan to embrace and uphold the principles of religious tolerance, gender equality, and equal protection under the law."

In December 1997, when the Pakistan Muslim League (PML) (q.v.) put forward Muhammad Rafiq Tarar (q.v.) as its candidate for president, Asma Jahangir joined the chorus of voices raised in protest at the party's choice. She opposed Tarar on account of his poor record in human rights while he was a magistrate and later a judge of the High and Supreme Courts. The opposition of human-rights activists did not prevent Tarar from being elected president.

ASSOCIATION OF PAKISTANI PHYSICIANS IN NORTH AMERICA (APPNA). The Association of Pakistani Physicians in North America—better known by its acronym APPNA—was established in 1978 by a group of Pakistani doctors working in Chicago. Its original purpose was to provide support to the professionals who had come from Pakistan to the United States. Over time, as Pakistani physicians from all over the United States and Canada joined the association, it broadened its objectives to include social work in Pakistan. It also sponsored a political action committee, Pak-pac, to protect what it saw as Pakistan's interests in the United States. APPNA holds two annual meetings, one in the summer in a major U.S. city and the other in the winter in a large Pakistani city. It operates out of Chicago.

ASSOCIATION OF PAKISTANI SCIENTISTS AND ENGINEERS IN NORTH AMERICA (APSENA). The Association of Pakistani Scientists and Engineers in North America was founded in 1984 to work as a lobby group for Pakistani professionals working abroad. Over time, APSENA also developed a work program to improve the quality of technical education being given by colleges and universities in Pakistan. A fund, Promotion for Education in Pakistan (PEP), was launched to provide financial assistance to those families in Pakistan that could not afford to send their children to the institutions operating in the private sector. The members of APSENA meet every year at the headquarters of one of its many chapters in North America.

ATTIQUR RAHMAN, LIEUTENANT GENERAL (RETIRED) (1928–1996). Attiqur Rahman was one of the many army generals who held important political positions after leaving active service. In 1970, he was appointed governor of West Pakistan by the government of President Agha Muhammad Yahya Khan (q.v.). Rahman replaced Air Marshal Nur Khan, who held that position for several months following the imposition of martial law in March 1969. Rahman was the last person to hold this job; it was during his tenure that the decision was made to break up West Pakistan into four provinces—Balochistan, the Northwest Frontier, Punjab, and Sindh (qq.v.).

AURAT FOUNDATION. The Aurat (Women's) Foundation was established in Lahore (q.v.) in January 1986 by a group of professional women under the leadership of Nigar Ahmed. It is one of the many organizations that sprang up in Pakistan during the time (1977–88) President Zia ul-Haq (q.v.) was in power. Zia had encouraged the conservative point of view that in a Muslim society the role of women was in the house as wives, mothers, and housekeepers. Even after President Zia left the political field, Pakistani society continued to be pulled in two different directions. Accordingly, the Aurat Foundation concentrated its energies and resources on imparting training to women and providing them with information on the economic opportunities available to them. The Foundation produced cassette tapes and videos women could use to acquire the skills they needed in the marketplace. It has also set up "Hamjoli," a producer cooperative, to market simple products women produced in their homes. The Foundation also conducted workshops to familiarize nongovernmental organizations working in Pakistan with the problems women faced in the country.

AWAMI LEAGUE (AL). The Awami League was formed in 1949 by a group of leaders from East Bengal (today's Bangladesh) who were not satisfied with the role they were playing in the evolving political structure in Pakistan. There was a widespread impression in East Pakistan that the leaders of West Pakistan were discriminating against the people of the eastern wing. The first set of leaders of the AL belonged to the left wing of the Muslim League (q.v.), the party that had fought successfully for the establishment of Pakistan. They took control of the new party with Maulana Bhashani (q.v.) as their leader. The AL was the most important component of the United Front (q.v.) that won the provincial elections of 1954 (q.v.) and effectively marginalized the Muslim League in East Pakistan. However, serious dissension within the ranks of the United Front leadership led to Bhashani's resignation and the election of H. S. Suhrawardy (q.v.) as president. Following Suhrawardy's death in 1963, Mujibur Rahman (q.v.) became the party's president. It was under Mujib that the party developed its Six Point Program (q.v.) for obtaining greater autonomy for the federating provinces of Pakistan. The program announced in 1966 prepared the ground for Awami League's extraordinary victory in the elections of 1970 (q.v.) Following the breakup of Pakistan in December 1971 and the return of Mujibur Rahman in January 1972 from imprisonment in West Pakistan, the Awami League came to power in Dacca, the capital of Bangladesh.

AWAMI NATIONAL PARTY (ANP). The Awami National Party was formed in 1986 following the merger of several left-leaning parties including the Awami Tahrik, the National Democratic Party, the Mazdoor Kissan Party, and a splinter group from the Pakistan National Party. Khan Abdul Wali Khan (q.v.) was appointed the new party's president. The party's formation was hailed by its sponsors as the first step toward an effective presence of the left in the politics of Pakistan. But the unity that was forced by Wali Khan and the cofounders of the ANP on the traditionally fractious left proved to be weak. Within a year of the new party's birth, splinter groups began to assert their independence. In the Northwest Frontier Province (q.v.), Wali Khan's political base, a group of ANP dissidents set up the ANP (Constitutional Group) as a separate organization while another group broke away to establish the Pakhtoon

Liberation Front. In spite of these divisions, the ANP retained an effective presence in the Northwest Frontier Province.

In the early 1990s it became a strong ally of the Pakistan Muslim League (PML) led by Mian Nawaz Sharif (qq.v.). It sided with Sharif when the Pakistan People's Party (PPP) assumed power in Islamabad under the leadership of Prime Minister Benazir Bhutto (qq.v.). The prime minister, upset by the ANP move, persuaded President Farooq Leghari (q.v.) to dismiss the ANP Cabinet and maneuver the PPP into forming the government. The president's action further cemented the ties between the PML and the ANP. The ANP was rewarded handsomely when the PML won decisively against the PPP in the elections of February 1997. It joined the PML-led governments in both Islamabad, the federal capital, and Peshawar (q.v.), the capital of the Northwestern Frontier Province. In 1995 an ailing Wali Khan surrendered the leadership of the ANP to Ajmal Khattak (q.v.), while his wife, Nasim Wali Khan (q.v.), took over the NWFP wing of the party. In 1998, following the development of serious differences with Nawaz Sharif, ANP left the coalition government in Islamabad.

AYODHYA MOSQUE. Ayodhya mosque—also known as the Babri mosque because it was constructed by Babar, the first Mughul emperor (q.v.) of India—had been the target of Hindu nationalism for a long time. The mosque was constructed in the sixteenth century by the Muslim conquerors of northern India on a site the Hindus believe to be the birthplace of the god Rama. The mosque had long been a symbol of Islamic repression for those Hindus who believed that the Muslims had been singularly insensitive about their religion. It became a symbol of Hindu nationalism when it was razed by Hindu zealots in December 1992. The demolition of the mosque was encouraged by the Hindu nationalist Bharatiya Janata Party (BJP) (q.v.).

The mosque's destruction led to the eruption of communal violence all over India. The tension between the Hindus and Muslims increased enormously and led to bloody riots in Bombay from December 1992 to March 1993 in which thousands of Muslims were killed. The Ayodhya mosque may have contributed to the poor showing of the Indian National Congress Party in the elections held in May 1996 when Prime Minister P. V. Narasimha Rao suffered a humiliating defeat, in part, it was said, because he lost the confidence of the important Muslim vote. Up until then, India's Muslims, constituting 12.5 percent of the population, had faithfully supported the Congress Party. They were comfortable with the secular stance of the party as against the more Hindu militancy of some of the opposition parties, in particular the BJP. Rao forfeited this trust in the way he handled the Ayodhya mosque incident, however. The loss of the Muslim vote was a major cause of the decline of the Congress Party as a political force in the country. In spite of strenuous efforts, the party failed to recover the ground it had lost in the elections of 1996 when the country went back to the polls in 1998.

AYUB, GOHAR (1937–). Gohar Ayub is the second son of General (later Field Marshal and first military president of Pakistan) Muhammad Ayub Khan. He was educated at St. Mary's in Rawalpindi (q.v.), where he graduated in 1953. The same year, he joined the Pakistan Military Academy (q.v.) as a "gentleman cadet." A year later he was selected to go for training to the Royal Military Academy, Sandhurst. On his return from England, he was commissioned as a second lieutenant in the Pakistan army.

Soon after his return from England, Gohar Ayub married the daughter of General Habibullah Khan. In 1962, he resigned from the army to join Gandhara Industries, a business house his father-in-law had founded a few years earlier. The business house owned a number of flourishing enterprises including textile mills in the Northwestern Frontier Province (NWFP) (q.v.) and an automobile assembly plan near Karachi (q.v.).

Gohar Ayub's first foray into politics was in January 1995 when he organized a street demonstration in Karachi to celebrate his father's success in the presidential election, the first to be held under the constitution of 1962 (q.v.). The celebration turned into a riot when Ayub's supporters were challenged by those who had voted in favor of Fatima Jinnah (q.v.), the opposition's candidate in the presidential poll. A number of people were killed and hundreds were injured. This incident was to leave a bitter memory in the minds of the people who had opposed Ayub Khan—a memory that contributed to the success of the anti-Ayub Khan movement of 1968–69.

President Ayub Khan also paid a heavy political price for the perception that Gohar Ayub and his father-in-law had benefited enormously from the favors granted them by the government, including the granting of precious licenses for setting up industries and importing raw materials and equipment, as well as gaining access to cheap capital from government-owned investment banks.

Gohar Ayub won a seat in the National Assembly from his native Haripur in 1990, was elected the speaker of the National Assembly, and, following the elections of 1997, was given the portfolio of foreign affairs in the Cabinet of Prime Minister Mian Nawaz Sharif (q.v.). He resigned from the Sharif Cabinet in April 1998 but was asked to stay on. He played an important role in the Pakistani decision to explode six nuclear devices in May 1998 following the tests carried out by India earlier in the month. In August 1998 Gohar Ayub left the ministry of foreign affairs and was appointed minister of water and power.

AYUB KHAN, FIELD MARSHAL MUHAMMAD (1907–1970). Field Marshal Muhammad Ayub Khan was born in Rehana, a village in the Northwest Frontier Province (NWFP) (q.v.) district of Hazara. He went to Aligrah College to prepare for a career in one of the several professions that were now attracting the Muslim middle classes. Noting his family background, his physique and bearing, and the fact that he belonged to a class that the British had designated as "martial," a number of his teachers urged Ayub Khan to join the military. This he did as a gentleman cadet in 1926; and, after a couple of years at the Royal Military Academy, Sandhurst, in England, he received the King's Commission in 1928.

Ayub Khan rose quickly in the ranks of the British Indian Army and commanded a battalion in World War II. When the British announced their decision to leave India, he had already attained the rank of brigadier general. Being one of the most senior Muslim officers in the army at the time of the partition of British India, he was appointed to the Punjab Boundary Commission. A year later, he was promoted to the rank of major general and sent to Dacca as the general officer commanding (GOC) of the army garrison in East Bengal (later East Pakistan and later still Bangladesh).

In 1950 Prime Minister Liaqat Ali Khan (q.v.) invited Ayub Khan to become the first Pakistani to lead the army as its commander in chief. He was appointed to a second five-year term as the commander in chief of the army in January 1955. By that time Ayub Khan had made the decision to remove the civilian government and place Pakistan under martial law. The near-collapse of civilian authority in 1958 was his reason for intervention, but he was not in any hurry to do so. He waited for 20 months before making his first move. He struck in October 1958 but moved cautiously. On October 7, Ayub Khan forced President Iskander Mirza (q.v.) to place Pakistan under martial law. The president issued a proclamation to that effect and appointed Ayub Khan as the chief martial-law administrator. Twenty days later, on October 27, Ayub Khan sent President Mirza into exile and appointed himself the president.

A tremendous amount of goodwill accompanied Ayub Khan's assumption of political power and motivated him to institute deep structural changes in Pakistan's society, economy, and its political structure. The system of Basic Democracies, the Constitution of 1962 (q.v.), the Land Reforms of 1959 (q.v.), the Family Laws Ordinance of 1961 (q.v.), and the launching of the Second Five Year Plan in 1960 were all significant departures from the way political and economic business had been conducted in Pakistan in the first postindependence decade. Political tranquillity, if only on the surface, and rapid economic growth were the consequences of these changes.

In September 1965 Pakistan went to war with India. The war was the consequence of a number of ill-advised moves made by Pakistan in the summer of 1965—including the launching of Operation Gibraltar in Kashmir (qq.v.)—the precise motives of which, despite a considerable amount of speculation, remain murky to this day. The war drained Pakistan of financial resources precisely at the time it was implementing its Third Five Year Plan. It brought to a sudden end the highly coveted U.S. military and economic aid that had been critical for Pakistan's economic expansion. It exposed the military vulnerability of East Pakistan and contributed to the secessionist sentiment that surfaced in 1966 in the form of Mujibur Rahman's Six-Point Program (qq.v.) for political and economic autonomy for the eastern wing of the country. And, finally, the signing of the Tashkent Declaration (q.v.) on January 10, 1966, exploded the myth of Pakistan's military invincibility. India exacted a heavy price for its willingness to restore the status quo, but the price was too high for the people of Pakistan. The Tashkent "let down" was exploited to the full by Zulfikar Ali Bhutto (q.v.) who, as foreign minister, was a member of the Pakistani delegation that Ayub Khan took to Tashkent, but Bhutto distanced himself immediately from the position taken by the president on returning to Islamabad (q.v.).

For the second time in four years, the opposition surprised Ayub Khan by its ability to organize itself. In the fall of 1964, the Combined Opposition Party (COP) (q.v.) had launched a credible challenge to Ayub Khan by nominating Fatima Jinnah (q.v.) as its candidate for the presidential elections of January 1965. In December 1968, the opposition parties came together again and organized the Democratic Action Committee (DAC) (q.v.) to mobilize and channel the growing resentment against the government. The formation of the DAC quickened the pace of the movement against Ayub; the government invited the opposition to participate in a "round table" discussion but before the negotiations had concluded, the army intervened under the leadership of General Agha Muhammad Yahya Khan (q.v.). On March 25, 1969, Ayub Khan surrendered power to Yahya Khan.

Allowed to languish in his house in Islamabad, Ayub Khan saw with dismay the dismantling of his system by Yahya Khan.

AZAD KASHMIR. Pakistan calls the small sliver of land it captured in the first Kashmir war with India (1948–49), Azad (free) Kashmir. Ever since 1949 when the United Nations adopted a resolution that brought an end to the brief war between the two countries and authorized Pakistan to administer this part of Kashmir (q.v.) pending a plebiscite to determine the political future of the entire state, Azad Kashmir has enjoyed some autonomy. It has a constitution of its own according to which the people of the territory elect their own assembly. Azad Kashmir has its own president as its chief executive. In actual fact, the administration in Muzaffarabad usually has the same party affiliation as the administration in power in Islamabad (q.v.), Pakistan's capital. Muzaffarabad is the capital of Azad Kashmir and its only significant city. The city is about 50 miles from Pakistan and 20 miles from the border that currently separates Azad Kashmir from Indian Kashmir.

The boundary between Azad Kashmir and the Indian state of Kashmir was defined twice, once in 1949 and the second time in 1972. The first definition essentially followed the position of the troops of India and Pakistan when the two countries accepted the cease-fire brokered by the United Nations. The second demarcation grew out of the Simla Accord (q.v.) signed by India and Pakistan on July 3, 1972. The fact that the Bharatiya Janata Party (BJP) (q.v.), which took power in Delhi following the elections of March 1998 in India, formally laid claim to Azad Kashmir may complicate once again the relations between Pakistan and India over the future of Kashmir.

AZAM KHAN, LIEUTENANT GENERAL MUHAMMAD (1908–1994). Of the three senior generals of the Pakistani army who helped Ayub Khan (q.v.) stage his coup d'etat in October 1958, Lt. General Muhammad Azam Khan was the most experienced in civilian affairs. He was the general officer commanding (GOC) Lahore garrison when, in 1953, Governor-General Ghulam Muhammad (q.v.) called on the army to bring the anti-Ahmadiya movement under control. Azam Khan, as martial law administrator, became the virtual governor of Punjab (q.v.) province. Not only did he move with dispatch and succeed in quickly reestablishing law and order, but the army under his command also performed a number of civic functions.

Ayub Khan brought Azam Khan into his Cabinet as "senior minister" and put him in charge of the Department of Refugee Rehabilitation. The problem of rehabilitating the refugees from India, in particular those who had settled in the rural areas of Pakistan had proved intractable up until then. The success of the operation launched by Azam Khan made him the most popular military figure in the martial government of Ayub Khan. With the refugees resettled, Azam Khan was ready to move onto other things. In 1960 President Ayub Khan sent him to Dacca as governor of East Pakistan.

The new governor not only put together a good administration in Dacca but also gained a great deal of respect for advancing Bengal's desire to meaningfully participate in government affairs. He concluded that political participation and not paternalism was a solution to East Pakistan's political problems. But Ayub Khan was not prepared to accept this assessment. He was also worried that Azam Khan, having become popular in both wings of the country, had the credibility to effectively challenge him politically. Azam Khan was called back to West Pakistan in 1962 and was succeeded by Abdul Monem Khan, a little-known Bengali politician.

In 1964, the Combined Opposition Party (COP) (q.v.) toyed with the idea of nominating Azam Khan as its candidate to oppose Ayub Khan in the presidential elections of January 1965. The ultimate candidate was Fatima Jinnah (q.v.), however, and Azam Khan, by campaigning for her with great enthusiasm, contributed to her relative success in the eastern wing of the country. After Fatima Jinnah's defeat, Azam Khan announced his retirement from politics.

AZIZ KHAN KAKA, ABDUL (1906–1987). Abdul Aziz Khan Kaka was born in Zaida Village in Swabi Tehsil of Mardan district. He was an active member of the Khudai Khidmatgar Movement (q.v.) and defeated Sir Sahibzada Abdul Qayyum Khan (q.v.) in the elections of 1936. Sahibzada was an established politician, knighted by the British in recognition for his services to his people. Aziz Kaka was a newcomer to the politics of the province, virtually unknown outside his district. Sahibzada's loss and Kaka's victory signaled the arrival of Khudai Khidmatgar as a potent political force on the province's political scene.

Kaka repeated his performance in the provincial elections of 1945 by defeating Abdul Qayyum Bacha of the Muslim League (q.v.). Kaka was imprisoned several times after the birth of Pakistan in 1947, spending a total of 21 years in prison for "political crimes." He joined the National Awami Party (NAP) (q.v.) and was elected in 1970 to the provincial legislature as a representative of the NAP. He died on October 3, 1987.

AZIZ, SARTAJ (1929–). Sartaj Aziz comes from the Northwest Frontier Province (NWFP) (q.v.). He was educated at the Hailey College of Commerce, Lahore (q.v.) and joined the Pakistan Military Accounts Service in 1952. He served in the Planning Commission for a number of years. It was during his tenure in the Commission that the Second and Third Five-Year Plans (qq.v.) were prepared. He attended Harvard University's Kennedy School in 1965 as a Mason Fellow. He left Pakistan in 1970 to join the Food and Agricultural Organization and, while in Rome, played an important role in launching the International Fund for Agricultural Development. He returned to Pakistan in 1980 at the invitation of President Zia ul-Haq (q.v.) and was appointed minister of agriculture. He served as finance minister in all Muslim League (q.v.) governments that were in office during the 1990s. In August 1998 Aziz moved from the ministry of finance to the ministry of foreign affairs.

↩ **B** ↪

BABAR, EMPEROR (1483–1530). Babar was the first of the six great Mughuls (q.v.) to rule India. His rule began in 1526 after the defeat of the army of Emperor Lodhi, the last Pathan ruler of the Delhi Sultanate. Lodhi's forces were defeated at the battlefield of Panipat near Delhi. Although the Mughuls ruled India for 331 years, from 1526 to 1857, they were most powerful under Babar and his five successors: Humayun (1530–1540 and 1555–1556), Akbar (1556–1605), Jahangir (1605–1627), Shahjahan (1627–1658), and Aurangzeb (1658–1707). *See also* Mughul Empire.

BABAR, LIEUTENANT GENERAL (RETIRED) NASEERULLAH KHAN (1929–). Babar was born in the Northwest Frontier Province (NWFP) (q.v.) and after being educated in the schools of the province, joined the Pakistan army as a commissioned officer in 1952. He distinguished himself during Pakistan's war with India in 1965. Impressed with Zulfikar Ali Bhutto's (q.v.) conduct during the war with India—Bhutto wanted the war to continue while Ayub Khan (q.v.) negotiated a peace agreement with India—Babar decided to join the Pakistan People's Party (PPP) (q.v.) on his retirement. from the army. He won a National Assembly seat from his native NWFP in the elections of 1993 (q.v.) and when Benazir Bhutto (q.v.) was invited to form a government in Islamabad (q.v.), he joined her Cabinet and was given the important portfolio of Interior.

As interior minister, Babar had the mandate to maintain law and order in the country. It was in pursuit of this mandate that he carried out a highly controversial policy of repression in Karachi (q.v.) against the activists of the Muhajir Qaumi Mahaz (MQM) (q.v.). The battle for Karachi began once the army was pulled out of the city in November 1995. The carnage that ensued claimed more than 1,800 lives in 1995 alone, many of those the result of the active pursuit of MQM activists by the forces under the command of the Interior Ministry.

The harsh measures adopted by Babar in dealing with the MQM brought relative calm to Karachi in the spring of 1996. Babar lost his position along with other members of the federal Cabinet when Prime Minister Benazir Bhutto was dismissed by President Farooq Leghari (q.v.) on November 5, 1996. He continued to defend Bhutto, her family, and her administration, however, when charges of corruption and mismanagement began to be leveled by the successor governments of caretaker Prime Minister Meraj Khalid (q.v.) and the elected government of Prime Minister Mian Nawaz Sharif (q.v.).

BABAR, ZAHEER (1928–1998). Zaheer Babar was one of a group of pioneering journalists who joined the Progressive Papers Limited (PPL), founded in 1950 by Mian Iftikharuddin. He edited *Imroze,* the Urdu-language newspaper published by PPL before General Ayub Khan (q.v.) brought Pakistan under martial law. He refused to accept the rigors imposed by the military government and was arrested. He was confined to the notorious Lahore Fort prison for some time. With the rise of the Pakistan People's Party (PPP) (q.v.), Zaheer Babar was able to go back to being active in journalism. In 1988, he was appointed chief editor of *Musawat,* an Urdu-language newspaper owned by the PPP.

Babar also wrote short stories in Urdu. Two collections of his stories—*Raat ki Roshni* and *Sheeshey key Aabley*—were published and well received by critics. He died in Lahore (q.v.).

BADR, JEHANGIR (1948–). Jehangir Badr started his political career as a student activist. In 1969, he ran for the presidency of the Punjab University Student Union but lost narrowly to the candidate of the Jamiat-e-Tuleba, the student organization affiliated with the Jamaat-e-Islami (q.v.). After finishing studies he became active in the Pakistan People's Party (PPP) (q.v.).

Badr was one of several young political activists given senior party positions by Benazir Bhutto (q.v.) when she returned to Pakistan in 1986 from self-imposed exile in London. Bhutto wanted to wrest the control of the party from the "uncles," friends of her father, Zulfikar Ali Bhutto (q.v.), who had managed party affairs during her absence from the country. Badr and his associates were given PPP tickets for the elections of 1988, the first poll to be held after the lifting of martial law. Badr won a National Assembly seat from Lahore (q.v.) and joined the Benazir Bhutto administration as energy and petroleum minister. He was elected to the Senate in 1996 and included in the federal Cabinet in the 1996, shortly before it was dismissed by President Farooq Leghari (q.v.) on November 5, 1996.

BAGHDAD PACT. *See* IRAQ–PAKISTAN RELATIONS.

BAHAUDDIN (1170–1270). Bahauddin was born in 1170 in Leiah, a small town in Punjab's (q.v.) southwest. He studied at Khorasan in Central Asia under Shahabuddin Suhrawardi, a well-known Islamic scholar and Sufi saint of his time. He returned to India in 1222, and eventually settled at Multan. He died at the age of 100 and was buried with great ceremony at Multan. His shrine is still visited by thousands of devotees from all over Pakistan. His descendants—the Qureshis of Multan—take care of his shrine.

BAHAWALPUR. Bahawalpur was one of the several "princely states" (q.v.) that opted to join Pakistan after the partition of British India in 1947. About the size of Denmark, it was founded by Nawab Bahawal Khan Abbasi I in 1748, exactly 100 years before the British occupation of Punjab (q.v.). Bahawal Khan came from Sindh (q.v.) but claimed descent from the Abbasid Caliphs of Baghdad. The state carved out by Nawab Bahawal lay between Punjab and Sindh. On the northwestern side its boundary ran along three rivers, the Sutlej, the Panjad, and the Indus (q.v.). For the most part, the southeastern boundary ran along the states of Bikanir and Jaisalmir in what was to become the state of Rajputana in independent India.

In 1833, fearing invasion by the Sikh ruler Raja Ranjit Singh, the ruling nawab of Bahawalpur turned to the British for protection. The British, as had been their practice with other similarly situated princes, acted with dispatch and declared Bahawalpur to be a protected princely state. In this way they not only kept the Sikhs out of Bahawalpur, they also ensured that their southern flank would be in friendly hands when they decided to march into Punjab.

Bahawalpur remained a princely state until 1947, when the British partitioned India. After slight hesitation, the ruler of the state was persuaded to accede to Pakistan in 1947. In 1955, the state was merged with the provinces and other princely states in the western part of Pakistan to create the One Unit of West Pakistan (q.v.). When the one unit was dissolved in 1969, Bahawalpur became part of the province of Punjab.

BAIT-UL-MAAL. The Bait-ul-Maal was established by the government of Prime Minister Mian Nawaz Sharif (q.v.) on February 6, 1992. By taking this step, the Sharif administration continued with the tradition started by President Zia ul-Haq (q.v.) to Islamize the economy. Zia ul-Haq, Sharif's mentor, had introduced a number of Islamic instruments into the economy, including taxes such as *zakat* and *ushr* (qq.v.). The government of Prime Minister Mian Nawaz Sharif continued with the program begun by Zia. Islamists trace the institution of Bait-ul-Maal to Caliph Hazrat

Umar who enjoined all well-to-do Muslims to contribute funds to the state for the welfare of the needy. Bait-ul-Maal survived the change in government in 1993 when Benazir Bhutto (q.v.) replaced Nawaz Sharif as prime minister. This was one of the few initiatives taken by her predecessor that she was prepared to keep in place. It would have been exceedingly difficult for her to dismantle an institution that had been established in the name of Islam.

BALAWAL ZARDARI (1988–). Born in Karachi, Balawal Zardari is the first child and the oldest son of Benazir Bhutto and Asif Ali Zardari (qq.v.). The couple named their principal residence in Karachi after their son. Balawal House has been the center of political activity in the country especially during the period when Bhutto was not in power in Islamabad as prime minister.

BALOCHISTAN. Balochistan is Pakistan's largest province in terms of area (347,000 square kilometers) and smallest in terms of population (6 million estimated for early 1998). With only 17 persons to a square kilometer, it has the lowest population density among Pakistan's four provinces. Much of the province is a high plateau, some 3,000 to 4,000 feet above sea level. The plateau is bounded by two mountain ranges: the Tabakkar range runs along the border with Afghanistan, whereas the Sulaiman range runs along the right bank of the Indus river (q.v.). To the south lies the inhospitable Mekran desert in which Alexander the Great almost succumbed as he was pulling his troops out of India. The Balochis, although constituting the majority of the province's population, share Balochistan with a number of diverse ethnic groups. These include the Brohis, the Pathans, and the Mekranis.

Present-day Balochistan was formed by the merger of a number of "princely states" (q.v.) that chose—or, in some cases, were forced—to join Pakistan. The province of Balochistan in its present form was created after the dissolution of the one unit of West Pakistan (q.v.) in 1969. The creation of the separate province of Balochistan was well received by the tribal sardars of the area who worked with Zulfikar Ali Bhutto (q.v.) to launch Pakistan's third constitution in 1973 (q.v.). The new constitution provided the federating provinces with a great deal of autonomy within the Federation of Pakistan. In 1973, soon after the promulgation of the new constitution, Bhutto's Pakistan People's Party (PPP) (q.v.) formed governments in Islamabad (q.v.) and in the provinces of Lahore and Sindh (qq.v.). The smaller provinces went to a coalition of the National Awami Party (NAP) and the Jamiatul-Ulemai Islam (JUI) (qq.v.). In 1974, however, Bhutto dismissed the Balochistan government on the charge of antistate activities. This action was resented by the sardars, some of whom started an armed insurrection against the central government. Bhutto had to call in the army to help put down the rebellion but the army remained engaged in the province for as long as Bhutto was in power in Islamabad. It was only after the military takeover in 1977 that the sardars laid down their arms and peace returned to the province. Some of the tribal leaders remained unhappy and continued to support various forms of political movements aimed at securing more autonomy, if not outright independence, for the province of Balochistan.

During the time President Zia ul-Haq (q.v.) was in power (1977–1988) he was able to keep peace in Balochistan by working closely with the tribal sardars of the province. This policy of accommodation was continued by the two Benazir Bhutto (q.v.) administrations (1988–1990 and 1993–1996) and by the two administrations headed by Prime Minister Nawaz Sharif (q.v.) (1990–1993 and 1997–). This approach brought tranquillity to the province after years of turbulence but its cost was the continued backwardness of the region. Today, Balochistan is by far the most backward province of Pakistan.

BANGLADESH–PAKISTAN RELATIONS. Pakistan was born with two "wings": the western wing was made up of the provinces of Punjab, Sindh, the Northwest Frontier, and Balochistan (qq.v.) The western wing also included dozens of princely states (q.v.). East Bengal comprised the "eastern wing" of the country, separated from the western part by more than 1,000 miles of often hostile Indian territory. Soon after the birth of Pakistan in 1947, the people of East Bengal gave a strong signal that the new state would be politically viable only if the leadership of the western wing was prepared to accommodate Bengali interests. The first response from the leaders of West Pakistan came in 1948 when Governor-General Muhammad Ali Jinnah (q.v.) visited Dacca, the capital of East Bengal. This was his first visit since his success in creating Pakistan, an independent state for the Muslims of British India.

Jinnah told his Dacca audience that for the sake of national unity he wanted only one national language: Urdu. In 1952, a similar suggestion from Prime Minister Khawaja Nazimuddin, himself from Bengal, led to bloody riots. The language riots of 1952 were to be the turning point in East Bengal's relations with the western wing. Within 24 hours of Nazimuddin's statement, the chief minister of East Bengal successfully carried through the provincial legislature a motion calling on the central government to adopt Bengali as one of the national languages. The full force of Bengali resentment at what was seen as the western wing's political and economic domination and the insensitivity of the leaders of the west toward Bengal's legitimate demands was felt by the country in 1954. In the provincial elections of 1954 the Muslim League (q.v.) was trounced by the United Front (q.v.).

From 1954 to 1971 Pakistan's two wings stayed attached but the union was uncomfortable. Some of the solutions sought served only to underscore the real nature of the relationship. For instance, in 1955 the leaders of the western wing agreed to merge all the provinces and the princely states in the west into the One Unit of West Pakistan (q.v.). In this way, the western leaders tried to balance Bengal with their part of Pakistan. From now on East Bengal was to be called East Pakistan and was to have an equal number of seats in the National Assembly even though its population was larger than that of the western wing. This was the formula of "political parity" that became the basis of the Constitution of 1956 (q.v.).

Parity between the country's two wings was retained in the constitution of 1962 (q.v.) promulgated by President Ayub Khan (q.v.), but the highly restricted political activity permitted within the new political framework was seen as a major step backward by the leaders of East Pakistan. By the close of the 1960s, however, Bengali nationalism began to reassert itself. On February 12, 1966, Mujibur Rahman (q.v.), the leader of the Awami League (q.v.) and East Pakistan's most popular politician, announced his Six Point Program (q.v.) for obtaining greater political and economic autonomy for his province.

Beginning in the spring of 1969, events moved rapidly. Ayub Khan resigned in March. He was succeeded by General Yahya Khan (q.v.), the commander in chief of the Pakistan army, who imposed martial law and abrogated the constitution of 1962. He also promulgated an interim constitution under the name of the Legal Framework Order (q.v.) that did away with the principle of political party and gave East Pakistan representation in the to-be-elected Constituent Assembly on the basis of population. Elections to the Constituent Assembly were held in December 1970 in which Mujibur Rahman's Awami League won a clear majority. Had Yahya Khan kept his word for transferring power to the majority party, Mujibur Rahman would have become Pakistan's first elected prime minister. If that had happened, Pakistan might have succeeded in keeping together its two wings. But Yahya Khan, encouraged by Zulfikar Ali Bhutto (q.v.), hesitated and postponed the convening of the Constituent Assembly. That was a big blow for the hopes of the people of East Pakistan. In a large public meeting held in Dacca on March 7, 1971, Mujibur Rahman made an emotional statement that virtually amounted to a declaration of independence. He was arrested soon after, flown to West Pakistan, and imprisoned in a town in Punjab (q.v.). The army followed these moves by attempting to quash the rebellion. The result was a civil war that lasted for nine months and led to the emergence of Bangladesh as an independent state on December 17, 1971.

Zulfikar Ali Bhutto, who took over as president from General Yahya Khan in December 1971, moved quickly to normalize relations with Bangladesh. Mujibur Rahman was released from prison and flown back to Dacca where he was installed as prime minister. On the eve of the Islamic summit held in Lahore (q.v.) in February 1974, Bhutto announced Pakistan's recognition of Bangladesh. In return for this gesture, Mujibur Rahman flew to Lahore to attend the meeting. Bangladesh went through a number of political traumas after its birth in December 1971. Mujibur Rahman was assassinated in 1975 and the military assumed power in the country. President Ziaur Rahman, the military leader, was himself assassinated in May 1981 and was followed by General Hussain Muhammad Ershad who ruled the country for six years before surrendering power to a civilian government led by Khaleda Zia, the widow of the slain president. The intense rivalry between Prime Minister Zia and Hoseina Wajid, the daughter of Mujibur Rahman, kept Bangladesh off balance for a number of years.

During these troubled times, however, Pakistan's relations with Bangladesh improved. The two countries began to work together within the framework of the South Asian Association for Regional Cooperation (SAARC) (q.v.) to forge closer economic ties between themselves.

BANK OF CREDIT AND COMMERCE INTERNATIONAL. *See* ABEDI, AGHA HASAN.

BANK OF PUNJAB. The Bank of Punjab was established on November 15, 1989, with its head office located in Lahore (q.v.) the capital of Punjab (q.v.) province. The main reason for the bank's establishment was to provide an additional source of credit for the entrepreneurial class of Punjab. The bank's creation was an act of desperation on the part of the provincial administration of Chief Minister Nawaz Sharif (q.v.). At the time of the bank's birth, the Punjab administration, under the control of the Islami Jamhuri Itehad (IJI), was engaged in a running political feud with the Pakistan People's Party (PPP) government headed by Prime Minister Benazir Bhutto in Islamabad (qq.v.). This dispute had economic ramifications including implicit constraints imposed by the central government on access to development banks by Punjab's entrepreneurial community. All development banks were controlled by the central government and the leaders of Punjab believed that Islamabad was discriminating against their province in not allocating sufficient investment bank financing. Accordingly, over the central government's serious objections, the government of Punjab decided to set up a bank of its own in the public sector. Tajammul Hussain, an experienced investment banker, was appointed the Bank of Punjab's first chairman.

In October 1993 Benazir Bhutto was back in power as prime minister and her party was also able to form a coalition government in Punjab. Despite this political change and the program of bank privatization launched by the new government, the Bank of Punjab remained under state control. Neither the Bhutto government nor the successor government of Nawaz Sharif revealed any plans to privatize the bank. It continues to operate in the public sector.

BANKS, NATIONALIZATION OF. The decision to nationalize the commercial banking sector was taken by the administration of Prime Minister Zulfikar Ali Bhutto (q.v.) and announced on December 31, 1973. The Banks (Nationalization) (Payments of Compensation) Rules of 1974 went into effect on January 1, 1974. The government took over the control and management of 14 commercial banks after issuing compensation bonds to their owners. The nationalized banks were regrouped and reorganized into five state-owned companies: the National Bank of Pakistan, the Habib Bank Limited, the United Bank Limited, the Muslim Commercial Bank Limited, and the Allied Bank of Pakistan. The Pakistan Banking Council was set up to look after the "performance and progress" of the nationalized banks.

Even though the government of President Zia ul-Haq (q.v.) did not share the socialist ideology of Prime Minister Zulfikar Ali Bhutto, it did not privatize the banks. It was only after Zia's death in 1988 and the induction into office of Prime Minister Benazir Bhutto (q.v.) that the government's policy toward the financial sector changed significantly. The Bhutto administration permitted the entry of private entrepreneurs into the financial sector. It was only under the first administration of Prime Minister Nawaz Sharif (q.v.) (1990–1993) that the government began a program of privatization of commercial banks, however. Two commercial banks—the Muslim Commercial Bank and the Allied Bank (q.v.)— were sold to the private sector. But the deals that were consummated proved to be controversial and their propriety was widely questioned. Benazir Bhutto's successor government (1993–96) did not reverse the decisions but succeeded in changing the management of one of the privatized institutions, the Allied Bank.

In October 1995 the government invited the private sector to bid for the United Bank, one of the three largest commercial banks in the public sector. The bank was sold to a Saudi Arabian group in the spring of 1996. This deal was not honored by the caretaker administration of Prime

Minister Meraj Khalid (q.v.). The caretakers decided that the first order of business should be to clean the portfolios of the banks. With this end in view a presidential ordinance was promulgated creating a new institution—the Resolution Trust Corporation of Pakistan (q.v.)—charged with the task of dealing with the nonperforming assets accumulated over the years by the nationalized banks. The government of Prime Minister Nawaz Sharif, which came to office in February 1997, adopted a different approach toward the nationalized banks. It chose to keep the nonperforming assets on the books of the nationalized banks but appointed a new set of managers and gave them the mandate to improve the quality of banking assets. The new managers were recruited from among the large cadre of Pakistanis working in foreign banks.

BASIC DEMOCRACIES (BD). The system of "Basic Democracies," launched by General Ayub Khan (q.v.) in 1960, was meant to serve two purposes: to constitute the electoral college for the president and the national and provincial legislatures and to bring his government closer to the people. The "Basic Democracies" was a system of local councils. Eight thousand Union Councils, 4,000 each in the provinces of East and West Pakistan, constituted the base of the system. Each Union Council had about 10 members and represented, on average, 1,000 people. The members of the Union Council were elected directly by the people; once elected they chose their chairman from among themselves. All Union Council chairmen in a *tehsil*—the lowest administrative unit in the government's structure—constituted the Tehsil Council. The Subdivisional Magistrate (SDM) was the chairman of the Tehsil Council. The representatives of various government departments working in the tehsil were appointed ex-officio members of the council. The Tehsil Councils elected the members of the District Council and the District Councils the members of the Divisional Councils. The District Councils were chaired by deputy commissioners and the Divisional Councils by commissioners. Like the Tehsil Councils, the District and Divisional Councils also drew membership from among government officials stationed in these jurisdictions. When the system was inaugurated, West Pakistan had a dozen divisions and about 50 districts. East Pakistan had four divisions and about 20 districts.

The first batch of 80,000 "basic democrats" was elected in January 1960, 40,000 each came from East and West Pakistan. In January 1965, Pakistan held its first presidential election under the constitution of 1965. This was the only occasion that the "basic democrats" were to serve as the "college" for electing the president. In 1969, General Yahya Khan dissolved the system of Basic Democracies.

BASIC PRINCIPLES REPORT. The Basic Principles Report was the culmination of three years of effort on the part of the First Constituent Assembly (q.v.) of Pakistan. It was published in 1950 and dealt with such issues as the role of religion in politics and governance, the role of Urdu as the country's only national language, and the division of power between the federal government and the provinces. The report was vigorously opposed by most politicians from East Bengal, Pakistan's eastern wing, which was later to separate from the country and become Bangladesh. Most political parties of East Pakistan were not prepared to accept Urdu as the only national language. They demanded equal status for Bengali, arguing that their language was spoken by a majority of Pakistan's population. East Bengal was also uncomfortable with the idea of a strong center governing over provinces with very limited power. The adoption of the report led to the electoral triumph of the United Front (q.v.) in the provincial elections of 1954 (q.v.).

BEG, GENERAL (RETIRED) MIRZA ASLAM (1931–). Originally from Azamgarh, United Provinces in undivided India, Beg was a teenager involved in the Pakistan movement when his family migrated to Pakistan, settling in Sindh (q.v.). He joined the sixth officer cadet course of the Pakistan Military Academy (q.v.) at Kakul in 1950, and was commissioned as an infantry officer on August 23, 1952, in the Baluch Regiment. In 1978 he was promoted to major general and given command of a division. Two years later he was posted as chief of the General Staff (GS) at General Headquarters (GHQ), Rawalpindi (q.v.), by General Muhammad Zia ul-Haq (q.v.), followed by a promotion to lieutenant general while still serving as CGS. He was given command of a corps in Peshawar (q.v.) in 1985. In March 1987 he was brought back to GHQ, promoted to general and replaced General Khalid Mahmud Arif as vice chief of the Army Staff under General Zia, who continued to retain concurrently the titles of president and chief of the Army Staff.

Beg would have completed his three-year term as a full general in 1990 had General Zia not died in an airplane crash near Bahawalpur (q.v.), along with the chairman of the Joint Chiefs of Staff Committee, General Akhtar Abdur Rahman (q.v.) and other senior military officers. Beg was elevated to the positions of chief of the Army Staff, a three-year term that ended August 16, 1991, when he was succeeded by General Asif Nawaz.

But General Beg did not fade away, activating the forum FRIENDS (the well-financed Foundation for Research on National Defence and Security), an organization that he set up while he was army chief and that included members of the local intelligentsia, such as former Foreign Minister Agha Shahi and pro-Iran columnist Mushahid Hussain. He continued to speak before public forums at home and abroad on political matters. In 1995, Beg formed his own "Awami Haqooq Party" (the Peoples Rights Party) but failed to arouse much public interest in the new organization.

BHARATIYA JANATA PARTY (BJP). The Bharatiya Janata Party first came to power in India following the national elections held in May 1996. Prime Minister Atal Bihari Vajpayee resigned less than two weeks later, however, unable to win the vote of confidence in the lower house, the Lok Sabha. The BJP had fought the election by emphasizing a combination of Indian nationalism and the revival of Hinduism. It promised a hard look at the arrival of all foreign capital into India. It promised to cultivate what it described as *Hindutva,* a kind of all-embracing Hindu-based culture to which all Indians, no matter what their religion, would be required to subscribe. It also advocated an uncompromising stance toward Pakistan.

It was reasonable for Pakistan to worry about the ascent of the BJP. The BJP had links with a well-armed Hindu militia that was responsible for tearing down a sixteenth-century mosque at Ayodhya (q.v.) in 1992, sparking riots that killed thousands of people, mostly Muslims. The BJP used the Ayodhya incident and its promise to construct a Hindu temple at the site of the mosque to its electoral advantage. Although the promise of Hindu revivalism in India was of concern to Pakistan, the Pakistani leaders were disturbed by another position taken by the BJP. It had been pushing the Indian leaders to openly develop nuclear arms and to use them, if the need arose, against Pakistan.

The BJP was back in power in March 1998, following a hard-fought campaign in India's twelfth elections. The BJP reneged on its previous promises; this time it also promised to remove the legislation that allowed Indian Muslims a separate status in that they could follow their own religion on matters pertaining to marriage and family formation. The party also pledged to force Pakistan out of Azad Kashmir (q.v.). After having secured a more comfortable position in the Lok Sabha and having also persuaded a dozen or so small regional parties to join hands with it, the BJP was able to form a government in New Delhi and win the vote of confidence in the Lok Sabha. Once again the BJP chose Atal Bihari Vajpayee to lead the government as prime minister. The prime minister, a moderate, had to deal with such hardliners as L. K. Advani. From Pakistan's perspective it was troubling that Advani was assigned the responsibility for Kashmir affairs.

On May 11, 1998 the government of India surprised an unsuspecting world by exploding three nuclear devices at a site close to Pakistan. The Indian action was widely condemned by the world but this reaction did not stop the BJP from ordering two more tests two days later at the same site. Pakistan was aghast at this turn of events. It did not follow immediately with nuclear tests of its own hoping that the western countries would impose severe sanctions on India. This did not happen at the G8 summit of eight industrial countries held in Birmingham, England on May 16–17. On May 18, a week after the nuclear tests, L. K. Advani, the Indian Home Minister, issued a stern warning to Pakistan concerning Kashmir (q.v.), indicating that India would not tolerate any Pakistani opposition to its rule over the state. On May 28, Pakistan responded to the Indian initiative by exploding five nuclear bombs of its own and followed up with one more test two days later. On April 18, 1999, the BJP government lost a vote of confidence in the parliament. Prime Minister Vajpayee resigned immediately following the defeat in the legislature. *See also* India–Pakistan Relations; Indo–Pakistan Nuclear Arms Race.

BHASHANI, MAULANA ABDUL HAMID KHAN (1885–1976). Born in the Tangail district of what was then the Bengal province of British India, Maulana Abdul Hamid Khan Bhashani was a prominent Muslim League (q.v.) leader during the campaign for Pakistan. He left the Muslim League soon after Pakistan was born and in 1949 formed the Awami League (q.v.), reflecting both his socialist ideology and his desire to attain greater autonomy for East Bengal. He was an active supporter of the United Front (q.v.), which decisively defeated the Muslim League in the East Bengal provincial elections of 1954 (q.v.). Major differences over foreign affairs with H. S. Suhrawardy (q.v.), the president of the Awami League, persuaded him to leave the party he had helped to create in favor of a new political organization that espoused a policy in favor of China and other socialist countries. The new organization, the National Awami Party (NAP), won Bhashani a great deal of support in Pakistan's western wing, in particular among the leaders of the smaller provinces of Balochistan and the Northwest Frontier (qq.v.). Bhashani, although opposed to Ayub Khan's (q.v.) domestic policies and not prepared to accept the political system established under the Constitution of 1962 (q.v.), supported the president's overtures to the People's Republic of China.

BHATTI, RAZIA (1955–1996). Razia Bhatti gained prominence as a journalist in the 1980s after starting *Newsline,* an English-language monthly newsmagazine that was published in Karachi. The magazine published a number of reports exposing corruption in high places. Its work contributed to the dismissal of the first administration of Prime Minister Benazir Bhutto in August 1990. The magazine continued with its independent policy even after the death of Bhatti.

BHUTTO, BENAZIR (1953–). Benazir Bhutto was the first child of Zulfikar Ali Bhutto and his second wife, Nusrat (qq.v.). She was educated in Murree, a hill station near Islamabad, in Karachi (qq.v.) and at Oxford and Harvard Universities. At Oxford, she was elected president of the Student Union. When Zulfikar Ali Bhutto became president of Pakistan, replacing General Yahya Khan (q.v.), Benazir Bhutto returned to Rawalpindi (q.v.) and began assisting her father on foreign policy issues. She was with Zulfikar Ali Bhutto in 1972 when he signed the Simla Accord (q.v.) with Indira Gandhi, India's prime minister.

Her first prominent role was bequeathed by her father who, shortly before his execution on April 4, 1979, appointed her co-chairperson of the Pakistan People's Party (PPP) (q.v.). Following Zulfikar Ali Bhutto's execution, both Nusrat and Benazir Bhutto were incarcerated for several months, either in jail or watched over by the authorities in their homes. Life in Pakistan was made intolerable for them and both decided to go abroad to live out Zia's martial law.

Benazir Bhutto's finest hour in public life came on April 10, 1986, when she returned to Pakistan after months of self-imposed exile in London. Notwithstanding Pakistan's long history of governments being toppled by street agitation, the Zia–Junejo government did not seem troubled either by the reception Benazir Bhutto received or by her insistence that the elections of 1985 could not be seen as signifying a return to democracy. On December 18, 1987 Benazir Bhutto married Asif Ali Zardari (q.v.) in Karachi; her wedding was attended by thousands of her followers.

A dramatic change occurred in Pakistan's political situation in August 1988. Zia ul-Haq (q.v.) was killed in an airplane crash and the senior leaders of the armed forces agreed to abide by the constitution and invited Ghulam Ishaq Khan (q.v.), chairman of the Senate, to take over the reins of the administration as acting president; Ishaq Khan announced that general elections would be held as scheduled in November 1988; and in September the Supreme Court ruled that political parties could participate in the elections. While these events were unfolding, Benazir Bhutto gave birth to her first child, a son, and named him Balawal (q.v.). She did not lose much time in getting back to active politics and launched a vigorous campaign all over the country. Her efforts were handsomely rewarded and the PPP emerged as the single largest group in the National Assembly, winning 92 out of 207 seats. The party won a clear majority in the Sindh (q.v.) legislature but lost Punjab (q.v.) to Islami Jamhuri Itehad (q.v.), a coalition of right-wing parties in which Mian Nawaz Sharif's Pakistan Muslim League (qq.v.) was the dominant player.

After some hesitation the Muhajir Qaumi Mahaz (MQM) (q.v.) announced its support for Bhutto and her party. This cleared the way for her to become prime minister. An invitation was issued to her to from a government in Islamabad and she was sworn in on December 2, 1988 as Pakistan's thirteenth prime minister. It soon become apparent, however, that to get that position she had accepted an informal arrangement according to which all important decisions that concerned Pakistan's security were to be taken by a "troika" (q.v.). The troika was to include, in addition to herself, the president, and the chief of the Army Staff. She also agreed to give the ministry of foreign affairs to Lt. General (retired) Yaqub Khan (q.v.), a trusted member of the Islamabad establishment.

By mid-year 1988, President Ghulam Ishaq Khan and General Aslam Beg (q.v.) had come to the conclusion that Pakistan was not safe in Benazir Bhutto's hands and that she had to be forced out of office. She was dismissed by Ishaq Khan in August 1990 on charges of corruption and incompetence. Asif Ali Zardari was imprisoned on numerous charges of corruption while a number of cases were filed against Ms. Bhutto.

In the elections of 1990 (q.v.), Bhutto and the PPP did less well, winning only 45 of the 206 seats in the National Assembly, less than half the number won in the 1988 elections. The elections of October 1993 (q.v.), held following the dismissal of the government of Prime Minister Nawaz Sharif by President Ghulam Ishaq Khan, went in favor of Benazir Bhutto and she was back in power as prime minister.

This time Benazir Bhutto found the environment in Islamabad to be more conducive. The "troika," which included the president, prime minister, and the chief of Army Staff, had survived but she was now clearly in command. She had managed to get Farooq Leghari (q.v.), her trusted lieutenant, elected president; General Abdul Waheed Kakar (q.v.), chief of the Army Staff, was not interested in politics. This favorable environment notwithstanding, Bhutto did not govern wisely. The economy (q.v.) performed poorly under her stewardship; Pakistan mismanaged its relations with Afghanistan; her inability to work with the MQM in Karachi resulted in a virtual civil war between the forces of the MQM and her government's law-and-order enforcement machinery; and there was widespread misuse of public funds by the functionaries of the government. Bhutto and the PPP quickly lost popularity and by the fall of 1995, with the economy in trouble and the people restive, there was a great deal of talk in the country of yet another intervention by the army. These rumors contributed to a delay in the nomination of new chief of the Army Staff. In early December 1995, President Farooq Leghari chose Lt. General Jehangir Karamat to succeed General Kakar. Karamat was the senior-most serving general and was widely respected. His appointment brought some stability to the government.

In the spring of 1996, the Supreme Court surprised Benazir Bhutto by issuing an order that questioned the basis on which her government had appointed dozens of judges to the Supreme Court and the Provincial High Courts. She was ordered to regularize these appointments by first consulting with the chief justices of the courts. In response, Bhutto was defiant and the country came close to another constitutional crisis. After considerable hesitation, Bhutto compromised with the court and stopped the country from moving toward yet another political abyss.

But it was a grudging accommodation and she continued to drag her feet. Her problem with the Supreme Court, the continued deterioration in the state of the economy, a sharp increase in the incidence of corruption, and a serious worsening of the law-and-order situation in the large cities of the country persuaded President Farooq Leghari, her onetime close associate, to use Article 58.2(b) (q.v.) of the constitution against her. Accordingly, on November 5, 1996, President Leghari dismissed Benazir Bhutto as prime minister, dissolved the National Assembly, and appointed a caretaker administration under Meraj Khalid (q.v.), a veteran PPP politician, to oversee another general election. The elections of 1997 (q.v.) were held on February 3 and resulted in a massive defeat of Bhutto's PPP by Mian Nawaz Sharif's Pakistan Muslim League (q.v.). The administration of Prime Minister Nawaz Sharif, which came into office following the 1997 elections, pursued the cases of corruption against Bhutto and other members of her family originally initiated by the caretaker administration of Meraj Khalid. In September 1997, the government of Switzerland, in response to a request by the Pakistan government, blocked a number of bank accounts held by the Bhutto family. Similar proceedings were begun in Great Britain where the Bhutto family was reported to own a number of properties including a large estate in Surrey. In July 1998, the Swiss and British courts authorized the authorities in their countries to provide assistance to the government of Pakistan to pursue its corruption case against Benazir Bhutto and Asif Ali Zardari. In April 1999, Lahore High Court accepted the government's case against Bhutto and sentenced her to five years in prison. She was also barred from holding public office.

BHUTTO, GHINWA. Ghinwa Bhutto, born in Lebanon but a citizen of Syria, married Mir Murtaza Bhutto (q.v.), Zulfikar Ali Bhutto's (q.v.) son, while the latter was living in self-imposed exile in Damascus from 1981 to 1993. Ghinwa was Mir Murtaza Bhutto's second wife. His first wife was an Afghani woman whom he had married when he was living in

Kabul, after leaving Pakistan in 1979. Ghinwa and Murtaza had one son, who was born in Damascus.

Ghinwa Bhutto accompanied her husband when he returned to Pakistan in 1993. She entered politics after her husband was killed in an encounter with the police on September 20, 1996. On September 25 she filed a petition with the High Court of Sindh (q.v.), alleging that her husband was "physically eliminated through a conspiracy hatched between the government functionaries, officials of the Intelligence Bureau and senior police officers of the province." Following the dismissal of the government of Prime Minister Benazir Bhutto (q.v.), Ghinwa Bhutto sought to continue her husband's program of finding space in Sindh politics for his party—the Pakistan People's Party (Bhutto Shaheed) (q.v.), a PPP faction formed by her husband. She contested for a seat in the National Assembly in the elections of 1997 (q.v.) but lost to a PPP candidate.

BHUTTO, MIR MURTAZA (1954–1996). Mir Murtaza Bhutto was born in 1954. He was the second child of Zulfikar Ali Bhutto and Nusrat Bhutto (qq.v.). He was only 23 years old when Zia ul-Haq (q.v.) staged a coup that forced his father out of office. When Zulfikar Ali Bhutto was executed two years later, Murtaza vowed to take revenge. He organized a group called Al-Zulfikar (q.v.), which carried out a number of terrorist operations in the country, including the hijacking of a Pakistan International Airlines plane in 1981.

Murtaza Bhutto spent several years in self-imposed exile in Damascus, Syria, where he met his second wife, Ghinwa (q.v.), a Lebanese citizen. He returned to Pakistan in 1994 and was promptly arrested. He remained in prison for several months and was eventually released on bail by the Sindh (q.v.) High Court. After being released, he formed his own faction of the Pakistan People's Party (PPP) (q.v.) and named it after his father. The PPP (Bhutto Shaheed) failed to gain much support even in rural Sindh. Murtaza was gunned down by a group of assailants on the night of September 20, 1996. His murder was one of several developments that led President Farooq Leghari (q.v.) to dismiss Benazir Bhutto and arrest Asif Zardari (q.v.), her husband. Zardari was charged with conspiracy to murder Murtaza Bhutto.

BHUTTO, MUMTAZ ALI (1936–). Mumtaz Ali Bhutto was educated at Christ Church, Oxford and entered active politics when his cousin Zulfikar Ali Bhutto (q.v.) launched the Pakistan People's Party (PPP) (q.v.). He was a member of the federal cabinet for a few months after Zulfikar Ali Bhutto became president and chief martial law administrator in December 1971. He was appointed governor of Sindh (q.v.) in 1972 and served in that capacity until 1974. He came back to Islamabad (q.v.) in 1974 as a federal minister. Mumtaz Ali Bhutto was arrested by the army in July 1977 along with a number of other PPP leaders when Zia ul-Haq (q.v.) moved against Zulfikar Ali Bhutto. Following Zulfikar Ali Bhutto's execution on April 4, 1979 he left Pakistan and stayed in London until 1986.

With Benazir Bhutto (q.v.) in full political command of rural Sindh, Mumtaz Bhutto became at best a minor player in politics. In November 1996, however, following the dismissal of Prime Minister Benazir Bhutto, President Farooq Leghari (q.v.) appointed Mumtaz Bhutto the caretaker chief minister of Sindh. In that capacity he had the satisfaction to witness the disastrous defeat of Benazir Bhutto in the elections of February 1997. Following the installation of Mian Nawaz Sharif (q.v.) as prime minister, Mumtaz Bhutto, once again, began to champion the cause of rural Sindh.

BHUTTO, NUSRAT (1928–). Nusrat Bhutto married Zulfikar Ali Bhutto (q.v.) in Karachi (q.v.) in 1950. She was his second wife. She entered politics during her husband's lifetime. She won a seat in the National Assembly in the elections of 1970 (q.v.) as a representative of the Pakistan People's Party (PPP) (q.v.). In 1979, after Zulfikar Ali Bhutto's execution, she was appointed chairperson of the PPP. After being confined to house arrest for several years by the administration of President Zia ul-Haq (q.v.), she was allowed to leave the country for Europe on medical grounds. She did not accompany her daughter, Benazir Bhutto (q.v.), when the latter returned to Pakistan 1986.

Begum Nusrat Bhutto was again elected to the National Assembly in the general elections of 1988 (q.v.) from a seat in Karachi. When Benazir Bhutto was invited to become prime minister, Nusrat Bhutto was appointed as "senior minister" in her daughter's Cabinet. She left Pakistan for Europe after her daughter and her Cabinet were dismissed by President Ghulam Ishaq Khan (q.v.) in August 1990. She returned to Pakistan a year later to launch a campaign to get her son, Mir Murtaza Bhutto (q.v.), permission to return to the country. She was elected to the National Assembly for the third time, but was not invited to join the second administration of Benazir Bhutto, which took office in October 1993.

Although unhappy with the way Benazir Bhutto and her husband, Asif Zardari (q.v.), had treated Murtaza Bhutto, her oldest son, and suspicious that Zardari may have had been involved in Murtaza'a murder in 1996, she agreed to represent her daughter's Pakistan People's Party in the elections of February 1997 (q.v.). She was one of the seventeen PPP candidates to be elected to the National Assembly but by that time she was too ill with Alzheimer's disease to play an effective political role.

BHUTTO, SHAHNAWAZ (1956–1986). Shahnawaz Bhutto was the third of the four children of Zulfikar Ali Bhutto and Nusrat Bhutto (qq.v.). He was born in Karachi (q.v.) and named after his grandfather, Shahnawaz Bhutto. He left Pakistan in 1979 following the execution of his father. He joined hands with his elder brother, Mir Murtaza Bhutto (q.v.), to found Al-Zulfikar (q.v.), an organization dedicated to avenging the execution of his father by the military regime headed by President Zia ul-Haq (q.v.). After spending several years in Afghanistan, Shahnawaz Bhutto moved to southern France where he died in 1986 under mysterious circumstances, perhaps of a drug overdose.

BHUTTO, ZULFIKAR ALI (1928–1979). Zulfikar Ali Bhutto was born at Larkana, a medium-size town on the right bank of the Indus River in the province of Sindh (qq.v.). His father, Sir Shahnawaz Bhutto, was one of Sindh's largest landlords, with extensive landholdings in the Larkana district. Khurshid, Zulfikar Ali's mother was a Hindu woman of low social standing who had converted to Islam before becoming Sir Shahnawaz's second wife. Zulfikar Ali was Sir Shahnawaz's only son; on his father's death in 1949, he inherited most of the Larkana estate. Zulfikar Ali was also to marry twice, the first time to a cousin and the second time, in 1950, to Nusrat Isphani, a woman of Iranian origin whom he met in Karachi (q.v.). He and Nusrat had four children; two of them, Benazir and Mir Murtaza (qq.v.), were to play active roles in Pakistan's politics.

Zulfikar Ali Bhutto was sent to Bombay for schooling and then to the University of California, Berkeley, and Christ Church, Oxford, for education in law. He returned to Karachi in 1953 and started legal practice at the Sindh High Court. In 1958, General Ayub Khan (q.v.) brought him into his Cabinet as the minister of fuel, power, and natural resources. Bhutto's big opportunity came in 1963, with the sudden death of Foreign Minister Muhammad Ali Bogra. Bhutto persuaded Ayub Khan to reassign him to the foreign ministry. Against the openly expressed unhappiness of Washington, Bhutto developed close ties with the People's Republic of China. Pakistan and China negotiated a border agreement, established commercial airline operations between them, and increased the flow of trade.

In the summer of 1965, Bhutto persuaded Ayub Khan to take a series of steps that eventually resulted in provoking a war with India. On September 23, barely 17 days after the war had begun, Ayub Khan announced a cease-fire agreement with India, which he negotiated with the help of the United Nations. Four months later, along with Prime Minister Lal Bahadur Shastri of India, he went to the Soviet city of Tashkent and negotiated what he believed would be a more durable agreement of peace between the two neighboring countries. Zulfikar Ali Bhutto accompanied Ayub Khan to Tashkent but appears not to have endorsed the substance of the agreement. A few months after their return to Pakistan, Ayub and Bhutto finally parted company, with the latter making much of his opposition to the Tashkent Declaration (q.v.) in public debate. Bhutto joined hands with a number of politicians from East and West Pakistan to launch a massive campaign against the government of President Ayub Khan. The president sought to negotiate his way out of his political problems but the opposition proved more stubborn than he had expected. On March 25, 1969, the army stepped in. It forced Ayub Khan to resign.

Bhutto had prepared himself well for the time when political power would pass from the army to the politicians. In 1967, a year after leaving the government of Ayub Khan and after weighing the offers from several opposition parties, Bhutto had decided to form his own political organization, the Pakistan People's Party (PPP).

Bhutto took office as president in December 1971 following the defeat of the Pakistani army in East Pakistan. Insofar as the conduct of domestic economic policies is concerned, the Bhutto era (December 1971 to July 1977) divides itself neatly into two periods: 1971 to 1974 and 1974 to 1977. During the first period, the Bhutto government pursued a socialist program, capturing for the government all the commanding heights of the economy (q.v.). In the second, starting with the departure of such socialist ministers as Mubashir Hasan and J. A. Rahim, Bhutto took control of the economy. The result was a total loss of orientation and whimsical decision-making that caused major economic disruption, reduced the rate of growth of the gross domestic product, increased the incidence of poverty, and did away with the fiscal and monetary discipline that had been the hallmark of economic management during the period of President Ayub Khan. Bhutto's economic legacy was to affect the pace and nature of Pakistan's economic development for a long time after his departure from the political scene.

In foreign affairs, Bhutto proved to be a much more imaginative and flexible manager. He negotiated the Simla Accord (q.v.) with Indira Gandhi in 1972, hosted the second summit of the Organization of the Islamic Conference (OIC) at Lahore (q.v.) in 1974, recognized Bangladesh as an independent state in 1974 and made some tangible advances in healing Pakistan's relations with Afghanistan. In keeping with the approach he had advocated during the Ayub period, he realigned Pakistan's foreign relations away from a close dependence on the United States.

In 1973, with his political skills once again on full display, Bhutto persuaded and cajoled the opposition into accepting a new constitutional arrangement for Pakistan. The constitution was passed by the National Assembly and became effective on August 14, 1973, which was Pakistan's 26th anniversary. Bhutto stepped down from the presidency and became prime minister. In January 1977, when Bhutto suddenly called national elections—the first to be held under the new constitution—he expected to catch the opposition unprepared. The opposition surprised him by preparing itself quickly: the Pakistan National Alliance (PNA) (q.v.) was born and a disparate set of parties agreed to compete with the PPP under a single political umbrella. The army took advantage of Bhutto's inability to settle his differences with the opposition. He was deposed by the military on July 5, 1977, sentenced to death by the Lahore High Court in 1978, his sentence confirmed by the Supreme Court in March 1978, and executed in Rawalpindi (q.v.) on April 4, 1979. *See also* Constitution of 1973; Indo–Pakistan War of 1965.

BIJARANI, KHIZAR KHAN (1948–). Khizar Khan Bijarani was among the new generation of provincial leaders to be given prominent positions in the Pakistan People's Party (PPP) (q.v.) in the late 1980s. This change in the senior personnel of the party was undertaken by Benazir Bhutto (q.v.) after she returned to Pakistan in April 1986 from self-exile in London. Bhutto wanted to replace the leadership that was associated with her father with people she could trust.

Bijarani was appointed president of the Sindh PPP and was entrusted with the task of reorganizing the party at the district level and preparing for the elections that were expected to be held in 1990. The party performed poorly in the local government elections held in 1987, however, and Bijarani was held responsible for the embarrassment suffered by Bhutto. She asked for his resignation, which she received in January 1988; in his letter of resignation, Bijarani blamed Ms. Bhutto for continuous interference in the affairs of the party. He maintained that in a democratic party setup, the affairs of the provincial chapter should be strictly the responsibility of the provincial president. The "Bijarani episode" demonstrated that the Benazir Bhutto style of leadership was similar to that of Zulfikar Ali Bhutto (q.v.), her late father. Like her father she did not believe in delegating much authority to party officials. This style of management was to cause considerable disaffection among the leaders of the party.

BIN LADEN, OSAMA. Osama bin Laden, a member of the Saudi royal family and a millionaire, came to the attention of the intelligence community in the late 1970s after he had begun to establish industries in

Sudan to manufacture materials that could be used by the Afghan mujahideen (q.v.) fighting against the Soviet Union in Afghanistan. After the withdrawal of the Soviet Union from Afghanistan in the late 1980s, bin Laden is said to have involved himself with the groups that opposed the Oslo peace accord concerning the Israel-occupied West Bank. Under pressure from the United States, the Sudanese expelled bin Laden and in 1996 he moved to Khost (q.v.), a small town close to the Pakistan–Afghanistan border. From this hideout bin Laden began operations against the United States and the countries he accused of supporting the "American campaign against Islam." The Taliban (q.v.) forces in Afghanistan received support from bin Laden as they consolidated their hold on their country.

On a visit to Pakistan in early 1998 the United States Secretary of State Madeleine Albright described bin Laden as "inimical to those of the civilized world" and called on Afghanistan to "stop harboring those considered terrorists." The Taliban ignored Albright and continued to provide sanctuary to the Saudi millionaire.

On August 7, 1998 terrorists bombs in Tanzania and Kenya exploded near the United States's embassies, claiming nearly 300 lives including 12 Americans. On the same day, the authorities in Pakistan arrested Muhammad Siddique Odeh, an alleged associate of bin Laden. Odeh was interrogated and linked the embassy attacks to a group operating out of Afghanistan and headed by bin Laden. On August 17 the United States ordered hundreds of its citizens to leave Pakistan. On August 20 the United States launched air attacks on the camp that housed bin Laden. The United States linked bin Laden not only to the embassy bombings in East Africa but also to the activities of people such as Ramzi Youssef (q.v.). The cruise missiles used by the United States in the attack on the bin Laden camp in Khost flew over Pakistani airspace, prompting Pakistan to lodge a protest with United Nations.

BOGRA, MUHAMMAD ALI (1901–1963). Muhammad Ali belonged to the Bogra district of Bangladesh. He came from a landowning family. He entered politics in the late 1930s and was elected to the Bengal provincial assembly in 1936. He won the provincial assembly seat in 1946 and was appointed parliamentary secretary in the Muslim League (q.v.) administration led by Khawaja Nazimuddin (q.v.). After the establishment of Pakistan, Bogra held a number of diplomatic positions including Pakistan's ambassador to the United States. He stayed in Washington for a year, from 1952 to 1953. In 1953 he was summoned back to replace his old mentor Nazimuddin as prime minister of Pakistan. He was the choice of Governor-General Ghulam Muhammad (q.v.), who wanted the position to remain with a Bengali politician.

Bogra reorganized his cabinet in 1954 to include a number of professionals including General Ayub Khan (q.v.), the commander in chief of the Pakistan army. He was dismissed as prime minister in 1955 and was sent back to Washington as ambassador, a position he held for three years. In 1962, following the promulgation of a new constitution, Bogra joined the first civilian cabinet put in office by President Ayub Khan. The president assigned him the important portfolio of foreign affairs in part because of the close relations he had developed with the United States. He died in office in 1963 and was succeeded by Zulfikar Ali Bhutto (q.v.) as foreign minister.

BONDED LABOR LIBERATION FRONT (BLLF). The Bonded Labor Liberation Front was organized in 1974 in Lahore (q.v.). Its main purpose is to improve the conditions of the people working in the unorganized sector. Most of its efforts were directed at children employed in such small-scale activities as carpet weaving and metal working. In Iqbal Masih (q.v.), himself once a child worker in a small carpet-weaving workshop, the organization gained a highly effective visible spokesman. Masih's murder in 1995 further highlighted the importance of the work undertaken by the BLLF.

BONUS VOUCHER SCHEME, EXPORT. The Export Bonus Voucher Scheme was one of the major economic policy innovations of the Ayub Khan (q.v.) period (1958–69). It was introduced in January 1959 at the suggestion of two German experts who had been invited by the government to help the country increase the value of its exports. The experts devised a simple mechanism for allowing importers and consumers of imports to subsidize exporters and producers of exports. In its original form, the Bonus Voucher Scheme granted "vouchers" to exporters equivalent to some prespecified proportion of the value of exports. Originally, only two different percentages were prescribed: 20 percent for commodities in "their natural state" (other than raw jute, raw cotton, leather, and hides) and 40 percent for all manufactured items.

The Bonus Voucher Scheme, therefore, introduced a system of multiple exchange rates, the range of which changed every day with the value of the premium quoted on the market for the vouchers. The scheme remained in effect for 13 years; it was abandoned in the spring of 1972 when Pakistan undertook a massive devaluation of its currency with respect to the U.S. dollar, from Rs.4.76 to Rs.11.

BRI-KOT-GHAWANDAI. Bri-Kot-Ghawandai is the site of a town dating back to the Greek period. It was discovered and excavated in 1987 by a joint team of Pakistani and Italian archeologists. The town is situated on the left bank of the Swat River. Archeologist Sir Aurel Stein and Professor Giuseppe Tucci identified the settlement as the town of Bazira, which was conquered by Alexander the Great in 327 B.C.

BROWN AMENDMENT, THE. The "Brown amendment," named for its chief sponsor, Hank Brown, the Republican Senator from Colorado, was passed by the U.S. Senate on September 21, 1995. Most of the senators from President Bill Clinton's Democratic Party opposed the amendment even though it had the approval of the White House. The Brown amendment, in effect, was a one-time waiver of the Pressler amendment (q.v.). The latter had the effect of virtually stopping all U.S. assistance, military as well as economic, from being received by Pakistan. The Brown amendment would allow Pakistan to receive $368 million worth of missiles and other military equipment for which it had already paid. Pakistan would still not be able to receive the 71 F-16 jet fighters for which it had also made a payment, however. In the same amendment, the Senate also agreed to authorize resumption of U.S. aid to and cooperation with Pakistan in the areas of counterterrorism, narcotics, and other law-enforcement fields.

BURKI, LIEUTENANT GENERAL WAJID ALI KHAN (1899–1989). Lt. General Wajid Ali Khan Burki was born in Jullundhur. After graduating from St. Andrews University in Scotland, he joined the Royal Army Medical Corps. He saw active service in Burma during World War II. In 1947, he opted to join the Medical Corps of the Pakistan Army and moved to Rawalpindi (q.v.). In 1955, he was appointed the director general of the corps.

Wajid Burki joined the first Cabinet of President Ayub Khan (q.v.) as minister for health, labor, and social development. A number of reforms were initiated under his watch and he worked closely with President Ayub Khan and served as his deputy after the departure of General Azam Khan (q.v.). He was appointed Pakistan's ambassador to Sweden in 1963. He returned to Pakistan three years later and devoted the rest of his life to developing modern medical institutions in the country, including Jinnah Post-Graduate Medical College in Karachi (q.v.).

BURKI, SHAHID JAVED (1938–). Shahid Javed Burki was born in Simla into a well-known Pathan family from Jullundhur, Punjab. After joining the Civil Service of Pakistan (q.v.) in 1960, he went to Oxford University a year later as a Rhodes Scholar. In 1967 he went to Harvard University as a Mason Fellow. In 1974 he joined the World Bank (q.v.) as senior economist and served in several positions in that organization, including Director of China Department and Vice President, Latin

America and the Caribbean Regional Office. In August 1993 he advised Moeen Qureshi, the caretaker prime minister, and took an active part in developing the reform program announced on August 19. In November 1996 he was invited by President Farooq Leghari (q.v.) to take over responsibility for the portfolios of finance, planning, and economic affairs in the caretaker cabinet that took office following the dismissal of the government of Prime Minister Benazir Bhutto (q.v.). He was credited with the formulation of an ambitious program of structural reforms that was to become the basis for assistance by the International Monetary Fund (q.v.). He returned to the World Bank after the elections of 1997 (q.v.), which resulted in the administration of Prime Minister Mian Nawaz Sharif (q.v.).

╰┐ C ┌╯

CABINET MISSION PLAN, 1946. The plan submitted by the "Cabinet Mission" sent by the British government called for the creation of three groups in India after the departure of the British. Two groups, in the northwest and northeast of the country, were to be made up of the provinces in which the Muslims constituted the majority, whereas the rest of India was to form the third group. The three groups, as well as the Indian Union, were to have their own legislatures. The Indian Congress Party wanted to control the provinces from the union legislature, which it knew it could dominate, whereas the Muslim League (q.v.) wanted the authority for the central government to flow from the group legislatures. The plan was accepted by the Muslim League but rejected by the Congress Party.

CAROE, SIR OLAF (1901–1992). Sir Olaf Caroe was appointed governor of the Northwest Frontier Province (q.v.) in September 1946 and held that position until the birth of Pakistan in August 1947. Sir Caroe stayed on as governor for less than two years; in August 1947, Governor General Muhammad Ali Jinnah (q.v.) replaced him with another British officer, Sir George Cunningham (q.v.). Sir Olaf Caroe returned to England but came back to the Northwest Frontier Province in 1956 to work on his study of the Pathans. *The Pathans* was published in 1958 and was immediately acclaimed as the most comprehensive history of the area ever written.

CENSUS OF 1941. The census of 1941, conducted in British India while Great Britain was engaged in fighting with Germany, holds special significance for Pakistan. It demonstrated that the Muslim community in India constituted an even larger minority than was generally believed. The Muslim population, with a higher total fertility rate (q.v.) than the non-Muslims, was growing at a faster pace than the rest of India. According to the census estimates, some 30 percent of the Indian population—about 100 million people in all—was Muslim. The census also provided the basis for the partition of the large provinces of Bengal and Punjab (q.v.) into Muslim and non-Muslim parts. Muslim Bengal was to become East Pakistan, Pakistan's eastern wing, which then attained independence as Bangladesh in 1971. The census was used by Sir Cyril Radcliffe (q.v.) to draw the line between the Indian and Muslim portions of Punjab in a way that left at least two Muslim majority provinces—Jullundhur and Gurdaspur—in Indian hands.

CENSUS OF 1951. Pakistan held its first census four years after its birth. The population count was taken in March 1951. The census estimated the population at 33.780 million of whom 27.761 million—or 82.2 percent of the total—lived in rural areas, whereas the remaining 6.019 million—or 17.8 percent—resided in towns and cities. The estimated rate of growth was 1.8 percent a year. The urban population had increased at a rate more than three times that of the rural population, 4.1 percent as against 1.3 percent for the areas that now make up Pakistan. Pakistan had added 5.458 million people to the population estimated in 1941. The increase was the result of both natural growth and migration of millions of people from India.

CENSUS OF 1961. The second Pakistani census was taken 10 years after the first. It showed the population to have grown at 2.4. percent a year, a rate considerably higher than the rate of increase estimated for the first post-independence decade. In 1961 the country's estimated population was 42.880 million. Of this, 33.226 million, or 77.5 percent of the total, lived in the countryside. The remaining 9.654 million people—22.5 percent—lived in towns and villages. The urban population was estimated to be increasing at a rate of 4.7 percent, whereas the rural population was growing at the rate of 1.8 percent.

CENSUS OF 1972. The third census in Pakistan's history was held in the fall of 1972 and estimated the country's population at 64.890 million. This meant that the country had added more than 22 million to its population over a period of slightly more than 11 years. Pakistan had doubled its population in 25 years. The rate of growth had increased to 3.5 percent a year, the largest increase recorded in Pakistan's 25-year history. Rural population, at an estimated 48.201 million, or 74.3 percent of the total, had increased at a rate of 3.1 percent a year. The increase in the urban population was estimated at 4.6 percent a year. It was estimated that 16.689 million people were now living in towns and cities.

CENSUS OF 1981. With the fourth census, held in February 1981, Pakistan returned to the decennial approach for counting its population. The size of the 1981 population was estimated at 84.254 million, of whom 60.413 million lived in the countryside and the remaining 23.841 million resided in towns and cities. The rural population accounted for 71.7 percent of the total while the proportion of the urban population was on the order of 28.3 percent. Overall, the population was estimated to have increased at a rate of 3.1 percent a year since the third census, held in 1972 (q.v.). The rural population had increased at a rate of 2.8 percent and that of the urban areas at a rate of 4.3 percent per annum. There were 44.232 million men and 40.022 million women in Pakistan's population. This means that there were 111 men to 100 women in the population, so the male–female ratio is 1.11:1, making Pakistan one of the few countries with more men than women.

CENSUS OF 1998. It took 17 years for Pakistan's politicians to muster enough political courage to hold another population census. Under normal circumstances a census should have been held in 1991, in keeping with the decennial approach, which the country was expected to follow along with most of the rest of the world. Also, the Constitution of 1973 (q.v.) had mandated that population censuses should be held every 10 years to provide the basis for the allocation of seats in the National Assembly and the sharing among the four provinces of revenues collected by the federal government. That did not happen since the government of Prime Minister Nawaz Sharif (q.v.) did not feel that it had enough political authority to overrule the objections of provinces and powerful socioeconomic groups that would have lost some political ground as a result of an accurate count of the population. Accordingly, the census was postponed. The successor government of Prime Minister Benazir Bhutto (q.v.), operating under the same set of constraints, also failed to hold a census while it held office, from October 1993 to November 1996. It was only with the decisive victory of Nawaz Sharif and his Pakistan Muslim League (q.v.) in the elections of February 1997 (q.v.) that a government came to office that felt it had sufficient political authority to go ahead with a census.

The census was held over a period of 18 days in March 1998. The military assisted the government by having soldiers accompany enumerators as they went from house to house gathering data. Preliminary results from the census were announced in June 1998, according to which Pakistan had a population of 137 million, 10 million less than the estimates of most demographers.

CENSUSES, POPULATION. Pakistan has been more irregular than most countries in holding population censuses. The first census was held in 1951, four years after the country's birth. The second was held on time, in 1961. The third census was delayed by a year on account of the crisis in East Pakistan, which lasted through most of 1971, and the war with India fought in December of that year. The third census was conducted in 1972. In 1974, the National Assembly passed the electoral law, which provided that a census be held regularly at 10-year intervals in order to apportion seats in the national and provincial assemblies. With the fourth census, taken in 1981, Pakistan attempted to get back to the 10-year plan but it was interrupted once again when the country failed to take the fifth census on time in 1991. It was scheduled to be held three times but was postponed every time. The first two postponements were due to political reasons. The last postponement was in October 1997 at the urging of the armed forces. The military (q.v.) wished to expand the scope of the census to include the gathering of information for defense purposes. The census was finally conducted in March 1998 with the active participation of the armed forces. *See also* Censuses of 1941, 1951, 1961, 1972, 1981, 1998.

CENTRAL TREATY ORGANIZATION (CENTO). *See* UNITED STATES–PAKISTAN RELATIONS.

CHARAR SHARIEF. The struggle of Muslim Kashmiris against the occupation of their state by India, which turned exceptionally violent in 1989, acquired a new symbol six years later. On May 11, 1995, a fire totally destroyed the shrine of Sheikh Nooruddin Wali at Charar Sharief, a town 30 kilometer southwest of Srinagar, the state's capital. The shrine had been built in the fifteenth century by the disciples of Wali, a saint who had brought Islam to this part of the world.

The Kashmiri Muslim freedom fighters blamed the Indian security forces for setting the shrine and the town of Charar Sharief on fire. The Indians claimed that the Kashmiri militants had deliberately destroyed the shrine to win more converts to their cause. Whatever the motives, the destruction of the shrine had some immediate consequences. It resulted in the postponement of the elections in Kashmir (q.v.) scheduled by the Indian government to be held in mid-July. It also evoked a bitter response in neighboring Pakistan. On May 18, Prime Minister Benazir Bhutto (q.v.) went on national TV to announce that the destruction of the shrine would be mourned officially in Pakistan on the following day. On Friday, May 19, President Farooq Leghari (q.v.) led "funeral" prayers for the mosque and the Kashmiris killed at Charar Sharief.

CHATTA, HAMID NASIR (1950–). Hamid Nasir Chatta belongs to an established political family of Punjab (q.v.). His differences with Nawaz Sharif (q.v.) were to shape Pakistani politics for a long time. These differences were not ideological; they were the result of an intense rivalry between the two politicians. Each wanted to be recognized as the leader of Punjab. Nawaz Sharif's effort to capture the Pakistan Muslim League (PML) (q.v.) following the death of its president, Muhammad Khan Junejo (q.v.), in 1993 brought about a rupture between the two. Chatta left the main PML and formed his own group and gave it the name of Pakistan Muslim League (Junejo) (PML[J]) (q.v.). He went on to associate himself with Benazir Bhutto's Pakistan People's Party (q.v.), which made it possible for the latter to hold power in both Islamabad, the federal capital, and Lahore, the capital of Punjab (qq.v.), from 1993 to 1996. Both Chatta and the PML(J) fared poorly in the elections of 1997 (q.v.), however.

CHHOR. The army cantonments of Pano Adil (q.v.) and Chhor were established over a 10-year period, starting in the mid-1980s. The principle purpose of these two centers in the remote parts of Sindh (q.v.) was not to deter aggression against Pakistan. Instead, these locations were chosen to station the army close to the areas that had experienced political instability. One lesson learned by the army in its efforts to help the civil authorities maintain law and order was that it needed to position itself physically close to the centers of perpetual political turbulence. The decision to locate a cantonment in Pano Adil, taken during the Zia years, was an unpopular one because it was widely advertised by the Pakistan People's Party (PPP) (q.v.) as a move by the military establishment to "colonize" the interior of Sindh (q.v.).

No resistance was mounted when the army began to develop Chhor for the simple reason that the decision to do so was made by a civilian rather than a military government. The decision to establish a cantonment in Chhor, a village in Sindh's Tharparker district, was made in 1992 by the government of Prime Minister Nawaz Sharif (q.v.), but major civil works were begun only in 1994 and 1995. By early 1996 Chhor had started to function as an army center and the army felt confident enough about the wisdom of its move to mount a major public-relations effort. A group of prominent journalists was invited to visit the new cantonment and they wrote glowing accounts of the positive changes that had resulted from the army's presence in this remote area.

CHINA–PAKISTAN RELATIONS. The Communists came to power in China on October 1, 1949. At that time, Liaqat Ali Khan (q.v.), Pakistan's prime minister, was trying to cultivate close relations with the United

States. Accordingly, China started official business with Pakistan by leaning toward India on the issue of Kashmir (q.v.).

It was only with the arrival of military rule in Pakistan that relations between the People's Republic of China and Pakistan began to improve. The initial overture to China was made by Zulfikar Ali Bhutto (q.v.), a member of the Ayub Khan (q.v.) Cabinet. Bhutto found China in a receptive mood. It had severed relations with the Soviet Union in 1961; Japan was still not prepared to work with Beijing; Taiwan remained an irritant, supported by the United States. Despite the close personal relations that had developed between Prime Ministers Jawaharlal Nehru and Zhou Enlai, India was inclined to support the Soviet Union in its dispute with China. That left Pakistan, a close ally of the United States, but a country at odds with both India (q.v.) and the Soviet Union.

The 1962 border war between China and India prompted President John Kennedy to get personally involved in South Asia. To bring pressure on Pakistan, Washington decided to withhold funding of some development projects. But the Pakistani leadership refused to buckle under this pressure. In January 1964, Pakistan and China announced that the two countries had agreed to demarcate the undefined 300-mile-long border between them. The border ran from the point where Afghanistan (q.v.), China, and Pakistan meet and included the strategic Khunjerab Pass (q.v.) in the Karakoram range. In August 1964, China and Pakistan announced an agreement to build a road connecting China's Xinjiang province with the northern areas of Pakistan. The United States retaliated by suspending all development assistance to Pakistan.

In 1965, Pakistan fought its second war with India over the state of Kashmir. The enormous investment Pakistan had made in cultivating a close relationship with China now paid off. Although the United States and the countries of Western Europe stopped all economic and military assistance to Pakistan and India, Pakistan was able to procure military supplies from China. Pakistan's close relations with China came in handy for the United States when, under President Richard Nixon, Washington decided to begin the process of normalization with Beijing. In July 1971 Pakistan facilitated the secret mission to China undertaken by Henry Kissinger, the U. S. secretary of state. Kissinger's first meeting with Chinese officials was on-board the Pakistan Airlines plane to Beijing.

China continued to figure in an important way in Pakistan's relations with the United States. The United States suspected that the two countries had worked closely on the development of a nuclear bomb by Pakistan. In addition to the complication caused by the United States in Pakistan's relations with China, one other irritant has emerged in the way the two countries are dealing with one another. As Pakistan sought to strengthen its relations with the Muslim republics of Central Asia, a number Islamic groups in the country began to work in these countries. But they did not confine their activities only to Central Asia. Some of them, in particular the Jamaat-e-Islami (q.v.), extended their reach to Xinjiang province of China as well. This type of activity did not sit well with the authorities in Beijing.

These irritants notwithstanding, Pakistan looked to China once again when on May 11, 1998, India tested three nuclear devices and followed the testing a week later with a strongly worded warning to its neighbor not to influence the ongoing agitation in Kashmir against Indian occupation of the state. Pakistan dispatched a high-powered delegation to Beijing to secure support and protection from the Chinese in its conflict with India. *See also* Indo–Pakistan Nuclear Arms Race.

CHRISTIANS IN PAKISTAN. Christianity arrived in the areas that now constitute Pakistan as a result of the work done by European missionaries in the sixteenth to the twentieth centuries. The missionaries concentrated their efforts mostly on the members of the scheduled castes (q.v.), who were receptive to their overtures given the low social status they occupied in the highly structured Hindu religion. When the Hindus and Sikhs left Pakistan at the time of partition of British India in 1947, the Christians stayed behind. Some of them played important roles in Pakistan; one of them, A. R. Cornelius (q.v.), became chief justice of the Supreme Court.

With Zia ul-Haq's (q.v.) program of Islamization—with the introduction, in particular, of the Hadud Ordinances (q.v.), which prescribed heavy punishment for defaming Islam—Pakistan became a progressively less-tolerant society, especially toward the minorities. Among the religious groups that were especially discriminated against were the Ahmadiyas (q.v.) and the Christians. Although no firm estimates are available, the former number about five million and the latter two million in a population estimated at 137 million during mid-1998.

An incident in the Punjab (q.v.) city of Sahiwal in May 1998 serves as an example of the kind of treatment suffered by the minorities. Ayub Masih, a young Christian, was accused of having spoken derogatorily of Islam and the Holy Prophet and praising the novelist Salman Rushdie (q.v.). Masih was tried and sentenced to death by a local court after proceedings that lasted for nearly two years. The sentence, not the first to be handed out by a court under the "blasphemy laws," shocked the Christian community. In an act of desperation, John Joseph, the Bishop of Faisalabad (q.v.), another Punjab city, went to Sahiwal on May 6, conducted a prayer ceremony for the condemned youth, and then put a pistol to his head and killed himself.

CHUNDRIGAR, ISMAIL IBRAHIM (1897–1960). I. I. Chundrigar was born in Bombay and obtained a degree in law from Bombay University. He began his legal career in Ahmadabad but on being elected to the Bombay Legislative Assembly in February 1937, moved his legal practice to Bombay. He was elected president of the Bombay Muslim League in 1940 for a period of five years. In 1943 he was elected to the All-India Muslim League (q.v.) Working Committee, which functioned as the policy-making body for the party. In 1946, he was one of the five members of the Muslim League (q.v.) to join the Interim Government headed by Jawaharlal Nehru.

After the establishment of Pakistan, Chundrigar moved to Karachi (q.v.) and was included as a minister in the first Cabinet under Prime Minister Liaqat Ali Khan (q.v.). He left the Cabinet in May 1948 to become Pakistan's first ambassador to Afghanistan (q.v.) but was recalled from Kabul in 1950 to assume the governorship of the Northwest Frontier Province (q.v.). In 1951, he was sent to Lahore as governor of Punjab (qq.v.). He resigned from this position in 1953 because of differences with Governor-General Ghulam Muhammad (q.v.) over the handling of the anti-Ahmadiya agitation. In 1955 he was invited back into the central Cabinet. When H. S. Suhrawardhy (q.v.) became prime minister, he was elected to lead the opposition in the National Assembly. On Suhrawardhy's dismissal by President Iskander Mirza (q.v.), I. I. Chundrigar was invited to become prime minister. He remained in office for only 54 days, from October 18 to December 11, 1957, one of the shortest tenures of any prime minister in the country's history. He was succeeded by Feroze Khan Noon as prime minister. *See also* Ahmadiyas, The.

CITIZEN'S VOICE. The launching of Citizen's Voice—a nongovernment organization sponsored by 18 prominent citizens of Karachi (q.v.)—was an indication that some segments of the Pakistani population were prepared to work toward the resolution of the problems that brought the country's largest city to a state of virtual paralysis. "We are a group of professional men and women" the sponsors announced in newspaper advertisements carried on December 27, 1995. "We believe that it is time for concerned citizens to step into the breach, erect obstacles along the path of violence and warfare, and create a climate of purposeful politics. Else the jeopardy to state and society in Pakistan shall augment." The sponsors were worried about the direction in which Pakistan's major political parties had taken the country. "Successive governments had failed to rein in corruption which is eating into the vitals of the society. The continuous criminalization of politics is widening the gulf between the state and the people." For this reason, the founders of the Citizen's

Voice implored "Pakistan's leaders to embark on a process of peace and civility, abjure confrontations and embrace compromise by negotiation, and take a decisive turn toward progressive and democratic reforms for a humane and prosperous future. Karachi is the appropriate starting point [for these efforts]."

The founders of the Citizen's Voice did not request financial contributions but only asked "all thoughtful and committed citizens who feel concerned over the deteriorating state of Pakistan in general and Karachi in particular" to join the organization.

CIVIL SERVICE OF PAKISTAN (CSP) AND THE ECONOMY. While Pakistan's postindependence politicians were busy squabbling over the form of government to give their new country, senior members of the civil bureaucracy took over the role of economic decision-making. For a period of four decades, from the late 1940s to the late 1980s, the civil servants, with few interruptions, remained in charge of economic decision-making. Interruptions came briefly in the late 1950s and the early 1970s: the first, when the military government of General Ayub Khan (q.v.) was still in the process of settling down; the second, when Prime Minister Zulfikar Ali Bhutto (q.v.) placed political ideologues into important economic positions. Even under Ayub Khan and Zulfikar Ali Bhutto, members of the Civil Service of Pakistan played important roles as economic decision-makers. M. M. Ahmad was in charge of Ayub Khan's Planning Commission. Qamarul Islam held the same position under Bhutto.

It was only with the return of democracy in November 1988 that politicians began to take over control of the economy. Even then the process proved to be a slow one. When President Ghulam Ishaq Khan called on Benazir Bhutto (qq.v.) to become prime minister he persuaded her to appoint Vaseem A. Jaffrey (q.v.) as her economic advisor. Vaseem Jaffrey played a low-key role in this capacity, a role not typical of the civil servants who had occupied similar positions in the past. As such, he may have set into motion a new trend in which the senior civil servants were expected to render advice but not make decisions.

The dismissal of the government of Prime Minister Benazir Bhutto in November 1996 brought a number of former CSP members into the caretaker administration inducted into office by President Farooq Leghari (q.v.), once a CSP member himself. Leghari was a member of the 1964 CSP class. He turned to a number of his former CSP classmates to take up important positions including Shahid Hamid, who was appointed defense minister, and Abdullah Memon, who was put in charge of the ministry of water and power. Shahid Javed Burki, who belonged to the 1960 CSP, was put in charge of finance, planning, and economic affairs.

COMBINED OPPOSITION PARTY (COP). The Combined Opposition Party was formed in the fall of 1964 to challenge President Ayub Khan (q.v.) at the presidential polls scheduled for December. This was the first election to be held under the constitution of 1962 (q.v.). The opposition to Ayub Khan had hoped to force the president to adopt a political structure more to its liking. It preferred a parliamentary system over the presidential form introduced by Ayub Khan in 1962. Once convinced that the president was not inclined to accept the demand of the opposition, a number of political parties chose to pool their resources and organize an electoral alliance of the type that had appeared before in the country's history. Among the more prominent parties that were assembled under the umbrella of the COP were the Council Muslim League, the Awami League, and the National Awami Party (qq.v.).

The COP leadership was able to persuade Fatima Jinnah (q.v.), the sister of Muhammad Ali Jinnah (q.v.) and a persistent critic of the system introduced by Ayub Khan, to become its candidate in the presidential election. In spite of her advanced years, Ms. Jinnah campaigned well and was able to win the support of more Basic Democrats than was thought possible by the government. The COP was disbanded after the elections were over. It was succeeded by the Pakistan Democratic Movement (PDM) (q.v.)—another opposition alliance—that was to successfully challenge Ayub Khan in 1968–69. *See also* Basic Democracies.

COMMISSION ON MARRIAGE AND FAMILY LAWS. *See* FAMILY LAWS ORDINANCE OF 1961.

COMPREHENSIVE TEST BAN TREATY (CTBT). Work on the Comprehensive Test Ban Treaty began in January 1994 and concluded on June 28, 1996. The treaty was opened for signatures soon after its adoption and by the time India and Pakistan conducted nuclear tests in May 1998, 149 countries had already signed it. Only 13 have fully ratified it. The treaty cannot come into effect unless ratified by 44 countries that have nuclear reactors. This includes India, Pakistan, and North Korea. Although the treaty was signed by Israel, it has yet to ratify it. The Western powers exerted a great deal of pressure on both India and Pakistan to sign the CTBT after the two countries conducted nuclear tests in May 1998.

CONFERENCE OF MUSLIM WOMEN PARLIAMENTARIANS. The first Conference of Muslim Women Parliamentarians was held in Islamabad (q.v.) on August 1 to 3, 1995, chaired by Benazir Bhutto (q.v.), Pakistan's prime minister. The idea of the conference was conceived by Ms. Bhutto to prepare for the Fourth World Conference on Women and to "give a correct view about the role of women in Muslim society to the West which often projects it negatively. We want to show that the Muslim women are playing a positive role in top decision-making levels as parliamentarians, journalists and in other fields." The conference was attended by over 100 delegates from 35 Muslim nations and adopted a declaration on the role of women and women's rights as envisioned in Islam.

CONSTITUENT ASSEMBLY, THE FIRST. The First Constituent Assembly of Pakistan was created by the Indian Independence Act of 1947. It started with 69 members, but after the accession of the states of Bahawalpur (q.v.), Khairpur, and Balochistan (q.v.) to Pakistan, the membership was increased to 74. Of the 61 Muslim members in the assembly, the Muslim League (q.v.), with 59 members, had a clear majority. The two members who did not belong to the League were Abdul Ghaffar Khan of the Northwest Frontier Province and A. K. Fazlul Haq (qq.v.) of East Bengal. The assembly met for the first time on August 10, 1947, in Karachi (q.v.). On August 11, three days before Pakistan achieved independence, it elected Muhammad Ali Jinnah (q.v.) as its president.

Jinnah became too ill in early 1948 to be able to guide the process of writing the constitution. He died on September 11, 1948, prompting a series of changes that brought Maulvi Tamizuddin (q.v.) of East Bengal to the presidency of the Constituent Assembly and Ghulam Muhammad (q.v.) as governor-general. Liaqat Ali Khan (q.v.) stayed on as prime minister. None of these individuals had Jinnah's charisma or his moral authority and, consequently, the process of constitution making got bogged down in endless political disputes. Agreement could not be achieved on two issues: the powers to be assigned to the provinces within the Pakistani federation and the role of religion in the state of Pakistan. Eventually, the assembly was able to pass a bill labeled the "Basic Principles" (q.v.), which was adopted to guide the process of creating the constitution.

Under the Indian Independence Act, the Constituent Assembly had two separate functions: to prepare a constitution, and to act as a legislative assembly. The assembly's legislative powers were to be exercised under the Government of India Act of 1935 (q.v.). Although the assembly failed in carrying out its first mandate, it functioned effectively as a legislative assembly until it was dissolved in 1954. On September 21, 1954, the assembly sought to limit the power of the governor-general by moving a bill to amend the Government of India Act of 1935. Sections 9, 10, 10A, and 10B of the act were amended, taking away from the governor-general powers to act independently except on the advice of his ministers, and requiring the choice of new ministers to be made only from among members of the assembly. But Governor-General Ghulam Muhammad moved before the assembly was able to adopt the bill: On October 24, 1954 he precipitated a constitutional crisis by dissolving the Constituent Assembly.

Maulvi Tamizuddin took the case to the federal court and challenged the governor-general's dissolution as unconstitutional. In a decision that was to have profound implications for Pakistan's political development, the Court refused to overturn the governor-general's action. It took cover under the "doctrine of necessity" (q.v.), arguing that by not endorsing the dissolution of the assembly, the Court could create a serious constitutional crisis. The Court ordered the governor-general to reconstitute the Constituent Assembly, however. *See also* Basic Principles Report.

CONSTITUENT ASSEMBLY, THE SECOND. The dissolution of the First Constituent Assembly (q.v.) resulted in a number of landmark decisions by the federal court. In Usif Patel's case, the federal court unanimously decided that the task of framing a constitution could not be assumed by the governor-general; it had to be performed by a representative body. On May 10, 1955 the federal court declared that the governor-general was not empowered to summon a constitutional convention, as was his intention, but had to form a Constituent Assembly to function under the provisions of the Indian Independence Act of 1947. Accordingly, the Second Constituent Assembly was elected in June 1955, and met for its first session in Murree on July 7, 1955. The session was presided by Mushtaq Ahmad Gurmani, the governor-general's nominee. The assembly's regular sessions were held later in Karachi (q.v.). As with the first assembly, it acted both as the federal legislature and as the body entrusted with the task of framing a constitution. In the former capacity it passed the Unification of West Pakistan Bill on September 30, 1955. On January 8, 1956, it produced a draft constitution, which, with some amendments, was adopted on February 29, 1956. On March 23, 1956, the Second Constituent Assembly reconstituted itself as the national legislature under the constitution it had adopted earlier. *See also* Constitution of 1956.

CONSTITUENT ASSEMBLY, THE THIRD. Pakistan's Third Constituent Assembly was convened in 1972 by President Zulfikar Ali Bhutto (q.v.) to draft a new constitution. The constitution of 1962 (q.v.), introduced by President Ayub Khan (q.v.), had been abrogated by the military when it assumed power in March 1969. The assembly was made up of the National Assembly members elected in December 1970. A new draft constitution was submitted to the assembly on December 31, 1972, and became effective on August 14, 1973. *See also* Constitution of 1973.

CONSTITUTION OF 1956. The Second Constituent Assembly (q.v.), which first met in 1955, was successful in drafting and promulgating Pakistan's first constitution. The principle of parity (q.v.), which gave equal representation to East and West Pakistan in the assembly, was adopted as the cornerstone of the new constitution. The provinces and states in the western wing of the country were merged to form the One Unit of West Pakistan (q.v.).

Hussain Shaheed Suhrawardhy and Chaudhri Muhammad Ali (qq.v.) were the principal architects of the constitution. Suhrawardhy was responsible for drafting the constitution bill when he was law minister in the Cabinet of Muhammad Ali Bogra (q.v.), but walked out of the assembly when the bill was put to vote in the National Assembly, proclaiming that East Pakistan's interests had not been duly protected. It was Chaudhri Muhammad Ali who, as prime minister, finally got the Constituent Assembly to pass the constitution bill. The constitution came into force on March 23, 1956, and Chaudhri Muhammad Ali became the first chief executive under the new setup.

The 1956 constitution created a federal republic in Pakistan with two units, East and West Pakistan. The president was to be the head of the republic. He was to be chosen by an electoral college made up of the National and Provincial Assemblies. The president was to select the prime minister from among the members of the National Assembly. The person most likely to command the confidence of the majority of the assembly members was to be chosen by the president to become prime minister. The prime minister was to be the head of the government who, along with his Cabinet, was responsible to the National Assembly. The National Assembly was to have 300 members, 150 each from East and West Pakistan. The provinces were to have a form of cabinet government similar in all essentials to that provided for the federation.

The federal court was to be reconstituted as the Supreme Court. The chief justice was to be appointed by the president and the other judges by the president after consultation with the chief justice. A judge could be removed by the president after advice of the National Assembly with two-thirds of the member concurring.

The constitution remained in force for only two-and-a-half years. Preparations to hold Pakistan's first general elections were started in early 1958 but the constitution was abrogated on October 7, 1958, by a proclamation issued by President Iskander Mirza (q.v.). Mirza's action was forced on him by General Ayub Khan (q.v.), who was commander in chief of the army at that time. Twenty days later, on October 27, 1958, Ayub Khan sent Iskander Mirza into exile and became Pakistan's first military president.

CONSTITUTION OF 1962. The process of consultation for devising a new constitution began in February 1960, when a constitutional commission was appointed to first elicit the views of the people on the structure of government and then to present its recommendations to the president. The commission, working under the chairmanship of Muhammad Shahbuddin, a senior judge of the Supreme Court, made its recommendations in a report to President Ayub Khan (q.v.) on May 6, 1961. Rather than accept the structure proposed by the commission, Ayub Khan entrusted the job of writing the new constitution to Manzur Qadir (q.v.), his foreign minister. Manzur Qadir produced a constitutional framework that used the system of Basic Democracies (q.v.) as its foundation. Adult franchise was confined to the election of 80,000 Basic Democrats, 40,000 for each for the provinces of East and West Pakistan. The Basic Democrats constituted the electoral college for the president and members of the national and provincial assemblies. The president appointed his own Cabinet whose members were not responsible to the National Assembly. The president was given extensive executive, legislative, and financial powers, including power to issue ordinances, declare emergencies, and call referendums in case of persistent differences with the National Assembly. The constitution could be amended by the National Assembly only with the approval of the president.

The constitution became effective on June 8, 1962 and was used immediately to legitimize Ayub Khan's administration. Two sets of elections were held under the new political structure erected by the constitution. The first, held in 1962 to elect the "Basic Democrats," then went on to reaffirm Ayub Khan as president and to choose the members of the National and Provincial Assemblies. The second, held in 1965, reelected Ayub Khan as president but not with the kind of majority he had hoped. Ayub Khan had to fight hard against Fatima Jinnah (q.v.), the candidate put forward by the Combined Opposition Party (q.v.).

The constitution failed its most important test, that of transfer of power. In 1969, a prolonged agitation against Ayub Khan led to the president's resignation. Under the constitution, Abdul Jabbar Khan, a politician from East Pakistan and speaker of the National Assembly, should have become acting president pending the election of a new head of the state by the electoral college. Instead, Ayub Khan invited General Yahya Khan (q.v.) to perform his "constitutional duty" and take over the administration. General Yahya Khan became president, placed Pakistan once again under martial law, abrogated the constitution, and dissolved the National and Provincial Assemblies.

CONSTITUTION OF 1973. Pakistan's constitutional history was complicated by its geography, but the situation was not eased by the secession of Bangladesh in December 1971. The new Pakistan that emerged in 1971 was reasonably homogeneous; it was geographically contiguous; its people, although speaking several different languages, shared a common history and were culturally more alike than was case with the people of East and West Pakistan. The dramatic political change that occurred as a result of the breakup of Pakistan did not resolve the differences among the provinces in what was once the western wing of the country, however. A number of problems that had inhibited the writing of the constitution in the 1950s resurfaced. The question of defining the role of Islam in Pakistan's economy and polity became even more difficult to resolve than in the earlier period. Religious parties (q.v.) had always been more powerful in the provinces of West Pakistan than in East Bengal. With East Pakistan not there anymore to lend a moderating hand, the religious parties demanded the establishment of an Islamic state in what was left of Pakistan.

The issue of the sharing of power between the federal and state governments that had occupied the attention of the politicians when Bengal was a part of Pakistan did not disappear with the departure of the eastern wing. To these two perennial problems, Zulfikar Ali Bhutto (q.v.) added a third: the role of the head of state. Bhutto was now the president. He had inherited all the political power that his military predecessors—Generals Ayub Khan and Yahya Khan (qq.v.)—had accumulated since 1958. He was not disposed to dilute the power of the presidency for as long as he could occupy the office.

The task of devising a new constitutional arrangement was entrusted to a Constituent Assembly—the Third Constituent Assembly (q.v.) in Pakistan's history. Its membership was made up of the people who had been elected to the National Assembly from the provinces of West Pakistan in the elections held in December 1970. The Pakistan People's Party (PPP) (q.v.) had a clear majority in the assembly, and it proceeded to elect Zulfikar Ali Bhutto as the assembly chairman. In keeping with the tradition established by the First and Second Constituent Assemblies (q.v.), the third assembly also functioned as the national legislature.

It took the assembly six months to draft a new constitution; agreement was reached between the PPP and the smaller political organizations represented in the constituent body because of Bhutto's willingness to yield ground to them on most of the important issues. On October 20, leaders of the parties represented in the National Assembly agreed on a new constitution, which provided for a two-chamber federal Parliament, a president, and a prime minister. The president was to be elected by a joint sitting of the National Assembly, the Senate, and the four Provincial Assemblies. The president was to invite the member of the National Assembly or the Senate most likely to command a majority in the national legislature to become the prime minister. The prime minister was required to choose his ministers from among the members of the Parliament. The four provinces were to have unicameral legislatures with chief ministers chosen from among the members of the assemblies. Provincial governors were to be appointed by the president on the advice of the prime minister. The new constitution came into effect on August 14, 1973, Pakistan's twenty-sixth anniversary.

The constitution of 1973 (q.v.) established a parliamentary system in which the prime minister was responsible to the National Assembly. The provincial legislatures, like the National Assembly, were to be elected directly by the people on the basis of adult franchise. Provincial chief ministers were to be responsible to the provincial legislatures. The president and provincial governors had very limited powers; all the executive authority was in the hands of the prime minister and the provincial chief ministers.

Islam had a more prominent presence in the 1973 constitution than in the constitutions of 1956 and 1962 (qq.v.). Apart from making reference to the "sovereignty of Allah" in the preamble, Article 2 declared that "Islam shall be the State religion of Pakistan." This phrase had not appeared in the earlier constitutions. Article 40 declared that the state "shall endeavor to preserve and strengthen fraternal relations among the Muslim countries based on Islamic unity."

In defining the powers to be exercised by the provinces, the 1973 constitution was more explicitly in favor of the federating units than the constitutions of 1956 and 1962. It was because of these provisions that Bhutto was able to obtain the support of the political parties that had a stronger provincial base than the PPP. The 1973 constitution made one significant departure from the traditions established in 1958 and 1962: it defined the role of the military and proscribed any intervention by the armed forces in the political life of the state. Article 245 stated that the military's role was to "defend Pakistan against external aggression or threat of war, and subject to law, act in aid of civil authority when called upon to do so." Article 6 defined the subversion of the constitution " by the use of force or show of force or by other unconstitutional means" to be an act of high treason and authorized the Parliament to provide punishment for those who ignored this provision. On September 14, 1973 the National Assembly passed a law that prescribed the death sentence or life imprisonment for the subversion of the constitution.

The 1973 constitution remained in force in its original form for four years. It remained suspended for eight years, from 1977 to 1985, when Pakistan was under marital law. The president's Revival of the Constitution 1973 Order (q.v.) of 1985 restored the constitution after amending 67 out of its 280 articles.

CONVENTION MUSLIM LEAGUE. The Convention Muslim League was formed in 1963, a year after the promulgation of Pakistan's second constitution (the Constitution of 1962) (q.v.). By that time President Ayub Khan (q.v.) had reached the conclusion that he had made a mistake by not allowing political parties to reenter the political arena. Accordingly, Ayub Khan's supporters in the National Assembly summoned a "convention" of Muslim Leaguers in May 1963. The convention, held in Rawalpindi (q.v.), agreed to revive the Muslim League (q.v.) and to offer the party's chairmanship to Ayub Khan. The president accepted the offer. However, several prominent Muslim Leaguers not invited to the convention in Rawalpindi refused to accept the legitimacy of this act. They convened their own "council" and declared that they too had revived the old Muslim League. By the middle of 1963, therefore, Pakistan had two Muslim Leagues and they came to be distinguished by the manner of their revival. The official party was informally named the "Convention Muslim League," whereas the party in opposition to President Ayub Khan was named the "Council Muslim League."

In keeping with Pakistan's political tradition, a political party need not have a program in order to attract support. All it required was official patronage. Once the Convention Muslim League was formed, it was able to attract a large following not because the people who joined the party believed in the program it had to offer. They came for the reason that had attracted them before to the officially sponsored political parties: they were in search of jobs and official patronage. Once again, they seem to have made the right calculation. In the elections to the National Assembly held in 1965, the Convention Muslim League won 124 out of 156 seats it contested, 69 of which were from West Pakistan and 55 from East Pakistan. Its overwhelming presence in the national legislature said little about its popularity, however.

The party was put to a real test in the general elections of 1970 (q.v.) when, with Ayub Khan no longer in power and without any support from the government, the Convention Muslim League polled only 3.3

percent of the total votes cast. The party's best showing was in Punjab (q.v.), where it received 5.5 percent of the vote and was able to win two seats in the National Assembly. During the period of Zulfikar Ali Bhutto (q.v.) (1971–1977), the Convention Muslim League played a marginal role in politics. It was dissolved along with other political parties when General Zia ul-Haq (q.v.) wrested the reins of government from Bhutto in July 1977. The party was resuscitated later as the Pakistan Muslim League (q.v.).

CORNELIUS, JUSTICE A. R. (1903–1991). A. R. Cornelius was born in Agra, India and studied at a college in Allahabad, Uttar Pradesh, and then went on to Cambridge University in England for further studies. He joined the Indian Civil Service (ICS) in 1926 and was transferred to the judicial branch of the service. Soon after the establishment of Pakistan, Cornelius was appointed to the Supreme Court of Pakistan. While on the Court's bench he displayed total independence, refusing to go along with his fellow judges in sanctioning political actions in terms of the "doctrine of necessity" (q.v.). He was the sole dissenting voice in two landmark constitutional cases that dealt with the legality of executive decisions, both of which had profound implications for the country's political development. In a dissenting opinion in the Maulvi Tamizuddin (q.v.) case, filed to challenge Governor-General Ghulam Muhammad's (q.v.) dissolution of the Constituent Assembly, Justice Cornelius agreed with the finding of the Sindh High Court. The Sindh court had declared the governor-general's action to be unconstitutional and ordered the restoration of the Constituent Assembly. In the Dosso case, filed to challenge the military takeover of the government under the leadership of General Ayub Khan (q.v.), he was once again the lone dissenting voice. He disagreed with the majority opinion that Ayub Khan's martial law was de jure by virtue of its being de facto.

These dissenting opinions notwithstanding, Justice Cornelius will be remembered most for the report on the reform of the civil administration he authored in 1964. The report was never released to the public; the government regarded its conclusions to be too radical for implementation. Despite the secrecy surrounding the report, it became widely known that Cornelius and his colleagues had recommended the abolition of the Civil Service of Pakistan (q.v.) and its replacement by a more broadly constituted administrative service that would not have a powerful influence on economic decision-making. In this respect, Cornelius had gone even further than the recommendations of Zahid Hussain in the First Five Year Plan (q.v.) document.

Pakistan had to wait another eight years before the main recommendation of the Cornelius Commission was implemented. In 1972 Prime Minister Zulfikar Ali Bhutto (q.v.) dissolved the Civil Service of Pakistan and introduced a system of recruitment that allowed broad representation to the people to the civil service.

COTTON. Although cotton has been cultivated in the Indus River (q.v.) valley for centuries, it was grown mostly for household consumption. Very little of it was marketed. It took four developments, the full import of which were not realized at the time they occurred, to make cotton one of the most important crops for the Indus plain. The first was the introduction of American cotton to Sindh and south Punjab (qq.v.); the second, the arrival of canal irrigation to the areas that could support the production of cotton; the third, the use of chemical fertilizer for cotton production; and the fourth, the use of chemical insecticides and pesticides for saving cotton from being damaged by disease and pests. The fourth development contributed to Pakistan's "second green revolution" (q.v.).

For the last 50 years—ever since the arrival of irrigation in Sindh and south Punjab—raw cotton exports have been important for the areas that now constitute Pakistan. It was because of the sharp rise in earnings from cotton exports during the Korean War period that Pakistan was able to finance its first industrial revolution. Cotton exports were handled by large privately owned companies; there was an impression, particularly among the socialist circles from which Zulfikar Ali Bhutto's Pakistan People's Party (qq.v.) drew its initial support, that the trading houses made large profits at the expense of the growers. Accordingly, on assuming power, Bhutto nationalized external trade in cotton and other agricultural commodities and established a public-sector trading company, the Pakistan Trading Corporation, to handle commodity exports. During the period of Zia ul-Haq (q.v.), private-sector activity was encouraged and large private entrepreneurs returned to industry, in particular to cotton-based manufacturing. In the 1980s and the early part of the 1990s, there was such a great deal of new investment in cotton-related industries that during lean years Pakistan was forced to import raw cotton. Another unhappy development in the early 1990s—the arrival of a highly destructive fungus called "cotton rust"—inflicted a heavy damage on the crop and hence on the economy.

COUNCIL FOR DEFENSE AND NATIONAL SECURITY (CDNS). The Council for Defense and National Security was established by

President Farooq Leghari (q.v.) in December 1996. It had 10 members, four from the armed forces and six from the civilian realm, including the president, who was its chairman. The armed forces were represented by the chairman of the Joint Chiefs of Staff, and the chiefs of staff of the Army, Air Force, and Navy. The civilian side was represented by the prime minister and the ministers of defense, finance, foreign affairs, and the interior.

The CDNS was created to provide a formal mechanism for the senior military officers to keep a watch on all matters concerning national security. Its establishment sought to formalize the "troika" (q.v.) arrangement that had existed since the death of President Zia ul-Haq (q.v.). The CDNS met three times during the tenure of the caretaker administration but was not convened by Prime Minister Nawaz Sharif (q.v.).

COUNCIL MUSLIM LEAGUE. The Council Muslim League was founded in 1963 after President Ayub Khan (q.v.) decided to revive political parties. The president's supporters reorganized the Muslim League (q.v.) at a convention held in Rawalpindi (q.v.), the interim capital. Although the party was formally called the Pakistan Muslim League (q.v.), it came to be known instead as the Convention Muslim League (q.v.) to distinguish it from the party that was organized by another group of former Muslim Leaguers. The latter party came to be called the Council Muslim League and drew the support of the members of the Pakistan Muslim League—the party the military government had ordered dissolved in 1958—which did not support Ayub Khan's political order but wished, instead, to see Pakistan return to parliamentary democracy. Among those who were attracted to the Council Muslim League were Fatima Jinnah (q.v.), Mian Mumtaz Daulatana (q.v.), and Chaudhri Muhammad Ali (q.v.). In 1964, the Council League joined a number of other opposition parties to form the Combined Opposition Party (COP) (q.v.). The COP put up Fatima Jinnah as its candidate for the presidential election held in December 1964. Ayub Khan won the contest but with a margin much smaller than generally expected. The Council Muslim League faded away after the resignation of Ayub Khan in March 1969.

CRICKET WORLD CUP, THE FIFTH. The fifth Cricket World Cup was played in 1992 in Australia and New Zealand. The Pakistani team was led by Imran Khan (q.v.), who had been summoned back to cricket after he had left the game. Although the team did poorly in the round-robin part of the tournament, it managed to reach the semifinals.

Pakistan played against New Zealand in the semifinals and won in an exciting match. It played against England in the finals and, against most expectations, won the cup by defeating a team that was regarded as much superior by most commentators. The "man of the match" award was won by Imran Khan who was credited with exceptional leadership in pulling together his team to win the tournament. The Pakistanis returned to their country as heroes and were given a warm reception by a very large crowd that gathered to receive them at the airport in Lahore (q.v.).

CRICKET WORLD CUP, THE SIXTH. The sixth Cricket World Cup was played in India, Pakistan, and Sri Lanka in February and March 1996. Twelve national teams participated in the tournament. There were high expectations that one of the three host countries would claim the cup. Pakistan did well in the round-robin part of the tournament. It entered the quarter finals but lost to India in the match played in Hyderabad, India. The Pakistani team was clearly intimidated by the hostility of the crowd. India went on to play the semifinals with Sri Lanka in Calcutta. When it became clear that India was going to lose the match, the crowd became unruly and invaded the field. The match was abandoned, with victory awarded to Sri Lanka. The other semifinal was played between Australia and the West Indies. Australia won the match. The final between Australia and Sri Lanka was played in Lahore (q.v.), and the underdog Sri Lankans won the cup.

CUNNINGHAM, SIR GEORGE. Sir George Cunningham served as the governor of the Northwest Frontier Province (NWFP) (q.v.) from 1937 to 1946 and again, at the invitation of Governor-General Muhammad Ali Jinnah (q.v.), from 1947 to 1948. Jinnah's mission in the Frontier Province was still not finished when Pakistan was born on August 14, 1947. At the time of Pakistan's birth, the province was still being administered by a government representing the Indian National Congress (q.v.). Dr. Khan Sahib (q.v.) was the chief minister. Jinnah called for Dr. Khan Sahib's resignation but the chief minister refused to oblige. Sir George Cunningham who was a year in retirement, was invited to come back as governor, being the man everyone trusted. He administered the last rites to the Khan administration on August 22, 1947, a week after Pakistan was born. Khan Abdul Qayyum Khan was invited to become chief minister. His mission accomplished, Sir George left the NWFP and Pakistan in 1948.

↩ **D** ↪

DACOITS OF SINDH. Sindh (q.v.) has always had *dacoits,* bands of robbers who harassed the countryside with the rural poor as their main victims. These bands sometimes worked for the *waderas,* the large landlords, extorting taxes on their behalf from the small peasants. However, it was only after the agitation launched in 1983 by the Movement for the Restoration of Democracy (MRD) (q.v.) against the martial-law government of General Zia ul-Haq (q.v.) that the dacoits turned to politics and began to receive arms, training, and organizational support from the political parties that opposed military rule.

The army was called in to eliminate the threat that was now posed by the dacoits to the national economy. But its operations seemed more costly to it in terms of personnel lost in the confrontation with the roving bands of dacoits than to the dacoits themselves. Despite the close proximity of the army, the dacoits continued to operate with impunity from the sanctuary offered by the *katcha,* the bed of the Indus River (q.v.), five to seven miles wide between the river's protective embankments. With the flow in the river controlled by the Tarbela Dam (q.v.), the bed now supported thick vegetation from which the dacoits could launch operations without much fear of detection. The army was reluctant to move into the katcha itself. For a number of years the dacoits were not only able to harass the local authorities but were also able to disrupt traffic on the national highway connecting Karachi (q.v.) with the interior. On a number of occasions they also disrupted traffic on the main railway line connecting Karachi and the province of Punjab (q.v.). They staged raids on the trains, carrying both passengers and goods, operating on the line. It was only after the return of representative government in the province of Sindh in 1988, and hence the withdrawal of support to them, that the dacoits were brought under control.

DAEWOO. Daewoo, a Korean *chaebol* (industrial–business conglomerate), won the contract to build the Lahore–Islamabad Motorway (q.v.). The contract was awarded in 1992 by the first administration (1990–93) of Prime Minister Nawaz Sharif (q.v.) on terms that were considered by many in Pakistan to be favorable to the Korean enterprise. Daewoo also indicated interest in building a large industrial estate near Karachi (q.v.) and in developing the land alongside the motorway for industry and commerce. The motorway project was expected to be completed in three years but, instead, took six years to finish. The delay was caused in part by the less-than-enthusiastic support given to the project by the second administration (1993–96) of Benazir Bhutto (q.v.).

DAULATANA, MIAN MUMTAZ MUHAMMAD KHAN (1916–1995). Daulatana, the scion of a well-established land-owning family of Central Punjab (q.v.), was educated at Oxford in England. He was elected to the Punjab legislative assembly in 1943 and went on to win seats in both the Provincial and National Assemblies in the elections of 1946. He was elected president of the Punjab Muslim League (q.v.) in 1948 and joined the government of chief minister Iftikhar Mamdot (q.v.) as finance minister in 1951. Later in the year he replaced Mamdot as Punjab's chief minister. In 1953, following his inability to control the anti-Ahmadiya movement, he stepped down as chief minister. He took an active part in organizing the Council Muslim League (q.v.) to challenge the Convention Muslim League (q.v.) that supported the military government of Field Marshal Ayub Khan (q.v.). He served as ambassador to England during the administration of Prime Minister Zulfikar Ali Bhutto in the early 1970s. He retired from politics following the completion of his tenure and lived in Lahore (q.v.) for the remaining years of his life.

DAWOODS, THE. The Dawoods got their name from Ahmad Dawood, the head of a Memon family that migrated to Pakistan from India at the invitation of Muhammad Ali Jinnah (q.v.), the country's founder. Like a number of other families that came to dominate the industrial sector in Pakistan, the Dawoods were originally merchants. The family belonged to the village of Batwa in the Kathiawar peninsula of what is now the Indian state of Gujarat. The family's initial success came from supplying commodities and equipment to the Indian armed forces fighting in World War II. The family established its headquarters in Karachi (q.v.) and participated enthusiastically in Pakistan's initial efforts at industrialization.

The Dawoods seized the opportunity presented by Pakistan's first trade war with India in 1949. The conflict with India over the question of the value of the Pakistani rupee persuaded the leaders of Pakistan to launch a massive industrialization drive to achieve self-sufficiency in basic consumer goods. Generous incentives were provided to private investors to set up such basic industries as jute and cotton textiles, leather goods, food processing, and building materials. A number of people, in particular those who had reaped rich benefits from the commodity boom associated with the war in Korea, took advantage of the incentives provided by the government. The Dawoods concentrated their investments initially in cotton and jute textiles. In selecting jute, they took a calculated risk in going to distant East Pakistan (today's Bangladesh). Ahmad Dawood's jute ventures turned out to be enormously profitable and encouraged him to diversify his holdings in East Pakistan. In the early

1960s, he purchased the massive Karanaphuli Paper Mills built in East Pakistan by the Pakistan Industrial Development Corporation (q.v.).

The loss of East Pakistan in 1971 and the nationalization of large industrial enterprises in 1972 by the administration of President Zulfikar Ali Bhutto (q.v.) dealt a severe blow to the fortunes of the Dawood family. Ahmad Dawood's extraordinary resilience and his ability to work with administrations of different ideological dispositions helped the family to recover, however. By the end of the 1980s the Dawoods had the satisfaction of counting themselves once again among the richest industrial families of Pakistan.

DEBT. Pakistan's debt burden, both internal and external, has mounted steadily over the years. In 1998, the two burdens taken together amounted to nearly 90 percent of the gross domestic product (GDP). The large burden of debt is the consequence of a very low domestic savings rate. In 1998 Pakistan's tax to GDP ratio was slightly more than 13 percent, whereas the public-sector expenditure was close to 19.5 percent. The difference between the two—the budgetary deficit—has been traditionally financed by both domestic and external borrowing. This has resulted in a progressive increase in the debt burden. Pakistan also has a large balance-of-payments deficit—the difference between total external earnings and expenditure. In the absence of large capital flows such as foreign aid and workers remittances, which Pakistan used to finance the external deficit in the past, the country now has to resort to heavy commercial borrowing. This has added to the debt burden. Servicing of debt is now the largest claim on the budget. In the 1997–98 fiscal year, debt servicing consumed 40 percent of government revenues. Servicing of external debt in the same year took up 38 percent of export earnings.

DEFENSE. Pakistan's military, estimated to number 587,000, is the fifth largest force in the developing world after China, India, North Korea, and South Korea. Some four-fifths of the military is accounted for by the army, whereas the remaining 20 percent is deployed in the navy and the air force. The country spends 6.5 percent of the gross domestic product (GDP) on defense, which is equivalent to $28 per capita. Defense expenditure comprises 125 percent of the combined expenditure on education and health. Successive governments have justified such a large outlay on defense because of the tensions with India. Pakistan and India have fought three wars since they gained independence in 1947.

While maintaining a large force in arms, Pakistan has not developed an indigenous defense industry. Consequently, a significant amount of expenditure is incurred procuring equipment from abroad. In 1995, the country spent $391 million on military imports, equivalent to 8 percent of total export earnings. The United States has been the major supplier for more than 40 years. Pakistan has had a close association with the United States on defense matters since the two countries entered into a number of agreements, including the Central Treaty Organization (CENTO) and Southeast Treaty Organization (SEATO) (qq.v.). Under these agreements Pakistan received a significant amount of military assistance from the United States. The United States also assisted Pakistan following the invasion of Afghanistan by the Soviet Union in 1979. However, this close relationship was interrupted by the sanctions imposed by Washington on Pakistan as a result of the Pressler amendment (q.v.), when Islamabad (q.v.) refused to accept the demand by the United States to stop the development of nuclear weapons (q.v.).

The defense establishment has played an important role in shaping Pakistan's political development. Generals Ayub Khan, Yahya Khan, and Zia ul-Haq (qq.v) kept the country under martial law for 25 years. Even when the generals were not directly in control, they were able to influence decision-making in important matters by participating in such informal arrangements as the "troika" (q.v.). *See also* India–Pakistan Relations; Indo–Pakistan Wars of 1948–49, 1965, 1971; Military, The.

DEMOCRATIC ACTION COMMITTEE (DAC). The Democratic Action Committee was formed in December 1968 by eight political parties to coordinate and guide the movement against the government of Ayub Khan (q.v.). The parties that gathered under the DAC umbrella included the Awami League (q.v.) (Mujibur Rahman group), the Awami League (Nawabzada Nasrullah Khan group), the Council Muslim League (q.v.), the National Awami Party (q.v.) (Requisionists), the Jamaat-e-Islami (q.v.), the Jamiatul-Ulemai-Islam (q.v.), and the Jamiatul-Ulemai-Pakistan. The Pakistan People's Party (q.v.) and the National Awami Party (Bhashani Group) did not join the DAC. In a meeting held on January 8, 1969, the DAC put forward eight demands including the replacement of the constitution of 1962 (q.v.) by a federal parliamentary system of government; full restoration of all civil liberties; and repeal of such "black laws" as the University Ordinance, the Press Act, and the laws that allowed the government to detain without trial such political prisoners as Zulfikar Ali Bhutto, Mujibur Rahman, and Khan Abdul Wali Khan (qq.v.); the withdrawal of all orders under Section 144 of the Criminal Procedure Code; and the return to their original owners of all newspapers nationalized by the government.

Ayub Khan's response to these demands was to invite the DAC to a round-table meeting with himself and his associates. The consensus that had developed among the constituent parties quickly disappeared, however, once the discussions got underway. The main issue was the type of federal structure the opposition wanted in place once Ayub Khan's constitution was abrogated. The parties from West Pakistan were not prepared to accept some of the demands pushed by the representatives from East Pakistan. The Awami League of East Pakistan wanted much greater political autonomy for the country's eastern wing than the West Pakistanis were prepared to grant. Ayub Khan was not able to capitalize on these differences among the DAC leaders, however. By the time the round-table discussions got seriously underway, the military had become restive. It decided to move in and imposed martial law on March 25.

As was the case with other political umbrella groups in Pakistan's political history, the DAC did not survive the achievement of its immediate purpose: the removal from office of President Ayub Khan. It disappeared from the political scene following the imposition of martial law by General Yahya Khan (q.v.).

DIRECT ACTION DAY (AUGUST 16, 1946). Convinced that his demand for the creation of Pakistan, a separate state for the Muslims of British India, had not been treated with enough seriousness by both the British and the Indian National Congress (q.v.), Muhammad Ali Jinnah (q.v.) asked the Muslim League (q.v.) legislators meeting in New Delhi on July 27 to call for a "direct action day." The meeting also endorsed a major change in the "Pakistan resolution" passed by the Muslim League at its annual meeting held in Lahore (q.v.) on March 23, 1940. The earlier resolution had called for the establishment of Muslim states. The resolution passed in 1946 by the legislators asked for the establishment of a single Muslim state called Pakistan.

The call for the observance of the day was heeded by the Muslim community all over India. *Hartals* (work stoppages) by Muslim businesses marked the day. Jinnah had appealed for calm while the day was being observed but that was not to be the case. There were serious clashes between Hindus and Muslims in Bengal, which resulted in scores of deaths. The "day" was a success in other ways. Its observance signaled the seriousness with which the Muslim community all over India viewed the creation of Pakistan.

DOCTRINE OF NECESSITY, THE. In 1954 Governor-General Ghulam Muhammad (q.v.) dissolved the first constituent assembly (q.v.). Maulvi Tamizuddin (q.v.), the assembly president, challenged the constitutionality of the governor-general's action in the Supreme Court under the Independence Act of India. In its judgment, the court upheld the governor-general's dismissal order on the basis of what it called the "doctrine of necessity." According to the doctrine, certain actions by politically powerful individuals created situations to which legal remedy could not be meaningfully applied. The court argued that it was operating under considerable constraints and had only a limited degree of real freedom available to it. The chief justice felt that declaring the action by the governor-general to be constitutionally invalid would have created political chaos. The justices believed that the only viable course they could adopt was not to nullify the governor-general's act but to force him to go back to the constitutional path. Accordingly, the court ordered Ghulam Muhammad to reconstitute the Constituent Assembly. This decision suited the governor-general as it provided him the opportunity to rid the assembly of the representatives who had refused to follow his dictate.

The "Tamizuddin case," built on the doctrine of necessity, was to significantly influence Pakistan's constitutional and political development. The doctrine was to be applied several times subsequently by the courts to validate military coups d'etat and other unconstitutional acts by a string of authoritarian leaders. It also weakened the development of an independent judiciary in the country. It was only in the 1990s that the judiciary began to take a course that was not totally subservient to the wishes of the executive. *See also* Judiciary, The.

DYARCHY. The term "dyarchy" was used to describe the system of government created by the Government of India Act of 1919 (q.v.). Elected members constituted a majority in the provincial councils established under the Act. Ministers, appointed by the governor to head the "nation-building departments"—agriculture, education, health, irrigation, and public works—were responsible to the provincial councils. A number of other departments—home, finance, and revenue—remained outside the purview of the councils, however. These departments were headed by executive councilors responsible only to the governor. This division of responsibility was captured by the term "dyarchy." The Government of India Act of 1935 (q.v.) created a system of provincial autonomy, thereby doing away with the system of dyarchy.

⇜ **E** ⇝

EAST INDIA COMPANY. The British East India Company was founded in 1600 and proved more durable than a number of similar enterprises created for the purpose of monopolizing trade in exotic products between countries of the East and the mercantile powers of the West. Although the company survived officially until 1874, it effectively ended after the Great Indian Mutiny (q.v.) of 1857. The company started as a commercial enterprise but went on to establish British dominion over India. This it did by first defeating the nawabs of Bengal (later East Pakistan and still later Bangladesh), by liquidating the remnants of the Delhi-based Mughul Empire (q.v.), and by annexing the provinces of Punjab and Sindh (qq.v.) of modern-day Pakistan.

ECONOMIC REFORM ORDER OF 1972. On January 1, 1972, only two weeks after assuming political power, President Zulfikar Ali Bhutto (q.v.) issued a presidential order entitled "The Economic Reform Order of 1972." The Order gave the government the authority to nationalize 31 large industrial units belonging to 10 categories of "basic industries." Its implementation brought about a major shift in the approach of the government toward industrialization. The Industrial Policy of 1948 and the policies pursued by the government of President Ayub Khan (q.v.) had assigned only a supportive role to the public sector. The Bhutto administration now required the public sector to scale the commanding heights of the economy. The impact of the 1972 nationalization and those that were to follow—the takeover of the vegetable oil industry in 1974 and that of the rice husking, cotton ginning, and wheat flour industries in 1976— were to completely reorder the industrial sector. Private initiative, cultivated assiduously since the country's independence, was discouraged to the extent that a number of prominent industrial families left Pakistan. Industrial efficiency suffered under state control.

ECONOMY, THE. Since independence in 1947, Pakistan's gross domestic product (GDP) has increased at a rate of 4.5 percent a year, which is one of the highest rates of growth in GDP in the developing world. But the performance of the economy during this period was not uniform; there were periods of exceptionally high growth rates as in the 1960s and the early 1970s, and periods of relative sluggishness as in the 1950s, the early 1970s, and in the 1990s. The governments were also not consistent in their approach to economic development, and in the choice of the sectors to be given special attention.

From 1947 to 1958 governments depended on the private sector to develop the economy. The trade dispute with India in 1949 caused a great deal of hardship in Pakistan. There was a serious scarcity of goods of daily consumption, which Pakistan used to import from India but now had to buy from other sources. The country did not have the foreign exchange to pay for these imports, however. Rapid industrialization, therefore, became a high priority. The government encouraged the merchant class to invest in industry. This encouragement took the form of subsidized credit, high tariffs against imports, and public investment in physical infrastructure.

The government's orientation toward economic development changed with the establishment of the first military government in 1958 under General Ayub Khan (q.v.). Ayub Khan believed that without rapid economic growth he would not be able to solve the country's basic economic problems: persistent poverty and dependence on foreign capital for investment. The economy responded to a number of initiatives taken by his government by growing at an unprecedented rate. The GDP grew at 6.7 percent a year during the Ayub Khan period (1958–69). By the time Ayub Khan was forced out of office, Pakistan had achieved near self-sufficiency in food. Having established an efficient consumer industry, it had also made impressive strides in such producer-goods industries as cement, steel, and machinery. The private sector continued to lead the effort in industrialization. Another, but at that time little-noticed accomplishment, was the development of the financial sector in both the private and public parts of the economy. During the Ayub period, private commercial banks expanded their penetration of the economy while specialized investment banks in the public sector began to function to fill the gap left by private entrepreneurship.

The third major shift in the government's approach toward economic development occurred in the early 1970s when Zulfikar Ali Bhutto and his Pakistan People's Party (qq.v.) assumed power. Large parts of the economy were brought under the control of the government through nationalization. This was a wrenching structural change for the economy for which the country paid a heavy price. The rate of growth slowed down to about the rate of population increase. Had the economies in the Middle East not taken off as a result of the "oil boom" produced by the sharp jump in the price of oil, Bhutto's socialist experiment would have resulted in a sharp increase in the incidence of poverty. With the Middle East offering millions of jobs for the unskilled and semi-skilled workers of Pakistan, however, the poor began to receive billions of dollars of remittances from their relatives who migrated to the Middle East. They used this largesse to meet their basic needs and to invest in the development of their human capital.

With the country going under martial law once again in 1977, the government was prepared to bring the private sector back as a major player in the economy. However, President Zia ul-Haq (q.v.), Pakistan's new military leader, did not have the political strength to be able to dismantle the public sector Bhutto had erected. The labor and the "economic bureaucrats" were not prepared to countenance the swift privatization of the "taken over" enterprises. Operating even under these constraints the government of Zia ul-Haq succeeded in returning the economy to the rate of economic growth achieved during the period of Ayub Khan. Industrial growth, which had stagnated under Zulfikar Ali Bhutto, significantly contributed to economic revival.

The end of military rule in 1988 and the reintroduction of democracy brought about another radical change in thinking about economic growth and development. First the government of Benazir Bhutto (1988–90) (q.v.), then the administration of Mian Nawaz Sharif (1990–93) (q.v.), and then again the government of Benazir Bhutto (1993–96) and the second Nawaz Sharif administration (1997–) were prepared to allow a great deal of space to both domestic and foreign private initiative. They were also able to overcome the resistance of labor and "economic bureaucrats" to begin the process of privatization of the economic assets that still remained in the hands of the government. All four administrations actively encouraged foreign capital to move into the sectors that had been starved of investment for more than a decade and half.

Much of Pakistan's economic success in the period since independence occurred because of large flows of foreign capital, which came in mostly as aid or remittances sent by the Pakistanis working abroad. These flows provided resources for sustaining a reasonable rate of domestic investment. A sharp decline in the flow of external capital in the 1990s slowed down economic growth to a rate not large enough to make a significant impact on the incidence of poverty. In Pakistan's case this translates into a growth rate of 6 percent a year. Without a major increase in domestic savings, Pakistan would not be able to obtain this level of growth. The nuclear arms race with India in the summer of 1998 and sanctions imposed by the United States and Japan further compounded the country's problems. By July Pakistan was close to bankruptcy and its leaders were threatening to default on the country's external obligations unless the United States agreed to lift the sanctions it had imposed. During a visit to Islamabad—his second in two months—U.S. Deputy Secretary of State Strobe Talbot indicated that his country would not oppose a major International Monetary Fund (q.v.) Program in Pakistan. *See also* Agriculture; Debt; Employment; Five Year Plans; Indo–Pakistan Nuclear Arms Race; Industry; Trade.

EDHI, ABDUL SATTAR (1946–). Abdul Sattar Edhi is Pakistan's most well-known social worker. Born in India, Edhi migrated to Pakistan shortly after the birth of the country. He started modestly, establishing a small dispensary in 1951 in Mithadar, a poor neighborhood in Karachi (q.v.), to honor the memory of his mother. Single-handedly—or more accurately, with the help of his wife, Bilquise—he turned this one small dispensary into a social-welfare organization that now operates 240 Edhi centers throughout Pakistan. The Edhi Foundation is responsible for running the centers. It employs more than 1,000 people and owns a fleet of 500 ambulances. The Foundation is funded entirely by donations received mostly from the poor and middle class. Edhi has avoided large donors. The emergency care provided by the Foundation is often all that is available to the poorly served people of Pakistan.

Edhi's work in a society in which the government had become dysfunctional was bound to attract a great deal of attention. It appears that an attempt was made in 1995 to recruit him as a member of a political movement, the main purpose of which was to introduce a new political order in the country. Edhi refused to get involved and when those who wanted him to lend his name and prestige to their movement persisted in their efforts, he panicked and fled the country. He stayed in London for a few weeks but returned to Karachi to resume his work. By opening a center in Canada in 1997, he extended his social work to the communities of Pakistani expatriates in North America.

EHETASAB. In Persian, "ehetasab" means accountability. The word entered Pakistan's political language in November 1996 following the dismissal of the government of Prime Minister Benazir Bhutto (q.v.). The government was dismissed by President Farooq Leghari (q.v.) on a number of charges, the most prominent of which were allegations of corruption. The president instructed the caretaker government that took office on November 5 to begin the process of accountability against the functionaries of the government suspected of having abused power in return for private gain.

The president's dismissal of Benazir Bhutto was a popular move; there was a widely shared sentiment that the caretaker government should concentrate its efforts on bringing to justice a large number of people who were thought to have indulged in corruption while Ms. Bhutto was in power. A number of influential people believed that if the elections promised for February 1997 had to be postponed to bring corrupt officials to justice that trade-off would be acceptable to most people. Ardeshir Cowasjee, a popular columnist who wrote for *Dawn*, a Karachi (q.v.) newspaper, published a series of articles in November and December advocating *ehetasab* before *intikhab* (elections). Although the president was not prepared to tinker with the election timetable—he was obliged by the constitution to hold elections within 90 days of the government's dismissal—he worked closely with the caretaker administration to set up a mechanism for bringing those who had indulged in malpractice to justice. An Ehetasab Ordinance was promulgated by the president in early December that called for the establishment of an Ehetasab Commission. Mujaddid Mirza, a retired judge of the Supreme Court, was appointed the first Ehetasab Commissioner. The task for preparing cases against corrupt officials was entrusted to the Ministry of Interior. The Ordinance required the commissioner to carefully examine all the cases submitted to him to ascertain if there was enough substance in them to warrant formal judicial proceedings.

On taking office and in presenting the presidential ordinance for approval by the National Assembly, the administration of Nawaz Sharif (q.v.) introduced some changes in the Ehetasab process. The most important of these was to exclude the period up to 1993 from investigation and to transfer the authority for preliminary work to an ehetasab cell established for this purpose in the prime minister's secretariat.

ELECTIONS OF 1954, EAST BENGAL. The first electoral contest of any significance since the establishment of Pakistan in 1947 was held in East Bengal, now Bangladesh (q.v.), in March 1954. By then the Muslim League (q.v.) had lost most of its popular support in the province. The opposition to the Muslim League government in Dacca was able to organize itself under the banner of the United Front (q.v.) led by A. K. Fazle Haq (q.v.). Election results were announced on March 19. The United Front captured 223 out of 309 seats in the provincial legislature. The Scheduled Caste Federation came in second with 27 seats, the Minorities United Front won 10 seats, and the Communist Party captured four seats. A number of small parties secured the remaining 11 seats. The United Front was expected to do well but a total rout of the Muslim League had not been predicted. From this time on and until the breakup of Pakistan in December 1971, no single political party was able to cultivate a large following in either of the two wings.

ELECTIONS OF 1970. The first direct elections to the National Assembly were held in 1970 under the Legal Framework Order (LFO) of 1970 (q.v.) promulgated by the martial law administration of President Yahya Khan (q.v.). The elections, initially scheduled for October 1970, had to be postponed until December because of a cyclone that struck the coastal areas of East Pakistan. Mujibur Rahman's (q.v.) Awami League (q.v.) won 162 of the 300 seats in the National Assembly. The Muslim League (q.v.) managed to capture only one seat in East Pakistan. Zulfikar Ali Bhutto's Pakistan People's Party (qq.v.) emerged as the largest single-party winner in West Pakistan with 81 seats. The elections polarized politics between the forces that wanted provincial autonomy and those that favored a strong central government. Mujib supported the first approach toward governance, Bhutto the second. The failure to reconcile these two points of view led to a civil war in East Pakistan in 1971 and the secession of East Pakistan from Pakistan later that year.

ELECTIONS OF 1977. In January 1977 Prime Minister Zulfikar Ali Bhutto (q.v.) decided to hold elections in order to seek a new mandate for himself and his organization, the Pakistan People's Party (PPP) (q.v.). These were to be the first elections held under the Constitution of 1973 (q.v.). The opposition, caught by surprise by this move, formed a coalition under the name of the Pakistan National Alliance (PNA) (q.v.). The PNA was able to mount an effective campaign and was confident of obtaining a sizeable presence in the National Assembly, if not an outright majority. The elections were held in February but the results announced by the administration were not acceptable to the opposition. According to the Election Commission, the PPP had won a comfortable victory. A frustrated opposition decided to launch a protest against the government. The protest turned violent; after dozens of people had been killed, the military, under the command of General Zia ul-Haq (q.v.), chief of the Army Staff, imposed martial law and forced Prime Minister Bhutto out of office.

ELECTIONS OF 1985. After having first promised and then postponed general elections a number of times, President Zia ul-Haq (q.v.) allowed the country to go to the polls in 1985 to elect a new National Assembly. The elections were not quite what the democratic forces in the country had been campaigning for ever since the proclamation of martial law in July 1977. Zia did not permit the participation of political parties in the contest. Participation was allowed only on an individual basis. Zia adopted this approach to keep the late Zulfikar Ali Bhutto's Pakistan People's Party (qq.v.) from coming back to power. The PPP, now under the leadership of Benazir Bhutto (q.v.), refused to put forward its candidates for the elections.

ELECTIONS OF 1988. The elections of 1988, held on November 17, represented the first time in 18 years that Pakistanis went to the polls to choose among parties and candidates. The last time people were allowed to fully exercise their rights was in December 1970. Political parties were not allowed to participate in the elections held in 1985. The election was a contest between the late Zulfikar Ali Bhutto's Pakistan People's Party (qq.v.) and the Islami Jamhuri Itehad (IJI) (q.v.), a right-wing coalition of parties including the Muslim League (q.v.), which sought to continue the policies of deceased president Zia ul-Haq (q.v.).

The Pakistan People's Party obtained 37.4 percent of the total vote and won 92 of the 204 seats contested. A new party, the Muhajir Qaumi Mahaz (MQM) (q.v.) swept the polls in Karachi (q.v.) and parts of Hyderabad city. It captured 11 out of 13 seats in Karachi and another two seats in Hyderabad. The IJI was unable to win any seat in Sindh (q.v.). Even Muhammad Khan Junejo (q.v.), who represented the Muslim League as its president, was not returned from what was regarded as a safe seat. With 54 seats, the IJI was the second largest party represented in the National Assembly.

ELECTIONS OF 1990. The dismissal of Prime Minister Benazir Bhutto by President Ghulam Ishaq Khan (qq.v.) in August 1990 led to another set of elections. Elections to the National and Provincial Assemblies were held in October. The elections pitted Bhutto's Pakistan People's Party (PPP) against Nawaz Sharif's Pakistan Muslim League (qq.v.). The League fought the elections as a part of a right-wing alliance called the Islami Jamhuri Itehad (IJI) (q.v.). The IJI won the most seats in the National Assembly—105 compared to 45 by the PPP—a narrow majority in a house of 206 members. The IJI also obtained a majority in Punjab (q.v.). The Muhajir Qaumi Mahaz (q.v.) retained its support in the muhajir-dominated areas of Sindh (q.v.). The IJI-led governments were formed in Islamabad (q.v.), the federal capital, and Lahore (q.v.), the capital of Punjab.

ELECTIONS OF 1993. Following a prolonged struggle between President Ghulam Ishaq Khan and Prime Minister Nawaz Sharif (qq.v.), which lasted for several months, the National Assembly was dissolved in July 1993 and the president and prime minister were forced out of office. These changes were the consequence of the army working behind the scenes. A caretaker government under Prime Minister Moeen Qureshi (q.v.) took office and organized another general election, which was held in October. The elections did not provide a clear mandate. The Pakistan People's Party, led by Benazir Bhutto (qq.v.), won 91 seats but did not obtain a majority. It was able to form a government in Islamabad (q.v.) with the help of the Pakistan Muslim League (Junejo) (PML[J]) (q.v.), a faction of the mainstream Pakistan Muslim League (q.v.), which, under the leadership of Nawaz Sharif (q.v.), was able to win only 54 seats. The Muhajir Qaumi Mahaz (MQM) (q.v.) won the usual 13 seats, 11 from Karachi (q.v.) and 2 from Hyderabad. The PPP was also able to form provincial governments in Punjab, Sindh, and the Northwest Frontier Province (qq.v.) although the Punjab government was led by a member of the PML(J).

ELECTIONS OF 1997. The elections of 1997, held on February 3, followed another dismissal of the prime minister by the president. On November 5, 1996, President Farooq Leghari (q.v.) used Article 58.2(b) (q.v.) of the constitution to remove Prime Minister Benazir Bhutto (q.v.) from office. The National Assembly was dissolved and another general election was ordered, the fourth in less than nine years. For the first time, voting for the National and four Provincial Assemblies was held on the same day.

There was some expectation that these elections would bring a new political force onto the political scene. Imran Khan's (q.v.) Tehrik-e-Insaf (q.v.) was expected to do well, in particular in the urban areas. The party had mounted a vigorous campaign against both the Pakistan People's Party (PPP) (q.v.) of Bhutto and Nawaz Sharif's Pakistan Muslim League (qq.v.). The results surprised most political observers. The PML, by winning 138 of 200 seats in the National Assembly, was given a mandate that was clear and unambiguous. The PPP, by seeing only 17 candidates return to the assembly, received the message that the people were very unhappy with the way it had governed while it held power. The PPP was completely wiped out from Punjab (q.v.), the largest province and the place of the party's birth.

EMPLOYMENT. Pakistan's 1998 population is estimated at 137 million. With a participation rate of 31 percent, this translates into a work force of 42.5 million people. The rate of participation is higher in the rural areas compared to the urban areas, 31.8 percent as against 29.8 percent. In all, 26.7 million people are in the work force in the countryside compared to 15.8 million in towns and cities. The lower rate of participation in the urban areas is the result of the much-lower proportion of women working in towns and cities. The number of men in the labor force is estimated at 37.4 million or 88 percent of the total work force while only 15 million women are counted as working or seeking work. This means that while 54.8 percent of men are in the work force, the proportion of women is only 21 percent.

Agriculture (q.v.) now provides employment to some 24 million people, about 48 percent of the total work force. Manufacturing accounts for another 6.8 million, or 16 percent. The remaining 15.3 million are employed in the service sector. As in other poor developing countries, the service sector picks up the workers who cannot find employment in the formal sectors of the economy.

The same problem can be looked at another way. Large-scale manufacturing and modern enterprises in the service sector employ only 1.5 million workers, all of them in the urban areas. This means that of the nearly 16 million workers in towns and cities, 14.5 million are employed either in small-scale enterprises or in informal parts of the service sector. It is this concentration of the work force in the less productive part of the economy that poses a serious economic and social problem for the country. This problem has become more acute in recent years with a marked slow down in the growth of the economy (q.v.). The economy is now generating new jobs at a rate that is less than half the rate of growth of the labor force, 1.4 percent a year compared to 3.0 percent. In the 15-year period between 1975 and 1990, massive out-migration to the Middle East was able to absorb a large proportion of the work force that could not be gainfully accommodated at home. That safety valve is no longer available, which compounds the employment problem.

ↄ **F** ↄ

FAISALABAD. Originally named Lyallpur by the British, Faisalabad is now Pakistan's third largest city, after Karachi and Lahore (qq.v.). Its 1998 population is estimated at 2.5 million. The British founded the city in the late-nineteenth century to service the agriculture sector, which had received a great boost as a result of the development of irrigation in central Punjab (q.v.). Lyallpur, named after Sir John Lyall, governor of Punjab, was situated in the heart of the areas colonized (settled by new owners working the irrigated land) by the British. Cotton was one of the favored crops of the farmers who settled in these areas. The partition of British India separated the cotton-growing areas of Punjab from the textile mills in India, most of which were located in the distant Gujarat and Maharashtara states. Pakistan adopted the policy of developing an indigenous textile industry based on home-grown cotton. Consequently, by the mid-1970s Lyallpur had become the most important textile center of Pakistan. Also in the mid-1970s, the authorities in Pakistan decided to change the name of the city to Faisalabad in the honor of King Faisal of Saudi Arabia who had developed very close relations with Pakistan.

FAIZ AHMAD FAIZ (1911–1984). Faiz Ahmad Faiz was born in Sialkot and joined the Education Corps of the British Indian Army during World War II. After the war was over he settled in Lahore (q.v.), where he became the central figure in a small but increasingly influential group that espoused socialist causes. The group included several politicians, including Mian Iftikharuddin (q.v.), a wealthy landlord and businessman who in the late 1940s founded an English-language newspaper, *The*

Pakistan Times. Faiz was appointed the newspaper's chief editor. The paper's initial aim was to promote the idea of Pakistan, a separate homeland for the Muslims of British India. Once it became clear that the idea of Pakistan was close to realization, the paper turned its attention toward the social objectives the new country should pursue. In recommending a course of action for Pakistan's first government, the editorial pages of the newspaper followed an approach close to that adopted by the Soviet Union and the countries of Eastern Europe.

Faiz Ahmad Faiz was deeply disappointed by the turn taken by Pakistani politics, especially after the death of Muhammad Ali Jinnah (q.v.), Pakistan's founder, and the new country's first governor-general. He and some of his associates were approached by a group of army officers to help them articulate a program for the social and political development that the army should pursue in the country if it were to assume power. These contacts led to the formation of a group of people drawn from the military and from Faiz's associates in Lahore, who began to conspire against the government. The result was the Rawalpindi Conspiracy (q.v.). Faiz and his fellow conspirators were arrested in early 1951 and were given long prison sentences by a military court. He was, however, released from prison in 1955 and went back to writing poetry.

The award of the prestigious Lenin Peace prize by the Soviet Union made Faiz even more suspect in the eyes of Pakistan's conservative establishment. During Zia ul-Haq's (q.v.) period of martial law, Faiz spent several years in self-imposed exile in the Soviet Union, Eastern Europe, and Lebanon. While in Beirut, he edited a journal to promote the Palestinian cause. He returned to Lahore, Pakistan in 1982 and died in 1984. Several of his books of poems have been translated into Western languages. *See also* Press and News Media.

FAIZUL ISLAM. Faizul Islam, Pakistan's largest orphanage, was started in 1943 by Raja Ghulam Qadir at Faizabad, near Rawalpindi (q.v.) in response to an appeal from Muhammad Ali Jinnah (q.v.). Jinnah asked Muslim philanthropists all over British India to come to assist the people who were suffering from famine in the provinces of Bengal and Bihar. Qadir heeded Jinnah's call and brought hundreds of Bengali Muslim children, orphaned by the famine, to Rawalpindi and housed them in a facility built for this purpose in the city's outskirts. He created an organization, Anjuman-e-Faizul Islam, to manage the orphanage. From these modest beginnings, the orphanage grew to be the largest institution of its kind in Pakistan. The Anjuman continues to manage the institution with the help of private donations.

FAMILY LAWS ORDINANCE OF 1961. Up until the promulgation of the Family Laws Ordinance by the government of President Ayub Khan (q.v.) in 1961, there was no legal requirement for the registration of *nikhanamas*—marriage contracts—and no legal obligation that a husband, in exercising his right to divorce, had to strictly follow the contract. It is not surprising that in a society in which less than one-tenth of the female population was functionally literate and in which the social status of women was very low, the Koranic injunctions about the rights of women (q.v.) entering marriage were not observed. The Family Laws Ordinance was one of several measures adopted by the martial-law government of Ayub Khan to deal with this situation. The Ordinance was based on the recommendations made by a long-forgotten Commission on Marriage and Family Laws. The Commission's report, presented to the government in 1956, had suggested the compulsory registration of nikhanamas, adoption of a minimum age below which both men and women were considered legally not competent to enter marriage, restrictions on the husband's right to divorce, and restrictions on men to enter multiple marriages. The Family Laws Ordinance stipulated that all marriage contracts had to be registered with the Union Councils; that the decision to divorce had to be announced by the husband to an Arbitration Council, which included representatives of both the husband and the wife he wished to divorce; and that the decision by a married man to take another wife could only be given by the Arbitration Council. The Ordinance also dealt with another thorny issue; the question of inheritance by the widow of the property left by the husband.

The provisions of the Ordinance were not popular with conservative forces. After martial law was lifted in 1962, a private-member bill was introduced in the National Assembly asking for its repeal. The bill would have been adopted but for the strong oppositions of a powerful coalition of women's organizations. Some political historians believe that the political agitation that succeeded in dislodging Ayub Khan in 1969 was fueled in part by the perceived wrong done by the Ordinance.

FAMILY PLANNING ASSOCIATION OF PAKISTAN (FPA). The Family Planning Association of Pakistan was founded in 1956 by a group of women (q.v.) who had begun to appreciate the importance of motivating couples to have smaller families and of providing them with information on modern family-planning practices. The Association received a major boost for its activities when it succeeded in persuading President Ayub Khan (q.v.) to attend a seminar on population held in 1959 in Lahore (q.v.). As the head of the armed forces and the chief martial-law administrator, Ayub had enormous power to make things happen. The seminar was addressed by a number of world-recognized authorities who spoke of the danger Pakistan faced if its leaders did not succeed in motivating the people to opt for smaller family size. The participants argued for an active role by the government in not only communicating this message to the people but also in making provision for the supply of family-planning services. Ayub Khan left the seminar fully persuaded that he had to incorporate family planning as an important element in his economic strategy and social modernization of the country.

The main result of Ayub Khan's conversion was the adoption of an ambitious plan of action aimed at bringing a significant decline in the rate of fertility. While the government-sponsored Family Planning Program held center stage, the FPA concentrated its efforts on education and dissemination of information. Its activities remained modest in scope and reach for as long as the government was willing to provide active support to family-planning activities. With the advent of the Zia ul-Haq (q.v.) era (1977–88), however, the government effectively withdrew from family-planning activities, leaving the field to such nongovernment organizations as the Family Planning Association. The Association took up the challenge. It invited Atiya Inyatullah, a well-known social worker and once a minister in one of the Cabinets of President Zia ul-Haq, to become its president. Under Inyatullah's leadership, the Association expanded its activities in the early 1990s and began to target its activities toward a number of socioeconomic groups. One novel feature of this approach was to reach the army *jawans* (enlisted men) not only to adopt family planning themselves but also to spread the word in the communities from which they were recruited that Pakistan was faced with a serious demographic crisis.

The Association's affiliation with the powerful Planned Parenthood Federation brought its activities to the notice of nongovernmental organizations outside Pakistan and helped Inyatullah to continue to put pressure on the government for providing some resources for family planning. She was also able to attract foreign funding, albeit in modest amounts, from the donor community.

FAZLE HAQ, LIEUTENANT GENERAL (1929–1992). Lieutenant General Fazle Haq hailed from the Northwest Frontier Province (NWFP) (q.v.) and came from a family with a tradition of military service. He was trained at the Pakistan Military Academy (PMA) (q.v.) at Kakul. He was one of the corps commanders of the Pakistan army when General Zia ul-Haq (q.v.) moved against the government of Prime Minister Zulfikar Ali Bhutto (q.v.) on July 5, 1977. During most of Zia ul-Haq's martial law, General Fazle Haq served as governor of the Northwest Frontier

Province. He was appointed to that position in 1978, a year after the imposition of martial law by Zia, and remained in this position until 1985 when Zia decided to lift martial law and allowed limited democracy to return to the country.

As the governor of the NWFP, Fazle Haq concentrated his considerable energies on promoting economic development in the province, at times working against the wishes of the central government. This approach helped him to develop a constituency of his own, which made it difficult for President Zia to sideline him. On leaving his official position, Fazle Haq decided to enter politics and toyed with the idea of joining one of the traditional political groupings in the province. To promote his political ambitions, he joined hands with some local entrepreneurs to launch an English-language newspaper, *The Frontier Post,* which quickly established itself as an independent voice in the politics of the NWFP. Zia ul-Haq brought Fazle Haq back to the center as a member of the caretaker Cabinet that he put into place after dismissing Prime Minister Muhammad Khan Junejo (q.v.). Zia's death in August 1988 and general elections in November provided Fazle Haq the opportunity to launch his political career. He stood as a candidate for the National Assembly but did not succeed. Fazle Haq was assassinated in Peshawar (q.v.).

FAZLI HUSAIN, SIR MIAN (1848–1936). Fazli Husain was born in Lahore (q.v.) and educated at Lahore's Government College and at Cambridge University, in England. He was called to the bar in 1901 and practiced law for more than two decades, becoming president of the Lahore High Court Bar Association. He strongly believed in communal harmony and saw no reason why the followers of India's major religions could not live together in peace. It was with the purpose of promoting understanding among the different communities of Punjab (q.v.) that he founded the Punjab Nationalist Unionist Party (q.v.)—commonly known as the Unionists—in 1923 and became its first president. He remained president of the party until his death in Lahore on July 9, 1936.

FAZLUL HAQ, ABUL KASEM (1873–1962). Fazlul Haq was one of the most prominent leaders of Muslim Bengal during the first half of the twentieth century. He joined the All-India Muslim League (q.v.) in 1913 and remained an active member until 1942, when a dispute with Muhammad Ali Jinnah (q.v.) led to his resignation. While still with the Muslim League he moved the "Pakistan Resolution" (q.v.) on March 23, 1940 at the annual meeting of the party in Lahore (q.v.). In 1954 he led the Krishak Sramik Party into a grand coalition with a number of other parties, including the Awami League, to challenge the Muslim League in the provincial elections of 1954 (q.v.). This United Front swept to victory and Fazlul Haq became the chief minister of East Pakistan. His government was dismissed within a few months of taking office by Governor-General Ghulam Muhammad (q.v.). The central government accused Fazlul Haq of working towards the establishment of an independent Bengal. A year later he was accepted into the mainstream of Pakistani politics and appointed as a minister in the central government. He served as governor of East Pakistan for two years (1956–58) but retired from politics when Ayub Khan (q.v.) declared martial law.

FEDERAL SECURITY FORCE (FSF). The government of Prime Minister Zulfikar Ali Bhutto (q.v.) organized the Federal Security Force to limit its reliance on the military. Before the creation of the FSF, governments had to depend on the armed forces to handle law-and-order problems that were beyond the capacity of the police force to tackle. Calling the army to aid civilian authorities had resulted in its politicization, however. For instance, in 1954 the army was summoned to deal with the anti-Ahmadiya riots in Punjab (q.v.) province. The army's success in dealing with that situation ultimately led to Ayub Khan's (q.v.) martial law. Similarly, Ayub Khan had relied on the army to bring order to the country when the campaign against his government turned violent in 1969. The army succeeded in restoring law and order but stayed on and imposed martial law for the second time in Pakistan's history.

Bhutto was determined not to repeat these past mistakes. He needed a force he controlled himself and that was independent of the military. The FSF was his answer. A number of retired army officers were brought into the force to provide training, while the services of some senior police officers were obtained to command the FSF units. The FSF command worked closely with the office of the prime minister. Once it was operational, the FSF's role changed and it began to gather intelligence about politicians and political organizations. It also began to interfere in political activities. Some personnel of the FSF were alleged to have been involved in the murder of a Bhutto political opponent, a charge for which the deposed prime minister was arrested in late 1977 and tried. Masood Mahmud, the director general of the FSF and one of the closest associates of Bhutto while he was in power, was also charged with the plot to kill the Bhutto opponent. Once the trial began, however, Mahmud entered into a plea-bargaining arrangement with the prosecution. It was his testimony against the former prime minister on which the prosecution based its case and the one that persuaded the Lahore High Court to sentence Bhutto to death. After Bhutto was executed on April 4, 1979, Masood Mahmud slipped out of Pakistan and did not return to the country.

The FSF was of no use to the government of Zia ul-Haq (q.v.). It was disbanded in 1977, soon after the declaration of martial law.

FISCAL DEFICIT. Pakistan's budgetary deficits, never very low, became the focus of great concern in the 1990s. The reason for growing worry was the government's inability to finance them. Earlier large flows of foreign aid and remittances sent by Pakistanis working abroad had made it possible for the government to manage large deficits. In the 1990s both flows declined precipitously and the government had to resort to expensive borrowing to meet its obligations. Poor credit ratings closed the cheaper options for the government; it had to turn to expensive sources of finance to meet its bills. This resulted in a rapid buildup of both internal and external debt (q.v.). This was not a sustainable situation.

The International Monetary Fund (IMF) (q.v.) made the reduction of the budgetary deficit its primary concern in the Standby Arrangements negotiated in October and December 1996 and in the IMF Extended Structural Adjustment Facility (ESAF) (q.v.) program agreed with the government in October 1997. In the Standby Arrangement the Fund endorsed a program of reform that would have aimed to reduce the fiscal deficit to 4 percent of the gross domestic product (GDP) by the end of June 1997. In the ESAF program, this target was revised to 5 percent and the deadline for achieving it was extended to the end of June 1998. These changes were made on the insistence of the government of Prime Minister Nawaz Sharif (q.v.), which felt that the lower target and the earlier date for achieving it were not politically feasible propositions. Even the 4 percent target was contingent on the government's ability to successfully undertake a program that included at least four features: extending the general sales tax (GST) (q.v.) to retail trade; collecting the tax on agricultural incomes that had been levied by the caretaker administration of Prime Minister Meraj Khalid (q.v.); overall improvements in tax collection; and having people respond positively to the tax amnesty announced in March 1997 by Nawaz Sharif.

In March 1998 the IMF carried out a review of the country's fiscal situation in preparation for the release of the second ESAF tranche. Although it agreed to release the tranche, the Fund expressed considerable concern about the government's fiscal performance. An example of poor performance was the lukewarm response by the people to the tax-amnesty initiative. India had introduced a similar scheme but had imposed a much higher tax on hidden incomes—30 percent compared to 7.5 percent by Pakistan. Although the amount collected by Pakistan was negligible, India was able to mobilize Rs.100 billion, equivalent to 0.5 percent of its GDP.

FIVE YEAR PLAN, THE FIRST (1955–1960). Pakistan made a hesitant start at medium-term planning. The Pakistan Planning Board was appointed in July 1953 but without a clear vision of the country's future economic and social structure. The Board drew up a five-year development plan for the period 1955–1960 but was able to publish it in draft form only in May 1956, after the first year of the plan period had already passed. However, the Planning Board had to wait for the arrival of the military government under the leadership of General Ayub Khan (q.v.) before being allowed to start implementing the plan. Ayub Khan reconstituted the Planning Board as the Planning Commission and assumed its chairmanship.

The First Five Year Plan in many ways was a radical document, which was one reason why it took so long for the establishment to give it its formal approval. The Plan document bore the imprint of Zahid Husain, the chairman of the Planning Board, who wrote the introduction as well as the chapters on land reform (q.v.) and public administration. Zahid Husain wanted a deep structural change in the Pakistani society and also in the way the government was organized. In the chapter on land reform he argued for a more equitable distribution of productive assets in the countryside. In the chapter on the organization of the government he recommended the creation of an administrative structure that would permit personnel from Pakistan's many technical services to hold senior management positions rather than leave the appointments at that level as the exclusive preserve of the elitist Civil Service of Pakistan (CSP) (q.v.).

If Zahid Husain's recommendations had been accepted and implemented, two of the most important elements in the establishment that ruled Pakistan at that time—the landed aristocracy and the civil bureaucracy in the shape of the CSP—would have seen some loosening in their grip on the levers of power. With political power gravitating back to the landed aristocracy and with the CSP comfortably settled in a partnership with the landed community, however, this was not the right time for the acceptance of such radical recommendations.

The Plan's overall targets were relatively modest: a 15-percent increase in per capita income over five years, which translated into a growth rate of only 2.8 percent a year in gross domestic product (GDP). Industry was to contribute significantly to the increase in national income. The sector was to receive 31 percent of the resources during the plan period. Housing and the settlement of the refugees from India were to get 20 percent of the resources, agriculture (q.v.) 7 percent, and transport and communication 6 percent.

Even these modest targets were not achieved, however. National income increased by a mere 13 percent over the 1955–60 period and with the population growing at a much faster rate than that envisaged by the planners, per capita income increased by less than 1 percent a year. At such a modest rate of increase, Pakistan added significantly to the number of people living in absolute poverty. Industry was the only sector that fared well but agriculture performed poorly; only 52 percent of the planned financial outlay was actually spent. It was during the period of the First Plan that Pakistan became a net importer of food grains.

FIVE YEAR PLAN, THE SECOND (1960–1965). One of the first moves made by the military government of President Ayub Khan (q.v.) was to strengthen the Planning Commission. Said Hassan, a senior civil servant, was appointed the commission's deputy chairman and given the responsibility for formulating the Second Five-Year Plan. Ayub Khan himself became the commission's chairman. The Plan did not put as much emphasis on poverty alleviation and increased social services as did the First Plan (q.v.); the Second Plan's principal objective was to accelerate the rate of economic growth. It provided the theoretical underpinning for Ayub Khan's preoccupation with achieving rapid economic growth in the country without much concern for income distribution.

The Plan envisaged a total outlay of Rs.29 billion ($6.1 billion at the rate of exchange then prevailing) of which 48 percent was to go to the public sector, 39 percent to the private sector, 10 percent for the Indus-basin replacement works, and 3 percent for rural works programs to be implemented by the local councils established under the system of Basic Democracies (q.v.). The largest amount of planned expenditure in the public sector was to be for the development of water and power (31 percent of the total), with transport and communications (22 percent) assigned the second highest priority. Agriculture (q.v.) was to receive 14 percent of the outlay in the public sector; housing and settlements 13 percent; industries, fuels, and minerals another 12 percent. The remaining 8 percent was to be spent on education, health, social welfare, and manpower development. These priorities reflected the martial-law government's economic philosophy: to leave industrial development in the hands of private entrepreneurs and to get the state to improve physical infrastructure so that the private sector could go about doing its business more efficiently.

The Plan succeeded in increasing the rate of economic growth well beyond the modest level achieved by the First Plan; Pakistan's gross domestic product (GDP) increased at a rate of 5.2 percent per year during 1960–65. With the rate of population increase greater than anticipated by the framers of the Plan, however, gross national product (GNP) per person increased by only 2.6 percent a year. The Plan also succeeded in narrowing the economic gap between East and West Pakistan.

The greatest success of the Second Five Year Plan was to discipline the use of public resources. An institutional structure was put in place for the approval of public expenditure. This structure allowed the representatives of different tiers of government and different "nation building" departments to participate in the process of public resource allocation.

FIVE YEAR PLAN, THE THIRD (1965–1970). Buoyed by the success of the Second Five Year Plan (q.v.), the government of Ayub Khan (q.v.) launched the Third Five Year Plan in June 1965. Its objectives were similar to those of its predecessor: to produce rapid economic growth and to reduce income disparities between the two wings of the country by undertaking massive public-sector investments in East Pakistan. In West Pakistan, the private sector was to play an even more significant role than it did in the early 1960s.

Compared to the Second Five Year Plan, there was some change in sectoral priorities: water and power remained the largest recipient, but with 26 percent of the total resources, transport and communication were still in second place with 20 percent of total commitment. The industry, fuel, and mineral sectors were to receive 17 percent of total public-sector outlays, 5 percentage points more than in the Second Plan. The reason for the increased priority assigned to this sector was to expedite the industrialization of East Pakistan. The public sector was to undertake the implementation of a number of large-scale industrial projects in the province. Agriculture (q.v.) was to receive 19 percent of the public-sector expenditure and the cluster of social sectors the remaining 18 percent. Out of its expenditure for social sectors, education was to receive 8.5 percent of the government-financed development expenditure compared to 6 percent in 1960–65; health was to receive 4 percent rather than 2.5 percent; social welfare and manpower was to see a near doubling in its share from 0.4 to 0.7 percent.

Soon after the Plan came into force, Pakistan went to war with India. More resources had to be committed to defense while the flow of economic assistance from abroad was interrupted. Despite these setbacks, the Plan's basic objectives were realized. GDP increased at the rate of 5.5 percent per year, and income per capita at the rate of 2.7 percent a year. *See also* Indo–Pakistan War of 1965.

FIVE YEAR PLAN, THE FOURTH (1970–1975). The formulation of the Fourth Five Year Plan was undertaken at an exceptionally difficult time for Pakistan. There was active debate among politicians and economists on two issues. First, there was a widespread perception that the rapid growth of the economy during the administration of President Ayub Khan

(1958–1969) (q.v.) had increased income inequalities in the country. A number of influential political figures—among them the most important being Zulfikar Ali Bhutto (q.v.)—demanded that the government should actively intervene in the economy to correct this situation. The "twenty-two families speech" (q.v.) by Mahbubul Haq (q.v.), the chief economist of the Planning Commission, lent credibility to this point of view. Second, there was a growing resentment in the country's eastern wing—present-day Bangladesh (q.v.)—that the domination of the national economy by West Pakistan meant a continuing subservient role for that province in economic matters. Again, powerful political forces wanted a direct role by the government to correct this imbalance.

The Planning Commission, working under the guidance of Mian Muzaffar Ahmad, its chairman, responded by setting up two panels of economic experts, one from East Pakistan and the other from West Pakistan, with the mandate to provide information on what had actually happened to "inter-regional income disparity" and what could be done within the framework of a five-year development plan to improve the situation if income disparities between the two provinces had indeed widened. The two panels could not agree on the Plan's priorities. The debate over the Plan document produced a political crisis when the government announced the allocation of public funds for fiscal 1970–71, the first year of the Fourth Plan period. Yahya Khan's (q.v.) Bengali ministers threatened to resign en bloc, and the president, succumbing to this political pressure, decided to send the Planning Commission back to the drawing board.

The Fourth Five Year Plan was formally launched on July 1, 1970. Its twin objectives of reducing interpersonal and interregional income disparities were given great prominence in the official proclamation that accompanied the launching of the Plan. Events in East Pakistan in 1971 made the Plan largely irrelevant, however. After the defeat of the army in East Pakistan and the emergence of Bangladesh, the administration of Zulfikar Ali Bhutto (q.v.), which took office in December 1971, did not revive medium-term planning and the Fourth Plan was shelved for good. *See also* Bangladesh–Pakistan Relations.

FIVE YEAR PLAN, THE FIFTH (1978–1983). The work on the Fifth Five Year Plan began in the winter of 1977–78 under the overall direction of Ghulam Ishaq Khan (q.v.), who at that time was the principal economic advisor to the martial-law administration of General Zia ul-Haq (q.v.). Vaseem A. Jaffrey (q.v.), secretary of planning, was assigned the responsibility for preparing the draft of the Plan for consideration by the military government. The Plan's principal objective was to restore the momentum of economic development that had been severely interrupted during the closing years of the administration of Prime Minister Zulfikar Ali Bhutto (q.v.). The Plan made three profound contributions to economic development in Pakistan. First, it instituted a set of policies aimed at rationalizing the role of the public sector in economic management and development. Second, it defined the role, scope, and speed with which the economy was to be Islamized. Third, it set the stage for the beginning of Pakistan's second "green revolution" (q.v.).

At the time of the promulgation of the Fifth Plan, the Zia government had three choices: it could have denationalized government-owned industries, curtailed further expansion of the public sector, or continued with the expansionary policies of the Bhutto administration. The Zia administration chose the second course. It limited the expansion of the public sector to the investments started during the Bhutto period. No new industrial investments were undertaken in the public sector during the Fifth Plan. The Plan adopted an equally conservative approach toward the development of physical infrastructure. Emphasis was placed on improving the operation of existing facilities rather than building new ones. A number of projects that were on the drawing board when Bhutto left the scene were either put on the back burner or were altogether abandoned.

The Plan adopted a cautious approach toward the Islamization of the economy. Although it accepted the recommendation of a panel of experts to introduce such Islamic taxes as *zakat* and *ushr* (qq.v.), it postponed to a later date, pending a careful study of the matter, the elimination of *riba* (interest) (q.v.) from the economy. It also reversed the Bhutto government's benign neglect of the agricultural sector by committing a significant amount of resources to input subsidies on agricultural chemicals, new irrigation works, reclamation of saline and water-logged land, and farm credit. It was hoped that by pursuing these approaches, the plan would reverse the virtual stagnation of the productive sectors of the economy during the Bhutto years. The gross domestic product (GDP) was expected to increase at a rate of 7 percent a year, made possible by an increase of agricultural output by 6 percent and of industrial production by 10 percent a year. These objectives were realized; during the Plan period (1978–1983), GDP increased at the rate of 6.8 percent a year, income per capita of the population by 3.7 percent, manufacturing output by 11 percent, and agricultural production by 4 percent. By the close of the Fifth Plan period, Pakistan's economy had regained the momentum it had lost during the years Zulfikar Ali Bhutto was in power. *See also* Agriculture.

FIVE YEAR PLAN, THE SIXTH (1983–1988). The Sixth Five Year Plan took 16 months to prepare; the work on it began soon after the return of Mahbubul Haq (q.v.) to Pakistan in February 1982. Haq's main objective was to use the Plan to bring about a major structural change in the economy, in particular to promote social development. In keeping with this promise, the Sixth Plan allocated Rs.20.5 billion for education and manpower development and Rs.14.6 billion for health. The two sectors together were provided Rs.35.1 billion worth of resources out of the Rs.242.49 billion that the public-sector expenditure envisaged for the five-year-plan period. This worked out to a share of 11.8 percent of total public resources. Had this amount of resource commitment been realized, the public sector would have spent 76 percent more on education and health compared to the actual outlay during the Fifth Plan (q.v.) period. It was hoped that the increase in public-sector expenditure would be accompanied by greater private-sector interest in social development and that private entrepreneurs would be induced to invest in those areas of education and health care for which the population was willing to pay for services provided.

The Plan also made an attempt to free Pakistan from excessive dependence on foreign savings—foreign borrowing and foreign aid—by aiming at a sharp increase in domestic savings. The gross investment rate was projected to increase from 16.4 percent realized in 1982–83, the last year of the Fifth Plan, to 19.4 percent in 1987–88, the last year of the Sixth Plan. At the same time, the national savings rate was to increase by four percentage points during the course of the plan, from 12.7 percent to 16.7 percent of gross domestic product (GDP).

The dependence on external capital resources was also to be reduced by following an export-led strategy. Although the plan projected a growth rate of 8 percent a year in the volume of exports, it expected export earnings to increase by almost twice as much, or 15 percent. The difference between volume exported and the value of exports was to result from a concentration of government and private effort on the sale abroad of high value-added products such as fashion garments rather than cotton yarn. Export receipts in current prices were expected to reach the level of $19.4 billion during the Plan's five years. Actual performance, however, was only 81.6 percent ($16.19 billion) of the target. The Plan was a success only in terms of continuing Pakistan's impressive growth performance. GDP increased at a rate of 6.6 percent, slightly higher than the target of 6.5 percent. In almost everything else the Plan failed. The structural transformation that it sought and attempted to bring about by redirecting public-sector expenditure did not take place.

FIVE YEAR PLAN, THE SEVENTH (1988–1993). The Seventh Five Year Plan (1988–93) was launched on July 1, 1988 by the caretaker government that took office after the dismissal on May 29 of the administration of Prime Minister Muhammad Khan Junejo (q.v.). Mahbubul Haq (q.v.), the architect of the Sixth Plan (q.v.), was back in office as the minister in charge of finance and planning. Five months after the launching of the Seventh Plan, there was another change of administration. On December 2, 1988 Benazir Bhutto (q.v.) was invited to form a government in Islamabad, returning the Pakistan People's Party (PPP) (qq.v.) to power for the second time in 20 years. Although the PPP government pursued an activist economic policy, it did not formally reformulate the Seventh Plan. The Plan's basic objectives and proposed policies were kept unchanged and the first annual development plan for the financial year 1989–90 was cast within the original framework.

The Sixth Plan had achieved a gross domestic product (GDP) growth rate of 6.6 percent a year, slightly higher than the target of 6.5 percent. The Seventh Plan went back to the target of the Sixth Plan. About 44 percent of the planned investment was to come from the private sector. This implied a rate of increase of 10.5 percent a year in private investment over that realized in the Sixth Plan. This rate of growth was also considerably higher than the 7.9 percent increase envisaged for public-sector investment. In other words, the planners were hoping to return to the pattern of investment that prevailed before the 1972 nationalization of private economic assets. Nationalization had not only significantly increased the economic role of the public sector, it had also discouraged new capital formation by the private sector.

As had been attempted repeatedly by the framers of five-year plans, those responsible for preparing the Seventh Plan also promised to provide a large flow of public resources for the development of social sectors. Education and health were to receive 10 percent of total public investment. The Plan recognized the precarious situation the country faced concerning its resources. The most striking feature of the budgetary performance during the Sixth Plan was the emergence of revenue deficits instead of the revenue surpluses that had been anticipated. Budgetary deficit as a proportion of GDP increased from less than 5 percent in 1982–83 to 8 percent in 1987–88. The Seventh Plan sought to address this situation and suggested a number of improvements in fiscal management. These included the requirement that all provinces must balance their current budgets by curtailing nondevelopment expenditure and raising additional tax revenues.

FIVE YEAR PLAN, THE EIGHTH (1993–1998). The work on the Eighth Five Year Plan began in earnest after Pakistan successfully dealt with an economic emergency in 1993. The emergency was caused by a serious political disagreement between President Ghulam Ishaq Khan and Prime Minister Mian Nawaz Sharif (qq.v.). The conflict between the two could not be resolved by constitutional means and a caretaker government under Moeen Qureshi (q.v.) had to be put into place to organize another general election. The caretaker administration was in power for three months and worked successfully on improving the country's fiscal and external situation. There was no time for the Planning Commission to work on formulating the Eighth Plan while the caretaker administration was in office.

The Planning Commission worked on the new Plan document in the winter of 1993–94 and made it public in the early months of 1994. At that time Benazir Bhutto (q.v.) had returned to office as prime minister and the Plan reflected her government's priorities. The Plan document went into considerable detail about the sectoral priorities that were to be assigned by the government, the amount of public resources that were to be committed to the realization of these objectives, and the role the private sector was to play in promoting development. The government did not indicate how it was going to achieve any of these objectives, however. The Plan remained a paper document; it was not acted on by the government.

↭ **G** ↭

GANDHARA. Some 2,000 years ago, the area now covered by the Peshawar and Rawalpindi (qq.v.) districts of modern-day Pakistan was known by the name of Gandhara. Its people were known as Gandharas. At one point the kingdom of Gandhara also included Kashmir (q.v.). In the third century B.C., it was a part of the empire of Asoka (c.273 B.C.–232 B.C.), the third emperor of the Maurya dynasty. Gandhara contained the two famous cities of Taxila and Pushkaravati. After the collapse of the Mauryan empire, Gandhara was parceled out among the Indo-Bactrian princes; still later it formed part of the Kushan dominions. It thus became a meeting point of Eastern and Western cultures and gave birth to what came to be called Gandhara art.

GENERAL SALES TAX (GST). The General Sales Tax was introduced as a federal tax by the first administration (1990–93) of Prime Minister Nawaz Sharif (q.v.) in the budget presented to the National Assembly in June 1991. The GST was a variant on the value-added tax (VAT) (q.v.), which had become the mainstay of the revenue raised by many developing countries. The authorities in Pakistan determined that it would have been premature to impose the VAT in the country as that would have required the transactions to be covered by the tax to be fully documented. For cultural reasons—and also because of the deep distrust of tax administration prevalent in the country—a very large number of transactions were not formally recorded.

The rationalization of the GST so that it included only a few rates and its extension to cover retail trade were among the many conditions agreed to by the government of Prime Minister Benazir Bhutto (q.v.) and Shahid Javed Burki, the caretaker advisor, with the International Monetary Fund (IMF), in return for Pakistan's access to the IMF's standby program (q.v.). In March 1997 the government of Mian Nawaz Sharif extended the GST to retail trade as a part of the structural-reform package it presented to the IMF so as to qualify for the IMF Extended Structural Adjustment Facility (q.v.).

GHAFFAR KHAN, ABDUL (1890–1989). Abdul Ghaffar Khan was born in 1890 in the village of Utmanzai near Peshawar in the Northwest Frontier Province (qq.v.). At an early age, Ghaffar Khan decided to involve himself with social causes and work for the betterment of the poor people of the region. The Khudai Khidmatgars (q.v.), a popular sociopolitical group of the area, offered him an opportunity to pursue his interests and he became one of its more enthusiastic members. He discovered that the Khidmatgars social philosophy had a great deal in common with the policies advocated by Mahatma Gandhi. Accordingly, he forged a close link between the Khidmatgars and the Indian National Congress (q.v.), which won him the title of the Frontier Gandhi. Although the title made him popular among the followers of Gandhi and the members of the Congress Party, it distanced him from the Muslims of the Frontier province, who had begun to subscribe to the "idea of Pakistan."

Pakistan's birth on August 14, 1947 posed a difficult political dilemma for Ghaffar Khan. He had no affinity for the new country or liking for its founder, Muhammad Ali Jinnah (q.v.). Immediately after the birth of Pakistan he began to espouse the cause of autonomy for the Pathan population. This campaign was often couched in a language that suggested to his detractors that he was working for the creation of an independent state for the Pathan population, which lived on both sides of the Afghanistan–Pakistan border. Such an entity was given the name of Pukhtunistan (q.v.) and it attracted support from large sections of the Pathan community in both Pakistan and Afghanistan (q.v.). For a long time, the idea of Pukhtunistan had the official support of the government of Afghanistan and was the cause of the uneasy relationship Pakistan had with its neighbor for more than 30 years, from 1947 to 1979. By endorsing the idea of Pukhtunistan, Ghaffar Khan could not join the mainstream of Pakistani politics. He had to endure long periods of incarceration at the hands of several regimes in Pakistan, which accused him of working against the integrity of the country. But Ghaffar Khan refused to either profess loyalty towards the country of which he was now a citizen or to agree not to work toward its dismemberment.

In 1979 the Soviet Union, by invading Afghanistan, presented another worrisome dilemma for the Pathan leader. Ghaffar Khan refused, however, to either condemn the Soviet move into Afghanistan or distance himself from the communist government in Kabul. In 1987, during one of his frequent visits to India, Ghaffar Khan suffered a stroke that immobilized him permanently. Even from his deathbed he managed to provoke controversy by suggesting that he did not wish to be buried in Pakistan. His wish was carried out and he was buried in Jalalabad, Afghanistan.

GHULAM ISHAQ KHAN (1915–). Ghulam Ishaq Khan was born in Bannu, then a small town in the Northwest Frontier Province (NWFP) (q.v.). He was educated at Peshawar's Islamia College. He joined the Provincial Civil Service in 1938. In 1958 President Ayub Khan (q.v.) nominated him as a member of the Land Reform Commission. Ishaq Khan opted for fairly radical land reforms but the majority of the commission chose to go for generous ceilings on ownership: 1,000 acres for nonirrigated and 500 acres for irrigated land. In 1962 President Ayub Khan launched Ghulam Ishaq Khan on a career path that thoroughly exposed him to economic management. He was appointed chairman of the West Pakistan Water and Power Development Authority (WAPDA) (q.v.). The WAPDA, under the chairmanship of Ghulam Ishaq Khan and that of Aftab Kazi, his successor, accomplished a great deal. It was particularly successful in implementing the gigantic Indus Water Replacement Works to bring water from the western rivers in compensation for that lost to India from the eastern rivers. One of Ghulam Ishaq Khan's proudest achievement of this period was the decision by the international community—taken reluctantly and after considerable persuasion by experts from Pakistan, including Ishaq Khan, that without the dam at Tarbela the objective of the replacement works would not be achieved—to construct the giant Tarbela dam on the Indus river (qq.v.).

In 1966 Ghulam Ishaq Khan was put in charge of the Ministry of Finance as its secretary. In 1971, he went to Karachi (q.v.) as governor of the State Bank of Pakistan; and in 1975, he was back in Islamabad (q.v.) as secretary-general of the Ministry of Defense. Within the space of a decade, Ishaq Khan was able to see the working of the central government from three very different perspectives: finance, development, and defense. The Ministry of Finance in Pakistan was always a very conservative institution inclined to keep in strict check public expenditure on both development and current (nondevelopmental) activities. Under Ishaq Khan's management it stuck to its original mandate and tradition. The State Bank of Pakistan, although not able to exercise much control over money supply, was nevertheless concerned about maintaining a watchful eye on the macroeconomic situation. While at the State Bank, Ishaq Khan began to get concerned about the free-wheeling ways of the government of Prime Minister Zulfikar Ali Bhutto (q.v.). He used the opportunity presented by the issuance of the State Bank's annual report on the health of the economy (q.v.) to question the wisdom of a number of policies that were being pursued by the Bhutto government at that time.

This statement did not endear him to the government and Ghulam Ishaq Khan was moved from the State Bank and appointed secretary-general in charge of the Ministry of Defense. This was an unusual but fortuitous appointment for a person who had spent most of his career in the government dealing with economic matters. It was while in this job that he was thrown into close contact with Zia ul-Haq (q.v.), the chief of staff of the army. General Zia, after removing Bhutto from office on July 5, 1977, appointed Ishaq Khan secretary-general. Ghulam Ishaq Khan held several different jobs in the government under President Zia ul-Haq. Although his titles changed, he functioned virtually as the prime minister and the economic czar from 1977 to 1985. In March 1985 Ishaq Khan was elected to the Senate from a seat in the NWFP and the Senate went on to elect him as its chairman. The portfolio of finance was given by President Zia ul-Haq to Mahbubul Haq (q.v.).

On August 17, 1988 President Zia ul-Haq was killed in a plane crash near the town of Bahawalpur in southern Punjab (qq.v.). General Aslam Beg (q.v.), the vice-chief of the Army Staff, and his senior colleagues met in Rawalpindi (q.v.) that same evening before announcing to the public the news of the president's death. General Beg revealed later that the meeting's attendees decided that it would be prudent to adopt the constitutional course and invite the chairman of the Senate to assume the presidency. Had the Senate chair been occupied by a person with less experience and prestige than Ghulam Ishaq Khan, the military might well have decided to take over the reins of government.

Ghulam Ishaq Khan's presidency lasted for a little less than five years. During this time he performed two very different functions. On three occasions—from August 17 to December 2, 1988, from August 6 to November 6, 1990, and from April 17 to May 28, 1993—he supervised the working of caretaker administrations appointed to hold general elections. During these periods, Ishaq Khan was the chief executive. For the rest of the time he kept a careful watch over the workings of the government. It was this watch that persuaded him to dismiss first the administration of Prime Minister Benazir Bhutto (q.v.) in August 1990 and then the administration of Prime Minister Nawaz Sharif (q.v.) in April 1993.

It was the second dismissal—that of Nawaz Sharif and the way he handled the circumstances created by the decision of the Supreme Court to declare the dismissal unconstitutional—that left a cloud over a career that was remarkable not only for its longevity but also for its dedication to the cause of Pakistan. It was clear that the decision to remove Nawaz Sharif was taken out of personal pique rather than on the basis of the prime minister's incompetence. Once the Supreme Court restored the prime minister, Ishaq Khan went on to subvert the functioning of the government by creating a difficult environment for the prime minister. This was done with the help of a group of loyal civil servants who made it impossible for the prime minister to function effectively. The result was a political and constitutional crisis that was resolved by the intervention of the military. General Abdul Waheed Kakar, the chief of the Army Staff, forced both Ishaq Khan and Nawaz Sharif to resign. A caretaker administration was appointed and elections were held in October 1993 (q.v.). The elections brought Benazir Bhutto back to power and Ishaq Khan went into retirement. After making a half-hearted attempt to contest the presidential election held in December 1993, he left Islamabad and settled in Peshawar.

GHULAM MUHAMMAD (1895–1955). Ghulam Muhammad was born in the small state of Kaparthula, which is now a part of the Indian province of Punjab (q.v.). After a distinguished academic career that included graduation from Aligarh University, he joined the Indian Accounts Service in 1920. He was deputized for two years (1930–32) to serve in the Bhopal State Service, from whence he returned to follow a successful career in the government of India's Finance and Supply Department. In 1938 he was appointed to the Indian Legislative Assembly as an official member. For four years, from 1942 to 1946, he held the office of minister of finance in the state government of Hyderabad (q.v.). In 1947 he was appointed minister of finance in the first cabinet to take office in Pakistan.

In 1951, when Liaqat Ali Khan (q.v.) was assassinated, Ghulam Muhammad engineered a bureaucratic solution to the deep political problem in which Pakistan suddenly found itself. Khawaja Nazimuddin was appointed prime minister while Ghulam Muhammad took Nazimuddin's position as governor-general. In April 1953 he dismissed Nazimuddin's government on grounds of ineptitude and, in October 1954, dissolved the First Constituent Assembly (q.v.). These actions stretched the powers of the governor-general beyond his constitutional power, thus plunging Pakistan into its first constitutional crisis. In *Tamizuddin vs. the Government of Pakistan,* the Supreme Court gave highly qualified support to the governor-general's action. The Supreme Court used the "doctrine of necessity" (q.v.) to justify the action of the governor-general but ordered him to reestablish the Constituent Assembly, which Ghulam Muhammad did by bringing in people who were more supportive of him. Rapidly failing health and the ascendancy of General Iskander Mirza (q.v.) forced Ghulam Muhammad out of office in 1955. He resigned as Pakistan's third governor-general on October 6, 1955.

GIK INSTITUTE OF ENGINEERING SCIENCES AND TECHNOLOGY. President Ghulam Ishaq Khan (q.v.) took an active interest in the promotion of science and technology in Pakistan. A scientist by training, he had come to recognize the importance of science and technology for economic development when he was appointed by General Zia ul-Haq (q.v.) to supervise Pakistan's nuclear program. Although Ishaq Khan was a strong believer in a prominent role of the state in economic and social management, the government's poor performance in these areas in the 1970s and 1980s seemed to have persuaded him to rely on private initiative. The success of the Lahore University of Management Sciences (LUMS) (q.v.) influenced his thinking. By the time he became president in 1988, following the death of Zia ul-Haq, he was prepared to accept a role for the private sector in the areas of special emphasis, including education, science, and technology.

In 1988 the Bank for Credit and Commerce International (BCCI) (q.v.) committed Rs.500 million to Ishaq Khan for the establishment of an advanced institution of learning in science and technology. The preparatory work for the design of the institution was done by Abdul Qadeer Khan (q.v.) and the launching of the institution was announced in Islamabad (q.v.) on January 7, 1991. The institution was to be located in Topi in the Swabi District of the Northwest Frontier Province (q.v.). The land for the institution was donated by the provincial government. The institution received its first class of students in 1993. The institution was designed to accommodate the graduation of 600 students every year. The program called for the establishment of a postgraduate facility after the year 2001.

GLOBAL ENVIRONMENT FACILITY (GEF). The Global Environment Facility was launched in 1990 with the objective of assisting the developing world in preserving the environment. The GEF was to provide developing countries with grants for launching environmental programs and undertaking the implementation of environmental projects, the impact of which went beyond their borders. The facility was managed jointly by three international institutions: the World Bank (q.v.), the United Nations Development Program (UNDP), and the United Nations Environment Program (UNEP). The facility was lodged at the World Bank's headquarters in Washington.

The pilot phase of the GEF lasted for two years; in 1994 the GEF was converted into a development institution under the joint management of the World Bank, the UNEP, and the UNDP. Pakistan is one of the several beneficiaries of the grants given by the GEF.

GOVERNMENT OF INDIA ACT OF 1909. The Government of India Act of 1909—also known as the Minto-Morley Act after Lord Minto, viceroy of India, and John Morley, secretary of state for India in the British Cabinet in London, respectively—was a major initiative taken by Great Britain toward the introduction of self-government in its Indian domain. The Act brought Indians into the viceroy's executive council and in similar bodies aiding provincial governors. The Act also provided for the election of Indians to the legislative councils at the central as well as provincial levels. Not all members of the legislative councils were to be elected, however. The Act allowed the government of India the authority to nominate people to the legislative councils.

The Act made a major concession to the Muslim community by accepting the principle of "separate electorates." This was a long-standing demand of the Muslim League (q.v.). Separate electorates meant that Muslim voters voted only for Muslim candidates, whereas the non-Muslims could vote for a candidate from any community.

GOVERNMENT OF INDIA ACT OF 1919. Also known as the Montagu–Chelmsford Act after Edwin Montagu, secretary of state for India in the British Cabinet, and Lord Chelmsford, the British viceroy of India, respectively, the Government of India Act of 1919 granted the Indians somewhat greater participation in managing their affairs by creating two legislative houses. In both houses, the Council of State and the Central Legislative Assembly, elected Indian representatives constituted a majority. The viceroy, however, who was nominated by the British government in London, had the final authority. The viceroy was allowed to appoint a Cabinet of seven members, called the Executive Council, three of whom were Indians. This structure was repeated at the provincial level with Indians constituting a majority in the legislative councils. The Act allowed the provinces some autonomy in decision-making. *See also* Dyarchy.

GOVERNMENT OF INDIA ACT OF 1935. The Government of India Act of 1935 granted provinces the right to govern themselves with some constraints. The legislative councils set up under the Government of India Act of 1919 (q.v.) were replaced with legislative assemblies. The provincial governor appointed a prime minister who, along with his Cabinet, was responsible to the provincial assembly. In the case of breakdown of the Cabinet government or in a financial emergency caused, for instance, by the failure of the assembly to pass a budget, the governor had the power to assume the functioning of the government. The Act envisaged a similar setup at the center provided the "princely states" (q.v.) could be brought into the constitutional structure created by the Act. This did not happen as most princes refused to accept what would have been a considerable encroachment on their authority. The 1935 Act, amended by the India Independence Act of 1947, served as the constitution of both India and Pakistan until each adopted its own constitution.

Two sets of provincial elections were held under the Act of 1935—one in 1937 and the other in 1946. In the first the Muslim League (q.v.) did very poorly; in the second, however, the League scored impressive electoral gains in most provinces in which the Muslims were in majority.

GRAND TRUNK ROAD. Grand Trunk Road was built by Emperor Sher Shah Suri during his brief rule of India. It was a marvelous feat of engineering. The road, some 2000 kilometers long, connected Peshawar (q.v.) in the northwest of Suri's domain, with Bengal in the southeast. Trees were planted to provide shade on both sides of the road. Wells were dug to provide water to the travelers using the road who could also use scores of *serais* (rest houses), which were constructed at suitable intervals along the road. The Grand Trunk Road—or GT Road as it is commonly called—remained the main communication artery for both West Pakistan and north India. It was only with the construction in the 1990s of the Lahore–Islamabad Motorway (q.v.) that an alternate route was developed in Pakistan.

GREAT GAME, THE. The Great Game—the term commonly used for the struggle among the world's great powers to dominate Central Asia—was played between two major imperial powers in the nineteenth century. Both Great Britain and Russia sought to gain the upper hand in the region; Britain, in order to protect its dominion over India from possible encroachment by Russia; Russia, in order to strengthen its soft southern belly against possible prodding by Britain. The Great Game became dormant after the emergence of the Soviet Union as a world power. The collapse of the Soviet Union in 1991 and the grant of independence to the Central Asian Republics revived the conflict, however, especially when it came to be realized that the region held vast amounts of oil reserves.

The Great Game of the 1990s—in all probability, the Game will continue to be played into the early years of the twenty-first century—was about the access by Russia and the West to the oil reserves of central Asia. As Western oil companies got involved in prospecting for oil in the region and marketing the oil brought to the surface, the question of the direction to be taken by the pipelines carrying oil became of paramount importance. Of the several routes being investigated, the Russians favored the one that terminated at Novorossiysk, their port on the Black Sea. The Western oil companies seemed inclined to bypass Russia altogether, taking the oil pipeline from Baku, the capital of Azerbaijan, through Georgia to the Turkish port of Ceyhan on the Mediterranean. The new Great Game and its outcome had tremendous significance for Pakistan. The countries involved included a number of Muslim countries to its northwest—Iran, Turkey, Azerbaijan, Kazakhstan, and Turkmenistan among them. There was also active interest in laying down a gas pipeline from Turkmenistan to Iran, Afghanistan, Pakistan, and India.

GREEN REVOLUTION, THE FIRST. The fortunes of the agricultural sector changed in the late 1960s with a suddenness that surprised most observers. This happened because of the advent of the "green revolution." The revolution arrived in the form of high-yielding varieties (HYVs) of wheat and rice in the late 1960s that came from laboratories in Mexico and the Philippines. The HYVs spread very quickly in Punjab and Sindh (qq.v.); wheat more rapidly than rice. In the four-year period between 1965–66 and 1969–70, the index of food-crop production increased from 107 to 177, a rise of 70 points. In this short period wheat production increased by 86 percent (an extraordinary rate of 16.8 percent a year), from 3.9 million tons to 7.3 million tons. Rice output increased by 54 percent (11.5 percent a year), from 1.3 million tons to 2.4 million tons.

There were two developments specific to Pakistan that explain the rapid spread of HYVs in the country. First, unnoticed by the government but indirectly encouraged by it, Pakistani farmers invested largely in sinking tubewells. The government's encouragement came in the form of the Salinity Control and Reclamation Projects (SCARPs) (q.v.), which it initiated in the late 1950s. These projects demonstrated to the farmers the profitability of the conjunctive use of surface and ground water. Once the farmers became aware of this they moved fast to install wells of their own. According to one estimate, farmers had installed about 25,000 wells in the irrigated districts of Punjab. Second, the introduction of the "Basic

Democracies" (q.v.) system of local government by the administration of President Ayub Khan (q.v.) in the early 1960s brought the middle farmers in close touch with the bureaucracy, particularly that part of it which had the direct responsibility for promoting economic development. With this easy access available to the functionaries of the government, the farming community was able to procure the public services it required for making a success of the HYVs.

The transformation of agriculture (q.v.) begun with the first green revolution was interrupted during the period Zulfikar Ali Bhutto (q.v.) was the prime minister, and resumed again with the start of the second green revolution (q.v.), which began in the mid-1980s.

GREEN REVOLUTION, THE SECOND. The second green revolution began in the mid-1980s and its consequence was the commercialization of agriculture (q.v.). It was centered around the use of modern inputs in agriculture—in particular farm chemicals and labor-saving machinery—and its beneficiaries were principally the producers of such cash crops as cotton (q.v.), fruits, and vegetables. There were three circumstances that led to the launching of the second green revolution. First, the migration of millions of people from Pakistan to the Middle East in the late 1970s. This movement of people created serious shortages of labor in the countryside of Punjab and the Northwest Frontier Province (qq.v.) and forced the farming community to mechanize some parts of their production process. Once the farmers came into the market to purchase and service machinery they were also exposed to other features of commercial agriculture. As was the case with the first green revolution (q.v.), it was the middle-sized farmer who led the agricultural sector in bringing its second revolution. Second, the nationalization of large-scale industry by the administration of Prime Minister Zulfikar Ali Bhutto (q.v.) in the early 1970s persuaded both old and new industrial entrepreneurs to concentrate their efforts in small industries. Denationalization of agroindustries by the government of President Zia ul-Haq (q.v.) in the late 1970s further encouraged these entrepreneurs. Most of these industries had strong links with the agricultural sector and required marketable agricultural surpluses as inputs, and they began to provide incentives to the farming community to produce them. Cotton growers were the first to respond to this increase in demand for their produce, and they were followed by other producers of cash crops. Third, the establishment of Pakistani communities in the Middle East, Western Europe, and the United States created a demand for Pakistani products, particularly processed food, giving further impetus to both the small industrialists and commercial farmers.

The second green revolution had a decisive impact on the cotton-growing areas of Punjab and Sindh (qq.v.). Before its advent, some 700,000 tons of cotton lint were being produced in these areas; by the early 1990s, output had increased to well over 1.5 million tons. As a consequence, Pakistan is now one of the major cotton-growing countries in the world, producing, in good years, as much as 10 percent of the world's total cotton crop. It has an even greater presence in world cotton trade; accounting, again in good years, for some 20 percent of the total world trade in cotton. There were large increases of output of fruits and vegetables as well; for instance, the production of citrus doubled over the 10-year period from the late 1970s to the late 1980s, increasing from an average of 723,000 tons to 1.51 million tons. There was a corresponding increase in exports of fruits from the country. In the late 1970s Pakistan exported on average some 74,000 tons of fruits, mostly to the markets in the Middle East. This increased to an average of 100,000 tons in the late 1980s.

GUL, LIEUTENANT GENERAL (RETIRED) HAMEED (1932–). Hameed Gul was born in Sargodah, a city in central Punjab (q.v.), and was commissioned in the armor corps on October 19, 1958. After a distinguished career that included the command of an armor division, he was appointed director general of the Interservices Intelligence (ISI), a position that had been held for several years by General Akhtar Abdur Rahman (q.v.). Under Rahman, the ISI had been deeply involved in training Afghani mujahideen in their war against the Soviets and in providing them with arms and equipment. Under Gul, however, the ISI's role in Afghanistan (q.v.) changed as it attempted to bring the various Afghan factions under one political umbrella. He was still engaged in these efforts when, in August 1988, he lost his mentor, General Zia ul-Haq (q.v.). Zia was killed in an airplane crash and a few months later Benazir Bhutto (q.v.) became prime minister.

The government of Benazir Bhutto was suspicious of the role played by both the ISI and its director general. Hameed Gul was transferred and appointed corps commander; his successor, General Shamsur Rehman Kallu, was a Bhutto loyalist. After the appointment of General Asif Nawaz (q.v.) as the chief of the Army Staff in August 1991, Gul was transferred once again, this time to Taxila as the commandant of a large military–industrial complex. Until then this position had been held by engineers; Gul clearly was not well equipped for it. Rather than move to his new assignment, he chose to retire from the army in early 1992.

After spending the mandatory two-year postretirement period out of public view, Hameed Gul reemerged. He was particularly interested in Pakistan taking the opportunity created by the war in Afghanistan to influence political development in that country. While retaining an active interest in foreign affairs, Hameed Gul decided that he could only influence the country's foreign policy if he were to develop a strong domestic political base for himself. The confidence that he could make some difference to the way Pakistan was to develop politically led him first to support Pasban, a social welfare organization affiliated with the Jamaat-e-Islami (q.v.) and then, in July 1995, to get involved in bringing the government and the Muhajir Qaumi Mahaz (MQM) (q.v.) to the conference table in order to find a solution to the rapidly deteriorating situation in Karachi (q.v.). In July, Gul met with Benazir Bhutto in Islamabad (q.v.), flew to hold talks with MQM's Altaf Hussain (q.v.) in London, and flew back to Karachi to announce that both the government and the MQM had agreed to dispense with their preconditions for holding talks and had decided to nominate teams that could begin immediate discussions. He had underestimated the ill will between Bhutto and Altaf Hussain, however, and his efforts did not bear fruit.

By the late summer of 1996 as the government of Benazir Bhutto became increasingly unpopular on account of numerous stories of corruption that began to circulate in the country involving her husband, Asif Ali Zardari (q.v.), and as the economy came under a great deal of pressure, Hameed Gul gave the impression of a person who wanted to get involved to cleanse the system but was still trying to figure out the best way of achieving that objective. He would have wanted to be actively involved in politics after President Farooq Leghari (q.v.) dismissed the Bhutto government in November 1996. Such an opportunity did not arise, however.

GUL HASSAN KHAN, LIEUTENANT GENERAL (1921–). Born in Quetta, Balochistan (qq.v.), to a middle-class family, Gul Hassan Khan joined the Indian Military Academy in 1941. He was stationed on the Assam–Burma sector during the closing years of World War II; and, in August 1947, he was appointed assistant to Muhammad Ali Jinnah (q.v.), Pakistan's first governor-general. In 1971, when the Pakistani army was fighting the Bengali separatists in East Pakistan, Gul Hassan occupied the important position of the chief of General Staff.

Gul Hassan Khan was appointed commander in chief of the Pakistani army on December 20, 1971 by President Zulfikar Ali Bhutto (q.v.). Earlier that day Gul Hassan had reluctantly accepted Bhutto's offer to take over as the commander in chief of a demoralized army that had suffered a humiliating defeat at the hands of the Indian army in East Pakistan. Gul Hassan did not serve Bhutto for long, however. His break with the new president came precisely because of the qualities Bhutto had underscored for choosing him in the first place. As Bhutto began to consolidate his hold over the country, he wanted the army to be led by a man who appreciated the imperatives of politics. But Gul Hassan was inclined to be a professional soldier, refusing to be drawn into politics. On March 3, 1972 he and Air Marshal Rahim Khan, the air force commander in chief, were summoned to the president's house, accused by the president of not being fully supportive of the civilian authority, and asked to resign. General Tikka Khan (q.v.) was appointed the new commander of the army. Unlike many of his predecessors, Gul Hassan Khan chose not to remain active in public life after his retirement from the army.

⟅ **H** ⟆

HABIB BANK LIMITED. Habib Bank Limited was established in Bombay on August 25, 1941 by the Habibs, a prominent Muslim family. The bank's creation was encouraged by Muhammad Ali Jinnah (q.v.) to provide a source of institutional credit to the Muslim community. Habib Bank not only helped the Muslim commercial classes; it also became the repository of the various fundraising schemes Jinnah launched to help the Muslim community of British India. After Pakistan was born on August 14, 1947, the bank moved its headquarters from Bombay to Karachi (q.v.), the capital of the new country. In Pakistan the bank rapidly expanded its activities. In the industrial boom that followed Pakistan's first trade with India in 1949, Habib Bank provided seed and operating capital to a number of new industrialists who came forward to take advantage of the opportunities the government offered. The Habibs themselves entered industry. The bank opened hundreds of new branches all over Pakistan, including East Pakistan, the eastern wing of the country, where banks were few.

The arrival of the socialist government of President Zulfikar Ali Bhutto (q.v.) in December 1971 suddenly changed the country's economic environment. Along with all the other private-sector banks, Habib Bank was nationalized by the new government on January 1, 1974. For the next two decades the bank was to be run by the government, its officers were appointed by the ministry of finance, and it was subjected to all kinds of pressures to lend money to the political supporters of whichever government happened to be in power. As was the case with other banks under the control of the government, Habib Bank's financial situation deteriorated progressively. By the middle of the 1990s the administration of Prime Minister Benazir Bhutto (q.v.), revived the program to privatize public-sector banks launched earlier by the government of Prime Minister Nawaz

Sharif (q.v.). By then, however, Habib Bank's nonperforming assets far exceeded its capital. In 1996, there was a widespread impression in the market that the bank—like the United Bank Limited (q.v.), another large public-sector commercial bank—was insolvent. This market perception made it difficult for the government of Prime Minister Benazir Bhutto to privatize the institution. The government of Nawaz Sharif that came to power in February 1997 took the position that professional managers appointed to public-sector banks with the mandate to improve the quality of their assets would be able to prepare the public-sector banks for privatization. Accordingly, Sharif appointed Shaukat Tareen, a respected Pakistani banker working for City Bank, as president of Habib Bank. *See also* Banks, Nationalization of.

HABIBS, THE. The Habib family came originally from Bombay. The Habibs were principally traders when World War II started and the British began to rely heavily on India for a number of commodities required by their troops. The family made good use of this opportunity as did a number of other established trading houses in Bombay and Calcutta. After the war, Muhammad Ali Habib was persuaded by Muhammad Ali Jinnah (q.v.) to help finance the Muslim League (q.v.) movement for the establishment of an independent Muslim state in British India. Habib Bank (q.v.) was started by Muhammad Ali as a part of this effort. The Habib family made generous donations to the various funds established by Jinnah for the benefit of his people. The family, for instance, led the drive to raise money for helping the victims of the communal riots in Bihar in which thousands of Muslims perished and hundreds of thousands were injured. The Habibs migrated to Pakistan after India's partition and set up their headquarters in Karachi (q.v.), the new country's capital. Like other trading families, they also moved into manufacturing when Pakistan began to industrialize. By the end of the Ayub Khan (q.v.) period (1958–69), the Habibs were counted among the 22 richest families in Pakistan. They paid a heavy price for the attention they received during the movement against Ayub Khan, when it was alleged that the bulk of the rewards of the rapid growth during his decade of development had been claimed by the "twenty-two families." Most of the industries owned by the Habibs as well as Habib Bank Limited were nationalized between 1972 and 1974 by the government of Zulfikar Ali Bhutto (q.v.). Unlike some other industrial families, however, the Habibs did not show much resilience and did not recover from the waves of nationalization that swept Pakistan during the Bhutto period (1971–77). By the mid-1990s, the family was no longer regarded as a major industrial player in Pakistan. *See also* Twenty-Two Families Speech, The.

HABIBULLAH KHAN, LIEUTENANT GENERAL (1916–1996). Born in the Northwest Frontier Province (q.v.), Habibullah Khan joined the British Indian army in 1937 and the Pakistani army in 1947. He rose rapidly in the army. He was a senior general at the time of Ayub Khan's (q.v.) coup d'etat. Among army circles he was considered to be highly competent and not without political ambitions of his own. President Ayub Khan had good reasons to be wary of Habibullah Khan even though his second son, Gohar Ayub (q.v.), was married to the general's daughter. From Ayub Khan's perspective, it was better to have Habibullah Khan out of the army and into a career from which he could not pose any real political threat to the president. Accordingly, Habibullah Khan was encouraged to move into industry, which he did by establishing Janana Demaluchoo, a large cotton-textile plant in Kohat, a town in the Northwest Frontier Province. The plant was very well managed and made money for its owner, which he invested in Gandhara Motors, an automobile assembly plant near Karachi (q.v.), set up with assistance from General Motors. Gandhara Motors was equally successful and also made a great deal of money for Habibullah Khan and Gohar Ayub, the latter, in the meantime having joined his father-in-law's business.

The rapidly rising fortune of Habibullah Khan and his family seemed to vindicate Ayub Khan's confidence in the ability of civil and military bureaucrats to become successful industrial entrepreneurs. A large number of Pakistanis saw Habibullah's rise to the position of wealth and prosperity as an example of governmental nepotism and corruption, however. At the time that Habibullah Khan began to count himself among Pakistan's wealthiest people, Mahbubul Haq (q.v.), the Planning Commission's chief economist, delivered his "twenty-two families speech" (q.v.) in which he accused the government of following a model of economic development that deliberately favored the rich over the poor. The speech had a great political impact and Habibullah Khan became the symbol of all that was considered wrong with Ayub Khan's economic philosophy. When Zulfikar Ali Bhutto (q.v.) took over the reins of government from the armed forces in December 1971, he exploited the sentiment against Ayub Khan and the distributive consequences of his economic policies by arresting Habibullah Khan and parading him handcuffed on national television. At the same time, the Bhutto administration nationalized Gandhara Industries and merged it with other automobile plants to form the Automobile Corporation of Pakistan.

Habibullah Khan survived Bhutto, however. He was appointed minister in charge of industry by President Zia ul-Haq (q.v.) in the first civilian Cabinet to take office under the new military president. The Cabinet was made up of technocrats. Habibullah Khan left the Cabinet a few months later when President Zia decided to replace experts with politicians. He went back to managing his large industrial empire, while Gohar Ayub, Ayub Khan's son and Habibullah Khan's son-in-law, entered politics.

HADUD ORDINANCES OF 1979. The Hadud Ordinances of 1979, promulgated by the government of President Zia ul-Haq (q.v.), concerned crimes related to sex—adultery, fornication, rape, and prostitution. The Ordinances were viewed with great concern by women (q.v.) not only because they termed criminal many activities that were regarded in most civilized societies as beyond the reach of law. Women in Pakistan were also apprehensive that the Ordinances would provide a new set of instruments to those in the Pakistani society who were determined to reduce the status of women. There was particular concern about two provisions in the Ordinances. One, in crimes relating to *zina* (adultery and fornication) and *zina-bil-jabir* (rape), the Ordinances required that there must be four Muslim male adult witnesses present when the crime was committed for it to be recognized. Two, the law did not draw any distinction between adultery and rape. It was the latter provision that gave an enormous amount of authority to the state to regulate even those relations that had the consent of the men and women involved.

HAIDER, SYED IQBAL (1946–). Born in Agra, India, Iqbal Haider migrated to Karachi (q.v.), Pakistan after the partition of India and the emergence of Pakistan. He entered Punjab University Law College in Lahore (q.v.) in 1964 and became active in student politics. He was present at the meeting in Lahore's YMCA hall in 1966 at which Zulfikar Ali Bhutto (q.v.) made the first public statement against the Tashkent Declaration (q.v.). He went to London's Lincoln Inn to study law. It was during his stay in London that he developed a close relationship with the Bhutto family. Iqbal Haider returned to Pakistan in 1971 and began to practice law in Karachi. Although given a ticket by the Pakistan People's Party (PPP) (q.v.), he lost from Korangi district in Karachi in the National Assembly elections of 1977 and 1988 (qq.v.). It was during this period that he turned his attention to another area of interest: human rights. In 1985 he joined hands with Asma Jehangir (q.v.) and other human-rights activists to establish the Human Rights Commission of Pakistan.

Iqbal Haider's loyal service to the PPP was rewarded in 1991, when Benazir Bhutto (q.v.), the party's chairperson, gave him the ticket to contest for a safe seat in the Senate. He won the seat and was brought to the cabinet by Prime Minister Bhutto as law minister in 1993. He resigned from the Cabinet in December 1994 over differences with the prime minister concerning her approach toward governance. He was back in the

Cabinet in September 1995, however, as minister in charge of human rights, a new ministry created as a result of the recommendations made to the prime minister by a commission headed by him. In October 1996 the prime minister appointed him attorney general as the controversy concerning her government's reluctance to implement the Supreme Court decision in the judges' case (q.v.) gathered steam. Benazir Bhutto was dismissed by President Farooq Leghari (q.v.) a month later and Iqbal Haider went back to Karachi to resume his law practice. In 1997 his term in the Senate was renewed by Bhutto, who retained for him a safe PPP seat.

HAMOODUR RAHMAN COMMISSION, THE. The Hamoodur Rahman Commission was appointed by President Zulfikar Ali Bhutto (q.v.) in 1972 to investigate the circumstances that led to the secession of East Pakistan and the emergence of Bangladesh as an independent state. The commission's appointment served to still the clamor for accountability in West Pakistan—now Pakistan—for the breakup of Pakistan in December 1971 and for the defeat of the Pakistan army at the hands of a combined force of the Indian army and Mukti Bahini (q.v.), the Bengali freedom fighters. Bhutto turned to Chief Justice Hamoodur Rahman of the Supreme Court, himself a Bengali, to lead the inquiry. The commission investigated for two years, interviewed a large number of people, and issued its report to the government. The report was not released to the public either by the Bhutto administration or by any of its many successor administrations. It is widely believed that the report portrays the army's performance in East Pakistan in a very unfavorable light. As such, the military leadership has succeeded in keeping the report under wraps for more than a quarter century.

HAQ, MAHBUBUL (1934–1998). Mahbubul Haq was born in Jammu, Kashmir (q.v.) and migrated with his family to Lahore (q.v.) after the partition of India and the emergence of Pakistan as an independent state. He was educated at Lahore's Government College and at Cambridge University in England. On his return from England in 1957, he joined the Planning Commission. His first assignment at the commission was to work on the Second Five Year Plan (1960–65) (q.v.). He became the principal author of the Plan, which was released to the public in the spring of 1960.

The Plan adopted the approach that a developing country such as Pakistan must first concentrate on increasing the rate of economic growth before attempting to solve the problems of poverty and poor distribution of income. Haq defended this approach in an influential book, *The Strategy of Economic Planning: A Case Study of Pakistan,* published in 1963. A few months later, however, he surprised the government by delivering what came to be known as the "twenty-two families speech" (q.v.). In this speech he argued that a significant part of the benefit of the rapid growth of the economy during the period of Ayub Khan (q.v.) accrued to no more than 22 industrial and commercial houses that had accumulated vast fortunes.

Haq joined the World Bank (q.v.) in 1968 and worked as the director of the Policy Planning Department until his resignation 13 years later. It was largely because of his influence that the bank began to address the problem of poverty by lending directly to the projects aimed at the poor and for meeting their basic needs. Haq left the bank in 1981 and was appointed deputy chairman of the Planning Commission by President Zia ul-Haq (q.v.). After supervising the preparation of the Sixth Five Year Plan (q.v.), he replaced Ghulam Ishaq Khan (q.v.) as finance minister. Following President Zia's death in 1988, Haq stayed on as a member of the caretaker government. He left Pakistan in 1988 and joined the United Nations Development Program and assumed the responsibility for launching the annual *Human Development Report*. He returned to Pakistan to establish the Human Development Center at Islamabad (q.v.). Haq died while on a visit to New York. *See also* Twenty-Two Families Speech, The.

HARIS. *Haris,* or tenants at will, constitute the majority of the agricultural work force in Sindh (q.v.) province. Their poverty was the subject of several government reports, the most detailed of which was produced by the Government Hari Enquiry Committee. The committee was established in 1947 and, after working for a year, submitted its report in 1948. One member of the committee, Muhammad Masud Khadarposh, was convinced that the only way to solve the problem of poverty faced by the haris was to give them the ownership of the land they cultivated. Other members of the committee were not prepared to accept such a radical approach. Their reluctance to go along with Khadarposh persuaded him to write his well-known "note of dissent."

Masud Khadarposh gave a vivid account of the plight of the haris. According to him, fear reigns supreme in the life of the hari—fear of imprisonment, fear of losing the land he is allowed to work on, fear of losing his children into servitude and his wife to the landlord, fear also of losing his life. The *zamindar* (landlord) can deal with him almost at will, unconstrained by law but encouraged by custom. He has enough political and social power to have the officialdom always on his side. Section 110 of the Criminal Procedure Court, which allows the police to detain any person for four weeks without trial, was the weapon most feared by the haris. The police had only to show the magistrate that the person in question was suspected of disturbing public peace. Although Khadarposh was not able to persuade the committee to adopt a radical solution to improve the situation of the haris, his note of dissent had a profound impact. It is read to this day by social and political workers.

HARRAPA. Harrapa is situated in the Sahiwal district of Punjab (q.v.). The ancient city was part of what is today called the Indus civilization. Archeological excavations have revealed a large, well-planned city with granaries, living quarters for workers, and a citadel with gates and cemeteries. Many seals discovered at the site have hieroglyphics that have yet to be deciphered.

HUMAN DEVELOPMENT INDEX. The United Nations Development Program (UNDP) defined a new index to measure human welfare. The index went beyond the gross domestic product (GDP), the standard measure used to gauge the size of an economy. This index has three components: longevity, knowledge, and decent living standards. The index, first developed in the 1991 Human Development Report issued by the UNDP, rated Japan and Barbados as the top performers among developed and developing countries, respectively, and Rumania and Sierra Leone as the poorest performers in these two categories of countries. Among the 160 countries ranked by the report, Pakistan was ranked at 120, India 123, Bangladesh 136, Nepal 145, and Afghanistan 157. In 1998 the UNDP placed Pakistan at 134 among 174, only one place above India. *See also* Haq, Mahbubul.

HYDERABAD STATE. *See* KASHMIR.

◁ | ▷

IFTIKHARUDDIN, MIAN MUHAMMAD (1907–1962). Mian Muhammad Iftikharuddin was one of the few Muslim politicians of preindependence Punjab (q.v.) who gained prominence without aligning himself with the Unionist Party (q.v.). He was born in Lahore (q.v.) into a prominent family and was educated at Government College, Lahore, and Oxford University. Family riches notwithstanding, he was attracted to socialist causes and decided that his personal objectives would be better served by joining the All-India Congress, which he did in 1936. Mian Iftikharuddin was elected to the Punjab Provincial Assembly in 1936 on the All-India Congress ticket. He was arrested by the Indian British administration for his political activities and remained in prison for three years (1942–45). On his release, he left the Congress and joined the Muslim League (q.v.) and devoted himself with his customary enthusiasm and energy to advancing the League's political objective of establishing a separate homeland for the Muslims of British India. In 1946, Mian Iftikharuddin spearheaded the Muslim League movement against the provincial government of Khizar Hayat Khan Tiwana (q.v.) and was sent back to jail. His conversion to the idea of Pakistan was now complete; convinced that the establishment of a separate homeland for the Muslims of India would be possible only if it was championed by the urban intelligentsia, he used his abundant wealth to found two newspapers, the *Pakistan Times* in English and *Imroze* in Urdu.

After the emergence of Pakistan, he served briefly as a minister in the Cabinet of Nawab Mamdot (q.v.). Not happy with the intrigue and infighting that characterized Muslim League politics in Punjab, he organized a "forward bloc" of his own within the League and used his newspapers to question the policies being pursued by the provincial government. These were not popular positions to take and he was expelled from the League in 1951. He founded the Azad Pakistan Party soon after leaving the League and then merged it with the National Awami Party (NAP) of Maulana Abdul Hamid Bhashani (qq.v.), a left-leaning politician from East Pakistan. The *Pakistan Times* and *Imroze* were nationalized in 1958 by the martial-law government of Ayub Khan (q.v.) and their holding company, Progressive Papers Ltd., was dissolved. These were severe blows for Mian Iftikharuddin and he never recovered from them.

INDEMNITY CLAUSE. The martial-law administration of General Zia ul-Haq (q.v.) faced one serious problem in its efforts to restore constitutional government in Pakistan. The Constitution of 1973 made intervention by the military a capital offense. This constitutional provision notwithstanding, General Zia ul-Haq had assumed power on July 5, 1977 by staging a successful coup d'etat against the government of Zulfikar Ali Bhutto (q.v.). Zia had to indemnify the actions taken by his government before he could lift martial law. Accordingly, by inserting Article 270-A as the eighth amendment (q.v.) to the Constitution, all acts by the martial government were indemnified. The amendment was passed by the National Assembly in October 1985. According to Section 2 of the new article: "All orders made, proceedings taken and acts done by any authority or by any person, which were made, taken or done, or purported to have been made, taken or done, between the fifth day of July 1977 and the date on which this Article comes into force, in exercise of the powers derived from any Proclamation, President's Orders, Ordinances, Martial Law Regulation, Martial Law Orders, enactments, notifications, rules, orders or by-laws, or in execution of or in compliance with any order made or sentence passed by any authority in the exercise or purported exercise of powers as aforesaid shall, notwithstanding any judgment of any court, be deemed to be and always to have been validly made, taken or done and shall not be called in question in any court on any ground whatsoever." Article 270-A came into force along with the amended Constitution on the withdrawal of martial law on December 30, 1985.

INDIAN NATIONAL CONGRESS. The Indian National Congress was formed in 1885 by Allan Octavian Hume, a retired member of the Indian Civil Service. It held its first session in Bombay in December 1885. The group's initial purpose was "the consolidation of the union between England and India by securing the modification of such conditions as may be unjust or injurious to the latter country." The formation of the organization—if not its stated official purpose—encouraged a group of younger politicians to begin to campaign for limited democracy, which would permit Indians to be elected to provincial councils. These efforts resulted in the Minto-Morley reforms of 1909.

The Congress adopted a more militant stance when, in 1920, its leadership was assumed by Mahatma Gandhi. The party now demanded a "Dominion status" within the British Empire, similar to that enjoyed by such former colonies as Australia and New Zealand. This campaign lasted for more than a decade and at times provoked the British administration in India to repress the party's activities and imprison its senior leaders, including Gandhi. Some progress was made, however. In 1935 the Government of India Act of 1935 (q.v.) expanded Indian participation in the legislative councils at the provincial and central levels. The Congress participated actively in the elections of 1936–37 held under the 1935 Act and succeeded in forming governments in 8 of the 11 provinces. Its failure to accommodate the Muslim League (q.v.) in these governments contributed to the latter's demand for the creation of Pakistan, an independent state for the Muslims of British India.

On the eve of the 1942 annual meeting, two years after the Muslim League had passed the Pakistan Resolution (q.v.) asking for the creation of a separate homeland for the Muslims, the Madras wing of the Congress party, under the leadership of C. Rajagopalacharia, asked for it to "acknowledge the All-India Muslim League's claim for separation [of the Muslim areas] should the same be persisted in for framing the future constitution of India." Had the Congress accepted this initiative, it might have prevented the total alienation of a vast number of Muslims from the majority Hindu population. That did not happen, however. Gandhi was not prepared to tolerate any attempt to break up "mother India." Instead of working on preserving the unity of India, the 1942 annual meeting of the Congress asked the British to leave India. Its "Quit India" movement led to a great deal of unrest in the country at the time Great Britain was locked in conflict with Germany, Italy, and Japan. The British administration did not appreciate this gesture on the part of the Congress' leadership. It reacted by imprisoning most of its senior leaders, including Gandhi and Jawaharlal Nehru.

The Muslims by and large kept out of the "Quit India" movement. Gandhi was released in May 1944; in September 1945, the party opted in favor of a constitutional approach for advancing its cause. It decided to participate in the elections to the central and provincial legislatures the British had promised to hold once the war in Europe was over. The elections were held in 1946 but this time around, the Muslim League gained ground in the Muslim majority provinces in the northwestern and northeastern parts of the country. Emboldened by its electoral success, the Muslim League pressed hard for the partition of India and the creation of Pakistan. On June 3, 1946 the Congress and the Muslim League accepted the plan put forward by Lord Louis Mountbatten (q.v.), the viceroy of India, to partition India into the two independent states of India and Pakistan. *See also* Government of India Act of 1909; Government of India Act of 1935.

INDIA–PAKISTAN RELATIONS. Muhammad Ali Jinnah's (q.v.) demand for the creation of a separate country for the Muslims of British India was bitterly opposed by the leaders of the Indian National Congress (q.v.). When they finally accepted his demand for the partition of India along communal lines, they did not look kindly on Pakistan, the country that was established in spite of their efforts to preserve Indian unity. India and Pakistan began their independent existence highly suspicious of each other. The suspicion persists to this day.

A number of developments soured the relationship between the two countries soon after they became independent. Partition resulted in a massive exchange of population between the two countries with Muslims leaving India for Pakistan and Hindus and Sikhs going in the other direction. About 14 million people were involved in this exchange of population; six million left Pakistan, while eight million arrived in the new country. The considerable bloodshed that occurred during this exchange affected the relations between India and Pakistan. In the fall of 1947, the government of India blocked payments to Pakistan from the joint sterling account that was set up by the departing British for the two countries. In 1948 India–Pakistan relations were complicated by the question of the accession of a number of princely states to the two countries. India encouraged Kashmir (q.v.)—a predominantly Muslim state ruled by a Hindu prince, the Maharaja of Kashmir—to join the Indian union. Pakistan worked with the ruling elite of Hyderabad (q.v.)—a predominantly Hindu state ruled by a Muslim prince, the Nizam of Hyderabad—to become an independent country. Kashmir shared boundaries with India and Pakistan; Hyderabad was a land-locked state in the south of India, more than a thousand miles from Pakistan. Geography of the two states ultimately dictated their political destinies.

The dispute over Hyderabad was resolved by a quick Indian military action undertaken in September 1948 while Pakistan was preoccupied with the situation created by the death of Muhammad Ali Jinnah. But Kashmir turned out to be a more difficult problem. India and Pakistan fought three wars over it; one in 1947, that led to the state's division between Azad Kashmir (q.v.) occupied by Pakistan and the state of Jammu and Kashmir, which became a part of India. The cease-fire line supervised by the United Nations became the boundary between the two parts of the state. Pakistan's attempt to gain the rest of the state in 1965 resulted in an all-out war between the two countries that was fought between September 6 and 23. The result was inconclusive and led to the signing of a peace accord—the Tashkent Declaration (q.v.) with the encouragement of the Soviet Union. India and Pakistan fought their third war in 1971 but this time, although Kashmir once again became one of the battle grounds, the immediate cause was the civil war in East Pakistan.

The Tashkent Declaration did not improve Pakistan's relations with India; there was a marked deterioration in 1971 when India, first covertly but then openly, sided with the secessionist forces operating in East Pakistan. When civil war broke out in East Pakistan, India supported the Mukti Bahini (q.v.) (the Bengali freedom fighters) and then sent in its troops to defeat Pakistan's forces in Bengal. In December 1971, the Pakistani contingent surrendered to the Indians and East Pakistan emerged as the independent state of Bangladesh (q.v.).

Zulfikar Ali Bhutto (q.v.), who succeeded Yahya Khan (q.v.) as Pakistan's president after the war in Bangladesh, went to the Indian city of Simla in April 1972 to conclude yet another treaty of understanding. The Simla Accord's (q.v.) immediate consequence was the redefinition of the cease-fire line in Kashmir. It also resulted in sufficiently improved relations between the two countries for India to release 90,000 prisoners of war it had taken after the surrender of the Pakistani army in East Bengal. But basic suspicions persisted, and were aggravated once again by the Indian explosion of a "nuclear device" in 1974. The explosion by India persuaded Bhutto to initiate Pakistan's own nuclear program. The program began in the mid-1970s and by the late 1980s had made enough progress to worry India as well as the United States.

In the early 1990s the citizens of the Indian-occupied Kashmir openly rebelled against India. India responded by sending 500,000 troops to the state and a bloody conflict ensued. India accused Pakistan of training the dissident forces in Kashmir and providing them with sanctuaries on its side of the border. The conflict in Kashmir took a heavy toll in terms of both lives lost and damage to the economy of the state. For six years, Indian Kashmir remained under the direct control of Delhi. In 1996 the Congress Party government led by Prime Minister Narasimha Rao decided to hold elections in the state. The Kashmiris refused to participate in the elections. Pakistan also opposed the Indian move, arguing that India was likely to use the elections to legitimize its hold over the state.

The Indian elections of February 1998 further complicated the relations between the two countries by introducing a new element, the Bharatiya Janata Party (BJP) (q.v.). The elections resulted in the formation of a government led by the BJP, the party that won the largest number of seats in the Lok Sabha, the lower house of the Indian parliament. The BJP had taken a very militant position against Pakistan in its election manifesto; it had argued for the open development of an Indian nuclear capability and its use against Pakistan if Pakistan continued to aid the Kashmiris in their struggle against India. The induction of the BJP government in Delhi caused a great deal of anxiety in Islamabad, which increased immeasurably on May 11, 1998, when India announced the successful test of three nuclear devices in the Rajasthan desert, close to the border with Pakistan. The fact that a few years earlier, India had successfully test fired long-range surface-to-surface missiles called Agni meant that it had now the capacity to hit Pakistan with nuclear weapons.

INDO-PAKISTAN NUCLEAR ARMS RACE. India carried out an underground nuclear test in 1974. This alerted Pakistan to the danger of being exposed to a country with which it had already fought three wars and that now seemed poised to arm itself with nuclear weapons. Pakistan's response came from Prime Minister Zulfikar Ali Bhutto (q.v.), who launched his country on an effort to close the nuclear gap. Much of Pakistan's endeavors were highly secret, led by Abdul Qadeer Khan (q.v.), a metallurgist trained in Germany and The Netherlands. Pakistan concentrated on developing the capacity to produce nuclear-weapon-grade material. India, protesting all the time that the 1974 explosion was not aimed at developing weapons but was intended to give the country the technology it needed to produce nuclear energy, went about achieving nuclear self-sufficiency. By the late 1990s India had built 10 commercial nuclear power stations, with 7 others under construction and 10 more in the planning stages. India also had four research reactors and was building a nuclear-powered submarine. The country also had an advanced missile development program.

Although the Congress Party-led governments—and also the government led by the United Front that held office in 1996–98—had kept the nuclear weapons program under wraps, the Bharatiya Janata Party (BJP) (q.v.), which came to power on March 17, 1998, indicated its intention of developing the capability to produce and deliver nuclear weapons. The Pakistani response to the voicing of this intention came immediately: It announced that it too would develop weapons if India took that route. The nuclear arms race between the two countries heated up when, on May 11, 1998, India exploded three nuclear bombs at a testing site in Rajasthan close to the Pakistan border. The tests took the world by surprise and were condemned by most Western countries as well as China and Russia. The United States imposed economic sanctions on India, but India was not deterred. It carried out two more tests on May 13. The world's attention then shifted to Pakistan and there was hope that it could be prevented from testing its nuclear devices by the promise of generous economic assistance. The leaders of Pakistan, however, were not satisfied with the quality of the Western response to the Indian tests. There was also a great deal of domestic pressure on Prime Minister Nawaz Sharif (q.v.) to follow India and claim the status of a nuclear power for Pakistan. Accordingly, Pakistan carried out six tests of its own on May 28 and May 30 in the Balochistan desert. The United States and Japan responded by imposing sanctions similar to those imposed on India.

A joint Western response to these development came on June 12, 1998, when the foreign ministers representing the G8 countries (Canada, France, Germany, Great Britain, Italy, Japan, Russia, and the United States) decided to oppose loans to both India and Pakistan by the International Monetary Fund, the World Bank, and the Asian Development Bank (qq.v.). *See also* India–Pakistan Relations; Missiles.

INDO–PAKISTAN WAR OF 1948–49. India and Pakistan were only a bit more than one year old as independent states when they confronted one an other on the battlefield over Kashmir (q.v.). The trouble began with Pakistan's unhappiness over the decision by the maharaja of Kashmir to join India. Pakistan's response took the form of encouragement given to thousands of Pathan tribesmen to invade Kashmir. The involvement of the Pakistan army was limited to advice and logistical support to the invading forces. The tribesmen were about to enter Srinagar, the capital of Kashmir, when India moved in troops in large numbers to aid the weak forces at the command of the maharaja. This confrontation between the two new countries could have flared up into a major conflagration had the United Nations not intervened. India and Pakistan decided to abide by the resolution passed by the U.N. Security Council asking the two countries to settle the issue of accession of the state by holding a plebiscite. *See also* India–Pakistan Relations.

INDO–PAKISTAN WAR OF 1965. The 1965 war between India and Pakistan was fought for 17 days, between September 6 and September 23. This was the second time India and Pakistan confronted each other on the battlefield over the issue of Kashmir (q.v.). The war began when India opened a number of fronts on its border with West Pakistan, including a major artillery and armor attack on Lahore (q.v.). The Indian action came as a response to the infiltration of mujahideen (freedom fighters) into Kashmir from Pakistan. India accused Pakistan of instigating the rebellion in Kashmir; initially Pakistan denied these charges but later accepted responsibility for supporting the mujahideen. Pakistan lost some ground to the Indian forces around Lahore while capturing some land on the border with Kashmir. There was no conflict on the border between East Pakistan and India. That notwithstanding, the Bengalis realized that Pakistan did not have enough resources to protect them against a possible Indian attack. This apprehension formed the basis of one of Mujibur Rahman's. Six Point Program (qq.v.), demanding the creation of a separate militia for East Pakistan. This particular conflict was settled when, under the auspices of the Soviet Union, India and Pakistan signed an agreement after a meeting held at Tashkent. *See also* India–Pakistan Relations; Tashkent Declaration.

INDO–PAKISTAN WAR OF 1971. Pakistan and India fought their third war in 22 years in December 1971. Unlike the two previous wars, the issue was not Kashmir (q.v.) but the political future of East Pakistan, Pakistan's eastern wing. By the time India decided to intervene directly, the civil war in East Pakistan between Mukti Bahini (q.v.)—the freedom fighters of Bengal—and the Pakistan army had gone on for seven months. During this period, India had provided covert support to the freedom fighters.

In late November, however, Prime Minister Indira Gandhi of India decided to intervene directly in the conflict by moving Indian troops into East Pakistan. The Indians advanced quickly and Dacca fell on December 16, 1971. In early December, Pakistan had responded by opening a number of fronts in the west but even here it was overwhelmed by Indian strength. Unlike the 1965 war, India was able to capture large chunks of

166 • Indus River

territory in West Pakistan. India might have pressed its advantage but for the United States's tilt toward Pakistan. India received the message and agreed to cease hostilities in West Pakistan after East Pakistan had declared independence as the new republic of Bangladesh.

Final settlement of the conflict was achieved at the Indian city of Simla, following a meeting between Prime Minister Zulfikar Ali Bhutto (q.v.) of Pakistan and Indira Gandhi. The Simla Accord (q.v.) was arrived at without a major power looking over the shoulders of the two countries as had happened at Tashkent (q.v.). Bhutto won the release of over 90,000 prisoners of war captured by India in East Pakistan and the withdrawal of Indian troops from the territory they had occupied in West Pakistan. *See also* India–Pakistan Relations; Simla Accord.

INDUS RIVER. The Indus River is Pakistan's longest river. It originates in the Kalias mountain range in Tibet and flows through Kashmir (q.v.) before flowing into Pakistan. It enters the great Punjab (q.v.) plane north of Tarbela dam (q.v.). Before entering Punjab, the Indus is joined by the Kabul River. In Punjab, it picks up five more tributaries, the Jhelum, the Chenab, the Ravi, the Sutlej, and the Beas. The Indus flows into the Arabian Sea through a delta south of Karachi (q.v.). The river is 3,060 kilometers long.

The Indus and its tributary rivers supply a great deal of water for land irrigation in Pakistan's three provinces, the Northwest Frontier, Punjab, and Sindh (qq.v.). For the last 100 years an extensive network of dams, barrages, and weirs was built on the river and its tributaries to water the plains of Pakistan. Without these irrigation works, today much of Pakistan would be desert. With these irrigation works obstructing the flow of water, the Indus is not used for navigation. If boats ply on the river, they are generally small and do not cover great distances. In fact, the Indus is the only one of the world's great rivers that is not used for transport.

INDUS WATERS TREATY. The Indus Waters Treaty was signed in Karachi (q.v.) on September 19, 1960 by President Muhammad Ayub Khan (q.v.) of Pakistan, Prime Minister Jawaharlal Nehru of India, and W. A. B. Iliff, vice-president of the World Bank (q.v.). It agreed to apportion the waters of the Indus river system on the basis of a formula that gave both countries access to the system. The treaty gave the use of the three eastern rivers—Ravi, Beas, and Sutlej—exclusively to India, whereas the waters of the three western rivers—Indus, Jhelum, and Chenab—were available exclusively for use by Pakistan, except for limited exploitation by India in the upstream areas in the Indian Kashmir (q.v.), and the Indian states of Punjab (q.v.) and Himachel Pradesh. The actual division of water was to be accomplished over a period of 10 years during which a system of "replacement works" was to be constructed. At Pakistan's request, the period of transition could be extended to 13 years.

The Indus replacement works were to cost $1,070 million in 1960 prices of which $870 million, or 81.3 percent, were to be spent in Pakistan. These works included two storage dams, one at Mangla (q.v.) on the Jhelum River with a capacity of 4.75 million acre feet (MAF) and the other on the Indus River (q.v.), with a capacity of 4.2 MAF. Tarbela (q.v.) was later selected as the site for the dam on the Indus. The works also included five barrages and eight "link canals," nearly 650 kilometers long, to be built to transfer water from the western to the eastern rivers. Although India argued that the expenditure under the treaty should be only for "replacement" works, the final agreement incorporated some developmental schemes as well. For instance, it was agreed that a power station would be built at Mangla with a total generating capacity of 800 megawatts (MW) of electricity.

The World Bank established an Indus Basin Development Fund to finance the works to be built in Pakistan. The work on the replacement system began in the early 1960s and was completed, 14 years later, with the commissioning of the Tarbela dam in 1974. The treaty made it possible for Pakistan to use 80 percent of the waters in the Indus river system, it extended the country's irrigation network thus preparing the ground for Pakistan's first "green revolution" (q.v.) in the late 1960s, and provided 3,000 MW of electric power at a time when the demand for energy was increasing very rapidly. The treaty did not fully resolve all disputes between the two countries. One particular problem occurred in the late 1980s when India decided to build a barrage at Wullar (q.v.) in the part of Kashmir (q.v.) it occupied. *See also* Indus River.

INDUSTRY. At the time of independence, Pakistan did not have an industrial sector of any significance. Two cement plants, one each in the provinces of Punjab and Sindh (qq.v.), and a few vegetable-oil factories made up the entire industrial sector, contributing no more than six percent to the gross domestic product (GDP). Agriculture (q.v.) was the predominant economic activity, producing not only enough food to feed the population, but leaving a significant amount for export to India. Agriculture also produced such cash crops as cotton (q.v.), sugar cane, and tobacco, which also were exported to India to be processed in the mills of Calcutta, Bombay, and Ahmadabad. The trade war between India and Pakistan fought in 1949 changed this relationship, however. From then on, with imports of consumer goods no longer coming from India, Pakistan was forced to industrialize, which it did with the help of the merchants who had made large profits exporting commodities during the boom years of the Korean War (1951–54).

Pakistan industrialized quickly during this period, with industrial output increasing at a rate of over 11 percent a year during the 1950s. By the time the military government of President Ayub Khan (q.v.) took office (1958), the country's need for basic manufactured goods was being met from domestic output. Ayub Khan's government changed the orientation of industrialization by giving much greater attention to the establishment of producer-goods industries. Because this type of industrialization needs a much larger amount of capital investment, the rate of increase in industrial output slowed down somewhat during the 1960s, although at more than 8 percent per year it was still well above the average for the developing world. By the end of the Ayub Khan period, industry contributed 18 percent to the GDP.

By nationalizing 31 large-scale industries (steel, cement, fertilizer, automotive, chemical, etc.) in January 1972, the Pakistan People's Party government of Zulfikar Ali Bhutto (1971–77) (qq.v.) introduced a profound change in the structure of the industrial sector. Public ownership of a significant proportion of output became the most prominent feature of the new structure. Because commercial banks and insurance companies were also nationalized two years later, a symbiotic relationship was established between finance and industry and was probably the cause for a considerable amount of wasteful expenditure in the sector. The rate of increase in the output of the industrial sector declined in this period to less than 2.5 percent a year.

The third military government under the leadership of President Zia ul-Haq (q.v.) (1977–88) went back to the model followed successfully during the 1960s: the private sector was encouraged once again to participate in the creation of new industrial capital while a serious attempt was made to improve the efficiency of public enterprises. But there was one difference in the approach toward industrialization during the Zia ul-Haq period compared to the approach taken by Ayub Khan. There was now greater reliance on market signals as against direct bureaucratic controls in the 1960s. For instance, by delinking the value of the rupee from that of the American dollar, the Zia government introduced an element of flexibility in the management of the exchange rate. This policy option had not been tried in the 1960s. Zia, however, did not privatize the industries taken over by Bhutto; he allowed them to remain with the public sector.

The growth rate in the output of the industrial sector picked up once again. From 1977 to 1988 industrial output increased at a rate of over 8 percent per year. In 1988 the share of industry in the country's GDP was over 25 percent. Benazir Bhutto's (q.v.) government, which took office in

December 1988, launched a program for the privatization of the industries and other assets that were still held by the public sector. This policy was continued with even greater vigor by Nawaz Sharif (q.v.) when he became prime minister in November 1990. A number of industries—in particular those producing cement—were privatized as were two commercial banks. Some of this momentum was lost when Benazir Bhutto returned to Islamabad as prime minister in October 1993, although her government actively implemented the policy of encouraging the private sector to invest in energy plants. Bhutto was dismissed in November 1996 and Sharif returned as prime minister in 1997. The political turmoil following Zia's death no doubt contributed to the slowdown of the growth in the output of the industrial sector. During the period 1988–97, industrial production increased by only 3.7 percent a year, less than half the rate of increase in the first four decades following independence.

INTERNATIONAL MONETARY FUND (IMF). The IMF was established in 1944 after a number of governments, meeting at a conference held at Bretton Woods, New Hampshire, decided to create two institutions to help the world recover from the devastation caused by World War II. The IMF was given the responsibility of stabilizing the economies of member countries in the case of shocks delivered by events over which they had little control. The types of shocks envisaged by the Bretton Woods conferees included changes in terms of trade and the need to make large payments to external creditors that required temporary relief. By providing this form of assistance, the IMF could help the member countries defend their exchange rates. The exchange rates were fixed to the U.S. dollar; the dollar, in turn, was fixed to the gold standard. This system of exchange rates collapsed in 1971, when the administration of President Richard Nixon decided to delink the dollar from gold.

The IMF acquired a new mandate in the early 1980s when a number of developing countries—many of them in Latin America—were not able to meet their external debt obligations. The IMF-funded "work-out arrangements" were to save dozens of economies from collapse. It has continued to perform that function. On a number of occasions the IMF came to the rescue of Pakistan by providing the country with assistance to meet external obligations. The latest IMF–Pakistan agreement was reached in October 1998.

INTERNATIONAL MONETARY FUND'S (IMF) EXTENDED STRUCTURAL ADJUSTMENT FACILITY (ESAF). The programs of structural adjustment supported by the IMF usually entail economic opening on the part of the countries agreeing to the conditions imposed by the institution. Economic opening implies cuts in the rates of tariff on imports, fewer obstacles for foreign direct investment, and greater freedom to the domestic banking sector to manage their resources without government intervention. These programs may initially result in increasing the balance of payments deficit on account of higher levels of imports permitted by them. The assumption is that over time, countries implementing these programs would become more competitive in the world markets and, with an increase in the level of their exports, would be able to narrow the gap between export earnings and the expenditure on imports. The IMF's Extended Structural Adjustment Facility was designed to help poor countries meet the additional burden imposed on them as a result of these programs. The resources from the facility have easy terms. The fund charges only 0.5 per percent interest a year. The amount lent is disbursed over a three-year period and is to be paid back over a period extending from 5.5 to 10 years.

The caretaker administration of 1996–97 developed a major program of structural reform. The program was announced by President Farooq Leghari (q.v.) in a televised address on December 25, 1996. It became the core of the program introduced later by the government of Prime Minister Nawaz Sharif (q.v.). In October 1997 the IMF pledged its support for the program by allowing Pakistan to access $1.8 billion from the ESAF facility. The first tranche of $250 million was released in November.

INTERNATIONAL MONETARY FUND'S (IMF) STANDBY PRO-GRAMS. The purpose behind the IMF's standby programs is to provide countries in economic distress access to resources on relatively easy terms. The funds are disbursed over an 18-month period and the recipients have to pay interest rates of about 4.5 percent a year. The amount of money received is to be returned over a period extending from 3.24 to 5 years. Disbursements are made following "reviews" by the Fund in which the institution's staff and its board of directors determine whether the country receiving help is successfully implementing the agreed program.

Pakistan has a long history of first negotiating standby arrangements with the Fund and then midway through the period of implementation seeing them canceled. The last two arrangements met the same fate. In October 1996 the government of Prime Minister Benazir Bhutto (q.v.) negotiated a standby arrangement in which she committed herself to reducing the fiscal deficit from 6.2 percent, estimated in fiscal year 1995–96 to be 4 percent of the gross domestic product, by June 30, 1997. This target was to be achieved by the government's adoption of a series of fiscal measures that included widening the tax base, extending the coverage of the general sales tax (q.v.), and reductions in public-sector expenditure. Following the fall of the Bhutto government in November

1996, the caretaker administration sent Shahid Javed Burki, its economic advisor, to Washington to renegotiate the arrangement. This was done in December. It was after a great deal of effort that the caretaker administration was able to meet the Fund's targets for the period ending December 31, 1996. These efforts by the caretakers resulted in the release of some $160 million by the fund at a time when the country's balance-of-payments situation was under a great deal of strain. In March 1997, however, the government of Prime Minister Nawaz Sharif (q.v.), following a review of the economic situation, determined that it would be politically difficult for it to meet the Fund's targets for the rest of the period. Accordingly, it withdrew from the arrangement opting, instead, for receiving assistance from the IMF under its Extended Structural Adjustment Facility (q.v.). *See also* International Monetary Fund's Extended Structural Adjustment Facility.

INTERSERVICES INTELLIGENCE (ISI). The Interservices Intelligence was originally established in the 1980s to counter the Research and Analysis Wing (RAW) of the government of India, which had managed to develop a strong presence in Pakistan. Unlike the RAW, which operated under the control of civilian authorities, the ISI was an organization managed by the Pakistani army. Over time, the attention of the ISI shifted from India to Afghanistan (q.v.) and other countries to the north of Pakistan. The ISI gained strength and prestige during the 10-year war in Afghanistan during which arms and equipment were channeled through it by the United States and Saudi Arabia to the mujahideen (q.v.) (freedom fighters) fighting the Soviet Union. The ISI also helped to organize training camps for the mujahideen. Most of them were located in the Pakistani provinces of Balochistan and the Northwest Frontier (qq.v.).

During this period the ISI was headed by General Akhtar Abdur Rahman (q.v.), a close associate of President Zia ul-Haq (q.v.). Rahman was succeeded by Lieutenant General Hameed Gul (q.v.), who was convinced that Pakistan could gain considerable influence in Central Asia following the collapse of the Soviet Union. Gul succeeded in reorienting the mission of the organization by convincing some of its senior operators that they could spearhead the Islamization of the areas in Central Asia vacated by the Soviet Union. There were reports that under Gul the ISI involved itself in supporting the insurrection in Indian-occupied Kashmir (q.v.). In 1989 Prime Minister Benazir Bhutto (q.v.) replaced Gul with General Shamsur Rahman Kallu, who was summoned back from retirement and was given the mission of cleansing the ISI of fundamentalist Muslim influence. Following the dismissal of Bhutto and the election of Nawaz Sharif as prime minister, however, the ISI was handed over to General Javed Nasir, an officer who was a strong believer in the mission initially launched by Gul.

During the war in Afghanistan the ISI was able to develop an identity of its own, independent of the army. The attempts by Generals Asif Nawaz, Waheed Kakar, and Jehangir Karamat (qq.v.), successive commanders of the army, to establish the control of the army establishment over the organization were only partly successful. For instance, the ISI continued to lend support to the Taliban (q.v.) in Afghanistan even when the government of Pakistan wished to distance itself from them.

IQBAL, SIR MUHAMMAD (1877–1938). Muhammad Iqbal was born in Sialkot, a city near the Punjab–Kashmir (qq.v.) border. He was educated at Lahore (q.v.), Cambridge, and Munich. He started his professional career as a teacher at Government College, Lahore. He went back to Europe after a brief stay in Lahore and in 1908 was appointed professor of Arabic at London University. He gained considerable reputation as a poet after publishing a long poem, *Asrari-i-Khudi,* in Persian in 1915. In spite of the success of this poem, he was to write most of his poetry in Urdu. He and Faiz Ahmad Faiz (q.v.) are generally regarded as the most prominent Urdu poets of the twentieth century. Iqbal also gained a reputation as a philosopher. His theme was the role of religion in the life of man. His philosophical essays were published in a collection entitled *Reconstruction of Religious Thought in Islam.* His poems and writings had a profound influence on Muslim India.

Iqbal was also to play an important role in the Muslim politics of British India. In 1930 he was invited to chair the annual session of the All-India Muslim League (q.v.). The session was held at Allahabad, and in his inaugural address he proposed the establishment of an autonomous Muslim state in northwest British India. He was one of the several prominent Muslim leaders who persuaded Muhammad Ali Jinnah (q.v.) to return to India from a self-imposed exile in London. Jinnah came back in 1931 and, in an exchange of letters with Iqbal that lasted for several years, the two discussed the future of the Muslim community in South Asia. Iqbal died in Lahore and was buried in the compound of Lahore's Badshah-i-Mosque. Pakistan observes April 21, the day of his death, as Iqbal Day.

IRAN–PAKISTAN RELATIONS. Iran is one of the few countries with whom Pakistan maintained warm relations throughout history. Reza Shah Pahlavi, the emperor of Iran, was the first head of state to visit Pakistan. The visit took place in 1950 and the Iranian monarch was received with great affection. Both Iran and Pakistan joined the defense agreements sponsored by the United States in the 1950s. The two countries also organized a regional arrangement called the Regional Cooperation for Development (RCD), which also included Turkey. The RCD, with head-quarters in Tehran, the capital of Iran, was meant to achieve closer economic cooperation among the non-Arab Muslim states of West Asia. The RCD was launched with much enthusiasm by President Ayub Khan (q.v.) in 1962 and survived for nearly two decades, but did not achieve anything of great significance. In 1965, when Pakistan went to war with India, Iran offered both political and material support.

Relations between the two countries cooled a bit after the Islamic revolution in Iran in 1976. The religious leadership in Iran sought to project Shia Islam, its brand of Islam, in the countries in which Shias constituted sizable minorities. Pakistan and Saudi Arabia were two such countries. Although Iran's relations with Saudi Arabia deteriorated to the point where the two countries broke all diplomatic contacts, Pakistan managed to retain reasonable contacts with Tehran. However, the success of the Taliban (q.v.) in Afghanistan and their effort to impose a very strict Sunni Islam in their country and Iran's strong belief that Pakistan was encouraging these moves created some tension between the two countries in the late 1990s. There was also an impression in Pakistan that Iran was providing assistance to the Shias in sectarian violence that claimed hundreds of lives in Pakistan during 1995–98. *See also* Indo–Pakistan War of 1965.

IRAQ–PAKISTAN RELATIONS. Pakistan's relations with Iraq go back to the early 1950s when Pakistan joined the Baghdad Pact, a U.S.-sponsored defense arrangement among the countries in the Middle East and West Asia. These countries had expressed a strong commitment to contain the spread of communism to their areas. The assassination of the King of Iraq in 1958 took Iraq out of the pact, which was renamed the Central Treaty Organization. In the quarter century after the revolution in Iraq, trade was the only contact between the two countries. Iraq continued to be an important market for basmati rice from Pakistan. In 1991, however, General Aslam Beg (q.v.), the chief of the Army Staff at that time, signaled a definite Pakistani tilt toward Iraq during the buildup of the Gulf War. Beg predicted heavy losses by the Allied forces led by the United States in case they chose to move against Iraq. He also implied that the action against Iraq was somehow a part of the West's desire to dominate the Islamic world. These reactions on the part of the head of the armed forces soured Pakistan's relations with the United States and Saudi Arabia. They also raised some serious issues about Beg's judgment on military strategy.

Beg's successors, Generals Asif Nawaz, Abdul Waheed Kakar, and Jehangir Karamat (qq.v.), sought to rebuild relations with Saudi Arabia and the United States. They met with limited success. In 1998, with some easing of the economic sanctions imposed by the United Nations on Iraq, Pakistan was able to resume commercial ties with that country. It entered an agreement to export 400,000 tons of basmati rice to Iraq.

ISKANDER MIRZA, GENERAL (1899–1969). Iskander Mirza belonged to the family of the nawabs of Murshidabad. He was the first Indian to graduate from the Royal Military Academy, Sandhurst although he did not serve for very long in the British Indian Army. He joined the Indian Political Service in 1931 and opted to serve in Pakistan after the partition of British India. He was appointed defense secretary in 1947 and held that position for seven years. It was in that capacity that he developed close relations with the senior officers of the Pakistani army, including General Ayub Khan (q.v.). Following the dismissal of the provincial government headed by A. K. Fazlul Haq in 1954, he was appointed governor of the province of East Pakistan. He returned to Karachi (q.v.) a year later and was appointed minister of defense. In 1955 he took over as governor-general from the ailing Ghulam Muhammad (q.v.). A few months later, after the promulgation of Pakistan's first constitution, the constitution of 1956 (q.v.), he was appointed president. He remained president until October 27, 1958, when General Ayub Khan, having proclaimed martial law, sent him into exile in London.

ISLAMABAD. Soon after placing Pakistan under martial law, General Ayub Khan (q.v.) decided to move the country's capital from Karachi (q.v.) to a place inland. Karachi did not suit the military regime. It was a 1,600 kilometers from Rawalpindi (q.v.), the general headquarters of the army. It was dominated by the business and industrial communities with which Ayub Khan at that point had little affinity. Culturally, linguistically, and ethnically Karachi had little in common with Pakistan military's homeland—the districts in Punjab's (q.v.) north and in the Northwest Frontier Province (NWFP) (q.v.). The decision to move the capital from Karachi, therefore, was a political one. The objective was to move the country's political center of gravity to a point located within indigenous Pakistan.

Having made the decision to move the capital, Ayub Khan appointed a commission under the chairmanship of General Yahya Khan (q.v.) to suggest a new site. The commission worked diligently, examined many sites, investigated the possibility of retaining Karachi as the seat of government, but finally came up with the not unsurprising conclusion that the area just north of Rawalpindi would be the most appropriate place. From the several names suggested (including Jinnahabad), Ayub Khan chose to call the new capital Islamabad—the city of Islam.

The constitution of 1962 (q.v.) confirmed Islamabad as the executive seat of the central government but located the legislative branch near Dacca, the capital of East Pakistan. A site named Ayubnagar was to be developed in the vicinity of Dacca as the seat of the legislative branch of the government, thus carrying to an absurd extent the concept of separation of powers. Construction on the new city of Islamabad began in 1961 and the city's first residents began to be accommodated in 1963. The Indo–Pakistan War of 1965 (q.v.) and the resultant constraint on resources slowed the city's development. The presidency and several other important departments were temporarily housed in Rawalpindi.

With Bangladesh (q.v.) becoming an independent country, Islamabad's ambiguous status as the national capital was finally resolved. There was no longer any need to physically separate the executive and legislative branches of the government. When Zulfikar Ali Bhutto (q.v.) summoned the national legislature in the spring of 1972, it met in Islamabad in a building constructed for the State Bank of Pakistan. It was from this building that the National Assembly, in 1973, produced Pakistan's third constitution of 1973 (q.v.). A new set of buildings to house the National Assembly was commissioned by the Bhutto government in 1974. Completed in 1986, it now houses the Senate and the National Assembly.

In the late 1970s a construction boom began in Islamabad and continues to this day. Karachi's ethnic problems and the breakdown in law and order in that city in the winter of 1986 induced hundreds of business and professional firms from Karachi to relocate in Islamabad. In 1998 Islamabad's population was estimated at 600,000 and was increasing at the rate of 6 to 7 percent per year.

ISLAMABAD NEW CITY. In August 1995 the government of Prime Minister Benazir Bhutto (q.v.) announced an ambitious plan to build a new city 12 kilometers south of Islamabad. The city was to be Pakistan's "Silicon Valley." Invitations were sent out to interested investors in Asia and Europe to buy land in the city and take "advantage of the rapidly growing demand in Pakistan for computer soft- and hardware." There was some expression of interest on the part of a few investors from Southeast Asia. Following the dismissal of Prime Minister Bhutto in November 1996, the caretaker administration that took office investigated the project and concluded that it was basically a scheme to milk money from a number of Pakistani banks and development institutions. The project was canceled by the caretakers in December 1996.

ISLAMI JAMHURI ITEHAD (IJI). The Islami Jamhuri Itehad (Islamic Democratic Alliance) was organized in September 1988 to challenge the

Pakistan People's Party (PPP) (q.v.) in the elections of November 1988. The alliance was made up of nine parties, including the two factions of the Muslim League (q.v.) into which the party President Zia ul-Haq (q.v.) had patronized split after his death. The IJI also included the powerful Jamaat-e-Islami as well as the Tehrik-e-lstiqlal (qq.v.). The alliance won only 53 seats in the National Assembly, against 92 secured by the PPP. Most of its seats were won in Punjab (q.v.). Most important IJI leaders lost the election; the only exception was Mian Nawaz Sharif (q.v.), Zia ul-Haq's protégé from Punjab. Nawaz Sharif resigned from his National Assembly seat and went to Lahore (q.v.), where he was able to form an IJI provincial government.

The IJI won the majority of National Assembly seats in the 1990 elections, which were held following the dismissal of the PPP administration by President Ghulam Ishaq Khan. It was invited to form the government with Nawaz Sharif as prime minister. The IJI government was dismissed by President Khan in April 1993 on charges of corruption and incompetence. The Supreme Court overturned the president's action, declaring it unconstitutional, and restored the government of Nawaz Sharif. The Supreme Court's action did not end the conflict between the president and the prime minister, however. Working behind the scenes, General Abdul Waheed Kakar, the army chief of staff, forced the president and the prime minister to resign. Another round of elections was held in October 1993 (q.v.) in which the Muslim League decided to participate independently rather than as a member of a coalition. This decision led to the demise of the IJI.

ISMAILIS. The Ismaili sect of Islam owes its origin to a series of disputes between the sons of a Shia *imam* (leader) in the eighteenth century. Ismail was one of the two sons. With their claims unsettled, the followers of Ismail became the Ismailis; the followers of his brother remained in the mainstream of Shiism. The Ismailis, fearing persecution, went into hiding for more than a century but emerged to establish sovereignty over Egypt and North Africa. The Ismaili missionaries traveled far and wide and established communities of their followers in a number of areas, including the northern parts of Pakistan, southern Russia, and western China. In the mid-1800s, the head of the Ismail community was forced to leave Iran. He took his followers to Sindh (q.v.), now a province of Pakistan, and proclaimed himself the Agha (father) Khan. His grandson, Sultan Agha Khan, played an active role in the Muslim politics of British India, was associated with the decision to form the All-India Muslim League (q.v.), and became a close associate of Muhammad Ali Jinnah (q.v.). After the death of Sultan Agha Khan, his grandson, Karim Agha

Khan was nominated to succeed him as the Agha Khan. Sultan Khan established a number of charitable organizations that work not only among the Ismaili communities but among other groups of poor Muslims as well. These organizations expanded a great deal under the leadership of Karim Agha Khan.

The Ismailis are estimated to number about 15 million, with their largest communities in Pakistan and India. There are also pockets of Ismailis in China, the Soviet Union, Afghanistan, Syria, and East Africa. In Pakistan, the largest communities of Ismailis are in Gilgit and Hunza. The Agha Khan Foundation and the Agha Khan Fund for Economic Development, both based in Geneva, established the Agha Khan Medical University in Karachi (q.v.) and are financing an imaginative program of rural development in Gilgit and Hunza.

↩ J ↪

JALIB, HABIB (c.1952–1994). Habib Jalib was a poet in the tradition of Faiz Ahmad Faiz (q.v.). Like Faiz, he used the idiom of poetry to communicate political messages to his diverse audience. Jalib's poetry called for an end to exploitation, feudalism, obscurantism, and imperialism. He gained prominence during the 1960s when Field Marshal Ayub Khan (q.v.), Pakistan's first military ruler, held power and succeeded in silencing all voices of dissent. Jalib's was one of the few voices that continued to challenge military authority by calling the poor and the underprivileged to fight for their economic, social, and political rights. Jalib was imprisoned several times for expressing views that ran counter to those of the government of the day. He continued to be out of favor even with the government of Zulfikar Ali Bhutto (q.v.), which succeeded the military regimes of Ayub Khan and Yahya Khan (q.v.). Jalib's view of the quality of governance provided by Bhutto and his Pakistan People's Party (q.v.) was no less critical.

JAM GHULAM QADIR KHAN OF LASBELA (c.1915–1994). Jam Ghulam Qadir Khan belonged to what was once the "princely state" (q.v.) of Lasbela in Balochistan (q.v.). His state became a part of the province of Balochistan. The Jam—as he was usually called—gained political prominence during the administration of Zulfikar Ali Bhutto (q.v.). In 1973 Bhutto had alienated all the major tribal *sardars* of Balochistan by dismissing the provincial government that had been formed by the National Awami Party (NAP) and the Jamiatul-Ulemai-Islam (JUI) (qq.v.). Bhutto accused the NAP–JUI coalition of antistate activities. The result of this action was open revolt against the central authorities and Bhutto had to call in the army to bring peace to Balochistan. Peace did not return for as long as Bhutto was in power, however. In these difficult circumstances, Bhutto needed the support of a reasonably well-placed tribal sardar to help him in the province. He turned to the Jam and appointed him chief minister of the province. The Jam served in that position for almost three years. He left office on December 31, 1975, when Bhutto once again brought Balochistan under "president's rule."

Jam of Lasbela returned to politics in 1985 when President Zia ul-Haq (q.v.) lifted martial law and appointed Muhammad Khan Junejo (q.v.) prime minister of Pakistan. Junejo, in turn, appointed civilian governments in the four provinces. The government in Balochistan was headed by the Jam, who served as the chief minister of the province for the second time. He was dismissed by President Zia on May 29, 1988, along with Prime Minister Junejo and all other provincial chief ministers. Jam Qadir Khan died in Karachi (q.v.) in 1994.

JAMAAT-E-ISLAMI. The Jamaat-e-Islami (Islamic Organization) was founded by Maulana Abul Maududi (q.v.) in 1941 as an ideological movement to reinculcate Islamic values among all Muslims, in particular those who lived in British India. The Jamaat's appeal was initially limited to a small number of people, all of them dedicated followers of Maulana Maududi. Its opposition to the idea of Pakistan—the creation of a separate homeland for the Muslims of British India—inhibited the Jamaat from expanding its presence among the Muslim masses. In 1940, by getting the Muslim League to pass the Pakistan Resolution, Muhammad Ali Jinnah (qq.v.) had succeeded in galvanizing the Muslim masses.

The Jamaat changed its position once it became obvious that Jinnah had succeeded in persuading both the British and the Hindu-dominated Indian National Congress (q.v.) to agree to the establishment of Pakistan. In 1947, following the birth of Pakistan, Maulana Maududi moved the headquarters of his organization to a suburb in Lahore (q.v.). Lahore at that time was the largest city in Pakistan and Maududi knew that the base of his support was basically among the more literate urban communities. Once in Lahore, the Jamaat's main objective was redefined as the establishment of an Islamic state in Pakistan.

In order to cleanse Pakistan of "aberrant and deviant" behavior, the Jamaat launched a campaign against the Ahmadiya (q.v.) community in 1953 in most large cities of Punjab (q.v.). The campaign resulted in thousands of deaths as the party's followers fought pitched battles with law-enforcement authorities in Lahore and other cities of Punjab. The Jamaat did not succeed in its purpose immediately, as the government was not prepared to declare the Ahmadiyas as a non-Muslim minority. It had to wait for two decades before this objective was realized and Prime Minister Zulfikar Ali Bhutto (q.v.) accepted its demand in 1974. The Bhutto administration moved a bill through the National Assembly that classified the Ahmadiya community as "non-Muslims" and deprived it of the right to practice its religion.

The Jamaat took part in a number of opposition movements against the government of the day. It supported the Combined Opposition Party (COP) (q.v.) in the presidential election of 1965 (q.v.); it worked with the Pakistan National Alliance (PNA) (q.v.) that agitated against the government of Zulfikar Ali Bhutto following the elections of 1977 (q.v.); it participated, off and on, in the Movement for the Restoration of Democracy (MRD) (q.v.) that worked against the government of President Zia ul-Haq (q.v.). In spite of all of this, the Jamaat did not succeed in expanding its political base. In the National Assembly elections of 1970 it won only four seats in a house of 300, all of them from West Pakistan. Out of the 33 million total votes cast in the elections, the Jamaat polled less than two million, one million each in East and West Pakistan. However, the entire contingent of 70 candidates it fielded in East Pakistan lost, whereas only 4 of the 78 it nominated in West Pakistan won in the elections. In the "party-less" elections called by the martial-law government of Zia ul-Haq, Jamaat was able to significantly increase its representation in the National Assembly. Of the 237 members in the house, 12 were said to be associated with the Jamaat.

Maulana Maududi resigned as the Jamaat's *amir* (president) in 1972 and was succeeded by the considerably less charismatic Mian Tufail Muhammad. Under the new leadership, the Jamaat attempted to work with the government of President Zia ul-Haq. The Jamaat supported Zia's program of Islamization. The party entered into an electoral alliance with the Pakistan Muslim League (q.v.) in 1988 and 1990 and joined the Islami Jamhuri Itehad (IJI) (q.v.) administration led by Prime Minister Nawaz Sharif (q.v.), which took office in November 1990. In the elections of 1993 (q.v.), however, the Muslim League decided to dissolve the IJI and the Jamaat once again had to fight the elections on its own. It did not fare very well, winning only three seats in the National Assembly.

JAMIATUL-ULEMAI-ISLAM (JUI). The Jamiatul-Ulemai-Islam was formed in 1919 in the wake of the Khilafat Movement. The Khilafat Movement, in turn, was the result of Turkey's war with Great Britain and the apprehension on the part of a segment of the Muslim leadership in India that the collapse of the Ottoman empire was the result of a Western conspiracy to subjugate Islam. Accordingly, the leadership of the JUI was intensely suspicious of the British, and its principal aim was to rid the subcontinent of British rule. The JUI did not initially align itself with the Muslim League (q.v.), the mainstream Muslim organization in British India, or support the idea of Pakistan, which was being espoused by the League under its president, Muhammad Ali Jinnah (q.v.). In November 1945, however, a group of Jamiatul-Ulemai-Hind (JUH) ulema left the organization to form a splinter group, named the group the Jamiatul-Ulemai-Islam, and declared their support for the idea of Pakistan.

The JUI went through a number of organizational changes after its leaders migrated to Pakistan in August 1947, most of whom settled in Karachi (q.v.), Pakistan's first capital. In the 1960s the party developed a strong presence in Balochistan and the Northwest Frontier Province (NWFP) (qq.v.). The JUI's support base was in the intensely conservative countryside of these two provinces. Its leaders, in particular Maulana Mufti Mahmud (q.v.) in the Northwest Frontier Province, used the Friday sermon as an effective way of communicating political messages. This grassroots work by the ulema in Balochistan and the Frontier paid off handsomely in the elections of 1970, when the JUI captured seven seats in the National Assembly.

In December 1971 the military handed over power to President Zulfikar Ali Bhutto (q.v.), and Bhutto allowed the formation of political administrations in the country's four remaining provinces—Balochistan, the Northwest Frontier Province, Punjab, and Sindh (qq.v.). The JUI joined hands with the National Awami Party (NAP) (q.v.) to put coalition governments in place in both Balochistan and the Frontier Province. Maulana Mufti Mahmud became the chief minister of the NWFP. Bhutto, however, not at ease with the provincial governments that he could not control, dismissed the JUI–NAP administrations in Balochistan and the NWFP on the pretext that they were acting against the integrity of Pakistan. The dismissal of the JUI– and NAP-headed administrations was to have many profound consequences for the evolution of democracy in Pakistan. The removal of the two provincial Cabinets sent the signal to the parties not aligned with Bhutto's Pakistan People's Party (PPP) (q.v.) that the prime minister was not prepared to tolerate any opposition to his rule. The opposition reacted by coming together, in spite of ideological differences.

In 1977 the JUI joined the Pakistan National Alliance (PNA) (q.v.) and organized to oppose the PPP in the elections that were held in February of that year (elections of 1977 [q.v.]). The ability of the religious parties to muster popular support—particularly after the Friday sermon—galvanized the opposition, put Bhutto on the defensive, and created an opportunity for the army to intervene once again in politics. The JUI played an important role in the campaign against Bhutto and inadvertently set the stage for Pakistan's third martial-law administration. When Maulana Mufti Mahmud died and was succeeded by his son, Maulana Fazlur Rahman (q.v.), an even closer relationship was forged between the PPP and JUI. Maulana Rahman's move caused a split in the party and resulted in its regionalization. The JUI (Fazl Group [F]) remained a force only in the NWFP, while the Balochistan wing of the party went its separate way.

In the elections of 1990 (q.v.) the JUI (F) captured six seats in the National Assembly, four of them from the Northwest Frontier. In the Frontier Provincial Assembly, the party took 15 seats in a house of 80 members. This performance was repeated in the elections of 1993 (q.v.). After 1993 Maulana Fazlur Rahman became a vocal supporter of Benazir Bhutto and was rewarded by her with the chairmanship of the Foreign Affairs Committee in the National Assembly. The elections of 1997 (q.v.) saw a considerable reduction in the base of support for the JUI both in the provincial and national legislatures. The tide seemed to have turned against the party in favor of the moderate but still conservative Pakistan Muslim League (q.v.).

JAMSHORO. Jamshoro in Sindh (q.v.) province is the site of the third largest thermal power station in the system developed by the Water and Power Development Authority (WAPDA) (q.v.). Guddu and Kot Addu (q.v.) are the largest plants in the system. The Jamshoro power plant houses four oil-fired units, each capable of generating 220 megawatts of electric power, thus providing the plant with a total capacity of 880 megawatts. In 1994 the government of Prime Minister Benazir Bhutto initiated a phased program for the privatization of the WAPDA. This program included the power plant at Kot Addu as well as the one at Jamshoro. The plant was privatized in 1996—it was sold to a consortium of companies led by a British firm.

JANSHER KHAN (1969–). In 1987, then only 18 years old, Jansher Khan of Pakistan took the world squash crown from Jehangir Khan, his countryman. World squash was dominated by two families, both from the Northwest Frontier Province (q.v.). Jansher Khan belonged to one of these families. Before he arrived on the scene, these families had provided such champions as Hashim Khan—considered by many to be the father of modern squash and the first person to win a world title—Azam Khan, Roshan Khan, and Mohibullah Khan. In 1995, eight years after winning his first world title, Jansher Khan made squash history by capturing seven world titles in succession. At 26 he reigned supreme. Jansher continued to rule the world of squash in 1996–98 by maintaining his extraordinary winning streak.

JAPAN–PAKISTAN RELATIONS. The collapse of communism in Eastern Europe and the Soviet Union's disintegration made Pakistan take greater notice of Japan and vice versa. During the Cold War Pakistan was concerned mostly with maintaining good relations with the United States and China. The United States provided economic and military assistance and China offered a good counterpoint to India. The end of the Cold War also coincided with the emergence of Japan as the largest source of bilateral economic assistance to the developing world.

Although Pakistan was anxious to move closer to Japan, the latter failed to assign a high priority to the country. Japan was deeply troubled by a number of developments in Pakistan. It viewed Pakistan's nuclear weapons program with great concern. It was not pleased that Pakistan continued to commit a large proportion of its gross domestic product to maintaining and equipping a sizable military force. It was unhappy with Pakistan's neglect of social development. These concerns were openly communicated to Pakistan in bilateral exchanges and in the pronouncements made by Japan in such multilateral institutions as the Asian Development Bank, the World Bank, and the International Monetary Fund (IMF) (qq.v.), and in such forums as the Aid to Pakistan Consortium (q.v.), where, in the 1980s and 1990s, Japan's influence continued to increase along with the increase in its development budget.

A number of governments in Pakistan made serious attempts to improve economic relations with Japan. The country was visited by General Zia ul-Haq, Prime Minister Mian Nawaz Sharif, and Prime Minster Benazir Bhutto (qq.v.). It was only with the visit of Benazir Bhutto in January 1996, however, that Japan began to show some understanding of Pakistan's geopolitical situation. While on this visit to Japan, Prime Minister Bhutto spoke with great passion about the need for creating a nuclear-weapons-free region in South Asia. Her approach resonated well with her hosts. She reminded the Japanese that it was India that continued to resist these moves and it was India that was now preparing to test a nuclear weapon and, again, it was India that was spending a large sum of money on developing ballistic missiles.

These arguments paid off and Benazir Bhutto returned from Japan with an assurance from Prime Minister Ryutaro Hashimoto that "Japan will work closely with Pakistan in expanding and promoting bilateral relationship in the ever deepening interdependence in the international community." During her visit, Japan and Pakistan signed a number of agreements for Japanese support of projects in Pakistan. Japan agreed to contribute $764 million for the construction of four important projects including the Ghazi–Barotha hydropower project, a 13-kilometer elevated light-rail-transit system in Lahore (q.v.), the national drainage project, and the Balochistan (q.v.) portion of the World Bank-sponsored Social Action Program (SAP) (q.v.). The amount pledged by Japan was 50 percent more than the previously indicated amount of $500 million. Prime Minister Benazir Bhutto also succeeded in persuading the business community in Japan that Pakistan had about the most liberal laws for foreign investment in South Asia. Once again, she managed to elicit a positive response although she was reminded that the continuing troubles in Karachi (q.v.), weak human resources, especially a poor educational system, and a dysfunctional legal system were some of the major obstacles in the way of increased direct foreign investment in Pakistan.

Bhutto's dismissal in November 5, 1996 did not sit well with the Japanese authorities. It demonstrated once again the weakness of Pakistan's democratic institutions. By canceling some highly visible development projects for which Benazir Bhutto had received Japanese funding during her visit to Tokyo, the caretaker administration led by Prime Minister Meraj Khalid (q.v.) added further to Pakistan's strained relations with Japan. The projects canceled by the caretaker administration included the Lahore elevated railway. In January 1996 Shahid Javed Burki, the advisor to Meraj Khalid and the caretaker's de facto finance minister, visited Tokyo to detail the caretaker's program for economic restructuring and to explain the decision to cancel some of the projects supported by Japan. He was listened to patiently but received a cold reception. Then, in early 1998, Prime Minister Nawaz Sharif (q.v.) signaled to the Japanese authorities that he was prepared to implement the entire program of assistance Tokyo had negotiated with Benazir Bhutto. After Pakistan exploded six nuclear devices in May 1998, Japan joined the Western nations and imposed economic sanctions on the country.

JATOI, GHULAM MUSTAFA (1934–). Ghulam Mustafa Jatoi is one of the largest landowners in Pakistan. According to one reckoning he and his family own more than 80,000 acres of land. Ghulam Mustafa entered the national political scene in 1956 when, following the merger of Sindh (q.v.) into the One Unit of West Pakistan (q.v.) and the dissolution of the Sindh Assembly, he inherited the Nawabshah seat from his father, Ghulam Rasool Jatoi. The 1962 election to the National Assembly created under the Constitution of 1962 (q.v.) took Ghulam Mustafa Jatoi to Rawalpindi (q.v.), Pakistan's interim capital, as a member from Nawabshah. When President Ayub Khan (q.v.) allowed the revival of political parties and joined the Convention Muslim League (q.v.), Jatoi followed him into the new organization. He remained with the party until the departure of his friend, Zulfikar Ali Bhutto (q.v.), from the Cabinet of Ayub Khan. He resigned from the Muslim League (q.v.) in 1968 and joined the Pakistan People's Party (PPP) (q.v.) founded by Bhutto. It was as a PPP candidate that Jatoi returned to the National Assembly, elected in December 1970. When Bhutto took over as president from Yahya Khan (q.v.) in December 1971, he invited Jatoi to join the federal Cabinet as a minister. In December 1973 Bhutto sent Jatoi to Karachi (q.v.) as the chief minister of Sindh province. He remained in that position until the declaration of martial law by General Zia ul-Haq (q.v.) on July 5, 1977.

In 1986, following the return of Benazir Bhutto (q.v.) from self-imposed exile in Europe, Jatoi was removed from the chairmanship of the Sindh PPP. In July 1986, following a convention held in Lahore (q.v.), Jatoi launched his own political movement under the banner of the National People's Party (NPP) (q.v.). The NPP was able to attract some of the "uncles"—including Ghulam Mustafa Khar (q.v.)—who had been forced out of the PPP earlier. Jatoi and the NPP fared very poorly in the elections held in 1988 (q.v.). He was unable even to win his traditional Nawabshah seat, losing it to a virtual newcomer to politics. Jatoi was able to get into the National Assembly in a seat vacated by his friend Ghulam Mustafa Khar, however.

In August 1990 Ms. Bhutto was dismissed by President Ghulam Ishaq Khan (q.v.). Jatoi became the caretaker prime minister and supervised the elections held in October 1990 (q.v.) in which Bhutto lost to a coalition that called itself Islami Jamhuri Itehad (IJI) (q.v.). Mian Nawaz Sharif's Pakistan Muslim League (PML) (qq.v.) was the most important component of this coalition. In November 1990 Sharif became prime minister and Jatoi receded into the background.

JINNAH, FATIMA (1893–1967). Fatima Jinnah was the youngest sister of Muhammad Ali Jinnah (q.v.), the founder of Pakistan. She was born in Karachi (q.v.) and was educated at Bombay and Calcutta. After graduating in dental science, she started clinical practice in 1923 but did not stay in the profession for very long. She moved in with her brother in 1929 when he lost his wife; she stayed by his side for nearly 20 years, right until his death on September 11, 1948. She provided invaluable support to him as he redefined his political objectives. Jinnah had initially worked for Hindu–Muslim unity within the context of one independent India. Once he decided to campaign for Pakistan, however—an independent Muslim country to be established in India once the British left the subcontinent of South Asia—Fatima Jinnah's untiring support proved critical for his success. She was always with him as he traversed India, persuading the Muslim community to join his efforts to establish Pakistan. She played an active role in organizing Muslim women to support Jinnah's efforts. In 1938 she was instrumental in getting the Muslim League (q.v.) to create a women's subcommittee headed by herself, which would include 30 women from every province as well as from Delhi.

After her brother's death Fatima Jinnah maintained an interest in politics. She opposed the imposition of martial law by General Ayub Khan (q.v.), arguing that her brother had fought for the establishment of a country that would be governed by democracy rather than by the military. She had little use for Ayub Khan's political philosophy of guided democracy, which curtailed what she viewed as fundamental human rights—the right to vote for a Parliament, the right to freely express oneself, and the right for free political association. Ayub Khan became weary of her constant opposition to his rule. That notwithstanding, he was surprised when she accepted the offer of the Combined Opposition Party (q.v.) to oppose him in the presidential elections of January 1965. Despite her advanced years and frail health, she campaigned vigorously and may have upset Ayub Khan in the polls had not the government thrown its entire weight into getting the president reelected. The margin of her defeat was narrow, particularly in East Pakistan. She died in Karachi and was buried in the compound of the mausoleum built in the city to honor her brother.

JINNAH, MUHAMMAD ALI (1876–1948). Muhammad Ali Jinnah was born into a Shia Muslim family that did business in Karachi (q.v.). In 1892, at the age of 16, Mahemdali Jinnahbai, went to London to acquire business experience. While in London, Jinnah decided to prepare himself for a legal rather than a business profession. It was also during this time that he changed his name from Mahemdali Jinnahbai to Muhammad Ali Jinnah. He was called to the bar in 1895, returned to Karachi in 1896, and in 1897 moved to Bombay to set up his law practice.

It took Jinnah some time to get acquainted with the aspirations of the Indian Muslim community because Bombay was remote from the center of Indian Muslim politics. Although Jinnah was based in Bombay, it was in Delhi and Aligarh that the Muslims were seeking to get themselves recognized politically. Once he moved to the center stage of Indian politics and had to rub shoulders with the leaders of Muslim India he began to appreciate that independence from the British rule was not the most important political objective of many of his co-religionists. Their principal objective was the protection of the political, social, and economic interests of the Muslims when the British finally departed from India.

Jinnah took a long time to make the transition from being an Indian nationalist to becoming an Indian Muslim politician. It took him 20 years to cover this distance and he did it in several small steps. He joined the All-India Muslim League (AIML) (q.v.) in 1913 without giving up the membership of the Indian National Congress (q.v.). As an active AIML member he began to interest himself in Muslim issues and took advantage of his membership in the Imperial Legislative Assembly to speak on these issues.

Jinnah was befuddled by the rapid developments in Indian politics as Gandhi gained ground in the Congress Party, as the Congress changed its tactics to employ more confrontational means for securing concessions from the British, and as religion began to assert itself in both Hindu and Muslim politics. Disenchanted by all these developments, he decided to leave the Indian political stage. In June 1931 he left for England and settled in London. The change in residence did not help to distance him from Indian politics. He came under intense pressure to return to India. Several Muslim leaders were looking for a person who could not only lead the Muslim League (q.v.) but also discipline the independent-minded leadership of the Indian Muslim-majority provinces. Jinnah was the obvious candidate to perform this task. He returned to India on April 1, 1935 and was given a warm reception by the Indian Muslim community. By now his own political objective had been defined clearly. He was no longer interested in working for Indian independence, as he had before he left. Instead, he wanted to work for the protection of the social, economic, and political rights of the Indian Muslim community once India gained independence.

In the early 1940s Jinnah persuaded the Muslim League—in particular the provinces in which Muslims were in a minority—to opt for the idea of Pakistan. His own experience dealing with the leadership of the Indian National Congress had convinced him that the only way the Muslim community could protect itself once the British left was to establish an independent country for themselves. Accordingly, on March 23, 1940, the Muslim League passed the historic "Lahore resolution" demanding the establishment of a separate homeland for the Muslims of British India. The Pakistan slogan won Jinnah and the Muslim League mass political support in the Muslim majority provinces. Jinnah was now in a powerful position with respect to the provincial leaders, able and willing to exert his authority over them and to bring them into line with his thinking. He was now the sole spokesman for India's Muslims.

The provincial elections of 1945–46 confirmed this position for Muhammad Ali Jinnah. The Muslim League polled 75 percent of the total votes cast by the Muslims compared to only 4 percent in the 1937 elections. This was a profound improvement. Jinnah and his demand for Pakistan had struck an exceptionally responsive chord with the Muslims of British India. The Pakistan bandwagon had now begun to roll. On June 3, 1947 the British government in India announced a plan to partition the country along religious lines. The idea of Pakistan was now a reality; the country to be created for the Muslim community was to have two wings separated by India. On August 14, 1947 Pakistan achieved independence and Muhammad Ali Jinnah was sworn in as the governor-general of the new country. Karachi became the new country's capital.

By the time Pakistan gained independence, Jinnah was a very sick man. He suffered from tuberculosis, a fact that had been kept closely guarded right up to the announcement of his death on September 11, 1948. Jinnah's death came as a great shock to the people of Pakistan. They were still struggling with the aftermath of the partition of British India and his sudden departure left a void that was never entirely filled.

JINNAH, RUTTIE (1901–1929). Ruttie Petit was born in Bombay on February 20, 1901. She was the daughter of Sir Dinshaw and Lady Dina Petit. Eighteen years after her birth she married Muhammad Ali Jinnah (q.v.), a prominent Muslim lawyer. Jinnah was 43 years old at that time. The marriage lasted for 11 years. It ended with Ruttie's death in Bombay on February 20, 1929. She was buried four days later in the Khoja Isna'asherio cemetery.

JIYE SINDH MOVEMENT. *See* SYED, G. M.

JUDGES' CASE, THE. The judges' case—the name given to an important Supreme Court decision announced on March 20, 1996—was to have a profound impact on Pakistan's political development. The case concerned the criteria for the appointment of judges to the provincial high courts and the Supreme Court. The case was brought to the Supreme Court by Wahabul Khairi, a lawyer from Islamabad (q.v.). Khairi wanted the court to stop the practice of packing the judiciary with hand-picked judges who could be relied on to rule in favor of the appointing authorities whenever they made decisions that were not strictly constitutional. Because such decisions had been made in Pakistan's history, it was important for the rulers to have a supportive judiciary.

The Supreme Court, under the leadership of Chief Justice Sajjad Ali Shah (q.v.), heard Khairi's petition in the early months of 1996 and came to the decision that limited the discretion of the executive in appointing judges to the courts. The Supreme Court held that the prime minister, in recommending people for appointment to the superior courts, had to be guided by the principle of seniority. The decision to bypass a judge had to be recorded and accepted by the chief judge of the court to which the appointment was being made. The application of the decision in the judges case was made retroactive and Prime Minister Benazir Bhutto (q.v.) was ordered to resubmit the names of the people she had appointed to the courts since assuming power. The prime minister's reluctance to implement the Court's order eventually led to her dismissal by President Farooq Leghari (q.v.) on November 5, 1996.

The judges' case also seriously soured the relations between Prime Minister Nawaz Sharif (q.v.) and Chief Justice Sajjad Ali Shah. The disagreement between the two led Pakistan to the brink of a deep constitutional crisis. The situation was saved by the resignation of President Leghari on December 2, 1997 and the removal of Chief Justice Sajjad Ali Shah by his fellow judges. *See also* Judiciary, The.

JUDICIARY, THE. Pakistan inherited a judicial system with limited autonomy. With independence, the judicial system became even more subservient to the executive. The tendency on the part of the executive branch of the government to disregard the constitution (q.v.) inevitably brought the judiciary and the executive into conflict but the judiciary accepted the final authority of the executive even on constitutional matters.

The effective subordination of the judiciary resulted in a number of landmark decisions given by the high courts. They started with the decision to uphold the dissolution of the First Constituent Assembly (q.v.) by Governor-General Ghulam Muhammad (q.v.) in 1954. The series continued with the acceptance of three martial-law regimes, imposed on the country in 1958, 1969, and 1977, and the validation of the dismissal of three prime ministers in 1988, 1990, and 1996.

It was only in 1993 that the Supreme Court took a position contrary to its tradition. Under Chief Justice Nasim Hasan Shah, the Court declared President Ishaq Khan's dismissal of Prime Minister Nawaz Sharif (qq.v.) and the dissolution of the National and Provincial Assemblies to be unconstitutional. The prime minister was restored only to be forced out of office by the military acting in concert with the president. Another general elections brought Benazir Bhutto (q.v.) back to power in October 1993 as prime minister. She decided to follow in the footsteps of General Zia ul-Haq (q.v.) by ensuring that the judges appointed to the Supreme Courts and the provincial high courts would not be tempted to follow the newly declared independence of the Nasim Hasan Shah court. Her government made 45 judicial appointments to the high courts but did not consult the chief justices of the courts as required by the constitution. The courts were now totally beholden to the executive, refusing even to grant bail to politicians who were incarcerated for political reasons. A lawyer, Wahabul Khairi, filed a petition in the Supreme Court, questioning the appointment of new judges. On March 20, 1996 the Supreme Court, meeting under the direction of Chief Justice Sajjad Ali Shah (q.v.), issued a short judgment declaring that "any appointment to a High Court made without consulting the Chief Justice of that High Court, the Chief Justice of Pakistan and the Governor of that province would violate the constitution and would, therefore, be invalid. In the case of the Supreme Court Judge, consultation with the Chief Justice of Pakistan was mandatory." The government was given 30 days to regularize the appointments of the judges that had not been reviewed and approved by the Chief Justices. The prime minister's reluctance to implement the court's decision was one of the charges leveled against her by President Farooq Leghari (q.v.) in his order of November 5, 1996, dismissing her.

In keeping with the tradition the dismissed prime minister challenged the president's decision in the Supreme Court. The Court, after intensive deliberation, upheld the constitutionality of the president's action. The conflict between the judiciary and the executive did not disappear after the induction of Nawaz Sharif (q.v.) as prime minister. By the fall of 1997 the differences between the two pillars of government created a deep constitutional crisis. The issue once again was the appointment of judges to the Supreme Court. It was finally resolved with the resignation of President Farooq Leghari, who had sided with the chief justice, and the subsequent removal of Chief Justice Sajjad Ali Shah. *See also* Judges' Case, The.

JUNAGADH STATE. *See* KASHMIR.

JUNEJO, MUHAMMAD KHAN (1930–1993). Muhammad Khan Junejo was born in Sindhri village in Sanghar district and attended Karachi's St. Patrick School before going to the Agricultural Institute at Hastings, Great Britain. He returned from Hastings, England with a diploma in agricultural sciences. He won a seat to the West Pakistan provincial assembly from his native Sanghar district in 1962. The 1962 elections were the first to be held under the constitution of 1962 (q.v.), which limited the franchise to 8,000 "basic democrats," 4,000 each from East and West Pakistan. After being elected to the provincial assembly, he was invited to join the provincial administration as minister in charge of railways and communications.

Junejo adopted a low political profile when General Yahya Khan (q.v.) brought back martial law to Pakistan in March 1969 and again when Zulfikar Ali Bhutto (q.v.) became president and later prime minister. He reappeared on the political scene in 1977 as a member of the Pakistan

National Alliance (PNA) (q.v.) organized by Bhutto's opposition to challenge him in the elections held that year. After Bhutto was overthrown by General Zia ul-Haq (q.v.), Junejo came to Islamabad (q.v.) as a minister in the Cabinet formed by the president in order to provide a civilian color to his martial-law administration. He did not stay long with Zia, however. A number of his PNA colleagues left the Cabinet once it became clear that Zia was in no particular hurry to hold elections in the country. Zia called general elections in 1985 (q.v.) but banned the participation of political parties in the polls. This arrangement was not acceptable to the Pakistan People's Party (PPP) (q.v.) but Junejo and his PNA associates decided to take part in the elections. Junejo was elected to the National Assembly and, after Zia agreed to lift martial law, agreed to serve as prime minister. Martial law was lifted on December 31, 1985.

A number of differences on important policy matters that developed between the president and the prime minister—in particular those concerning Pakistan's stance toward Afghanistan (q.v.)—led to the dismissal of Junejo by Zia on May 29, 1988. Zia chose his moment well. Junejo had just returned from a visit to China and Japan (qq.v.) and was given the news of his dismissal shortly after landing at the Islamabad airport. Along with Junejo went not only his Cabinet but also the National and Provincial Assemblies. In dismissing Junejo, Zia invoked Article 58.2(b) (q.v.) of the constitution. As required by the constitution, Zia promised fresh elections within 90 days of the dismissal order. Zia made an attempt to maneuver Junejo out of the chairmanship of the Pakistan Muslim League (q.v.) but Junejo refused to oblige. As had happened on so many previous occasions in the history of the Muslim League, the party promptly split into two factions, one that supported Junejo and the other that favored Zia ul-Haq. The party failed to reunite even after the death of Zia ul-Haq and went to the polls in November 1988 as two opposing groups.

Muhammad Khan Junejo died in Washington, where he had gone for treatment. His death was to lead to another constitutional crisis in the country, prompted by the move by Nawaz Sharif (q.v.) to take over as the president of the Muslim League. This move was not endorsed by President Ghulam Ishaq Khan (q.v.). The president interpreted it as an effort by the prime minister to consolidate his power. *See also* Basic Democracies.

↩ **K** ↪

K-2. At 8,611 meters (28,250 feet) Karakoram (more commonly known as K-2) is the second highest peak in the world. It is only 219 meters short of Mount Everest in Nepal, the world's tallest mountain. K-2 is Pakistan's highest mountain peak located on the border with China (q.v.). It was first climbed in 1954 by two Italian mountaineers, Lino Lacedelli and Achille Comagnoni.

KALABAGH DAM. Unlike several other countries with large river systems, Pakistan was able to construct a number of water-diversion projects without meeting serious opposition from environmental groups or from the people residing in the lower reaches of the rivers. This relatively complacent attitude toward large water-usage projects changed in the early 1980s when the country initiated preliminary works on the Kalabagh dam. Kalabagh is a site downstream of Tarbela (q.v.). At Kalabagh, the Indus River (q.v.) leaves the hills of the northern areas and enters the plains of Punjab (q.v.).

With the people of Sindh and the Northwest Frontier Province (qq.v.) opposed to the construction of the Kalabagh dam, not much progress was made on the project in the 1980s and 1990s. The dam was opposed on a number of grounds. Its opponents argued that a large dam in Punjab would deprive the farmers in the lower reaches of the river with adequate supply of water, cause grave environmental damage to the Indus delta, and displace hundreds of thousands of people by submerging the city of Nowshera (q.v.). The first administration of Prime Minister Mian Nawaz Sharif (1990–93) (q.v.) was of the view that by getting the four provinces to agree on a formula to apportion the waters in the Indus river system, it had set the stage to begin work on the dam. That did not happen. The government of Benazir Bhutto appointed Ghulam Mustafa Khar (q.v.) minister in charge of water and power. Khar was in favor of constructing the dam but his enthusiasm for the project could not overcome the political difficulties the project continued to face.

Prime Minister Nawaz Sharif tried to revive the Kalabagh dam project when he returned to power in February 1997. In a nationally televised speech announcing the news that Pakistan had tested six nuclear devices in Balochistan (q.v.) on May 28 and 30, the prime minister promised to begin work on the dam as a way of eliminating Pakistan's dependence on imported fuel. Once again, however, the opposition to the dam by Sindh and the Northwest Frontier Province stalled the government's efforts.

KALABAGH, AMIR MUHAMMAD KHAN (1900–1970). Amir Muhammad Khan, the nawab of Kalabagh, achieved political prominence in the early 1960s. Up until then he was well known only in his native district of Mianwali in northern Punjab (q.v.), where he had extensive landholdings. He had made little effort to use his local position to carve out a prominent political position for himself either in Punjab or in national politics. This political detachment was not typical of landlords of his size and local prominence. He had stayed out of active politics largely because of the role he had played as a Unionist (q.v.) in the period before the emergence of Pakistan. The Unionists had opposed the idea of Pakistan and although a number of them were able to regain entry into politics once Pakistan became a reality, Amir Muhammad Khan preferred to stay quiet.

Appointed by President Ayub Khan (q.v.) in 1960, Amir Muhammad Khan served as governor of West Pakistan for six years. However, his style of governance alienated a large number of important people and by about the middle of the decade President Ayub Khan had come to the realization that the nawab was no longer a political asset but, instead, was quickly becoming a liability. The governor was blamed for the heavy-handed way in which the civil bureaucracy was alleged to have interfered in the presidential elections of 1965. The nawab was persuaded to resign and was replaced in 1966 by General Muhammad Musa (q.v.). Amir Muhammad Khan went back to his lands in Mianwali. In 1970 he was murdered by his son over a dispute concerning the management of his large estate.

KANSI, MIR AJMAL (1964–). On January 26, 1993 Mir Ajmal Kansi shot dead two employees of the U.S. Central Intelligence Agency as they were waiting in their cars to enter the agency's vast office complex located in Langley, outside Washington. At least one of Kansi's two victims—Frank Darling—had worked in Pakistan, as a communications expert during the height of the Afghan–Soviet war. Mir Ajmal Kansi was born in Quetta, Balochistan (qq.v.), the only child of Abdullah Jan Kansi, a Pathan tribal malik. He took up residence at Herndon, a suburb in Virginia and only a few minutes by car from CIA's Langley headquarters. After drifting for a while, he found a job as a courier with Excel Courier Inc., a firm that worked with the CIA.

On the evening of January 26, 1993, within hours of having committed the murders, Kansi boarded a Pakistan International Airlines (PIA) flight from New York to Karachi (q.v.). Arriving in Karachi twenty-two hours later, he picked up a connecting PIA flight to Quetta, his hometown, and went underground. While the Federal Bureau of Investigation, working with the officials from Pakistan, made some efforts to trace Kansi, some people, including the wife of Frank Darling, believe that the CIA did not wish to pursue this case. Kansi's name was later to be linked with Ramzi Youssef (q.v.), accused of participating in the bombing of the World Trade Center in New York. Kansi was arrested in Pakistan in 1996 and deported immediately to the United States. A court in Virginia sentenced him to death.

KARACHI. Before becoming Pakistan's capital in 1947, Karachi was a small port city with a population of only 200,000. The choice of Karachi as Pakistan's first capital was the result, in part, of its geographical location. The city expanded rapidly but haphazardly after 1947, largely on account of migration by people seeking to avail themselves of the opportunities it seemed to offer. Migration was to play an important role in Karachi's growth, more so than in other cities of Pakistan. Migrants arrived in three distinct waves: the first movement involved people displaced by the partition of British India and the creation of Pakistan; the second was comprised of the people who arrived a few years later to seek jobs in the rapidly expanding economy of the city; the third wave consisted of Afghans who sought both shelter and jobs in the city after their country was invaded by the Soviet Union (q.v.).

While the migrations associated with these waves added significantly to the growth in the population of Karachi, regular movement of people into the city from towns, cities, and villages also added hundreds of thousands of the people to its population. In 1961 Karachi had a population of 1.9 million; by 1972 the population was estimated at 3.5 million; it grew to 5.1 million by 1981. In 1992, when Pakistan should have taken its fifth population census, Karachi had 6.7 million living within its boundaries. By the end of 1997, 50 years after the creation of Pakistan, Karachi's population had crossed the 9-million mark; the census of 1998 (q.v.) estimated the city's population at 9.3 million.

In the 1980s the *muhajir* (refugees from India who arrived in Pakistan after the country gained independence in 1947) community organized itself into an effective political force under the banner of the Muhajir Qaumi Mahaz (MQM) (q.v.). The MQM won an impressive victory in the local elections held in November 1987 and went on to repeat its performance in the national elections held a year later. Its electoral triumph in the national elections was at the expense of two powerful but competing political forces: the Pakistan People's Party and the Jamaat-e-Islami (qq.v.). It was clear that the MQM had drawn a large number of people from these two parties. In the national elections of October 1990 (q.v.), the MQM repeated its performance. It was clear that the MQM was now a potent political force that had to be dealt with. The MQM went on to capture most of the seats on the National and Provincial Assemblies from Karachi in the elections of October 1993 and February 1997 (qq.v.).

KARAKORAM HIGHWAY. The Karakoram Highway—also known as KKH—connects the northern parts of Pakistan with the Chinese province of Xinjiang. The road follows the Indus river (q.v.) from Abbotabad in Pakistan to Hunza, also in Pakistan. From Hunza it goes along the Hunza river, a tributary of the Indus. It crosses into China at the Khunjerab Pass (qq.v.) and then cuts across the great Pamir Plateau in Xinjiang. It ends in the ancient city of Khashkar, now called Kashi. The road's alignment is generally the same as the old Silk Road that was supposedly taken by Marco Polo, the Italian explorer. The decision to build the road was taken after China and Pakistan demarcated their border in the early 1960s. It took a dozen years to build, from the late 1960s until the early 1980s. The Chinese provided assistance to Pakistan's Frontier Works Organization in completing the Pakistani side of the road.

KARAMAT, GENERAL JEHANGIR (1941–). On December 8, 1995 President Farooq Leghari (q.v.) appointed Lt. General Jehangir Karamat chief of Army Staff (COAS). On January 8, 1996 General Karamat took over the command of the army from General Abdul Waheed Kakar, becoming the twelfth person to command the army and the tenth Pakistani to get this position. His appointment was well received. Even though he may not have wished to be involved in politics, a number of developments in 1996–97 thrust Karamat onto the center of the political stage. In November 1996, he supported President Farooq Leghari's (q.v.) decision to dismiss Prime Minister Benazir Bhutto (q.v.). A year later he tried to mediate between President Leghari and Prime Minister Nawaz Sharif (q.v.) in their dispute over the role of Chief Justice Sajjad Ali Shah (q.v.) of the Supreme Court. Karamat failed in his efforts and President Leghari resigned on December 2, 1997. Karamat resigned from the army in October 1998 after giving a speech in Lahore that was critical of the government of Nawaz Sharif. *See also* Judges' Case, The.

KARDAR, ABDUL HAFEEZ (1925–1996). Abdul Hafeez Kardar was born in Lahore (q.v.) on January 17, 1925. He was the youngest member of the Indian cricket team that went to England in 1946 for the first post-war tour of that country by an Asian side. The first three of the 26 "test matches" he was to play in were played for India. After the tour was over, he stayed in England, changed his name to Abdul Hafeez Kardar, went to Oxford to study philosophy, politics, and economics, and played cricket for Oxford University. He returned to Pakistan in 1949 and led the country's cricket team in test victories against England at The Oval, London, over Australia in Karachi, over India in Lucknow, and over the West Indies in Port of Spain.

Kardar joined Zulfikar Ali Bhutto's Pakistan People's Party (PPP) (qq.v.) soon after it was formed, won a seat in the Punjab (q.v.) provincial assembly in the elections of 1970, and served as minister of food and education in the PPP government. His last government appointment was as Pakistan's ambassador to Switzerland from 1991 to 1993.

KASHMIR. The state of Kashmir lies to the northeast of Pakistan. When, in August 1947, the British left India in the hands of the successor states of India and Pakistan, Kashmir had a population of some four million, 75 percent of whom were Muslim, the remaining were Hindus. The Hindus were concentrated in the Jammu district in the state's southwest, close to the border with Pakistan. Although the state was predominantly Muslim, it had been ruled by a Hindu maharaja for as long as the British ruled India.

The British decision to leave India was taken without any clear indication as to the political future of the hundreds of princely states (q.v.) that dotted the South Asian subcontinent. The assumption was that the princes would seek association with either India or Pakistan depending on the geographical location of their areas. This policy did not pose a problem for most states as the princes decided to join the country that was the closest to them. This did not happen in the case of two large states, Hyderabad (q.v.) and Kashmir, however, and one small one, Junagadh. The case of Hyderabad was clear; while ruled by a Muslim— the Nizam of Hyderabad—its population was predominantly Hindu. When the Nizam showed some hesitation in joining India, the Indian government simply took over the control of the state in 1948 by sending in its army in what it euphemistically called a "police action." Junagadh was also annexed by India in the same way.

The problem of Kashmir proved to be more difficult to resolve, however. Hyderabad was surrounded by India; Kashmir, on the other hand, shared borders with both India and Pakistan. Pakistan clearly expected the Hindu maharaja to file the instruments of accession in its favor. When it seemed that the maharaja was deliberately stalling for time, Pakistanis encouraged a force of Pathan tribesmen to move into the state. The Pathans advanced quickly toward Srinagar, the state capital, in the spring of 1948 and would have conquered it had the Indians not moved in their troops following the formal accession by the maharaja to India. The Indian troops, airlifted into the state, were able to push the Pathans back but not completely out of the state. At this point Pakistan formally joined the fighting, thus launching the First Indo–Pakistan war (q.v.). In January 1949, the Indian and Pakistani governments agreed to a United Nations-sponsored cease-fire with the promise that a plebiscite would be held in the state in order to ascertain whether the Kashmiris wished to join India or Pakistan. They were not given the choice to opt for independence.

The Kashmir case was referred to the U.N. Security Council almost every year, mostly by Pakistan but Indians gradually changed the status of the state by applying to it the provisions of their constitution and holding elections to the state assembly. The Indians argued that by holding elections in the state they had fulfilled the United Nations' demand for a plebiscite.

The Chinese invasion of India in 1962 seemed to create an environment for the possible resolution of the issue. With the United States and Great Britain pushing hard, Jawaharlal Nehru, India's prime minister, agreed to hold talks with Pakistan. Five rounds of talks were held in 1962–63 but no progress was made, which provoked Pakistan to encourage the citizens of Kashmir to rebel against the occupation of their state by India. "Operation Gibraltar" (q.v.), launched in the summer of 1965, infiltrated commandos from the Pakistan army into Kashmir. The Indians retaliated by invading Pakistan on September 6, 1965, thus starting the Second Indo–Pakistan War (q.v.) over the state. Once again the United Nations intervened and the Indian and Pakistani troops returned to the positions they had occupied before the start of the war.

The Third Indo–Pakistan War (q.v.), fought in November–December 1971 was not over Kashmir but over the future of East Pakistan. By signing the Simla Accord (q.v.) in July 1972, however, Zulfikar Ali Bhutto (q.v.) accepted the Indian demand that the issue of Kashmir should be resolved by bilateral discussions. The Indians understood that by accepting this provision of the accord, Pakistan had agreed not to go back to the United Nations. In other words, Pakistan seemed to have given up the demand to determine the future of the state by holding a plebiscite. The Simla accord also established a new border between the Indian and Pakistani held parts of the state. It was called the "line of control" (LOC).

In the early 1990s some Kashmiris, inspired by the success of the Afghan mujahideen in expelling the Soviet Union from their country, decided to launch a struggle of their own against Indian occupation. India responded by sending hundreds of thousands of troops into the state but was not able to suppress the movement. In May 1998, when India exploded five nuclear devices and Pakistan followed two weeks later with six explosions of its own, Kashmir once again drew the world's attention. By then some 10,000 Kashmiris had been killed in battles with the 50,000-strong Indian force, which was determined to keep the Indian hold over the state. Pakistan seemed ready to hit back with nuclear weapons if the Indian troops invaded its territory in pursuit of Kashmiri freedom fighters. In the summer of 1998 there was considerable apprehension that the unresolved Kashmir problem could lead to a nuclear war between India and Pakistan. In July 1998, in conversations with Strobe Talbot, deputy secretary of the U.S. State Department, Prime Minister Nawaz Sharif (q.v.) requested the United States to help resolve the Kashmir dispute.

KAYANI, CHIEF JUSTICE MUHAMMAD RUSTAM (1902–1962). Muhammad Rustam Kayani was born in 1902 in the village of Shahpur in Kohat district, Northwest Frontier Province (q.v.). He joined the Indian Civil Service (ICS) in 1922 and then went to Cambridge University for training in law and administration. He joined the judicial branch of the ICS early in his career and held several judicial positions in Punjab (q.v.) and the Northwest Frontier Province. Soon after the establishment of Pakistan he was appointed to the Lahore Court as an associate judge.

In 1953 Justice Kayani was appointed the head of the commission set up by the government of Pakistan to inquire into the circumstances that resulted in the anti-Ahmadiya riots in Punjab. In April 1958 Kayani was appointed chief justice of the Lahore (q.v.) High Court. He used this position to speak openly about what ailed Pakistan at that time. In a number of speeches given around the country, he spoke about social justice and the importance of the rule of law.

It was inevitable that the outspoken chief justice of the Lahore High Court, the most prestigious of Pakistan's superior courts, would come into conflict with the military when Pakistan was placed under martial law by General Muhammad Ayub Khan (q.v.) in October 1958. His open criticism of many facets of martial law cost him elevation to the Supreme Court. He retired from the Lahore High Court in October 1962 and died in Chittagong in November of the same year while on a visit to East Pakistan. *See also* Ahmadiyas, The.

KHAD. Following the Soviet invasion of Afghanistan (q.v.) in December 1979, the security services in the country were reorganized. The KAM, the Workers Intelligence Department, was rechristened as the KhAD, the State Information Department. It soon became obvious that the Communist rulers of Afghanistan would rely extensively on the KhAD not only to keep a watchful eye on their citizens but also to intimidate Pakistan. While Pakistan was actively supporting the Afghan mujahideen in the struggle against the communist rulers and their Soviet supporters, the KhAD mounted a series of attacks in the major cities of Pakistan. In carrying out this mandate it came into direct conflict with Pakistan's Inter-services Intelligence (ISI) (q.v.). The war between the two intelligence agencies was to take a heavy toll in both countries.

The KhAD worked in Pakistan by getting its agents to infiltrate the Afghan refugee camps in Pakistan and the Afghan communities in such major cities as Karachi and Peshawar (qq.v.). It made use of the weapons found in the armories of all intelligence agencies in the countries of the former Soviet bloc; the KhAD murdered people it suspected of collaborating with Pakistan and the mujahideen and set off car bombs in Pakistan's cities. In 1987 alone, bomb explosions in Pakistan's major cities claimed 350 lives.

The withdrawal of the Soviet Union from Afghanistan in 1989 and the collapse of the communist regime soon thereafter resulted in the demise of the KhAD. Most of its personnel were either killed or went underground. With the demise of the agency, Afghanistan lost the capability of creating trouble in Pakistan.

KHAKSARS, THE. *See* MASHRIQI, ALLAMA INYATULLAH KHAN.

KHALID, MERAJ (1915–). Meraj Khalid was born in Lahore (q.v.) into a family of modest means. He chose to pursue a legal career and attended Lahore's Law College, from where he obtained a bachelor degree. His principal interest was in politics, however. He pursued this interest first at the local level, taking advantage of the dissolution of authority that was part of the design of the system of Basic Democracies (q.v.) introduced by the government of President Ayub Khan (q.v.) in 1962. In 1967 he joined a number of people in Lahore with socialist leanings to support Zulfikar Ali Bhutto's (q.v.) efforts to bring a new force into Pakistani politics. The Pakistan People's Party (PPP) (q.v.) was the consequence of these efforts. The PPP was formally launched in 1969 and almost immediately after its creation the socialist bandwagon began to roll. The general elections of 1970 (q.v.)—the first to be held in Pakistan on the basis of adult franchise—brought unanticipated victory to the PPP. The party's electoral triumph—it won 81 out of the 139 seats in West Pakistan—launched a number of political careers, including that of Meraj Khalid.

Meraj Khalid held a number of important political positions while Bhutto was in power (December 1971–July 1977). Bhutto's removal by the military in July 1977 sent Meraj Khalid back to grassroots politics. He remained loyal to the PPP and its new chairperson, Benazir Bhutto (q.v.), during the period Pakistan was under military rule, from July 1977 to August 1988. When Benazir Bhutto returned to Pakistan in 1987 from self-exile in London, however, she dispensed with the "uncles"—her term for her father's old associates—in favor of a younger group of politicians. Meraj Khalid was one of the few uncles to be awarded the party's ticket for the elections of October 1988 (q.v.). He won a seat in the National Assembly from Lahore and, in the first sitting of the assembly, was elected its speaker. Bhutto's dismissal in August 1990 sent Meraj Khalid back to Lahore. He returned with her three years later in October 1993, when Bhutto became prime minister for the second time. He was not given a political position, however. Instead, he was appointed as rector of the International Islamic University in Islamabad (q.v.).

Meraj Khalid watched Benazir Bhutto's performance as prime minister from fairly close quarters and was terribly disappointed with the way she conducted herself. He made no secret of his unhappiness with the prime minister's performance and shared it with President Farooq Leghari (q.v.), an old PPP associate. He did not hesitate when, on November 5, 1996, the president called him to take over as caretaker prime minister following the dismissal of Benazir Bhutto. He was caretaker prime minister for 104 days, from November 5, 1996 to February 17, 1997. During this time his administration concentrated its attention on three things: promulgating the legislation and creating the institutional infrastructure to hold all public officials accountable for their actions, stabilizing the economy, and organizing another general election. The elections supervised by the caretaker administration were held on February 3, 1997 and resulted in the massive defeat of Benazir Bhutto's PPP at the hands of Mian Nawaz Sharif's Pakistan Muslim League (qq.v.). Nawaz Sharif became prime minister on February 17 and brought back Meraj Khalid as rector of the Islamic University in Islamabad.

KHAN, IMRAN (1954–). Imran Khan belongs to a famous cricketing family from Pakistan that has produced three "test" captains. In 1986 his team won the test series against England in England and against India in India. His ambition to crown his career by winning the World Cup for Pakistan in 1987 was not realized when the Pakistanis, having played very well in the league matches, lost to Australia in the semifinals played at Lahore (q.v.), Imran Khan's hometown. Australia went on to win the cup by defeating England in the finals at Calcutta. Khan retired from the game following the World Cup series and was replaced as captain of the Pakistani side by his deputy, Javed Miandad. But Miandad's team performed very poorly in 1988 and Imran Khan was persuaded to return as captain by President Zia ul-Haq (q.v.), who was also the patron of Pakistan Cricket Control Board.

The president's decision was vindicated and Imran Khan's ambition was finally realized in 1992 when the team led by him came from behind and won the Fifth Cricket World Cup (q.v.). The series was held in Australia and New Zealand and at one point it seemed that Pakistan would not be able to make it even to the semifinals. This extraordinarily thrilling series brought new prominence to Imran Khan and he and his team received an extremely warm welcome on their return to Pakistan. The crowds that greeted them at Lahore's airport matched in size and enthusiasm the crowds that had received Benazir Bhutto (q.v.) in 1986 when she returned to Pakistan from a period of self-imposed exile. After this victory, Khan once again announced his retirement from the game.

Even though he left the game of cricket, Imran Khan remained in the public eye as he launched an ambitious program to raise funds for building a cancer treatment and research center in Lahore in memory of his mother, who had succumbed to the disease at a relatively young age. Imran brought the same level of commitment to this enterprise as he had done to the game of cricket and the people of Pakistan, both native and emigrant, responded with an equal amount of enthusiasm. Fundraising for the Shaukat Khan Memorial Trust Hospital brought Imran Khan in direct contact with hundreds of thousands of people as he traveled the country. During this long crusade, he decided that it would be appropriate for him to play a political role in the country. In reaching this decision he was encouraged by General (retired) Hameed Gul (q.v.) and Pasban, a social-service organization associated with the Jamaat-e-Islami (q.v.).

With this shift in ambition also came a shift in his political and social outlook. In 1994 Imran Khan gave a number of interviews in which he projected the image of a born-again Muslim, resentful of the influence of the West on Muslim cultures. He also alienated Pakistan's upper-class women by suggesting that in a Muslim society such as Pakistan's, the most appropriate role for women was in the household as housewives. It was with considerable surprise, therefore, that the people of Pakistan received the news of his marriage to Jemima Goldsmith (q.v. Khan), the daughter of a prominent Jewish businessman from England. On April 25, 1996 Imran Khan announced the launching of a political movement rather than a party. He called the movement Tehrik-e-Insaf (Movement for Justice) (q.v.) and focused on corruption as the most serious problem confronting the country. Both Khan and his party were not prepared for the general elections called by President Farooq Ahmad Khan Leghari (q.v.) following the dismissal of the government of Prime Minister Benazir Bhutto. The Tehrik performed very poorly in the elections held on February 3, 1997. It did not win a single seat in the National or Provincial Assemblies. Imran himself contested half a dozen seats but lost in all of them.

KHAN, JEMIMA GOLDSMITH (1974–). Jemima Goldsmith, the daughter of Sir James Goldsmith, an Anglo–French tycoon, married Imran Khan (q.v.) in 1995. At the time of their wedding, she was only 21, whereas Imran Khan was 42 years old. She was Jewish but had converted to Islam to be able to wed Imran. He was a born-again Muslim who seemed to have become even more devout in pursuing the religion he had rediscovered. She abandoned her Western dress in favor of the Pakistani *shalwar-kamiz.* He had already gone "native" in his dress. The Khan–Goldsmith wedding was celebrated on the front pages of all Pakistani and most British newspapers. Jemima took an active part in politics when, in the summer of 1996, her husband decided to launch a new political party called the Tehrik-e-Insaf (q.v.). Both Khan and the Tehrik did poorly in the elections of February 1997 (q.v.), however, thus ending—at least for the time—Jemima's foray into the political life of her adopted homeland.

KHAN SAHIB, DR. (1882–1956). Dr. Khan Sahib, one of the "two Khan brothers"—the other being Abdul Ghaffar Khan—was born in the Northwest Frontier Province (qq.v.). His initial inclination was to pursue a career in medicine rather than in politics. Accordingly, he studied medicine, received a degree from London University, and began clinical practice in Peshawar (q.v.). He did not pursue the medical career for long and joined his brother in promoting the objectives of the Khudai Khidmatgar Movement (q.v.). The movement, also known as the Red Shirts, had caught the imagination of a large number of people in the Northwest Frontier Province largely because of the work done by the Khan brothers.

Unlike Abdul Ghaffar Khan, Dr. Khan Sahib was not averse to holding public office. After the provincial elections of 1937 in which he associated his movement with Gandhi's Indian National Congress (q.v.) and won an impressive victory for the Congress Party, he was invited to become the province's chief minister. He resigned two years later along with all other Congress provincial chief ministers to protest the entry of British India in the war against Germany. He was back as the chief minister of the Frontier Province after leading the Congress–Khudai Khidmatgar coalition to another electoral triumph in the elections of 1946. This victory was even more impressive than the one in 1937 because in the interim Muhammad Ali Jinnah (q.v.) and his demand for the establishment of an independent homeland for the Muslims of British India had begun to draw a great amount of support from the Muslims of the country. With the Muslims accounting for 95 percent of the province's total population, the Northwest Frontier Province was expected to follow Jinnah and the rest of Muslim India in favoring the idea of Pakistan.

The Khan brothers and their Khudai Khidmatgar supporters had vigorously opposed the idea of Pakistan and their opposition to Jinnah was strong enough for the British administration to insist that a referendum should be held in order to ascertain whether the people of the Frontier Province wished to join Pakistan. The referendum was held and the supporters of Pakistan won easily and the Khan brothers lost their bid to keep their province out of Pakistan. That notwithstanding, Dr. Khan Sahib refused to leave office. When Pakistan was born on August 14, 1947, Dr. Khan Sahib was still the province's chief minister. This situation was clearly unacceptable to Governor-General Jinnah who intervened by ordering the governor of the province to dismiss the Khan administration and order Abdul Quyyum Khan (q.v.) to form a new government.

The emergence of Pakistan did not put an end to Dr. Khan Sahib's political career. In 1955 he reappeared as a member of the federal Cabinet headed by Muhammad Ali Bogra (q.v.). In 1955, when the four provinces and the princely states (q.v.) in the country's west wing were merged to form the one unit of West Pakistan (q.v), Governor-General Iskander Mirza (q.v.) sent Dr. Khan Sahib to Lahore (q.v.) to head the new administration as West Pakistan's first chief minister. This was a shrewd move on the part of the governor-general as the creation of West Pakistan had been opposed by the smaller provinces, in particular by Balochistan (q.v.) and the Northwest Frontier. These provinces were afraid of total domination by Punjab (q.v.), the largest province in Pakistan's western wing. At the same time, Dr. Khan Sahib's decision to accept the governor-general's offer represented a significant shift in his position because he had spent his entire political career in promoting a separate identity for the Pathan people.

In April 1956 he joined hands with Governor-General Iskander Mirza to start a new political organization, the aim of which was to provide the Pakistani establishment with a political vehicle that it could dominate. The Muslim League (q.v.) was too large an organization to be dominated by one faction. Iskander Mirza and his associates called their group the Republican Party of Pakistan. Dr. Khan Sahib remained the chief minister of West Pakistan. He was murdered in Lahore by a young Pathan while still in office.

KHAR, GHULAM MUSTAFA (1934–). Ghulam Mustafa Khar, a landlord with large holdings in South Punjab (q.v.), was one of the founding fathers of the Pakistan People's Party (PPP) (q.v.), the political organization created by Zulfikar Ali Bhutto (q.v.) in 1967. Khar served Bhutto in several capacities, including governor of Punjab, Pakistan's largest province. He remained with the party after Bhutto's removal by the military in 1977 and his execution two years later. Zulfikar Ali's death brought Benazir Bhutto (q.v.), the late prime minister's daughter, to the center stage of politics in Pakistan. She was elected the PPP's chairperson with the support of her father's old associates, including Khar.

In 1986 Benazir Bhutto, after spending several years in self-imposed exile in London, returned to Pakistan. Buoyed by the very warm reception she received, she decided to reshape her father's party in her own image. She sidelined the first generation of leaders, including Mustafa Khar. Not happy with this move, Khar joined hands with Ghulam Mustafa Jatoi (q.v.), another leader who had suffered at the hands of Benazir Bhutto, to form the National People's Party (q.v.). The party was unsuccessful in the elections of 1988 (q.v.), the first to be held after the return of democracy in Pakistan.

Khar returned to the fold of the PPP, following the party's win in the elections of 1993 (q.v.). Benazir Bhutto included him in her Cabinet and gave him the important portfolio of water and power. There was an expectation that Khar would succeed in producing the political consensus needed to start the construction of another dam on the Indus river (q.v.) at a place called Kalabagh on the border of Punjab and the Northwest Frontier Province (q.v.). Success eluded Khar, however. He had made little progress by the time President Leghari (q.v.) dismissed the Bhutto government on November 5, 1996. Khar contested in the elections of 1997 (q.v.) and won a seat for himself from south Punjab.

KHARIAN. *See* MUTUAL DEFENSE AGREEMENT.

KHIZAR HAYAT KHAN TIWANA (1900–1986). Sir Khizar Hayat Khan Tiwana was born in 1900 into the politically powerful Tiwana family of Shahpur (Sargodah) in northwest Punjab (q.v.). He was educated at Oxford and briefly served in the British Indian Army in the closing days of World War I. He was elected to the Punjab assembly in 1937 and served as minister of public works in the Unionist (q.v.) cabinet headed by Sir Sikander Hayat Khan (q.v.). In 1942, following the death of Sir Sikander, he was elected president of the Unionist Party, a development that was to profoundly effect not only the politics of his native Punjab but of the entire Muslim community of British India.

Khizar took the Unionist Party out of the Muslim League (q.v.) in 1946 and decided to fight the elections held that year on a platform that supported the concept of a united India, presumably under continuing British rule. The Muslim League won a plurality in the Provincial Assembly but did not have enough seats to form a government on its own. Khizar refused to cooperate with the League; instead, he aligned the Unionists with the Hindu-dominated Indian National Congress (q.v.) and the Sikh-dominated Akali Dal to form a coalition government in April 1946. These moves, including the decision to ban the Muslim League National Guards as a paramilitary organization, won him the permanent wrath of the majority of Muslims in Punjab. A mass agitation was launched against him by the Muslim League and hundreds of thousands of people came out in the streets all over the province. Jails were soon filled with agitators and Khizar was unable to cope with the situation. He resigned in March 1947, a few weeks before the British announced their intention to leave India after partitioning it into the independent states of India and Pakistan. *See also* Tiwanas, The.

KHOST. Khost is a small town in a plain of that name west of Pakistan's border with Afghanistan. Mujahideen (q.v.) forces besieged Afghan and Soviet garrisons in Khost almost from the beginning of the war in December 1979. The Soviet forces tried hard to dislocate the mujahideen from Khost while Pakistan and the United States provided the mujahideen with heavy equipment by land and by air. Once the mujahideen were equipped with such sophisticated antiaircraft weapons as stinger and blowpipe missiles, the supply of the garrison by air became hazardous. In December 1987 the Soviet and Afghan troops launched a massive operation to open the 120-kilometer road through the mountains to the plain of Khost. The battle for Khost was the most important land battle to be fought during the Soviet occupation of Afghanistan.

After the departure of the Soviet troops from Afghanistan, Khost became an important training center for the "soldiers of Islam" who fought in several conflicts around the world including those in Bosnia-Herzegovina, Chechnya, Kashmir (q.v.), and Kosovo. The people receiving training in the camps at Khost were also allegedly involved in several acts of terrorism (q.v.), including the bombing in August 1998 of the United States embassies in East Africa. On August 20, 1998 U.S. President Bill Clinton ordered missile attacks on Khost. *See also* bin Laden, Osama.

KHUDAI KHIDMATGAR MOVEMENT, THE. The Khudai Khidmatgar Movement, or the Servants of God Movement, was launched in the 1930s. Its main political purpose was to obtain some form of autonomy for the Pathan population living in the Northwest Frontier Province (q.v.) of British India. The movement was backed by uniformed but unarmed shock troopers who wore homespun and hand-woven garments dyed a dirty red. The color of the uniform gave the Khudai Khidmatgars (KK) another name: the Surkhposhan, or the Red Shirts.

The Red Shirts operated at two different levels: first, they mobilized the landless peasants and village workers against the khans or the large landlords of the Northwest Frontier Province. They also appealed to the urban intelligentsia to campaign against the British rule of India. The movement's popularity with the less privileged segments of the Pathan society gave it a distinct socialist—almost Marxist—flavor and its anti-British stance brought it close to Mahatma Gandhi and his Indian National Congress (q.v.). These two antiestablishment orientations—against the landlords and against the British—explain why the movement was to be drawn toward the Hindu-dominated Congress Party and why it developed a strong antipathy toward the Muslim League (q.v.).

The Khan brothers—Dr. Khan Sahib and Abdul Ghaffar Khan (qq.v.)—were the movement's most prominent leaders, and their politics made them close associates of Gandhi and Jawaharlal Nehru. In the critical elections of 1946 the Khan brothers guided the Congress Party to an impressive win. With the help of other non-Muslim League members of the provincial legislature, the Red Shirts were able to form a government with Dr. Khan Sahib as the chief minister. The Red Shirt government was still in power when Pakistan was born on August 14, 1947. The administration was dismissed by Governor Sir George Cunningham (q.v.) on August 22, 1947, and Abdul Quyyum Khan (q.v.), president of the provincial Muslim League, was invited to form a new administration. This change resulted in the political demise of the Khudai Khidmatgars.

KHUDA-KI-BASTI. The establishment of Khuda-ki-Basti—or God's village—was one of the initiatives taken in 1987 by the government of Prime Minister Muhammad Khan Junejo (q.v.). The initiative was designed to address the problems posed by hundreds of squatter settlements in Karachi (q.v.). The enormous and unrelenting increase in Karachi's population since 1947, when the city was chosen to become Pakistan's first capital, had not been matched by the supply of suitable living space for the migrants who came in search for jobs. This led to the development of *katchi abadis*—or temporary settlements—in all parts of the city. These abadis were usually located on public lands and resembled squatter settlements in all major cities of the developing world.

The establishment of Khuda-ki-Basti, first in Hyderabad (q.v.) and then in Karachi, was one response to the problem of urban spread in south Sindh (q.v.). The concept was pioneered by Tawfiq Siddiqui, a civil servant, who gave operational meaning to the concept originally promoted by Prime Minister Junejo. The *bastis* survived even after the departure of Junejo. The troubles in Karachi in most of the 1990s encouraged the provincial government to keep focusing on the basti concept for depressed shanty towns in Karachi and other parts of Sindh.

KHUNJERAB PASS. The Karakoram Highway (KKH) (q.v.) leaves Pakistan and enters China through the Khunjerab Pass. The pass is located at a height of 5,000 meters in the Karakoram mountain range. The pass was opened to the public by the Pakistani and Chinese authorities on May 1, 1986. Since then it has become a popular attraction for the tourists who take the KKH from northern Pakistan into Kashgar in China's Xinjiang province.

KHYBER PASS. The Khyber Pass is the main pass in the mountain range that runs along Pakistan's border with Afghanistan (q.v.). It has been traveled extensively for centuries. Bringing Afghanistan under their influence was an important part of the "Great Game" (q.v.) played by the British once they were the masters of India. This meant turning the Khyber Pass into an important military artery through which troops and equipment could be easily moved. Accordingly, the British laid an all-weather road that traversed the pass and also built a railway that connected the city of Peshawar (q.v.) with Landikotal, a small town on the Indian side of the pass. A number of forts were constructed all along the Khyber road and railway.

It was only after the establishment of Pakistan that the Khyber became an important crossing point for commerce—mostly goods smuggled into Pakistan from Afghanistan. However, military action returned to the Khyber Pass after the invasion of Afghanistan by the Soviet Union (q.v.) in 1979. Millions of refugees used the pass to enter Pakistan from Afghanistan while hundreds of thousands of Afghan mujahideen used the pass to launch military operations into their country. The unsettled conditions all along the pass during the Afghan war turned it into a route for the transport of drugs, mostly heroin manufactured in hundreds of crude workshops that sprung up all along the pass. Even after the withdrawal of the Soviet troops, Khyber remained an active place for the manufacture, trade, and transport of drugs.

KOREA (SOUTH)–PAKISTAN RELATIONS. The economic decision-makers in Pakistan were (and probably still are) only vaguely familiar with the circumstances that led to the economic success of Korea. In fact, even in the late 1970s, they were much more enamored of the northern half of the county: in 1979 Prime Minister Zulfikar Ali Bhutto (q.v.) lavished large amounts of public funds to receive Prime Minister Kim Il Sung of North Korea in Islamabad (q.v.). It was only during the administration of Prime Minister Nawaz Sharif (q.v.) that Pakistan began to take serious note of the Republic of (South) Korea. This interest was not directed at understanding the set of circumstances that had produced the Korean miracle, however. Instead, it was aimed at attracting Korean private capital for investment in Pakistan.

The Korean response to Prime Minister Nawaz Sharif's overtures was encouraging. In February 1992 Daewoo (q.v.) of Korea signed an agreement with the government of Pakistan to construct a $2-billion motorway between Lahore and Islamabad (qq.v.). During the same month a high-powered delegation visited Pakistan to explore the possibility of setting up a Korean industrial estate on a site near Karachi (q.v.). The Koreans requested Pakistan to set aside a site measuring 500 acres near Port Kasim for investment by industries from their country. This effort was stymied by the change in government in July 1993 when Nawaz Sharif resigned, first to be replaced by the caretaker administration of Prime Minister Moeen Qureshi (q.v.), and then by the administration of Prime Minister Benazir Bhutto (q.v.). Bhutto had no interest in continuing with the projects started by Sharif. She incurred the displeasure of the Koreans by putting the completion of Lahore–Islamabad Motorway (q.v.) on the back burner. In 1995 Bhutto made an effort to improve relations with the Korean private sector. She sent Asif Ali Zardari (q.v.), her husband, to Korea to hold discussions with the large industrial houses but was rebuffed. She paid a state visit to Korea in 1996 but it was only with the return of Nawaz Sharif as prime minister in February of 1997 that Pakistan's relations began to warm with Korea. However, the East Asian financial crisis of 1997–98 and the stress it caused to the Korean private sector put on hold the new plans for investment that began to be developed after the return of Sharif as prime minister.

KOT ADDU. In 1994 the government of Prime Minister Benazir Bhutto (q.v.) began to implement a plan to privatize the Water and Power Development Authority (WAPDA) (q.v.), Pakistan's largest public-sector corporation. The first phase of the plan called for the transfer of two thermal power plants, the 1,600-megawatt plant at Kot Addu and the 880-megawatt plant at Jamshoro (q.v.). The government's plan for the privatization of the Kot Addu plant envisaged a phased transfer of ownership to the private sector. In the first stage all financial obligations of the WAPDA, including an outstanding debt of $756 million, were to be taken over by the Kot Addu Power Company (KAPC), an entity legally separate from the Authority. The second stage included the transfer of 26 percent of the company's assets, along with the responsibility for its operation, to a strategic investor selected on the basis of international competitive bidding. Four foreign companies entered the last phase of the bidding process. Britain's National Power was the successful bidder. It took over the management of the power station in 1996.

⤿ **L** ⤾

LAHORE. The first few decades of the twenty-first century may see the reemergence of Lahore as Pakistan's premier urban center. If the present trends continue, by 2010 Lahore may overtake Karachi (q.v.) in terms of both the size of its population and its contribution to the national economy. There is also the possibility that Lahore may evolve a cultural identity of its own, quite separate from that of Karachi. Finally, the political center of gravity may also shift toward Lahore. The last trend is already visible; it may gather momentum as some of the forces that have surfaced in urban Pakistan begin to move the city ahead of its competitors and take it toward greater prominence.

Lahore would have been Pakistan's most prominent city but for the way Lord Radcliffe (q.v.) drew the boundary between the Indian and Pakistani Punjab (q.v.). In 1947, the year Pakistan was born, Lahore would have been the most obvious choice to become the capital of the new country. However, Radcliffe drew the border too near the city of Lahore to justify locating the country's capital in what was then Pakistan's largest city. Apart from its size, Lahore, more than Karachi, had most of the infrastructure required by the capital of a country; it was well connected with the provinces in the western wing of what was now Pakistan, had a sound economic base on which the urban economy could be built, and possessed the bureaucratic skills around which the new administration could be structured. Lord Radcliffe's dispensation permanently disabled Lahore; it could not become the seat of the Pakistani government for as long as India and Pakistan continued to view each other with suspicion and hostility.

In the fifty-year period since independence, Lahore has grown in size. In 1947, the year of Pakistan's birth, the city had a population of 500,000. In the census of 1998 (q.v.) its population was estimated at five million. Its boundaries now include a number of small towns that were once separated from it by farmland. It is now the second largest industrial city, accounting for one-fifth of industrial output.

LAHORE FORT. The Lahore Fort is the most elaborate structure to be built by the Mughul emperors of India. It was not conceived as one building erected for one purpose. It evolved instead over time as a mini-city on the outskirts of Lahore (q.v.), the capital of Mughul Punjab (q.v.). Four Mughul emperors were to contribute to the development of the fort. The site for the fort was selected by Akbar the Great in the middle of the sixteenth century. He chose the left bank of the Ravi River that flowed through Lahore to construct a series of buildings to be located within the walls of a fort. The fort was meant to provide residences for the emperor and the members of his court, places for giving audience to the emperor's courtiers and to the public, places of worship, palaces for the women in the harem, and quarters for the soldiers. Akbar laid the foundation stone of the fort but it was his son, Jahangir, who had a special fondness for the city of Lahore, and who undertook the first phase of the fort's construction.

It was Akbar's grandson and Jahangir's son, Emperor Shahjahan, however, who brought to the fort his genius for building and his flair for magnificence. Shahjahan's most important contribution to the cluster of buildings located within the periphery of the fort is the Diwan-i-Khas, or the hall of private audience, and the Sheesh Mahal, or the Mirror Palace. The Mirror Palace has a marble dado, carved marble screens, and the mosaic is made of tiny convex mirrors of many colors set in arabesques. West of the Sheesh Mahal stands the Naulakha Pavilion, or the pavilion of 900,000, so named because its walls are studded with 900,000 precious stones. The main gate to the fort faces the Badshahi Mosque. It was Aurangzeb, the last great Mughul emperor of India, who put the final touches to the Fort as it now stands. *See also* Mughul Empire.

LAHORE–ISLAMABAD MOTORWAY. The idea of constructing a motorway linking Lahore with Islamabad (qq.v.) along an entirely new alignment, scores of kilometers west of the existing highway, was first put forward by Nawaz Sharif (q.v.) when he was the chief minister of Punjab (q.v.). The feasibility report prepared for the project estimated its cost at Rs.8.2 billion. The proposal did not advance very far; the Islamabad administration, then under Prime Minister Benazir Bhutto (q.v.) and hostile to the provincial administration of Nawaz Sharif, showed little interest in the project. The idea was revived, however, when Nawaz Sharif replaced Benazir Bhutto as prime minister. The motorway was identified as one of the several projects included in the multibillion-dollar-highway-construction program developed by the Nawaz Sharif government soon after it assumed office. The program—the motorway included—received the government's approval in a special meeting of the Cabinet on October 10, 1991. Three months later, on January 10, 1992, Mian Nawaz Sharif performed the groundbreaking ceremony of the motorway.

The contract for the construction of the 340-kilometer motorway was given to Daewoo of Korea (qq.v). The project was to be completed over a period of three years. With the return of Benazir Bhutto as prime minister in October 1993, however, the project suffered a major setback. The new government stopped payments to Daewoo while yet another investigation was carried out. Ultimately the government decided to proceed with the construction of the highway but on a schedule considerably longer than the original. It was only after the return of Sharif as prime minister in February 1997 that the project once again received the government's attention. The motorway was opened for public use in November 1997.

LAHORE RESOLUTION. *See* PAKISTAN RESOLUTION.

LAHORE UNIVERSITY OF MANAGEMENT SCIENCES (LUMS). The Lahore University of Management Sciences was founded in 1980 by a group of industrialists headed by Syed Babar Ali. By the time the institution had been established, large industrial and commercial houses had begun to recruit professional managers for their enterprises. The LUMS was designed to meet this burgeoning demand. It fashioned itself after the Harvard Business School, borrowing the HBS's case method for teaching. Having started in rented buildings in Gulberg, Lahore (q.v.), the LUMS moved to a permanent campus, financed in part by a grant from the U.S. Agency for International Development (AID), near the Defense Housing Society on the outskirts of Lahore.

Initially, the LUMS focused on training students in managerial sciences, awarding degrees in Master's of Business Administration after two years to students selected after they had finished three years of college. Later, in 1994, the institution decided to add undergraduate teaching. It also established an executive-training program, once again patterned after the program run by the Harvard Business School.

LAND ALIENATION ACT OF 1901. The Land Alienation Act of 1901 was promulgated by the British administrators of Punjab (q.v.) to protect the Muslim peasantry from Hindu moneylenders.The Act prohibited the transfer of agricultural land from the group of people it defined as "agriculturists" to those it identified as "nonagriculturalists." Agriculturalists were mostly Muslims and non-agriculturists were mostly non-Muslims. The Act proved to be a significant piece of legislation. It restored social peace and harmony among the communities of rural Punjab. It also permanently bound the Muslim landed class of Punjab to the British. The fact that the Muslim community of Punjab never became restive under British rule and did not actively participate in the movement to create Pakistan, a separate homeland for the Muslims of British India, can be largely attributed to the Land Alienation Act of 1901 and its successful application.

LAND REFORMS OF 1959. The Land Reforms of 1959, introduced by the military government of General Ayub Khan (q.v.) in the form of a martial-law regulation (Martial Law Regulation [MLR] 64), prescribed two ceilings on land holdings: 500 acres for irrigated and 1,000 acres for non-irrigated (*barani*) land. The owners of resumed land were to be compensated through the issue of long-term (20 years) interest-bearing (3 percent a year) bonds. The resumed area was to be distributed to small peasants against payment stretched over several years. MLR 64 departed from Ayub Khan's original thinking on land reforms in two areas. These concerned *jagirs* (land grants) and the relationship between owners and cultivators. All jagirs were abolished without compensation to their owners. And all tenants were to be provided with legal protection against eviction. At the same time, the owners were prohibited from levying any other charge, except rent, on the cultivators. *Begar,* or forced labor extracted from cultivators by owners, was made illegal.

Slightly more than one million hectares of land were resumed under the Land Reforms of 1959. Of this land, 896,000 hectares were allotted to 183,266 persons. The beneficiaries, on average, received 4.9 hectares of resumed land. A significant proportion of the land resumed came from Punjab (q.v.); the province provided 503,000 hectares or slightly more than one half of the total. Sindh (q.v.) provided 9.3 percent; the Northwest Frontier Province (q.v.) 2.4 percent; and Balochistan (q.v.) 1.3 percent. The Land Reforms of 1959 affected only 5 percent of the total farm area in Pakistan.

LAND REFORMS OF 1972. The Pakistan People's Party (PPP) (q.v.) in its "Foundation Papers" and in the manifesto it issued for the elections of 1970 (q.v.), promised radical land reforms. The party promised that its reforms would go much beyond those introduced by the administration of President Ayub Khan (q.v.) in 1959. The PPP contended that Ayub Khan's reforms had been insignificant in scope as they sidestepped the issue of inequality in the distribution of rural assets. The PPP promised to remedy that situation once it came to power.

On March 1, 1972 President Zulfikar Ali Bhutto (q.v.), acting as the chief martial-law administrator, promulgated the Martial Law Regulation (MLR) 115 of 1972, which specified a new ceiling on land holding. In spite of the promise made in the Foundation Papers, the reforms proved not to be any more radical than those undertaken in 1959 by the government of Ayub Khan; they only advanced the process of structural change in land ownership that had begun with the earlier reforms. As in the case of the 1959 reforms, this effort also aimed to achieve greater equality but not a radical change in equality in land distribution. A new and lower ceiling was prescribed: 150 acres for irrigated land and 300 acres for nonirrigated land. The land owned in excess of these ceilings was to be resumed by the state without payment of compensation to the affected landlords. The resumed land was to be provided to landless peasants and small landholders without charge. A total of 1.3 million acres was resumed under the reforms, of which 900,000 acres were distributed to 76,000 small cultivators. *See also* Land Reforms of 1959.

LAND REFORMS OF 1977. The third attempt to address persistent inequities in land distribution in West Pakistan was made in 1977. On January 7, 1977, acting on the advice of Prime Minister Zulfikar Ali Bhutto (q.v.), President Fazal Elahi Chaudhry promulgated the Land Reform Ordinance of 1977 (Ordinance II of 1977). These reforms, like those attempted in 1959 and 1972, had a marginal effect on land distribution.

The land reforms of 1977 had three significant features: they reduced the ceiling on land holdings to 100 acres of irrigated land; allowed compensation to the people who were required to surrender land in the form of long-maturity government bonds; and the land assumed by the government was offered without charge to landless peasants and small landholders. About 1.8 million acres of land were surrendered to the government under the reforms, of which 900,000 acres were distributed among 13,143 persons.

LATIF, KHALID. See ALLIED BANK LIMITED.

LATIF OF BHIT, SHAH ABDUL (1609–1672). Shah Abdul Latif of Bhit occupies a special place of honor among the "saints of Sindh" (q.v.), a group of religious leaders who first brought Islam to the lower Indus valley. Shah Abdul Latif was born in 1609 in Hela Haveli. His family had migrated to Sindh from the city of Herat in Afghanistan. Shah Abdul Karim of Bulri, Latif's great-grandfather, had been recognized in his own time both as a poet and a saint. Latif followed in the family tradition. Not much is known about Latif's formal education, but the scope and sweep of his verse, composed mostly in his native Sindhi, suggests considerable familiarity not only with Persian and Arabic—languages that all reasonably literate Muslims were expected to know—but also with such vernacular dialects as Balochi, Punjabi, and Seraiki. Shah Abdul Latif's *urs* (death anniversary) brings tens of thousands of devotees to the mausoleum that was built at Bhit Shah by Ghulam Shah Kalhoro, the ruler of Sindh, in the middle of the eighteenth century.

LAW REFORM COMMISSION OF 1958. As President Ayub Khan (q.v.) was to explain later in his political biography, the principal purpose of his coup d'etat (he called it "my revolution") was to bring Pakistan into the twentieth century by modernizing its institutional structure. Although he had his own ideas about the changes he wished to introduce, he nevertheless freely sought advice from people he considered more knowledgeable than himself. One way of receiving this advice was to appoint commissions of inquiry with clear terms of reference. A Law Reform Commission was among the dozens of commissions appointed by Ayub Khan in 1958–59. It was convened in November 1958 with the injunction to study the entire legal infrastructure and to suggest how it could be modernized.

As instructed, the Commission reported back in one year, but its recommendations were less epoch-making than had been expected. It made

368 recommendations dealing with legal procedures, legal conduct, and the structure of the legal system. It also covered the area of family laws. Its suggestion that special family courts should be established influenced the content of the Family Laws Ordinance of 1961 (q.v.).

LEGAL FRAMEWORK ORDER (LFO) OF 1970. The Legal Framework Order was promulgated by the martial-law government of General Agha Muhammad Yahya Khan (q.v.) on March 20, 1970. Its main purpose was to fill the legal vacuum that was left by the abrogation of the Constitution of 1962 (q.v.) by the martial-law government when it took office on March 29, 1969. The LFO was to serve as a quasi-constitution until a new constituent assembly came up with a new constitutional structure for the country.

The political structure prescribed by the LFO was entirely different from the one that supported the Constitution of 1962. The principle of parity (q.v.) was dispensed with. The LFO established a Constituent Assembly of 300 members with provincial representation determined on the basis of the shares of the provinces in total population. East Pakistan was allocated 162 seats, whereas West Pakistan was given 138 seats. Unlike the Constitution of 1962, the Legal Framework Order opted for direct elections of the president and the National and Provincial Assemblies. Under the LFO, general elections were to be held on October 5, 1970, and the National Assembly elected by the people was to be given 120 days to write a new constitution. This provision was put in the LFO in order not to repeat the experience of the First Constituent Assembly (1947–54) (q.v.), which labored for more than seven years without agreeing on a constitution. If the assembly failed to write a constitution within the stipulated period it was to be dissolved by the president and another election was to be held to reconstitute it.

The military was not prepared to grant full constitution-making powers to the Constituent Assembly, however. It was fearful of two possible outcomes. One, it did not wish the assembly to come up with a constitution that granted so much autonomy to the provinces that the unity of the state of Pakistan would be undermined. Two, it did not want provisions in the constitution that would put unacceptable constraints on the role of the army.

The elections (q.v.) promised by the LFO were held on December 7, 1970, two months after the time indicated in the order. The delay was caused by a cyclone that devastated the coastline of East Pakistan on November 12, 1970, leaving more than a million people dead and causing inestimable damage to property.

LEGHARI, SARDAR FAROOQ AHMAD KHAN (1941–). Farooq Ahmad Khan Leghari, Pakistan's eighth president, comes from Baloch-Pathan stock. His father, Muhammad Khan Leghari, was from Balochistan (q.v.), whereas his mother belonged to the Northwest Frontier Province (q.v.). He was born in Tank, a small town in the Northwest Frontier Province but was brought up in Lahore (q.v.), where his father lived most of his life. He was educated first at Lahore's renowned Aitcheson College, briefly attended Forman Christian College also in Lahore, and then, in 1961, went to St. Catherine's College, Oxford. He joined the Civil Service of Pakistan (CSP) in 1964 but did not stay in government service for very long. He joined the Pakistan People's Party (PPP) (q.v.) in 1970 and won a seat from Dera Ghazi Khan, the seat of his family, in the elections of 1970 as well as 1977 (qq.v.).

The 1977 victory brought him a seat in the Cabinet headed by Prime Minister Zulfikar Ali Bhutto (q.v.). But the Cabinet had a very short life. On July 5, 1977 Bhutto was removed from office by General Zia ul-Haq (q.v.), the chief of staff of the army. Zia put Pakistan under martial law. Leghari, along with several members of the PPP, decided to actively oppose the imposition of martial law. Following Bhutto's execution on April 4, 1979, his wife, Nusrat Bhutto, and his daughter, Benazir Bhutto (qq.v.), became the PPP's co-chairpersons. Leghari was given the important position of the party's secretary-general. He spent several months in prison when Zia came down hard on the movement that was launched by the PPP and a number of other parties to force the military president to hold elections and return democracy to Pakistan.

In the elections of November 1988 (q.v.) Leghari won seats in the National Assembly as well as in the Punjab Provincial Assembly. The PPP was returned to power at the center in Islamabad (q.v.) but did not do well in Punjab (q.v.), the country's largest province. Benazir Bhutto became prime minister but chose not to include Leghari in the federal cabinet; instead, he was asked to resign his National Assembly seat, go to Lahore and stop Nawaz Sharif (q.v.) from forming a government in Lahore, Punjab's capital. Leghari did not succeed in his efforts, Sharif managed to secure the support of a majority of the Punjab assembly members and became the chief minister of the province. Leghari returned to Islamabad (q.v.) and the National Assembly and, although he would have preferred the portfolio of finance, he was brought into the Cabinet as minister in charge of water and power.

Bhutto's dismissal from office in August 1990 sent her and her associates into opposition once again as the PPP lost to Nawaz Sharif's Islami Jamhuri Itehad (IJI) (q.v.) in the elections (q.v.) that were held in October. Bhutto and Leghari refused to accept the legitimacy of Sharif's elections. They accused the interim government of Ghulam Mustafa Jatoi (q.v.) of rigging the elections with the tacit approval of President Ghulam Ishaq Khan (q.v.) and the active involvement of the armed forces. While Sharif was prime minister, Leghari led noisy agitations against the government, including an effort in December 1991 to prevent Ishaq Khan from giving the annual state of the country address to the joint sitting of the Senate and the National Assembly. The PPP did not win an outright majority in the elections held in October 1993 (q.v.) but emerged as the largest single party in the National Assembly. Benazir Bhutto was once again in the position to form a government in Islamabad, which she did with the help of a number of small parties. Leghari was given the portfolio of foreign affairs. In the effort to gain the presidency for her party, however, Bhutto turned to Leghari and put him forward as the PPP candidate. Leghari won a comfortable victory with 274 votes against Waseem Sajjad, who received 168 out of 446 valid votes cast by the electoral college. Leghari announced his resignation from the Pakistan People's Party after being sworn in as president. He wanted to be a nonparty president, responsible to the constitution and not to any particular party affiliation. By the summer of 1996, Pakistan had slipped into serious economic difficulties, the government of Benazir Bhutto was accused of massive corruption and mismanagement, and the law-and-order situation had deteriorated remarkably. Leghari was clearly upset with these developments as with the reluctance of the government to implement the judgment awarded by the Supreme Court in what had come to be called the "judges' case" (q.v.).

Leghari dismissed the Bhutto government on November 5, 1996, using Article 58.2(b) (q.v.) of the constitution. Elections were held again in February 1997 (q.v.) in which Nawaz Sharif and the Pakistan Muslim League (q.v.) won a decisive victory. Sharif became prime minister and used his vast majority in the National Assembly to amend the constitution twice. Article 58.2 (b) was dropped. In the fall of 1997 Sharif and the judiciary (q.v.) clashed, the latter upset over some remarks made by the prime minister about the justices of the Supreme Court. To save Pakistan from plunging into a deep constitutional crisis, Leghari resigned as president on December 2, 1997.

After his resignation, Leghari moved to Lahore and began discussions with his supporters to chart out his political future. In a number of press interviews he criticized both Benazir Bhutto and Nawaz Sharif for having failed to provide good leadership. He claimed that the two had plundered the country while in power and had amassed vast personal fortunes through corruption. It was clear that Leghari was hoping to present the people with an another alternative to Sharif and Bhutto. On August 14,

1998—Pakistan's fifty-first birthday—Leghari launched a new party. Named the Millat (q.v.), the party's foundation papers were aimed at the middle classes, who were by then deeply concerned about the country's mounting political and economic problems.

LIAQAT ALI KHAN (1885–1951). Liaqat Ali Khan was born in Karnal, Punjab (q.v.), and was educated at Aligarh, Allahabad, and Oxford Universities. He took the bar examinations in 1922 and joined the All-India Muslim League (q.v.) soon after returning to India. He was a member of the United Provinces' Legislative council from 1926 to 1940, secretary of the All-India Muslim League from 1936 to 1947, and chairman of the Muslim League Central Parliamentary Board in 1945. He joined Muhammad Ali Jinnah (q.v.) in all the important discussions that were held by the British to resolve India's constitutional dilemma. These included the Simla Tripartite Conferences (q.v.) held in 1945 and 1946.

In October 1946 Liaqat led the Muslim League group into the "interim government" formed by the British under Prime Minister Jawaharlal Nehru of the Indian National Congress (q.v.) and was given the portfolio of finance. On August 14, 1947, Pakistan became a reality, and Liaqat Ali Khan was sworn in as the country's first prime minister. But even then, he remained in Jinnah's shadow. As governor-general, Jinnah wielded more power than had been given to him under the Government of India Act 1935 (q.v.) and the India Independence Act of 1947—two documents that together served as the new country's constitutions. It was only after Jinnah's death on September 11, 1948 that Liaqat emerged as the principal leader of Pakistan and the de facto head of the Pakistan government. He invited Khawaja Nazimuddin to succeed Jinnah as governor-general and Maulvi Tamizuddin (q.v.), another politician from Bengal, to become president of the first Constituent Assembly (q.v.).

Liaqat devoted considerable energy to foreign affairs. He concluded the war in Kashmir (q.v.) by signing a cease-fire agreement with Jawaharlal Nehru, India's Prime Minister, in January 1949 but failed to get India to follow up on its terms. His effort to maintain neutrality in the U.S.–Soviet conflict, while claiming to be India's equal in the international arena, resulted in both superpowers giving Pakistan the cold shoulder. Liaqat moved out of this difficult situation by tilting toward the United States. In 1950 he visited Washington and met with President Harry Truman.

By the time of his death on October 16, 1951 Liaqat had begun to lose ground in domestic politics. Punjab (q.v.) and Bengal were restive under the control of the Muslim League, and several factions in Sindh were engaged in endless infighting within the Muslim League. It was only in the Northwest Frontier Province that Abdul Qayyum Khan (qq.v.), the Muslim League chief minister, had succeeded in cultivating support for himself and his party. Liaqat's approach to these developments was to bypass the provincial political bosses and go directly to the people. In 1950 and 1951 he began to build a constituency for himself by traveling all over the country and using his great oratorical skills to address large audiences. It was while he was addressing a mammoth public meeting in Rawalpindi's (q.v.) Company Bagh that he was assassinated. His assailant, Said Akbar (q.v.), was killed by the police soon after he had fired the fatal shot at the prime minister.

LOCAL BODIES ELECTIONS OF 1987. The first local bodies elections under the system introduced in 1987 were held in November of the same year, after President Zia ul-Haq (q.v.) had surrendered some power to an elected government and Muhammad Khan Junejo (q.v.) had become prime minister. The elections chose members of 4,467 local councils including 11 municipal corporations, 127 municipal committees, 186 town committees, 65 *zila* (district) councils, and 3,971 union councils. Punjab (q.v.) had 2,627 local councils of which 7 were municipal corporations (Lahore, Faisalabad, Rawalpindi [qq.v.], Multan, Gujranwala, Sargodah, and Sialkot), 67 municipal committees, 135 town committees, 29 zila councils, and 2,392 union councils. Sindh (q.v.), Pakistan's second-largest province, had 767 local councils of which there were only two municipal corporations (Karachi and Hyderabad [qq.v.]), 33 municipal committees, 108 town committees, 13 zila councils, and 653 union councils. The Northwest Frontier Province (q.v.) had 706 local councils with one municipal corporation (Peshawar [q.v.]), 17 municipal committees, 23 town committees, 13 zila councils, and 653 union councils. Finally, Balochistan (q.v.), Pakistan's smallest province in terms of population but its largest in terms of geographical area, had one municipal corporation (Quetta [q.v.]), 10 municipal committees, 20 town committees, 19 zila councils, and 315 union councils, making a system of 365 local councils. In 1987, the entire system had 61,000 elected members.

LOCAL BODIES ELECTIONS OF 1991. The second local council elections were held in 1991 while Mian Nawaz Sharif was prime minister and his Pakistan Muslim League (qq.v.) was the dominant player in the administration in Islamabad (q.v.). This was the first time in Pakistan's history that political parties contested local council elections and put up candidates with clear party affiliations. The Muslim League did well in the elections, particularly in the provinces of Punjab and the

Northwest Frontier (qq.v.); the Pakistan People's Party dominated the local councils in rural Sindh (q.v.), while the Muhajir Qaumi Mahaz (MQM) (q.v.) triumphed in Karachi and had a strong presence in Hyderabad (q.v.), Sindh's second largest city. Tribal *maliks* (chiefs) continued to hold rural Balochistan (q.v.) in their grip. The 1991 elections returned a member of the Muhajir Qaumi Mahaz as mayor of Karachi, whereas the mayors of Lahore, Rawalpindi, and Faisalabad (qq.v.) were from the Muslim League.

The local councils elected in 1991 were dissolved in July 1993 by the caretaker government of Moeen Qureshi (q.v.). In a landmark decision given by the Lahore High Court in the spring of 1996, the dissolution of the local councils by Qureshi was declared to be an unconstitutional act. The Court instructed the government to restore the councils dissolved in 1993. A day after the decision was announced, however, the Punjab Provincial Assembly, acting under the direction of Prime Minister Benazir Bhutto (q.v.), passed an act dissolving the resurrected local councils.

LOCAL COUNCILS. In 1978 the government of President Zia ul-Haq (q.v.) adapted and simplified the system of Basic Democracies (BDs) (q.v.) introduced by the administration of President Ayub Khan (q.v.) in 1962. Unlike the BD structure that had interlocking councils at several levels, the system introduced by Zia had only two tiers in both the rural and urban areas. Union councils and town committees constituted the lowest rung of the system as they had in the BD structure. The *zila* (district) council in the rural areas, municipal committees in medium-sized towns, and corporations in large cities constituted the second tier. All local council members were directly elected by the people; the chairpersons of the local bodies were not directly elected but were chosen by the members of the councils. Elections to the local councils were to be held every four years. Having created the system, Zia, however, was in no great hurry to hold elections.

◠ **M** ◠

MADRASAS. *Madrasas*—the word derives from Arabic and means schools—have always played an important role in providing education in Muslim societies. Some of them have been operating in South Asia for decades and have educated hundreds of thousands of students. Soon after he took over the reins of government in Pakistan in 1977, however, President Zia ul-Haq (q.v.) began an Islamization program that created a highly supportive environment for the growth of madrasa education. Not only did the state look with favor on the style of instruction the madrasas provided, it was prepared to fund them by using a significant part of the accumulated resources of the *zakat* (q.v.) fund. The number of madrasas operating in the country during Zia's 11-year (1977–88) rule increased significantly. The madrasas filled an important gap in such areas as the tribal districts of Balochistan and the Northwest Frontier Province (qq.v.), where the state had not set up its own schools.

Madrasas in Balochistan and the Northwest Frontier acquired a new significance with the Soviet Union's invasion of Afghanistan. Both the leadership in Pakistan that aided the Afghan mujahideen in their struggle against the Soviet Union as well as the mujahideen themselves gave a religious color to their efforts. In the minds of many Muslim communities all over the world, the struggle against the Soviet occupation of Afghanistan was a *jihad* (holy war) against the infidel. As such Afghanistan attracted a large number of Muslim fundamentalists who fought alongside the mujahideen. This form of international support also influenced the type of education that was provided to the Afghan refugees in the camps located in the northwestern parts of Pakistan. A large number of madrasas were set up to educate the refugees from Afghanistan.

The departure of the Soviet troops from Afghanistan did not end the involvement of the Pakistani madrasas in Afghan affairs. The most vivid illustration of this was the appearance of *taliban* (q.v.)—an Arabic word meaning students—who were able to conquer most of the Afghan territory within a few months. A large number of taliban was the product of madrasas in the Northwest Frontier Province of Pakistan. The taliban success in Afghanistan further increased the power, prestige, and importance of the madrasas in Pakistan. They were now significant not only as institutions that provided education, they also began to acquire considerable political importance.

MAHMUD, MASOOD. *See* FEDERAL SECURITY FORCE.

MAMDOT, NAWAB IFTIKHAR HUSAIN KHAN OF (1905–1969). Iftikhar Husain Khan was born in Mamdot, in the part of Punjab (q.v.) that served as the cultural and linguistic boundary between Punjab and the United Provinces (today's Uttar Pradesh) of British India. He migrated to Pakistan in 1947 and became the first chief minister of Pakistan's Punjab, appointed to the position by Muhammad Ali Jinnah and Liaqat Ali Khan (qq.v.). He resigned in 1949 and in 1950, he left the Muslim League (q.v.) to form a party of his own, the Jinnah Muslim League. He came back to the Muslim League in 1953 and was rewarded by Governor-General Ghulam Muhammad (q.v.), who appointed him governor of Sindh (q.v.) province. Mamdot held this position for two years but left in 1955 after Ghulam Muhammad departed from the political scene. After Ghulam Muhammad's departure, Mamdot was once again back in the political wilderness. He reappeared later during the early years of the Ayub Khan (q.v.) period (1958–69) when he joined hands with a number of other veteran Muslim Leaguers to convene a meeting to express support for the military leader. The Convention Muslim League (q.v.) was the product of these efforts and Mamdot became its deputy leader. He died in Lahore (q.v.) in 1969.

MANDAL, JAGENDRA NATH (1892–1962). Jagendra Nath Mandal was the only prominent non-Muslim politician to support the demand for the creation of a separate homeland for the Muslims of British India. He was a lawyer from Bengal and belonged to one of the "untouchable castes"—the "scheduled castes" (q.v.)—as the British preferred to label them. He was inducted in the "interim Cabinet" formed by Lord Louis Mountbatten (q.v.) in 1946 to prepare the transition to Indian independence. He joined the Cabinet as one of the five members representing the Muslim League and was given the portfolio of law. Muhammad Ali Jinnah's (q.v.) decision to include Mandal in the Cabinet scored an important tactical point as the All-India Congress contingent included a prominent Muslim, Maulana Abul Kalam Azad.

Pakistan's first Constituent Assembly (q.v.) came into being on August 10, 1947, four days before the country gained independence. Mandal was called on to chair the first session at which Jinnah was elected the president. For three years, from August 1947 to September 1950, Mandal served as minister in a series of Cabinets that took office in Karachi (q.v.), Pakistan's first capital. In September 1950 Muhammad Ali Bogra (q.v.), the second Bengali to become prime minister, dropped Mandal from the cabinet. Disappointed by this move, Mandal chose not to stay on in Karachi or go back to East Pakistan. Instead he migrated to India, where he died.

MANGLA DAM, THE. The Mangla Dam on the Jhelum River was built as part of the Indus Waters Treaty (q.v.) between India and Pakistan. It was constructed in the early 1960s by a consortium of American companies that worked under the supervision of the Water and Power Development Authority (WAPDA) (q.v.). The dam is 3,500 meters (11,000 feet) long and has an "above river" height of 119 meters. Including the power house and other ancillary works; the dam cost $540 million to build. It is built of rock and sand and has one giant spillway that operates during the flood season. The lake formed by the dam covers an area of 160 square kilometers and initially stored 4.75 million acre-feet of water. A canal takes off from the left side of the river at Mangla and transfers water into Chenab to compensate Chenab for the water it lost to India by way of a dam in its upper reaches. The Mangla dam also generates electricity. As of 1996 the dam's powerhouse had the capacity to generate 1,000 megawatts of electricity.

MARTIAL LAW OF 1953, THE. In 1953 a number of religious leaders decided to take advantage of the political turmoil in Pakistan to press their campaign against the Ahmadiya (q.v.) community. Their aim was to persuade the government of Prime Minister Khawaja Nazimuddin to declare the Ahmadiyas to be outside the pale of Islam. Nazimuddin's government had already been weakened by its inability to control the province of Punjab (q.v.). The religious leaders—in particular those active in the Jamaat-e-Islami (q.v.)—decided that the conflict between the central government and the government in Punjab provided them with a good opportunity to mount an agitation against the Ahmadiyas. Once the agitation was started, however, it got out of hand, particularly in the large cities of Punjab, where the crowds turned violent. The mounting violence in the cities of Punjab persuaded Governor-General Ghulam Muhammad (q.v.) to call in the army to restore law and order. Punjab was put under martial law with Lieutenant General Azam Khan (q.v.) as the martial-law administrator. The proclamation introducing martial law in Punjab was issued by the governor-general on March 6, 1953. Punjab was to stay under martial law for 69 days; martial law was lifted on May 14, 1953.

MARTIAL LAW, THE FIRST. Pakistan's first general martial law was imposed on October 7, 1958 by Governor-General Iskander Mirza (q.v.). The proclamation issued by the governor-general abrogated the Constitution of 1956 (q.v.), dissolved the National and Provincial Assemblies, and dismissed the government of Prime Minister Feroze Khan Noon (q.v.). All political parties were banned. Twenty days later, Ayub Khan (q.v.) sent President Iskander Mirza out of office and assumed the position himself. The first martial law remained in force for 1,339 days. It was lifted on June 8, 1962 with the promulgation of the Constitution of 1962 (q.v.).

MARTIAL LAW, THE SECOND. Pakistan's second general martial law was imposed on March 29, 1969 when President Muhammad Ayub Khan (q.v.) was persuaded to resign by the commander in chief of the army, General Yahya Khan (q.v.). Yahya put the country under martial law, and appointed himself president and chief martial-law administrator. The second martial law remained in force even after the resignation of President Yahya Khan on December 20, 1971. On the same day Zulfikar Ali Bhutto (q.v.) became president and chief martial-law administrator. President Bhutto kept the martial law in place for four more months. He lifted the martial law on April 21, 1972, when an interim constitution was promulgated. The second martial law remained in place for 1,020 days.

MARTIAL LAW, THE THIRD. Pakistan's third—and longest lasting—general martial law was imposed by General Zia ul-Haq (q.v.) on July 5, 1977. Although the National and Provincial Assemblies were dismissed, the Constitution of 1973 (q.v.) was not abrogated. It was merely suspended during the life of the martial law. General Zia ul-Haq retained Fazal Elahi Chaudhry as president, appointing himself the chief martial law administrator. Return to civilian rule under the constitution of 1973 was promised in 90 days after which the military said it would go back to the barracks. The chief justices of the four provincial high courts were appointed governors of the provinces. It was only in September 1978, 15 months after the country was brought under the rule of the military, that Zia's military shed its civilian clothes. Zia ul-Haq became president and replaced the provincial governors with army generals. Martial law lasted for 3,100 days. It was lifted on December 30, 1985 when Muhammad Khan Junejo (q.v.) was appointed prime minister. Zia ul-Haq stayed on as president, however, and retained the powerful position of chief of Army Staff.

MASHRIQI, ALLAMA INYATULLAH KHAN (1888–1963). Allama Inyatullah Khan Mashriqi was one of the more colorful and eccentric political figures of Muslim India. He graduated in mathematics from Cambridge University in England. On returning from Cambridge, he joined the Indian Educational Service and rose to become principal of Islamia College, Peshawar (q.v.). Islam had a strong presence in both Peshawar and Islamia College, the city's most prominent educational institution. It was during his stay in Peshawar that Mashriqi decided to devote his life to improving the economic well-being of the Muslims of India.

Mashriqi decided to resign from the Indian Educational Service and joined the Khilifat movement—an effort made by the Muslims of British India to provide assistance to the Ottoman Turks. After the Khilifat movement collapsed, he founded his own party, the Khaksars (q.v.), or the "humble ones." The Khaksars was a paramilitary organization; as such it was looked on with disfavor by the British administration in India. Like a number of other Islamic scholars, Mashriqi also believed that the best way to help the Muslims of British India was not to create a separate homeland for them but to improve the economic and social conditions of Muslims the world over, including those living in all parts of British India. Accordingly, he did not support the idea of Pakistan. Once Pakistan came into being, however, he brought his followers to the new country and began to work for the establishment of an Islamic order. He founded the Islamic League but the party attracted little support and Mashriqi became politically irrelevant. He was largely ignored by the new leaders of Pakistan.

MASIH, IQBAL (1979–1995). Pakistan's use of child-bonded labor in industries such as carpet weaving was brought to light in a vivid way in early 1995 by the murder near Lahore (q.v.) of Iqbal Masih, a spokesman for the Bonded Labor Liberation Front (BLLF) (q.v.). Masih himself had worked in the carpet industry. He was sold into bonded labor by his mother when he was only 10 years old. Chained to the loom on which he worked, he came to the attention of the BLLF when its representatives visited the village in which he was working. Taken to Lahore, he received some education in a special school run by the organization and then went on to become an untiring and eloquent spokesman for the organization. In 1994 he received the Reebok Foundation award for his long-time crusade against bonded labor. He was also awarded a fellowship by Brandeis University in the United States.

While preparing to leave for the United States, Iqbal Masih was murdered in his village near Mureedke, a town 25 kilometers north of Lahore and well known for its carpet industry. The murder was widely publicized in the West by the BLLF and led to the suspension of carpet imports from Pakistan by a number of Western countries, including Australia, Austria, and Sweden. An impression was created that Iqbal Masih had been killed by the representatives of the carpet industry, an accusation that was vehemently denied by carpet makers. After a detailed investigation carried out by its staff, the Human Rights Commission of Pakistan came to the conclusion that the carpet industry was not involved in Masih's murder; rather the killing was an act of random violence. At the same time the government ordered a judicial inquiry into the murder; a commission was set up under the chairmanship of a judge of the Lahore High Court to investigate the circumstances that led to the killing of Iqbal Masih. But the murder and the coverage it received in the Western media achieved what Iqbal Masih had set out to do: to inform the world that a great deal of carpet weaving in Pakistan is done on hand looms that involves children working in inhuman circumstances.

MATERNAL MORTALITY. Pakistan has a very high rate of maternal mortality, estimated by the World Bank (q.v.) at 600 for every 100,000 live births in 1980. Although the rate is considerably less than that for some of the African countries, Pakistan's performance is poor compared to that of several Asian countries. The rate for India is estimated at 500, for the Philippines at 80, and for China at only 44. Maternal deaths occur for a combination of reasons: frequent births, births at a very early age, or at a very late age. In countries with a high incidence of maternal deaths, the period between a woman's first pregnancy and her last may span more than half her lifetime. Pakistan's failure to address this problem reflects the failure of policy in a number of areas. It has still to launch an effective family-planning program; the access to family-planning services is limited to a very small number of women. No attempt has been made to deal with the issue of poor female health in a comprehensive way. Finally, the social status of women remains very low. *See also* Women.

MAUDUDI, MAULANA ABUL ALA (1903–1979). Maulana Abul Ala Maududi started his public career when he was only 24 years old. He published a collection of essays entitled *Al-Jihad fi al-Islam* ("Jihad in Islam") that caused a stir among Islamic scholars. In 1933 he took over as editor of a monthly magazine, *Tarjuman al-Quran.* The magazine offered an interpretation of the Koran that emphasized that Islam as revealed to Muhammad, its prophet, did not draw a distinction between the spiritual and the temporal worlds. In 1941 Maududi decided to enter politics by establishing the Jamaat-e-Islami (JI) (q.v.) (the Party of Islam). For six years, however, from 1941 to 1947, Maududi and the JI opposed Muhammad Ali Jinnah (q.v.), his All-India Muslim League (q.v.), and their demand for the creation of Pakistan, a homeland for the Muslim population of British India.

Maududi's opposition to the idea of Pakistan was based on the belief that nation states could not be reconciled with the concept of the Muslim *ummah* (community) that included all Muslims. The *ummah* could not be divided by borders that separated nation-states. Once Pakistan was born, Maududi decided to move to the new country and established himself and the JI in Lahore (q.v.). Once in Pakistan, he turned his attention to creating an Islamic state in the country created by Jinnah and the Muslim League. Maududi's program consisted of two parts. First, he wished to define strictly the meaning of being a Muslim, excluding all those who deviated even slightly from subscribing to what he defined as the basic tenets of Islam. Second, he wanted Pakistan to adopt an Islamic political system rather than the systems borrowed from the West.

Maududi's first serious confrontation with the state of Pakistan came in 1953 when he led a movement against the Ahmadiya (q.v.) community. The movement turned violent and martial law (q.v.) had to be imposed before law and order was restored in the country. A military court sentenced Maududi to death but the sentence was later reduced. Maududi had to wait more than 20 years before the Ahmadiyas were declared to be non-Muslims. This action was taken in 1974 by the administration of Prime Minister Zulfikar Ali Bhutto (q.v.). It was during the early years of the regime of President Zia ul-Haq (q.v.) that Maududi's views had the greatest impact on Pakistan. Zia made several attempts to introduce Islam into the country's political and economic structures. Although Zia was not successful in the area of politics, he introduced a number of Islamic financial instruments. These included the imposition of taxes such as *zakat* and *ushr* (qq.v.).

MEMON, JUSTICE BACHAL. Justice Bachal Memon was a member of the Sindh (q.v.) Chief Court (now the Sindh Court) bench that heard the case filed by Maulvi Tamizuddin (q.v.) in 1954 against the dismissal of the constituent assembly by Governor-General Ghulam Muhammad (qq.v.). The governor-general had taken this action in order to preempt the Constituent Assembly from limiting the powers that were given to him by the India Independence Act of 1947 (q.v.). The Sindh Chief Court not only admitted the case against the governor-general, it went on to declare the governor-general's dismissal of the assembly as unconstitutional. This was one of the rare occasions that Pakistan's judiciary (q.v.) was to act totally independent of the executive. The Sindh Court's judgment was written by Justice Bachal Memon but, on appeal by the government, was overturned by the federal court presided over by Chief Justice Muhammad Munir (q.v.).

MILITARY, THE. As with other things, Pakistan also had to carve out its military from what remained of the British Indian army after the end of World War II. It was not an exceptionally difficult task as Muslim representation in the force went well beyond their share in the Indian population. Most of the serving Muslims opted to join the Pakistan army, navy, and air force. Muhammad Ali Jinnah (q.v.), for want of physical space in Karachi (q.v.), the capital of the new country, chose to locate the army headquarters in Rawalpindi (q.v.), a British garrison town in northern Punjab. The air force was found a place in Peshawar (q.v.), and the headquarters of the navy was located in Karachi. Although Pakistan was able to attract enough soldiers to serve in the military, it was short of senior officers. Accordingly, the first generation of commanders of the three services were British. It was only in 1951 that a Pakistani—General Muhammad Ayub Khan (q.v.)—was appointed to head the army. Ayub Khan would not have been appointed to this job in 1951 had two senior officers not been killed in an air crash in 1950.

The military establishment was still in the process of settling down when Pakistan fought the First Indo–Pakistan War in 1948–49 (q.v.) over the state of Kashmir (q.v.). The war was inconclusive as Pakistan was not able to obtain by force what it had not succeeded in getting by persuasion. The ruler of Kashmir, after hesitating for a while, opted to take his state into India leaving behind a small sliver that Pakistan had occupied. The first war with India left a deep impression on Pakistan's military leadership. It realized that it had to quickly equip itself with modern weapons in order to deal with the Indian threat. This realization led to the development of a close relationship between the defense establishments of Pakistan and the United States. Prodded by Ayub Khan, Pakistan signed a defense agreement with Washington that provided access to American weapons and technical assistance. By allowing Ayub Khan a great deal of autonomy, the politicians laid the ground for the imposition of martial law in October 1958. Ayub Khan appointed himself martial-law administrator and president, thus inaugurating military rule of the country that, with one brief interruption, lasted for four decades.

The interruption in military rule occurred in 1971 when General Yahya Khan (q.v.), Pakistan's second military president, was forced out of office by his younger colleagues following the defeat of the army in East Pakistan in the Second Indo–Pakistan War (q.v.). Zulfikar Ali Bhutto (q.v.) succeeded Yahya and governed for less than six years. He was removed from office in July 1977 by the chief of the Army Staff, General Zia ul-Haq (q.v.). Zia was Pakistan's third military president and ruled for a little over 11 years.

Even when the military establishment finally surrendered power to politicians in 1988, after Zia was killed in an aircrash, it retained considerable influence over decision-making. This was exercised through an informal arrangement that was given the name of the "troika" (q.v.). This arrangement was put together in December 1988 when Benazir Bhutto (q.v.) was invited to become prime minister provided she consulted President Ghulam Ishaq Khan and General Aslam Beg (qq.v.) on all important matters. In January 1997 President Farooq Leghari (q.v.) formalized this arrangement by appointing a 10-member Council for Defense and National Security (CDNS) (q.v.). The military was represented by the chairman of the Joint Chiefs of Staff as well as by the chiefs of the three forces.

There was some diminution in the political influence of the military when the elections of 1997 resulted in a landslide in favor of Mian Nawaz Sharif's Pakistan Muslim League (qq.v.). Sharif became prime minister; although he did not dissolve the CDNS, he did not summon it for consultation during the first 26 months of his second tenure as prime minister. The political equation may change following the testing of nuclear bombs by India in May 1998 and the decision taken by Pakistan to test its own bombs a few days after the explosions set off by India. In 1998 Pakistan had some 540,000 persons in uniform and spent more that 6.5 percent of its gross domestic product on the military. *See also* India–Pakistan Relations; Indo–Pakistan Nuclear Arms Race; Martial Law of 1953, The; Martial Law, The First; Martial Law, The Second; Military and the Economy.

MILITARY AND THE ECONOMY. A dozen or so military officers have made important contributions to Pakistan's economy. These officers belonged to three categories. The first group included the three commanders in chief of the Pakistan army—Generals Ayub Khan, Yahya Khan, and Zia ul-Haq (qq.v.). All three became president after staging successful military coup d'etats against civilian governments. As presidents, all three left a deep impression on the economy.

The second category was made up of the officers who were assigned important political positions by the country's three soldier presidents and, from these positions, made singular contributions to the development of the economy. This category included Lieutenant Generals Wajid Ali Burki and Azam Khan (qq.v.), Air Marshal Nur Khan, and Admiral Abul Ahsen. Burki and Azam were the members of the military Cabinet that took office after Ayub Khan assumed political control in October 1958. Azam Khan went on to become the governor of East Pakistan, whereas Burki was appointed special assistant to the president after the adoption of the constitution of 1962 (q.v.). Air Marshal Nur Khan and Admiral Abul Ahsen were the members of the martial-law government that assumed office after Yahya Khan's coup of March 1969. A few months later, Nur Khan was appointed governor of West Pakistan while Ahsen was sent to East Pakistan as the province's governor.

The third category consists of the people who were assigned important administrative and economic positions because of their technical competence. Lieutenant Generals Saeed Qadir (q.v.) and Zahid Ali Akbar Khan and Admiral Khalid Janjua belonged to this category. Saeed Qadir and Khalid Janjua were appointed Cabinet ministers by President Zia ul-Haq and made responsible for the portfolios of production and agriculture, respectively. After retiring from the army, Zahid Khan, an engineer, served as the chairman of Water and Power Development Authority (q.v.) for five years.

MILLAT PARTY (MP). The Millat Party was launched by Farooq Ahmad Khan Leghari (q.v.) on August 14, 1998, Pakistan's 51st birthday. Leghari, as president, had worked closely with the senior leaders of Pakistan's main parties, the Pakistan Muslim League (PML) and the Pakistan People's Party (PPP) (qq.v.). This experience persuaded him that neither party could be expected to provide good and honest government to the citizens of Pakistan. Before inaugurating the party, Leghari had criticized both Benazir Bhutto and Nawaz Sharif (qq.v.) and claimed that as prime ministers they had used public resources for personal gains. He was convinced that people, in particular those living in the rapidly growing towns and those in the country, were now looking for a third political option. The Millat Party was designed to appeal to these people.

The inaugural session of the party was attended by more than 500 persons from all provinces of Pakistan. Leghari promised a new form of federalism in which the provinces would be granted a great deal of autonomy to manage their affairs. He also indicated that the party's leadership would be democratically elected, something that had not been done by the PML and the PPP. After launching the party, Leghari began touring the country on a campaign to win support for the new organization. *See also* Leghari, Sardar Farooq Ahmad Khan.

MINTO-MORLEY REFORMS. *See* GOVERNMENT OF INDIA ACT OF 1909.

MISSILES. In the 1990s both India and Pakistan, having made advances in the field of nuclear development, began to concentrate their attention and resources on the development of missiles. India's efforts were largely indigenous, supported by its scientific establishment and local industry. Pakistan started work in the 1980s on the development of the Hatf series of missiles but also seems to have relied on a considerable transfer of technology from China. There was a great deal of concern that China may have provided Pakistan with the wherewithal to manufacture the M11 missile. In 1996, India successfully test-fired the Prithvi (q.v.), a surface-to-surface missile with a range of 150–250 kilometers. India also let it be known that work was proceeding on the development of the much longer ranged Agni, which could travel 2,000 kilometers. In 1998 Pakistan announced the successful test of the Ghauri, a medium-range missile with a range of 1,500 kilometers.

The missile race between the two countries took a serious turn when, on May 11, 1998, India announced the successful testing of three nuclear bombs at a site close to the Pakistani border. A few days later, Athal Bihari Vajpay, the Indian prime minister announced that his country was working on the development of nuclear weapons that could be deployed on medium- and long-range missiles. Pakistan followed with its own tests on May 28 and 31 and also announced that it was preparing to arm its missiles with nuclear weapons. *See also* Indo–Pakistan Nuclear Arms Race.

MOENJODARO. Moenjodaro, or the "mound of the dead," was excavated in 1922 by Sir John Marshall, a British archaeologist. It is one of the 400 cities that are said to have flourished in the Indus plain some 4,000 years ago. The Indus civilization represented by Moenjodaro existed at the same time as the civilizations of Egypt and Mesopotamia. Moenjodaro has buildings that date back more than 4,000 years, to 2,500 B.C. The Indus River was the main transportation highway that linked the cities of the empire of which Moenjodaro was a part. The other main urban areas of the period were Harapa in Punjab (q.v.) on the banks of the River Ravi and an unexcavated city on the banks of the River Ghaggar, also in Punjab. The Indus cities traded actively with the cities in Egypt and Mesopotamia exporting cotton (*sindu* in Mesopotamia and *sindon* in Greek) in exchange for some perishable commodities. The cities of the Indus plain practiced a simple religion before the arrival of Buddhism. Moenjodaro was abandoned in about 1,500 B.C. after being overrun by the Aryans who came into India from Europe and established their dominion over the subcontinent in second-century B.C.

MONEM KHAN, ABDUL (1899–1971). Abdul Monem Khan belonged to the Mymensingh district of Bengal. He was born in 1899 and joined the Muslim League (q.v.) in 1935. He became a member of the Constituent Assembly (q.v.) when it was reconstituted in 1954. He was elected to the National Assembly in 1962 as a member from East Pakistan. He was appointed minister of health, labor, and social welfare in 1962, succeeding Lieutenant General Wajid Ali Burki (q.v.).

Later in 1962 President Ayub Khan (q.v.) picked Abdul Monem Khan to succeed another general and close associate, Lieutenant General Azam Khan (q.v.). He stayed on as governor for seven years—the longest tenure in that job in the province's history. He lost his job only with the change in government in March 1969 when President Ayub Khan resigned and General Yahya Khan (q.v.) became president. His long and loyal service to Ayub Khan had not endeared Monem Khan to the nationalist elements in East Pakistan. They took their revenge in 1971, shortly after the Pakistani army moved against the Awami League (q.v.). He was assassinated by the members of the Mukti Bahini (q.v.), the Bengali freedom fighters.

MOUNTBATTEN, LORD LOUIS (1900–1979). Lord Louis Mountbatten was the last viceroy of British India and the first governor-general of independent India. He was appointed viceroy in 1946 by the Labour government of Prime Minister Clement Attlee and given the mandate to guide India toward independence. Soon after arriving in India, he developed a warm relationship with Jawaharlal Nehru, a prominent leader of the Indian National Congress (q.v.). He was, however, cool toward Muhammad Ali Jinnah (q.v.). He was reluctant to agree to the partition of India. He told his biographers that had he known about Jinnah's sickness, he could have avoided partitioning India by waiting for his death. Once having accepted the Muslim demand for an independent homeland, he let it be known that he wished to be appointed governor-general of both independent India and Pakistan. Jinnah refused to accommodate him and chose to become the first governor-general of Pakistan himself. The Muslim League (q.v.) leadership suspected Mountbatten's hand in drawing the line that separated Indian and Pakistani Punjabs (q.v.). The demarcation was unfavorable for Pakistan since it provided access to India to the Muslim majority state of Kashmir (q.v.).

MOVEMENT FOR THE RESTORATION OF DEMOCRACY (MRD). The Movement for the Restoration of Democracy was launched in February 1981 to put pressure on the military government of President Zia ul-Haq (q.v.) to hold elections and bring back democracy to the country. The movement was joined by 11 political parties: the Awami Tehrik, the Jamiatul-Ulemai Islam (JUI) (q.v.), the National Awami Party (NAP) (q.v.) (Pakhtunkhawa group), the National Democratic Party (NDP), the Pakistan Mazdoor Kisan Party, the Pakistan Muslim League (PML) (q.v.) (Khairuddin group), the Pakistan National Party, the Pakistan People's Party (PPP) (q.v.), the Qaumi Mahaz-i-Azadi, and the Tehrik-e-Istiqlal (q.v.). The MRD went to work immediately after it was launched. A campaign was started in February 1981 and seemed to be gaining momentum but suffered a serious setback when a group of terrorists led by Murtaza Bhutto (q.v.), the son of Zulfikar Ali Bhutto (q.v.), hijacked a Pakistan International Airlines plane. The hijackers belonged to a group called Al-Zulfikar (q.v.). The plane was taken first to Kabul, Afghanistan, where the hijackers killed one passenger, an army officer from a well-known family from the Northwest Frontier Province (NWFP) (q.v.). The hijackers then forced the plane to go to Damascus, Syria. They released the passengers held hostage after President Zia ul-Haq agreed to set free scores of political prisoners. Although the PPP disassociated itself from Al-Zulfikar, the MRD was not able to recover from the incident.

The MRD launched another campaign in the summer of 1983, this time under the direction of Ghulam Mustafa Jatoi (q.v.), an associate of Zulfikar Ali Bhutto. The movement did not spread beyond Sindh (q.v.); in Sindh, its supporters were involved in an number of bloody clashes with the police. The campaign was called off after the loss of hundreds of lives and after its organizers were convinced that the government of Zia ul-Haq was not prepared to yield ground. The MRD remained dormant for five years, not able to come up with an effective strategy for challenging the Zia administration. It was dissolved after the elections of October 1988, which saw the return of PPP to power under Benazir Bhutto (q.v.).

MUBASHIR HASAN, DR. (1920–). Mubashir Hasan, an engineer who had a flair for politics, was one of the founding fathers of the Pakistan People's Party (PPP). The first PPP convention was held in the front yard of his modest home in Gulberg, Lahore (q.v.). He made significant contributions to the party's Foundation Papers, which firmly laid down the socialist road the PPP was to take if it ever came to political power. Dr. Hasan won a National Assembly seat from Lahore in the elections held in 1970 (q.v.) and was given the important portfolio of finance when Zulfikar Ali Bhutto (q.v.) was invited by the military to form a civilian government in December 1971.

Dr. Mubashir Hasan had a significant impact on economic policymaking. His influence was felt in the government's decision to nationalize large-scale industries in January 1972, to extend nationalization to the commercial banking industry in January 1974, to provide a generous compensation package to industrial workers under the Labor Policy of 1972, and to bring the small-scale business and industrial sector under fiscal discipline. Most of these policies alienated powerful economic interests and led to an anti-Mubashir movement even within PPP circles. In order to placate these interests, Zulfikar Ali Bhutto removed Mubashir Hasan from his Cabinet in 1974, and asked him to devote his time to the affairs of the party. Mubashir's departure brought a nonideological slant to the policies of the Bhutto administration. Once he was out of office, Mubashir Hasan's influence steadily declined.

Mubashir Hasan tried to get close to Benazir Bhutto (q.v.), Zulfikar Ali Bhutto's daughter, after she returned to Pakistan to renew her battle against President Zia ul-Haq (q.v.) and reclaim her political mantle. But Ms. Bhutto was not prepared to give much political space to her father's associates. She discarded the "uncles" in favor of the younger members of the party. Like most of the "uncles"—including Mumtaz Bhutto, Ghulam Mustafa Jatoi (qq.v.), and Abdul Hafeez Pirzada—Mubashir Hasan remained on the margins of politics even after the return of the PPP, the party he had helped to found, to office in 1988 and again in 1993.

MUDIE, SIR FRANCIS. Sir Francis Mudie was appointed governor of Sindh (q.v.) province in January 1946. He was one of several British officials with whom Muhammad Ali Jinnah (q.v.) had developed a comfortable relationship. Sir Francis had endeared himself to Jinnah when he interpreted the inconclusive results of the Sindh provincial elections of 1946 in favor of the Muslim League (q.v.). Not taking heed of the advice he had received from the central government in New Delhi, he invited Hussain Hidayatullah of the Muslim League and a close associate of Jinnah, to become the province's prime minister. When the Hidayatullah ministry seemed about to collapse after the defection of several members from the Muslim League, Mudie dissolved the Provincial Assembly and appointed a "caretaker" government headed by the League. Jinnah paid back the debt when, after Pakistan had been established, he appointed Sir Francis Mudie as the first governor of Punjab (q.v.). Sir Francis remained in this position for two years. He resigned in 1949 and returned to England.

MUFTI MAHMUD, MAULANA (1909–1981). Mufti Mahmud was born in the Northwest Frontier Province (q.v.) of present-day Pakistan. He received his education in Islamic *madrasas* (q.v) (schools) run by the Deobandi *ulema* (scholars). He joined the order himself and by virtue of his learning earned the right to use the title of Maulana. His interest in politics took him into the Jamiatul-Ulemai-Islam (JUI) (q.v.) and he became the organization's president in the late 1960s. The JUI did well in the elections of 1970 (q.v.). In 1972, following the return of democracy, Maulana Mufti Mahmud was called to lead the coalition government formed in the Northwest Frontier Province by the JUI and the National Awami Party (NAP) (q.v.). The government was allowed to remain in office for only a few months. It was dismissed by the central government headed by Zulfikar Ali Bhutto (q.v.) on the ground of "anti-state activities." Following his death, his son, Maulana Fazlur Rahman (q.v.), succeeded him as the president of the JUI.

MUGHUL EMPIRE. The Mughul Empire lasted for more than three centuries, from 1526 when Babar, the first emperor, defeated Ibrahim Lodhi (the last Pathan ruler of Delhi) at the battle of Panipat to 1857 when the British formally proclaimed their dominion over India. The Mughuls not only controlled most of modern Bangladesh, India, and Pakistan, their domain also included Afghanistan (q.v.). The first six Mughul rulers left a lasting impression on the entire history of South Asia. They included Babar, the founder, who ruled from 1526 to 1530, Humayun (1530–1540 and 1555–1556), Akbar (1556–1605), Jahangir (1605–1627), Shahjahan (1627–1658), and Aurangzeb (1658–1707). The last emperor dissipated his energy in an effort to introduce Islam into the Indian society and also to expand his control over the southern areas of India. After his death, a string of weak rulers presided over the empire as the British gained more ground in India.

The long Mughul rule over India was to profoundly effect the lives of hundreds of millions Muslims living in the subcontinent of South Asia. By far, the most important consequences were political. Centuries of Muslim domination over India created a rift between the Muslim and Hindu communities that reverberates to this day. The demolition of the mosque at Ayodhya (q.v.) in 1991—the mosque called Babri was built by the first Mughul emperor—is one symptom of the resentment still felt by a large segment of the Hindu population. Also, the British treatment of the Mughul rulers and their court created a deep sense of frustration among the Muslims and laid the ground for the Muslim demand for the creation of Pakistan.

MUHAJIR QAUMI MAHAZ (MQM). The Muhajir Qaumi Mahaz was formed on March 18, 1984, with Altaf Hussain (q.v.) as its president. Hussain traces the origin of his organization to student politics, when he and his fellow *muhajir* (the term means "refugee," but in the context of politics in Pakistan came to be associated with the refugees who migrated to Pakistan from the Indian provinces of Uttar Pradesh, Bihar, and Delhi) students in Karachi University felt the need for a body to represent their interests. Accordingly, the All Pakistan Muhajir Students Organization (APMSO) (q.v.) was formed in 1978. The APMSO converted itself into a grassroots organization in the early 1980s.

The MQM played an important part in the ethnic riots that paralyzed large parts of Karachi (q.v.) during the winter of 1986–87. It was at that point that the leadership of the MQM decided to convert the MQM into a political party. The Karachi riots pitted the Pathan community in the city against the muhajirs, leaving hundreds of people dead and several Pathan and muhajir *muhallas* (neighborhoods) in ruin. The disturbances lent further strength to the MQM and moved the political spotlight from Karachi's old and established politicians to such political newcomers as Altaf Hussain.

The full political weight of the MQM was felt in the general elections of November 1988 (q.v.) when its candidates won 11 out of Karachi's 13

National Assembly seats. The MQM also won two seats in Hyderabad (q.v.), the second largest city in Sindh (q.v.). With 13 seats in a chamber of 207, the MQM became the third largest group in the National Assembly after the Pakistan People's Party (PPP) and Islami Jamhuri Itehad (qq.v.). It was the decision by the MQM to lend its support to the PPP that made it possible for Benazir Bhutto (q.v.) to become prime minister on December 2, 1988. The MQM withdrew its support from the PPP a few months later, however. This break with the Bhutto government led to an open confrontation in Karachi between the MQM activists and law-enforcement authorities. The MQM's relations with the authorities did not improve with the change in government in Islamabad (q.v.) following the dismissal of Bhutto as prime minister in August 1990. Another election in 1990 (q.v.) reconfirmed MQM's authority in the urban areas of Sindh.

In late 1992 Nawaz Sharif (q.v.), the new prime minister, called the army to assist the civil authorities in restoring law and order in Karachi. Bhutto was back in power in 1993 after yet another election in which the MQM retained its hold over Karachi and maintained some presence in Hyderabad. This time around, Bhutto increased the pressure on the MQM by giving extraordinary powers to the police and paramilitary forces to hunt down MQM activists. The result was the arrest of a very large number of MQM functionaries and the death of hundreds of them in encounters with the authorities. There was a high political cost to this approach but it brought peace to Karachi—1996 turned out to be the most tranquil year for the city in some time.

Bhutto's second dismissal in November 1996 and another general election in February 1997 (q.v.) resulted in the formation of a coalition between the MQM and the Muslim League (q.v.). As a result the MQM entered both the federal government as well as the Sindh provincial government. In an effort to enter the mainstream of Pakistani politics, the Muhajir Qaumi Mahaz changed the name of their movement to Muttahida Qaumi Movement (United National Movement). However, in 1998 MQM left the coalition government and went into opposition to Nawaz Sharif.

MUHAJIR QAUMI MAHAZ (HAQIQI). On June 19, 1992 the Muhajir Qaumi Mahaz (MQM) (q.v.) splintered into two groups, the original led by Altaf Hussain, the other by Afaq Ahmed (qq.v.). It was widely believed that this division was the consequence of the enormous amount of work done by the army intelligence agencies among the MQM members. The authorities, having convinced themselves that the MQM could not be destroyed by the use of force, decided to try and control it from within. But the split in the MQM did not diminish Altaf Hussain's popularity. If the aim was to bring peace to the troubled city of Karachi (q.v.) by creating a political force that could lead the city's people away from violence, that purpose also was not achieved. In fact, the creation of the MQM (Haqiqi) made Altaf Hussain even more popular among his followers. And, the arrival of a rival organization persuaded the original MQM to direct its wrath first against its own dissidents. What followed was a bloodbath of the type Karachi had not seen before. The new organization battled not only with its parent body, it also fought with the police and other "law and order" forces. This three-way conflict led to the killing of 1,800 persons in Karachi in 1995, the bloodiest year in the city's history. When the government in Islamabad (q.v.) finally sat down to negotiate with the MQM in early 1995, it invited Altaf Hussain's Group to the table. The Haqiqis were left out in the cold. The negotiations did not bridge the gap between the government of Benazir Bhutto and the MQM led by Altaf Hussain but they certainly alienated the Haqiqis. In 1997 the tension between the two branches of MQM flared up again and Karachi once again reverted to turbulence.

MUHAMMAD ALI, CHAUDHRI (1905–1985). Muhammad Ali was born in Jullundhur, a city in the northern part of what is now the Indian state of Punjab (q.v.). After gaining a master's degree in chemistry from Punjab University, Lahore (q.v.), Ali joined the Indian Audit and Accounts Service in 1928. In 1931 he was deputized by the government of India to serve as accountant general in the state of Bahawalpur. In 1935, after serving in Bahawalpur for four years, Muhammad Ali went to the central government in New Delhi and rose quickly in the department of finance. It was while serving as Additional Finance Secretary that he came to the attention of Muhammad Ali Jinnah (q.v.).

Muhammad Ali was appointed to advise Finance Minister Liaqat Ali Khan (q.v.) in the interim government formed in New Delhi in 1946. The British decision to accelerate their departure from India put an enormous administrative burden on the two designated successor governments of Pakistan and India. For Pakistan, a large portion of this burden fell on Muhammad Ali, who, as a member of the two-man steering committee of the Partition Council, was responsible for building Pakistan's administrative structure. After partition, Muhammad Ali moved to Karachi (q.v.), Pakistan's first capital, and was appointed secretary-general in the new administration. In October 1951, following the assassination of Prime Minister Liaqat Ali Khan, Muhammad Ali became Pakistan's second finance minister, succeeding Ghulam Muhammad (q.v.). In August 1955 he was called on by Governor-General Ghulam Muhammad to become Pakistan's fourth prime minister.

Muhammad Ali's main achievement as prime minister was to give Pakistan its first constitution—the Constitution of 1956 (q.v.). Pakistan, now declared a republic, chose Iskander Mirza (q.v.) as its first president; he, in turn, decided to strengthen his political base by overseeing the formation of a new political party, the Republican Party. Muhammad Ali refused to abandon the Muslim League (q.v.) and Iskander Mirza (q.v.) chose a more trusted associate to succeed him. After leaving the government Muhammad Ali also came to the conclusion that not much political life was left in the Muslim League. In 1957 he launched a new movement under the banner of Tehrik Istikham-i-Pakistan (Movement for the Preservation of Pakistan), which in 1958, merged with the Nizam-i-Islam Party. Muhammad Ali was elected the party's president.

In 1959 President Ayub Khan (q.v.) appointed a Constitution Commission to advise him on a new political structure for the country. Muhammad Ali wrote a long memorandum for the commission on the subject of democracy and its relevance for Pakistan. The memorandum was given wide circulation by the press and, consequently, won Muhammad Ali Ayub Khan's displeasure. In 1964, when the first presidential election was held under the Constitution of 1962 (q.v.), Muhammad Ali was active in organizing the Combined Opposition Party (COP) (q.v.) and in persuading Fatima Jinnah (q.v.) to challenge Ayub Khan at the polls. Later, in 1967, at the height of the political agitation that ultimately resulted in the resignation of Ayub Khan, Muhammad Ali played a central role in attempting to find a constitutional way out of the impasse that had developed between the president and the opposition.

Muhammad Ali did not expect that his efforts to restore democracy in the country would result in Pakistan's second military administration, civil war between East and West Pakistan, the breakup of Pakistan, and the emergence of East Pakistan as independent Bangladesh. He died in Lahore at age of 80.

MUJAHIDEEN. Mujahideen, or "freedom fighters," led the resistance to the occupation of Afghanistan by the troops of the Soviet Union. The Soviet occupation lasted for 10 years, from 1979 to 1989. The mujahideen, helped by Pakistan, Saudi Arabia, and the United States, were able to make the Soviet Union withdraw its troops from Afghanistan in early 1989. The Soviet defeat in Afghanistan contributed to its collapse two years later. The mujahideen did not fight as a unified force, however. They were divided into a number of factions, each led by a powerful warlord. The failure of the mujahideen leaders to work together after the withdrawal of the Soviet Union prolonged the war in Afghanistan for another 10 years and provided the opportunity for another group, the Taliban (q.v.), to conquer most of the country in the early 1990s.

MUJIBUR RAHMAN, SHEIKH (1921–1975). Sheikh Mujibur Rahman began to take an active interest in Muslim politics at a very early age. In 1940 he joined the Muslim Student's Federation, an arm of the All India Muslim League (q.v.). Soon after the establishment of Pakistan on August 14, 1947, he joined Hussain Shaheed Suhrawardhy (q.v.) in founding the Awami League (q.v.). Mujibur Rahman opposed the imposition of martial law by General Ayub Khan (q.v.) and was imprisoned by the military government. After the death in 1963 of Suhrawardhy, his political mentor, Mujibur was elected president of the Awami League. In 1964 he joined hands with the opposition leaders from West Pakistan to found the Combined Opposition Party (COP) (q.v.). The COP's main objective was to challenge Ayub Khan at the polls. Fatima Jinnah (q.v.), the COP's candidate, lost the election, however.

Mujibur Rahman offered his Six Point Program (q.v.) in 1966 in a meeting of the opposition parties held in Lahore (q.v.), West Pakistan. This was too large a dose of provincial autonomy for Ayub Khan to swallow. Even the leaders of West Pakistan, who otherwise opposed Ayub Khan, were troubled by the direction the East Pakistani leadership was taking under the guiding hand of Mujibur Rahman. He was arrested and charged with undermining the integrity of the state of Pakistan. The result was the Agartala Conspiracy Case. The case dragged on for several months. It was eventually overtaken by political developments, including the launching of a campaign against the government of Ayub Khan. The president decided to negotiate and as gesture of good will the Agartala Conspiracy against Mujibur Rahman was withdrawn.

In the elections of 1970 (q.v.)—the first to be held in Pakistan to directly elect the National Assembly—Mujib's Awami League won a decisive victory in East Pakistan. The party captured all but two seats from the eastern wing. The leaders of West Pakistan refused to hand over power to Mujib. The result was a brutal civil war between the Mukti Bahini (q.v.), Bengal's freedom fighters, and the Pakistan army. On December 16, 1971 the Pakistani army surrendered to a joint Indian and Mukti Bahini force and East Pakistan became the independent state of Bangladesh. Mujibur Rahman was still in a West Pakistani prison, however. Mujib was released in January 1972 and returned to Dacca, the capital of Bangladesh and was appointed prime minister—later president—of the new state. He was assassinated by a group of disgruntled army officers on August 15, 1975, along with his wife and several other members of his family. Four years later, Bhutto was to meet a similar fate at the hands of the army in Pakistan. *See also* Indo-Pakistan War of 1971.

MUKTI BAHINI. The Mukti Bahini—meaning "freedom fighters" in Bengali—was a paramilitary force organized to oppose the Pakistan army in East Pakistan. The Mukti Bahini surfaced following an action launched somewhat unexpectedly by the units of the Pakistani army stationed in East Bengal, then called East Pakistan. The Pakistani army began its operation on March 25, 1971 and arrested a large number of supporters of Mujibur Rahman (q.v.). Hundreds of people were killed. The Bengali members of the Pakistani army who managed to escape to India when the West Pakistanis began their operation formed the core of the Bengali force. India took the Mukti Bahini under its wing when it decided to aid the Bengalis in their struggle against West Pakistan. The Bengali militia entered East Pakistan along with the Indian forces and participated in the ceremony in which the commander of the Pakistani force surrendered to the Indians. Some members of the Mukti Bahini were later incorporated into the armed forces of independent Bangladesh, whereas others joined the civil service of the new state. *See also* Indo–Pakistan War of 1971.

MUNIR, CHIEF JUSTICE MUHAMMAD. Muhammad Munir was a lawyer from Punjab (q.v.) who gained prominence by publishing *Principles and Digest of the Law of Evidence.* The book appeared in 1936 and established Munir's reputation not only as a lawyer but also as a profound thinker on legal matters. He was appointed to the federal court of Pakistan soon after Pakistan became independent. After a few months on the bench he was appointed to head the court as the chief justice. When the Court was reconstituted as the Supreme Court of Pakistan following the adoption of the constitution of 1962 (q.v.), Muhammad Munir was appointed chief justice.

A number of landmark decisions were issued by the Supreme Court under the guidance of Chief Justice Muhammad Munir. These included the Usif Patel and Maulvi Tamizuddin (q.v.) cases, both of which were to have a profound impact on Pakistan's political development. In the Tamizuddin case, the court used the "doctrine of necessity" (q.v.) to endorse the dissolution of the Constituent Assembly by Governor-General Ghulam Muhammad (qq.v.). Chief Justice Munir headed several inquiry commissions, including the commission appointed by the governor-general to investigate the circumstances that led to the anti-Ahmadiya riots in 1953.

Justice Muhammad Munir retired from the Supreme Court in 1960 and was succeeded by Chief Justice A. R. Cornelius (q.v.). Munir wrote extensively after retirement; one of his books, *From Jinnah to Zia,* went into several printings. When the book was first published, his main argument ran counter to the one that was being espoused by President Zia ul-Haq (q.v.). Munir maintained in the book that Pakistan was not created to become an Islamic state. Its purpose, according to Muhammad Ali Jinnah (q.v.), the country's founder, was to establish a country from the Muslim community of India to be run as a modern democracy in which followers of all religions would have equal rights as citizens. *See also* Ahmadiyas, The; Munir Report, The.

MUNIR REPORT, THE. *The Report of the Court of Inquiry into the Punjab Disturbances of 1953* was published in 1954 and has come to be called the "Munir Report." The report is so named because the two-man Court of Inquiry appointed by the governor-general to investigate the government's handling of the anti-Ahmadiya riots was headed by Chief Justice Muhammad Munir (q.v.) of the Supreme Court. Justice Muhammad Rustam Kayani (q.v.) was the Court's other member. The report issued by the Court of Inquiry is important for two reasons. First, it offered an opinion on the role of religion in state and politics. Second, it advised the government on an appropriate role for the elitist Civil Service of Pakistan (CSP) in the country's economic and political development. *See also* Ahmadiyas, The; Munir, Chief Justice Muhammad.

MUSA, GENERAL (RETIRED) MUHAMMAD (1915–). Muhammad Musa was born in the province of Balochistan (q.v.) and joined the British Indian Army while still in his teens. He took part in the operations carried out by the British Indian Army from 1936 to 1939 in Wazirstan, in the northwest of India. Musa saw action in Africa during World War II. He rose quickly in the ranks of the new Pakistani army and became a two-star general in 1950, succeeding General Ayub Khan (q.v.) as the general commanding officer of the Army Garrison in East Pakistan. When, in 1951, Ayub Khan was appointed as the first Pakistani to command the Pakistani Army, General Musa was summoned back to Rawalpindi (q.v.) and appointed deputy chief of staff. In 1955 he became chief of staff of the army and when Ayub Khan put Pakistan under martial law, Musa was appointed commander in chief. He was the fourth person, but only the second Pakistani, to command the Pakistani army.

It was under General Musa's command that Pakistan fought its second war with India in September 1965. He retired from the army in October 1966, after having served for eight years as commander in chief. President Ayub Khan rewarded him for his loyal service by appointing him governor of West Pakistan. He held this position until March 1969. In January 1986 General Musa was recalled from retirement and appointed governor of Balochistan by Prime Minister Muhammad Khan

Junejo (q.v.). Musa was retained in this position when Benazir Bhutto (q.v.) became prime minister in December 1988, a position he held until the prime minister's dismissal in August 1990. *See also* Indo–Pakistan War of 1965.

MUSHARAF, PERVEZ (1943–). Lieutenant General Pervez Musharaf was appointed chief of Army Staff (COAS) in October 1998 following the resignation of Jehangir Karamat (q.v.), who left office after giving a speech at the Naval Staff College in Lahore in which he criticized the government of Prime Minister Mian Nawaz Sharif (q.v.) for failing to seriously address the country's many problems. Musharaf is the thirteenth person to command the Pakistani army. He is the second member of the muhajir community to lead the army.

MUSLIM LEAGUE, THE (1906–1958). The formation of the All-India Muslim League in 1906 established a political tradition in Muslim India that survives to this day in Pakistan. The tradition is to set up a political organization for the pursuit of narrowly defined political objectives. Once the objectives are achieved, the sponsoring organization tends to wither away. This was to be the fate of the Muslim League. The organization was to be transformed several times to pursue the issue of the day. It was also to fragment into factions that remained active for as long as the sponsoring person or group remained on the scene. The Pakistan Muslim League (q.v.) of the mid-1990s has little resemblance to the party that was created in 1906.

Founded in Dacca, Bengal, in December 1906 by Nawab Viqar ul-Mulk, the League's main objective was to get the British to accept that the political interests of the Muslim community did not always coincide with those of the majority Hindu community. The Hindu leadership was anxious to get the British to leave India; the League, on the other hand, wanted the British to prolong their stay if only to protect the minorities. The Muslim League remained a weak organization during the time that it failed to define a broad set of objectives that would win it the support of the diverse Indian Muslim community, in particular those who lived in the Muslim-majority provinces. It also needed a leader who could get the provincial Muslim leaders to accept the discipline of a national party. These two objectives were realized when Muhammad Ali Jinnah (q.v.) took over as president of the League in 1934. With Jinnah as its leader, the League found a good organizer; he was also respected for the selfless way in which he had served the interests of the Muslim community even when he was associated with the Indian National Congress (q.v.). Despite Jinnah's activism, however, the League did poorly in the provincial elections of 1937, especially in the Muslim-majority provinces in the northwest.

The Muslim League's 1940 annual session, held in Lahore (q.v.) on March 23, 1940, turned its fortune around. The assembled delegates approved the "Pakistan Resolution" (q.v.) demanding the creation of a separate homeland for the Muslims of British India. The resolution gave the League a tangible objective to pursue, which it did with remarkable tenacity unfamiliar to those who had observed the course of Indian Muslim politics. Within a few years of the passage of the Pakistan Resolution, the League was converted from a party of a few notables to one with a growing following. By 1944 the League had a membership of some three million people. It had begun to penetrate even the Muslim-majority provinces. In Bengal, the League claimed a membership of 500,000; Punjab and Sindh (qq.v.) had 200,000 members each. These successes were translated into electoral victories in 1946. The results of the provincial elections of 1946 surprised even the leaders of the League. Muhammad Ali Jinnah was now in the position to challenge the provincial leaders who had resisted his attempts to bring them and their provinces under the umbrella of the Muslim League. The provincial leaders read the tea leaves and several joined the party, whereas those who continued to resist—such as Khizar Hayat Tiwana (q.v.) of Punjab—were crushed by the League's steamroller. After the elections, the League and Muhammad Ali Jinnah were able to proclaim, with some justification, that they alone represented the interests of the Muslims of British India. First the British, and later the Indian National Congress, accepted this position and both agreed to the creation of Pakistan, an independent state for the Muslims of British India.

The question of the League's future arose as soon as the British announced the decision to leave their Indian domain in the hands of two successor states. Should the All-India Muslim League transform itself into the All-Pakistan Muslim League or should it be divided also into two parts, one for India and the other for Pakistan? Recognizing that independent India would continue to have a large Muslim minority, Jinnah and his associates decided in favor of two Leagues. The one for Pakistan was to function under Jinnah, whereas Nawab Ismail was to head the League in India.

With Pakistan achieved and Jinnah dead within a year of Pakistan coming into existence, the Muslim League lost its mission and its sense of direction. Liaqat Ali Khan's (q.v.) death in October 1951 dealt a further blow. In the provincial elections in East Bengal, the Muslim League suffered a humiliating defeat at the hands of the United Front (q.v.). In 1956, soon after Pakistan adopted its first constitution, President Iskander

Mirza (q.v.) formed the Republican Party, attracting a large number of Muslim Leaguers into the fold of the new organization. In September 1957 another tradition was broken. Hussain Shaheed Suhrawardhy (q.v.), who had been long gone from the Muslim League, was invited to form a government in Karachi (q.v.). He thus became the first non-Muslim Leaguer to become Pakistan's prime minister. The military takeover of October 1958 and the decision by President Muhammad Ayub Khan (q.v.) to ban all political parties finally killed the Muslim League.

MUSLIM LEAGUE AGRARIAN REFORM COMMITTEE, THE. See LAND REFORMS OF 1959.

MUTTAHIDA QAUMI MOVEMENT. See MUHAJIR QAUMI MAHAZ (MQM).

MUTTAHIDA SHARIAT MAHAZ (MSM). The Muttahida Shariat Mahaz, or the Joint Shariat Front, was formed in 1986 to work for the passage of the Shariat bill. The MSM's main support came from the Jamaat-i-Islami (q.v.) and the religious leaders of the Northwest Frontier Province (q.v.). It did not include the two Jamiats—the Jamiatul-Ulemai-Islam and the Jamiatul-Ulemai-Pakistan. In a big public rally held in Peshawar (q.v.) on February 6, 1987, the Mahaz issued an ultimatum to the government threatening direct action if it did not succeed in getting the National Assembly to pass the Shariat Bill. The Mahaz set Ramzan 27, 1407 A.H. as the deadline for the government, choosing a date on the Islamic calendar to signify the fortieth anniversary of Pakistan. The Peshawar meeting was described as the first large gathering of the ulemai Islam (Islamic scholars) in 66 years since the Allahabad meeting of 1920, called by the All-India Khilifat Conference. The Allahabad conference had endorsed the movement against the British and had decided to create a force of volunteers to help Turkey in its struggle against Great Britain.

The Mahaz's threat to launch a massive street campaign against the government of Prime Minister Muhammad Khan Junejo (q.v.) was not carried out even though the Shariat Bill was not enacted into law. The bill passed the Senate but remained under discussion in the National Assembly until its dismissal by President Zia ul-Haq (q.v.) in May 1988. The bill was finally approved by the National Assembly in 1991 when Mian Nawaz Sharif (q.v.) became prime minister. Its purpose secured, the MSM went out of business.

MUTINY, THE GREAT INDIAN. According to a celebrated phrase, much of the British Indian empire was acquired "in a fit of absence of mind." The British first came to India as traders in the early years of the seventeenth century, but through purchases, bribery, conquest, treaties with land owners and princes, and sheer intimidation, their domain over India kept expanding rapidly. By the middle of the nineteenth century, Great Britain controlled almost all of India either directly or as a result of having persuaded sometimes willing and sometimes reluctant princes to sign treaties of protection that effectively made them the subjects of India's new rulers.

A reaction came in 1857 in the form of a *sepoy* (enlisted men) mutiny. It was provoked by the introduction of a new kind of Enfield rifle (provided by the East India Company), which used ammunition in the form of cartridges that had to be greased not with vegetable oil, as was the case before this unfortunate innovation, but with animal fat. The fat provided to the *sepoys* came either from cows or from pigs—or at least so went the rumor. This offended both the Muslims, who considered pigs dirty and therefore forbidden to be used for food, and the Hindus, for whom the cow was a sacred animal. When 85 sepoys were thrown into jail for refusing to use the new cartridges, their enraged colleagues stormed the jail and launched the Great Indian Mutiny. A good deal of blood, both Indian and British, was to flow before the mutiny was brought under control. The British had to import troops from the northern areas of India—from Punjab and the Northwest Frontier (qq.v.)—before they were able to bring order back to the areas that had been affected by the uprising. Once law and order had been restored, the East India Company (q.v.) was dissolved and the government of Great Britain took over all responsibility for administering the Company's territories in India. Thanks to the Great Indian Mutiny, India formally, and from the perspective of the British, legally and constitutionally became a colony of Britain.

MUTUAL DEFENSE AGREEMENT (MDA). The Mutual Defense Agreement (MDA) was signed between Pakistan and the United States in 1954. General Muhammad Ayub Khan (q.v.), at that time commander in chief of the Pakistan army, was the main force in Pakistan for entering into this alliance with the United States. Pakistan entered into the agreement in order to help secure U.S. assistance in building its defenses against India. The United States was interested in obtaining the support of Pakistan in its effort to contain the spread of communism in Asia. The agreement led to the massive flow of military assistance from the Unites States, including the construction of two military bases (cantonments) in Kharian and Multan (q.v.). However, given the fact that the two countries had entirely different interests in entering into the MDA, it did not survive the war between India and Pakistan in September 1965. Pakistan believed that it was entitled to receive support from the United States during this difficult period; the United States, on the other hand, imposed an embargo on the export of military equipment to Pakistan, arguing that the MDA was aimed only at containing the spread of communism to Asia. *See also* South-East Asia Treaty Organization.

ᔛ **N** ᔛ

NADWAT AL-ULEMA (NU). Nadwat al-Ulema (the Council of Islamic Scholars), established in Lucknow, India, in 1893 was to have a profound influence on the umbrella of religious-school organizations founded in Pakistan. The NU continued to flourish even after the partition of British India and the loss of millions of Muslims to Pakistan from Uttar Pradesh, the home state of the organization. The organizations in Pakistan maintained strong links with the NU. In the 1990s the NU oversaw 60 affiliated schools, managed mostly by the graduates of its seminary in Lucknow. More than 13,000 students received education in these schools with a teaching body of some 3,300. The seminary in Lucknow had 2,000 students of whom 1,500 lived on campus.

NASRULLAH KHAN, NAWABZADA (1922–). Born in Muzaffargarh in south Punjab (q.v.), Nawabzada Nasrullah was one of the few politician from Punjab who did not join any one of the major political parties that were to dominate the political scene. He stayed away from the Unionist Party (q.v.), which launched scores of political careers before Pakistan was born. Nasrullah opted to work for the Ahrar party and supported its campaign against British rule. A number of Unionist politicians abandoned their party in favor of the Muslim League (q.v.) when they realized that Muhammad Ali Jinnah's (q.v.) demand for Pakistan would become a reality. Nasrullah Khan remained with the Ahrar and after Pakistan was born moved into the Awami League (q.v.) and became a close associate of Hussain Shaheed Suhrawardhy (q.v.), the party's founder and leader. The Awami League was to be the only large political organization Nasrullah Khan was associated with; he left the party when Mujibur Rahman (q.v.), the party's new head, put forward a "Six Point Program" (q.v.) for gaining autonomy for East Pakistan.

Nasrullah Khan was resolute in his opposition to the "militarization" of Pakistani politics, first under General Ayub Khan and later under Generals Yahya Khan and Zia ul-Haq (qq.v.). He was one of the principal architects of the Combined Opposition Party (q.v.), which was cobbled together in 1964 to fight Ayub Khan in the presidential election of

1964 and actively opposed Ayub Khan once again in 1967 when he, along with several other prominent leaders, launched a campaign to democratize the constitution of 1962 (q.v.). He cooperated with Zulfikar Ali Bhutto (q.v.) in giving Pakistan its most democratic constitution in 1973 (q.v.) but turned against the prime minister when he and several other opposition politicians believed that the prime minister had stolen the elections of 1977 by gross misuse of administrative power. Nasrullah Khan remained in opposition throughout President Zia ul-Haq's 11 years in power. He was one of the prominent figures associated with the Movement for the Restoration of Democracy (MRD) (q.v.). It was only toward the close of his political career that he chose to work for the government in power rather than against it. He supported the return of Benazir Bhutto (q.v.) to power in 1993 and was rewarded with the chairmanship of the Foreign Affairs Committee of the National Assembly.

NASIM WALI KHAN. Nasim Wali Khan, the wife of Abdul Wali Khan (q.v.), became politically active in the early 1990s following the withdrawal of her husband from the political scene on account of illness. She was appointed chairperson of the provincial branch of the Awami National Party (ANP) (q.v.) in which capacity she was active in the deliberations with Prime Minister Nawaz Sharif's Muslim League (qq.v.) on the issue of renaming the Northwest Frontier Province (q.v.) as Pakhtunkhawa.

NATIONAL AWAMI PARTY (NAP). The National Awami Party was founded by Maulana Abdul Hamid Khan Bhashani (q.v.) in the early 1950s. The left-of-center politics of the party attracted leaders and people from both East and West Pakistan. It was one of the few political parties that gained a sizable following in both parts of Pakistan. Over the years the NAP grew in influence in the smaller provinces of the western wing, in particular in the Northwest Frontier Province (NWFP) (q.v.). In the NWFP, Abdul Wali Khan (q.v.) led the provincial wing of the party for several years and saw it win enough seats in the elections of 1970 (q.v.) to be able to form a government in the province in 1972. In 1973, Prime Minister Zulfikar Ali Bhutto (q.v.) dismissed the NAP-led provincial governments in the NWFP and Balochistan (q.v.) and banned the party. The NAP was revived by Wali Khan and his associates in 1986 under the name of Awami National Party (q.v.). This decision was taken after President Zia ul-Haq (q.v.) agreed to restore political activity in the country.

NATIONAL COMMISSION ON AGRICULTURE (NCA). The National Commission on Agriculture was appointed by Prime Minister Muhammad Khan Junejo (q.v.) in 1986 under the chairmanship of Sartaj

Aziz (q.v.), minister of agriculture. The tradition of appointing commissions to make recommendations to the government on agricultural policy goes back more than a century. The NCA was the last of several such commissions. It presented its report to the government in March 1988. Its reach and recommendations were comprehensive in that it argued for the radical transformation of the agricultural sector. It was of the view that the way the sector was organized, it would not be able to realize its full economic potential. That potential was large but could only be achieved if the government was prepared to undertake some major changes in the way land was owned, water supplied, inputs marketed, surpluses sold, and taxes collected. The commission's report was made public only a few months before the government of Muhammad Khan Junejo was dismissed by President Zia ul-Haq (q.v.). In the political uncertainty in which Pakistan has functioned since that time no government has had the time or the inclination to think through the recommendations by the Commission. *See also* Agriculture.

NATIONAL DEFENSE COLLEGE (NDC). The National Defense College was established at Rawalpindi (q.v.) in 1972 to provide instruction to middle-level officials of the armed forces in military and social sciences. The college was housed on the premises once occupied by the National Assembly. The college offers two courses every year. A "War Course" is attended by the officers from all branches of the military and is focused principally on military matters. A "National Defense Course" also brings in middle-level officials from the federal secretariat who sit with military officers to be instructed in defense strategy. Giving a broader interpretation to "strategy," the course teaches economics and political science along with military strategy. At the end of each Defense Course, the students are required to present a "national strategy" to the college on a subject considered to be of vital interest to the country at that point in time. This paper is known to be read by the senior echelons of the military and is said to have influenced their policies on several occasions.

NATIONAL FINANCE COMMISSION AWARD (1991), THE FOURTH. The Constitution of 1973 (q.v.) showed some sensitivity to the need for an institutional arrangement for the distribution of financial and other resources among the provinces. It required the formation of two bodies for this purpose: a Council of Common Interests (CCI) to resolve all disputes among the provinces and a National Finance Commission (NFC) to distribute financial resources from the center to the provinces and to allocate them among the provinces on the basis of an agreed formula. Although the CCI was to be a "standing body" to be called into session by the prime minister whenever the need was felt for deliberations among the provinces, the NFC was to be convened every five years. The first NFC under the 1973 constitution was set up soon after the promulgation of the constitution and went on to announce its award in 1975. Two more commissions were formed, one in 1979 and the other in 1985, but neither was able to reach agreement over the distribution of resources among the provinces. The Fourth National Finance Commission was appointed by President Ghulam Ishaq Khan (q.v.) during the first administration of Prime Minister Benazir Bhutto (q.v.) (December 1988–August 1990). The Commission was not able to complete its work during Benazir Bhutto's tenure, however; it was reconstituted with the change in government and the appointment of Mian Nawaz Sharif (q.v.) as prime minister. The reconstituted commission announced its award on April 20, 1991.

The award took effect on July 1, 1991, the first day of the 1991–92 financial year. It made a number of changes in the country's fiscal system. For instance, it discontinued the practice of meeting the budgetary deficits of the provinces or requiring them to surrender their budgetary surpluses. All strategic projects executed in the provinces or any development activity undertaken on the directives of the president or prime minister were to be fully funded by the federal government. The award of the National Finance Commission, by making the provinces virtually autonomous in the fiscal field, was expected to have a profound developmental effect. For the first time in the country's history, it provided incentives to the provinces to use the tax authority available to them under the constitution to generate resources for their development. Also, by establishing the principle of payment of rent for the exploitation of natural resources, the award also set the stage for the construction of large hydroelectric projects in the upper reaches of the Indus. *See also* Indus Waters Treaty.

NATIONAL INDUSTRIAL COOPERATIVE FINANCE CORPO-RATION (NICFC). The National Industrial Cooperative Finance Corporation was established in 1964 in Lahore (q.v.) and was registered under the Punjab Cooperative Act of 1925. Its aim was to help its members, mostly the province's rural elite, to diversify into activities other than agriculture (q.v.). The institution grew rapidly in the latter part of the 1960s when the "green revolution" (q.v.) in Punjab (q.v.) resulted in considerable prosperity in the province's countryside. It lay dormant in the 1970s when the government of Zulfikar Ali Bhutto (q.v.) banned private commercial banking but revived in the 1980s, particularly after the induction into office of Benazir Bhutto (q.v.) as prime minister and Mian

Nawaz Sharif (q.v.) as chief minister of Punjab. A serious political conflict between the two deprived Nawaz Sharif and the Iteffaq Group of Industries, owned by his family, access to the commercial and investment banks controlled by the central government. Sharif and his associates turned to the Punjab's cooperatives for the funds they required. By the time of its collapse on account of a large number of nonperforming loans, the NICFC had grown into Punjab's largest cooperative bank. In August 1991 the government withdrew the operating license of the NICFC and closed down its operations. The government of Benazir Bhutto launched an investigation accusing the Sharif family and their associates of plundering the bank. The investigation did not result in a court trial and the responsibility for what came to be called the "Punjab cooperatives scandal" was not determined.

NATIONAL LANGUAGE AUTHORITY. The Constitution of 1973 (q.v.) adopted Urdu as Pakistan's national language and provided for the establishment of a National Language Authority to promote the use of Urdu in the country. The framers of the constitution believed that with the departure of Bengali-speaking East Pakistan from the fold of Pakistan, they were no longer dealing with an explosive issue. They also believed that as Urdu was the mother tongue of a small proportion of the population, its use had to be promoted by special state effort. Hence the need for a Language Authority.

It soon became obvious that the framers of the constitution had misread public sentiment. They had not fully realized that language remained a burning issue in at least one part of Pakistan, the major cities of Sindh (q.v.) province in which millions of Urdu native speakers had settled in the late 1940s and the early 1950s after migrating from India. The native Sindhis were becoming increasingly apprehensive that their ancient culture and equally ancient language—Sindhi—were being threatened by Urdu and the *muhajir* (refugees from India) community. They were disappointed that Prime Minister Zulfikar Ali Bhutto (q.v.), himself a Sindhi, would forsake their language by giving such prominence to Urdu in the constitution he piloted through the National Assembly. The language riots of 1974 in Karachi (q.v.) were the result of Sindhi resentment against the government's language policy in general and what was considered to be the growing influence of the muhajir community in particular. Scores of people were killed in the riots as angry demonstrators clashed with the police in several parts of Karachi.

Prime Minister Bhutto received the message delivered by the riots in Karachi and did not appoint the National Language Authority as stipulated in the constitution. That constitutional hole was plugged by the martial-law government of President Zia ul-Haq (q.v.) when, in October 1979, it set up the Language Authority under the chairmanship of Ishtiaq Hussain Qureshi. Qureshi was a highly respected figure: He was a well-known historian who had served his country in several important positions, including as vice chancellor of Karachi University. In November 1987 Jameel Jalibi, a noted scholar and former vice chancellor of Karachi University, became the third chairman of the Language Authority under Prime Minister Muhammad Khan Junejo (q.v.).

NATIONAL LOGISTICS CELL (NLC). The National Logistics Cell was established in 1984 as a transport unit within Pakistan Army's Electrical and Mechanical Corps (EME). Its initial mandate was to organize the transport of a million and a half tons of wheat that Pakistan had to import and distribute because of the massive failure of the wheat crop of 1983–84. This task was entrusted to General Saeed Qadir (q.v.) by the government of President Zia ul-Haq (q.v.). After the successful completion of the task, Qadir decided to keep the cell in business. In time, the NLC became the largest public-sector transport company in Pakistan.

NATIONAL PEOPLE'S PARTY (NPP). The National People's Party (NPP) was founded in 1986 by Ghulam Mustafa Jatoi (q.v.), an old associate of Zulfikar Ali Bhutto (q.v.) and one of the founding fathers of Bhutto's Pakistan People's Party (PPP) (q.v.). Jatoi's decision to launch a new organization was provoked by the treatment meted out to the first generation of PPP leaders by Benazir Bhutto (q.v.), Zulfikar Ali Bhutto's daughter and his successor as the chairperson of the party. Benazir Bhutto's treatment of Jatoi reflected her intention to turn to a younger generation of leaders in redefining the party.

The NPP was launched with great hope and there was considerable expectation that Jatoi would succeed in attracting not only Zulfikar Ali Bhutto's political associates but also the landed community of Sindh (q.v.). That did not happen and the party fared poorly in the elections of 1988, the first to be held after the revival of democracy in Pakistan. Even Jatoi did not succeed in winning his ancestral seat in Nawabshah.

NIKAI, ARIF. Arif Nikai, a little-known politician from a small town near Lahore (q.v.), achieved sudden prominence when, on September 13, 1995, the Provincial Assembly of Punjab (q.v.) elected him as the province's chief minister. He secured 152 votes in the 248-member Provincial Assembly. Nikai's election was the outcome of intense politicking on the part of both the Pakistan People's Party (PPP) and the

Pakistan Muslim League (PML) (qq.v.) following the dismissal of Chief Minster Manzoor Wattoo by President Farooq Leghari (qq.v.). The PPP's efforts to get the coveted position for itself did not succeed because the splinter Pakistan Muslim League (Junejo group) (PML[J]) threatened to walk out of the coalition government at the center in Islamabad (q.v.) if the PPP denied it the chief ministership. The PML(J) won the support of the mainstream Muslim League, which was also anxious to keep the chief minister's job from going to the PPP.

Nikai's election was not well received by the people of Punjab as they felt the province, given its size and importance, deserved a more experienced chief executive. With Nikai's elevation to chief ministership, the conflict between the PPP and the PML took a heavy toll in terms of the quality of governance in the province. While Nikai was in office, effective power passed into the hands of Major General (retired) Saroop, governor of the province.

NISAR ALI KHAN, CHAUDHARY (1950–). Chaudhary Nisar Ali Khan belongs to Punjab's (q.v.) Campbellpur district. He gained prominence as one of the "young Turks" in the first administration of Prime Minister Mian Nawaz Sharif (q.v.) (November 1990–April 1993). He was not only a close confidante of Prime Minister Nawaz Sharif but also wielded considerable power in the Muslim League (q.v.). He was in charge of the powerful petroleum ministry in the first Sharif administration, a position from which he was able to influence economic policymaking during the period. As a "young Turk" he was consulted on all important matters by the prime minister and was instrumental in persuading the latter to begin to hew a course independent of President Ghulam Ishaq Khan (q.v.) in the spring of 1993. This advice led to the confrontation between the president and the prime minister and, ultimately, to the resignation of both. Elections were held in October 1993, which brought Benazir Bhutto (q.v.) back to power as prime minister. Nisar won back his seat in the National Assembly and played an active role from the opposition benches. After winning a seat in the National Assembly in the elections of 1997 (q.v.), he returned as a minister in the second Sharif administration, which took office in February 1997. He continued to play an important role in the new government.

NISHTAR, SARDAR ABDUR RAB (1899–1961). Abdur Rab was born in Peshawar (q.v.). He acquired the pen name of Nishtar, probably while he was a graduate student at Aligarh. He practiced law for a few years but took up serious politics when he joined the All India Congress in 1929. He resigned from the Congress in 1931 to join the Muslim League (q.v.)

and was elected to the legislative assembly of the Northwest Frontier Province (q.v.) in 1937. In 1943 he joined the Cabinet of Aurangzeb Khan and was given the portfolio of finance. He left the provincial Cabinet in 1945 when, with the defection of Sardar Bahadur Sadullah Khan, the Aurangzeb government fell.

Muhammad Ali Jinnah (q.v.) included Nishtar in the four-person Muslim League (q.v.) delegation that attended the Simla Tripartite Conference (q.v.) of May 5–12, 1946. He was also one of the five ministers to join the interim government under Jawaharlal Nehru later that year. In the interim government, Nishtar held the portfolios of posts and air communications. Even more significant was Muhammad Ali Jinnah's invitation to Nishtar to join himself and Liaqat Ali Khan (q.v.) as the Muslim League representatives in the decisive meetings held on June 2 and 3 by Lord Louis Mountbatten (q.v.) to apply final touches to the plan to partition India. A four-member Partition Committee was set up to prepare for India's division with Vallahbhai Patel and Rajandra Prasad representing the Congress and Liaqat Ali Khan and Abdur Rab Nishtar representing the Muslim League.

Nishtar joined Liaqat Ali Khan's first postindependence Cabinet as the minister of communications but left in August 1949 to become the governor of the politically troubled province of Punjab (q.v.). Once Pakistan was born, the Punjab Muslim League disintegrated into a number of feuding factions competing for power in the province. Liaqat Ali Khan needed a strong presence in Lahore (q.v.), Punjab's capital, to get the faction leaders to work together. He chose Nishtar for the job. He was called back in October 1951 to the central cabinet by Khawaja Nazimuddin, Pakistan's second prime minister, as a part of a complicated political maneuver that left much political power in the hands of such bureaucrats turned politicians as Ghulam Muhammad, Chaudhri Muhammad Ali, and Iskander Mirza (qq.v.). Khawaja Nazimuddin was dismissed from office by Governor-General Ghulam Muhammad in April 1953, an action that for all practical purposes also ended Abdur Rab Nishtar's political career. For another two years, Nishtar remained on the sidelines but was unable to come to terms with the new generation of politicians or to reestablish himself in the Northwest Frontier Province (NWFP) (q.v.), his province of origin. In 1956 he agreed to assume the presidency of the Muslim League but the party had lost most of its luster and Nishtar could do little to revive it.

NONGOVERNMENTAL ORGANIZATIONS (NGOS). Although the NGO type of activity had always existed in the countries of the third world, the work of local NGOs began to gain greater prominence and importance in the 1980s. Sometimes this happened because of the encouragement by the developed-country NGOs but also because of the frustration of the people with the government's inability to provide such basic services as primary education and health care. With the government becoming increasingly dysfunctional in Pakistan, a number of NGOs began to provide services normally reserved for the government. Among the NGOs most active in Pakistan are the Edhi Foundation, the Agha Khan Foundation, and several associations working to promote women's welfare. See also Edhi, Abdul Sattar.

NOON, SIR FEROZE KHAN (1893–1970). Born in Punjab (q.v.), Feroze Khan Noon held a number of important positions in the government of that province before the partition of India and the birth of Pakistan. In 1936 he was appointed high commissioner to London, a position he held for five years. Upon returning to India in 1941 he was appointed to the Viceroy's Council. Under the Government of India Act of 1935 (q.v.), the Council worked as a cabinet. He became a member of the First Constituent Assembly (q.v.) of Pakistan. He served as governor of East Pakistan (1950–53), chief minister of Punjab (1953–55), and foreign minister (1956–57) in the Cabinet headed by Prime Minister H. S. Suhrawardhy (q.v.). President Iskander Mirza (q.v.) invited him to become prime minister in 1957, a position he held until the declaration of martial law by General Ayub Khan (q.v.) on October 7, 1958.

NOORIABAD. The Nooriabad Industrial Estate, located midway between Karachi and Hyderabad (qq.v.), was established to stem the departure of industries from Karachi to the areas around Lahore (q.v.). Industries had begun to leave Karachi because of the law-and-order problem in the city during the late 1970s and the 1980s. The Nooriabad Estate was established in 1983 on 1,450 hectares of land. It was planned to accommodate 1,000 industrial units and could take in another 2,500 enterprises by expanding into Dadu district. Fully developed, the estate could stretch over an area of 6,600 hectares. By 1992 it had managed to attract only 66 industrial units with a total investment of Rs.6 billion, however.

NORTHWEST FRONTIER PROVINCE (NWFP). The Northwest Frontier Province contains an area of 75,000 square kilometers, a population of 13.7 million, and a population density of 182 persons/square kilometer. Of Pakistan's four provinces, the Northwest Frontier Province is the only one without a historical name. Punjab, Sindh, and Balochistan (qq.v.) have been so named for hundreds of years. The NWFP acquired its name only in 1901 when Lord Curzon, the viceroy of India, persuaded the British government to separate the Pathan districts of Punjab to form a separate province. The British could have called the new province Pathanistan or Pukhtunistan (q.v.), but, instead, they chose the name "Northwest Frontier Province." Most often, the province was just called the "Frontier." The British reluctance to call the new province by the name of the majority of its population was dictated in part by the uneasy relations they had had with Afghanistan (q.v.) and the Pathan tribes that lived on their side of the border. Had the NWFP been given the name Pukhtunistan, it would have saved Pakistan a great deal of trouble when the leaders of the new country had to contend with Pathan (or Pukhtun) nationalism.

The establishment of the NWFP did not entirely endear the British to the Pathans. The Pathans continued to resent the British presence in their midst and this resentment gave birth to a movement—the Khudai Khidmatgar (KK) (q.v.)—that combined Pathan nationalism and socialism. The Khudai Khidmatgar's political program was closer to that of the Indian National Congress (q.v.) than to that of the Muslim League (q.v.). The KK entered into an electoral alliance with the Congress that resulted in the Congress gaining a strong presence in the NWFP. It took a referendum conducted on July 17, 1947, in which almost 99 percent of those who voted cast their vote for Pakistan, to dislodge the Congress from the Frontier Province. Less than a month later, on August 14, 1947, the NWFP joined other Muslim majority provinces and areas of British India to form the state of Pakistan. Eight days later, on August 22, Governor-General Muhammad Ali Jinnah (q.v.) dismissed the Congress/Khudai Khidmatgar provincial ministry and installed a Muslim League administration with Abdul Qayyum Khan (q.v.) as chief minister.

Qayyum Khan remained the province's chief minister for six years, from 1947 to 1953, and during this period the NWFP made impressive economic strides. He launched and completed a number of large public-sector projects, including the Warsak dam on the Kabul River, and encouraged private entrepreneurs to invest in agriculture (q.v.) and set up industry. Qayyum Khan was succeeded first by Sardar Abdur Rashid, a policeman turned politician, and then by Sardar Bahadur Khan. The latter was the younger brother of General Ayub Khan (q.v.); he led the NWFP into the One Unit of West Pakistan (q.v.). Most residents of the province considered the creation of the One Unit a serious infringement of their political rights. There was reason for their unhappiness. The province suffered economically during the One Unit period. The One Unit was dissolved by the military government of General Yahya Khan (q.v.) on July 1, 1970 and the NWFP reemerged as a province.

The national elections of December 1970 (q.v.) saw the emergence of the Jamiatul-Ulemai-Islam (JUI) of Maulana Mufti Mahmud (qq.v.), the Qayyum Muslim League, and the National Awami Party (q.v.) (Wali Khan Group) as the main political parties. The JUI and the NAP together won 10 seats to the National Assembly, out of the 25 allotted to the province and secured 34 percent of the total votes cast. In 1972 Zulfikar Ali Bhutto (q.v.) invited the JUI–NAP coalition to form a government. The coalition appointed Arbab Sikander Khalil of the NAP as governor and Maulana Mufti Mahmud (q.v.) as chief minister. The JUI–NAP government resigned a year later to protest the dismissal of a similar coalition in Balochistan. Political turmoil ensued and Bhutto was not able to fully establish his political control over the province.

In 1978 General Zia ul-Haq's (q.v.) martial-law government appointed Lt. General Fazle Haq (q.v.) the governor of the NWFP. Fazle Haq stayed in the job for seven years and adopted Qayyum Khan's approach toward economic development and political management. Under him, the province once again went through a period of rapid economic growth under highly centralized management in spite of the fact that it had also to accommodate more than two million refugees who poured in after the arrival of the Soviet troops in Afghanistan. After martial law was lifted in 1985, Arbab Jehangir Khan of the Muslim League was appointed chief minister.

In the elections of November 1988 (q.v.), the Muslim League and other political parties that had been associated with Zia ul-Haq performed poorly. The Pakistan People's Party (PPP) (q.v.) was able to control the provincial legislature with the help of a number of minor parties for two years. In the elections of 1990 (q.v.), however, power passed into the hands of the IJI. The PPP was back in power following the elections of 1993 (q.v.) but lost to the Muslim League in the 1997 elections (q.v.).

NOWSHERA. At Nowshera, a middle-sized city of about 200,000 people in the Northwest Frontier Province (q.v.), the Indus River (q.v.) briefly enters a narrow gorge that runs as far as Kalabagh in Punjab (q.v.). If a dam is built at Kalabagh, the impounded water would submerge a good part of Nowshera. This is unacceptable to the people of the Frontier Province, who are prepared neither to lose a city of significant size nor to accommodate the people who would be displaced. Their opposition to the construction of the dam put the project on hold. In the meantime Nowshera continues to grow in size.

NUCLEAR NON-PROLIFERATION TREATY (NPT). The Nuclear Non-Proliferation Treaty came into being in 1970. Originally negotiated for a period of 25 years, it was renewed in 1995. It has been signed by 186 states: only Brazil, Cuba, India, Israel, and Pakistan still remain opposed. The treaty divided the world into parts: the countries that possessed nuclear weapons (Great Britain, China, France, the Soviet Union, and the United States) and those that did not. The five recognized nuclear powers promised to work toward nuclear disarmament as part of an effort toward general and complete disarmament. The nonnuclear states agreed not to acquire nuclear weapons on their own but were promised help with their civilian nuclear industry. India decided against joining the NPT on the ground that it discriminated among countries. It wanted all states, nuclear and nonnuclear, to give up nuclear weapons. Pakistan did not sign because of India's refusal to do so.

The International Atomic Energy Commission (IAEC) was given the responsibility of enforcing the provisions of the treaty, in particular keeping an inventory of the fissionable material stockpiled by nonnuclear states. The ability of some countries, in particular Iraq and North Korea, to acquire weapon-grade material in spite of the inspections carried by the IAEC resulted in the strengthening of the powers of the agency. The new protocol to the NPT incorporating the additional powers given to IAEC came into force in 1997. That the treaty failed to stop the spread of nuclear weapons was demonstrated vividly by the 11 nuclear tests—five by India and six by Pakistan—in May 1998. By testing their weapons, neither India nor Pakistan broke any international law but seriously undermined the principal objective of the NPT. *See also* Indo–Pakistan Nuclear Arms Race.

NUCLEAR WEAPONS. *See* INDO–PAKISTAN NUCLEAR ARMS RACE.

NUR KHAN, AIR MARSHAL (1927–). Nur Khan was the second Pakistani to command the air force of Pakistan. (Air Marshal Asghar Khan (q.v.) was the first person of Pakistani origin to occupy that position.) At the time of his appointment he had already distinguished himself as the chairman of Pakistan International Airlines, the public-sector airline that had built an impressive record for itself. Nur Khan took over the air force shortly before the Indo–Pakistan war of 1965 (q.v.) and is credited with the exceptional performance of the air force against India. In March 1969, following the imposition of martial law by General Yahya Khan (q.v.), Nur Khan was inducted into the Cabinet and was assigned the portfolio of health, education, and social welfare. In the summer of 1970 he left the Cabinet and was appointed governor of West Pakistan. Assisted by his principal economic advisors, including Vaseem

Jaffrey and Shahid Javed Burki (qq.v.), Nur Khan developed an ambitious program of economic reform for West Pakistan. However, by that time serious differences had developed between him and the Yahya government in Islamabad (q.v.), which led to his resignation in June 1971. He was elected to the National Assembly in the elections of 1977 (q.v.) but was unable to establish a political role for himself. He resurfaced briefly in 1993 when he was appointed to chair the prime minister's Commission on Education by the caretaker administration of Moeen Qureshi (q.v.).

NUSRAT FATEH ALI KHAN (1949–1997). Nusrat Fateh Ali Khan belonged to a famous family of *qawals*—singers of religious, Sufi music. Originally from Jullundhur, Punjab (q.v.) the family migrated to Faisalabad (q.v.) following the partition of India. Nusrat's father and grandfather had practiced the art of *qawali* in India and gained a considerable reputation for themselves. Nusrat learned the art from his father and became the head of the group after his father's death. He was introduced to Western audiences by Imran Khan (q.v.), who invited him to participate in fundraising concerts in Great Britain and North America. Nusrat's talent as a singer of exceptional quality was recognized in the West and contributed to his fame in his native country. He died in London while preparing for another concert.

⊷ O ⊶

OJHRI CAMP. The Ojhri Camp was an ammunition depot built by the British in the vicinity of Rawalpindi (q.v.). The depot became an active storage-and-supply station for the arming of the Afghan *mujahideen* (q.v.) during their war with the Soviet Union that started in 1979. The depot was managed by the Interservices Intelligence (ISI) (q.v.) of the armed forces. On April 10, 1988 a big explosion in the depot destroyed thousands of tons of ammunition and killed hundreds of people in the depot and in the neighboring cities of Rawalpindi and Islamabad (q.v.). The government of Prime Minister Junejo (q.v.) ordered an inquiry into the incident. The inquiry reportedly pinned the responsibility on some senior army officers. Had the report been made public it would have caused a great deal of embarrassment to the senior officers of the armed forces. President Zia ul-Haq (q.v.) decided to act before the report could be presented to the National Assembly. He dismissed Prime Minister Junejo and dissolved the National Assembly.

ONE UNIT OF WEST PAKISTAN. West Pakistan in the early 1950s was still not a "wing." Pakistan was made up of three provinces (the Northwest Frontier, Punjab, and Sindh [qq.v.]), a number of princely states (Bahawalpur [q.v.], Kalat, and Khairpur being the largest among them), and the large, centrally administered, territory of Balochistan (q.v.). The assembly of all these diverse administrative parts into "One Unit," or one wing, was therefore a precondition for the acceptance of the principle of parity (q.v.), the basis of the Constitution of 1956 (q.v.). According to the principle of parity, seats in the National Assembly were divided not on the basis of population but equally between East and West Pakistan. To apply this principle neatly it was important to create one administrative unit in the western wing. This was done on September 30, 1955 with the establishment of the One Unit of West Pakistan. Lahore (q.v.) was designated the capital of the new province and Dr. Khan Sahib (q.v.) was appointed chief minister.

The creation of the One Unit of Pakistan did not sit well with the smaller provinces of the western wing. These provinces resented the loss of autonomy implied by its creation. From the day the One Unit came into being, the smaller provinces started the campaign to undo it. Their demand was finally accepted by the military government of President Yahya Khan (q.v.), which took office in March 1969. On November 28, 1969 he accepted Bengal's demand for representation on the basis of population and the demand of the smaller West Pakistan provinces for the dissolution of the "One Unit." Because the principle of parity was not to be the basis of the new constitution promised by Yahya Khan, retention of the One Unit of West Pakistan was no longer necessary. The military government accepted this logic; the One Unit (Reorganization) Committee was set up on December 10, 1969, under the chairmanship of Mian Muzaffar Ahmad, deputy chairman of the Planning Commission, to reorganize West Pakistan into the four provinces of Baluchistan, Northwest Frontier, Punjab, and Sindh. The committee concluded its work in June 1970, and on July 1 the One Unit of West Pakistan was divided into four provinces.

OPERATION FAIRPLAY. Operation Fairplay was the code name given to the move made by the armed forces on the night between July 4 and 5, 1977 to arrest prime minister Zulfikar Ali Bhutto (q.v.) and place Pakistan under martial law. The decision to move against Bhutto was taken after a number of senior officers refused to fire on the crowds that kept coming out on the streets of Pakistan's major cities—in particular Lahore (q.v.)—despite the government's orders of "shoot to kill." It was later claimed by those who put the operation in place that had they not acted, some officers involved in restoring law and order in the cities might have mutinied against their commanders.

OPERATION GIBRALTAR. Military planners in Pakistan used the code name "Operation Gibraltar" for infiltrating commandos across the border into the Indian-occupied state of Kashmir (q.v.). The operation began in the summer of 1965 and was launched in the belief—mistaken though it turned out to be—that the commandos would be able to incite rebellion by the Muslim population of the state against the occupying forces of India. The operation led to a full-scale war between India and Pakistan. *See also* Indo–Pakistan War of 1965.

OPPOSITION ALLIANCES. Pakistan's political history is punctuated with the appearance and disappearance of numerous political alliances. Most of these alliances addressed particular situations—the need to mount an effective opposition to an unpopular leader who was prepared to use the instruments of state to curb those not in his favor, the need to challenge the ruling party in the general elections, the need to educate the people about some particular issue. Most of these alliances were short lived; they disappeared once their immediate objective had been achieved. Some of them appeared briefly and left little impression on political developments.

Among those that had some impact on history was the United Front (UF) (q.v.) organized by a number of political groups to challenge the Muslim League (q.v.) in the elections held in 1954 in East Bengal. The UF defeated the Muslim League and laid the foundation for the ultimate secession of East Pakistan as the independent state of Bangladesh. The Combined Opposition Party (COP) (q.v.) of 1964 was formed to challenge President Ayub Khan (q.v.) in the presidential elections of 1965 and contributed to his fall three years later. The Pakistan National Alliance (PNA) (q.v.) was put together to fight the elections of 1977 called by Prime Minister Zulfikar Ali Bhutto (q.v.). The PNA's refusal to accept the results of the elections led to the military take over in July 1977. The Movement for the Restoration of Democracy (q.v.), sought to challenge the military government of President Zia ul-Haq (q.v.) and campaigned for the restoration of the Constitution of 1973 (q.v.). The Islami Jamhuri Itehad (q.v.) was an effort mounted by the right-of-center parties to block the reemergence of the Pakistan People's Party (PPP) (q.v.) as a dominant political force. The Pakistan Awami Itehad (q.v.), with the PPP as its main component, was assembled in 1998 to check the authoritarian tendencies displayed by Prime Minister Nawaz Sharif (q.v.) when he returned to power in February 1997.

ORANGI. Orangi is one of Karachi's (q.v.) several squatter settlements. It was settled by *muhajirs*—refugees who came from India after Pakistan became independent—in the 1950s. It has received public attention for two reasons: First, it was the scene of a major ethnic disturbance in Karachi when thousands of Pathans from the neighboring ghetto of Sohrab Goth (q.v.) attacked the muhajir population of Orangi. Second, Akhtar Hamed Khan, a well-known Pakistani social worker, made the township the center of his urban-revival project, which emphasized the importance of community participation.

OVERSEAS PAKISTANIS INSTITUTE (OPI). The Overseas Pakistanis Institute, founded in September 1994, is the brainchild of some Pakistani expatriates working in Saudi Arabia. More than 5,000 associations of overseas Pakistanis as well as thousands of individuals from Pakistan living and working abroad were contacted by the sponsors of the OPI before it was launched. Its purpose is to introduce Pakistan—its history, language, culture, and traditions—to the rapidly growing community of younger expatriates and, conversely, to introduce them to Pakistan, the country of their parents. The organization held its first annual meeting in Islamabad (q.v.) in August 1995. The OPI has launched a number of programs including the acquisition of land in Islamabad to help overseas Pakistanis to build retirement homes in the capital city of their home country. The OPI is also hoping to hold a census of overseas Pakistanis to develop a better statistical profile of the numerous expatriate communities that have developed in the Middle East, Europe, and North America.

The 1996 annual conference, again held in Islamabad, was attended by a number of overseas Pakistanis. Its theme was the contribution the community of overseas Pakistanis could make to the economic, cultural, and political development of their homeland. The 1997 conference dealt with the issue of political instability in Pakistan, which had become a subject of major concern for Pakistanis living abroad.

↩ P ↪

PAKISTAN AWAMI ITEHAD (PAI). The Pakistan Awami Itehad was formed in the spring of 1998 when Benazir Bhutto (q.v.), chairperson of the Pakistan People's Party (PPP) (q.v.), decided that she needed to align herself with a religious grouping to mount an effective challenge to Prime Minister Nawaz Sharif's Pakistan Muslim League (qq.v.). The League's decisive victory in the elections of 1997 (q.v.) had reduced the

PPP to the status of a minor party in Punjab (q.v.), Pakistan's largest province. The PPP chose Tahir-ul-Qadri and his Awami Tehrik Party to be the principal partner in this new alliance. However, to broaden the appeal of the new grouping the organizers invited 11 other minor parties to come under the umbrella of the new alliance. Among the parties attracted was Mirza Aslam Beg's (q.v.) Qiadat Party. The PAI organized its first "mass contact" event in Gujranwala, Punjab. Held on March 20, 1998, the Gujranwala meeting attracted a large number of people. In the speeches made at the meeting, Bhutto promised to abandon the program of privatization that was being followed at the time by the Sharif government. Tahir-ul-Qadri indicated that he was in favor of introducing a pragmatic form of Islam in Pakistan while Beg stressed the importance of a strategic alliance among the Muslim countries of West and Central Asia to meet the challenge posed by the West to Islam.

PAKISTAN DEMOCRATIC ALLIANCE (PDA). The Pakistan Democratic Alliance was formed in 1990 in anticipation of the elections scheduled for that November (q.v.). The parties coming together under the umbrella of the alliance included the Pakistan People's Party (PPP), the Tehrik-e-Istiqlal, and the Pakistan Muslim League (Junejo group) (qq.v.). The PDA fared poorly, winning only 45 seats in the National Assembly compared to 105 secured by the Islami Jamhuri Itehad. Differences soon emerged between the Tehrik and the PPP and the former left the alliance in 1991.

PAKISTAN DEMOCRATIC MOVEMENT (PDM). The Pakistan Democratic Movement was formed on May 1, 1967 by the Awami League, the Council Muslim League, the Jamaat-e-Islami (qq.v.), and the Nizam-i-Islami Party. The movement's program included the reintroduction of a parliamentary system of government, direct elections to the National and Provincial Assemblies, and a federal structure. By agreeing that the federal government's jurisdiction should be limited only to defense, foreign affairs, currency, and communications between Pakistan's two provinces, the PDM sought to accommodate Bengal's growing apprehension about West Pakistan's political and economic domination. The PDM parties agreed to transfer the headquarters of the Pakistan navy to Dacca, to seek equal representation for East and West Pakistan in all government services, and to maintain separate accounts of foreign exchange earnings of exports from the two provinces. This avowedly pro-East Pakistan sentiment in the PDM program won it a great deal of sympathy in Bengal but little support in the western wing. In December 1968, at the height of the movement against Ayub Khan (q.v.), the PDM parties joined hands with a number of other political organizations to form the Democratic Action Committee (q.v.). The PDM participated in the inconclusive "round table" discussions convened by Ayub Khan in March 1969. It was dissolved following the army takeover later in the same month.

PAKISTAN INDUSTRIAL DEVELOPMENT CORPORATION (PIDC). The Pakistan Industrial Development Corporation was established in 1950 as a public-sector enterprise. Its mandate was to establish large projects, preferably outside Karachi (q.v.) and, if possible, in the more underdeveloped parts of the country. Preference was to be given to the projects that faced long gestation periods between conception and completion, required more investment than could be mustered by individual entrepreneurs, and needed the types of management skills that were not readily available to the new industrial families. This mandate constrained the scope of the corporation's activities. Accordingly, it was some three years after its establishments that the PIDC undertook its first substantial investment. It was only in 1956–57, six years after it commenced operations, that the investments undertaken by the PIDC, exceeded 10 percent of total industrial assets.

In the latter half of 1960s the corporation's role as an investor of last resort meant that it had to concentrate its energies on the industrial development of East Pakistan. In the western part of the country, industrial entrepreneurship had developed to the extent that private investors, with the help of the by now fairly well-developed capital markets, could undertake projects requiring large investments and complex technologies. The situation was different in East Pakistan, where the original role of the PIDC still remained relevant. It was logical for the PIDC to be split into two corporations, one for each wing of the country. The original PIDC, therefore, spawned two public-sector corporations, the East and the West Pakistan Industrial Development Corporations.

With the nationalization of large industries by the government of Zulfikar Ali Bhutto (q.v.) in January 1972 and the setting up a number of sectoral corporations, the PIDC lost its raison d'etre. It stayed in business a while longer but was liquidated in 1985.

PAKISTAN MILITARY ACADEMY (PMA). The Pakistan Military Academy was established in 1947 at Kakul, a small military station outside Abbotabad in Northwest Frontier Province (q.v.). The academy was fashioned after the Indian Military Academy (IMA) at Dera Dun. The class of Muslim students already enrolled at the IMA was the first group to be trained at the PMA. The academy admitted its first class of cadets in September 1948, graduating it two years later in September 1950. By the spring of 1999, the PMA had received 101 cadet classes and had graduated more than 20,000 men into the Pakistan army as "commissioned officers." In addition to its regular class, the PMA began training men who had received college education. These cadets were commissioned into the army after spending only one year at the academy. The Pakistan army does not enroll women into its officer class. General Mirza Aslam Beg (q.v.) was the first PMA-trained officer to command the Pakistan army.

PAKISTAN MUSLIM LEAGUE (PML), THE. What is now called the Pakistan Muslim League shares little but its name with the All-India Muslim League (q.v.), which successfully campaigned for the creation of Pakistan; or the Convention Muslim League (q.v.), which was founded by the supporters of President Ayub Khan (q.v.) in 1963; or the rival Council Muslim League (q.v.), which was formed by the opposition to Ayub Khan. The PML of the late 1980s and 1990s owes its existence to President Zia ul-Haq (q.v.), who encouraged those who supported him to form a political party. The party was founded and given the name of the Pakistan Muslim League. Zia ul-Haq chose not to join the new organization himself, however.

When President Zia allowed elections to be held in 1985 (q.v.), he decided to hold them on a "partyless" basis. This decision was motivated essentially by the president's wish not to give an opportunity to the Pakistan People's Party (PPP) (q.v.) to win power in the National Assembly. By boycotting the elections, the PPP fell into the trap dug by Zia. The majority of the people elected to the National Assembly were affiliated with the PML. This allowed President Zia to call on Muhammad Khan Junejo (q.v.), the PML president, to take over as prime minister.

Zia's death on August 17, 1988 opened the political field to political parties once again and in the elections of 1988 (q.v.), in which political parties were allowed to contest, the PPP emerged as the single largest party in the National Assembly. The PML, not confident that it would do well in a direct contest with the PPP, encouraged the formation of an alliance of conservative and religious parties under the banner of Islami Jamhuri Itehad (IJI) (q.v.). Although Junejo remained as president of the PML, the IJI coalition was headed by Mian Nawaz Sharif (q.v.). Following the elections of 1988, the PPP, headed by Benazir Bhutto (q.v.), took office in Islamabad (q.v.) whereas the IJI, under the leadership of Sharif, was called on to form the government in Punjab (q.v.).

The elections of 1990 (q.v.) brought the IJI to power in Islamabad and Nawaz Sharif became prime minister. Junejo's death in January 1993 prompted Nawaz Sharif to claim the PML leadership for himself. This attempt was interpreted by President Ghulam Ishaq Khan (q.v.) as an effort by the prime minister to concentrate power in his hands. The president worked behind the scenes to split the PML. The split did occur and a faction headed by Hamid Nasir Chatta was formed and named PML (Junejo) (PML[J]). The PML(J) joined hands with the PPP to form the government at Islamabad following the elections of 1993 (q.v.). The PPP–PML(J) coalition government was headed by Benazir Bhutto, who was also able to keep Sharif and the PML out of power even in Punjab by getting Manzoor Wattoo (q.v.) elected the chief minister of the province.

Bhutto's poor performance during her second administration (October 1993–November 1996) resulted in another general election in which the PML, under Nawaz Sharif won a massive victory, wiping out both the PPP and PML(J) from Punjab and reducing the presence of the former from the provinces of Balochistan and the Northwest Frontier (qq.v). By February 1997, when Sharif became prime minister for the second time, the PML had emerged as the largest political party in the country. *See also* Convention Muslim League; Council Muslim League; Muslim League, The.

PAKISTAN MUSLIM LEAGUE (CHATTA) (PML[C]). The Pakistan Muslim League (Junejo) (PML[J]) (q.v.) was renamed the Pakistan Muslim League (Chatta) in March 1998 following a split in the former faction of the Pakistan Muslim League (q.v.). The split was the result of a decision made by a number of Sindhi politicians affiliated with the PML(J), including the son and daughter of Muhammad Khan Junejo (q.v.), not to agree to the move by Hamid Nasir Chatta (q.v.) to align the PML(J) with the Pakistan People's Party (PPP) (q.v.) and several other parties in the opposition in a new grouping called the Pakistan Awami Itehad (q.v.). The split was also the consequence of active wooing by Mian Nawaz Sharif (q.v.) to win back some of the prominent PML(J) leaders to Nawaz Sharif's mainstream Pakistan Muslim League.

PAKISTAN MUSLIM LEAGUE (JUNEJO) (PML[J]). The emergence of the Pakistan Muslim League (Junejo) in the spring of 1993 was in keeping with a time-honored tradition in Pakistani politics. As had happened on numerous occasions, disagreement between two prominent politicians within a political party led to the creation of factions that remained politically active for as long as differences remained or for as long as the leader of the splinter group remained in active politics. This process of constant splintering affected parties with weak ideologies. The Pakistan Muslim League (q.v.) was particularly subjected to it since the party had failed to redefine itself after the emergence of Pakistan.

The formation of the PML(J) was the consequence of the struggle between Mian Nawaz Sharif and Hamid Nasir Chatta (qq.v), two young politicians from Punjab (q.v.) who were brought to prominence by President Zia ul-Haq (q.v.). Zia was interested in breaking the hold of the Pakistan People's Party (PPP) (q.v.) on the politics of Punjab and was looking for people who could mount an effective challenge to Benazir Bhutto's (q.v.) party. Sharif and Chatta fitted the bill very well. The two came from very different backgrounds and between them they covered a wide spectrum of Punjabi politics. Chatta was from a prominent landed political family. His father was active in Punjab politics for a number of years following independence, representing the interests of the landed community. Nawaz was a relative newcomer to politics. He belonged to an industrial family with vast holdings in and around Lahore (q.v.). His main concern was the promotion and protection of the interests of the urban classes.

Uneasy peace was maintained between the two protagonists from Punjab for as long as Zia was in power. After Zia's death, Sharif and Chatta began to drift apart but were persuaded to work together by Muhammad Khan Junejo (q.v.), who feared that an open rift between the two would provide an opening for the PPP in Punjab. A compromise was achieved following the elections of 1990 (q.v.), with Nawaz becoming prime minister and Junejo taking over the presidency of the Pakistan Muslim League. Nawaz included Chatta and his associates in the federal Cabinet. Junejo's death in early 1993 introduced a new complication into the equation, however. Nawaz made an attempt to consolidate his power by putting himself forward as successor to Junejo. This move was not acceptable to the Chatta group, which wanted to retain the PML's presidency. In these endeavors Chatta and his associates had the support of President Ghulam Ishaq Khan (q.v.), who was also not willing to see Sharif consolidate his power. When Sharif refused to relent, Chatta and his colleagues resigned from the cabinet and formed the Pakistan Muslim League (Junejo). Their departure provided the president the pretext for the dismissal of Sharif and his Cabinet.

The PML(J) fielded separate candidates in the elections of 1993 (q.v.) and won enough seats in the National and Punjab Provincial Assemblies to deny a majority to Nawaz Sharif's Pakistan Muslim League in both houses. The PML(J) joined Benazir Bhutto's PPP in a political alliance called the Pakistan Democratic Alliance (PDA) (q.v.). The PDA was able to muster majorities in both the National Assembly and in the Punjab Provincial Assembly. It was thus able to form the government in both Islamabad (q.v.) and Lahore. The PPP–PML(J) alliance was maintained for the elections of February 1997 (q.v.) but this time around the PML(J) was of no help whatsoever to Bhutto and her party since it was not able to secure a single seat. The PML(J) dropped the suffix "Junejo" and became the Pakistan Muslim League (Chatta) (q.v.) in March 1998 when Muhammad Khan Junejo's son and daughter decided to leave the party and join the mainstream Pakistan Muslim League headed by Prime Minister Nawaz Sharif.

PAKISTAN NATIONAL ALLIANCE (PNA). The Pakistan National Alliance was formed in January 1977 to face the Pakistan People's Party (PPP) (q.v.) in the elections that were called by Prime Minister Zulfikar Ali Bhutto (q.v.). The alliance included a number of religious parties and political groupings that had bitterly opposed Bhutto's economic and social policies. Air Marshal Asghar Khan (q.v.) of the Tehrik-e-Istiqlal (q.v.) was among the more prominent members of the alliance. The alliance parties had done poorly in the elections of 1970 (q.v.) and as such Bhutto was initially not inclined to treat them seriously. However, their ability to attract large crowds to their meetings surprised the administration and persuaded it to put a somewhat greater effort into the campaign leading up to the elections. According to the PNA, this effort included the mobilization of the civil bureaucracy to aid the candidates fielded by the PPP.

The results of the elections shocked the PNA leadership. It had expected a much better showing by its candidates. Not satisfied with the results announced by the Election Commission, the PNA launched a countrywide campaign against the government, demanding that it hold a new poll. The campaign resulted in a great deal of violence and the military (q.v.) had to be called in to restore law and order in a number of cities. Bhutto, after receiving a strong message from the high command of the army that it was not prepared to fire on its own citizens, decided to call the leaders of the opposition to the negotiating table. Bhutto concluded an agreement with the PNA on July 3, 1977. By that time, however, the army high command under chief of Army Staff (COAS) General Zia ul-Haq (q.v.) had already decided to act and put the country under martial law (q.v.). In this they had been encouraged by Air Marshal Asghar Khan who had openly invited the armed forces to intervene once again in Pakistani politics.

The PNA survived the imposition of martial law and some of its members joined the first of several civilian administrations Zia was to put into office during his 11-year rule. The decision by some PNA parties to work with Zia split the alliance, however. Some of its constituents later joined the PPP to organize the Movement for the Restoration of Democracy (q.v.).

PAKISTAN PEOPLE'S PARTY (PPP). The inaugural convention of the Pakistan People's Party was held in Lahore (q.v.), on November 30, 1967 at the residence of Mubashir Hasan (q.v.), a left-wing intellectual. The party was created to provide Zulfikar Ali Bhutto (q.v.) with a political vehicle to use to return to politics. The convention adopted the party's ethos as "Islam is our faith; democracy is our polity; socialism is our economic creed; all power to the people." This proved to be a heady brew for the underprivileged segments of the Pakistani population. Unlike scores of parties that had appeared on Pakistan's political scene before the advent of the PPP, Bhutto's organization was remarkably successful in gaining the electoral support of many groups of people. It triumphed in the elections of 1970 (q.v.), winning a clear majority of seats allocated to West Pakistan. It was because of the strong support received by the PPP in the elections that Bhutto was able to take the position that the PPP should not be treated merely as a party that would occupy the opposition benches in the newly elected National Assembly. Instead, the PPP demanded that it should be considered equal to Mujibur Rahman's Awami League (qq.v.), which had won an even more impressive victory in Bengal, Pakistan's eastern wing. This stance of the PPP ultimately contributed to the breakup of Pakistan in December 1971 and the emergence of Bangladesh (q.v.) as an independent state.

Once in power in December 1971, the PPP leaders carried out their promise of bringing most large-scale industry, commerce, and finance under the direct control of the government. The nationalization of privately owned economic assets carried out by the PPP government in 1972–74 led to a fundamental restructuring of the economy (q.v.). It also produced a sharp decline in the rate of growth of the gross domestic product, which contributed to the fall of Bhutto in July 1977.

The PPP remained a potent political force throughout the 1980s despite its unpopularity with the military (q.v.). It was at the center of the Movement for the Restoration of Democracy (q.v.) launched by the opposition against the military government of President Zia ul-Haq (q.v.). Zia's sudden death in August 1988 resulted in the return of the PPP to political power in December of the same year under the leadership of Benazir Bhutto (q.v.), who had become the party's chairperson following her father's execution in April 1979. The party survived another attempt by the military to send it into the wilderness when Benazir Bhutto was dismissed by President Ghulam Ishaq Khan (q.v.) on charges of corruption and mismanagement. Although the PPP performed poorly in the elections of 1990 (q.v.), which brought Nawaz Sharif and the Islami Jamhuri Itehad (IJI) (qq.v.) to power in Islamabad (q.v.), the party improved its performance in the elections of 1993 (q.v.). In October

1993, with Benazir Bhutto once again sworn in as prime minister, the party was back in power to rule Pakistan for the third time in 20 years.

It was during the second tenure of Benazir Bhutto as prime minister, however, from October 1993 to November 1996, that the PPP eventually lost favor with the people. It suffered a massive defeat at the hands of the Pakistan Muslim League (q.v.) in the elections of 1997 (q.v.). There were many reasons for the precipitous decline of the PPP. Scores of stories published in the press (q.v.) about the corrupt practices of the senior functionaries of the second Bhutto administration as well as members of her family contributed to the party's loss of favor with the public. These stories figured in particular the prime minister's husband, Asif Ali Zardari (q.v.). Bhutto's authoritarian style of management as well as the lack of party discipline also contributed to its decline. The PPP was not helped by the poor performance of the economy during Benazir Bhutto's second term.

PAKISTAN PEOPLE'S PARTY (BHUTTO SHAHEED) (PPP[B-S]). The only serious threat to the political authority of the Pakistan People's Party (PPP) (q.v.) and its unity came in 1995 when Mir Murtaza Ali Bhutto, Zulfikar Ali Bhutto's (qq.v) only surviving son, returned to Pakistan and founded the Pakistan Peoples Party (Bhutto Shaheed). He added the suffix "Bhutto Shaheed" ("Bhutto the Martyr") to underscore the point that he and not his sister had inherited his father's political mantle. In this effort Murtaza had the full support of his mother, Begum Nusrat Bhutto (q.v.), who was also of the view that her husband's political legacy should be inherited by his son and not his daughter. For all these reasons Murtaza was bitterly opposed by his sister, Benazir Bhutto and her husband, Asif Ali Zardari (qq.v).

The dispute between the Bhutto siblings heated up in September 1996 when the government arrested one of Murtaza's staunch supporters. Murtaza reacted by sending a well-armed team of his followers to obtain the release of his associate. The police were ordered to confront Murtaza and to force him and his followers to surrender their arms. This confrontation led to Murtaza Bhutto's death at the hands of police gunmen on the evening of September 20, 1996. Murtaza's wife, Ghinwa Bhutto (q.v.), took over as the party's chairperson. She took part in the elections of 1997 (q.v.) but failed to win a seat in the National Assembly.

PAKISTAN RESOLUTION. On March 23, 1940 the All-India Muslim League (AIML) (q.v.) met in the city of Lahore (q.v.) for its annual session. The session began in a charged political atmosphere. The All-India Congress (q.v.) had refused to support the British war effort against the

Germans; however, the AIML's decision to help the British effort did not result in any tangible reward for them from the rulers of India. The AIML was clearly disappointed at the failure of the British government to specify how, once the war was over, it proposed to deal with the Muslim community's demand for the protection of their economic and political rights in an independent India. Muhammad Ali Jinnah (q.v.), the president of the Muslim League, had, up until then, resisted the pressure exerted by the more radical elements of the party to demand the creation of an independent Muslim state in British India. All along Jinnah had been a strong advocate of a united India.

In 1940, as the Lahore session began, it was clear to him that he could no longer avoid this pressure. Always a consummate tactician, he also felt that such a demand would give the British government a very strong signal that the Muslim community was not likely to be appeased by anything short of iron-clad guarantees aimed at protecting the rights of the Muslims in India. Accordingly, he authorized the movement of the resolution demanding the creation of "independent Muslim states" in the areas of British India in which the Muslims were a majority. The resolution was moved on March 23, 1940 by A. K. Fazlul Haq (q.v.), a veteran Bengali politician, and received the overwhelming support of the delegates. Thus was laid the foundation of the state of Pakistan. The Pakistan resolution is also referred to as the Lahore resolution.

PANO ADIL. *See* CHHOR.

PARITY. The principle of parity—that is, political equality between East and West Pakistan—was the basis of the Constitutions of 1956 and 1962 (qq.v.). Given East Pakistan's larger population, one man–one vote would have meant providing it with a permanent majority in the national legislature. This the powerful political elite of West Pakistan was not prepared to accept and was one reason why it took the First Constituent Assembly (q.v.) so long to reach an agreement on the Constitution of 1956. Politicians from West Pakistan found a solution to this problem; they came up with the principle of parity according to which seats in the National Assembly were to be divided equally between the two wings of the country, East and West Pakistan. The Bengalis gave the principle the name of "fifty-fifty," claiming that this formula had to be applied not only to the apportionment of seats in the National Assembly but also to jobs in government, recruitment to the army, division of government resources, and investment by the private sector. This wider application of the formula was not acceptable to West Pakistan. Instead of solving what came to be known as the "East Pakistan problem," therefore, the principle of parity made it more complex and ultimately led to the creation of Bangladesh as an independent state.

PARVEZ, ARSHAD Z. Arshad Z. Parvez, a Canadian citizen of Pakistani origin, was arrested in the United States in mid-July 1987 on charges of seeking to illegally provide Pakistan with sensitive materials used in making nuclear weapons. He was accused of applying for a license to export to Pakistan maraging 350 steel, a rare alloy used almost exclusively in uranium processing. The export of the alloy is tightly controlled by the U.S. government. The Parvez case complicated Pakistan's relations with the United States because of the "Solarz amendment," passed by the U.S. Congress in 1985, which mandated a cutoff of U.S. aid to any country that illegally imports nuclear-weapon materials from the United States. The case surfaced at the time Pakistan had successfully negotiated a six-year aid package with the United States valued at $4.02 billion. On December 17, 1987 a Philadelphia jury found Parvez guilty of the charge but the jury's verdict did not affect the U.S. aid program to Pakistan for the year 1987–88. It was much later and by a different law—the Pressler amendment (q.v.)—that the flow of economic and military aid to Pakistan was to be affected by the United States' concerns over Pakistan's nuclear program.

PATEL, DURAB (1920–1997). Durab Patel was a prominent lawyer practicing law in Karachi (q.v.). He was also a well-known jurist who served several years as a judge of Pakistan's Supreme Court. He displayed a remarkable sense of independence while sitting on the Supreme Court bench. He refused to confirm the death sentence given to Zulfikar Ali Bhutto (q.v.) by the Lahore High Court when the sentence was appealed to the Supreme Court. He also refused to take the oath under the Provisional Constitutional Order promulgated by President Zia ul-Haq (q.v.). Those judges who agreed to take the oath "were violating the oath they had taken under the Constitution of 1973" (q.v.), he told an interviewer while discussing the implications of the tension between the Supreme Court and the government of Benazir Bhutto (q.v.) over the appointment of judges to the provincial high courts and the Supreme Court. The position taken by him in the Bhutto murder case not only cost him his seat on the Supreme Court. He also gave up the opportunity to become the Chief Justice of Pakistan.

Durab Patel also took a clear position on the question of the appointment of judges to the courts when this issue became the source of a major disagreement between the judiciary and the executive. He maintained that it was correct for the Supreme Court to insist on consultation although not to claim that the chief justices of the Supreme Court and provincial high courts had the constitutional right to approve these appointments. He was also of the view that the practice of letting chief justices serve in acting capacities, although allowed by the constitution, was against the intent of those who had included that provision and had been misused by a number of administrations including those headed by Zulfikar Ali Bhutto (q.v.), Zia ul-Haq, and Benazir Bhutto. *See also* Judges' Case, The; Judiciary, The.

PATTALA. Pattala, a city on the banks of the Indus River (q.v.), was an important port at the time that Alexander the Great invaded India. The city, now called Thatta (q.v.), was destroyed by floods and rebuilt in later centuries.

PATWARI. Pakistan and many parts of India inherited the office of *pat-wari*—land registration clerk—from the Mughuls (q.v.) who ruled India for three centuries. Although the patwari was the central figure in the land-administration system developed by the Mughuls, he was, in fact, part of an elaborate hierarchical system. He was responsible to the *kanungoh,* literally the "law giver," who was responsible for adjudicating between the patwari and the people with some claim on land. The *tehsildar,* the official next in line, was responsible for land and civil administration in *tehsils,* a jurisdiction that included several hundred villages. *Ziladar* was the next in line and so forth.

The patwari was responsible for maintaining up-to-date records on land ownership in the area for which he was in charge, usually a large village or a cluster of small villages. All land transfers to be recognized by the state to have taken place legitimately had to be entered in the patwari records. The patwari also recorded births and deaths in his areas in order to deal with issues of inheritance. He was also responsible for maintaining a record of crops grown and animals kept on the land in his areas. He also estimated the level of output of various crops and other agricultural output. Most of this information was needed by the Mughuls to collect "revenue," or tax, from the countryside. The patwari maintained a map of his areas showing the division of property among different owners on a piece of cloth. The record of ownership was kept in a book called *khotani* and transfer of land either because of inheritance or sale was called *intiqal.*

The land-administration system introduced by the British after they established their control over India continued to rely on the same hierarchy of officials and the patwari remained the key official. The British instituted the system of fixing the amount of revenue to be collected by the state by undertaking "settlements" at regular intervals, every 10 to 20 years. This system was kept in place by Pakistan. The patwaris were also called on to perform other functions for the state when a large number of trained officials were needed. For instance, they were critical in the enumeration effort undertaken by Pakistan as a part of the population census held in 1998 (q.v.).

It was inevitable that the considerable authority wielded by the patwari would tempt him into corruption. In fact, corruption became so much associated with patwaris—as it did with the *thanadar,* the officer in charge of the local police station—that exactions by them were not resented by those who needed their services.

PESHAWAR. Of Pakistan's dozen large cities, Peshawar was the only one that did not immediately benefit from independence. Its population declined after 1947, the result of a large outflow of non-Muslims that was not compensated by the arrival of migrants from India. In 1941 Peshawar's population was estimated at 173,000 and in 1951, according to the first census (q.v.) taken after Pakistan was established, the city had only 151,000 people. The 1955 merger of West Pakistan's four provinces in the "One Unit" of West Pakistan (q.v.) dealt Peshawar another blow as its status was reduced from that of provincial headquarters to that of the residence of a divisional commissioner. The decision in 1970 to dissolve West Pakistan's "one unit" and recreate the old provinces was a welcome one for Peshawar but the city had to wait until the late 1970s to see its fortunes really change. In 1978 the Soviet move into Afghanistan brought millions of refugees pouring into Pakistan; a large number of these settled in and around Peshawar. Also in 1978 General Zia ul-Haq (q.v.) appointed Lt. General Fazle Haq (q.v.) governor of the Northwest Frontier Province (NWFP) (q.v.). The new governor proved to be a dynamic leader and under his leadership Peshawar began to develop rapidly as the center of commerce and industry in Pakistan's northwest. Not counting the refugees from Afghanistan, it is now a city of over one million people.

POPULATION. In 1947, the year Pakistan gained independence, the country had a population of 32 million; in 1985 it crossed the 100-million mark. In 1997, when the country celebrated its fiftieth anniversary, its population was estimated to be 127 million. Between 1947 and 1997 the average rate of growth was 2.2 percent per year. The population census of 1998 (q.v.), conducted in March of that year, estimated the population at 130.5 million. In the last decade (1980–90) the population increased by 2.7 percent per annum. It is estimated that by the year 2000,

Pakistan will have a population of 138 million. At 5.5, Pakistan's total fertility rate (TFR) (the number of children born per woman) was considerably higher than the rates for India (4.2), Sri Lanka (2.5), and China (2.3). The TFR is not declining as rapidly as the other countries of Asia. There is, therefore, a built-in demographic dynamism in Pakistan that will contribute to further rapid growth in population over the next two to three decades. *See also* Censuses, Population.

PRESS AND NEWS MEDIA. The press played an active role in mobilizing political support for the Muslim League (q.v.) and its demand for the establishment of Pakistan, a separate homeland for the Muslims of British India. Four newspapers, two writing in English—*Dawn,* published from Delhi and the *Pakistan Times,* published from Lahore (q.v.) —were aimed at the well-educated Muslim middle and upper classes. Two Urdu-language newspapers—*Jang,* published from Delhi and *Nawa -i-Waqt,* published from Lahore—were read mostly by the people who had sought to maintain their Muslim identity. Neither the All-India Muslim League nor its rival, the Hindu-dominated All-India Congress, had access to electronic media, which were controlled by the government. The first news bulletin by the All-Pakistan Radio was made on midnight August 14, 1947, a few hours before Muhammad Ali Jinnah (q.v.) was sworn in as Pakistan's governor-general.

Following the partition of India and the birth of Pakistan, *Dawn* and *Jang* moved their operations to Karachi (q.v.), the country's first capital. Both papers continued to support Jinnah and the Muslim League. The *Pakistan Times,* under the direction of its owner, Mian Iftikharuddin and its editor, Faiz Ahmad Faiz (qq.v.), moved to the left and began to espouse socialist causes, whereas the *Nawa-i-Waqt* moved to the right of the political spectrum and began to work for the Islamization of the institutions of government. Recognizing that without an Urdu-language newspaper it would be difficult to reach a mass audience, Iftikharuddin founded the *Imroze,* which began to appear from Lahore in 1949.

Ayub Khan (q.v.), Pakistan's first military president (1958–69), did not believe in free speech. He was of the view that it was only with the help of a government-controlled press that he would be able to introduce some order in Pakistan's chaotic political life. His government nationalized Progressive Papers Ltd., the publishing house responsible for the *Pakistan Times* and *Imroze,* promulgated the Pakistan Press Ordinance to curb the freedom of expression of all print media. Television came to the country in the mid-1960s, and along with the state-controlled radio, continued to voice the views of the government. This situation did not change for 30 years. It was only after the death of President Zia ul-Haq (q.v.) in August 1988 and the assumption of power by Prime Minister Benazir Bhutto (q.v.) in December 1988 that the print media obtained the freedom for which it had campaigned for three decades. Over the past decade, several news magazines have become important independent voices. Two news monthlies, the *Herald,* published from Karachi, by the Dawn Group and *Newsline,* also published from Karachi, have done serious investigative exposés, concerned particularly with government corruption. The *Friday Times,* a weekly published from Lahore and read with great interest by the Islamabad (q.v.) establishment, has become an influential voice in recent years. Several new newspapers have also begun to appear in both English and Urdu. These include the *Muslim,* published from Islamabad, the *Nation,* published by the Nawa-i-Waqt group from Lahore and Islamabad, and the *News,* published by the Jang group from Karachi, Lahore, and Islamabad. An independent English-language newspaper, *Business Recorder,* represents the interest of the business community. *Khabrain,* an Urdu-language newspaper published simultaneously from several urban centers has developed a large readership since its appearance.

Although the government of Prime Minister Benazir Bhutto loosened the government's grip over the print medium, it kept radio and television under its firm control. The opposition was prevented from accessing the electronic media. This tradition was maintained by all governments that succeeded the Bhutto administration. It was only in November 1996 under the caretaker administration headed by Prime Minister Meraj Khalid (q.v.) that points of view other than those of the government were voiced on the air.

PRESSLER AMENDMENT, THE. In 1986 U.S. Senator Larry Pressler (R.-South Dakota) successfully attached an amendment to a foreign-aid bill in which all assistance from the United States to Pakistan had to be stopped if there was reason to believe that the country was developing a nuclear bomb. The Pressler amendment was signed into law after a provision was included that gave the U.S. president the authority to waive the penalty against Pakistan on grounds of the United States's strategic interests. Such waivers were granted for as long as Pakistan was engaged in the Afghan effort; President George Bush refused to use this provision in 1992, which resulted in blocking all U.S. aid to Pakistan. It took Pakistan nine years of intensive lobbying in Washington to obtain some relief under the provision of the Brown amendment (q.v.). The Brown amendment was a one-time deal, however; it did not repeal the Pressler amendment.

PRINCELY STATES. It took the British almost 100 years before they were able to establish their dominion over India. Their advance was made in fits and starts, sometimes by conquest, sometimes by agreements reached with the ruling princes. What emerged out of all of this was a patchwork that included provinces directly administrated by the British and 562 princely states that retained some degree of autonomy from British rule. The political future of the princely states had become an issue when the Indian politicians began to campaign actively for independence. The British administration had set up a Chamber of Princes to involve the states in government. If the princes had hoped that they would receive some protection from the British as they abandoned their rule in India, these hopes were dashed on July 25, 1947. In a conference of princes convened by Lord Louis Mountbatten (q.v.), the last viceroy of India, it was explained that by August 15, when British paramountcy would cease, the princes should have acceded either to India or Pakistan, as geographic proximity dictated.

As India marched toward independence, it was clear that the Indian National Congress (q.v.) had no interest in preserving the princely states in any autonomous form. They were to be treated as any other part of British India. The position of Muhammad Ali Jinnah and his Muslim League (qq.v.) was somewhat more ambiguous. This may have encouraged some of them to toy with the idea of some form of autonomy or even independence. Even the ruler of Bahawalpur (q.v.) flirted with the idea of acceding to India before he was persuaded that such a move would be imprudent. Some other states gave Pakistan more problems. It was only after military action that the Khan of Kalat agreed to surrender sovereignty to Pakistan. The problem of Kashmir (q.v.), unresolved to this day, was one serious and unanticipated consequence of the British policy that left the question of accession to India or Pakistan to the discretion of the princes.

PRITHVI MISSILE. The Prithvi is a medium-range missile successfully tested by India for the fifteenth time in January 1995. It was inducted into service in January 1996. The missile has a range of 150 to 250 kilometers and can carry a payload of one ton of conventional or nuclear warhead. Prithvi's deployment met with criticism from both the United States and Pakistan.

Prithvi (a Hindi word meaning "earth") is an important part of an ambitious missile-development program launched by India in 1983. The program includes the development and deployment of five types of missiles including the Agni (fire), a ballistic missile which has a range of 2,500 kilometers and carries a small nuclear warhead. India is said to have spent more that $800 million in 1983–95 on its missile-development program. The Indian program for the development and deployment of medium- and long-range missiles evoked the expected response from Pakistan, including the launching of an alleged program to develop local capability for manufacturing the Chinese M11 missile. The allegation that Pakistan had embarked on that course was made off and on by U.S. intelligence agencies. In April 1998 and again in April 1999 Pakistan tested the Ghauri, its own medium-range missile. *See also* Missiles.

PROXIMITY TALKS. The "proximity talks" between the governments of Afghanistan (q.v.) and Pakistan began in Geneva in 1982 under the auspices of the United Nations. The government of Pakistan, not having recognized any of the many regimes that were established in Kabul following the Soviet invasion of Afghanistan, refused to sit with the Afghans at the same conference table. To overcome this problem, a formula was devised by Diego Cordovez, undersecretary for political affairs at the United Nations, for holding talks without the two delegations coming face to face. Cordovez shuttled between the two delegations, which sat in different but proximate rooms in Geneva, hence these negotiations became known as "proximity talks."

Between the summer of 1982 and February 1988 10 rounds of discussions had been held. Agreement was arrived at fairly quickly on three basic principles: the need for the Soviets to withdraw their troops from Afghanistan; the need to stop the flow of arms to the mujahideen once fighting had stopped; and the need for all refugees to return to their homes in Afghanistan. The only point that required considerable negotiation concerned the period of time over which the Soviet Union would complete the process of withdrawal. After a great deal of diplomatic activity in the spring of 1988, even this issue was resolved.

The talks lasted six years in all. An agreement signed in Geneva on April 14, 1988 brought an end to the involvement of the Soviet Union in the affairs of Afghanistan. Pakistan, Afghanistan, the Soviet Union, and the United States put their signatures on the final document. The Soviet Union agreed to withdraw its troops by the end of the year, whereas the United States promised to stop supporting the Afghan mujahideen once the Soviet troops were out of Afghanistan.

PUKHTUNISTAN. Pakistan's birth on August 14, 1947 posed a difficult political dilemma for a number of Pathan leaders. They had little affinity for the new country or liking for Muhammad Ali Jinnah (q.v.), the man who was responsible for its creation. Immediately after the birth of

Pakistan a number of them, most notably Ghaffar Khan (q.v.), began to espouse the cause of autonomy for the Pathan population. This campaign was often couched in a language that suggested to their detractors that this group was working for the creation of an independent state for the Pathans who lived on both sides of the Afghanistan–Pakistan border. That notwithstanding, the campaign for the establishment of Pukhtunistan—a homeland for the Pukhtuns or Pathans—attracted support from large sections of the Pathan community in both Pakistan and Afghanistan. For a long time, the idea of Pukhtunistan had the official support of the government of Afghanistan and was the cause of the uneasy relationship Pakistan had with its neighbor for more than 30 years, from 1947 to 1979. By endorsing the idea of Pukhtunistan, Ghaffar Khan (q.v.) and his associates could not join the mainstream of Pakistani politics. Some of them endured long periods of incarceration at the hands of several regimes in Pakistan, which accused them of working against the integrity of the country. In 1979 the Soviet Union, by invading Afghanistan and alienating the Pathan population, effectively killed the idea of Pukhtunistan.

PUKHTUNKHAWA. Pukhtunkhawa means the home of the Pukhtuns or Pathans. It is the name the Awami National Party (ANP) (q.v.) wanted to give to the Northwest Frontier Province (NWFP) (q.v.). The ANP leaders claimed that an agreement had been reached between them and Nawaz Sharif (q.v.) before the elections of 1997 (q.v.), that this change in the name of the NWFP would occur if Sharif's party, the Pakistan Muslim League (PML) (q.v.), returned to power in Islamabad (q.v.). It was because of this understanding that the ANP had joined the Muslim League and formed a coalition with Sharif's party in the NWFP. The support of the NAP was critical for the PML in the province. Sharif became prime minister in February 1997 but, fearful that a change in the province's name would not be popular with the non-Pathan residents, failed to act. The ANP, disappointed by the breach in promise, left the PML-dominated government in Peshawar (q.v.), the capital of the NWFP, in 1998.

PUNJAB. With a population in 1998 of some 72.6 million people—or 55.6 percent of the total—Punjab is Pakistan's largest province. Its area of 205,344 square kilometers is equivalent to 25.8 percent of the total. It has a population density of 354 persons per square kilometer. The province produces two-thirds of Pakistan's gross domestic product. Until recently, agriculture (q.v.) was the most important sector of the provincial economy. Since the mid-1980s, Punjab has been industrializing rapidly.

"Punj" is a Punjabi/Sanskrit word for "five" and "aab" means water in Persian. "Punjab" therefore means "five waters," or the "land of five rivers." The etymology of the word "Punjab" reflects the rich cultural heritage of the area that lies between the Indus River (q.v.) in the north and the Jumna River in the south. This land of five rivers, watered by the Jhelum, the Chenab, the Sutlej, the Ravi, and the Beas, is agriculturally rich.

Punjab afforded easy access to the riches of India to the invaders who came in from the northwest either by land, by sea, or through the passes in the mountains that shield the area from west Asia and Europe. Punjab was invaded by the Greeks under Alexander the Great, the Arabs under Muhammad Ibn Qasim, the Mongols under Timurlane, the Afghans under Mahmud of Ghazni and Mohammad Ghauri, the Turks under Babar, and the Persians under Nadir Shah. Some of these invaders plundered the cities of the river plains of Punjab and then went back home; some of them went deep into India, taking the Punjabis with them; and some of the conquerors simply stayed. These invaders brought many different religions into the area; Punjab was successively Hindu, Buddhist, and Muslim. It also produced a religion of its own—Sikhism. Only the British entered the province from the south; and only the Sikhs were able to establish a kingdom in this area that Punjab could truly call its own.

In 1947 Punjab was divided into two parts: one became the Indian state of Punjab, whereas the other became the Pakistani province of Punjab. The demise of the Unionist Party (q.v.) in 1946–47 left Punjab in Pakistan with a discredited political elite that could not match the popularity and power of the Karachi-based urban *muhajir* (refugees from India) community. The militarization of politics in Pakistan took power away from the muhajir community but did not give it to Punjab. In 1955 Punjab was merged with other provinces and princely states (q.v.) of the country's western wing to form the One Unit of West Pakistan (q.v.). Lahore (q.v.) became the capital of the new province. The creation of One Unit was not a popular step and the military government headed by President Yahya Khan (q.v.) decided to disband it. West Pakistan was divided into four provinces: Balochistan, the Northwest Frontier Province (q.v.), Punjab, and Sindh (q.v.).

The rise of Zulfikar Ali Bhutto (q.v.) in the early 1970s moved the political center to Sindh. Bhutto's removal by the military under the command of General Zia ul-Haq (q.v.), a Punjabi military officer, did not benefit Punjab. Zia was originally from the part of the province that had gone to India. After migrating from India, his family chose to settle in Peshawar (q.v.), the capital of the Northwest Frontier Province, rather than in Punjab. It was only with the ascendancy of Mian Nawaz Sharif (q.v.), who was prime minister of Pakistan twice (1990–93 and 1997–), that Punjab gained political authority. In fact, in 1998 Punjabis held the four most important positions in the country with Muhammad Rafiq Tarar (q.v.) as president, Nawaz Sharif as prime minister, General Jehangir Karamat (q.v.) as chief of the Army Staff, and Waseem Sajjad as the chairman of the Senate.

PUSHTOON ULASI QAUMI JIRGA (PUQJ). Perhaps because of the absence of an institutional base that can help people to redress their grievances, people in Pakistan have a tradition of creating "one issue" organizations that come into being to deal with a specific problem and disappear once the problem has been resolved. The Pushtoon Ulasi Qaumi Jirga arrived on the national scene at the time Pakistan began work on the population census of 1998 (q.v.). The organization was opposed to the census in the belief that the population count would indicate a much smaller proportion of the Pathan population in the province of Balochistan (q.v.) than was claimed by the organizations and political parties that represented the Pathans in the province. The PUQJ had the support of the Pushtoonkhwa Milli Awami Party, which claimed to represent Balochistan's Pathan population. Working together, the two organizations were able to stop work in the province on March 21–22, 1998 while the census was being conducted.

↜ **Q** ↜

QADEER KHAN, ABDUL (1935–). Abdul Qadeer Khan, generally credited with having led Pakistan's effort to develop nuclear weapons, received training in metallurgy in the Netherlands. Summoned back to Pakistan in the early 1970s to head the effort to equal the advances made by India in the nuclear field, Khan organized and led a team of scores of nuclear scientists and started work in makeshift laboratories in Kahuta, a small town near Islamabad (q.v.). Khan and his team of experts concentrated their attention on producing weapon-grade nuclear material from the fuel available from the small reactor that was operating at Nilor, near Islamabad. By the early 1990s Pakistan had stockpiled enough enriched uranium to make at least a dozen bombs. With the help of a series of well-managed news leaks, Pakistan let it be known that it had developed the capacity to build nuclear bombs. This revelation was meant to deter India from taking military action against Pakistan as the Kashmiris launched a campaign to free their state of Indian occupation.

Pakistan's advance in the nuclear field caused sanctions to be imposed on the country under the Pressler amendment (q.v.) passed by the United States in 1986. From 1990 on, Pakistan stopped receiving assistance from the United States. In the early 1990s Khan and his associates began work on developing missiles (q.v.) for delivering nuclear weapons. Most of the work was undertaken at Kahuta in the laboratories now named A. Q. Khan Laboratories. The scientists announced their success by launching the Ghauri in 1997, a medium-range missile. In May 1998 India tested five nuclear bombs and Pakistan followed with its own tests a few days later. *See also* Indo–Pakistan Nuclear Arms Race; Kashmir; Missiles; United States–Pakistan Relations.

QADIR, LIEUTENANT GENERAL (RETIRED) SAEED (1930–). Saeed Qadir was trained as an engineer, and joined the Electrical and Mechanical (EME) Corps of the Pakistan army. He rose rapidly in the army and was the first EME officer to attain the rank of lieutenant general. He left active service in 1977 and joined the first martial-law government of Zia ul-Haq (q.v.) as minister in-charge of production. The Ministry of Production was created by Prime Minister Zulfikar Ali Bhutto (q.v.) to look after the industries his government had nationalized in three phases in the four-year period between 1972 and 1976. The ministry was also made responsible for new industrial investments by the public sector. Accordingly, when Saeed Qadir became minister he was by far the biggest industrial entrepreneur in the country.

In 1983–84 Pakistan suffered a catastrophic decline in wheat production as the result of a fungus ("wheat rust") that spread quickly and destroyed a large acreage of wheat as it was waiting to be harvested. The news of the loss came late to the government; it moved quickly once it was recognized that a million and a half tons of wheat would have to be imported in order to prevent famine in the country. General Qadir was entrusted with the task of organizing the transport of this quantity of wheat from Karachi (q.v.) to the major consumption centers in-land. He responded by turning to the EME Corps of the army and entrusted it with the task of organizing the logistics for this operation. The EME established a logistics transport cell by importing thousands of large haulage trucks from abroad. Once these trucks were deployed, the EME, under Lt. General Qadir's supervision, moved a million and a half tons of imported wheat within a few months. Even when the crisis was over, the Logistics Cell remained in operation and went on to become the largest goods-transport company in Pakistan.

General Qadir's next important assignment came from the administration of Prime Minister Nawaz Sharif (q.v.) when, in early 1991, he was appointed chairman of the Privatization Commission to dispose off the economic assets acquired by the government of Zulfikar Ali Bhutto. The commission was asked to implement the privatization program in less than a year. It did not succeed and some of its decisions—such as the privatization of the Muslim Commercial Bank—led to considerable controversy. That notwithstanding, the commission's performance was commendable in the sense that privatization in Pakistan was undertaken with greater dispatch and efficiency than in most other countries where similar attempts were made.

Benazir Bhutto (q.v.) returned to power as prime minister in October 1993 and moved quickly against a number of initiatives taken by her predecessor. She was determined to demonstrate to the people that the government of Nawaz Sharif had indulged in corrupt practices. Sharif's privatization program was singled out as one area in which her administration thought that it had solid evidence of wrongdoing by Sharif and his associates. As a part of this campaign, Lt. General Saeed Qadir was arrested and imprisoned. Because the courts refused to grant bail to Qadir, he spent several months in prison.

QADIR, SHEIKH MANZUR (1913–1974). Manzur Qadir was born in Lahore (q.v.) and educated at Lahore's Government College and Cambridge University, in England. He was called to the bar in 1935 at London's Inn. He gained national prominence by defending General Akbar Khan (q.v.) and his associates in the Rawalpindi Conspiracy case (q.v.). He became foreign minister in the first Cabinet appointed by General Ayub Khan (q.v.) following the imposition of martial law in October 1958. He also served Ayub Khan as chairman of the Cabinet subcommittee that wrote the draft of the Constitution of 1962 (q.v.). Qadir left the administration following the promulgation of the constitution on March 23, 1962 and was appointed chief justice of the West Pakistan High Court. He resigned from the court in 1963 and went back to private practice. He was called back to public service to represent Pakistan in its case against India at the International Court of Justice at The Hague over the demarcation of the boundary in the Rann of Kutch. The case was decided in Pakistan's favor in 1967. Qadir's last high-profile legal assignment was in 1968–69 when he argued the government's case against Sheikh Mujibur Rahman (q.v.) in what came to called the Agartala Conspiracy. Rahman had been accused by the government for conspiring with India to break up Pakistan. The case was withdrawn after the resignation of Ayub Khan and the imposition of martial law by General Yahya Khan (q.v.).

QAMAR, SYED NAVEED. Syed Naveed Qamar, a member of the National Assembly, belongs to the Pakistan People's Party (PPP) (q.v.). He was appointed finance minister in the Cabinet of Prime Minister

Benazir Bhutto (q.v.) on October 28, 1996, two days after a team from the International Monetary Fund (IMF) (q.v.) began discussions in Islamabad (q.v.) on reviving the standby agreement that was on hold. The IMF, not satisfied with Pakistan's program to bring about a major reduction in fiscal deficit, had refused to disburse funds from the $600 million standby agreement the Bhutto government had negotiated earlier. The Fund, along with its sister organization, the World Bank (q.v.), had asked Bhutto to assign the portfolio of finance to a full-time minister. Bhutto had kept the portfolio for herself in her first administration (December 1988–August 1990) as well for the first three years of her second administration (October 1993–November 1996). Naveed Qamar's appointment was viewed as a major concession by Bhutto to international financial institutions. He was still a member of the Bhutto Cabinet when it was dismissed on November 5, 1996.

QAYYUM KHAN, KAHN ABDUL (1901–1981). Qayyum Khan was born in Peshawar (q.v.) and educated at Aligarh and London. He returned to Peshawar in 1927 to practice law. He joined the Indian National Congress (q.v.) and was elected to the assembly of the Northwest Frontier Province (NWFP) (q.v.) in the elections of 1937. He switched to the Muslim League (q.v.) in 1945 and was elected as a League representative to the Provincial Assembly in the elections of 1946 and played an active role in turning out the vote in favor of Pakistan in the plebiscite held in July 1947. On August 22, following the dismissal of the provincial government led by Congress Party's Dr. Khan Sahib (q.v.), he became the NWFP chief minister. Qayyum stayed on in this position for six years and was responsible for the economic turnaround of the province. He left the province in 1953 and briefly served as a minister in the Cabinet headed by Muhammad Ali Bogra (q.v.). He was elected president of the Muslim League in 1957 and began to campaign actively for the party for the elections scheduled for early 1959 under the constitution of 1956 (q.v.). The campaign was suspended after General Ayub Khan (q.v.) imposed martial law in October 1958.

Qayyum adopted a low profile while the country was under martial law from October 1958 to March 1962. When political parties were revived in 1962, however, he decided to join neither the Convention Muslim League (q.v.) headed by Ayub Khan, nor the Council Muslim League (q.v.) sponsored by those who opposed military rule. Instead, he created his own party and called it the Qayyum Muslim League (QML). The QML proved to be the most popular party in the NWFP in the elections of 1970 (q.v.), winning seven of the 25 National Assembly seats allocated to the province. In 1972, when Zulfikar Ali Bhutto (q.v.) took over as president, the QML opted to work with the Pakistan People's Party (PPP) (q.v.). He served as a minister in the cabinet headed by Prime Minister Bhutto but retired from politics following his defeat in the elections of 1977 (q.v.).

QUAID-E-AZAM. The title of Quaid-e-Azam (the "Great Leader") was formally bestowed on Muhammad Ali Jinnah (q.v.) by the Constituent Assembly (q.v.) of Pakistan at its first session held on August 12, 1947, two days before the country became independent and Jinnah was sworn in as its first governor-general.

QUETTA. Quetta is the capital of Balochistan (q.v.) province and the largest city in the northwestern part of Pakistan. The census of 1998 (q.v.) estimated the city's population at 560,000. It houses a corps of the Pakistan army and a number of military institutions including the Army Staff College. The present city was built on the ruins of the city completely destroyed by the earthquake of 1932, which left 23,000 people dead. Although the Quetta of today is a new city with no building more than 65 years old, its history goes back a thousand years, at least to the time of Mahmud of Ghazni, an Afghan general who raided India several times in the early eleventh century and occupied the city for a while. Quetta was an outpost of the Mughul Empire (1526–1756) (q.v.). It was occupied by the British in 1876. It was only after the birth of Pakistan that Balochistan acquired the status of a province and Quetta became a provincial capital. The war in Afghanistan (1979–89) brought a large number of Afghan refugees into Balochistan. Many of them became active in the economic life of Quetta. The Afghan incursion turned Quetta into a Baloch–Pathan city.

QURESHI, MOEENUDDIN AHMAD (1931–). Moeenuddin Ahmad Qureshi—more commonly known as Moeen Qureshi—was born in Lahore (q.v.). He belonged to a distinguished family from Kasur, a small town southeast of Lahore. Qureshi was educated at Government College, Lahore, where he studied economics. After being awarded a Fulbright Fellowship, he went to the United States for postgraduate work. On receiving a Ph.D. in economics from Illinois University, he returned to Pakistan in 1955 and joined the Planning Commission. He left the Planning Commission a year later to join the International Monetary Fund (IMF) (q.v.).

Qureshi rose rapidly in the ranks of the IMF. His tenure at the IMF included a stint as economic advisor to Ghana. In the 1960s he was persuaded to move "across Nineteenth Street" to the International Finance

Corporation (IFC), a World Bank affiliate. In the early 1970s he was appointed to head the IFC and later still was invited by Robert McNamara, the World Bank president, to become the Senior Vice President of Finance. In 1987, after a major reorganization at the World Bank, Qureshi was appointed Senior Vice President of Operations. He retired from the World Bank in November 1991 and founded Emerging Markets Associates, his own investment company.

While visiting Singapore in July 1993 to raise funds for his company, he received a call from Ghulam Ishaq Khan (q.v.), Pakistan's president, asking him to go to Islamabad (q.v.) and form a government of technocrats with himself as the caretaker prime minister. The offer came as a part of the solution that had been proposed by General Abdul Waheed Kakar (q.v.), chief of Army Staff, to solve the constitutional crisis into which the country had been thrown as a result of the deepening antipathy between the president and Prime Minister Nawaz Sharif (q.v.). Qureshi accepted the offer with some reluctance. He stayed in Islamabad for three months during which he began the implementation of a program of economic reform aimed at introducing a number of long-postponed structural changes. He also made some efforts to improve governance in the country: his main focus was to introduce a "culture of payment" by making public the names of the people who had defaulted in paying back loans obtained from public-sector banks. He also published a list of taxpayers in the country that showed clearly not only the small tax base but also the very small amounts paid into the country's exchequer by the rich.

The main task of the Qureshi administration, however, was to hold another round of national and provincial elections. These were held in the first half of October 1993 (q.v.) and resulted in the return of Benazir Bhutto (q.v.) as prime minister and, a few weeks later, in the election of Farooq Ahmad Khan Leghari (q.v.) as president. Leghari belonged to Bhutto's Pakistan People's Party (PPP) (q.v.) and had been a close political associate of hers ever since the execution of her father on April 4, 1979. With the PPP controlling the offices of the heads of state and government, political tranquillity was expected to return to Pakistan. Qureshi was widely credited for bringing this about as well for his success in introducing a semblance of order in the management of the economy. He returned to Washington and to his business in late October 1993 after having been seen off from the Islamabad airport by Benazir Bhutto, the new prime minister.

QURESHIS, THE. The Qureshis of Multan trace their ancestry to the twelfth-century saint named Bahauddin (q.v.). They gained great wealth first as the guardians of the shrine of Bahauddin and later as owners of land granted to them by various rulers of the area. However, the family suffered a great deal at the hands of the Sikh rulers who occupied Multan in 1818. In 1857 Makhdum Shah Mahmood, the *sajadanashin* (the keeper) of the shrine of Bahauddin at that time, rendered excellent service to the British rulers of India during the Great Mutiny of India (q.v.). Shah Mahmood was awarded a *jagir* (estate) as a reward for his services. In 1860, on the occasion of the visit by the British viceroy to Lahore (q.v.), the Makhdum received a personal grant of a garden, the Banghiwala Bagh.

The Makhdum's descendants continued this tradition of loyal service to the British until the time the British departed from the subcontinent. Later, in Pakistan, they developed close ties with the succession of military rulers who governed the country. In the politically turbulent years following the death of President Zia ul-Haq (q.v.), the Makhdums first served the Muslim League (q.v.) governments in both Lahore, the capital of Punjab, and Islamabad (qq.v.), the federal capital. Later, however, Shah Mahmood Qureshi, the current sajadanashin, left the Muslim League and joined the Pakistan People's Party (q.v.) government headed by Prime Minister Benazir Bhutto (q.v.).

↪ R ↩

RAANA LIAQAT ALI KHAN, BEGUM (c.1916–1991). Raana Liaqat Ali Khan was the second wife of Prime Minister Liaqat Ali Khan (q.v.). She played an active role in the movement that led to the creation of Pakistan. She worked with Fatima Jinnah (q.v.), the sister of Muhammad Ali Jinnah (q.v.), in getting the upper-class Muslim women to give up their secluded lives and participate actively in politics. After the birth of Pakistan, she carved out a niche for herself as a strong advocate for women's rights. It was for this reason that she joined hands with a number of other women (q.v.)—mostly the wives of senior officials—to organize the All-Pakistan Women's Association (APWA) (q.v.).

Raana Liaqat Ali Khan went into virtual seclusion after the assassination of her husband on October 16, 1951 at Rawalpindi (q.v.). It was more than two decades after her husband's death that she was persuaded to accept public office. In 1973 Zulfikar Ali Bhutto (q.v.) appointed her governor of Sindh (q.v.), a position she occupied for three years. Bhutto was in search of a person who would command the respect of the *muhajir* (refugees from India) community in the province of Sindh. Raana filled that description very well. She stayed as governor for three years. She resigned in 1976.

RADCLIFFE, SIR CYRIL (1899–1977). Sir Cyril Radcliffe, a British lawyer, was appointed in 1947 to head the Punjab Boundary Commission and was entrusted with the task of drawing a line to separate the Indian and Pakistani Punjabs (q.v.). The demand for Pakistan as a separate homeland for the Muslims of British India sought to include the entire province of Punjab within Pakistan. In finally accepting the demand for Pakistan, the Indian National Congress (q.v.) applied the same logic to Punjab that Muhammad Ali Jinnah and the Muslim League (qq.v.) had used for partitioning India. The Congress maintained that as the Hindus and Sikhs constituted a significant minority in Punjab, the province should be partitioned into Muslim and non-Muslim parts. Jinnah accepted the Congress demand and also agreed to entrusting the task of partitioning the province to Radcliffe and his commission.

Radcliffe knew very little about India and even less about Punjab. He used the population data from the census of 1941 (q.v.) to draw the line that became the boundary between India and Pakistan. The line drawn by him became controversial the moment it was announced. The Muslim community claimed that Radcliffe had awarded the district of Gurdaspur to India in order to provide India access to the state of Kashmir (q.v.) and had included the district of Jullundhur in order to give Amritsar, the holy city of the Sikhs, to India. The people in Pakistan continue to lay the responsibility for the unresolved Kashmir dispute on Radcliffe's doorstep.

RAHIM, J. A. (1900–1982). J. A. Rahim was born in Calcutta and was educated at Cambridge University and the University of Munich. He joined the Indian Civil Service in 1926 and, in 1947, opted for service in Pakistan. In Pakistan, he transferred to the Pakistan Foreign Service and held numerous ambassadorships and other diplomatic posts. He came to know Zulfikar Ali Bhutto (q.v.) when the latter was appointed foreign minister in 1963 by President Muhammad Ayub Khan (q.v.). Bhutto resigned from the government of Ayub Khan in 1966 and Rahim retired from service in July 1967. In November 1967 the two became the founding members of the Pakistan People's Party (PPP) (q.v.).

Rahim was the author of several of the PPP's foundation papers in which he argued for the introduction of a socialist economy in Pakistan to be brought about by the government's occupation of the economy's commanding heights. It was as the party's secretary-general that he was able to attract a number of influential socialists to join the new movement. After the government's acquisition of large-scale industries in January 1972, President Zulfikar Ali Bhutto appointed Rahim to be in charge of the new ministry of production. His mandate was to organize and develop the expanded public sector. Rahim and Bhutto started to drift apart in 1974 when the president, in an effort to accommodate Pakistan's political elites, in particular the landed interests, began to move the government and the party to the right. Rahim objected to these moves and was dismissed in December 1974 both from the Cabinet and from his position as the PPP's secretary-general. Rahim died in Karachi (q.v.).

RAHMAN, MAULANA FAZLUR (1953–). Fazlur Rahman succeeded his father, Maulana Mufti Mahmud (q.v.), to the leadership of the Jamiatul-Ulemai-Islam (JUI) (q.v.). In 1986 he was appointed the convener of the multiparty Movement for the Restoration of Democracy (MRD) (q.v.). In appointing the Maulana to this position, the MRD, an alliance of mostly leftist parties, took an unusual step in turning to a leader of the right. As the MRD convener, Maulana Fazlur Rahman toured the country extensively, emphasizing that the alliance's aim was "the realization of a limited objective, namely, the solution of the constitutional and political issues." Even after stepping down as the convener of the MRD, the Maulana remained active in opposition politics. After the collapse of the MRD in 1988 he retained some political influence. In the elections of November 1988, October 1990, and October 1993 (qq.v.) he won a seat for himself in the National Assembly from a constituency in the Northwest Frontier Province (q.v.). When Benazir Bhutto's Pakistan People's Party (qq.v.) was not able to win a majority in the elections of 1993, Fazlur Rahman joined hands with a number of parliamentarians from the smaller parties to provide Bhutto with enough votes to be elected prime minister. Benazir Bhutto rewarded the Maulana by appointing him chairman of the National Assembly's Foreign Affairs Committee. His party did not do well in the elections of 1997 (q.v.).

RAHMAT ALI, CHOUDHARY (1897–1951). Choudhary Rahmat Ali remains a shadowy figure in the politics of Muslim India. He was born in Hoshairpur, Punjab (q.v.) and was educated at Jullundur, Lahore (q.v.), and Cambridge University, in England. He was a prolific pamphleteer; in one of his pamphlets, written while he was a student at Cambridge, he proposed the creation of a Muslim state, to be carved out of the Muslim-majority provinces in the northwest of British India. He called the state "Pakistan" and explained that in choosing the name he had drawn letters from the names of the provinces that would ideally constitute such a state. Thus, "P" in Pakistan stood for Punjab (q.v.), "A" for Afghan (Pathan areas) of British India, "K" for Kashmir, "S" for Sindh, and "Tan" for Balochistan (qq.v.). Even though Muhammad Ali Jinnah and his Muslim League (qq.v.) put forward the demand for the creation of a separate

Muslim state in the League's annual meeting of 1940, the resolution that was endorsed by the party membership did not give the name of Pakistan to the state being demanded. Some modern historians believe that the Muslim League did not immediately adopt the name "Pakistan" in order not to give credit to Rahmat Ali for having first proposed the establishment of a Muslim country in British India.

Rahmat Ali returned to Pakistan in 1948, a year after the country was founded, but was not given the warm reception he considered his due. He went back to England and died in Cambridge, a bitter and disappointed man.

RAHU, FAZIL (?–1987). Fazil Rahu was assassinated in his hometown of Golrachi in Sindh (q.v.), 120 kilometers south of Hyderabad (q.v.). At the time of his death, he was the central vice president of the Awami National Party (q.v.) and was a close associate of Rasul Bakhsh Paleejo. Rahu and Paleejo belonged to a long-established tradition of socialist politics in Sindh that sought to challenge the powerful landed interests in the province. Rahu emerged on the national political scene in 1983 when he helped to organize the agitation launched by the Movement for the Restoration of Democracy (q.v.) against the military government of President Zia ul-Haq (q.v.). He was arrested for his participation in the agitation and sentenced to a three-year jail term by a military court. He was released from prison in July 1986.

RAIWIND. Raiwind, in Lahore's (q.v.) suburb, was chosen by the Tablighi Jamaat (q.v.) as its headquarters after Pakistan became independent. The Jamaat's success in attracting millions of followers turned Raiwind into an important center of religious activity in the country. In 1996 the Sharif family relocated itself to Raiwind and built itself a large estate in the city. After becoming prime minister in 1997, Nawaz Sharif (q.v.) began the practice of holding important meetings in Raiwind about once every week.

RAWALPINDI. Rawalpindi is now a bustling, crowded, somewhat unkempt city of two million people, which is in the process of being eclipsed by Islamabad (q.v.), the capital of Pakistan. Islamabad's "zero point" is only 20 kilometers from the heart of Rawalpindi. Pindi, as the city is commonly called, was probably built some 400 to 500 years ago by the Ghakkar tribe of north Punjab (q.v.). It came into some prominence when Emperor Sher Shah Suri built a highway in the 1500s to connect Peshawar with Lahore (qq.v.), Delhi, and Bengal. Rawalpindi was a convenient watering point for the caravans that plied the Grand Trunk Road (q.v.), situated as it is between the Margalla pass to the northwest and the Salt range to the south. The Ghakkars lost the city to the Sikhs in 1763, and the Sikhs lost it to the British in 1849; it remained a British possession for 98 years.

The British turned Rawalpindi into a major cantonment, or military base, by stationing their northern command in the city's vicinity. For them, Rawalpindi was strategically located, barely 80 kilometers from Kashmir (q.v.) in the east and 250 kilometers from the Khyber Pass (q.v.) in the northwest. One of the largest British cantonments in all of British India was constructed next to the city to house the British soldiers, their families, and to provide offices for the northern command. It was the availability of this infrastructure that persuaded Muhammad Ali Jinnah (q.v.) to locate the army's general headquarters in Rawalpindi rather than in Karachi (q.v.), which became Pakistan's capital in 1947.

It was in Rawalpindi that a conspiracy was hatched by a leftist clique of middle-ranking army officers to overthrow the government of Prime Minister Liaqat Ali Khan (q.v.). It was also in Rawalpindi that the following incidents took place: Liaqat Ali Khan was assassinated on October 16, 1951; General Ayub Khan (q.v.) launched his coup d'etat in October 1958; the first person was killed at the start of an agitation that resulted in the resignation of General Ayub Khan and the promulgation of Pakistan's second martial law; and Zulfikar Ali Bhutto (q.v.) was hanged on April 4, 1979, after having been condemned to death for the murder of a political opponent. In spite of this history, Rawalpindi has remained an apolitical city, following, rather, the political trends set in places such as Karachi, Lahore, and Peshawar. It has not been able to develop a political life of its own. *See also* Rawalpindi Conspiracy.

RAWALPINDI CONSPIRACY. In 1951 a conspiracy involving a number of senior officers was brought to light by the government of Prime Minister Liaqat Ali Khan (q.v.). The event, which became known as the Rawalpindi Conspiracy, was planned on February 23, 1951 at the Rawalpindi residence of Major General Akbar Khan (q.v.). A number of prominent civilians with leftist leanings were also involved. These included the poet Faiz Ahmad Faiz (q.v.) and Saijad Zaheer, a member of the Communist Party. General Akbar Khan (q.v.), in an article published in 1972 when he was serving the government of Zulfikar Ali Bhutto (q.v.) as minister of state for national security, revealed that the conspiracy's objective was to overthrow the government of Liaqat Ali Khan and establish in its place a military council consisting of senior generals. Once installed in power, the military government was to reconstitute the Constituent Assembly (q.v.) after holding elections on the basis of adult franchise.

There were a number of reasons for discontent among the senior ranks of the army, which persuaded some of them to conspire with General Akbar Khan. Rapid promotion following independence had raised unreasonable expectations of quick advance on the part of most young officers. This could not be realized once the army had reached what was then considered to be its stable size. Akbar Khan, who had been active in the Kashmir (q.v.) campaign, was also dissatisfied with the way the government of Liaqat Ali Khan had conducted itself in its attempts to resolve the Kashmir dispute with India. Akbar Khan believed, and his fellow conspirators no doubt agreed with him, that it was possible to dislodge India from Kashmir by force. Finally, the officers were disillusioned with the lack of progress made by the politicians in giving the country a viable set of political institutions. The rapid progress made by India in this respect did not go unnoticed by the army officers. A special tribunal was constituted to try the conspirators. The conspirators were given long sentences, with the longest awarded to General Akbar Khan. Most of them were released in 1955.

REFUGEES FROM AFGHANISTAN. Refugees from Afghanistan began pouring into the frontier regions of Pakistan after the movement of the Soviet troops into their country in the winter of 1979. Camps to provide temporary shelter to the refugees were set up in Pakistan's northern areas. By the winter of 1980–81, some 3.5 million people, a majority of whom were women and children, were living in these camps. Pakistan received external assistance to provide for the basic needs of the refugee population. The presence of such a large number of refugees had a profound political impact on Pakistan, however. Their presence also affected the economic situation in the areas around the camps in which they were housed. Growing urban violence in Pakistan was attributed to the easy availability of automatic weapons, which were supplied to the Afghan mujahideens (q.v.) by their Western supporters but found their way into Pakistan's crowded cities via the refugee camps. Several ethnic riots in Pakistan's largest city, Karachi (q.v.), in the winter of 1986–87, were also blamed in part on the presence of the refugees.

By early 1988, the patience of the population that hosted the refugees began to be exhausted. "When the Afghans first came, they were welcomed. People even gave them land for their homes. That has changed now," according to one report prepared by a foreign visitor. This change in the attitude of the host population toward the refugee population combined with the unease created by repeated "car bombings" in Pakistan's cities also convinced the Pakistani leadership to become more willing to accommodate Soviet interests in the Geneva Proximity Talks (q.v.) on the Afghan issue. The end of the conflict with the Soviet Union in 1989 did not bring peace to Afghanistan and Pakistan's expectation that the majority of the refugees would return to their country after the withdrawal of the Soviet troops was not realized. Million of Afghans continue to live in Pakistan. See also Afghanistan–Pakistan Relations.

REFUGEES FROM INDIA. See MUHAJIR QAUMI MAHAZ (MQM).

REGIONAL COOPERATION FOR DEVELOPMENT (RCD). See IRAN–PAKISTAN RELATIONS.

RELIGION. In 1998 Pakistan's population was estimated at 130.5 million, 95 percent of it Muslim. The remaining 5 percent is made up of a number of minorities that include Christians (q.v.), Hindus, and Parsees. Orthodox Muslims have always regarded the Ahmadiya (q.v.) community as a non-Muslim minority, a position accepted by the government of Zulfikar Ali Bhutto in 1976 when it moved legislation through the National Assembly declaring the Ahmadiyas to be non-Muslims. This act increased the proportion of non-Muslims in the population to 9 percent.

The vast preponderance of Islam in today's Pakistan was the consequence of "religious cleansing" that occurred soon after the British announced their intention to leave their domain in India to two successor states: India, with a Hindu majority and Pakistan, with a Muslim majority. In 1947, before the mass transfer of population that followed the partition of India, today's Pakistan had a population of 30 million, seven million of which was non-Muslim. Of the non-Muslim population, some six million people moved across the border to India, whereas Pakistan received eight million Muslims from India. This exchange left Pakistan with a population of 32 million, of whom one million were non-Muslims. Within a few months, the proportion of Muslims in the areas that now constitute Pakistan increased from 67 percent to slightly below 97 percent. The proportion of non-Muslims has increased as a consequence of the higher rate of fertility among these people, most of whom are among the poorest people in the country.

Muhammad Ali Jinnah (q.v.), Pakistan's founder, and his associates fought for the creation of Pakistan not to establish an Islamic state in the Indian subcontinent but to create a state in which the Muslims of British India would be able to practice their religion without fear of the Hindu majority. This position was accepted by most citizens of the new country but a small minority wished to formally introduce Islam into the state. This minority had more influence in West Pakistan—today's Pakistan—than in

East Pakistan—today's Bangladesh (q.v.). Therefore, as long as the two wings of Pakistan remained together, it was possible to keep the pressure of the "Islamists" in check. The breakup of Pakistan in December 1971 and the imposition of martial law in July 1977 by General Zia ul-Haq (q.v.), a devout Muslim, created an environment in which those who favored the Islamization of Pakistani society gained a great deal of influence.

This influence was exercised in a number of ways. President Zia encouraged the Islamization of the economy, the judicial system, and the political structure. He was partially successful in the first two areas but failed in the third. In the late 1970s the government introduced such Islamic taxes as the *zakat* and *ushr* (qq.v.). It also issued injunctions against *riba* (usury) (q.v.) and encouraged commercial and investment banks to respect Islamic principles. Zia established the Shariat Court (q.v.), equal in status to the Supreme Court, and empowered it to rule on the conformity of all legislation passed by the National and Provincial Assemblies to Islamic principles. Finally, Zia sought to replace elected assemblies with appointed *Shura*, assemblies of people nominated by a ruler with the selection of the individuals based on their dedication to Islam. A *Shura* was convened in 1979 but Zia had to abandon the idea in the face of considerable opposition.

The next impetus for the Islamization of Pakistan came from two different sources. The invasion of Afghanistan in December 1979 brought Islamic resistance to communist rule to the surface. The *jehad* (holy war) in Afghanistan was supported by both the United States and Saudi Arabia. The Afghan mujahideen (q.v.) fought gallantly and with great enthusiasm against the occupation by the Soviet Union. Their triumph resulted not only in the withdrawal of the Soviet troops from their country, it also brought respectability to militant Islam. The mujahideen themselves as well as their supporters gained considerable influence in Pakistan. They also expanded their reach into other areas with similar conflicts such as Bosnia–Herzegovina, Algeria, Egypt, and Kashmir (q.v).

The second reason for the increasing influence of Islam in Pakistan concerned the collapse of the state in the 1990s; in particular, its inability to provide such basic services as education, health, and security to the people. The increasing importance of the *madrasas* (q.v.) in providing basic education to the people is the consequence of the failure of the state to provide this important function. The madrasas have already produced one profound development, the taliban (q.v.) of Afghanistan. Although not much is known about the taliban, there is no doubt that a number of them received education in the madrasas strung along the Afghan–Pakistani border.

Another development of great concern to Pakistan is the increase in sectarian violence, involving the Sunnis and Shia organizations, supported by Saudi Arabia and Iran, respectively. Hundreds of people were killed in the 1990s as a result of this conflict. Sectarian conflict has added yet another element of volatility to Pakistan.

RELIGIOUS PARTIES. All three religious parties most active in Pakistan's politics today were formed in the 1940s—the Jamaat-e-Islami (JI) (q.v.) in 1941, the Jamiatul-Ulemai-Islam (JUI) (q.v.) in 1945, and the Jamiatul-Ulemai-Pakistan (JUP) in 1948. When the Muslim League's (q.v.) campaign for the establishment of an independent homeland for the Muslims of British India picked up momentum in the mid-1940s, the Muslim leadership was forced to define its position with respect to the role of Islam in politics and the position of the Muslim community when India would become free of British control. The religious leadership (*ulema*) responded in three different ways. The result was the establishment of three religious parties founded on three different political philosophies. Once Pakistan came into being, these three religious groups carved out three different political niches for themselves.

The ulema of the Deobandi School put forward a theory in which the spheres of religion and government did not overlap. Maulana Hasan Ahmad Madani was the most articulate spokesman of this school. He was also very influential because Deoband had considerable support among the Muslim middle classes. Madani argued that religion was a personal domain in which the state need not—in fact, should not—interfere. As such, the Muslims could live in a society in which the majority was not made up of their co-religionists, as was the case with India under the British and would be the case after the departure of the British from the subcontinent. This view was not shared by Muhammad Ali Jinnah's (q.v.) Muslim League. Because the League needed the support of the ulema in order to reach the Muslim masses, Jinnah worked hard to win some of them over to his side. He succeeded in 1945 when, under the leadership of Maulana Shabbir Ahmad Usmani (q.v.), some ulema broke from the mainstream of Deobandi thought and founded the Jamiatul-Ulemai-Islam. The JUI in Pakistan retained its Deobandi coloring and did not campaign for the Islamization of the Pakistani society through state action. It did not, therefore, sympathize with the program launched by General Zia ul-Haq (q.v.) to Islamize Pakistan. In 1981, the JUI joined the Movement for the Restoration of Democracy (q.v.), the main purpose of which was to pressure General Zia to move toward a more representative form of government.

The second response to the question of Muslim nationalism raised by the Muslim League's campaign came from the Barelvi ulema, so called because of the writings of Maulana Ahmad Raza Khan Barelvi. For the

Barelvi ulema, the domain of religion is not confined to the individual. The individual needs a guiding hand. But the hand that guides is provided not by the state but by the people who have demonstrated their piety. This view of Islam sat very comfortably with the rural folk, particularly in the northwestern provinces of British India where the veneration of saints and *pirs* (living saints) was commonplace. The Barelvis, by accepting nondivine intercession, were comfortable with Sufism (q.v.), which the Deobandis found particularly abhorrent. It was largely because of the intense rivalry between the Deobandi and Barelvi schools that the latter founded the Jamiatul-Ulemai-Pakistan. The JUP was founded to counter the influence of Maulana Shabbir Ahmad Usmani (q.v.) and his JUI. In independent Pakistan, JUP's political influence was confined to Karachi (q.v.), which attracted a large number of Muslims who left India and migrated to the new country. The JUP lost a good deal of its political authority with the rise of the Muhajir Qaumi Mahaz (MQM) (q.v.) in Karachi, however. The MQM drew its political base from the community that had given political support to the JUP.

Although an intense rivalry existed between the Deobandi and the Barelvis, and clashes between the followers of the two schools were not uncommon in Punjab and Sindh (qq.v.), the two groups of ulema did agree on one fundamental issue: the immutability of Islamic doctrine. These ulema did not accept *ijtihad,* or the effort to arrive at a consensus on the reinterpretation of religious issues. For the traditionalist ulema, the Islamic doctrine was fixed for eternity. There were some ulema, however, who believed that there was a need to reinterpret the Islamic doctrine in view of the changes that had occurred in the environment in which the Muslim communities lived. The concept of ijtihad was the cornerstone in the doctrine espoused by Pakistan's third religious party, the Jamaat-e-Islami, founded in 1941. The Jamaat was the brainchild of Maulana Maududi (q.v.), an Islamic scholar of great repute. The Jamaat's political doctrine did not recognize any separation between state and religion. Islam was an all-encompassing religion that provided guidance not only in the spiritual field but also in economics and statecraft. But to keep the Islamic doctrine current, these ulema accepted the concept of ijtihad. To achieve ijtihad, however, the ulema had first to gain control over the state. Maulana Maududi moved to Pakistan after the country gained independence. He established his party in a suburb of Lahore (q.v.). The party gained a large and committed following in Karachi and the large cities of Punjab and the Northwest Frontier Province (NWFP) (q.v.). Like the JUP, however, it lost its political support to the MQM but continued to retain influence in Punjab and the NWFP.

RESOLUTION TRUST CORPORATION OF PAKISTAN (RTC). The presidential ordinance establishing the Resolution Trust Corporation of Pakistan was issued in January 1997 by the caretaker administration of Prime Minister Meraj Khalid (q.v.). The RTC concept was introduced by Shahid Javed Burki, who was in charge of finance and planning in the caretaker government. The RTC was entrusted the task of taking over the nonperforming assets accumulated by the commercial banks since the nationalization of the banks (q.v.) in 1974. The caretaker administration was of the view that the government would get a much better price for the public-sector banks if they were sold without being encumbered by a very large number of nonperforming loans. The government of Prime Minister Nawaz Sharif (q.v.), which came into office in February 1997, decided instead to appoint a new set of professional managers and gave them the mandate to aggressively improve the quality of banking assets. Accordingly, it allowed the presidential ordinance establishing the RTC to lapse.

REVIVAL OF THE CONSTITUTION 1973 ORDER (RCO). The Revival of the Constitution 1973 Order was promulgated by President Zia ul-Haq (q.v.) on March 2, 1985. The RCO, by amending 67 out of 280 articles in the Constitution of 1973, introduced a number of significant changes in the political structure that had been erected by Zulfikar Ali Bhutto (q.v.). Two changes were especially important: The RCO strengthened the Islamic provisions of the 1973 Constitution by including the preamble relating to the sovereignty of Allah in the body of the amended constitution. A new article—Article 2A—was added, which effectively gave the Shariat Court the authority to veto legislation that was not found to be in conformity with the basic tenets of Islam. It is still too early to know the full significance of this change as a number of cases have been brought before the courts to test the precise implication of this provision for existing laws.

The other change concerned presidential powers and prerogatives. The original constitution had made the president the head of the republic but had given all executive functions to the prime minister. The RCO gave the president the authority to appoint and remove the prime minister, chiefs of the armed services, provincial governors, and judges of the Supreme and high courts. The president could dissolve the National Assembly without consulting the prime minister. The RCO also incorporated the referendum of December 1984 in the constitution, thus providing legitimacy to the continuation of Zia's presidency from 1985 to 1990, which he would have availed himself of had he lived. The RCO also provided constitutional protection to all presidential orders, martial-law (q.v.) regulations, and the actions undertaken by the martial-law authorities as of July 5, 1977. Finally, the RCO stipulated that the president had the sole authority to interpret the scope of his discretionary powers.

RIBA. Although agreeing that Islam bans *riba* (usury), Islamic scholars continue to differ on the meaning of the term. Does riba mean simple or compound interest; are there indications in the sayings of the Prophet that could be interpreted to mean that the lenders of money are allowed to receive back from the borrower at least the "real" value of the amount lent; does Islam allow capital to be lent and borrowed or is this concept of movement of capital totally alien to Islamic *fiqh* (law)? These and other questions became important not only for the scholars of Islam but for all citizens of Pakistan since, on November 14, 1991, the Federal Shariat Court (q.v.) gave a historic verdict declaring 20 federal laws to be against the principles of Islam. The laws found by the court to be contrary to the teachings of Islam as contained in the Koran and interpreted from the Hadith include the State Bank of Pakistan Act, the Agricultural Development Bank of Pakistan Rules of 1961, the Banking Companies Rules of 1963, the Banks Nationalization Act of 1974, the Banking Companies (Recovery of Loans) ordinance of 1979, and the General Financial Rules of the Federal Government. The Shariat Court judgment, therefore, threatened to twist out of shape the financial system as it had operated in Pakistan. If the judgment had remained in place it would have completely changed the shape of the financial structure in the country. One immediate impact of the court's pronouncement was to create a situation that would have made it impossible for the country's commercial and investment banks to recover loans.

Although the financial bureaucracy in Pakistan may have been taken aback by the Shariat Court's ruling, it did not come as a surprise to the Islamic scholars in Pakistan. The government was now faced with two serious questions: One, how to meet the deadline of June 30, 1992 set by the Shariat Court for making the laws identified by it conform to the teachings of Islam. Two, to save the banking system from suffering serious losses in case the debtors decided not to meet their obligations because they were not seen to be sanctioned by Islam.

For a while the government did not have a clear strategy of how to deal with the issue. It was now up to the government and the Parliament to carry out its injunction. In January 1992 the Muslim Commercial Bank, probably at the government's encouragement, appealed to the Supreme Court to extend beyond June 30, 1992, the period allowed by the Shariat Court for its judgment to take effect. A number of other references were also made to the Supreme Court, where the case has remained unresolved.

RICE. Rice has been cultivated in the Indus plains since the dawn of history but it never became the staple diet of the people of the region. Wheat was and remains the preferred crop for most locals. That notwithstanding, rice has always been grown in large quantities, mostly for export. One indigenous variety, the basmati—a fragrant, thin-grained rice highly valued in the Middle East—is grown by the farmers in Punjab (q.v.). For a time exports of basmati rice won handsome rewards in terms of foreign exchange for the country.

The advent of the first green revolution (q.v.) in the late 1960s heralded by the arrival of the high-yielding rice varieties from the Philippines made rice a very attractive commercial crop and the Pakistani farmers took full advantage of the economic benefit provided by it. The new varieties were particularly suited to the hot and humid climate of upper and middle Sindh (q.v.), which quickly became a major rice-producing area. In the 1996–97 season, rice was grown on 2.3 million hectares of land devoted to food crops. In the same year, 1.7 million tons of rice were exported, earning the country $435 million.

RUSHDIE, SALMAN (1947–). In February 1989 Salman Rushdie published *The Satanic Verses,* a novel peopled with several characters that closely resembled Prophet Muhammad, his wives, and associates. A few weeks after its publication, an Indian Muslim politician condemned the novel and declared that it blasphemed Islam and called for it to be banned. A few days later, Ayatollah Khomeini issued an edict, or *fatwa,* against the novelist and offered a $1.6-million award for the author's assassination. The fatwa forced Rushdie into hiding and contributed to the further souring of relations between Iran and the West. In spite of the intense pressure brought by the Western countries on Iran and even after the death of the Ayatollah, Iran refused to lift the death sentence imposed on Rushdie. It was more than six years before Rushdie was able to make a public appearance.

The Moor's Last Sigh, the first novel written by Rushdie since the publication of *The Satanic Verses,* also led to controversy. Some Hindu fundamentalists from Bombay, the city of Rushdie's birth, were incensed by the description of a character they said was based on Bal Thackerey, a powerful local politician who, it was generally believed, had inspired the Hindu–Muslim riots that had rocked the Indian city in 1992. The Hindu-fundamentalist reaction to the latest Rushdie novel persuaded his publisher not to release the book for distribution in Bombay.

Although born in Bombay, India, Rushdie had strong links with Pakistan. One of his maternal uncles, General Shahid Hamid, had served as an aide to Lord Louis Mountbatten (q.v.), India's last viceroy, and had become very familiar with the story of British India's partition. After India was partitioned, General Hamid and most members of the family to which Rushdie belonged migrated to Pakistan. In Pakistan, General Hamid became a close associate of General Muhammad Ayub Khan (q.v.). Some of the family's experiences were dutifully recorded by Rushdie in *Midnight's Children,* the novel that won its author the coveted Booker prize and international fame. General Hamid appeared as a major character in the novel. Rushdie went on to write *Shame,* a novel that chronicled President Zia ul-Haq's (q.v.) rise to power and his conflict with the Bhutto family. This interest in Pakistan notwithstanding, Rushdie retained considerable antipathy toward Pakistan. He believes in racial harmony—a subject that received a great deal of attention in both *The Satanic Verses* and *The Moor's Last Sigh*—and viewed the creation of Pakistan as a step in the wrong direction.

ᕦ S ᕤ

SADIQ ALI, JAM (1937–1991). Jam Sadiq Ali was born in rural Sindh (q.v.) and was educated in Karachi (q.v.). He belonged to a well-to-do, landed family that took an active interest in politics. He associated himself with Zulfikar Ali Bhutto (q.v.) when the latter left the government of President Ayub Khan (q.v.) and started out on his own. Bhutto's removal by the military in 1977 and his execution two years later convinced Sadiq Ali that it was prudent to leave Pakistan. Accordingly, he spent several years in exile in London. His stay in London coincided with that of Benazir Bhutto (q.v.), who had also left Pakistan for much the same reason. Differences developed between the two and when they returned to Pakistan in the late 1980s, however; they found themselves on opposite sides of the political divide. Jam's antipathy toward Benazir Bhutto was sufficient reason for President Ghulam Ishaq Khan (q.v.) to turn to him for his support when, in August 1990, he dismissed Bhutto as prime minister. Sadiq Ali served as the chief minister of Sindh during this critical period.

SALINITY CONTROL AND RECLAMATION PROGRAM (SCARP). In developing the vast Indus irrigation network, the British administration in India emphasized bringing water to the fields but not on its drainage. Water was brought from the rivers to the farms but no provision was made for draining it. The Pakistani engineers and administrators continued with this tradition. Consequently, vast areas of central Punjab (q.v.) began to show signs of salinity and of being waterlogged. The situation was perceived to be serious enough for President Ayub Khan (q.v.)

to raise it with President John Kennedy during his state visit to Washington in 1961. Kennedy responded by sending a team of experts to Pakistan under the leadership of John Revelle, a Harvard University geologist. Revelle submitted a report to the White House in which he suggested to the government of Pakistan that it extend its successful Salinity Control and Reclamation Project to other affected areas of the country. The first SCARP was completed in 1961 and covered an area of 500,000 hectares. By the end of 1990, when the SCARP program in its original form was discontinued, it had covered 3.7 million hectares with 22,000 deep-water tubewells installed in both saline and fresh-water areas.

SAQI, JAM (1939–). Jam Saqi of Sindh (q.v.), born in a village near Chachchro in the Tharparkar district, exposed a number of social problems faced by the poor and the underprivileged segments of the population in his province. His campaign to bring some relief to these people did not go well with the authorities and he was imprisoned by the governments of Zulfikar All Bhutto and General Zia ul-Haq (qq.v.). His detention lasted for more than eight years. On being released from prison in 1986, he announced that he would reorganize the Hari Committee and tour the country to meet like-minded people, and after that determine his future strategy. *See also* Haris.

SATTAR, FAROOQ (1961–). Farooq Sattar was born in Karachi (q.v.) and graduated in medicine from a medical school in the city. He joined the Muhajir Qaumi Mahaz (MQM) (q.v.) as a student activist and played an important role in helping the organization expand its base of support among the *muhajirs* (refugees from India) of Karachi. On January 9, 1988, Sattar was elected unopposed by the Karachi Municipal Corporation as the mayor of Karachi. The general elections of November 1988 (q.v.) brought Benazir Bhutto's Pakistan People's Party (PPP) (qq.v.) to power with the support of the MQM; Sattar, as the mayor of Karachi, had the full support of the federal government. The PPP–MQM alliance proved to be short lived, however. As the MQM drifted away from the ruling party, its emphasis shifted to "street politics" and Karachi plunged into ethnic violence. A number of MQM activists went underground or were imprisoned by the authorities. Farooq Sattar was one of the few leaders of the organization who remained present on the political scene.

The MQM decided to boycott the national elections of October 1993 (q.v.) but reversed itself and took part in the provincial elections held a few days later. Farooq Sattar won a seat for the MQM in the Provincial Assembly and was elected the leader of the opposition in the Sindh (q.v.) Legislature. Sattar again won a seat in the Provincial Assembly in the elections of 1997 (q.v.) and was included as a senior minister in the provincial Cabinet headed by Pakistan Muslim League's (q.v.) chief minister, Liaqat Jatoi.

SCHEDULED CASTES. Untouchable castes in India came to be called scheduled castes because their names were included in a piece of legislation passed by the British administration to give them some protection against abuse by the superior castes. Gandhi chose to call them the *harijans*. Later, in independent India, they chose to call themselves *dalits*. Jagendra Nath Mandal (q.v.), a prominent scheduled-cast lawyer from Bengal, joined the All-India Muslim League (q.v.), supported the demand for the creation of Pakistan, and was awarded a seat in the interim cabinet formed in 1946 under the leadership of Jawaharlal Nehru.

There is no particular name given to people of similar stature in Pakistan. They make up about 2 percent of Pakistan's population. Most of them are Christians (q.v.) and work either in agriculture or in the service sector.

SHAH, SAJJAD ALI (1933–). Sajjad Ali Shah was born in Sindh (q.v.). His father served for several years as the registrar of the Sindh High Court. In 1954 Shah senior created judicial history by accepting the petition filed by President of the Assembly Tamizuddin Khan (q.v.) challenging the dismissal of the First Constituent Assembly (q.v.) by Governor-General Ghulam Muhammad (q.v.). The petition was registered despite the executive branch's pressure on the high court not to entertain it.

After working as a judge in the Sindh High Court, Sajjad Ali Shah was elevated to the Supreme Court and continued in the tradition established by his father of being totally independent of all political pressures. He refused to side with the majority in 1990 when Benazir Bhutto (q.v.) brought a case to the Supreme Court against the presidential order for her dismissal. When Bhutto returned as prime minister in 1993 she appointed Shah the chief justice of the Supreme Court, bypassing several senior judges. It was widely believed that his appointment was her reward for the position he had taken three years earlier. It did not take long for Justice Shah to demonstrate that he was not beholden to the prime minister, however.

The question of the qualification of judges and their appointment was reviewed by the Supreme Court in early 1996 following a petition filed by Wahabul Khairi, a lawyer from Islamabad. On March 20 the Supreme Court bench headed by Justice Shah issued its opinion, holding that the prime minister could not ignore the principle of seniority in making her recommendation to the president for the appointment of judges. The Court's opinion was based on the tradition that had been established in

British India and was followed in the successor states of India and Pakistan. The Supreme Court held that the appointment of scores of judges had to be regularized in light of its finding. The prime minister was not happy with the decision and chose to ignore it. The Court's insistence that its decision had to be implemented contributed to the prime minister's dismissal by President Farooq Leghari (q.v.) on November 5, 1996. In the summer of 1997 Chief Justice Shah once again locked horns with the prime minister, this time with Mian Nawaz Sharif (q.v.), who had succeeded Benazir Bhutto. The issue, once again, was the appointment of a fresh batch of judges. The new prime minister was not willing to abide by the seniority rule either, as that would have meant elevating at least one judge to the Supreme Court who was not considered sympathetic to him and his program. The ensuing conflict between the prime minister and the chief justice brought Pakistan to the brink of a major constitutional crisis. It was only resolved with the resignation of president Farooq Leghari (q.v.) on December 2, 1997. The president had supported the chief justice; his departure led to the move by 10 judges of the Supreme Court to rule that under the seniority rule Sajjad Ali Shah's own appointment as the chief justice of the Supreme Court had to be vacated. Shah was removed from the Court and Justice Ajmal Mian, the senior-most judge of the Supreme Court, was appointed chief justice.

SHALIMAR GARDENS. Shalimar Gardens were built in 1642 by Emperor Shahjahan (1627–1658), the fifth great Mughul emperor of India. The gardens were laid in the outskirts of Lahore (q.v.) as a recreational place for the royal family. They were prepared by the emperor's chief architect, Ali Mardan, following the Persian style. They have a triple-terraced garden with marble pavilions, three lakes, and a marble waterfall. The lakes and the waterfall are surrounded by 400 water fountains. During the time of the Mughul empire (q.v.), the principal access to the Gardens ran outside the city wall of Lahore. A road was built to connect the Gardens with the Lahore Fort (q.v.), where the emperors lived and held court. The Shalimar Gardens are now open to the public and are also used for state functions by the government of Pakistan.

SHARIAT COURT. Pakistan's Federal Shariat Court is the highest Islamic law-making body in the country. It was set up in 1980 by President Zia ul-Haq (q.v.), who amended the constitution to allow for the Islamization of the legal structure. The Shariat Court was empowered to entertain requests for the review of existing laws to see whether they were "repugnant to Islam." Zia, after causing the court to be set up, constrained its authority; he excluded the laws relating to fiscal, procedural, or family matters from its jurisdiction until 1990.

Since 1982 the Federal Shariat Court has reviewed 1,511 laws and declared 267 to be wholly or partly "repugnant to Islam." In June 1990, while Benazir Bhutto (q.v.) was prime minister, the court's "period of exclusion" expired and it acquired the right to examine fiscal matters. A number of requests were made to the court to examine financial laws and, on November 14, 1991 it gave an opinion concerning 20 laws dealing with a variety of institutions and issues. The government was told to amend these laws by June 30, 1992, failing which "the various provisions of the laws discussed in judgment and held repugnant to the injunctions of Islam will cease to have effect." In January 1992 the Muslim Commercial Bank appealed to the Supreme Court to extend beyond June 30, 1992, the period allowed by the Shariat Court before its judgment came into effect. The bank's request was accepted and, as a result, Pakistan continues to live in a legal cul-de-sac, with little clarity as to which legal system is paramount.

SHARIF, MIAN NAWAZ (1950–). In March 1986 President Zia ul-Haq (q.v.) chose Mian Nawaz Sharif, a young industrialist turned politician, to become Punjab's (q.v.) chief minister. What distinguished Sharif was not only his youth—he was in his late thirties when he became chief minister and as such was the youngest of Pakistan's four provincial chief executives appointed by Zia ul-Haq—but also the fact that he belonged to an entirely new breed of politicians. The local bodies elections of November 1987 (q.v.), by returning a large number of supporters of Nawaz Sharif to the municipal committees all over Punjab, strengthened the chief minister's political position and also gave the signal that urban Pakistan had finally produced a political force of its own.

In the elections of November 1988 (q.v.), held after the death of Zia ul-Haq, Nawaz Sharif emerged as the most powerful politician outside the ranks of the Pakistan People's Party (PPP) (q.v.). He was the only political figure of any consequence from the time of Zia ul-Haq to survive the reemergence of the PPP. In December 1988, while the PPP formed a government in Islamabad (q.v.) under the leadership of Prime Minister Benazir Bhutto (q.v.), Nawaz Sharif was invited to lead the administration in Lahore (q.v.), which was centered around the Islami Jamhuri Itehad (IJI) (q.v.). What ensued was a bitter political dispute between Prime Minister Benazir Bhutto, operating out of Islamabad, and Chief Minister Nawaz Sharif, working out of Lahore. Each tried to unseat the other and both failed in their attempts. Finally, on August 6, 1990, President Ghulam Ishaq Khan (q.v.) dismissed all administrations—those at the center as well as those in the four provinces. In the elections held in October 1990 (q.v.), the IJI won the most seats in the National Assembly and Nawaz Sharif became Pakistan's twelfth prime minister.

Nawaz Sharif decided to free himself from the control still exercised on him by the "troika" (q.v.), a power-sharing arrangement among three actors—the president, the chief of the Army Staff, and the prime minister. This arrangement was put together prior to the induction of Benazir Bhutto as prime minister in December 1988. Ghulam Ishaq Khan struck back in April 1993 by dismissing Nawaz Sharif, his Cabinet, and the national and provincial legislatures. Nawaz Sharif responded by going to the Supreme Court and challenging the president's move as unconstitutional. The Court, to the great surprise of the president, agreed with Sharif, who was reinstated as prime minister. The president refused to surrender, however. He persuaded a faction of the Pakistan Muslim League (PML), led by Hamid Nasir Chatta (qq.v.), to leave the PML. All these maneuverings brought political paralysis to the country and the army decided to intervene. The military forced both the president and the prime minister to resign. Elections were held in October 1993 (q.v.) under the supervision of the interim administration and Benazir Bhutto and her Pakistan People's Party were back in power in Islamabad. With the help of Chatta and his group, Bhutto was able to keep Nawaz Sharif out of power in Punjab as well. This ushered in a period of considerable political instability as the opposition, led by Sharif, refused to work with the government.

The dismissal of Prime Minister Benazir Bhutto's government by President Farooq Leghari (q.v.) on November 5, 1996, followed by another general election on February 3, 1997 (q.v.), dramatically changed the political fortunes of the Sharif family. Nawaz Sharif led the Pakistan Muslim League to a massive electoral victory, capturing most of the seats in the National Assembly and in the Provincial Assembly of Punjab. For the first time in decades, the PML had a credible presence in Sindh (q.v.).

Taking over as prime minister on February 17, 1997, Sharif acted quickly to consolidate his position. He took advantage of the very comfortable majority in the National Assembly to move two constitutional amendments. The thirteenth amendment (q.v.) took away from the president the power to dissolve the assembly without being advised to do so by the prime minister. The fourteenth amendment made it unlawful for legislators to cross the floor in the National and Provincial assemblies. Now politically secure, Sharif moved against the judiciary (q.v.). Defying the Supreme Court's order, delivered in the "judges' case" (q.v.) of March 1996, that it had the authority to appoint judges to the superior courts, the prime minister refused to allow five men identified by the chief justice of the Supreme Court to be appointed as judges to his court. What followed was a deep constitutional crisis that was resolved only after the resignation of the president on December 2, 1997 and the removal of Sajjad Ali Shah (q.v.), the chief justice. On December 31 Muhammad Rafiq Tarar (q.v.), a close associate of the Sharif family, was elected president. Preoccupied with politics, the prime minister had little time for economics. The economic difficulties inherited from the Bhutto period continued to take their toll. Although the government adopted a program of structural reforms that had been initially introduced by the caretaker administration of Meraj Khalid (q.v.) and was supported by the International Monetary Fund (q.v.), the economy (q.v.) did not respond. The situation became more serious after the imposition of economic sanctions by the Western nations following the explosion of six nuclear devices by Pakistan in late May 1998. The country came close to bankruptcy in July of that year.

SHERPAO, HAYAT MUHAMMAD KHAN (1935–1975). Hayat Muhammad Khan Sherpao of the Northwest Frontier Province (NWFP) (q.v.) was one of several young politicians whom Zulfikar Ali Bhutto (q.v.) attracted to the Pakistan People's Party (q.v.) as its "founding members." Sherpao came to the party with no political background and baggage and was fully committed to implementing the new party's socialist program. In that respect he was more in line with the politics of the Khudai Khidmatgars (KK) (q.v.), although he had very little affection for Wali Khan (q.v.), who had inherited the KK mantle from Abdul Ghaffar Khan (q.v.). When Bhutto came to power in December 1971 he appointed Sherpao governor of the NWFP. Sherpao moved to Islamabad (q.v.) as a minister in the central Cabinet when a National Awami Party/Jamiatul-Ulemai-Islam (NAP–JUI) (qq.v.) government took office in Peshawar (q.v.) in 1972. On February 8, 1975 Sherpao was assassinated while addressing a public meeting in the university town of Peshawar. The government reacted by arresting a number of opposition leaders, including Wali Khan, and declaring the NAP an illegal organization.

SHOAIB, MUHAMMAD (1906–1974). Muhammad Shoaib was one of the many civil servants to have occupied important economic positions in Pakistan. Shoaib was a member of the Pakistan Accounts Service and was serving as an executive director at the World Bank (q.v.) when General Ayub Khan (q.v.) staged his military coup d'etat in Pakistan. He was summoned back to Pakistan and appointed minister of finance, a position he held for six years (1961–67). It was during his tenure as finance minister that Pakistan's economy (q.v.) performed exceptionally well. He went back to the World Bank in 1967 and was appointed vice president in charge of administration. He died in Washington in 1974.

SIACHEN GLACIER. The Siachen Glacier, located east of Pakistan's district of Baltistan, measures 75 kilometers in length and is about five to eight kilometers wide. It is the second-largest glacier in the world, and through Bilfond La and Sia La offers access to the peaks of the Karakoram range. The control of the glacier remains disputed between India and Pakistan; the two countries failed to reach agreement on the precise location of the line of control in the glaciated area in 1949 when the first cease-fire line was drawn in Kashmir (q.v.) and in 1973 when the line was redemarcated. In 1984 India occupied the glacier but was not able to dislodge the Pakistanis from the two passes. In 1985 and again in 1986 and 1987 the glacier saw a lot of military activity on both sides. According to the government of India, an exceptionally bitter but inconclusive battle was fought in September–October 1987 over the control of some parts of the glacier that left hundreds of soldiers dead on both sides. The dispute remains unresolved.

SIKANDER HAYAT KHAN, SIR (1892–1942). Sikander Hayat Khan was born in a family from Wah, a small town in north Punjab (q.v.). His father is said to have helped the British in their battles against the "sepoy mutineers" and is also said to have assisted in bringing back the body of General John Nicholson, who was killed in action during the uprising. The grateful British helped the Hayat family and contributed to Sikander's success in Punjab politics. British aid notwithstanding, Sikander was an able politician who played an important role in producing an unusual degree of communal harmony within Punjab among three religious groups: the Muslims, Hindus, and Sikhs. He empathized with the Punjab elite's desire to chart a political course that would have kept Punjab united. He believed that only such an approach would avoid a political upheaval and help to escape the communal tensions that were building up in other Indian provinces. At the same time, he was shrewd enough to realize the impracticality of such a course because it would not be possible for Punjab to become independent once the British left India. Therefore, he walked a thin line between the multireligious orientation of Punjab's politics and Muhammad Ali Jinnah's (q.v.) ambitions to carve a separate homeland for the Muslims of India. He succeeded Fazli Husain (q.v.) as the leader of the Punjab Unionist Party (q.v.) and arrived at an arrangement with Jinnah that allowed him membership of the Muslim League (q.v.) while preserving the separate identity of the Unionist Party. He led the Unionists to victory in the elections of 1937 and was appointed Punjab's first prime minister the same year. He held this position until his death.

SIMLA ACCORD. The Simla Accord was signed on July 3, 1972 between Prime Minister Indira Gandhi of India and President Zulfikar Ali Bhutto (q.v.) of Pakistan. The accord settled a number of outstanding matters between the two countries following the third Indo–Pakistan war (q.v.) fought in November–December 1971. India agreed in principle to release and send back to Pakistan 93,000 prisoners it had captured after the fall of Dacca in December 1971. It also agreed to vacate 5,000 square miles of territory it had captured in what was left of Pakistan. Although no agreement was reached over the future of Kashmir (q.v.), Pakistan accepted India's demand not to raise the matter in international fora. This last provision in the accord was interpreted by the Indian side as Pakistan's agreement not to ask for the implementation of the Security Council resolution passed in 1949, which required the two countries to hold a plebiscite in Kashmir to ascertain whether the people of the state wished to join Pakistan or India.

SIMLA TRIPARTITE CONFERENCE, 1946. Viceroy Lord Wavell and the British government's Cabinet Mission to India invited eight Indian leaders, four each from the All-India Congress (Maulana Azad, Jawaharlal Nehru, Sardar Vallabhai Patel, Abdul Ghafar Khan [q.v.]) and the All-India Muslim League (Muhammad Ali Jinnah, Liaqat Ali Khan, Sardar Abdur Rab Nishtar [qq.v], and Nawab Ismail Khan) to meet with them to find a solution to the Indian constitutional crisis. The tripartite conference opened at Simla on May 5, 1946 and collapsed seven days later on May 12. After seven days of proposals and counterproposals the conference broke down over the issue of "group powers," which according to Jinnah was "the whole guts" of the problem. *See also* Cabinet Mission Plan, 1946.

SINDH. With a population of 30 million in 1998, Sindh is Pakistan's second largest province. Its total area is 141,000 square kilometers, which means a moderate population density of 213 persons per square kilometer. Karachi (q.v.), with nearly 10 million people, is the province's largest city, its capital, and one of its two ports. The province derives its name and a great deal of its economic wealth from the Indus River (q.v.). The river is called Sindhu in Sindh, it enters the province from the northeast of Kashmore and leaves it via an extensive delta in the southwest from where it flows into the Arabian Sea. An extensive network of irrigation canals brings the water of the Indus to the fields of Sindh. The British constructed a barrage on the river at Sukkur in 1933, and Pakistan built another barrage downstream at Kotri in the 1950s. Of the total cultivated area of 5.34 million hectares, 3.26 million hectares are irrigated, 2.63 million hectares by the canals of the Indus system.

Of Pakistan's four provinces, Sindh has the richest history. Its recorded history goes back to the Indus civilization (2300 B.C. to 1750 B.C.), manifestations of which exist at the archeological sites of Moenjodaro (q.v.), Amri, and Kot Diji. From the third to the seventh centuries A.D., Sindh was under the dominion of Persia, which yielded the province to the Arabs in 712 A.D. With the Arab conquest of Sindh began the province's Islamic period. Sindh passed under the control of the Mughuls (q.v.) in the sixteenth century. The British conquered Sindh in 1843 and made it a part of the Bombay presidency. In 1934 the British created the province of Sindh and appointed Karachi as its capital.

The powerful political families of Sindh did not clearly articulate their position with respect to the province's future once the British announced their decision to leave India in the hands of the Indians. The result was an exceptionally turbulent period in which the politically influential groups allowed themselves to be pulled in different directions by Muhammad Ali Jinnah's Muslim League, the Indian National Congress (qq.v), and the British administration.

After the establishment of Pakistan, Sindh remained politically restive. Seven governments were formed and collapsed in the eight-year period between 1947 and 1955, three of them under one individual, Muhammad Ayub Khuhro. In 1955 Sindh was merged into the One Unit of West Pakistan (q.v.) and was governed for 15 years from Lahore (q.v.). The province was reestablished on July 1, 1970. For five years it was under the control of the Pakistan People's Party (q.v.) whose chairman, Zulfikar Ali Bhutto (q.v.), was from one of the most prominent landed families of the province and whose cousin, Mumtaz Ali Bhutto (q.v.), served as the province's chief minister for three years.

In the 1980s the Sindh's *muhajir* community—millions of refugees who arrived in the province from India in 1947 and settled in its large cities, in particular Karachi and Hyderabad (q.v.)—began to assert themselves and formed a coalition with the indigenous Sindhis to work against the Pathans and the Punjabis who migrated to the province after the mid-1960s. This four-way ethnic distribution of Sindh's population—the indigenous Sindhis, the Muhajirs, the Pathans, and the Punjabis—brought things to a boil in the winter of 1986–87, when ethnic riots in Karachi claimed hundreds of lives. The Pakistan People's Party, dominated by rural Sindh and, therefore, by the original inhabitants of the province, came to political power after the elections of 1988 (q.v.). It was initially supported by the Muhajir Qaumi Mahaz (MQM) (q.v.), which had won decisively in Karachi and parts of Hyderabad. But the two parties drifted apart. The political conflict between the PPP and the MQM resulted in a great deal of violence as the supporters of the muhajir party fought the law-enforcement agencies controlled by the PPP-led government. The demise of the PPP government in August 1990 did not bring peace to the province, however. The government of prime minister Nawaz Sharif (q.v.) brought in the army to fight the MQM. The army stayed for three years. It was pulled out of the province in late 1994 by the government of Benazir Bhutto (q.v.), a year after she returned as prime minister. The army's withdrawal resulted in the bloodiest year in the history of Karachi in 1995 when nearly 2,000 persons were killed in street battles fought by the MQM activists and the forces of government. A concerted effort by the Bhutto government that involved the use of considerable (according to the muhajir leadership, ruthless) force brought peace to Karachi but at some political price. Bhutto's PPP performed poorly in the province's urban areas in the elections of February 1997 when the MQM, once again, captured most of the seats from Karachi in the National and Sindh assemblies. The MQM joined the governments formed by Nawaz Sharif's Pakistan Muslim League (q.v.) in both Karachi and Islamabad (q.v.) but left the coalition in 1998.

SINDH PUNJAB ABADGAR WELFARE ASSOCIATION (SPAWA). The Sindh Punjab Abadgar Welfare Association was formed by the small Punjabi landowners who had settled in the province of Sindh (q.v.). The small Punjabi settler (*abadgar*) in rural Sindh (q.v.) became the target of Sindhi nationalists as well as the *dacoits* (highway robbers) of Sindh (q.v.). Most of the Punjabi settlers came to Sindh looking for virgin land or for holdings larger in size than those they had cultivated in the crowded villages of their own province. Although precise statistics are not available, it appears that most of the land the Punjabi settlers cultivate was purchased from the "allotees"—the people who were given land by the government either in return for the holdings they had abandoned in India at the time of partition, or in recognition of meritorious military service. The SPAWA decided to involve itself in issues beyond the immediate welfare of its members after the success of the Muhajir Qaumi Mahaz (MQM) (q.v.) in mobilizing political support against the new migrants to Sindh. In March 1987 Chaudhri Niaz Ahmad, the president of the SPAWA, was ambushed and killed by a group of dacoits. The SPAWA responded by holding a well-attended condolence meeting in Roshanabad, a town on the national highway, thereby signaling the arrival of yet another political organization on the crowded political arena of Sindh province.

SINDHUDESH. The name Sindhudesh was used by G. M. Syed (q.v.), a Sindhi politician, to give meaning to his campaign for greater autonomy for the province of Sindh (q.v.) within the Pakistani federation. The use of this name evoked unhappy memories in the minds of those who suspected Syed to be working for Sindh's independence. This was so because the Bengali nationalists called their country Bangladesh once East Pakistan gained independence.

SIRHOEY AFFAIR, THE. In 1989 Prime Minister Benazir Bhutto (q.v.) made an effort to extract herself from the controls that had been placed on her by president Ghulam Ishaq Khan and Aslam Beg (qq.v.), chief of the Army Staff. She was obliged to discharge her duties as a member of an informal arrangement that came to be called the "troika" (q.v.) and included the president, the army chief, and herself. Her plan to dismantle this arrangement involved the appointment of Aslam Beg as chairman of the three Joint Chiefs of Staff, a post that did not carry much weight. Once Beg had been moved out, she planned to bring in an officer of her choice to become the army chief. The position of Joint Chiefs was occupied at that time by the Pakistani navy's Admiral Sirhoey. She asked the president to make these changes; the president, claiming that the constitution gave him the right to make these appointments, refused. What followed was a bitter dispute between the president and the prime minister that ultimately led to the latter's dismissal in August 1990. This episode came to be known as the Sirhoey Affair.

SIX POINT PROGRAM, THE. Sheikh Mujibur Rahman (q.v.) unveiled his "Six Point Program" for gaining autonomy for the province of East Pakistan in a meeting held in Lahore (q.v.) on February 12, 1966. The program's announcement was to have a dramatic effect on Pakistan's future as a nation state. Its announcement holds the same significance in Pakistan's history as the All-India Muslim League's (q.v.) resolution, passed on March 23, 1940, demanding the creation of Pakistan. That resolution was also proposed and passed in Lahore.

SOCIAL ACTION PROGRAM (SAP). In the early 1990s several members of the Aid to Pakistan Consortium (q.v.) conditioned their economic support on greater emphasis by the government to social development. These efforts by the donors resulted in the formulation of the Social Action Program in association with the World Bank (q.v.). The SAP was a comprehensive program for improving the quality of life in the country's poorer areas.

The SAP has a number of unique features. Built into it are provisions to ensure that the government would continue to provide support to the program. Initially, the government agreed to implement the program for three years, from the 1993–94 to 1995–96 financial years, at an expenditure of $4,020 million, of which $3,050 million, or 76 percent, was to be provided by Pakistan from its own resources. The World Bank agreed to lend $200 million for the program, another $100 million came from the Asian Development Bank (q.v.), while the Netherlands provided $13 million. Because the program was implemented in a reasonably satisfactory way, the World Bank agreed to seek the remaining $105 million from external sources. In 1996 the program was extended for a period of two years, to the 1997–98 financial year. The total expenditure over the five-year period was estimated at $7,731 million. In 1998 Pakistan and the donor community agreed to launch SAP II at a cost of $10 billion to cover the 1998–2002 period.

SOCIÉTÉ GÉNÉRALE DE SURVEILLANCE (SGS). The Société Générale de Surveillance has been used by a number of countries the world over to undertake preshipment inspection of goods being imported. With the help of such inspections, countries have been able to obtain import taxes levied on the true value of goods arriving from abroad rather than on the basis of their declared value. In those countries in which customs officials could collude with importers there could be a sizable loss of revenues because of undervaluing of imports. The SGS was hired to do preshipment inspection in Indonesia, the Philippines, and Pakistan. It was revealed, however, that the company had paid commissions to a Geneva lawyer to "start up the Pakistani contract." The contract was won by Cotecna, an SGS subsidiary. It was alleged by the authorities in Pakistan that the Swiss lawyer who had received payment from the SGS was working as an agent of Asif Ali Zardari (q.v.), the husband of Prime Minister Benazir Bhutto (q.v.). It was during Bhutto's second tenure as prime minister that the SGS was awarded the contract by Pakistan. The contract was, however, canceled by the caretaker administration that took office following the dismissal of Bhutto as prime minister in November 1996. The SGS admitted making the payment to the Swiss lawyer and sold Cotecna, but in March 1998 decided to sue the Islamabad (q.v.) government over the cancellation of the contract.

SOHRAB GOTH. In 1978 a Pathan entrepreneur set up a store in Sohrab Goth, a village on the outskirts of Karachi (q.v.), selling imported merchandise smuggled into the country through illegal channels. Soon after,

Sohrab Goth became the site of a *"bara"* market, so called because of a similar bazaar in a village of that name that operated near Peshawar (q.v.) selling smuggled imported goods. In 1981 thousands of refugees from Afghanistan moved to Karachi and settled in the vicinity of Sohrab Goth. With the refugees came arms and drugs into the "bara" market of Sohrab Goth. With the emergence of Pakistan as a source of heroin for Europe and America, Sohrab Goth became an important link in the drug-supply chain. This troubled the U.S. administration and, with the use of heroin spreading quickly among Pakistan's affluent classes, the government of General Zia ul-Haq (q.v.) also began to show concern. Pressure mounted on the government to move against the drug merchants of Sohrab Goth.

On December 12, 1986 the Sindh (q.v.) administration launched "Operation Cleanup." Bulldozers moved to the village and leveled shops and houses. Reaction to the operation came quickly: on December 14, 1986 the residents of Sohrab Goth descended on the neighboring Orangi Colony and unleashed "acts of reprisal" against the *muhajir* (q.v.) (refugee) community. The "Black Sunday" left dozens of people dead. What ensued was ethnic violence of the type Pakistan had not known in its history. It left 170 dead and thousands injured. For several days the government seemed to have lost control over Karachi's outskirts. Peace was restored by army action and on December 22, 1986 the Pathans were moved into three camps south of Sohrab Goth on the national highway.

SOLARZ AMENDMENT. *See* PARVEZ, ARSHAD Z.

SOUTH ASIAN ASSOCIATION FOR REGIONAL COOPERATION (SAARC). The South Asian Association for Regional Cooperation was the brainchild of President Ziaur Rahman of Bangladesh (q.v.). Formally launched in December 1985 in Dacca at the summit of leaders from Bangladesh, Bhutan, India, the Maldives, Nepal, Pakistan, and Sri Lanka, its purpose is to improve relations among the countries of South Asia and to provide a forum for the discussion of regional issues. All decisions are to taken on the basis of consensus. The SAARC has a small secretariat that operates out of Khatmandu, the capital of Nepal.

SOUTH ASIAN PREFERENTIAL TRADING ARRANGEMENT (SAPTA). After ratification by Pakistan, the South Asian Preferential Trading Arrangement came into being on December 8, 1995. It was expected that the formation of the SAPTA would provide some impetus for growth of regional trade in South Asia. Trade between the countries of the region amounted to only 3 percent of the total in the first half of the 1990s. The items covered by the SAPTA agreement were a small fraction of even this modest exchange, however. The government of Pakistan decided to move with extreme caution in implementing SAPTA. It allowed duty relief on only 38 items (spices, fibers, medicinal herbs, leather, chemicals, etc.), whereas India gave concessions to 106 items to be imported from Pakistan. Also, the duty on imports of specified items from the members of the South Asian Association for Regional Cooperation (SAARC) (q.v.) other than India was to be equivalent to 85 percent of the prevailing rate compared to 90 percent for imports from India. At the tenth annual meeting of SAARC that foreign ministers held in New Delhi on December 19, 1995, the decision was made to create a free trade area after the turn of the century but no later than 2005.

SOUTH-EAST ASIA TREATY ORGANIZATION (SEATO). SEATO, established in 1956, was the brainchild of John Foster Dulles, the Secretary of State in the administration of the U.S. President Dwight D. Eisenhower (1953–61). It was a defense alliance that included the United States and a number of countries from Southeast Asia, all of whom being apprehensive about the encroachment of communism. Pakistan, having signed the Mutual Defense Agreement (q.v.) with the United States in 1954, joined SEATO, in which, in addition to the United States, it was the only nonregional member of the alliance. Pakistan's membership in the alliance was important because the country was already a member of the Central Treaty Organization (CENTO) and thereby provided the link between the two alliances. Turkey, by being the member of both CENTO and the North Atlantic Treaty Organization (NATO), was another link in the chain built by Dulles to contain the spread of communism in Europe and Asia. *See also* United States–Pakistan Relations.

SOVIET UNION–PAKISTAN RELATIONS. Pakistan's emergence as an independent state in August 1947 was not treated with enthusiasm by any major political power, least of all by the Soviet Union. Each country had its reason for not according the new country a warm welcome: in the case of the Soviet Union it was particularly distasteful to see a "religious nationality" break away from the state to establish a separate political entity of its own. The Muslim republics in central Asia had never shown a great deal of satisfaction at being included in the Russian empire— either in Czarist Russia or in the Union of Soviet Socialist Republics (USSR). By granting the Muslims of British India the right to secede from the motherland, London had accommodated the forces of separation that Moscow had resisted in its own domain for so long. Besides,

Pakistan was not very far from the USSR's southern border and some of the ethnic groups in the new country had historical ties with the Muslims in the Central Asian Soviet republics. An unqualified and warm reception to Pakistan's birth would have meant giving a form of recognition to the problem of Soviet nationalities. For understandable reasons, the Soviets were not prepared to do this.

This set the stage for two foreign-policy decisions taken by the Pakistani leadership in the early 1950s. First, to stay out of the non-aligned movement; second, to side unequivocally with the Western countries in the Cold War with the Soviet bloc. Both decisions dismayed the Soviets, who, with the assumption of power by Nikita Khrushchev, began to openly side with India on a number of disputes between Indian and Pakistan. This pronounced Soviet tilt toward India was corrected somewhat when Zulfikar Ali Bhutto (q.v.) became foreign minister in the government of Ayub Khan (q.v.). In the early 1960s Pakistan signed an oil-exploration agreement with the Soviets; in 1966, at the invitation of Soviet Prime Minister Aleksei Kosygin, India and Pakistan signed the Tashkent Declaration (q.v.); and in the second half of the 1960s, Pakistan invited Soviet assistance for setting up a steel mill in Karachi (q.v.). This thaw in the relationship lasted until 1971, when the Soviets once again supported India in the third Indo–Pakistan War (q.v.), Pakistan's war over Bangladesh (q.v.).

The entry of Soviet troops into Afghanistan in December 1979 pitted Pakistan and the Soviet Union on opposite sides of the Afghan conflict. The 1980s saw a sharp deterioration in relations as Pakistan permitted the use of its territory not only to accommodate 3.5 million refugees from Afghanistan but also to channel military and economic assistance to the Afghan mujahideens (q.v.), who successfully battled the Soviet troops in their country. In January 1988 Mikhail Gorbachev announced that the Soviet troops would be pulled out of Afghanistan if Pakistan and the communist regime of Afghanistan could sign an agreement at Geneva before March 15, 1988. Pakistan and Afghanistan signed an agreement that met this deadline and the Soviet Union pulled out its troops from Afghanistan.

The collapse of the Soviet Union in 1991 and its replacement by the Russian Republic brought a significant change in Moscow's attitude toward South Asia, including India and Pakistan. Preoccupied with its own economic problems, Russia was now only marginally interested in South Asia. It was now more interested in carving a role for itself as a member of the community of industrial and developed nations. Its ambition was rewarded when in June 1998 the G7 grouping of industrial nations became the G8, with Russia included. In the very first G8 meeting held in Birmingham, England, Russian joined with other industrial countries to agree to a freeze in lending by international financial institutions to sanction both India and Pakistan after the two countries carried out nuclear bomb tests in May. A few days after agreeing with the G8 position, Russia announced its intention to supply two heavy-water reactors to India, a development that drew instant criticism from the Western countries and seemed to suggest that the country was not playing entirely by the rules its was now expected to follow.

STOCK MARKETS. Pakistan has three stock markets operating in Karachi, Lahore, and Islamabad (qq.v.). At one point in the country's history—in the 1960s during the presidency of Ayub Khan (q.v.)—the evolution of capital markets in Pakistan was much more advanced compared with countries at the same level of development. Zulfikar Ali Bhutto's (q.v.) reforms introduced in the early 1970s, including the nationalization of large-scale industries and financial institutions working in the private sector, dealt a severe blow to capital-market development, however.

The stock markets showed some life in the early 1990s when Mian Nawaz Sharif (q.v.) was in office as prime minister for the first time. In 1992 the KSE-100 index crossed the 2000 mark for the first time in the history of the Karachi Stock Exchange. The economic downturn during the second tenure of Benazir Bhutto (q.v.) as prime minister depressed the markets, however. When she was dismissed in November 1996, the KSE-100 index had dipped to below 1300. The index recovered somewhat with Nawaz Sharif's assumption of office in February 1997. It crossed the 2000 mark once again. In May 1998, however, following the testing of nuclear bombs by India and the prospect that Pakistan may follow suit, the index showed a sharp decline. The business community feared that if Pakistan also tested nuclear weapons, the imposition of economic sanctions by Western nations would have a serious economic effect. On May 22 the index lost 350 points to close at 1202, a 10-year low. On May 23 the index was hit again but for different reasons: the government's unhelpful approach toward independent power producers who were providing electricity to the Water and Power Development Authority's (WAPDA) (q.v.). national grid. The index registered another record low at 1157. There was near panic in the market following the announcement by Pakistan that it carried out nuclear tests on May 28; the KSE-100 index closed at 1032, and the government, using the emergency powers it had acquired, shut down the market for one day. When the markets opened on May 30 the index dropped below 1000. It declined to 850 in August 1998 when Pakistan began to indicate that failing action by the industrial countries to remove the sanctions imposed after the nuclear tests might force it to default on its external obligations.

SUFISM. Sufism reflects the softer, reflective side of Islam. It is much more tolerant of local traditions and much less committed to fundamentalism or orthodoxy. The word "Sufism" is probably derived from *suf,* the Arabic word for wool, a fabric sometimes used by the Prophet Muhammad. The Sufis aim to emulate the Prophet's concern for humanity without focusing on Islamic dogma or rituals. Khwaja Mohiuddin Chisti is the greatest Sufi saint of South Asia. His mausoleum in Ajmer, Rajasthan, draws thousands of pilgrims every year. The Urs at Ajmer, to commemorate the anniversary of Chisti's death, is the most important pilgrimage for the Muslims of South Asia. Several shrines in Pakistan—in particular, those of Khwaja Farid in Pakpattan, Data Ganj Baksh in Lahore (q.v.), Shah Abdul Latif in Bhit—keep the Sufi tradition alive in the country. The shrines' devotees come mostly from the poorer segments of the population that have yet to be affected by the growing move in the country toward Islamic fundamentalism.

SUHRAWARDHY, HUSSAIN SHAHEED (1893–1963). Hussain Shaheed Suhrawardhy was born in Midnapur, Bengal and was educated at Calcutta and Oxford. He entered politics in the mid-1920s and was a member of the Bengal Legislative Council from 1924 to 1945. The launching of the Khilafat movement by the Indian Muslim leadership introduced Suhrawardhy to mass politics. In 1936 Suhrawardhy was appointed to the powerful position of secretary of the Bengal Muslim League. He used this position to advance his political career beyond Bengal. In 1940, at the historic meeting of the All-India Muslim League (q.v.) held in Lahore (q.v.), he seconded the "Pakistan Resolution" (q.v.) demanding the establishment of an independent state for the Muslims of India.

Suhrawardhy took an active part in the Pakistan movement and, after having been elected as the parliamentary leader of the Muslim League Party in Bengal's Legislative Assembly, he was invited to become the province's chief minister in 1946. He held back his support for the British plan of June 3, 1947 to partition the provinces of Bengal and Punjab (q.v.) and, for a few weeks, actively canvassed the idea of a united but independent Bengal. It appears that Suhrawardhy's campaign for the creation of an independent Bengal may have had the blessing of Muhammad Ali Jinnah (q.v.), but it did not endear him to other leaders of the Muslim League. His growing influence in Muslim politics was resented in particular by Liaqat Ali Khan (q.v.), who teamed up with Khawaja Nazimuddin to deny Suhrawardy the chairmanship of the East Bengal Muslim League, formed after the partition of Bengal and the establishment of Pakistan. But Suhrawardy was too active a politician to be sidelined for very long; he reasserted his role in Bengal in 1949 by founding the Awami Muslim League (AML). The AML joined hands with Fazlul Haq's (q.v.) Krishak Sramik Party in 1954 to defeat the Muslim League in the first election held in Bengal after partition. In September 1955 Suhrawardy was elected the leader of the opposition in the Second Constituent Assembly (q.v.). He used this position to seek constitutional protection for East Pakistan in any political arrangement to be devised by the Constituent Assembly. After declaring that the Constitution of 1956 (q.v.) had secured "95 percent autonomy for East Pakistan," he accepted President Iskander Mirza's (q.v.) call to become Pakistan's prime minister, a position he held for just over a year, from September 1956 to October 1957. He opposed the martial-law government of General Ayub Khan (q.v.) and campaigned openly and actively against the military government's plans to introduce a new constitutional arrangement. This led to his incarceration in 1962 for about six months. He died in Beirut on December 5, 1963.

"SURREYGATE." The story that the Zardaris—Asif Ali Zardari and his wife, Benazir Bhutto (qq.v.), the prime minister of Pakistan—may have purchased an estate in Surrey, near London, was first carried by the *Sunday Express* in late May 1996. The news was instantly communicated to the people in Pakistan and a question pertaining to the alleged deal was raised in the National Assembly by Mian Nawaz Sharif (q.v.), the leader of the opposition, and vehemently denied by the prime minister. The opposition's accusations and the prime minister's angry denial earned the developing story the name of "Surreygate."

Ms. Bhutto tried to get out of the situation created by the opposition's changes by first denying them angrily. The story, however, refused to go away. On August 21, 1996 Nawaz Sharif took the floor of the National Assembly once again, this time armed with a long list of damaging facts that seemed to lend credence to the accusation that a private firm, Roomina Property, registered in the Isle of Man, in October 1995 had purchased the Rockwood estate in Surrey. The Surrey house was being furnished with tons of freight carried by Pakistan International Airlines at no charge. The purchase of the house by the Zardaris in Surrey was one of the charges leveled against the prime minister in the dismissal order issued by President Farooq Leghari (q.v.) on November 5, 1996.

SYED, G. M. (1903–1992). G. M. Syed was born in the Dadu district in Sindh (q.v.) and remained active in politics for more than four decades, often at odds with the government in power. He was among several prominent leaders of British India who initially resisted Muhammad Ali Jinnah's (q.v.) attempt to create a strong political organization for the entire Indian Muslim community. Like Khizar Hayat Khan Tiwana and Sir Sikander Hayat Khan in Punjab, Abdul Ghaffar Khan in the Northwest Frontier, and Fazlul Haq (qq.v.) in Bengal, he believed that Muslim interests in the Muslim-majority provinces could be best served by a loose federation of Indian provinces. Although he joined the All-India Muslim League (q.v.) in the 1940s, became a cosponsor of the "Pakistan Resolution" (q.v.) in 1940, and, for a brief period (1942–46), was a member of the Central Working Party of the All-India Muslim League (1942), he never won the full trust of Muhammad Ali Jinnah.

After independence, Syed moved into the opposition and began to mobilize support for his efforts to gain greater autonomy for Sindh within the state of Pakistan. It was for this reason that he opposed the incorporation of Sindh in the One Unit of West Pakistan (q.v.) and suffered long periods of imprisonment for launching an anti-One Unit campaign in the province. His disillusionment with the course of political development grew and resulted in the launching of the Jiye Sindh (Long live Sindh) and Sindhudesh (qq.v.) (Land of the Sindhis) movements, which were seen by his detractors as secessionist in nature. The governments of Zia ul-Haq and Muhammad Khan Junejo (qq.v.) were more tolerant toward Syed and allowed him greater freedom of movement and expression. He was allowed to travel in India and speak openly in public. Newspapers carried extensive coverage of Syed's activities, leading to speculation that the government may have been using him to create another force in Sindh besides Benazir Bhutto's Pakistan People's Party (qq.v.).

↩ T ↪

TABLIGHI JAMAAT. The Tablighi Jamaat (organization for the spread of God's word) began in Delhi, India in 1880. The organization operated out of an office located near the shrine of Sufi saint Nazimuddin Aulia in a suburb of Delhi. In the 1940s Muhammad Ilyas, a Muslim reformist scholar, gave the movement its present-day form. After the establishment of Pakistan, the Jamaat set itself up in the new country, using Raiwind near Lahore (qq.v) as its headquarters. The Tablighi Jamaat is different from other major religious organizations in Pakistan in that it neither has regular membership nor any identified leadership. All Muslims can participate in its activities as long as they fulfill certain requirements. Those wishing to join the Jamaat's traveling missions must demonstrate that they have made arrangements to have their dependents looked after during their absence. The Jamaat's main purpose is to establish contact with both Muslims and non-Muslims and teach them correct Islamic practices. The task of proselytizing involves members of the Jamaat, both male and female, leaving home in small groups for varying periods of time, ranging from three to 40 days. All expenses for these trips must be borne by the members themselves. Only those who have already performed a four-month-long domestic mission and two 40-day local tours are allowed to embark on foreign trips. After the resurgence of Islam in Pakistan in the 1970s and 1980s, the Tablighi Jamaat's attraction increased enormously. Now hundreds of thousands of people attend its annual meeting held in Karachi's (q.v.) Madani mosque. According to some estimates, 2 million people are currently associated with the Jamaat in Pakistan. The organization remains active in India and has established itself in the United States, Europe, and Africa.

TALIBAN. The emergence of the Taliban—the Arabic word for "students"—as a major political and military force in Afghanistan caught most observers, in particular those from the West, by surprise. In November 1994 the Taliban marched out of their camps in the northwestern areas of Pakistan, organized themselves into a potent military force, and, in a short span of a few weeks, conquered one-third of Afghanistan. The size of the force increased as it got closer to Kabul; en route the Taliban also picked up sophisticated weapons and acquired an air force. In March 1995 they arrived at the doorstep of Kabul.

Few guerrilla leaders chose to stand up and fight the Taliban; some joined them while others, like Gulbuddin Hekmatyar, just melted away into the hills, leaving the territory they controlled and the arms they had collected in the hands of the advancing force. By attacking the city of Kabul the Taliban lost their moral authority, however. Their rapid advance toward Kabul without shedding much blood had distinguished them from other guerrilla forces that had ravaged the country in their hunger for power and territory. The Taliban assault on Kabul was as vicious and destructive as the relentless campaign conducted for years by Hekmatyar, however. In the end the Taliban failed to capture the city, which was protected by Ahmad Shah Masoud, the most successful guerrilla chief in the days when the Afghans were fighting the Russians rather than each other.

In September 1995 the Taliban changed their tactics and returned to doing what they had done so effectively before their advance on Kabul. They brought more territory under their control including the city of

Herat in the western part of the country, largely by bribing or cajoling faction leaders to join them. Although they now controlled nearly one-half of the Afghan territory, by bringing Herat into their domain they picked a new enemy, Iran. Herat was located in the Shia part of Afghanistan and Iran was not prepared to let its fellow Shias be subjected to rule by the Pathan Sunnis. The Taliban's entry into Herat also soured Pakistan's relations with Iran.

The entry of the Taliban into the Afghan picture complicated Pakistan's relations with the country it had helped for so long and at a great cost to itself. On September 6, 1995 a mob burned down Pakistan's embassy in Kabul. An embassy official was killed and others in the building, including the ambassador, were injured. The mob was protesting Pakistan's alleged support of the Taliban, something the Pakistani government had denied.

The final assault by the Taliban came in 1996 when they were able to buy their way into Meraj Sharif, the last stronghold of the forces that had sought to slow down their conquest of Afghanistan. With Meraj Sharif under their control, the Taliban were able to claim that they were the legitimate rulers of Afghanistan. This claim was accepted by Pakistan and Saudi Arabia, who recognized the Taliban government. Soon after this recognition, however, the Taliban forces were driven out of Meraj Sharif and reconfined once again to about two-thirds of the country.

While continuing to do battle in the northeast of the country, the Taliban government in Kabul introduced an exceptionally rigid style of government in the areas they occupied. Girls were prohibited from attending school, women were barred from employment outside their homes, music was banned, men were ordered to grow beards, and women were instructed to cover themselves from head to toe whenever they left home. These dictates were first ignored by the Western world, but in late 1997 a number of countries, most notably the United States, began to openly express concern to Pakistan about the way the Taliban were governing Afghanistan. During a brief visit to Islamabad (q.v.), Madeleine Albright, the U.S. Secretary of State, told her Pakistani hosts that the United States expected Pakistan to exercise its influence over the Taliban to get them to relax their rule over their country.

By August 1998, following the conquest of Mazar Sharif, the last stronghold of the opposition, the Taliban could claim to have taken all of Afghanistan. They might have gained international recognition but for the attack on the United States embassies in Kenya and Tanzania for which the Americans held Osama bin Laden (q.v.), based in Khost (q.v.), Afghanistan, to be responsible.

TAMIZUDDIN KHAN, MAULVI (1889–1963). Born in Bengal, Tamizuddin Khan became active in Muslim politics of the province at an early age. He was elected to the Bengali Provincial Assembly in 1937 from a Muslim seat and in 1938 joined the Krishak Praja—the Muslim League (q.v.) coalition administration of Fazlul Haq. After the partition of British India in 1947 and the establishment of Pakistan, Tamizuddin left Bengal and moved to Karachi (q.v.), the capital of the new country. The Muslim League elected him deputy president of the Constituent Assembly (q.v.). Muhammad Ali Jinnah (q.v.) was the assembly's president. After Jinnah's death in September 1948, Tamizuddin became the president of the Constituent Assembly. Under his leadership the assembly spent a great deal of its time debating the "basic principles" that should govern constitution-making but failed to write a constitution for the country. The assembly was unable to agree on such issues as the sharing of power between the federation and the provinces and the role of Islam in politics. In 1954, seven years after having been in existence, it was able to agree on one important issue, however: that the governor-general wielded too much power under the existing legal structure. A bill was moved and passed to curtail the chief executive's power, but Governor-General Ghulam Muhammad (q.v.) moved before the bill became law. He dissolved the Constituent Assembly.

As the president of the assembly, Tamizuddin filed a suit in Sindh High Court questioning the legality of the governor-general's move. The court accepted the argument but, on appeal by the government, its decision was overturned by the Supreme Court. Chief Justice Muhammad Munir (q.v.), in writing the majority opinion, argued in favor of the government on the basis of the "doctrine of necessity" (q.v.), or the judicial need to rectify an act, even if it is a priori unlawful, once a new government has come into being following the act. *Tamizuddin vs. the Government of Pakistan* remains a landmark case in the legal and political history of Pakistan. The "doctrine of necessity" was to be invoked a number of times by the courts to give legal cover to coup d'etats and other unconstitutional moves.

Tamizuddin Khan returned to politics after General Ayub Khan (q.v.) had consolidated his hold over Pakistan. In 1962 he joined Ayub Khan's Pakistan Muslim League (q.v.) and was unanimously elected speaker of the National Assembly constituted under the Constitution of 1962 (q.v.). By accepting the political order that was put into place by the military coup led by Ayub Khan in 1958, Tamizuddin Khan implicitly accepted the "doctrine of necessity."

TANZIM NIFAZ SHARIAT-I-MUHAMMADI (TNSM). Tanzim Nifaz Shariat-i-Muhammadi, or the organization for the promulgation of the legal system endorsed by Prophet Muhammad, scored its first success in the spring of 1994 when the government agreed to the enforcement of *Sharia* (Islamic law) in Malakand, a remote, mountainous district in the northwest of Pakistan. The TNSM, responding to a call for action by Maulana Sufi Muhammad, a highly respected Islamic scholar from the area, had launched a violent campaign directly challenging the authority of the state. It blocked the Malakand Pass on the Mardan–Buner highway, a busy road that connected this remote area with the rest of Pakistan. A dozen people were killed when the government's law-enforcement agencies tried to open the highway. On May 17 the administration of Benazir Bhutto (q.v.) accepted the TNSM's demand and agreed to establish a new system of *kazi* (magistrates with knowledge of Islam and therefore able to apply the Islamic legal system) courts.

A number of TNSM activists were not satisfied with the slow pace at which the government was implementing the agreement it had signed with their organization, however. Accordingly, in November 1994, another demonstration was organized that resulted in the loss of 21 lives, this time in the adjoining district of Swat. This was the second time that the TNSM's armed followers had confronted the government during the course of the year. Among those killed was Badiuzzaman, a Pakistan People's Party member of the Northwest Frontier Province (qq.v.) Provincial Assembly. The government now took a more aggressive position and arrested Maulana Sufi Muhammad. It also declared that it had no intention of moving faster than it had planned in bringing the new legal structure to the area.

TARAR, MUHAMMAD RAFIQ (1929–). Muhammad Rafiq Tarar entered politics after a long career in the judiciary (q.v.). He was born in the Punjab (q.v.) city of Gujranwala and studied law at Lahore Law College. After serving as a civil judge for a number of years, he was elevated to the Punjab High Court and from there went to the Supreme Court of Pakistan. He retired from the Supreme Court in 1994 and, three years later, received a ticket from Prime Minister Mian Nawaz Sharif's Pakistan Muslim League (PML) (qq.v.) to contest for a seat in the Senate. He won the seat. In December 1997 he was chosen by the Pakistan Muslim League to be the party's candidate for the presidency.

Tarar was sworn in as Pakistan's ninth president on January 1, 1998. He was elected the day before by a joint sitting of the National Assembly, the Senate, and the four provincial assemblies. Representing the PML, Tarar received 374 votes compared to 58 votes cast for Aftab Shahban Mirani, the candidate of the Pakistan People's Party (PPP) (q.v.). Jamiatul-Ulemai-Islam's Maulana Fazlur Rahman (qq.v.) received 26 votes.

TARBELA DAM. The Tarbela Dam is one of the largest earth-filled dams in the world and the largest dam in Pakistan. It was constructed at a site some 80 kilometers north of Islamabad (q.v.), Pakistan's capital. The dam rises to a height of 150 meters above the river bed and is 2,800 meters long. The reservoir area is 132 square kilometers; the Tarbela lake formed by the dam is 80 kilometers long. The initial size of the reservoir is over 11.1 MAF (million acre feet), although this capacity is being rapidly eroded by the heavy silting of the lake. Like the Mangla Dam (q.v.) on the Jhelum River, Tarbela is a multipurpose project. It provides electric power as well as water for irrigation. Once the Tarbela powerhouse is completed, it will have the capacity to generate 4,000 megawatts (MW) of electricity. In 1996 it had reached the capacity of 3,478 MW.

After some questioning and hesitation, the international community of donors agreed to finance the project out of the financial resources that had been mobilized to implement the Indus Waters Treaty (q.v.) between India and Pakistan. By the middle of 1966 the World Bank (q.v.), which managed the Indus Basin Development Fund on behalf of the donor community, had been persuaded that the dam on the Indus (q.v.) at Tarbela made economic sense, although the economic rate of return from the project was not very high. The dam's construction started in 1968, four years later than originally planned; it took six years to build and was commissioned in 1974. It was constructed by a consortium of European companies, led by an Italian firm, that worked under the name of Tarbela Joint Ventures (TJV). The TJV managed to outbid the consortium that had constructed the Mangla dam.

In retrospect, the dam has made a very significant contribution to Pakistan's economic development. The low rate of return originally estimated by the World Bank was no longer valid after the Organization of Petroleum Exporting Countries in the 1970s increased the price of oil manifold. Pakistan, an oil-importing country, needed its own sources of power supply. The power generated by Tarbela became much more critical for the country than had been originally envisaged.

TASHKENT DECLARATION. Immediately after India and Pakistan had accepted the United Nations resolution calling for a cease-fire in the Indo–Pakistan War of 1965 (q.v.), Aleksei Kosygin, the Soviet Prime Minister, invited Muhammad Ayub Khan (q.v.), President of Pakistan and Lal Bahadur Shastri, the Prime Minister of India to Tashkent to begin the process of reconciliation between the two countries. The choice of

Tashkent, the capital of the southern republic of Uzbekistan in the Asian part of the Soviet Union, underscored the Soviet interest in the area in which both India and Pakistan were located. The Tashkent Declaration was signed after a week of intense negotiations between the two delegations. Kosygin and his associates took an active part in the discussions. Prodded and encouraged by the Soviet leadership, the two South Asian leaders affirmed "their obligation under the [United Nations] Charter not to have recourse to force and to settle their disputes through peaceful means." Pakistan and India agreed to withdraw their troops to the positions they had occupied on August 5, 1965, when Pakistan had launched its Operation Gibraltar (q.v.) to encourage an uprising in the Indian part of Kashmir (q.v.). Prime Minister Shastri's death of a heart attack soon after the signing of the Tashkent Declaration added a dramatic touch to the entire episode.

Although the Tashkent Declaration did little to improve the relations between India and Pakistan, it had a profound impact on political developments in Pakistan. It proved to be the turning point for the administration of Ayub Khan. It quickly became known that Foreign Minister Zulfikar Ali Bhutto (q.v.) had not supported the declaration. He resigned his post soon after returning from Tashkent, alleging that Ayub Khan had given up at Tashkent what had been gained on the battlefield. Bhutto's position on Tashkent, which he never spelled out in detail, won him many admirers in Punjab (q.v.), Pakistan's largest province. "Tashkent" proved to be a potent political slogan. It attracted the powerful anti-India lobby to the fold of Zulfikar Ali Bhutto's Pakistan People's Party (q.v.) and contributed to the party's triumph in the elections of December 1970 (q.v.).

TAXILA. Taxila is one of the most important archeological sites in Pakistan. It is about 30 kilometer northwest of the twin cities of Rawalpindi and Islamabad (qq.v.), a couple of kilometers beyond the Margalla Pass. The cluster of three cities now called Taxila was built over a period of more than a thousand years, from 600 B.C. to 600 A.D. These cities together constituted a highly developed cultural, religious, and economic center situated at the confluence of the trade routes that linked China, India, Central Asia, and Europe. Buddhism evolved in these cities and spread to other parts of Asia. Asoka, the grandson of Chandragupta of the Mauryan empire, embraced Buddhism while serving his grandfather as the viceroy of Taxila. It is probable that the large stupa of Dharmarajika at Taxila was erected by Asoka to house a portion of Buddha's ashes.

The first of Taxila's three cities is now called Bhir Mound. It was built in the sixth century B.C. and lasted for 400 years, to the second century B.C. Alexander the Great visited Bhir Mound in 326 B.C. and with the help of three interpreters held a prolonged philosophical discourse with the intellectuals of the area. Sirkap, the second city, was founded by the Bactrian Greeks who were descendants of Alexander's army. The city lasted for 260 years, from 180 B.C. to 80 A.D. In about 60 A.D. the Kushans invaded Taxila and began work on a new city, Sirsukh, which lasted for about 600 years. It was sacked and buried by the White Huns in 455 A.D. but was rebuilt, although not to its previous grandeur.

Most of the archeological work at Taxila was done by Sir John Marshall around 1912. The three cities yielded a rich harvest of stone sculptures, coins, implements, household utensils, and ornaments that are now to be found in museums all over the world. The best Pakistani collections are in the museums at Taxila, Peshawar, and Lahore (qq.v.).

TEHRIK-E-INSAF. Imran Khan (q.v.) launched a movement on April 25, 1996 to fight corruption and injustice he said were rampant in the country. He called the movement Tehrik-e-Insaf, or the Justice Movement. That Imran Khan would start a political movement had been speculated for a long time. The actual announcement of the launching came 10 days after a big bomb extensively damaged the hospital he had built in memory of his mother, Shaukat Khanum.

Imran Khan provided few details of his program other than to say that he planned to set up committees to advise him on improvement in the areas that included justice and legal affairs, human rights, health, education, economy, youth employment, women's affairs, and the environment. The Tehrik was still struggling to organize itself when in November 1996 President Farooq Leghari (q.v.) dismissed the government of Prime Minister Benazir Bhutto (q.v.) and ordered general elections to be held in February 1997 (q.v.). Khan and the Tehrik launched an active campaign and fielded some 300 candidates for the National and Provincial Assemblies. Imran Khan contested for half a dozen seats himself. He chose to fight from Lahore (q.v.), his native city; Mianwali, the native city of his father; and from the cities where he thought he had a firm base of support. The Tehrik's failure to win a single seat surprised most political observers. The elections were a major setback for the Tehrik and Imran Khan's ambition to carve a solid political base for himself. He continued his efforts to develop grass-root support once Nawaz Sharif and his Pakistan Muslim League (qq.v.) assumed power.

TEHRIK-E-ISTIQLAL. The Tehrik-e-Istiqlal was founded in 1969 by Air Marshal (retired) Asghar Khan (q.v.) with the aim of providing Pakistan's rapidly growing middle classes an organizational vehicle for articulating their political, economic, and social aspirations. It was his belief that the established parties were either too far to the right of the political spectrum or too much on the left to be attractive to the constituency he sought to cultivate. The Pakistan Muslim League (q.v.) of that time was dominated by the landed aristocracy, the Jamaat-e-Islami (q.v.) by Islamic fundamentalists, and the Pakistan People's Party (PPP) (q.v.) was then under the influence of urban intellectuals who espoused various leftist causes. According to this analysis, therefore, there was a lot of space in the center of the political spectrum that a party such as the Tehrik could occupy.

The Tehrik's program attracted a sizable following from the urban professional classes: a number of lawyers, doctors, and engineers joined the party. The party's senior office holders were mostly retired government officials or influential lawyers from Lahore, Karachi, and Rawalpindi (qq.v.). The Tehrik failed to develop a strong grass-root following, however. None of the candidates it fielded in the national elections of 1970 and 1977 (qq.v.) were elected to the National Assembly. Asghar Khan, the party's chairman, was defeated in 1970 by a relatively unknown PPP politician from Rawalpindi.

In order to improve its political standing and gain a wider basis of support for itself, the Tehrik joined the other opposition parties in 1981 to launch the Movement for the Restoration of Democracy (MRD) (q.v.). Because the MRD was dominated by the PPP, a party with which the Tehrik had a difficult relationship all along, its stay in the movement was not a comfortable one. The Tehrik quit the MRD in 1986 and launched on its own once again. This decision and the visit by Air Marshal Asghar Khan to Kabul in the summer of 1967—an effort aimed at bringing peace to Afghanistan by negotiating with Najibullah, the Afghan president whose government Pakistan had refused to recognize—caused him to lose support among the members of his constituency. It resulted in a number of defections from the party, particularly from the province of Balochistan and the Northwest Frontier Province (qq.v.).

The Tehrik surprised political observers by joining the PPP to form the Pakistan Democratic Alliance (PDA) (q.v.) to fight the elections of 1990 (q.v.). The alliance with the PPP did not produce tangible results for the Tehrik and was terminated after the elections. The elections of October 1993 (q.v.) did not improve Tehrik's standing as none of its members were elected either to the National Assembly or to any of the four Provincial Assemblies. In the spring of 1996 Asghar Khan resigned from the leadership of the party but was persuaded to stay on. The party fielded a few candidates in the elections of 1997 (q.v.) but failed to win any seat.

TEHRIK ITEHAD-E-QABAIL. The Tehrik Itehad-e-Qabail (the Movement for Tribal Cooperation) was founded by a number of tribal leaders from the Northwest Frontier Province (q.v.). Its main objective was to reconcile the differences between the Pashtun tribes supporting the Afghan mujahideen (q.v.) and those that favored the Kabul government. The Tehrik's central leaders were arrested by the provincial government on February 17, 1987, when they declared their intention of traveling by road from Peshawar (q.v.) to Kabul on a "peace mission." The tribal leaders said that this mission was intended to set the stage for the Geneva "proximity talks" (q.v.) of February 1987 by showing that the tribal people of Pakistan and Afghanistan could reach an understanding on the differences that continued to fuel the rebellion in Afghanistan. These efforts did not produce any tangible results as the tribal leaders continued to battle one another, even after the troops of the Soviet Union withdrew from Afghanistan.

TERRORISM. One consequence of the ten-year Afghan struggle against the occupation of their country by the Soviet Union was to turn Pakistan into both a target of terrorism as well as a base for the training of terrorists. The ground for these developments was laid in the mid-1980s when the U.S. Central Intelligence Agency (CIA) worked with Pakistan's Interservices Intelligence (ISI) (q.v.) to establish training bases for the Afghan mujahideen (q.v.) on both sides of the Afghanistan–Pakistan border. The most important of these bases was in Khost (q.v.), a small town south of Kabul, near the Pakistan border. The CIA built an elaborate network of training camps at Khost. Some of these facilities were lodged deep in the mountains to protect them against air attacks by the Soviet Union.

Following the departure of the Soviet Union from Afghanistan in 1989 and the withdrawal of CIA operators from Pakistan, the mujahideen training camps were taken over by a number of different groups that continued to fight in the prolonged civil war in Afghanistan. The camps on the Pakistani side helped train young graduates from the *madrasas* (q.v.) (religious schools) who were to form the backbone of the Taliban (q.v.) movement that gradually extended its sway over Afghanistan. The Khost facilities were acquired by Osama bin Laden (q.v.), a Saudi millionaire, to train and equip hundreds of people to participate in various conflicts that pitched the forces of radical Islam against a variety of opponents. People trained in the camps run by bin Laden were said to have taken part in the conflicts in Bosnia–Herzegovina, Chechnya, Kosovo, Kashmir (q.v.), the Philippines, Somalia, and Sudan.

On August 7, 1998 terrorist bombs placed outside the United States embassies in Kenya and Tanzania killed nearly 300 persons including 12 Americans. On the same day, Pakistan arrested Muhammad Siddique Odeh, a young Palestinian at the airport in Karachi (q.v.) while on his way from Nairobi to Peshawar (q.v.). During interrogation, Odeh linked the bombings to Osama bin Laden. On August 20 the United States launched missile attacks on the bin Laden camps in Afghanistan and on a factory in Khartoum, the capital of Sudan, which was said to be producing chemicals that could be used in weapons of mass destruction. In explaining the attacks, President Bill Clinton linked bin Laden to a number of terrorist attacks including those on U.S. and Pakistani troops in Somali in October 1993; plans to bomb six American 747s over the Pacific; the plot to assassinate President Hosni Mubarak of Egypt in Ethiopia in June 1995; the bombing of the Egyptian embassy in Islamabad (q.v.), Pakistan in November 1995, and the gunning down of German tourists in Luxor, Egypt in November 1997.

Osama bin Laden's support of the insurgency in Kashmir with the possible help from Pakistan's ISI brought Pakistan very close to being declared a terrorist state by the United States in 1996 and 1997. It was only after Pakistan gave a firm assurance to the United States that it would sever all contacts with Harakat Ansari, a shadowy group deeply involved in the conflict in Kashmir, that the United States agreed to take Pakistan off the list of countries suspected of harboring terrorists. It was the need to establish a clean record for itself in the field of terrorism that persuaded Pakistan to arrest and extradite Ramzi Youssef (q.v.), accused of masterminding the February 1993 bombing of the World Trade Center in New York, and Mir Ajmal Kansi (q.v.), accused of killing two CIA employees outside the agency's headquarters in Langley, Virginia. The arrest and extradition of Odeh in August 1998 was also a part of this effort.

The authorities in Pakistan believe that Osama bin Laden, a devout Sunni Muslim, might also have contributed to the escalation of the Sunni–Shia strife that claimed hundreds of lives in the country in the 1990s. Terrorist activities in Pakistan were not confined to the work of Muslim fundamentalists in Pakistan, however. Several attacks in which scores of people died were often attributed by the authorities to the Research and Analysis Wing (RAW)—the intelligence agency of the Indian government. The operations by the RAW in Pakistan were said to have been in retaliation for the alleged involvement of the Pakistani intelligence agencies in the Indian state of Punjab (q.v.) in the 1980s and in the Indian occupied areas of Kashmir in the 1990s.

THATTA. Today's Thatta is a small town of less than 100,000 people, located on the right bank of the Indus River (q.v.) some 80 kilometers northeast of Karachi (q.v.). But Thatta has seen better times. According to legend, it was the city of Pattala where Alexander the Great rested his army before he crossed the Mekran desert on his way back to Greece. In the fourteenth century Thatta was the capital of the Muslim dynasties that governed Sindh. For 400 years, from the fourteenth to the eighteenth centuries, Thatta was an important administrative and commercial center for lower Sindh (q.v.). Its location on the Indus turned it into a busy port not only for the ships that moved up and down the river but also for small seafaring vessels. These ships and vessels connected the city with the centers of commerce on the Arabian side of the Arabian Sea. They not only brought goods and commodities to Thatta from the Arab world: Easy communication between Arabia and lower Sindh also brought Islamic culture to the city.

As has happened to many cities in the lower reaches of the world's great rivers, Thatta lost its significance when the Indus changed its course. The population of the city declined precipitously, from the high point of 200,000 reached in the middle of the eighteenth century to only 20,000 a century later. The region's fertile cotton and wheat (qq.v.) fields were reduced to wasteland. Thatta's second revival commenced under Prime Minister Zulfikar Ali Bhutto (q.v.) when his administration began to restore the city's many monuments and brought sugar and cotton-ginning industries to the town. Bhutto, a Sindhi and proud of his heritage, was anxious to restore his province to its past glory. Thatta benefited a great deal from his efforts.

TIKKA KHAN, GENERAL (RETIRED) (1917–). Tikka Khan was born in the Jhelum district of Punjab (q.v.), a favorite area for recruitment by the British Indian Army. He joined the army in 1937. Tikka, as he was commonly called, earned some notoriety while serving the administration of President Yahya Khan (q.v.) in East Pakistan (today's Bangladesh [q.v.]) as the general officer commanding the army garrison stationed in the province. The Bengalis called him the "butcher of Bengal" because he adopted a hard-line approach toward the secessionist elements in East Pakistan. This approach contributed to increasing Bengal's alienation with Pakistan and eventually led to civil war in East Pakistan.

In 1972 Zulfikar Ali Bhutto (q.v.) appointed Tikka Khan chief of Army Staff (COAS), replacing General Gul Hassan (q.v.). On Tikka Khan's retirement in March 1976, General Zia ul-Haq (q.v.) was appointed chief of the Army Staff. It was Tikka Khan who brought Zia ul-Haq to Bhutto's attention. Zia proved to be less loyal to Bhutto than his predecessor, however. General Zia forced Bhutto out of office on July 5, 1977, an act by a former and trusted colleague that brought Tikka into politics. He joined Zulfikar Ali Bhutto's Pakistan People's Party (PPP) (q.v.) and soon became the organization's general-secretary.

Tikka remained active in the PPP during the time General Zia ul-Haq was in power (1977–88). He was given the PPP ticket to fight the national elections of October 1988 (q.v.) from a seat in Rawalpindi (q.v.). He lost the election to an Islami Jamhuri Itehad (q.v.) candidate but was rewarded for his long and loyal service to the PPP. In December 1988 Prime Minister Benazir Bhutto (q.v.) appointed him governor of Punjab, a position he held until August 1990. He retired from politics after the dismissal of Bhutto's government in August 1990.

TIWANAS, THE. The Tiwanas of Shahpur district in northwest Punjab (q.v.) were one of the score or so landed families that benefited enormously from the British rule of their province. The complex irrigation system built by the British included "private canals" that drew water from the main rivers of the province during the rainy season. A number of these inundation canals were located in the riverian tract of the Jhelum River and, from 1860 onward, were given over to the area's large landlords for management. These were not the only concessions granted by the British to the landed families of Punjab. Land was also awarded under a number of other schemes, including land for maintaining stud farms to provide horses and mules needed by the British armed forces in India. Under the patronage of the British, the Tiwanas were able to vastly expand their holdings.

This was a good investment by the British rulers: the Tiwanas and other landed aristocrats provided the rulers with much needed loyalty in an area in which opposition to British rule could have been both embarrassing and expensive. The British recruited a large number of soldiers from Shahpur to put down the disturbances associated with the Great Indian Mutiny of 1857 (q.v.). They also turned to Shahpur and neighboring districts to feed manpower to the British Indian Army during World Wars I and II. And, finally, when much of India became openly hostile to British rule—a development that shook the Indian subcontinent in the 1930s and 1940s—Punjab remained steadfastly loyal to its rulers. Under Khizar Hayat Khan Tiwana (q.v.), the prime minister of Punjab, the landed interests of the province also held out against Muhammad Ali Jinnah (q.v.) and his demand for establishing Pakistan, an independent homeland for the Muslims of British India. Khizar Hayat Khan Tiwana became so closely associated with the anti-Pakistan movement in Punjab that the Tiwanas paid a heavy political price once Pakistan came into being. Whereas other landed families were able to find their way back into the mainstream of Punjabi politics in Pakistan, the Tiwanas did not fully recover their prominence. Khizar was never invited back into the corridors of power in Lahore (q.v.).

TOTAL FERTILITY RATE (TFR). The Total Fertility Rate is defined as the average number of children that would be born alive to a woman during her lifetime if, during her childbearing age, she were to have children at the prevailing age-specific fertility rates. For the purpose of making population policy, it is useful to investigate the difference between fecundity, which is the physiological capacity to produce a live birth, and the TFR. Demographers assume fecundity at 17 children, which means that on average a woman exposed to fertilization during her entire reproductive period could have that number of children. This biological limit is never attained for the entire population. In Pakistan, the TFR reached as high as 6.4 but is estimated to have declined to about 5.3 by 1998. According to a 1975 study carried out in Pakistan, contraception use accounted for only 4 percent of the difference between fecundity and fertility. Breast-feeding is the most important factor in Pakistan, responsible for 41 percent of the difference, whereas marriage delay explains another 21 percent. *See also* Population.

TRADE. In 1996–97, the latest year for which data are available, the value of Pakistan's exports was estimated at $8.1 billion, whereas imports were valued at $11.2 billion, leaving a trade deficit of $3.1 billion, or 5.2 percent of gross domestic product (GDP). Exports and imports combined amounted to $19.1 billion, equivalent to 31 percent of GDP. Since 1950–51, the value of exports has increased more than four times in real terms, whereas imports have increased by a factor of five.

In the last 45 years Pakistan has had a trade surplus in only two years, in 1950–51 and 1972–73. The first time Pakistan ran a trade surplus was because of the war in Korea when the demand as well as the price for the country's commodity exports—in particular cotton (q.v.) and wool—climbed to unprecedented levels. The surplus in 1972–73 was because of the diversion of trade from East Pakistan to international channels. With East Pakistan having gained independence as Bangladesh (q.v.), Pakistan had to find new markets for its exports to what was once the eastern wing of the country.

Pakistan has been unable to diversify its exports. Manufactured exports account for 68 percent of the total, whereas the share of primary products is 14 percent. Cotton remains the most important source of export revenues, with nearly a third of the value coming from cotton and cotton products. Among imports, petroleum products, wheat (q.v.), and edible oil account for 29 percent of the total.

TRADE UNIONS. Pakistan is a signatory of the 1948 International Labour Organisation Convention on the right of workers to organize, as well as of the 1949 Convention on Collective Bargaining. That notwithstanding, union membership claims only a small proportion of the local work force. With 3.5 percent of the labor force of 52 million enlisted in about 9,000 unions, Pakistan is one of the least-unionized countries in Asia. Only Bangladesh (q.v.) (with about 3 percent) and Thailand (with about 1.1 percent) have smaller proportions of workers in organized unions. Union activity is almost entirely confined to the urban sector; trade unions claim almost 1.5 million members out of an estimated industrial work force of about 2.5 million. The political and economic power of the unions has suffered over the years; they were powerful in the 1950s and 1960s but successive martial-law (q.v.) regimes have tended to look at them with suspicion. The 1969 Industrial Relations Act regulates union activity, including the right to appoint collective bargaining agents.

The Labor Act of 1972, passed by the government of Zulfikar Ali Bhutto (q.v.), provided some further rights to labor, including the right to social security payments, health care, and pensions. While General Zia ul-Haq's (q.v.) martial law (1977–85) did not change basic labor laws, certain overriding regulations were issued. Under one of these, unions were banned outright at the country's flag carrier, Pakistan International Airlines, Pakistan Television Corporation, and Pakistan Broadcasting Corporation. Since the lifting of martial law (December 30, 1985), unions have begun to assert themselves once again.

Most of the unions are established on the basis of individual enterprises, which makes it difficult for them to work together to promote the welfare of workers. National labor federations have developed in recent years, however, and some of them have acquired strong links with political parties. Eight of these unions claim two-thirds of the total union membership. These include the right-wing All-Pakistan Federation of Trade Unions and the Pakistan National Federation of Trade Unions— both affiliated with the Islamic National Labour Federation, which serves as the labor wing of the Jamaat-e-Islami (q.v.), and the Pakistan Federation of Trade Unions, affiliated with the left-wing World Federation of Trade Unions. Women workers have a very low representation in unions. Some of their leaders—most notably Kaneez Fatima—have played important political roles, however.

The unions became actively involved in the process of privatization that was begun by the first administration of Benazir Bhutto (q.v.) (December 1988–August 1990), continued by Prime Minister Nawaz Sharif (q.v.) (1990–93) and by the second Bhutto administration (October 1993–November 1996). They sought adequate compensation for their members. The most successful effort in this context was launched by the labor union representing the workers of the Water and Power Development Authority (q.v.), who made the government change in a very significant way the terms on which the Kot Addu (q.v.) power plant was privatized.

TROIKA. The term "troika" came into currency in the early months of 1989. It was used to describe the informal grouping made up of the president, the prime minister, and the chief of the Army Staff who governed Pakistan after the death of General Zia ul-Haq (q.v.). The "troika" as an informal governing arrangement evolved over time as a response to the twists and turns in the country's political history. From 1989 to 1996 Pakistan saw six "troikas," each with its own peculiar dynamics and each with a different distribution of power among its three members.

The first troika came into being gradually as Pakistan adjusted to the situation caused by the death of President Zia ul-Haq. Zia died in a plane crash on August 17, 1988, leaving behind an immense political vacuum that had somehow to be filled. Of the two formal positions held by him, that of chief of the Army Staff went to General Aslam Beg (q.v.), who was Zia's deputy at the time of his death. Ghulam Ishaq Khan (q.v.), chairman of the Senate, took over as acting president but in appointing a caretaker administration to function until an elected government could be put into place, he did not nominate a prime minister. Ishaq invited Aslam Beg to participate in the deliberations of the caretaker administration, thus laying the ground for the formation of the "troika." The third member of the arrangement was still to emerge, however.

There was no clear winner in the elections of November 1988 (q.v.). Benazir Bhutto's Pakistan People's Party (qq.v.) won the largest number of seats but was well short of a majority. This inconclusive result gave the president and the chief of the Army Staff a powerful bargaining hand, which they used to great effect. The tacit agreement reached with Ms. Bhutto created the troika; it also reduced her degree of freedom. Bhutto agreed to be guided by Ghulam Ishaq Khan and Aslam Beg in the areas they considered critical for Pakistan's security. These included nuclear policy—in particular decisions with respect to the development of a nuclear bomb and the capability to deliver it; the country's stance toward Afghanistan and Kashmir (q.v.); and relations with India. Bhutto also agreed to let the army look after its own affairs. The troika had thus evolved as an institution for overseeing decision-making in the country.

From 1988 until December 1997 Pakistan saw many changes in the membership of the "troika," but the informal institution retained its importance. With the resignation of President Farooq Leghari (q.v.) and the election of Muhammad Rafiq Tarar (q.v.) as president, Prime Minister Nawaz Sharif (q.v.) had concentrated so much power in his hands that the troika arrangement became redundant.

TUFAIL MUHAMMAD, MIAN (1914–). Mian Tufail Muhammad was elected the *amir* (president) of the Jamaat-i-Islami (q.v.) on November 2,

1972, following the resignation of the ailing Maulana Maududi (q.v.), the party's first leader. Tufail belonged to the first generation of leaders of the Jamaat. Like Maulana Maududi, he had migrated from East Punjab to the Pakistani part of Punjab (q.v.) after the partition of British India. Being a refugee, he did not have a strong geographical base of his own. His place, therefore, was in the party's secretariat rather than in one of its field offices. Before becoming president, he served as the party's secretary-general (*qayyim*) for several years with competence and dedication. His election as amir was more the result of the influence he exercised over the party machine than on its general membership.

Tufail served as amir for 15 years. It was under his stewardship of the party that the Jamaat forged a close relationship with President Zia ul-Haq (q.v.). Tufail and Zia had developed a good understanding, in part because both of them were from Jullundhur, a city in the part of Punjab that went to India. Tufail's willingness to work with Zia did not improve his standing in the party. Gradually he lost the confidence of the younger members of the organization. On October 15, 1987 the Jamaat elected Qazi Husain Ahmed as its amir. Ahmed was 24 years younger than Tufail and was also the first Jamaat amir not to have come to Pakistan as a *muhajir* (refugee) from India.

TWENTY-TWO FAMILIES SPEECH, THE. On April 24, 1968 Mahbubul Haq (q.v.), the chief economist of the Planning Commission, delivered what came to be called the "twenty-two families speech." He chose an influential audience in Karachi (q.v.) to speak about the extent of asset concentration that had taken place during the 1960s, the years in which Pakistan put into operation Ayub Khan's (q.v.) highly acclaimed model of economic development. The data Haq presented dealt with the accumulation of assets by the families that owned, managed, or controlled the firms listed on the Karachi Stock Exchange. Haq's conclusions were dramatic but not strictly accurate. He implied that just 22 families owned 66 percent of the industrial wealth in the country and controlled 87 percent of the assets of the banking and insurance industries. This may have been the case for the assets of the firms listed on the Karachi Stock Exchange, but certainly did not include the nonincorporated medium and small firms that had been extremely dynamic during the Ayub Khan period and had added significantly to the country's industrial wealth.

The speech had a profound political and economic impact. Its precise statistics and methodology were soon forgotten, but a general impression was created that in the 1960s the poor in Pakistan had become poorer, whereas the rich had become fabulously rich. From the government's perspective, Haq could not have chosen a worse time for making his pronouncements. From the point of view of the growing political opposition to Ayub Khan, the timing of the speech could not have been better. The speech was given while the government's program for celebrating Ayub Khan's "Decade of Development" was still at an early stage. Moreover, it served to reinforce the widespread feeling that had been created by a number of scandals concerning influence peddling that surfaced during President Ayub Khan's waning years. Some of these scandals involved the sons of the president. They left the strong impression that, notwithstanding government propaganda, the Ayub regime was not concerned with advancing the general welfare of the people. It appeared that it had instead promoted the economic interests of the persons closely connected with it. As a result of the speech, the expression "twenty-two families" became synonymous with government-promoted income and wealth concentration and economic exploitation in Pakistan.

Haq's findings were used to great political effect by Zulfikar Ali Bhutto (q.v.) in his campaign to discredit the economic policies of Ayub Khan. Once Bhutto was in control in Islamabad (q.v.), his government lost little time in launching a concerted campaign to reduce the economic power of the large industrial families and banking and insurance houses identified by Haq as the members of the exclusive "twenty-two families" club. Within days of becoming president, Bhutto began the process of profoundly restructuring the Pakistani economy. His government nationalized 31 large industries in January 1972 and later took control of all private banks and insurance companies.

↪ **U** ↩

UMBRELLA ORGANIZATIONS OF RELIGIOUS SCHOOLS. Schools basing their teaching on religion proliferated in Pakistan following the country's birth in 1947. A number of religious organizations, feeling the need for some discipline and control on the schools that were being run under their auspices, set up regulatory bodies. The most important task of these regulatory organizations was to prescribe the curricula that could be taught in the schools that sought to affiliate with them. Most of these bodies functioned on the lines followed by the well-known *Nadwatal-Ulama* (the council of Islamic scholars) that had been established in Lucknow, India in 1893. The Deobandis in Pakistan set up the Wafaq al Madaris al-Arabia in Multan in 1959. In the same year, the Barelvis founded the Tanzim al-Madaris al-Arabiya in Dera Ghazi Khan. Also in the same year, the Shia community established the Majlis-e-Nazarat-e Shia Arabiya in Lahore (q.v.). The Ahle Hadith already had a functioning organization by then, having established the Markaz-e Jamiat Ahl-i Hadith in Faisalabad (q.v.) in 1955. The Jamaat-e-Islami (q.v.) followed much later, with Rabita al-Madaris established in Lahore in 1982.

UNIONIST PARTY. The Nationalist Unionist Party, most commonly known as the Unionist Party, was founded in 1923 by a group that included Mian Fazli Husain (q.v.), a prominent urban professional, who invited the Muslims as well as the non-Muslims to cooperate politically in order to prepare for the transfer of power from the British to the Indians. The process had begun in 1911 with the Minto-Morley reforms (q.v.), and in Fazli Husain's estimate, was likely to gather pace quickly. The party's principal purpose was to protect the political and economic interests of all the communities of Punjab (q.v.): the Hindu merchant class, the Hindu and Muslim urban professionals, the Muslim landed aristocracy, and the Hindu *bania* (shopkeepers) in the countryside.

Sir Fazli Husain died in 1936 and the mantle of leadership moved onto the shoulders of Sir Sikander Hayat Khan (q.v.), the scion of a landholding family from northern Punjab. This change in leadership brought the Muslim landed community more deeply into politics. It was under Sir Sikander's leadership that the Unionists fought the first provincial elections, held in 1937 under the Government of India Act of 1935 (q.v.). The Unionists triumphed, winning 95 seats in a legislature of 175. What was even more impressive about the Unionists' success was that they secured 74 seats of the 88 allocated to the Muslims. The All-India Muslim League (q.v.) was left in disarray, winning only one seat. Sikander Hayat Khan was invited to form a government and became Punjab's first prime minister.

As Punjab's prime minister, Sikander Hayat Khan established a dialogue with Muhammad Ali Jinnah (q.v.) and joined the Muslim League while still retaining the leadership of the Unionist Party and maintaining its separate identity. Sikander Hayat Khan's death in 1942 changed the fortunes of the Unionist Party, however. Khizar Hayat Khan Tiwana (q.v.), the new leader, was much less cosmopolitan in his political orientation: He did not see any great need for the forging of alliances that extended beyond the boundaries of Punjab. He responded to Jinnah's increasing pressure to obtain a larger role for the Muslim League in provincial politics by removing the Unionists from the Muslim League shortly before the elections of 1946. Compared to their 1936 performance the Unionists fared poorly, this time obtaining only 21 seats in all in a legislature of 175 persons. The Unionists' formed an alliance with the All-India Congress and the Akali Dal, parties dominated by the Hindu and Sikh communities, respectively. Although this arrangement kept Khizar in office for a few more months, it was an act of extreme political desperation. It ensured Khizar's political death as well as the death of the Unionist Party. The All-India Muslim League won favor with Punjab's Muslim population as the campaign for Pakistan gained momentum in 1946. The League launched a highly effective movement of civil disobedience against the Unionist government headed by Khizar. At one point during the campaign so many Muslim League followers had courted arrest that the government ran out of jail space to accommodate all of them. The Punjab prime minister had to resign to restore peace and order in the province. Pakistan was born in August 1947 and the Unionist Party was dissolved soon after.

The Unionists were a much more broad-based political party than the Muslim League in Punjab. Unlike the League, its program had a wider reach. The League was a one-issue organization—the establishment of Pakistan—whereas the Unionists sought to represent and articulate a broad coalition of interests. But for Khizar's poor tactics, the Unionists might well have survived long after the Muslim League, in its original incarnation, had ceased to exist in Punjab.

UNITED BANK LIMITED (UBL). The United Bank Limited occupies a special place in Pakistan's economic and financial development. It was the first large commercial bank to be established by an industrial group, the Saigols. It was perceived, however, that the close links among the owners of industrial financial assets illustrated by the rapid growth of the UBL had contributed to the massive consolidation of wealth in only a few hands. This impression contributed to the campaign against the government during the closing years of the Ayub Khan (q.v.) administration. It also resulted in the nationalization of large-scale industry and private financial institutions by the government of Zulfikar Ali Bhutto (q.v.). The UBL also occupies an important place in Pakistan's economic history because it launched the impressive career of Agha Hasan Abedi (q.v.), who was later to be associated with the Bank of Credit and Commerce International (BCCI) (q.v.).

The UBL, along with other public-sector banks, was misused during the two administrations of Benazir Bhutto (1988–90 and 1993–96), resulting in the massive accumulation of nonperforming loans. An effort was made in 1996 to privatize the bank but the offers received were well below the value anticipated by the government of Benazir Bhutto. That notwithstanding, the Bhutto administration decided to sell the bank to a Middle Eastern group. The deal was not consummated by the caretaker administration that succeeded the Bhutto administration in November 1996. In 1997 the government of Prime Minister Nawaz Sharif (q.v.)

appointed a new set of managers and gave them the mandate to improve the asset base of the institution.

UNITED FRONT. The United Front was organized in East Bengal—later East Pakistan and still later Bangladesh (q.v.)—in 1954 to challenge the Muslim League (q.v.) in the provincial Elections of 1954 (q.v.). The Front consisted of the Awami League (q.v.), the Krishak Sramik Party, the Nizam-i-Islam, Ganotanrik Dal, and a number of small political organizations. The Front's 21-point election manifesto called for the recognition of Bengali as one of Pakistan's national languages, greater administrative autonomy for the province of East Bengal, and rejection of the Basic Principles Committee report (q.v.) as the basis for a constitutional structure for Pakistan.

The Front was inspired by the leadership of two veteran Bengali leaders—Fazlul Haq and Maulana Bhashani (qq.v.). It campaigned vigorously and won a decisive victory, capturing 237 seats in the Provincial Assembly of 309 members. The Muslim League won only 10 seats. The United Front was invited to form a government, which it did in April 1954. The administration lasted for less than two months. It was dismissed in May 1954 by the central government led by Governor-General Ghulam Muhammad (q.v.).

UNITED STATES–PAKISTAN RELATIONS. The administration of President Franklin D. Roosevelt in the United States supported the Indian aspiration for independence but not the demand for dividing British India into two states—one Hindu, the other Muslim. The United States wished India to remain united. Pakistan's emergence therefore was not greeted with enthusiasm by Washington. The visit by Liaqat Ali Khan (q.v.), Pakistan's first prime minister in 1950 notwithstanding, American indifference toward Pakistan persisted throughout the Truman presidency. It was only after the Eisenhower administration took office in 1953 that the U.S. government began to get anxious about the spread of communism to Asia, and the foreign-policy establishment in Washington began to take an interest in Pakistan. It suddenly began to appreciate Pakistan's geopolitical situation. This recognition culminated in the Mutual Defense Agreement signed in 1954 between Pakistan and the United States. Ayub Khan (q.v.), commander in chief of the Pakistan army and minister of defense in the Cabinet of prime minister Muhammad Ali Bogra (q.v.), was the principal architect of the agreement on the Pakistani side.

There was a further strengthening of the relationship with the United States as Pakistan entered the Southeast Asia Treaty Organization (SEATO) in 1955 and the Baghdad Pact—renamed the Central Treaty

Organization (CENTO) after Iraq left the pact—in 1956. With the North Atlantic Treaty Organization (NATO), CENTO, and SEATO, the United States had erected a chain around the Soviet Union and China in order to contain the spread of communism. Pakistan linked the SEATO and CENTO parts of the chain. The United States rewarded Pakistan with generous amounts of economic and military assistance. The Kharian and Multan cantonments were constructed with the aid of the United States and a secret air-force base was built at Badabir near Peshawar (q.v.). It was from this base that Gary Powers took off on his U-2 reconnaissance flight over the Soviet Union. The plane was shot down by the Soviets and an embarrassed Ayub Khan had to acknowledge the existence of the secret base.

The United States military program was terminated after the Indo–Pakistan War of 1965 (q.v.). Military assistance was revived 16 years later following the assumption of office by President Ronald Reagan in Washington. The United States decided to use Pakistan as a conduit for supplying assistance to the Afghan mujahideen (q.v.) fighting the Soviet troops in Afghanistan. The two countries signed a $3.2 billion program of economic and military assistance to cover a period of six years, 1981–87. The program was kept in place in spite of the United States's anxiety over the intensive work begun by Pakistan to develop the capability to produce nuclear weapons. Pakistan had decided to take this route following the explosion of a nuclear device by India in 1974. These misgivings intensified in the program's concluding months and for some time it seemed that Washington would not be able to pledge to assist Pakistan economically and militarily. To do so would have required the U.S. president to indicate that for strategic reasons the application of the Pressler amendment (q.v.), which required sanctions against Pakistan because of its nuclear program, had to be waived. The president issued the waiver and in December 1987 the U.S. Congress renewed the program of support for another six years (1987–93). An amount of $4.02 billion was pledged for this period. Presidential waivers were granted for two more years.

The dramatic change in Pakistan's geopolitical situation following the withdrawal of Soviet troops from Afghanistan in 1989 and the collapse of the Soviet Union in 1991 reduced Pakistan's importance in the eyes of Washington, however. President George Bush decided to apply the Pressler Amendment (q.v.) to Pakistan in 1990. Its most serious consequence was that even the military purchases made and paid for by Pakistan, including 36 F-16 fighter-bombers, were not shipped.

For a few days following the testing of five nuclear devices by India on May 11 and 13, 1998, it seemed that Pakistan was back in favor in Washington. There was intense diplomatic traffic between the capitals of the two countries, including four telephone conversations between Prime Minister Nawaz Sharif (q.v.) and President Bill Clinton. The United States failed to dissuade Pakistan from testing its nuclear bombs, however. Islamabad (q.v.) announced that it carried out two series of tests on May 28 and 30. On May 30 the United States imposed fresh sanctions on Pakistan. Following the visit to Islamabad in July by Strobe Talbot, Deputy Secretary of the U.S. State Department, Washington announced some easing of the sanctions in order to save Pakistan from bankruptcy.

UNNAR, GHULAM HUSSAIN (?–1995). Ghulam Hussain Unnar came from Larkana, Sindh (q.v.). He entered politics in the 1970s and became chairman of the District Council Larkana. He came to public attention when, in 1990, a corruption case was registered against Asif Ali Zardari, husband of Benazir Bhutto (qq.v.). Unnar maintained that Zardari had him abducted and forced him to pay a large sum of money in order to win his release. The incident alleged by Unnar took place during Ms. Bhutto's first administration and resulted in her husband's incarceration. Zardari was to spend nearly two years in jail before winning release on bail.

Unnar paid a heavy price for having filed a case against Zardari. Benazir Bhutto returned to power as prime minister in October 1993. A case was registered against Unnar in February 1994 by the anticorruption department and he was arrested on March 22. He was to spend 22 months in jail. A new case was filed against him every time he was granted bail by the courts. In all, Unnar had to go through 61 cases before he was finally released on bail by the Supreme Court on December 20, 1995. He did not enjoy his freedom for too long, however. He died in Karachi (q.v.) of a massive heart attack a few days later.

URBANIZATION. Pakistan has had one of the most rapid rates of urbanization in the third world. In 1947—the year Pakistan was born—no more than three million people lived in urban areas. This was equivalent to only 10 percent of the total population. According to the census of 1998 (q.v.), urban areas now account for 32.5 percent of the population. This translates into an urban population of 42 million. Two cities—Karachi and Lahore (qq.v.)—together house more than 15 million people. Karachi is on the verge of qualifying as a "mega-city," defined by demographers as urban conglomerates with more than 20 million people.

There are several reasons for the rapid growth of the urban population in Pakistan, some of which are unique to the country. These include a rapid and reasonably steady growth in the economy (q.v.). For more than 40 years Pakistan's gross domestic product (GDP) increased at a rate of nearly

6 percent a year, twice as much as the increase in population. This level of GDP growth inevitably means a high level of rural-to-urban migration and Pakistan was no exception. A fairly significant restructuring of the economy so that the nonagricultural sector now accounts for a greater proportion of the GDP than is common for the countries at Pakistan's level of development also contributed to a high level of urbanization.

Immigration of millions of people, first from India soon after independence and later from Afghanistan in the early 1980s, added to the size of the Pakistani cities. Karachi was the most seriously affected city as a result of the arrival of millions of foreigners in search of jobs and security. The development of an urban-based "underground" economy, fed by remittances sent by the Pakistanis working in the Middle East, trade in drugs, and the leakage from the supply of arms from the United States to the mujahideen (q.v.) fighting in Afghanistan also added to the rate of growth of urban population. Although most of the urban growth was the consequence of the rapid increase in the population of such large cities as Karachi, Lahore, Faisalabad, Hyderabad (qq.v.), and Multan, scores of small towns have also contributed to rapid urbanization. The growth in the size of small towns occurred because of the increase in agricultural output during the two "green revolutions" (q.v.).

URUGUAY ROUND OF TRADE NEGOTIATIONS. The Uruguay Round—so called because the first set of ministerial discussions on global trade and tariff reforms were held at a resort near Montevideo, the capital of Uruguay, and were chaired by Enrique Iglesias, then Foreign Minister of Uruguay—was started in 1986. The conferees set an ambitious agenda and gave themselves four years within which to reform the world trading system. The timetable agreed on in Uruguay called for the completion of the Round by December 1990. The ministers sought to rationalize trade in agriculture, to stiffen penalties against the violation of intellectual and copyright infringements, and to bring trade in services under the aegis of General Agreement on Tariffs and Trade. These were all highly controversial issues. Contention was not only between developed and developing countries but also among the countries of the industrial world. It was the first issue—trade in agricultural products—that nearly caused the collapse of the Uruguay Round in December 1991.

The Uruguay Round was concluded in 1994 with a meeting held in Marrakesh, Morocco. Pakistan successfully applied for membership in the World Trade Organization (WTO) that was established to implement the agreement signed by the signatories. All WTO members committed themselves to the new rules of trade, including treating all members of the new organization on an equal footing. It was this provision that India could have invoked had Pakistan not agreed to move toward a trade regime that did not discriminate against India's interests.

USHR. *Ushr* is a tax on agricultural income. Levied at the rate of 5 percent a year, it is enjoined by Islam together with *zakat* (q.v.). Zakat, a tax on accumulated wealth, does not count agricultural property among the taxpayers' assets. The Zakat and Ushr Ordinance was promulgated by President Zia ul-Haq (q.v.) on June 20, 1980. Although zakat was levied from the day of the promulgation of the Ordinance, collection of ushr began several years later. The delay in introducing ushr was the result, in part, of the government's failure to abolish the existing land revenue, a tax on gross agricultural income originally imposed by the Mughuls (q.v.) and incorporated by the British into the fiscal system during their rule of India. The powerful landed aristocracy argued successfully that the imposition of ushr along with the levy of land revenue would be tantamount to double taxation. The landlords were finally persuaded that ushr was a lighter burden to carry than an income tax on agricultural incomes, from which they had been exempt since the days of the Mughuls and British.

USMANI, MAULANA SHABBIR AHMAD (1885–1963). Shabbir Ahmad Usmani was born in 1885 and educated at Darul Ulum, Deoband. He taught at the institution after graduating with distinction. After 18 years (1910–28) at Darul Ulum, Deoband, he took up a teaching assignment at Jamia Islamia, Deoband (1928–32), and went on to become the institution's principal (1932–35). He was an early recruit to Muslim politics; in 1919 he took an active interest in the Khilafat movement. In 1945, having been influenced by the political thinking of Muhammad Ali Jinnah (q.v.), he parted company with the majority of the Deobandi *ulema* (Islamic scholars) and established the Jamiatul-Ulemai-Islam (JUI) (q.v.). The JUI turned away from the Jamiatul-Ulemai-Hind of the Deobandi ulema because the latter did not see any reason to campaign explicitly for the political rights of the Muslim community. According to the Deobandis of the traditional school, the Muslim was no different from a non-Muslim; what made him different was only the pursuit of Islam. What mattered was personal piety, which, in turn, depended on a profound understanding of the basic tenets of Islam.

Usmani's disregard of this philosophy and his decision to establish the JUI lent the Muslim League (q.v.) support at a critical time when the latter needed to reach the Muslim masses. With Usmani's efforts the JUI established a strong presence in the Northwest Frontier Province (NWFP) (q.v.) and campaigned successfully for Pakistan in the referendum conducted in 1947 in the NWFP. Jinnah rewarded Usmani for his efforts by inviting him to hoist the Pakistani flag on August 14, 1947 at the ceremony held in Karachi (q.v.) to launch the new Muslim state. Usmani joined the First Constituent Assembly in 1947 (q.v.) and remained an active member until his death in Karachi.

UTILITY STORES CORPORATION. The Utility Stores Corporation was set up by the government in 1962 to provide items of daily consumption at moderate prices to the not-so-well-to-do segments of the population. The corporation's establishment was one manifestation of President Ayub Khan's (q.v.) belief that middlemen were reaping very large profits and that prices could be moderated by eliminating them. It was the same belief that had led the martial-law government of General Ayub Khan to adopt draconian measures against "profiteers" and "price gougers" when it took office in October 1958. The government of Zulfikar Ali Bhutto (q.v.) breathed new life into the corporation; in 1977 it had 700 stores doing business all over the country. However, the martial-law government of General Zia ul-Haq (q.v.), displaying greater confidence in market forces, scaled down the corporation's operations by cutting back the number of utility stores from 700 to 319. The government of Muhammad Khan Junejo (q.v.) reversed the trend and decided to open 70 new stores, most of them in small towns and aimed at helping poor government employees.

During the two administrations headed by Benazir Bhutto (q.v.), the number of stores managed by the corporation increased and some of them, in particular those in Islamabad (q.v.), were scaled up to cater to the needs of upper-income groups. This approach, however, increased the burden on the budget. Consequently, the corporation's operations were scaled back considerably by the caretaker administration of Prime Minister Meraj Khalid (q.v.), which took office in November 1996.

⇜ **V** ⇝

VALUE-ADDED TAX (VAT). Pakistan's inability to improve its resource situation is in part the result of the tax instruments used by the government, which cannot tap the more-dynamic sectors of the economy. The possibility of adding the "value-added tax" to the armory of instruments has been examined on several occasions by the government but no action has been taken to date. The VAT is an indirect tax imposed on each sale at the start of the production-and-distribution cycle and culminating with the sale to the consumer.

The VAT has become a popular tax instrument over the last twenty-five years and has become a major source of revenue for a number of countries. The introduction of a comprehensive consumption tax such as the VAT has been recommended to Pakistan by the International Monetary Fund as well as the World Bank (qq.v.) as a way of increasing the government's tax receipts and reducing the large fiscal deficit the country has lived with for many years. But the introduction of the tax has been resisted by the powerful business community on the ground that it would place an enormous administrative burden on them. In 1993 the government adopted an expanded General Sales Tax (GST) (q.v.) as the first step toward the introduction of the VAT.

VASEEM A. JAFFREY (1927–). Born in Allahabad, India, Jaffrey joined the elitist Civil Service of Pakistan in 1949 soon after independence, and following a brief tenure as a district officer, moved to the West Pakistan secretariat in Lahore (q.v.) to hold senior economic positions. While Lahore was the capital of West Pakistan, Vaseem Jaffrey held the positions of secretary of finance, additional chief secretary of planning and development, and chairman of the planning board. In 1971 he was transferred to the central government, where he served as secretary of commerce, secretary of planning, and, finally, as governor of the State Bank, Pakistan's central bank. Some policy differences with Mahbubul Haq, President Zia ul-Haq's (qq.v.) finance minister, led him to resign from the State Bank in the summer of 1988. In December 1988, following the assumption of office by Benazir Bhutto (q.v.), Vaseem Jaffrey was appointed economic advisor to the prime minister.

He left office on August 6, 1990 following the dismissal of the government of Benazir Bhutto, but returned to the position he had held in Benazir Bhutto's first administration when she returned to power as prime minister in October 1993. This time, Jaffrey had to share even his advisory position with a number of other officials who were influential in different ways. The group included Shahid Hassan Khan, who was the prime minister's advisor on energy and power; Qazi Alimullah, the deputy chairman of the planning commission; and Javed Talat, secretary of the finance division. This division of power among so many different people produced a sense of drift on economic matters during Benazir Bhutto's second tenure in office. It was widely believed that Asif Ali Zardari (q.v.), the prime minister's husband, exercised the real authority on economic decision-making. Vaseem Jaffrey left the government following the dismissal of Prime Minister Benazir Bhutto on November 5, 1996 by President Farooq Leghari (q.v.).

ᓭ **W** ᓭ

WAHEED KAKAR, GENERAL (RETIRED) ABDUL (1934–). On January 13, 1993 General Abdul Waheed Kakar became the eleventh person to command the Pakistani army. For the army and for the country—and most certainly for Waheed himself—this was an unexpected appointment. The three-year term of General Asif Nawaz (q.v.), his predecessor, was to end in August 1994, a year after Lieutenant General Waheed was scheduled for retirement. The army's General Headquarters had already announced the names of half a dozen lieutenant generals who were to retire in the summer of 1993. The list included Waheed Kakar, who then commanded an army infantry corps stationed in Quetta (q.v.). General Asif Nawaz died of a massive heart attack on January 6, 1993, however, and a week later President Ghulam Ishaq Khan (q.v.) selected Waheed as the chief of the Army Staff.

On July 17, 1993 Waheed Kakar, taking a strictly neutral position in the conflict between President Ghulam Ishaq Khan and Prime Minister Nawaz Sharif (qq.v.), forced both to resign from office. A caretaker administration was appointed under Moeen Qureshi (q.v.); its assigned task was to hold another general election in the country. Elections were held in early October 1993 (q.v.) and, later that month, Benazir Bhutto (q.v.) was back in power as prime minister for the second time. Soon after Bhutto took office she was able to get Farooq Leghari (q.v.), her trusted lieutenant, elected president.

The Bhutto–Leghari–Waheed "troika" (q.v.) settled into an easy relationship. Waheed was quite content to be the most junior partner in this combination as long as the prime minister and the president followed a course that protected the interests of the armed forces. On December 18, 1995 President Farooq Leghari (q.v.) announced the appointment of General Jehangir Karamat (q.v.) as the new chief of the Army Staff. Waheed relinquished his position on January 12, 1996 and went into retirement.

WALI KHAN, KHAN ABDUL (1921–). Khan Abdul Wali Khan built his political career on two traditional foundations of Pathan politics: the antiestablishment approach adopted with great effectiveness by the Khudai Khidmatgars (q.v.), and the intense Pathan nationalism of his father, Abdul Ghaffar Khan (q.v.). He entered politics in 1942 at the height of the Quit India Movement launched by Mahatma Gandhi's Indian National Congress (q.v.). After Pakistan was born the Khan brothers—Ghaffar Khan and Dr. Khan Sahib (qq.v.)—and Abdul Wali Khan suffered long periods of incarceration. After several spells of confinement, Wali Khan finally emerged from jail in 1953 and three years later, in 1956, he joined the National Awami Party (NAP) formed by Maulana Bhashani (qq.v.). Following the military takeover of 1958, Wali Khan found himself back in prison.

The NAP split into two factions in 1965 and Wali Khan became the president of the pro-Moscow wing of the party. He and his faction took an active part in the anti-Ayub Khan (q.v.) movement of 1968–69. In Pakistan's first general election, called by General Yahya Khan (q.v.), Ayub Khan's successor, Wali Khan's NAP gained six seats in the National Assembly, three each from Balochistan and the Northwest Frontier Province (qq.v). With the restoration of civilian rule in 1972 the NAP formed coalition governments in Balochistan and the Northwest Frontier Province, joining hands with the Jamiatul-Ulemai-Islam (JUI) (q.v.). The NAP–JUI governments were dismissed a few months after they had taken office, however. Zulfikar Ali Bhutto (q.v.) accused the two provincial administrations of working against the integrity of the state of Pakistan, a charge that was upheld by the Supreme Court. Wali Khan was once again back in prison and the NAP was banned as a political organization. He had to wait for Bhutto's departure from the political scene before he could get back into active politics. He was released from prison in 1978. Not impressed with the state of socialist politics in Pakistan, he persuaded four small organizations to join forces under the umbrella of a new organization, the Awami National Party (ANP) (q.v.) in 1986. The ANP elected him president.

In the political realignment that took place after Zia ul-Haq's (q.v.) death in 1988, Wali Khan decided to work with the Pakistan Muslim League (PML) (q.v.), the party he had opposed throughout his political life. He joined hands with Mian Nawaz Sharif (q.v.), the president of the League, to fight against the Pakistan People's Party (PPP) of Benazir Bhutto (qq.v.). He stayed with Nawaz Sharif through four elections—in 1988, 1990, 1993, and 1997 (qq.v.). The ANP was in the coalition that governed the Northwest Frontier Province from 1990 to 1993 when Nawaz Sharif's PML was in power in Islamabad (q.v.). It stayed in office for a brief period after the elections of 1993 but was maneuvered out by Benazir Bhutto. In 1995 Wali Khan decided to step aside as the president of the ANP, leaving the organization to be managed by Ajmal Khattak (q.v.) and by his wife, Nasim Wali Khan (q.v.).

WAQFS. The Islamic tradition encourages—and the Muslim *fiqh* (law) allows—the setting up of charitable trusts, called *waqfs*, the profits from which can be used by the trustee, his family, his community, for any purpose designated by him. Such a broad interpretation of the legitimate use of waqf profit was bound to result in a great deal of misuse, and it did. Corruption traditionally associated with the management of religious properties was one of the many social problems sought to be addressed by the government of General Muhammad Ayub Khan (q.v.) when it assumed office in October 1958.

A large number of waqfs were set up in British India to administer mosques, shrines, and other religious properties. Donations to the waqfs came mostly from devotees and the waqfs were administered by individuals who, either by tradition or by inheritance, had the right to oversee religious properties. A great deal of corruption had crept into the way the waqfs were managed. This was investigated by a commission set up by the Ayub government, which recommended the establishment of the West Pakistan Auqaf (plural for waqf) Department to administer the properties hitherto run by trustees. This step, in fact, resulted in the nationalization of religious properties and became a source of abiding resentment against Ayub Khan on the part of the religious leaders who had lost an important source of income. Successor administrations continued government control of waqfs but did not expand the reach of the provincial auqaf departments to the properties that were not nationalized by the Ayub administration.

WATER AND POWER DEVELOPMENT AUTHORITY (WAPDA). The Water and Power Development Authority was established in 1958 to develop and maintain Pakistan's extensive irrigation system, to reclaim the land being lost to salinity and waterlogging, and to generate, transmit, and distribute electric power. Up until the creation of the WAPDA, these tasks were carried out by several ministries and departments in the federal and provincial governments. These overlapping responsibilities among ministries and departments had created a great deal of red tape and slowed the progress Pakistan needed to make in these vital sectors of the economy. The WAPDA was given the mandate to develop a strategy for the development of Pakistan's abundant water resources for irrigation as well as power generation.

The WAPDA was initially presided over by a number of exceptional men, including Ghulam Faruque (1959–62), Ghulam Ishaq Khan (1962–65) (q.v.), and A. G. N. Kazi (1965–69). The advent of martial law in 1977 turned WAPDA into a preserve of the army corps of engineers, however. Zia ul-Haq (q.v.) appointed Lieutenant Generals Fazle Raziq, Safdar Butt, and Zahid Ali Akbar, all from the Army Corps of Engineers, as chairmen. During Benazir Bhutto's (q.v.) second tenure in office, starting in 1993, the WAPDA Act was amended to make the authority and its chairman subject to greater control by the government.

Since its inception, the WAPDA has implemented a large number of irrigation and power-development schemes. These include the massive works built under the Indus Waters Replacement program, including the construction of two large dams—the Mangla and the Tarbela (qq.v.)—the Guddu Barrage, and a system of "link canals" that transferred water from the Indus River (q.v.) to the Jhelum, from the Jhelum to the Chenab, and from the Chenab to the Ravi. These achievements notwithstanding, by the late 1980s the WAPDA had begun to exhibit all the symptoms typical of large public corporations in the developing world. It had become a bloated organization, employing a much larger work force than needed. Employment had increased because of political pressures; like other corporations in the public sector, the WAPDA was the employer of last resort to which the politicians turned to obtain jobs for their constituents. The WAPDA was also incurring large losses in its power-transmission and -distribution system. It also failed to keep its power-development program proceeding in pace with the enormous growth in electricity consumption. The result was "load shedding"—or power rationing— particularly during the periods when the flow of water in the Indus River system was low.

The answer to all these woes was to downsize the WAPDA by starting a process of gradual privatization of some of its assets. In the early 1990s the authorities in Pakistan made the decision to privatize two power plants owned by the WAPDA—the plants at Jamshoro and Kot Addu (qq.v.)—and one system of power distribution, in the city of Faisalabad (q.v.). At the same time, it was decided to end the monopoly of the public sector over new power generation. In 1993 the government of Pakistan announced an energy policy that encouraged the participation of the private sector in power generation.

By the time Benazir Bhutto left office in November 1996 the WAPDA was effectively bankrupt. It owed large amounts of money to the government, to a number of public-sector corporations that supplied it with fuel, to the railways that transported fuel to its power stations, and to thousands of private business people who provided it all kinds of services. The caretaker administration of Prime Minister Meraj Khalid (q.v.), which took office after Bhutto's departure, made an effort to restore financial health to the WAPDA. Increasing power tariffs and improving operational efficiency were two important parts of this strategy. The government of Nawaz Sharif (q.v.) that came to power in early 1997 was initially reluctant to further increase tariffs, however, but was persuaded to reverse its decision in March 1998 on the insistence of the World Bank (q.v.), which had financed several programs of development undertaken over the years by the WAPDA.

WATTOO, MANZOOR AHMAD. Up until the Elections of 1993 (q.v.) Wattoo was a little-noticed small-town politician from central Punjab (q.v.). Shortly before the elections he decided to abandon Nawaz Sharif and the Pakistan Muslim League (PML) (qq.v.) in favor of a splinter group that was organized by Nasir Chatta, Sharif's rival. Chatta gave his splinter group the name of Pakistan Muslim League (Junejo) (PML[J]) in memory of Muhammad Khan Junejo (qq.v.), who had served as Zia ul-Haq's (q.v.) prime minister after the lifting of martial law in December 1985. Wattoo became a prominent member of the PML(J).

In the 1993 elections neither Benazir Bhutto's Pakistan People's Party (PPP) (q.v.) nor Mian Nawaz Sharif's Pakistan Muslim League returned to the National Assembly and the Provincial Assembly of Punjab with a clear majority. Both were dependent on the support of minor parties, splinter groups, and independents. The Pakistan Muslim League (Junejo) was one such splinter group that chose to support the PPP. In return, the PML(J) was awarded the chief ministership of Punjab, a position that went to Manzoor Wattoo. Wattoo had maneuvered himself into the right place at the right time. Once in office, Wattoo proved a difficult person to manage for the PPP. Under his stewardship the Punjab government also earned a reputation for corruption and incompetence and, after a number of skirmishes with Benazir Bhutto, it was dismissed by President Farooq Leghari (q.v.) on September 5, 1995. The president suspended the Provincial Assembly for two months and imposed direct rule through the governor.

WATTOO, MUHAMMAD YASIN KHAN. Yasin Khan Wattoo began his professional career as a lawyer in the Sahiwal district court. He joined the Convention Muslim League of General Ayub Khan (qq.v.) in 1963, was elected to the West Pakistan Provincial Assembly in 1965, and was appointed minister of basic democracies and local government in the same year. Muhammad Khan Junejo (q.v.) was also a minister in the same cabinet and the two formed a good working relationship, which helped Wattoo when Zia ul-Haq (q.v.) chose Junejo to become prime minister. In the 1970s Wattoo switched parties, joined Zulfikar Ali Bhutto's Pakistan People's Party (qq.v.), and was elected to the National Assembly in the controversial Elections of 1977 (q.v.). He briefly held a cabinet appointment at the center but lost the position with the promulgation of martial law on July 5, 1977. In the party-less elections of February 1985 (q.v.) Wattoo won a seat in the National Assembly from Sahiwal district. With Junejo appointed prime minister, Wattoo was called in to take charge of education. In 1986 he replaced Mahbubul Haq (q.v.) as minister of finance. Wattoo lost his job when Prime Minister Junejo was dismissed by President Zia ul-Haq in May 1988. Wattoo was defeated in the Elections of 1988 (q.v.), but won a seat in the National Assembly in the Elections of 1990 (q.v.).

WHEAT. Wheat is Pakistan's main staple and by far its most important crop. Of the country's total cultivated area of 22.93 million hectares, more than a third (36.6 percent 1997–98) is used to grow wheat. In 1997–98, the latest year for which crop data are available, wheat was cultivated on 8.4 million hectares. Both the output of wheat as well as the area occupied by it have increased several-fold (the area by almost twice as much, and production by four-and-a-half times) since Pakistan achieved independence. The yield per hectare has increased considerably since independence. Average output per hectare in 1950–55 was only 780 kg.; fifty years later it had increased to nearly 2.2 tons. The most spectacular growth came in the ten-year period between 1965 and 1975—the period of the first "green revolution" (q.v.)—when the yield of wheat per hectare increased from 995 kg to 1.2 tons or, considered another way, increased at an annual rate of nearly 2 percent.

The changes in wheat-yield per hectare of land were the consequence of both government policy and private initiative. Even after the green revolution was over—that is, after all the areas that could profitably use the new high-yielding wheat varieties were already doing so—wheat output and the productivity of land devoted to wheat continued to increase. This was largely because of the progressive commercialization of agriculture (q.v.). Although the second green revolution had its most dramatic impact on the cotton (q.v.) crop, it changed the environment in which all farmers—not just those growing cotton—were making production decisions. Agriculture was no longer directed at subsistence farming; its aim was now to produce for the market. And the signals that began to be received from the market in the late 1980s and 1990s did not indicate that continued emphasis on wheat was to Pakistan's overall comparative advantage.

WINGS OF PAKISTAN. Pakistan has existed as a nation-state for more than fifty years, but not in the shape and form in which it was created. It was born as a country with two "wings": the one in the west was made up of the provinces of Balochistan, the Northwest Frontier, Punjab, and Sindh (qq.v.); the other in the east included the Muslim part of Bengal and the district of Sylhet in Assam. The term "wings" to describe the two parts of the country, separated by 1,700 kilometers of Indian territory, became popular soon after the establishment of Pakistan in August 1947. The use of the term "wings" lost its relevance once Bangladesh (q.v.) gained independence from Pakistan in December 1971.

WOMEN. Statistics such as the female rate of literacy, female enrollment rates in schools and colleges, the rate of female infant mortality, maternal mortality, fertility rate, and so on all point vividly to the very low social status of Pakistani women. This applies particularly to the poorer segments of the society, where women suffer from all manner of deprivation. The social status of women in Pakistan is even lower than in the countries at comparable levels of development. At fifty-five years in 1996, Pakistan's female life-expectancy at birth was five years less than the average for all poor countries. The first time that female life expectancy in Pakistan was reported to be equal to male life expectancy was in 1988: in developed and most developing countries, women tend to outlive men by about five years. In 1997, at 35 percent, Pakistan's female primary-school enrollment ratio was among the lowest in the world. There were only eight countries with lower ratios and, apart from Bhutan, all the other were in Africa. The women of Pakistan carry a very heavy reproductive burden. The average age of marriage is seventeen; although it is increasing somewhat, it is still very low. With the incidence of marriage at 98 percent, exposure to possible pregnancy on average is 33 years. Since only 11 percent of women of childbearing age use contraception, this long exposure results in a very high total fertility rate (TFR) (q.v.). In Pakistan, the TFR for 1996 was estimated at 5.6, one of the highest in the world. Pakistan has one of the lowest gender ratios in the world, and it has declined over time. In 1985 there were only 91 women in Pakistan's population for every 100 men. This low and declining ratio is caused by two factors: high mortality rates for women and improving mortality rates for men.

For a variety of reasons, economic as well as social, women belonging to the upper strata of the society are acquiring education and skills that are comparable—in some cases even better—than those possessed by men. This has happened because of the rapid modernization and urbanization of the society since the mid-1970s, which pulled men prematurely into the work force. This had a significant impact on the enrollment rates for women in colleges and universities. Because society was still not prepared to accept women into most workplaces, they stayed on in colleges and universities. On graduation, a large number of women moved into professions where their presence will have a profound impact on the country's social and political development. Journalism, particularly in the English language, and politics attracted a number of talented women, for example. The fact that Benazir Bhutto (q.v.) became Pakistan's prime minister, not once but twice, and two women (Abida Hussain and Maleeha Lodhi) have served as ambassador to the United States are good indications of the emancipation of women belonging to the upper strata of society.

The Islamization of society ordered by Zia ul-Haq (q.v.) profoundly affected Pakistani women, producing a reaction that contributed to their politicization. Women's reactions to the policies adopted by Zia resulted in the establishment of scores of women's groups that adopted a wide variety of objectives: economic, social, and political. The most important of these organizations was an umbrella group, Khawateen Mahaz-e-Amal (Women's Action Forum) (WAF) (q.v.), founded in Karachi (q.v.) in 1981. The WAF opened branches all over the country and, within two years of its establishment, boasted a membership of 15,000 women.

Although keeping in some check the conservative elements of the society, the work done by women's organizations has not improved their situation after the death of Zia and the introduction of democracy. Much greater effort is needed to bring about a significant improvement in the status of women. The state must get directly involved. The rise of the Taliban (q.v.) in Afghanistan has added another source of pressure on the women of Pakistan.

WOMEN'S ACTION FORUM (WAF). The Women's Action Forum was formed in 1981 as Zia ul-Haq's (q.v.) program for the Islamization of the legal system gathered pace. Women were especially concerned with the Hadud Ordinances of 1979 (q.v.), the 1984 Law of Evidence, and the law of Qisas and Diyas. Women—in particular professional women working in large cities—were concerned that the changes in the legal system that had been introduced or were being contemplated by the government of Zia ul-Haq would reduce their status in the society to the point at which they would have to abandon their careers. Though most of the WAF's members identified themselves as Muslims, they viewed religion as a private matter and did not believe that it ought to shape public policies.

The WAF was successful in slowing the pace of change although it failed in removing the Hadud Ordinances from the statute books. In February 1983 the WAF sponsored a series of protests against the changes proposed by the Zia administration in the Law of Evidence. These changes proposed that in all cases other than those covered by the Hadud Ordinances, two male witnesses and in the absence of two male witnesses, one male and two female witnesses would be required for proving a crime against a woman. The WAF was of the view that these changes had nothing to do with Islam but reflected the obscurantism of the regime. On February 12 a clash between women activists and police in Lahore (q.v.) led to a number of injuries and arrests. This incident was a defining moment for women's movements in Pakistan. It not only slowed down the government's efforts at Islamization, but also sent a message to all politicians in the country that women's issues had to be taken seriously.

WORLD BANK, THE. The World Bank was established in 1944 as a part of the Bretton Woods system developed to restore economic health to the countries ravaged by World War II. Along with the International Monetary Fund (IMF) (q.v.), its sister institution, the World Bank was designed to provide assistance to developing countries. While the IMF concentrated its resources on stabilizing the economies suffering from external shocks, the World Bank was given the task of promoting structural change. Over time, the World Bank acquired new subsidiaries, including the International Finance Corporation (IFC), the International Development Agency (IDA), and the Multilateral Investment Guarantee Agency (MIGA). Of this World Bank Group, the IFC provides resources to the private sector; the IDA assists poor countries with concessional funds; and the MIGA guarantees private investments against risks, including government expropriation. All subsidiaries of the World Bank Group have provided assistance to Pakistan. *See also* World Bank Group and Pakistan.

WORLD BANK GROUP AND PAKISTAN. The World Bank was created in 1944. In its initial form—the International Bank for Reconstruction and Development (IBRD)—it focused on rebuilding the war-ravaged countries of Europe. It also provided large amounts of assistance to Japan. It was only after this task had been accomplished that the bank turned its attention to development. Two more affiliates were added to the original IBRD: The International Finance Corporation (IFC) was established in the 1950s to provide help to the private sector in the developing world. In 1960 the International Development Association (IDA) was created to provide "soft" funding to the poor countries. Whereas the IBRD and IFC raised most of their resources in the international financial markets, the IDA was funded by grants from the rich industrial countries. In the late 1980s a third affiliate was added to the bank: Called the Multilateral Investment Guarantee Association (MIGA), it provides insurance to the companies against political risks in the developing world. The IBRD, IFC, IDA, and MIGA together have come to be known as the World Bank Group. All four affiliates of the World Bank Group have been active in Pakistan.

The World Bank's association with Pakistan began in 1952. For the first eight years, the bank financed projects on close to market terms, but with the creation of the IDA, poor countries such as Pakistan gained access to soft credits. In the period since 1952 Pakistan has received 68 loans and credits amounting to a total of over $7 billion. Nearly 39 percent of the assistance provided by the World Bank has gone into agriculture (q.v.), 28 percent into energy, and 17 percent into industry (q.v.). The bank played a major role in getting Pakistan and India to agree to the division of the waters of the Indus River (q.v.) system. The resources required for the execution of the Indus Replacement Works were mobilized with the help of the World Bank. The bank also assisted Pakistan in setting up a number of development finance corporations, including the Pakistan Industrial and Commercial Investment Corporation, the Industrial Development Bank of Pakistan, and the National Development Finance Corporation.

WULLAR BARRAGE. The Indus Waters Treaty (q.v.) of 1960 succeeded in removing ambiguity over the riparian rights of Pakistan and India with respect to the Indus River (q.v.) system. The treaty's success notwithstanding, disputes occasionally arose over its precise interpretation on the use of the waters in the upper reaches of the Indus River. Pakistan's problem with the Indian plan to construct a barrage in the Wullar lake area is an example of the type of disputes that arose in spite of the treaty. In the mid-1980s India undertook the construction of the Tulbal Navigation Project to improve navigation in the Wullar Lake. A barrage on an important inlet into the lake was included in the "navigational facilities" to be constructed. India planned to spend 18 crore rupees (equivalent to $15 million at the time) on the project. Pakistan, however, saw the construction of the barrage as a violation of the Indus Waters Treaty because the project would result in some impounding of water. A series of discussions was held between the officials of the two governments to resolve the issue; the last session was held in Islamabad (q.v.) but the two governments were not able to reach an agreement. Pakistan threatened to take the matter to the International Court of Justice for arbitration. Such a reference to the court is allowed by the Indus Treaty. The issue was, however, resolved after India agreed to make some adjustments to the design of the dam at Wullar.

↳ Y ↲

YAHYA KHAN, GENERAL AGHA MUHAMMAD (1917–1980). Yahya Khan was born in the Northwest Frontier Province (q.v.) and joined the British Indian Army. He opted for service in Pakistan following the partition of India. With his career under the active sponsorship of General Ayub Khan (q.v.), Yahya Khan rose rapidly in the officer ranks of the Pakistan army. He received the ultimate reward of his loyal service to Ayub Khan when, in September 1966, he was promoted to the rank of full general and appointed to succeed General Muhammad Musa (q.v.) as commander in chief of the Pakistan army. Two-and-a-half years later, at the height of the anti-Ayub Khan movement, Yahya Khan decided to act against his mentor. He forced Ayub Khan out of office and nominated himself president and chief martial-law administrator. The Yahya administration took two important steps: It dissolved the One Unit of West Pakistan (q.v.) and promulgated the result of this reengineering as the Legal Framework Order (LFO) of 1970 (q.v.). The LFO turned back Pakistan's constitutional clock by more than two decades. It discarded the principle of representational parity (q.v.) between East and West Pakistan. With this important change, it was now possible for an East Pakistani political party to gain a comfortable majority in the National Assembly and thus form a government without assistance from the representatives of West Pakistan. Yahya Khan and his advisors, banking on the perpetuation of the fractious politics of East Pakistan, did not think that such an outcome would ever be possible.

The elections of 1970 (q.v.), held under the LFO, proved all these calculations wrong. Mujibur Rahman's Awami League (qq.v.), by winning 160 seats in a house of 300, was now in a position to dictate its terms to West Pakistan. Yahya Khan panicked, and in this he was encouraged by Zulfikar Ali Bhutto (q.v.). On the night between March 25 and 26, 1971 Yahya Khan ordered the military to restore law and order in East Pakistan. Mujibur Rahman was arrested and sent to a prison in West Pakistan and the Awami League was banned. What followed was an exceptionally bloody civil war in which hundreds of thousands of people were killed. Millions of Bengalis fled from East Pakistan and took refuge in neighboring India (q.v.). India used the arrival of the refugees in its territory as the pretext for intervening in the civil war. Aided by the Indian troops, the Bengali resistance force entered Dacca on December 16, 1971. The Pakistan army surrendered to the commander of the Indian army on the same day. Four days later, following a turbulent session with senior- and middle-level officers of the Pakistan army held in the General Headquarters Lecture Hall at Rawalpindi (q.v.), President Yahya Khan agreed to resign and hand over power to Zulfikar Ali Bhutto. Yahya Khan's role in the East Pakistan crisis was investigated by a commission set up by the government of Zulfikar Ali Bhutto under the chairmanship of Chief Justice Hamoodur Rahman. The commission's report was not released to the public. *See also* Hamoodur Rahman Commission, The.

YAQUB KHAN, LIEUTENANT GENERAL (RETIRED) SAHIB-ZADA (1910–). Born in the United Provinces of British India (today's state of Uttar Pradesh in India), Yaqub joined the British Indian Army before the British decided to leave the subcontinent. After the creation of Pakistan, he opted to work for the new Muslim state. To do so, he and his family had to leave their ancestral home and migrate to Pakistan. He rose quickly in the ranks of the Pakistani army. He came to the attention of the public at large during Pakistan's second general martial law imposed by General Yahya Khan (q.v.). In 1970 he was dispatched to Dacca to take over the command of the Pakistani armed forces stationed in the eastern wing of the country. As governor, Yaqub took the position that some of his predecessors had also taken. Like General Azam Khan (q.v.), who was the governor of East Pakistan during the first few years of Ayub Khan's martial-law administration, Yaqub Khan came to the conclusion that the use of force was not a viable solution to the problem of Bengal. When it became clear to him that Yahya Khan was determined to force the Bengalis to submit to the will of West Pakistan, Yaqub Khan asked for retirement from the army. He returned to Karachi (q.v.), having been replaced by Lieutenant General A. K. Niazi.

General Zia ul-Haq (q.v.) appointed Yaqub Khan to be Pakistan's ambassador to the United States. Zia was obviously happy with the job Yaqub Khan performed in Washington. When the military president decided to bring civilian professionals into his cabinet, he asked Yaqub Khan to take the portfolio of foreign affairs. He served many years in this position and was back in the foreign office as minister even after the induction of Benazir Bhutto (q.v.) as prime minister in December 1988. This appointment came as a total surprise, since Bhutto was not kindly disposed to any associate of Zia. It was obvious that Yaqub's appointment was one part of the deal Benazir Bhutto had struck with President Ghulam Ishaq Khan (q.v.) and the army to gain power. Yaqub remained with Bhutto until her dismissal in August 1990, after which he left active political life. He carried out a few assignments for the United Nations (UN) and was considered for a senior UN position at one point. He retired in Islamabad (q.v.) but returned as foreign minister in the caretaker cabinet that took office after the dismissal of the second administration of Prime Minister Benazir Bhutto.

YAQUB, MUHAMMAD (1939–). Muhammad Yaqub was born in Faisalabad (q.v.) and educated at Lahore (q.v.) and Yale University in the United States. He joined the International Monetary Fund (q.v.) in 1969, took early retirement, and returned to Pakistan in 1990. He was appointed special secretary in the Ministry of Finance and a year later became governor of the State Bank of Pakistan. His term at the central bank was renewed in January 1997 by the caretaker administration of Prime Minister Meraj Khalid (q.v.). In the spring of 1998, however, he developed major differences with the administration of Prime Minister Nawaz Sharif (q.v.) and tendered his resignation.

YOUSSEF, RAMZI. Ramzi Youssef is a shadowy figure with unknown nationality and a set of confused objectives. He was arrested by the Pakistani authorities in 1995, obviously on the basis of information provided by the U.S. intelligence agencies, and promptly deported to the United States to stand trial on two counts: conspiracy to blow up a U.S. civilian aircraft over the Pacific and for participating in the 1993 bombing of New York's World Trade Center. Youssef was accused of working with a number of different groups. His activities in the Philippines involved a number of Pakistanis who had participated in the war in Afghanistan against the Soviet Union. In the United States he was accused of working with a group of Arab activists whose principal aim was to punish the United States for providing support to Israel. Tried in New York in the World Trade Center bombing case, he was sentenced to death in 1997. Following the missile attack on Afghanistan in August 1998, the U.S. authorities revealed that Youssef might have worked for Osama bin Laden (q.v.), a Saudi businessman-turned-terrorist.

YUNIS KHALID, MAULVI. Maulvi Yunis Khalid headed Hizb-e-Islami, one of the seven groups of Afghan mujahideen (q.v.). These groups were formed after the Soviet Union invaded Afghanistan in December 1979. They operated out of Peshawar (q.v.), the capital of Pakistan's Northwest Frontier Province (q.v.). In the summer of 1984 the Hizb-e-Islami joined hands with the other six groups to coordinate their efforts against the Soviet troops in Afghanistan. He did not play a prominent role in Afghan politics after the signing of the Geneva peace agreement and the departure of the Soviet troops from Afghanistan.

↔ **Z** ↔

ZAKAT. *Zakat* is an Islamic tax on wealth; it is levied at the rate of 2.5 percent on accumulated wealth and assets in excess of Rs.2,000 (not including principal residence and agricultural land) and, in Pakistan, is deducted on the twenty-seventh day of the month of Ramadan. President Zia ul-Haq (q.v.) promulgated the Zakat and Ushr Ordinance on June 20, 1980. The provisions of the Ordinance concerning zakat came into operation from the date of its promulgation, while the provisions relating to *ushr* were to become operative at a later date. The Ordinance prescribed the system to be followed for the collection of zakat and its disbursement to *mustahequeen* (the deserving) under the Islamic Sharia (law).

Its Islamic origins notwithstanding, the introduction of zakat did not go unchallenged. The Shia community objected strongly to the promulgation of the Zakat Ordinance on religious grounds. According to the Fiqh-i-Jafariah—the legal code accepted by the Shias—zakat should not be levied on capital and trade. The Shias also believe that the payment of zakat and the purpose for which it is to be used are the responsibility of the individual, to be exercised without any state interference. After considerable agitation by the Shia community, the government amended the Ordinance and exempted the Shia community from the levy of zakat.

The distribution of zakat is entrusted to an elaborate network of committees, called Zakat Committees, elected by local communities throughout the country. The principal function of the committees is to identify the mustahequeen eligible for receiving zakat funds. Some 32,000 Zakat Committees now operate under a national body called the Zakat Council. As with most other functions performed by government agencies in recent years, the process for the collection and distribution of zakat was not without controversy. There was a growing feeling among the people that the mustahequeen identified by the Zakat Committees were not always the most deserving and that the local functionaries of both political parties, the Pakistan People's Party and the Pakistan Muslim League (qq.v.), were using some of the zakat funds to win votes for themselves and their organizations. The use of zakat resources for funding religious institutions also unleashed a dynamic, the full extent of which was not appreciated when the decision was taken to use these funds for this purpose.

ZARDARI, ASIF ALI (1950–). Asif Ali Zardari entered the center stage of Pakistani politics in the summer of 1987 after his engagement to Benazir Bhutto (q.v.) was announced in London. Belonging to a family of Sindhi landlords, he was born and brought up in Karachi (q.v.). After Zardari and Bhutto were married in Karachi on December 18, 1987, he promised not to become active in politics. He did not, however, keep his word and thus cast a long shadow on Prime Minister Benazir Bhutto's first administration. Although he was not assigned a formal position in the administration, a number of his close associates joined the prime minister's secretariat. Stories began to circulate about the way Zardari was influencing government decisions. There was a suspicion that he was involved in a number of deals in which government procurement of expensive items and the awarding of building contracts by the government had led to his receiving large commissions.

There was enough talk going around about his activities for the recently liberated press in Pakistan to choose Zardari as a subject for investigative reporting. The press coverage received by Zardari contributed no doubt to the dismissal of his wife's administration by President Ghulam Ishaq Khan (q.v.) in August 1990. The president mentioned "rampant corruption" as one of the reasons for his drastic move against Bhutto. In September 1990 Zardari was arrested on charges of corruption and extortion. One of the cases in which he was implicated—the Unnar Case—revolved around a London-based Pakistani business-man who was allegedly forced to write a check for a large sum of money. The caretaker government of Ghulam Mustafa Jatoi (q.v.), which took office after the dismissal of Benazir Bhutto, charged Zardari for having been involved in this case of extortion.

Zardari took part in the elections of 1990 (q.v.) as a candidate representing the Pakistan People's Party (PPP) (q.v.). Having been denied bail by the judge presiding over his case and, therefore, unable to leave jail, Zardari could not actively campaign for his own election. That notwithstanding, he won a seat in the National Assembly from the Lyari district of Karachi (q.v.). The elections brought Mian Nawaz Sharif and his Pakistan Muslim League (qq.v.) to power in Islamabad (q.v.). The new government was not inclined to give any space to Zardari; it was convinced that if he was allowed out of jail, he would flee the country. Thus Zardari languished in jail for two years, but was allowed to be freed on bail when Prime Minister Sharif's relations with President Ishaq Khan (q.v.) began to sour in the winter of 1993.

By October 1993 another general election (q.v.) had been held and Benazir Bhutto was back in power as prime minister. As if she and her husband had learned a valuable lesson from the way they had conducted themselves the first time she was prime minister, Zardari initially adopted a low profile. He once again won a seat in the National Assembly and for a few months was quite content to serve as a PPP back-bencher. But this new attitude did not persist for very long. Once Prime Minister Bhutto felt she was settled in her job, Zardari reemerged, with a profile even more prominent than the one he had adopted in 1988–90. He also began to amass a vast amount of official power. His wife gave him the job of chairman of the Environment Commission. In a surprising move in July 1996, Bhutto brought Zardari into her cabinet as the minister in charge of investment. This move was not appreciated by President Farooq Leghari (q.v.), who on November 5, 1996 dismissed the prime minister, her cabinet, and dissolved the National Assembly.

Once again, as had happened after Bhutto's first dismissal, Zardari found himself behind bars, accused of using his position in the government to amass vast amounts of wealth. Among the accusations that received the most attention was the purchase of a large mansion in Surrey, outside London. The cases against Zardari were investigated by the Ehetasab (q.v.) cell operating out of the office of Prime Minister Nawaz Sharif. In January 1998 the *New York Times* published a long story carefully documenting the misdeeds allegedly committed by Zardari while his wife was prime minister. *See also* "Surreygate."

ZARDARI, HAKIM ALI. Hakim Ali Zardari was a little-known Karachi (q.v.) businessman before his son, Asif Ali Zardari (q.v.), married Benazir Bhutto (q.v.). The son's marriage to Ms. Bhutto also brought the father into the political spotlight. He took part, as a Pakistan People's Party (q.v.) candidate, in the general elections of 1988 (q.v.) and won a seat from Sindh (q.v.). On being elected prime minister, Benazir Bhutto appointed her father-in-law as chairman of the Public Accounts Committee of the National Assembly. Zardari used this position to good political effect, focusing a great deal of the committee's time and effort on highlighting the alleged misdeeds of the administration of Zia ul-Haq and Prime Minister Muhammad Khan Junejo (qq.v.).

His own business dealings after his daughter-in-law's assumption of office came under scrutiny as a result of the investigative efforts of the press, however. Two Karachi-based newsmagazines, *Herald* and *Newsline,* took a great deal of interest in Hakim Ali Zardari's business practices. In its August 1990 issue, *Newsline* devoted its cover story to the way public-sector financial institutions—commercial and investment banks—had been used to lend large sums of money to those with close links to Prime Minister Benazir Bhutto, including Hakim Ali Zardari. These allegations were used by President Ghulam Ishaq Khan (q.v.) in dismissing Bhutto from office in August 1990. When she returned to power in October 1993 as prime minister, Hakim Ali Zardari did not play any significant political role.

ZIA UL-HAQ, GENERAL MUHAMMAD (1923–1988). Zia ul-Haq was born in Jullundur and was educated there and at St. Stephen's College in Delhi. He joined the British Indian Army in 1943 and was trained in the Officer Training School. After the establishment of Pakistan in 1947 he opted for service in the Pakistani army. He received training in the United States, served as an advisor to the government of Jordan in 1974–75, and was promoted to the rank of lieutenant general in 1975. He was commanding the army corps stationed in Multan when Prime Minister Zulfikar Ali Bhutto (q.v.) appointed him chief of the Army Staff (COAS). In selecting Zia to succeed General Tikka Khan (q.v.) as the COAS, Bhutto was influenced by a number of factors: Zia had the reputation of being a professional soldier with little interest in politics. He belonged to Jullundur and not to one of the northern districts of Pakistan, which had been the favorite recruiting areas for the British Indian and Pakistani armies. As such he did not have a strong rank-and-file following in the army. He was from the Arain caste, which had little representation in the army. From Bhutto's perspective this was a safe appointment. Zia would not come in with a political agenda of his own; unlike General Ayub Khan (q.v.), he was not known to have strong political views. He did not have strong community ties with the members of the army's officer corps. Ayub Khan and Yahya Khan (q.v.) were Pathans, and the Pathans had a strong presence in the armed forces. There were few Arains in the army. There were some other things about Zia's background that were known to Bhutto, however, but to which he seems not to have attached much importance. Among them was his belief that Islam presented Pakistan with a model of statecraft that it would do well to follow. He was also known to be tenacious.

Following a long and bitter confrontation between Bhutto and the Pakistan National Alliance (PNA) (q.v.), a coalition formed to challenge the Pakistan People's Party (PPP) (q.v.). The army, under the leadership of General Zia, decided to intervene. It assumed control on July 5, 1977 but did not abrogate the constitution as Generals Ayub Khan and Yahya Khan had done in 1958 and 1969, respectively. The Constitution of 1973 (q.v.) was merely suspended. The army's main objective for intervening was to create an environment in which fair general elections could be organized. The army set a limit of ninety days for the completion of this intervention, known as Operation Fairplay (q.v.).

Zia and his fellow army commanders might have stuck to this schedule had Bhutto not responded with such belligerence toward the leadership of the armed forces. Once allowed to address public meetings, he promised his followers that those who had engineered the military takeover in July would have to face the full legal consequences of their actions. The Constitution of 1973 had been explicit in defining coup d'etat against the government as a capital offense, punishable by death. Bhutto made it absolutely clear that it was his intention to implement this provision once he was back in power. The army therefore could not permit Bhutto to return to power. Tried for the murder of a political opponent, he was sentenced to death by the Lahore High Court in the summer of 1978, a sentence that was appealed but upheld by the Supreme Court in early 1979. Bhutto refused to appeal to Zia for clemency and was hanged in Rawalpindi (q.v.) on April 4, 1979.

Once the decision had been made to send Bhutto to the gallows, it was obvious that the army could not let his party, the Pakistan People's Party, regain power. The six-year period from 1979 to 1985 was devoted to restructuring the political system in such a way that the PPP and its new leader, Benazir Bhutto (q.v.), would not be able to return to power. In pursuit of this objective, Zia was prepared to take many risks, including the cancellation of elections promised for November 1979, the organization of a national referendum in December 1984 to award him five more years as president, and the development of close ties with the political forces that totally opposed the PPP and Bhutto. This strategy paid off. The PPP decided to boycott the Elections of 1985 (q.v.), which gave Zia the opportunity to put in place a civilian government that he could trust. Thus began the Zia–Junejo political era on March 23, 1985, which lasted for over three years. Zia and Muhammad Khan Junejo (q.v.) felt confident enough about their situation to lift martial law (Martial Law, The Third [q.v.]) on December 30, 1985. But Zia decided to stay on as the chief of the Army Staff, thus ensuring a role for the military in the further evolution of the political experiment he had launched with the referendum of December 1984.

The Zia–Junejo political experiment ended suddenly on May 29, 1988 when the president dismissed the prime minister and dissolved the National Assembly. Extreme incompetence, growing corruption, and the failure to further the process of Islamization were offered by Zia as the reasons for his decision. In actual fact, however, Zia had been long resentful of the efforts Junejo was making to distance himself from the president and many of his policies. Zia's death on August 17 in a plane crash near the city of Bahawalpur also destroyed the political model he had constructed with such care and diligence. Among Zia's abiding legacies were the formal introduction of Islam into the country's economic and social structures and the assistance provided to the Afghan mujahideen (q.v.) in their struggle against the Soviet Union.

Bibliography

Introductory Essay

Pakistan has not attracted a great deal of scholarship. Even when the country celebrated its fiftieth birthday on August 14, 1997, the event was marked by silence. On the other hand, a great deal was written and said about India when it turned fifty, a day after Pakistan did. A number of books on Indian history appeared and several journals and magazines published special issues or surveys.

Interest in Pakistan has been confined to a few periods in its turbulent history. The Pakistan Movement, which concerned the campaign to create an independent homeland for the Muslim community of British India, is the period that has attracted the most interest. The subject was often dealt with in the context of the Indian independence movement. Among the notable works belonging to this genre are two recent books: Patrick French's *Liberty or Death: India's Journey to Independence and Division* and Anthony Read and David Fisher's *The Proudest Day: India's Long Road to Independence*. This recent attention to the subject was not entirely the result of the fiftieth-anniversary celebration, however. A number of works have appeared on this subject over the last fifty years. These include Chaudri Muhmmad Ali's *The Emergence of Pakistan*. Ali was a close associate of Muhammad Ali Jinnah, Pakistan's founder, and Liaqat Ali Khan, the country's first prime minister. Khalid bin Sayeed's *Pakistan: The Formative Phase* provides a detailed account of the way Jinnah guided the Pakistan movement. Ayesha Jalal's *The Sole Spokesman: Jinnah, the Muslim League and the Demand for Pakistan* provides an entirely different interpretation of Jinnah's role in creating Pakistan. She argues that Jinnah wanted Pakistan to get a better deal for the Muslim community of British India from the Indian National Congress led by Mahatama Gandhi and Jawaharlal Nehru. Had such a deal been made, Jinnah might not have pressed on with the idea of Pakistan to the point at which India had to be partitioned.

Muhammad Ali Jinnah attracted few biographers. Among the more competent works are Stanley Wolpert's *Jinnah of Pakistan* and Sharif Al Mujahid's *Quaid-e-Azam Jinnah: Studies in Interpretation.* This latter book has a detailed chronology of Jinnah's political life. The National Archives of Pakistan is publishing the *Jinnah Papers* under the direction of Z. H. Zaidi, a Pakistani historian. Akbar S. Ahmad, a Pakistani anthropologist, is directing a project out of Cambridge University, England, that includes the production of a documentary on the life of Jinnah as well as a feature film.

The arrival of military rule in Pakistan in October 1958 and President Ayub Khan's political experiment, as well as his success with accelerating the rate of economic growth, excited considerable academic interest. This was helped by the presence of Harvard University's development experts in the Planning Commission, a number of whom wrote important books. Among these are Gustav Papanek's *Pakistan's Development: Social Goals and Private Incentives,* and Stephen R. Lewis's *Economic Policy and Industrial Growth in Pakistan.* This period was also covered by some Pakistani economists. Mahbubul Haq's *The Strategy of Economic Planning: A Case Study of Pakistan* provided useful insights into the model of planning pursued by the Planning Commission in formulating and implementing the highly successful Second Five Year Plan.

The conflict with East Pakistan that led to a civil war in 1971 and the breakup of Pakistan was also the subject of several useful works. Rounaq Jahan's *Pakistan: Failure in National Integration* examined the circumstances that led to the conflict between the two wings of the country. A more recent book, Hassan Zaheer's *The Separation of East Pakistan: The Rise of Bengali Muslim Nationalism,* presents a highly competent analysis of the entire episode. Zaheer was a senior civil service official at the time of the civil war and served several months as a prisoner of war in India.

Zulfikar Ali Bhutto's charisma and style of governance interested a number of scholars. Bhutto attracted more biographers than any other Pakistani leader. Among the books dealing with this extraordinary figure in Pakistan's history are Stanley Wolpert's *Zulfi Bhutto of Pakistan: His Life and Times,* Salman Taseer's *Bhutto: A Political Biography,* and Shahid Javed Burki's *Pakistan Under Bhutto, 1971–77.* The book by Benazir Bhutto, Zulfikar Ali Bhutto's daughter, *Daughter of the East: An Autobiography,* dealt with her father's rise and fall from power. Zulfikar Bhutto wrote a defense of himself while he was in prison waiting to be tried for the murder of an opponent. The manuscript of *If I Am Assassinated . . .?* was smuggled out of the prison in Rawalpindi and published in India.

Zia ul-Haq, Pakistan's third military president, has been largely ignored by Western scholars. The war in Afghanistan against the invasion of that country by the Soviet Union in which Zia ul-Haq took a personal interest was to become the subject of some inquiry. Among the better books written on this subject are Riaz M. Khan's *Untying the Afghan Knot: Negotiating Soviet*

Withdrawal and Diego Cordovez and Selig S. Harrison's *Out of Afghanistan: The Inside Story of the Soviet Withdrawal.* Both books deal with the long negotiations, much of it personally directed by President Zia, between the Soviet Union, the United States, Afghanistan, and Pakistan, which finally led to the Soviet Union's withdrawal after ten years of bitter struggle. One of the better books on the Zia period is General K. M. Arif's *Working with Zia.* Arif was a close associate of the president and, as such, was a participant in most of the important decisions made by the military government.

Pakistan's fiftieth birthday provided an occasion for one publisher, Oxford University Press, Karachi, to publish extensive material on the country's history. Among the books included in the series are Omar Noman's *Economic and Social Progress in Asia: Why Pakistan did not Become a Tiger; Just Development: Beyond Adjustment with a Human Face,* a book edited by Tariq J. Banuri, Shahrukh Rafi Khan, and Moazam Mahmood; Lawrence Ziring's *Pakistan in the Twentieth Century: A Political History;* Dicky Rutnagar's *Khan Unlimited: A History of Squash in Pakistan;* Sydney Friskin's *Going for Gold: Pakistan at Hockey;* and Mushtaq Gazdar's *Pakistan Cinema, 1947–1997.*

The best continuous source for the analysis of various aspects of the Pakistani economy is *Pakistan Development Review,* published by the Pakistan Institute of Development Economics (PIDE). PIDE also holds an annual conference in Islamabad and publishes its proceedings. The government of Pakistan's *Pakistan Economic Survey,* published annually, provides information on the year under review and carries time series on several economic indices including growth in gross domestic product, national income accounts, external trade, money supply, internal and external debt, population, and employment. Economic data are also available in the World Bank's annual *World Development Report,* the International Monetary Fund's monthly *International Financial Statistics,* and the United Nations Development Program's annual *Human Development Report.* Mahbubul Haq established the Human Development Center at Islamabad in 1995. Its annual report has become an important source of information and data on social development.

Pakistan does not publish a serious journal devoted to politics and history. Most of the academics, both Pakistanis and foreigners, publish their work in foreign journals. Among these are *Asian Survey, The Middle East Journal, Modern Asian Studies, Orbis,* and *Pacific Affairs.* Three Pakistani newsmagazines, *Herald, Newsline,* and *The Friday Times* carry useful articles and features on current affairs.

The bibliography is organized as follows:

I. History

A. Memoirs and Biographies

Aga Khan. *The Memoirs of Aga Khan: World Enough and Time.* London: Cassell, 1954.

Ahmed, Akbar S. *Jinnah, Pakistan and Islamic Identity.* London: Routledge, 1997.

Akhund, Iqbal. *Memoirs of a Bystander: A Life in Diplomacy.* Karachi: Oxford University Press, 1997.

Al-Nahal: A Quarterly Publication of Majlis Ansarullah. *Muhammad Abdus Salam (1926–1996).* Washington, DC: 1998.

Arif, K. M. *Working with Zia.* Karachi: Oxford University Press, 1995.

Aziz, K. K. *Ameer Ali: His Life and Work.* Lahore: Publishers United, 1966.

Bence-Jones, Mark. *Clive of India.* New York: St. Martin's Press, 1974.

Bhutto, Benazir. *Daughter of the East: An Autobiography.* London: Hamish Hamilton, 1988.

Bhutto, Zulfikar Ali. *If I Am Assassinated . . .?* Delhi: Vikas, 1976.

Chaudhuri, Nirad C. *Clive of India.* London: Barrie and Jenkins, 1975.

Collins, K. J. *Lord Wavell (1883–1941).* London: Hodder and Stoughton, 1948.

Connell, John. *Auchinleck.* London: Cassell, 1959.

Douglas, Ian Henderson. *Abdul Kalam Azad: An Intellectual and Religious Biography.* Delhi: Oxford University Press, 1993.

Durrani, Tehmina. *My Feudal Lord.* Lahore: Tehmina Durrani, 1991.

Findly, Ellison Banks. *Nur Jahan: Empress of Mughul India.* New York: Oxford University Press, 1993.

Galbraith, John Kenneth. *Ambassador's Journal.* Boston: Houghton Mifflin, 1969.

———. *A Life in Our Times: Memoirs.* Boston: Houghton Mifflin, 1981.

Hasan, Mushirul, ed. *Mohamed Ali in Indian Politics: Selected Writings,* Vols. I & II. New Delhi: Atlantic Publishers, 1982.

Hough, Richard. *Mountbatten.* New York: Random House, 1981.

Jafri, Rais Ahmad, ed. *Ayub: Soldier and Statesman.* Lahore: Mohammad Ali Academy, 1966.

Jalal, Ayesha. *The Sole Spokesman: Jinnah, the Muslim League and the Demand for Pakistan.* London: Cambridge University Press, 1985.

Khan, Field Marshal Muhammad. *Friends Not Masters: A Political Autobiography.* London: Oxford University Press, 1997.

Khan, Lt. Gen. Gul Hassan. *Memoirs.* Karachi: Oxford University Press, 1993.

Khan, Muhammad Zafrullah. *Servant of God.* London: Unwin Brothers, 1983.

Khan, Sardar Shaukat Hayat. *The Nation That Lost Its Soul: Memoirs.* Lahore: Jung Publishers, 1995.

Khuhuhro, Hamida. *Mohammed Ayub Khuhro: A Life of Courage in Politics.* Lahore: Ferozsons, 1998.

Kissinger, Henry. *White House Years.* Boston: Little, Brown, 1979.

Malik, Hafeez. *Iqbal: Poet-Philosopher of Pakistan.* New York: Columbia University Press, 1971.

Mohammad, Shan, ed. *Writings and Teachings of Sir Syed Ahmad Khan.* Bombay: Nachiketa Publications, 1972.

Moon, Penderel, ed. *Wavell: The Viceroy's Journal.* Karachi: Oxford University Press, 1997.

Mujahid, Sharif Al. *Quaid-e-Azam Jinnah: Studies in Interpretation.* Karachi: Quaid-e-Azam Academy, 1981.

Nehru, Jawaharlal. *An Autobiography.* New Delhi: Oxford University Press, 1982.

Niazi, Lt. Gen. A. A. K. *The Betrayal of East Pakistan.* Karachi: Oxford University Press, 1998.

Noon, Firoz Khan. *From Memory.* Islamabad: National Book Foundation, 1993.

Taseer, Salman. *Bhutto: A Political Biography.* New Delhi: Vikas, 1980.

Wolpert, Stanley. *Jinnah of Pakistan.* New York: Oxford University Press, 1984.

———. *Zulfi Bhutto of Pakistan: His Life and Times.* New York: Oxford University Press, 1993.

Yunus, Mohammad. *Persons, Passions and Politics.* New Delhi: Vikas, 1980.

Zaidi, Z. H. *Jinnah Papers.* Islamabad: National Archives of Pakistan, Quaid-e Azam Project, 1993.

B. Pre-British

Ali, Chiragh. *The Proposed Political, Legal and Social Reforms in the Ottoman Empire and Other Mohammedan States.* Bombay: Longmans, 1883.

Possehl, Gregory, ed. *Ancient Cities of India.* New Delhi: Vikas, 1979.

Richards, John F. *The Mughul Empire.* New York: Cambridge University Press, 1993.

Sharar, Abdul Halim. *Lucknow: The Last Phase of an Oriental Culture.* Boulder, Colo.: Westview Press, 1975.

Sherwani, H. K. *Cultural Trend in Medieval India.* London: Asia Publishing House, 1968.

Singh, Khushwant. *A History of the Sikhs, Vol. I, 1469–1839.* Princeton, N.J.: Princeton University Press, 1963.

———. *A History of the Sikhs, Vol. II, 1839–1964.* Princeton, N.J.: Princeton University Press. 1966.

C. British Period

Ali, Imran. *The Punjab Under Imperialism, 1885–1947.* New York: Columbia University Press, 1988.

Bayly, C. A. *Empire and Information: Intelligence Gathering and Social Communication in India, 1780–1870.* Cambridge: Cambridge University Press, 1996.

Candler, E. *The Sepoy.* London: John Murray, 1919.

Case, Margret H. *South Asia History, 1750–1950: A Guide to Periodicals, Dissertations, and Newspapers.* Princeton, N.J.: Princeton University Press, 1968.

Chirol, Valentine. *Indian Unrest.* London: Macmillan, 1960.

Choudhury, Mohammad Ali. *The Emergence of Pakistan.* New York: Columbia University Press, 1967.

Cohen, S. P. "Subhas Chandra Bose and the Indian National Army." *Pacific Affairs* 36, no. 4 (winter 1963–64): 411–29.

————. "Issue, Role, and Personality: The Kitchener–Curzon Dispute." *Comparative Studies in Society and History* 10, no. 3 (April 1968): 337–55.

————. "The Untouchable Soldier: Caste Politics and the Indian Army." *Journal of Asian Studies* 28, no. 3 (May 1969): 453–68.

Colyer, W. J. "Tackling the Refugee Problem in the Western Punjab." *Army Quarterly* 56, no. 2 (July 1948): 72–98.

Coupland, Reginald. *The Indian Problem, 1833–1935.* London: Oxford University Press, 1942.

————. *Indian Politics, 1936–1942.* London: Oxford University Press, 1943.

————. *The Future of India.* London: Oxford University Press, 1944.

Cross, Cecil. *The Development of Self Government in India, 1858–1914.* Chicago: University of Chicago Press, 1922.

Davies, C. Colin. "British Relations with the Afradis." *Army Quarterly* 23, no. 2 (January 1932): 21–32.

Das, M. N. *India Under Morley and Minto: Politics Behind Revolution, Repression and Reform.* London: George Allen and Unwin, 1964.

Das, T. S. *Indian Military Its History and Development.* New Delhi: Sagar Publications, 1969.

Elliott, J. G. *A Roll of Honour.* London: Cassell, 1965.

————. *The Frontier 1839–1847.* London: Cassell, 1968.

Frere, Bartle. *The Means of Ascertaining Public Opinion in India.* London: John Murray, 1871.

Gale, Sir Richard. "Progress and Special Problems of India and Pakistan." *Journal of Royal United Services Institution* 96 (February 1951): 34–44.

Gallagher, John, ed. *Locality, Province and Nation: Essays on Indian Politics, 1870–1947.* Cambridge: Cambridge University Press, 1973.

Gopal, S. *The Viceroyalty of Lord Ripon, 1880–1884.* London: Oxford University Press, 1953.

————. *British Policy in India, 1858–1905.* Cambridge: Cambridge University Press, 1965.

Griffiths, Sir Percival. *The British Impact on India.* London: MacDonald, 1952.

Gupta, S. C. *History of the Indian Air Force 1933–45.* Delhi: Orient Longmans, 1961.

Gutteridge, W. "The Indianisation of the Indian Army, 1918–45." *Race* IV, no. 2 (May 1963): 39–48.

Gwyer, Sir Maurice, and A. Appadorai, eds. *Speeches and Documents on the Indian Constitution 1921–47.* London: Oxford University Press, 1957.

Hodson, H. V. *The Great Divide.* Karachi: Oxford University Press, 1969.

Inden, Ronald. "Orientalist Constructions of India." *Modern Asian Studies* 20, no. 3 (January 1969): 389–412.

Irwin, S. F. "The Indian Army in Partition." *Army Quarterly* 56, no. 2 (July 1948): 177–92.

Ismay, Lord. *The Memoirs of General Lord Ismay.* London: Heinemann, 1940.

Jacob, Sir Claud W. "The Defense of India." *India Monthly* 5, no. 5 (November 1930).

————. "The Indian Army and Its Future." *English Review* (February 1931): 169–74.

James, Morrice. *Pakistan Chronicle.* New York: St. Martin's Press, 1993.

Jeffrey, Robin. "The Punjab Boundary Force and the Problems of Order, August 1947." *Modern Asian Studies* 8, no. 4 (October 1974): 491–520.

Kabir, Humayun. *Muslim Politics 1906–47 and Other Essays.* Calcutta: Firma K. L. Mukhopadhyay, 1969.

Kaye, John William. *A History of the Sepoy War in India, 1857–58.* London: W. H. Allen, 1880.

Keith, A. B. *A Constitutional History of India 1600–1935.* London: Macmillan, 1956.

Khan, Abdul Waheed. *India Wins Freedom: The Other Side.* Karachi: Pakistan Educational Publishers, 1961.

Kirby, S. W. *The War Against Japan.* London: Collins, 1961.

Kopf, David. *British Orientalism and the Bengal Renaissance: The Dynamics of Indian Modernization, 1773–1835.* Berkeley: University of California Press, 1969.

Lawford, J. P., and W. E. Solah. *Punjab.* Aldershot, Hampshire, England: Gale and Polden, 1967.

Lumby, E. W. R. *The Transfer of Power in India.* London: Allen and Unwin, 1954.

MacMunn, Sir George. *The Martial Races of India.* London: Sampson Low, 1933.

Magnus, Philip. *Kitchener: Portrait of an Imperialist.* London: John Murray, 1958.

Marshall, P. J. "Warren Hastings as Scholar and Patron." In *Statesmen, Scholars and Merchants,* ed. Anne Whiteman et al. London: Oxford University Press, 1973.

Mason, Philip. *A Matter of Honour: An Account of the Indian Army; Its Officers and Men.* London: Holt, Rinehart and Winston, 1974.

Mayo, Katherine. *Mother India.* New York: Blue Ribbon Books, 1927.

McLane, John R. *Indian Nationalism and the Early Congress.* Princeton, N.J.: Princeton University Press, 1977.

Menon, V. P. *The Transfer of Power in India.* London: Orient Longmans, 1957.

Mittal, S. C. *Freedom Movement in Punjab, 1905–1929.* Delhi: Concept Publishing, 1977.

Muir, Ramsay. *The Making of British India, 1756–1858.* Lahore: Al-Biruni, 1978.

O'Brien, A. "The Reforms and the Indian Army." *Nineteenth Century and After* 605, no. 12 (July 1927): 22–41.

Omissi, David. *The Sepoy and the Raj. The Indian Army, 1860–1940.* London: Macmillan, 1994.

Panikkar, K. M. *India and the Indian Ocean.* London: Allen and Unwin, 1959.

Philips, C. H., and M. D. Wainwright, eds. *The Partition of India: Policies and Perspectives 1935–47.* London: Allen and Unwin, 1967.

Poplai, S., ed. *Select Documents on Asian Affairs: India 1947–50.* Bombay: Oxford University Press, 1963.

Prasad, Bishehwar. *Defence of India: Policy and Plans.* London: Orient Longmans, 1963.

Prasad, Nandan, ed. *Expansion of the Armed Forces and Defence Organization, 1939–45.* London: Orient Longmans, 1956.

Preston, A. "The Indian Army and Indo–British Political and Strategic Relations, 1745–1947." *USI Journal* (India) 421 (Oct.–Dec. 1970): 351–89.

Rawlinson, H. G. *The British Achievement in India.* London: William Hodge, 1948.

Schweinitz Jr., Karl de. *The Rise and Fall of British India.* London: Methuen, 1983.

Seal, Anil. *The Emergence of Indian Nationalism: Competition and Collaboration in the Later Nineteenth Century.* Cambridge: Cambridge University Press, 1968.

Shaikh, Farzana. *Community and Consensus in Islam: Muslim Representation in Colonial India, 1860–1947.* New York: Cambridge University Press, 1989.

Singh, Jewan. "Some Aspects of the Indian Army and Its Indianization." *Army Quarterly* XXII, no. 2 (July 1931): 347–79.

Singh, Nagendra. *The Theory of Force and Organisation of Defence in Indian Constitutional History From Earliest Times to 1947.* New York: Asia Publishing House, 1969.

Spear, Percival. *A History of India,* Vol. II. Baltimore: Penguin Books, 1956.

Stokes, Eric. *The Peasant and the Raj: Studies in Agrarian Society and Peasant Rebellion in Colonial India.* Cambridge: Cambridge University Press, 1978.

Strachey, John. *The End of Empire.* New York: Praeger, 1959.

Strettel, Sir Dashwood. "The Indian Army Before and After 1947." *Journal of the Royal Central Asian Society* 35, no. 11 (April 1968): 119–30.

Sundaram, Lanka. *India's Armies and Their Costs.* Bombay: India Publishing, 1946.

Superintendent Government Printing Press. *The Army in India and Its Evolution.* Calcutta: Government Printing Press, 1924.

Tinker, Hugh. *South Asia: A Short History.* New York: Praeger, 1966.

———. *Viceroy: Curzon to Mountbatten.* Karachi: Oxford University Press, 1997.

Tomlinson, B. R. *The Indian National Congress and the Raj: 1929–1942.* London: Macmillan, 1976.

Tucker, Sir Francis. "Defence of India and Pakistan." *Manchester Guardian* (December 15, 1949): IV.

———. *While Memory Serves.* London: Cassell, 1950.

Venkateshwaran, A. L. *Defence Organisation in India.* New Delhi: Publication Division, Ministry of Defence, 1969.

Wasti, S. R. *Lord Minto and the Indian Nationalist Movement.* Oxford: Clarendon Press, 1964.

Wolpert, Stanley. *Tilak and Gokhale: Revolution and Reform in the Making of Modern India.* Berkeley: University of California Press, 1961.

———. *A New History of India.* New York: Oxford University Press, 1977.

Woodruff, Philip. *The Men Who Ruled India: The Founders.* London: Jonathan Cape, 1953.

———. *The Men Who Ruled India: The Guardians.* London: Jonathan Cape, 1954.

Yeats-Brown, F. *Martial India.* London: Eyre and Spottiswoode, 1945.

Zakaria, Z. H. *Rise of Muslims in Indian Politics: An Analysis of Developments from 1885 to 1906.* Bombay: Somaiya Publications, 1970.

D. Independence Movement

Azad, Maulana A. K. *India Wins Freedom.* Calcutta: Orient Longmans, 1959.

Aziz, K. K. *The Making of Pakistan: A Study in Nationalism.* London: Chatto and Windus, 1967.

Birdwood, Lord. *A Continent Decides.* London: Robert Hale, 1959.

Bryant, Arthur. *The Turn of the Tide.* London: Collins, 1957.

Campbell-Johnsons, A. *Mission with Mountbatten.* London: Robert Hale, 1951.

French, Patrick. *Liberty or Death: India's Journey to Independence and Division.* London: HarperCollins, 1997.

Hasan, K. Sarwar. *The Transfer of Power.* Karachi: Pakistan Institute for International Affairs, 1966.

Hasan, Mushirul. *India's Partition: Process, Strategy and Mobilization.* Delhi: Oxford University Press, 1993.

Ikram, S. M. *Modern Muslim India and the Birth of Pakistan.* Lahore: Shaikh Muhammad Ashraf, 1970.

Khaliquzzaman, Choudhry. *Pathway to Pakistan.* Karachi: Longman, 1961.

Lumby, E. W. R. *The Transfer of Power in India.* London: George Allen and Unwin, 1954.

Mansergh, N., and E. W. R. Lumby. *The Transfer of Power 1942–47* (5 vols.). London: Her Majesty's Stationery Office, 1970–71.

Mehrotra, S. R. *Towards India's Freedom and Partition.* New Delhi: Vikas, 1979.

Merriam, Allen Hayes. *Gandhi vs. Jinnah: The Debate Over the Partition of India.* Calcutta: Minerva, 1980.

Moore, R. J. *The Crisis of Indian Unity, 1917–1940.* London: Oxford University Press, 1974.

Moraes, Frank. *Witness to an Era: India 1920 to the Present Day.* New York: Holt, Rinehart and Winston, 1973.

Morris, James. *Pax Britannica: The Climax of an Empire.* New York: Harcourt, 1964.

———. *Heaven's Command: An Imperial Progress.* New York: Harcourt, Brace, Javanovich, 1973.

———. *Farewell the Trumpets: An Imperial Retreat.* New York: Faber and Faber, 1978.

Mujeeb, M. *The Indian Muslims.* London: George Allen and Unwin, 1967.

Nanda, B. R. *Gokhale, Gandhi and the Nehrus: Studies in Indian Nationalism.* New York: St. Martin's Press, 1973.

Page, David. *Prelude to Partition: The Indian Muslims and the Imperial System of Control, 1920–1932.* Delhi: Oxford University Press, 1982.

Pandey, B. N. *The Break–Up of British India.* London: Macmillan, 1969.

———. *The Indian Nationalist Movement, 1885–1947: Selected Documents.* London: Macmillan, 1979.

Philips, C. M., and Mary Doreen Wainwright. *The Partition of India: Policies and Perspectives, 1935–1947.* Cambridge, Mass.: MIT Press, 1970.

Read, Anthony, and David Fisher. *The Proudest Day: India's Long Road to Peace.* New York: W. W. Norton, 1997.

Robinson, Francis. *Separation Among Indian Muslims: The Politics of the United Provinces' Muslims, 1860–1923.* Cambridge: Cambridge University Press, 1974.

———. "Islam and Muslim Separatism." In *Political Identity in South Asia,* ed. David Taylor and Malcolm Yapp. London: London School of Oriental and African Studies, 1979, 78–112.

E. Pakistan

Bahadur, Lal. *The Muslim League: Its History, Activities, and Achievements.* Lahore: Book Traders, 1979.

Burki, Shahid Javed. *Pakistan Under Bhutto, 1971–77.* London: Macmillan, 1980.
——. *Pakistan: A Nation in the Making.* Boulder, Colo.: Westview Press, 1986.
——. *Pakistan: Continuing Search for Nationhood.* Boulder, Colo.: Westview Press, 1991.
——. *Historical Dictionary of Pakistan.* Metuchen, N.J.: Scarecrow Press, 1991.
Burki, Shahid Javed, and Craig Baxter, eds. *Pakistan Under the Military: Eleven Years of Zia ul-Haq.* Boulder. Colo.: Westview Press, 1991.
Burki, Shahid Javed, and R. Laporte, eds. *Pakistan's Development Priorities.* Karachi: Oxford University Press, 1984.
Callard, K. *Pakistan: A Political Study.* London: George Allen, 1958.
Caroe, Sir Olaf. *The Pathans 550 B.C.–A.D. 1957.* Karachi: Oxford University Press, 1958, 1983.
Chopra, Pran. *Contemporary Pakistan: New Aims and Images.* New Delhi: Vikas, 1983.
Choudhury, G. W. *Democracy in Pakistan.* Dhaka: Green Book House, 1963.
——. *Constitutional Development in Pakistan.* London: Longman, 1969.
——. *The Last Days of United Pakistan.* Bloomington: Indiana University Press, 1975.
——. *Pakistan: Transition from Military to Civilian Rule.* London: Scorpion Publishing, 1988.
Feldman, Herbert. *Revolution in Pakistan: A Study of the Martial Law Administration.* Karachi: Oxford University Press, 1967.
——. *From Crisis to Crisis: Pakistan 1962–1969.* Karachi: Oxford University Press, 1972.
——. *The End and the Beginning, 1969–1972.* Karachi: Oxford University Press, 1972.
Henderson, Gregory Lebow, Richard Ned, and John G. Stoessinger, eds. *Divided Nations in a Divided World.* New York: McKay, 1974.
Hussain, J. *A History of the Peoples of Pakistan.* Karachi: Oxford University Press, 1997.
Jahan, Rounaq. *Pakistan: Failure in National Integration.* New York: Columbia University Press, 1972.
James, Morrice. *Pakistan Chronicle.* New York: St. Martin's Press, 1993.
Lamb, Christina. *Waiting for Allah: Pakistan's Struggle for Democracy.* New York: Viking, 1991.
Munir, Muhammad. *From Jinnah to Zia.* Lahore: Vanguard, 1980.
Niazi, Lt. Gen. A. A. K. *The Betrayal of East Pakistan.* Karachi: Oxford University Press, 1998.
Qureshi, Ishtiaq Hussain. *The Struggle for Pakistan.* Karachi: University of Karachi Press, 1965.
Sayeed, Khalid Bin. *Pakistan: The Formative Phase.* London: Oxford University Press, 1960.
——. "Historical Origins of Some of Pakistan's Persistent Political Problems." In *The States of South Asia: Problems of National Integration,* ed. A. Jayaratnam Wilson and Dennis Dalton. New Delhi: Vikas, 1982.
Schofield, Victoria. *Old Roads New Highways: Fifty Years of Pakistan.* Karachi: Oxford University Press, 1997.

Sisson, Richard, and Leo Rose. *War and Succession: Pakistan, India, and the Creation of Bangladesh.* Berkeley: University of California Press, 1990.

Von Vorys, K. *Political Development in Pakistan.* Princeton, N.J.: Princeton University Press, 1965.

Weeks, R. V. *Pakistan: Birth and Growth of a Muslim Nation.* Princeton, N.J.: Van Nostrand, 1964.

Zaheer, Hassan. *The Separation of East Pakistan: The Rise and Realization of Bengali Muslim Nationalism.* Karachi: Oxford University Press, 1994.

———. *The Times and Trial of the Rawalpindi Conspiracy, 1951: The First Coup Attempt in Pakistan.* Karachi: Oxford University Press, 1998.

Ziring, Lawrence. *Pakistan in the Twentieth Century: A Political History.* Karachi: Oxford University Press, 1997.

F. Afghanistan

Ahmed, Samina. "Afghanistan: The Rocky Road to Peace." *Newsline* (May 1998): 68–73.

Cordovez, Diego, and Selig S. Harrison. *Out of Afghanistan: The Inside Story of the Soviet Withdrawal.* New York: Oxford University Press, 1995.

Gregorian, Victor. *The Emergence of Modern Afghanistan. Politics of Reform and Modernization.* Stanford, Calif.: Stanford University Press, 1969.

Harrison, Selig S. *In Afghanistan's Shadow: Baluch Nationalism and Soviet Temptations.* New York: Carnegie Endowment for International Peace, 1981.

Kakar, M. Hasan. *Afghanistan: The Soviet Invasion and the Afghan Response, 1979–1982.* Berkeley: University of California Press, 1995.

Khan, Riaz M. *Untying the Afghan Knot: Negotiating Soviet Withdrawal.* Durham, N.C.: Duke University Press, 1991.

Newell, Richard S. *The Politics of Afghanistan.* Ithaca, N.Y.: Cornell University Press, 1972.

Rose, Leo, and Kamal Matinuddin. *Beyond Afghanistan: The Emergence of U.S.–Pakistan Relations.* Berkeley, Calif.: Institute of East Asian Studies, 1989.

Rubin, Barnett R. *The Fragmentation: State Formation and Collapse in the International System.* New Haven, Conn.: Yale University Press, 1995.

Weinbaum, Marvin G. "Pakistan and the Resolution of the Afghan Conflict." In *Pakistan: 1992,* ed. Charles H. Kennedy. Boulder, Colo.: Westview Press, 1993: 109–32.

G. Kashmir

Akbar, M. J. *Kashmir: Behind the Vale.* New Delhi: Penguin Books, 1991.

Ashraf, Fahmida. "The Kashmir Dispute: An Evaluation." *Strategic Studies* (Islamabad) 13, no. 4 (summer 1990): 61–77.

Brecher, Michael. *The Struggle for Kashmir.* New York: Oxford University Press, 1953.

Cheema, Pervaiz Iqbal. "A Solution for Kashmir Dispute?" *Regional Studies* (Islamabad), 4, no. 4 (autumn 1986): 3–15.

Das-Gupta, J. B. *Jammu and Kashmir.* The Hague: Martinus Nijhoff, 1968.

Ganguly, Sumit. "Avoiding War in Kashmir." *Foreign Affairs* 69, no. 5 (winter 1990/91): 65–79.

Government of Jammu and Kashmir, India. *Statement of Facts on Gilgit, Hunza, Nagar, Yasin, Ponial, Chitral, and Skardu.* Srinigar, Kashmir: N.p., 1983.

Gupta, Sisir. *Kashmir: A Study in Indo–Pakistan Relations.* Bombay: Asia, 1966.

Hasan, K. Sarwar, ed. *The Kashmir Question: Documents on the Foreign Policy of Pakistan.* Karachi: Pakistan Institute of International Affairs, 1966.

Higgins, Rosalyn. *United Nations Peacekeeping, 1946–1967, Documents and Commentary II: Asia.* London: Oxford University Press, 1970.

Human Rights Watch. *Human Rights in India: Kashmir Under Siege, an Asia Watch Report.* New York, May 1991.

India Today. "Kashmir: Wages of Manipulation." A Round Table Discussion. New Delhi (August 31, 1991): 47–59.

Korbel, Josef. *Danger in Kashmir.* Princeton, N.J. : Princeton University Press, 1966.

Lamb, Alastair. *Kashmir: A Disputed Legacy, 1846–1990.* Hertingfordbury, England: Roxford Books, 1991.

Miller, Lynn H. "The Kashmir Dispute." In *International Law and Political Crisis: An Analytical Casebook*, ed. Lawrence Scheinman and David Wilkinson. Boston: Little, Brown, 1968.

Moore, Molly, and Kamran Khan. "Kashmir is Flash Point of Indo–Pakistani Tension." *Washington Post* (June 3, 1998): A1 & A18.

Nicholson, Mark, and Farhan Bokhari. "A Small Strip of the Himalayas Put on Top of the World Agenda." *Financial Times* (June 6, 1998): 4.

Subramanyam, K. "Kashmir." *Strategic Analysis* 13, no. 2 (May 1990): 132–47.

Thornton, Thomas Perry. *The 1972 Simla Agreement: An Asymmetrical Negotiation.* Washington, D.C.: Foreign Policy Institute, Johns Hopkins University, 1988.

Varshney, Ashutosh. "India, Pakistan, and Kashmir: Antinomies of Nationalism." *Asian Survey* 31, no. 11 (November 1991): 988–1006.

Wirsing, Robert G. "Kashmir Conflict: The New Phase." In *Pakistan 1992*, ed. Charles H. Kennedy. Boulder, Colo.: Westview Press, 1993: 133–66.

———. *India, Pakistan and the Kashmir Boundary Dispute: The Search for Settlement.* New York: St. Martin's Press, 1996.

Zutshi, U. K. *Emergence of Political Awakening in Kashmir.* New Delhi: Manohar Publications, 1986.

II. Government and Politics

A. Administration

Ahmad, Emajuddin. "Exclusive Bureaucratic Elites in Pakistan Their Socioeconomic and Regional Background." *Indian Political Science Review* XV, no. 1 (January 1981): 52–66.

Ahmad, Muneer. *Aspects of Pakistan's Politics and Administration.* Lahore: South Asia Institute, 1974.

Braibanti, R. "The Civil Service of Pakistan: A Theoretical Analysis." *South Atlantic Quarterly* LVIII, no. 2 (1959): 258–304.

————. *Research on the Bureaucracy of Pakistan.* Durham, N.C.: Duke University Press, 1966.

Burki, Shahid Javed. "Twenty Years of the Civil Service of Pakistan." *Asian Survey* 9, no. 4 (April 1969): 239–54.

Goodnow, H. F. *The Civil Service of Pakistan: Bureaucracy in the New Nation.* Karachi: Oxford University Press, 1969.

Gorvine, Albert. "The Civil Service Under the Revolutionary Government in Pakistan." *Middle East Journal* XIX, no. 2 (summer 1965): 321–36.

Sayeed, Khalid Bin. "The Political Role of Pakistan's Civil Service." *Pacific Affairs* 31, no. 2 (June 1958): 131–46.

B. Defense and Military

Ahmad, Mohammad (Colonel). *My Chief.* Lahore: Longmans, 1960.

Ahmad, Saeed (Major). *Indo–Pak Clash in Rann of Kutch 1965.* Rawalpindi: Army Education Press, 1973.

Akhtar, Ali. *Pakistan's Nuclear Dilemma: Energy and Security Dimensions.* Karachi: Economist Research Unit, 1983.

Akhtar, Hameed Saeed. *A Study of Pakistan Military Law.* Sialkot, Pakistan: Modern Book Depot, 1977.

Akhtar M. A. "Pakistan: The Way Ahead From Martial Law." *South Asian Review* 3, no. 1 (October 1969): 23–30.

Alam, Captain K. M. "The Maritime Compulsions of Pakistan." *Pakistan Times* (September 6, 1975): 3.

Alavi, Hamza. "The Army and the Bureaucracy in Pakistan." *International Socialist Journal* 3, no. 14 (March–April 1966): 149–81.

Ali, Tariq. *Pakistan: Military Rule or People's Power?* London: Jonathan Cape, 1970.

Asghar Khan, Air Marshal. *Generals in Politics: Pakistan 1958–82.* New Delhi: Vikas, 1983.

Atiqur Rahman, Lt. General M. *Leadership: Senior Commanders.* Lahore: Ferozsons, 1973.

————. *Our Defence Cause.* London: White Lion Publishers, 1976.

————. *The Wardens of the Marches: A History of the Piffers 1947–71.* Lahore: Wajidalis, 1980.

Babar, Sabihuddin. "Law and Martial Law." *Newsline* (Karachi), July 1990: 24–25.

Bains, J. S. *India's International Disputes: A Legal Study.* London: Asia, 1962.

Bhutto, Z. A. *The Myth of Independence.* London: Oxford University Press, 1969.

Birdwood, Lord. *Two Nations and Kashmir.* London: Robert Hale, 1956.

Bordewich, Fergus M. "The Pakistan Army: Sword of Islam." *Asia* (September–October 1982): 16–23, 48–53.

Brines, Russel. *The Indo–Pakistan Conflict.* London: Pall Mall, 1968.

Brown, W. Norman. *The United States and India, Pakistan, Bangladesh.* Cambridge, Mass.: Harvard University Press, 1972.

Burke, S. M. *Pakistan's Foreign Policy: An Historical Analysis.* Karachi: Oxford University Press, 1973.

————. *Mainsprings of Indian and Pakistani Foreign Policy.* Karachi: Oxford University Press, 1975.

Butt, Major General G. S. "Role of Armed Forces in National Development." *Muslim* (September 6, 1982): 4.

Buzan, Barry, and Gowher Rizvi. *South Asian Insecurity and the Great Powers*. New York: St. Martin's Press, 1986.

Chang, D. W. "The Military and Nation Building in Korea, Burma and Pakistan." *Asian Survey* 9, no. 11 (November 1969): 818–30.

Chaudhury, Brigadier Amiad Ali. *September 1965, Before and After*. Lahore: Ferozsons, 1977.

Chaudri, Vice Admiral H. M. Siddiq. "Defence Set-up Priorities." *Pakistan Times* (February 11, 1972): 3.

Cheema, Pervaiz Iqbal. *Pakistan's Defense Policy, 1947–58*. Basingstoke, U.K.: Macmillan, 1990.

Cohen, Stephen P. *The Indian Army. Its Contribution to the Development of a Nation*. Berkeley: University of California Press, 1971.

———. *The Pakistan Army*. Berkeley: University of California Press, 1984.

———. "Pakistan: Army, Society and Security." *Asian Affairs: An American Review* 10, no. 2 (summer 1983): 1–26.

———. *The Security of South Asia*. Urbana: University of Illinois Press, 1987.

Dar, Major General E. H. "Pakistan Army in the Eighties." *Daily Nawa-i-Waqt* (Lahore) (January 4, 1985): 2.

Eliot, Theodore, and Robert Pfaltzgraff. *The Red Army on Pakistan's Borders: Implications for the United States*. Washington, D.C.: Pergamon-Brassey's, 1986.

Ganguly, Sumit. *The Origins of War in South Asia: Indo–Pakistan Conflicts Since 1947*. Boulder, Colo.: Westview Press, 1990.

Fricker, John. *Battle for Pakistan: The Air War of 1965*. London: Ian Allen, 1979.

Haqqani, Hussain. "Politics of Defense." *Far Eastern Economic Review* (January 1986): 24–28.

Hashmi, Bilal. "Dragon Seed: Military in the State." In *Pakistan: The Roots of Dictatorship*, ed. H. Gardezi and J. Rashid. London: Zed Press, 1983, 148–72.

Husain, S. Murtaza. "Peace-Time Role of Armed Forces." *Dawn* (September 6, 1972): 13.

Hussain, Asaf. "Ethnicity, National Identity and Praetorianism: The Case of Pakistan." *Asian Survey* XVI, no. 10 (October 1976): 918–30.

Hussain, Mushahid. "Pakistan Army: A Profile." *Friday Times* (November 25, 1992): 10.

Hussain, Syed Shabbir, and M. Tariq Qureshi. *Proof: The Pakistan Air Force 1947–82*. Karachi: PAF Press, 1982.

Hussain, Zahid, and Amir Mir. "Army to the Rescue." *Newsline* (May 1998): 18–23.

Isphani, Mahnaz. *Pakistan: The Dimensions of Insecurity*. London: Brassey's International Institute for Strategic Studies, 1990.

Jane's Defense Weekly. "Country Survey: Pakistan." Couldson, England (November 7, 1992): 29–42.

Janjua, M. K. "Was the Rawalpindi Conspiracy a Myth?" *Outlook* 1, no. 41 (January 13, 1973): 12.

Khan, M. Akbar. "Pahli Jang-i-Kashmir ki Fire-Bandi aur Pindi Sazish Case [Urdu]." *Monthly Hikayat* 5, no. 1 (September 1972).

Khan, Major General Fazal Muqeem. "In the Service of the Country as Soldiers." *Dawn* (January 9, 1961): 13.

———. *The Story of the Pakistan Army.* Karachi: Oxford University Press, 1963.

———. *Pakistan Crisis in Leadership.* Rawalpindi: National Book Foundation, 1973.

———. *The First Round: Indo–Pakistan War 1965.* Lahore: Tabeer Publishing, 1979.

Khan, Major General M. Akbar. *Raiders in Kashmir.* Karachi: Pak Publishers, 1975.

Khan, Muhammad Asghar. *Generals in Politics, 1958–1982.* New Delhi: Vikas, 1983.

Longer, V. *Red Coats to Olive Green: A History of the Indian Army, 1600–1974.* New Delhi: Allied, 1974.

Majeed, Commander Tariq. "Navy in Indian Ocean Strategy." *Pakistan Times* (September 6, 1974): 6.

Malik, Brigadier S. K. *The Quranic Concept of War.* Lahore: Wajidalis, 1979.

Menezes, S. L. *Fidelity and Honour: The Indian Army from the Seventeenth to the Twenty-First Century.* New Delhi: Viking, 1993.

Mir, Amir. "Soldiers of Fortune." *Newsline* (May 1998): 27–28.

Moore, R. A. "The Army as a Vehicle for Social Change in Pakistan." *Journal of Developing Areas* 11 (October 1967): 57–74.

———. "The Use of the Army in Nation Building: The Case of Pakistan." *Asian Survey* 9, no. 6 (June 1969): 447–56.

———. "Military and Nation Building in India and Pakistan." *World Affairs* 132, no. 3 (December 1969): 219–34.

———. *Nation-Building and the Pakistan Army, 1947–69.* Lahore: Aziz Publishers, 1979.

Mujahid Shairf-al. "Pakistan Armed Forces in 1947." *Muslim* (September 6, 1980): 7.

Musa, General Mohammad. *My Version, Indo–Pakistan War, 1965.* Lahore: Wajidalis, 1983.

———. *Jawan to General.* Karachi: East and West Publishing, 1984.

Naseeruddin, Brigadier Saiyed. "The Muslim Soldier." *Muslim* (September 6, 1980): 5.

Nur Khan, Air Marshal Mohammad. "Organization for Higher Defence Policy in Pakistan." *Sun* (Karachi) (May 21, 1972): 4.

O'Ballance, E. "The Indo–Pakistan Campaign, 1965." *Journal of the Royal United Services Institution* CXI, no. 644 (November 1966): 2.

Observer. "Army's Assistance in Development of Baluchistan and Chitral." *Dawn* (September 6, 1975): 13.

Outlook (Karachi). Staff Study. "What Was the Rawalpindi Conspiracy Case?" 2, no. 32 (11 November 1972): 11.

———. "The War Commission and the Surrender." 3, no. 8 (25 May 1974): 16.

Panaforce. "Armed Forces Role in Nation Building." *Dawn* (September 6, 1974): 13.

———. "Armed Forces and National Development." *Pakistan Times* (March 23, 1983): 3.

———. "Training in the Armed Forces." *Pakistan Times* (September 6, 1984): 3.

Rahman, S. M. "Motivation: The Ultimate Weapon." *Muslim* (September 6, 1984): 5.

Riza, Shaukat. *The Pakistan Army, 1: War, 1965.* Lahore: Army Education Press, 1984.

———. *The Pakistan Army, 2: 1966–71.* Lahore: Army Education Press, 1990.

Rizvi, Hasan-Askari. "The Formative Phase of the Pakistan Armed Forces." *Journal of History & Political Science* 1, no. 1 (1971–72): 25–40.

———. "The Military and Nation Building in the Third World." *Defence Journal* 2, nos. 1–2 (January–February 1976): 35–48.

———. "Pakistan's Security Consideration and Defence Industry." *Defence Journal* 9, no. 9 (September 1983): 25–32.

———. "The Paradox of Military Rule in Pakistan." *Asian Survey* 24, no. 5 (May 1984): 534–55.

———. "Pakistan." In *Arms Production in Developing Countries,* ed. J. E. Katz. Lexington, Mass.: Johnathan Heath, 1984, 265–78.

———. *The Military and Politics in Pakistan.* Delhi: Konark, 1988.

———. "The Legacy of Military Rule in Pakistan." *Survival* 31, no. 3 (May–June 1989): 255–68.

———. *Pakistan and the Geostrategic Environment: A Study of Foreign Policy.* New York: St. Martin's Press, 1993.

Rizvi, Brigadier S. Haider Abbas. *Veteran Campaigners.* Lahore: Wajidalis, 1987.

Salik, Brigadier Siddiq. *Witness to Surrender.* Karachi: Oxford University Press, 1979.

Sarfaraz, Lt. Commander N. "Development of the Navy: Three Fundamental Principles." *Dawn* (September 6, 1974): 13.

Sayeed, Khalid Bin. "The Role of the Military in Pakistan." In *Armed Forces and Society,* ed. J. V. Doorn. The Hague: Mouton, 1968, 274–97.

Sher Ali Khan Pataudi, Nawabzada (Major General). *Soldiering and Politics in India and Pakistan.* Lahore: Wajidalis, 1978.

Sieveking, O. "Pakistan and Her Armed Forces." *Military Review* 43, no. 6 (June 1963): 91–97.

Singh, D., and K. Singh. "The Military Elites and Problems of National Integration in India and Pakistan." *Indian Journal of Politics* 5, no. 2 (July–December 1973): 165–76.

Tahir-Kheli. Shirin. "The Military in Contemporary Pakistan." *Armed Forces and Society* 6, no. 4 (summer 1980): 639–53.

Tetley, Brian. *Defenders of Pakistan.* Lahore: Ferozsons, 1988.

Tiwari, Chitra K. *Security in South Asia: Internal and External Dimensions.* Lanham, Md.: University Press of America, 1989.

Wirsing, Robert G. *Pakistan's Security Under Zia, 1977–1988: The Policy Imperatives of a Peripheral Asian State.* New York: St. Martin's Press, 1991.

C. Foreign Policy and External Affairs

Ali, Meharunnisa. "Soviet–Pakistan Ties Since the Afghanistan Crisis." *Asian Survey* XXIII, no. 9 (September 1983): 1025–42.

Ayub Khan, Mohammad. "Essentials of Pakistan's Foreign Policy." *Pakistan Horizon* 14, no. 4 (fourth quarter 1961): 263–71.

———. "The Pakistan American Alliances: Stresses and Strains." *Foreign Affairs* 42, no. 2 (January 1964): 195–209.

Brodkin, E. L. "United States Aid to India and Pakistan." *International Affairs* 43, no. 4 (October 1967): 664–77.

378 • Bibliography

Chaudhri, Mohammad Ahsan, ed. *Pakistan and Regional Security.* Karachi: Royal Books, 1984.

———. "Pakistan's Relations with the Soviet Union." *Asian Survey* 6, no. 9 (September 1966): 492–501.

Cheema, Pervaiz Iqbal. "The Afghanistan Crisis and Pakistan's Security Dilemma." *Asian Survey* 23, no. 3 (March 1983): 227–43.

Choudhury, G. W. *Pakistan's Relations with India, 1947–66.* London: Pall Mall, 1968.

Cohen, Stephen P. "U.S. Weapons and South Asia: A Policy Analysis." *Pacific Affairs* 49, no. 1 (spring 1976): 49–69.

———. "Pakistan." In *Security Policies of Developing Countries,* ed. E. A. Kolodziej and R. E. Harkavy. Lexington, Mass.: D.C. Heath, 1982.

———. "South Asia and Afghanistan." *Problems of Communism* (January–February 1985): 18–31.

Franck, D. S. "Pakhtunistan: Disputed Disposition of a Tribal Land." *Middle East Journal* VI (winter 1952): 49–68.

Hasan, K. Sarwar. *China, India, Pakistan: Documents on the Foreign Relations of Pakistan.* Karachi: Pakistan Institute of International Affairs, 1966.

Hasan, Masuma, ed. *Pakistan in a Changing World.* Karachi: Pakistan Institute of International Affairs, 1978.

Hasan, Zubeida. "United States Arms Policy in South Asia, 1965–67." *Pakistan Horizon* 20, no. 2 (second quarter 1967): 76–98.

———. "Soviet Arms Aid to Pakistan and India." *Pakistan Horizon* 21, no. 4 (fourth quarter 1968): 54–68.

Jones, R. W., and B. Roberts. "Pakistan and Regional Security." *Journal of South Asian Affairs* 7, no. 3 (summer 1976): 56–76.

Khan, Rais Ahmad, ed. *Pakistan–United States Relations.* Islamabad: Area Study Centre for Africa, North and South America, Quaid-i-Azam University, 1983.

Khan, Rashid Ahmad. "Security in the Gulf: Pakistan's Perspective" In *Pakistan–United States Relations,* ed. Rais Ahmad Khan. Islamabad: Quaid-i-Azam University, 1983: 139–65.

Khan, Shaheen Irshad. *Rejection Alliance: A Case Study of U.S.–Pakistan Relations, 1947–1971.* Lahore: Ferozsons, 1976.

Khan, Sultan Mohammad. "Pakistani Geopolitics: The Diplomatic Perspective." *International Security* 5, no. 1 (summer 1980): 26–36.

Naghmi, Shafqat Hussain. "Pakistan's Public Attitude Toward the United States." *Journal of Conflict Resolution* 26, no. 3 (September 1982): 507–23.

Pakistan Horizon XX, no. 2 (second quarter 1967). Special Issue on India–Pakistan Arms Race.

Palmer, N. D. "The Defence of South Asia." *Orbis* IX, no. 4 (winter 1966): 45–65.

———. *South Asia and United States Policy.* Boston: Free Press, 1966.

Razvi, Mujtaba. *The Frontiers of Pakistan.* Karachi: National Publishing House, 1971.

Rizvi, Hasan-Askari. *Politics of the Bomb in South Asia.* Lahore: Progress. 1975.

———. *Internal Strife and External Intervention: India's Role.* Lahore: Progressive Publishers, 1981.

———. "Pakistan and the Indian Ocean." *Modern Studies* IV, no. 4 (summer 1981): 30–42.

———. "Superpowers, India, Pakistan and the Indian Ocean." *Defence Journal* 7, no. 9 (September 1981): 7–16.

———. "Pakistan's Defence Policy." *Pakistan Horizon* 36, no. 1 (first quarter 1983): 31–56.

———. "Pakistan: Ideology and Foreign Policy." *Asian Affairs* 10, no. 1 (spring 1983): 48–59.

———. "Afghan Refugees in Pakistan: Influx, Humanitarian Assistance and Implications." *Pakistan Horizon* 37, no. 1 (first quarter 1984): 40–61.

———. "Problems and Prospects of South Asian Regional Cooperation." *Regional Studies* 2, no. 2 (spring 1984): 13–24.

———. "Pakistan and the Post-Cold War Environment." In *Pakistan: 1997,* ed. Craig Baxter and Charles Kennedy. Boulder, Colo.: Westview Press, 1998: 37–60.

Rose, Leo E. "The Superpowers in South Asia: A Geostrategic Analysis." *Orbis* 22, no. 2 (summer 1978): 395–413.

Siddiqi, Aslam. *Pakistan Seeks Security.* Lahore: Longmans, 1960.

———. *A Path for Pakistan.* Karachi: Pakistan Publishing House, 1964.

Simon, S. W. "The Kashmir Dispute in Sino–Soviet Perspective." *Asian Survey* 7, no. 3 (March 1967): 176–87.

Spain, J. W. "Military Assistance for Pakistan." *APSR* 48, no. 3 (September 1954): 738–51.

Syed, Anwar Hussain. *China and Pakistan: Diplomacy of Entente Cordiale.* Amherst: University of Massachusetts Press, 1974.

Tahir-Kheli, Shirin. "Iran and Pakistan: Cooperation in an Area of Conflict." *Asian Survey* XVII, no. 5 (May 1977): 477–90.

———. *The United States and Pakistan: The Evolution of Influence.* New York: Praeger, 1982.

Thornton, Thomas P. "Between the Stools: U.S. Policy Towards Pakistan in the Carter Administration." *Asian Survey* 20, no. 10 (October 1982): 955–77.

———. *Pakistan: Internal Developments and the U.S. Interest.* Washington, D.C.: Foreign Policy Institute, 1987.

———. "U.S.–Pakistan Relations." *Foreign Affairs* 68, no. 3 (Summer 1989): 142–59.

Vertzberger, Yaacov. *The Enduring Entente: Sino–Pakistan Relations 1960–80.* The Washington Papers, no. 95. New York: Praeger, 1983.

Wilcox, Wayne A. *India, Pakistan and the Rise of China.* New York: Walker, 1964.

Wirsing, R. G. "The Arms Race in South Asia: Implications for the United States." *Asian Survey* XXV, no. 3 (March 1985): 265–91.

Wirsing, R. G., and J. M. Roberty. "The United States and Pakistan." *International Affairs* 58, no. 4 (Autumn 1982): 588–609.

Ziring, Lawrence, ed. *The Sub-Continent in World Politics,* rev. ed. New York: Praeger, 1982.

D. Law and Judiciary

Azfar, Kamal. "Constitutional Dilemmas in Pakistan." In *Pakistan Under the Military: Eleven Years of Zia ul-Haq,* ed. Shahid Javed Burki and Craig Baxter. Boulder, Colo.: Westview Press, 1991.

Kennedy, Charles H. "Judicial Activism and Islamization After Zia: Toward the Prohibition of Zia." In *Pakistan: 1992,* ed. Charles H. Kennedy. Boulder, Colo.: Westview Press, 1993: 57–74.

Mannan, M. A. *Judgments on the Constitution, Rule of Law, and Martial Law in Pakistan.* Karachi: Oxford University Press, 1993.

Pakistan Legal Decisions (Federal Court). *The Federation of Pakistan vs. Maulvi Tamizuddin Khan.* Karachi, 1955.

Pakistan Legal Decisions (Quetta Section). *Muhammad Anwar Durrani vs. Province of Baluchistan.* Karachi, 1988.

Pakistan Legal Decisions (Supreme Court). *State of Pakistan vs. Dosso.* Karachi, 1958.

———. *Government of Punjab vs. Miss Asma Jilani.* Karachi, 1972.

———. *Begum Nusrat Bhutto vs. Chief of Army Staff.* Karachi, 1977.

———. *The Federation of Pakistan vs. Saifullah Khan.* Karachi, 1988.

———. *The Federation of Pakistan vs. Malik Ghulam Mustafa Khan.* Karachi, 1988.

———. *Benazir Bhutto vs. Federation of Pakistan.* Karachi, 1988.

Shah, Nasim Hasan. "Judiciary in Pakistan: A Quest for Independence." In *Pakistan: 1997,* ed. Craig Baxter and Charles Kennedy. Boulder, Colo.: Westview Press, 1998: 61–78.

Winkel, Eric. *Islam and the Living Law.* Karachi: Oxford University Press, 1997.

E. Nuclear Policy

Ahmad, Eqbal. "Hawks Make Strange Bedfellows." *Dawn* (May 24, 1998): 13.

———. "When the Mountains Die." *Dawn* (June 4, 1998): 13.

Ahmed, Sultan. "Bracing up for Hard Times." *Dawn* (June 4, 1998): 13.

Aijazuddin, F. S. "Pokhran Has Changed the Course of History." *Dawn* (May 29, 1998): 13.

Akhtar, Shameem. "Delhi's New Threat Perception." *Dawn* (May 17, 1998): 13.

Anderson, John Ward. "Confusion Dominates Arms Race: Deceit, Doubt Fuel South Asian Drama." *Washington Post* (June 1, 1998): A1 & A14.

Anderson, John Ward, and Kamran Khan. "Pakistani Politicians' Rallying Cry: 'Let Them Eat Grass.'" *Washington Post* (June 11, 1998): A30.

Bhatty, Maqbool Ahmad. "Our Moment of Truth." *Dawn* (May 26, 1998): 13.

Cheema, Pervaiz Iqbal. "Pakistan's Nuclear Option." *Journal of South Asian & Middle Eastern Studies* 7, no. 4 (summer 1984): 52–72.

Cohen, Stephen. "India's Strategic Misstep." *New York Times* (June 3, 1998): A29.

Coll, Steve. "The Force of Fear in South Asia." *Washington Post* (May 31, 1998): C1.

Cooper, Kenneth J., and John Ward Anderson. "A Misplaced Faith in Nuclear Deterrence." *Washington Post* (May 31, 1998): A23.

Economist. "The New Nuclear Stand-Off" (May 30, 1998): 16.

Elliot, Michael. "A Bomb in Every Backyard." *The Times* (London) (June 6, 1998): 17–18.

———. "Bombs, Gas and Microbes." *The Times* (London) (June 6, 1998): 23–25.

———. "Out of Pandora's Box." *Newsweek* (June 8, 1998): 20–21.

Fatima, Mahnaz. "N-Tests: Where There is a Will." *Dawn* (June 6, 1998): 11.

Fidler, Stephen, and Mark Nicholson. "The Fearful Symmetry." *Financial Times* (London) (May 30, 1998): 6.

Harrison, Selig S. "India's Muscle Flexing is Over: Let the Bargaining Begin." *Washington Post* (May 17, 1998): C1 & C7.

Hirsh, Michael, and John Barry. "Nuclear Jitters." *Newsweek* (June 8, 1998): 22–27.

Hoagland, Jim. "Nuclear Notice to be Ignored." *Washington Post* (May 13, 1998): A17.

Hoodbhoy, Pervez. "Living with the Bomb." *Dawn* (June 6, 1998): 13.

Ijaz, Mansoor. "Benign Neglect is a Dangerous Nuclear Policy." *Los Angeles Times* (April 10, 1998): 14.

Ikle, Fred C. "India: The Nuclear Age Continues." *Washington Post* (May 17, 1998): C9.

Kazmin, Amy Louise, and Quentin Peel. "Explosion of Self-Esteem." *Financial Times* (May 13, 1998): 11.

Kelly, Michael. "Nuclear Notice to be Ignored." *Washington Post* (May 13, 1998): A17.

Khan, Aamer Ahmed. "Testing Times." *Herald* (May 1998): 38–40.

Khlilzad, Zalmay. "The Nuclear Sub-Continent." *Wall Street Journal* (May 29, 1998): A14.

Kissinger, Henry. "India and Pakistan: After the Explosions." *Washington Post* (June 9, 1998): A15.

Lifschultz, Lawrence. "Doom Thy Neighbour." *Far Eastern Economic Review* (June 4, 1998): 30–34.

Manning, Robert A. "Civilization and the Bomb." *Far Eastern Economic Review* (June 4, 1998): 36.

Masood, Lt. Gen. (retired) Talat. "Pokhran Tests: Our Options." *Dawn* (May 26, 1998): 13.

Mian, Zia, and Frank von Hippel. "The Alternative to Nuclear Tests." *Washington Post* (May 31, 1998): C7.

Myers, Steven Lee. "It's a Test, Not a Weapon: But That's Awfully Close." *New York Times* (May 31, 1998): 4.

Nayar, Kuldip. "Talks are Still the Only Way Out." *Dawn* (May 26, 1998): 15.

Palit, Maj. Gen. D. K., and P. K. S. Namboodhri. *Pakistan's Islamic Bomb.* New Delhi: Vikas, 1979.

Rashid, Ahmad, and Shiraz Sidhva. "Might and Menace." *Far Eastern Economic Review* (June 4, 1998): 27–29.

Rosenfeld, Stephen S. "New Nuclear Arrangements." *Washington Post* (June 5, 1998): A31.

Rosenthal, A. M. "The Shout From India." *New York Times* (May 15, 1998): A29.

Schaffer, Teresita, and Howard B. Schaffer. "After India's Tests, and Now Pakistan's." *Washington Post* (May 29, 1998): A27.

Siddiqui, Aziz. "The Love of the Bomb." *Dawn* (May 31, 1998): 13.

Sokolski, Henry. "A Blast of Reality." *New York Times* (May 13, 1998): A27.

Spector, Leonard. *Nuclear Weapons and South Asian Security.* Washington, D.C.: Carnegie Endowment for International Peace, 1988.

Sullivan, Kevin. "Nagasaki Survivors Have a Message for India and Pakistan." *Washington Post* (June 2, 1998): A1.

Thakar, Sankarshan. "Undiplomatic Offensive." *Herald* (May 1998): 42–43.

Umar, Maj. Gen. (retired) Ghulam. "Pakistan Must Not Give Up N-Option." *Dawn* (May 28, 1998): 13.

Warnke, Paul. "The Unratified Treaty." *New York Times* (May 14, 1998): A29.

Weisman, Steven R. "Nuclear Fear and Narcissism Shake South Asia." *New York Times* (May 31, 1998): 4.

Zakaria, Fareed. "Facing Up to Nuclear Reality." *Newsweek* (June 8, 1998): 28.

F. Politics

Afzal, M. Rafique. *Political Parties in Pakistan 1947–58.* Islamabad: National Commission on Historical & Cultural Research, 1976.

Ahmad, Manzooruddin, ed. *Contemporary Pakistan: Politics, Economy and Society.* Durham, N.C.: Carolina Academic Press, 1980.

Ahmad, Mushtaq. *Government and Politics in Pakistan.* Karachi: Space Publishers, 1970.

———. *Politics Without Social Change.* Karachi: Space Publishers, 1971.

Alavi, Hamza. "The State in Post-Colonial Societies: Pakistan and Bangladesh." *New Left Review* 74 (July–August 1972): 59–81.

Ali, Tariq. *Can Pakistan Survive?* New York: Penguin, 1983.

Anderson, D. D. "Pakistan's Search for National Identity." *Yale Review* 55, no. 4 (summer 1966): 552–69.

Asghar Khan, Air Marshal. *Pakistan at the Cross-Roads.* Lahore: Ferozsons, 1969.

Ayub Khan, Mohammad. "A New Experiment in Democracy in Pakistan." *Annals* 348 (March 1965): 109–13.

Aziz, K. K. *Party Politics in Pakistan 1947–58.* Islamabad: National Commission on Historical & Cultural Research, 1976.

Baxter, Craig "Pakistan Votes—1970." *Asian Survey* XI, no. 3 (March 1971): 197–218.

———. *Zia's Pakistan: Politics and Stability in a Frontline State.* Boulder, Colo.: Westview Press, 1985.

Baxter, Craig, and Syed Razi Wasti. *Pakistan Authoritarianism in the 1980s.* Lahore: Vanguard, 1991.

Bertocci, P. J. "East Pakistan: The Harvest of Strife." *South Asian Review* 5, no. 1 (October 1971): 11–18.

Bhutto, Z. A. *The Great Tragedy.* Karachi: People's Party, 1971.

Cohen, Stephen P. "State Building in Pakistan." In *The State, Religious, and Ethnic Politics: Afghanistan, Iran, and Pakistan,* ed. Myron Weiner and Ali Banuazizi. Syracuse, N.Y.: Syracuse University Press, 1986.

Dobell, W. M. "Ayub Khan as President of Pakistan." *Pacific Affairs* XLII, no. 3 (fall 1969).

Dunbar, David. "Pakistan: The Failure of Political Negotiations." *Asian Survey* 12, no. 5 (May 1972): 444–61.

Edger, A., and K. R. Schuler. *Public Opinion and Constitutionmaking in Pakistan 1958–62.* East Lansing: Michigan State University Press, 1967.

Gardezi, H., and J. Rashid, eds. *Pakistan: The Roots of Dictatorship.* London: Zed Press, 1983.

Gough, K., and H. Sharma. *Imperialism and Revolution in South Asia.* New York: Monthly Review Press, 1973.

Harrison, Selig S. *In Afghanistan's Shadow: Baluch Nationalism and Soviet Temptations.* Washington, D.C.: Carnegie Endowment, 1981.

Hayes, Louis D. *Politics in Pakistan: The Struggle for Legitimacy.* Boulder, Colo.: Westview Press, 1984.

Heeger, Gerald A. "Politics in the Post-Military State: Some Reflections on the Pakistani Experience." *World Politics* 29, no. 2 (January 1977): 242–62.

Hussain, Asaf. *Elite Politics in an Ideological State: The Case of Pakistan.* Folkestone, Kent, England: Dawson, 1978.

Jahan, Rounaq. *Pakistan: Failure in National Integration.* New York: Columbia University Press, 1972.

Jalal, Ayesha. "The State and Political Privilege in Pakistan." In *The Politics of Social Transformation in Afghanistan, Iran, and Pakistan,* ed. Myron Weiner and Ali Banuazizi. Syracuse, N.Y.: Syracuse University Press, 1994: 152–84.

———. *Democracy and Authoritarianism in South Asia.* Cambridge: Cambridge University Press. 1995.

Kennedy, Charles H. "Politics of Ethnic Preference in Pakistan." *Asian Survey* XXIV, no. 6 (June 1984): 688–703.

Khalizad, Zalmay. "The Politics of Ethnicity in Southwest Asia: Political Development or Decay." *Political Science Quarterly* (winter 1984–85): 657–79.

Laporte, Robert. "Succession in Pakistan: Continuity and Change in a Garrison State." *Asian Survey* 9, no. 11 (November 1969): 842–61.

———. "Pakistan in 1971: The Disintegration of a Nation." *Asian Survey* 12, no. 2 (February 1972): 221–30.

———. *Power and Privilege: Influence and Decision Making in Pakistan.* Berkeley: University of California Press, 1975.

Lodhi Maliha. "Pakistan in Crisis." *Journal of Commonwealth & Comparative Politics* 26, no. 1 (March 1978): 60–78.

Mahmud, Safdar. *Pakistan Divided.* Lahore: Ferozsons, 1984.

Mehdi, Haider, ed. *Essays on Pakistan.* Lahore: Progressive Publishers, 1970.

Morris-Jones, W. H. "Pakistan Post-Mortem and the Roots of Bangladesh." *Political Quarterly* 43, no. 2 (April–July 1972): 187–200.

Mujahid, Sharif-al. "Pakistan's First Presidential Elections." *Asian Survey* 5, no. 6 (June 1965): 280–94.

———. "The Assembly Elections in Pakistan." *Asian Survey* 5, no. 11 (November 1965): 712–32.

———. "The 1977 Pakistani Elections: An Analysis." In *Contemporary Pakistan,* ed. M. Ahmad. Durham, N.C.: Carolina Academic Press, 1980.

Munir, Muhammad. *From Jinnah to Zia.* Lahore: Vanguard, 1979.

Muniruzzaman, Talukdar. "National Integration and Political Development in Pakistan." *Asian Survey* 7, no. 12 (December 1967): 17–32.

Naqvi, M. B. "Pakistan: Revolution Without a Plan." *Asian Review* (UK) 2, no. 4 (July 1969): 267–76.

Newman, K. J. "Pakistan's Preventive Autocracy and Its Causes." *Pacific Affairs* XXXII, no. 1 (March 1959): 18–33.

Qureshi, Saleem M. "Party Politics in the Second Republic of Pakistan." *Middle East Journal* XX, no. 4 (autumn 1966): 456–72.

Rehman, Inamur. *Public Opinion and Political Development in Pakistan.* Karachi: Oxford University Press, 1982.

Richter, William L. "Persistent Praetorianism: Pakistan's Third Military Regime." *Pacific Affairs* 51, no. 3 (fall 1978): 406–26.

———. "The Political Dynamics of Islamic Resurgence in Pakistan." *Asian Survey* XIX, no. 6 (June 1979): 547–77.

———. "The 1990 General Elections in Pakistan." In *Pakistan: 1992,* ed. Charles H. Kennedy. Boulder, Colo.: Westview Press, 1993: 19–42.

Rizvi, Hasan-Askari. *Pakistan People's Party: The First Phase 1967–71.* Lahore: Progressive Publishers, 1973.

———. "Pakistan's Political Culture." *Journal of Political Science* 2, no. 2 (1975–76): 22–33.

Sayeed, Khalid Bin. "Collapse of Parliamentary Democracy in Pakistan." *Middle East Journal* 13, no. 4 (autumn 1959): 389–406.

———. "Religion and Nation Building in Pakistan." *Middle East Journal* 17, no. 3 (summer 1963): 279–91.

———. "Pathan Regionalism." *South Atlantic Quarterly* 63 (1964): 478–504.

———. *The Political System of Pakistan.* Karachi: Oxford University Press, 1967.

———. *Politics in Pakistan: The Nature and Direction of Change.* New York: Praeger, 1980.

Siddiqui, Kalim. *Conflict, Crisis and War in Pakistan.* London: Macmillan, 1972.

Suhrawardhy, H. S. "Political Stability and Democracy in Pakistan." *Foreign Affairs* 35, no. 3 (April 1957): 23–34.

Syed, Anwar. "Z. A. Bhutto's Self-Characterizations and Pakistani Political Culture." *Asian Survey* 18, no. 12 (December 1978): 1250–66.

Tinker, Hugh. *Ballot Box and Bayonet.* London: Oxford University Press, 1964.

———. *India and Pakistan: A Political Analysis,* rev. ed. London: Pall Mall, 1967.

Waseem, Mohammad. "Pakistan Elections 1997: One Step Forward." In *Pakistan: 1997,* ed. Craig Baxter and Charles H. Kennedy. Boulder, Colo.: Westview Press, 1998: 1–16.

Weinbaum, M. G. "The March 1977 Elections in Pakistan: Where Everyone Lost." *Asian Survey* 17, no. 7 (July 1977): 599–618.

Wheeler, Richard S. *The Politics of Pakistan: A Constitutional Quest.* Ithaca, N.Y.: Cornell University Press, 1970.

Wilcox, W. A. *Pakistan: The Consolidation of a Nation.* New York: Columbia University Press, 1964.

———. "The Pakistan Coup d'Etat of 1958." *Pacific Affairs* 38, no. 2 (summer 1965): 142–63.

———. "Pakistan in 1969: Once Again at the Starting Point." *Asian Survey* 10, no. 2 (February 1970): 73–81.

Wriggins, W. H., ed. *Pakistan in Transition.* Islamabad: University of Islamabad Press, 1965.

Yusuf, Hamid. *Pakistan in Search of Democracy 1947–77.* Lahore: Afrasia Publications, 1982.

Zafar S. M. *Through the Crisis.* Lahore: Book Center, 1970.

Ziring, Lawrence. *The Ayub Khan Era: Politics in Pakistan 1958–69.* Syracuse, N.Y.: Syracuse University Press, 1971.

———. "Pakistan: The Campaign Before the Storm." *Asian Survey* 17, no. 7 (July 1977): 581–98.

———. *Pakistan: The Enigma of Political Development.* Boulder, Colo.: Westview, 1980.

———. "From Islamic Republic to Islamic State in Pakistan." *Asian Survey* 24, no. 9 (September 1984): 931–46.

———. "Dilemma and Challenge in Nawaz Sharif's Pakistan." In *Pakistan: 1992,* ed. Charles H. Kennedy. Boulder, Colo.: Westview Press, 1993: 1–18.

Ziring, L., R. Braibantir, and H. Wriggins, eds. *Pakistan: The Long View.* Durham, N.C.: Duke University Center for Commonwealth & Comparative Studies, 1977.

III. Economics

A. General

Ahmad, Ehtisham, David Coady, and Nicholas Stern. "A Complete Set of Shadow Prices for Pakistan: Illustrations for 1975–76." *Pakistan Development Review* 27, no. 1 (spring 1988): 7–44.

Ahmad, Ehtisham, Stephen Ludlow, and Nicholas Stern. "Demand Response in Pakistan: A Modification of the Linear Expenditure System for 1976." *Pakistan Development Review* 27, no. 3 (autumn 1988): 293–308.

Alvi, Imtiaz. *The Informal Sector in Urban Economy.* Karachi: Oxford University Press, 1997.

Ayub Khan, Mohammad. "Pakistan's Economic Progress." *International Affairs* 43, no. 1 (January 1967): 1–11.

Banuri, Tariq J., Shahrukh Rafi Khan, and Moazam Mahmood. *Just Development: Beyond Adjustment with a Human Face.* Karachi: Oxford University Press, 1997.

Burki, Shahid Javed. "Ayub's Fall: A Socio-Economic Explanation." *Asian Survey* 12, no. 3 (March 1972): 201–12.

———. "Pakistan's Development: An Overview." *World Development* 9, no. 3 (March 1981): 301–14.

———. "Economic Policy After Zia ul-Haq." In *Pakistan: 1992,* ed. Charles H. Kennedy. Boulder, Colo.: Westview Press. 1993: 43–56.

———. "Is Pakistan's Past Relevant for its Economic Future?" In *Pakistan: 1997,* ed. Craig Baxter and Charles H. Kennedy. Boulder, Colo.: Westview Press, 1998: 17–36.

Dixit, Avinash K. *The Making of Economic Policy: A Transaction–Cost Politics Perspective.* Cambridge, Mass.: MIT Press, 1996.

Drazen, Allan, and Vittorio Grilli. "The Benefit of Crises for Economic Reforms." *American Economic Review* 83, no. 3 (1993): 598–607.

Fernandez, Racqul, and Dani Rodrick. "Resistance to Reform: Status Quo Bias in the Presence of Individual-Specific Uncertainty." *American Economic Review* 81, no. 5 (1991): 1146–55.

Government of Pakistan. *The Fifth Five Year Plan, 1978–1983.* Islamabad: Planning Commission, 1978.

———. *The Sixth Five Year Plan, 1983–1988.* Islamabad: Planning Commission, 1983.

————. *The Seventh Five Year Plan, 1988–1993.* Islamabad: Planning Commission, 1988.

Haq, Mahbubul. *The Strategy of Economic Planning: A Case Study of Pakistan.* Karachi: Oxford University Press, 1965.

Hasan, M. Ayunal, S. Ghulam Kadir, and S. Fakhre Mahmud. "Substitutability of Pakistan's Monetary Assets under Alternative Monetary Aggregates." *Pakistan Development Review* 27, no. 3 (autumn 1988): 317–26.

Hasan, Parvez. *Pakistan's Economy at the Crossroads: Past Policies and Present Imperatives.* Karachi: Oxford University Press, 1998.

Hirschman, Albert O. *Exit, Voice, and Loyalty: Responses to Decline in Firms, Organizations and States.* Cambridge, Mass.: Harvard University Press, 1970.

Jones, Jonathan D., and Nasir M. Khan. "Money Growth, Inflation, and Causality (Empirical Evidence for Pakistan, 1973–1985)." *Pakistan Development Review* 27, no. 1 (spring 1988): 45–58.

Khan, Ashfaque H. "A Macroeconomic Study of the Growth Prospects of Pakistan's Economy." Unpublished Ph.D. dissertation. Baltimore: Johns Hopkins University, 1987.

————. "Macroeconomic Policy and Private Investment in Pakistan." *Pakistan Development Review* 27, no. 3 (autumn 1988): 277–92.

Khilji, Nasir M. "Growth Prospects of a Developing Economy: A Macroeconomic Study of Pakistan." Unpublished Ph.D. dissertation. Hamilton, Ont.: McMaster University, 1982.

Knack, Stephen, and Philip Keefer. "Institutions and Economic Performance: Cross-Country Tests Using Alternative Institutional Measures." *Economics and Politics* 7, no. 3 (1995): 207–27.

————. "Why Don't Poor Countries Catch Up? A Cross-National Test of an Institutional Explanation." *Economic Inquiry* 35 (July 1997): 590–602.

————. "Does Social Capital Have an Economic Payoff? A Cross-Country Investigation." *Quarterly Journal of Economics* 112 (November 1997): 1251–88.

Kochanek, Stanley A. *Interest Groups and Political Development: Business and Politics in Pakistan.* Karachi: Oxford University Press, 1983.

LaPorte, Robert, Jr., and Muntazar Bashir Ahmed. *Public Enterprises in Pakistan: The Hidden Crisis in Economic Development.* Boulder, Colo.: Westview Press, 1989.

————. "Liberalization of the Economy Through Privatization." In *Pakistan: 1997,* ed. Craig Baxter and Charles H. Kennedy. Boulder, Colo.: Westview Press, 1998: 79–100.

Mauro, Paolo. "Corruption and Growth." *Quarterly Journal of Economics* 110 (1995): 681–712.

Naqvi, Syed Nawab Haider, Ather Maqsood Ahmed, and Ashfaque H. Khan. "Possibilities of Regional Trade Expansion: A Link Model for Pakistan, India, Bangladesh and Sri Lanka." *Pakistan Development Review* 23, no. 1 (spring 1984): 1–34.

Naqvi, Syed Nawab Haider, Ashfaque H. Khilji Khan, and A. M. Ahmed. *The P.I.D.E. Macro-Econometric Model of Pakistan's Economy.* Islamabad: Pakistan Institute of Development Economics, 1983.

Noman, Omar. *Pakistan: Political and Economic History Since 1947.* London: Kegan Paul, 1990.

———. *Economic and Social Progress in Asia: Why Pakistan Did Not Become a Tiger.* Karachi: Oxford University Press, 1997.

Papanek, Gustav F. *Pakistan's Development: Social Goals and Private Incentives.* Cambridge, Mass.: Harvard University Press, 1967.

Posner, Richard A. "Creating a Legal Framework for Economic Development." *World Bank Research Observer* 13, no. 1 (1998): 1–12.

Sarmad, Khwaja. "The Functional Form of the Aggregate Import Demand Equation: Evidence from Developing Countries." *Pakistan Development Review* 27, no. 3 (autumn 1988): 309–16.

Sen, Amartya. *What's the Point of a Development Strategy?* London: London School of Economics and Political Science, 1997.

Stiglitz, Joseph E. *Economics of the Public Sector.* New York: W.W. Norton, 1986.

———. *Whither Socialism?* Cambridge, Mass.: MIT Press, 1994.

Tommasi, Mariano, and Andres Vealso. "Where Are We in the Political Economy of Reform?" *Journal of Policy Reform* 1 (1996): 187–238.

Williamson, Oliver. *The Institutions and Governance of Economic Development and Reform.* Washington, D.C.: World Bank, 1994.

B. Agriculture

Ahmad, Manzoor, and Rajan K. Sampath. "Irrigation Inequalities in Pakistan 1960–1980." *Pakistan Development Review* 33, no. 1 (spring 1994): 53–74.

Ahmad, S. *Class and Power in a Punjab Village.* London: Monthly Review Press, 1977.

Akmal, Muhammad. "The Production and Consumption of Livestock Foods in Pakistan: A Look into the Future." *Pakistan Development Review* 33, no. 1 (spring 1994): 1–18.

Akram, M. "Socio-Economic Effects of Industrialization of Lyallpur, Town on the Surrounding Rural Areas." Unpublished M.Sc. thesis. Lyallpur: Department of Agricultural Economics, West Pakistan Agricultural University, 1962.

Alavi, Hamza. "The Rural Elite and Agricultural Development in Pakistan." In *Rural Development in Bangladesh and Pakistan,* ed. Robert D. Stevens, Hamza Alavi, and Peter J. Bertocci. Honolulu: University of Hawaii, 1976.

Aslam, M. M. "Some Comparative Aspects of Production and Profit Functions: Empirical Applications to a Punjab District." *Pakistan Development Review* 17, no. 2 (summer 1978): 321–44.

Bose, S. R., and E. H. Clark. "Some Basic Considerations on Agricultural Mechanization and West Pakistan." *Pakistan Development Review* 8, no. 3 (autumn 1969): 273–308.

Braverman. A., and J. E. Stiglitz. "Share-Cropping and the Inter-Linking of Agrarian Markets." *American Economic Review* 72, no. 4 (September 1982): 34–58.

Burki, Shahid Javed. "The Development of Pakistan's Agriculture: An Interdisciplinary Explanation." In *Rural Development in Bangladesh and Pakistan,* ed. Robert D. Stevens, Hamza Alavi, and Peter J. Bertocci. Honolulu: University of Hawaii, 1976.

Byerlee, Derek. "Technical Change and Returns to Wheat Breeding in Pakistan's Punjab in the Post-Green Revolution Period." *Pakistan Development Review* 32, no. 1 (spring 1993): 69–86.

Dubashi, P. R. *Policy and Performance: Agriculture and Rural Development in Post-Independence India.* New Delhi: Sage Publications, 1986.

Eckert, J. B. *Rural Labour in Punjab.* Lahore: Planning and Development Department, Government of Punjab, 1972.

Eckert, J. B., and D. A. Khan. *Rural–Urban Migration in Pakistan.* Lahore: Punjab Economic Research Institute, 1977.

Finney, C. E. *Farm Power in West Pakistan.* Development Study No. 11. Reading, England: University of Reading, Department of Agricultural Economics and Management, October 1972.

Gotsch, Carl, and Gilbert Brown. *Prices, Taxes and Subsidies in Pakistan Agriculture, 1970–76.* World Bank Staff Working Paper No. 387. Washington, D.C.: World Bank, April 1980.

Government of West Pakistan. *Report of the Land Reforms Commission for West Pakistan.* Lahore: Government Printing Press, 1959.

Hamid, N. "Dispossession and Differentiation of the Peasantry in the Punjab During Colonial Rule." *Journal of Peasant Studies* 10, no. 1 (1982): 17–29.

Haque, Nadeemul, and M. Mahmood. "Size–Productivity Relationship Revisited." *Pakistan Development Review* (1981): 39–53.

Herring, R. H. *Land to the Tiller.* New Haven, Conn.: Yale University Press, 1983.

Herring, R. H., and M. G. Chaudhry. "The 1972 Land Reforms in Pakistan and Their Implications." *Pakistan Development Review* 13, no. 3 (autumn 1974).

Hoque, Asraul. "Allocative Efficiency and Input Subsidy in Asian Agriculture." *Pakistan Development Review* 32, no. 1 (spring 1993): 87–100.

Joshi, P. C. "Land Reform and Agrarian Change in India and Pakistan Since 1947." *Journal of Peasant Studies* 1, no. 2 (January 1974): 164–85.

Khan, Mahmood Hasan. *The Economics of Green Revolution in Pakistan.* New York: Praeger, 1975.

———. *Underdevelopment and Agrarian Structure in Pakistan.* Boulder, Colo.: Westview Press, 1981.

Kurosaki, Takashi. "Government Interventions, Market Integration, and Price Risk in Pakistan's Punjab." *Pakistan Development Review* 35, no. 2 (summer 1996): 129–44.

Lowdermilk, M. K. "Diffusion of Dwarf Wheat Production Technology in Pakistan's Punjab." Unpublished Ph.D. thesis. Ithaca, N.Y.: Cornell University, 1972.

Mahmood, Moazam. "Growth and Distribution of Agrarian Assets in the Punjab." *Pakistan Development Review* 30, no. 4 (winter 1991): 1007–27.

McInerney, John P., and Graham F. Donaldson. *Consequences of Farm Tractors in Pakistan.* World Bank Staff Working Paper No. 210. Washington, D.C.: World Bank, 1975.

Nabi, Ijaz. "Rural Factor Markets in Pakistan." Unpublished Ph.D. thesis. Coventry, England: University of Warwick, 1981.

———. *Rural Factor Market Imperfections and the Incidence of Tenancy in Agriculture.* Discussion Paper 17. Coventry, England: Development Economics Research Centre, University of Warwick, 1982.

———. "Aspects of Technological Change in Pakistan." *Pakistan Economic and Social Review* (autumn 1982): 44–69.

———. *Contracts Resource Use and Productivity in Sharecropping.* Discussion Paper 34. Coventry, England: Development Economics Research Centre, University of Warwick, 1983.

Sabot, Richard H. "Human Capital Accumulation in Post-Green Revolution Pakistan." *Pakistan Development Review* 30, no. 1 (spring 1991): 13–31.

WAPDA. *Agricultural Economics Survey of the Indus Basin.* Lahore: WAPDA, 1977.

Yasin, C. G. *Socio-Economic Effects of Land Reforms of 1959.* Punjab Board of Economic Inquiry Publication No. 151. Lahore, 1972.

Zahid, Shahid Naeem. "Factor Markets, Land Tenure and Agrarian Development: A Study of Sind." Unpublished Ph.D. dissertation. Stanford, Calif.: Stanford University, 1982.

———. "Differences Between Share-Cropped and Owner-Operated Farms in Sindh, Pakistan: Some Theoretical and Empirical Observations." *Pakistan Journal of Applied Economics* II, no. 2 (winter 1983): 41–72.

C. Employment and Immigration

Addleton, J. S. *Undermining the Centre: The Gulf Migration and Pakistan.* Karachi: Oxford University Press, 1992.

Ahmed, Ather Maqsood, and Ismail Sergeldin. "Socio-Economic Determinants of Labour Mobility in Pakistan." *Pakistan Development Review* 32, no. 2 (summer 1993): 139–58.

Amjad, Rashid. "Impact of Workers' Remittances from the Middle East on Pakistan's Economy: Some Selected Issues." *Pakistan Development Review* 24, no. 4 (winter 1985): 757–85.

———, ed. *To the Gulf and Back: Studies on the Employment Impact of Asian Labour Migration.* New Delhi: ILO/ARTEP, 1987.

Arif, G. M., and M. Irfan. "Return Migration and Occupational Change: The Case of Pakistani Migrants Returned from the Middle East." *Pakistan Development Review* 32, no. 1 (spring 1993): 1–38.

Ballard, R. "The Political Economy of Migration: Pakistan, Britain and the Middle East." In *Migrants, Workers, and the Social Order,* ed. J. Eades. London: Tavistock Publications, 1987: 17–40.

Gilani, I. "Pakistan." In *Middle East Interlude: Asian Workers Abroad,* ed. I. M. Abella and Y. Atal. Bangkok: UNESCO Regional Office, 1986.

Gilani, I., F. Khan, and M. Iqbal. *Labour Migration from Pakistan to the Middle East and its Impact on the Domestic Economy.* Islamabad: Pakistan Institute of Development Economics (Research Report No. 126), 1981.

Guantilleke, G., ed. *Migration to the Arab World: The Experience of Returning Migrants.* Tokyo: United Nations University Press, 1991.

Gulati, Leela. *In the Absence of Their Men: The Impact of Male Migration on Women.* New Delhi: Sage, 1993.

ILO/ARTEP. *Impact of Out and Return Migration on Domestic Employment in Pakistan.* Vol. II: *Reabsorption of Return Migrants in the Domestic Economy.* New Delhi: ILO/ARTEP, 1987.

———. *Impact of Out and Return Migration on Domestic Employment in Pakistan.*

Vol. V: *Survey of Return Migrants Sample Design and Field Work.* New Delhi: ILO/ARTEP, 1987.

Jamal Haroon. "Explanation of Off-Farm Work Participation in Rural Pakistan." *Pakistan Development Review* 35, no. 2 (summer 1996): 139–48.

Kazi, S. "Domestic Impact of Overseas Migration: Pakistan." In *To the Gulf and Back: Studies in Asian Labour Migration,* ed. R. Amjad. New Delhi: ILO/ARTEP, 1987.

Khan, F. M. "Migrant Workers to the Arab World: The Experience of Pakistan." In *Migration to the Arab World: The Experience of Returning Migrants,* ed. G. Guantilleke. Tokyo: United Nations University Press, 1991: 195–237.

Philips, Mike, and Trevor Philips. *Windrush: The Irresistible Rise of Multicultural Britain.* London: HarperCollins, 1998.

Wambu, Onyekachi. *Empire Windrush: Fifty Years of Writing About Black Britain.* London: Victor Gollancz, 1998.

D. Energy, Manufacturing, and Industry

Abbas, Azhar. "Power Politics." *Herald* (May 1998): 23–37.

Ahmad, Nuzhat. "Choice of Mode for the Workshop in a Third World City: Karachi." *Pakistan Development Review* 34, no. 2 (summer 1995): 149–64.

Ali, M. "Frontier Migration to Industrial Areas of West Pakistan: A Case of Temporary Migration with Return Flow of Funds." Unpublished Ph.D. dissertation. Pullman: Washington State University, 1973.

Battese, George E., and Sohail Malik. "Estimation of Elasticities of Substitution for CES and VES Production Functions using Firm-Level Data for Food Processing Industries in Pakistan." *Pakistan Development Review* 27, no. 1 (spring 1988): 59–72.

Government of Pakistan. *Census of Manufacturing Industries, 1969–70.* Karachi: Statistics Division, 1973.

Government of Pakistan. *Census of Manufacturing Industries, 1970–71.* Karachi: Statistics Division, 1977.

Government of Pakistan. *Census of Manufacturing Industries, 1975–76.* Karachi: Statistics Division, 1980.

Government of Pakistan. *Census of Manufacturing Industries, 1976–77.* Karachi: Statistics Division, 1982.

Haque, Ihtashamul. "True Confessions: Crusade Against the Independent Power Projects." *Herald* (May 1998): 38–39.

Kazi, S., Z. S. Khan, and S. A. Khan. "Production Relationships in Pakistan's Manufacturing." *Pakistan Development Review* 9, no. 3 (autumn 1970): 406–21.

Kazmi, N. *Substitution Elasticities in Small and Household Manufacturing Industries in Pakistan* (Research Report Series, No. 109). Islamabad: Pakistan Institute of Development Economics, 1976.

Kemal, A. R. "Consistent Line Series Data Relating to Pakistan's Large-Scale Manufacturing Industries." *Pakistan Development Review* 15, no. 1 (spring 1976): 28–63.

———. "Substitution Elasticities in the Large-Scale Manufacturing Industries of Pakistan." *Pakistan Development Review* 20, no. 1 (spring 1981): 1–36.

Lewis, Stephen R. *Economic Policy and Industrial Growth in Pakistan*. London: George Allen & Unwin, 1969.

Meekal, A. "Substitution Elasticities in the Large-Scale Manufacturing Industries of Pakistan: A Comment." *Pakistan Development Review* 21, no. 1 (spring 1982): 73–82.

Shahid, Saleem, and Zaigham Khan. "Running Out of Energy." *Herald* (May 1998): 56–57.

E. Population and Urbanization

Afzal, Mohammad. "Disability Prevalence and Correlates in Pakistan: A Demographic Analysis." *Pakistan Development Review* 31, no. 3 (autumn 1992): 217–58.

Burki, Shahid Javed. "Rapid Population Growth and Urbanization: The Case of Pakistan." *Pakistan Economic and Social Review* XI, no. 3 (autumn 1973).

―――. *Population Bulletin: Pakistan: A Demographic Report*. Washington, D.C.: Population Reference Bureau, 1973.

Butt, Sabihuddin Mohammed, and Jamal Haroon. "Determinants of Marital Fertility in Pakistan: An Application of the 'Synthesis Framework.'" *Pakistan Development Review* 32, no. 2 (summer 1993): 199–200.

De Tray, Dennis N. "Child Quality and the Demand for Children." *Journal of Political Economy* 81, part 2 (1973): S70–S90.

D'Souza, Victor S. *Economic Development, Social Structure and Population Growth*. New Delhi: Sage Publications, 1985.

Government of Pakistan. *Population Census of Pakistan*. Islamabad: Census Organization, 1960.

Government of Pakistan. *Population Census of Pakistan*. Islamabad: Census Organization, 1972.

Haque, Ihtashamul. "Population Figures of Census Released: Population Swells to 130.58 million." *Dawn* (July 9, 1998): 13.

Ibraz, Tassawar Saeed. "The Cultural Context of Women's Productive Invisibility: A Case Study of a Pakistani Village." *Pakistan Development Review* 32, no. 1 (spring 1993): 101–26.

Nabi, Ijaz. "An Empirical Analysis of Rural–Urban Migration in Less-Developed Economies." *Economics Letters* 8 (1981): 193–99.

Qadeer, Mohammad A. "An Assessment of Pakistan's Urban Policies, 1947–1997." *Pakistan Development Review* 35, no. 4 (winter 1996): 443–66.

Ridker, Ronald, ed. *Population and Development: The Search for Selective Interventions*. Baltimore, Md.: Johns Hopkins University Press, 1976.

Schultz, T. W. "The Value of Children: An Economic Perspective." *Journal of Political Economy* 81, no. 2, part 2 (1973): S2–S13.

Siddiqui, Rehana. "The Impact of Socio-Economic Factors in Fertility Behaviour: A Cross-Country Analysis." *Pakistan Development Review* 35, no. 2 (summer 1996): 107–28.

Yotopolous, Pan A., and Yoshimi Kuroda. "Equilibrium Approach to the Value of Children in the Agricultural Household." *Pakistan Development Review* 27, no. 3 (autumn 1988): 229–76.

Zafar, Muhammad Iqbal. "Husband–Wife Roles as a Correlate of Contraceptive and Fertility Behaviour." *Pakistan Development Review* 35, no. 2 (summer 1996): 145–70.

F. Poverty and Social Development

Alauddin, T. "Mass Poverty in Pakistan: A Further Study." *Pakistan Development Review* 14, no. 4 (winter 1975): 431–50.

Ali, M. Shaukat. "Poverty Assessment: Pakistan's Case." *Pakistan Development Review* 34, no. 1 (spring 1995): 43–54.

Altaf, Mir Anjum, Aly Ercelawn, Kaiser Bengali, and Abdul Rahim. "Poverty in Karachi: Incidence, Location Characteristics and Upward Mobility." *Pakistan Development Review* 32, no. 2 (summer 1993): 159–78.

Amjad, Rashid, and A. R. Kemal. "Macroeconomic Policies and Their Impact on Poverty Alleviation in Pakistan." *Pakistan Development Review* 36, no. 1 (spring 1997): 39–68.

Amus, P., and Carole Rakodi. "Urban Poverty: Issues for Research and Policy." *Journal of International Development* 23, no. 4 (1966): 12–34.

Behrman, Jere R., and Ryan Schneider. "An International Perspective on Pakistani Human Capital Formation in the Last Quarter Century." *Pakistan Development Review* 32, no. 1 (spring 1993): 1–68.

Brockerhoff, Martin, and Ellen Brennan. "The Poverty of Cities in Developing Regions." *Population and Development Review* 24, no. 1 (March 1998): 75–114.

Burki, Shahid Javed. "Pakistan's Six Redistributive Crises." *Muslim* (Islamabad) (March 11–14, 1989).

———. "The State and the Political Economy of Redistribution in Pakistan." In *The Politics of Social Transformation in Afghanistan, Iran, and Pakistan,* ed. Myron Weiner and Ali Banuazizi. Syracuse, N.Y.: Syracuse University Press, 1994: 270–329.

Dasgupta, Partha. *The Economics of Poverty in Poor Countries.* London: London School of Economics and Political Science, 1998.

Foster, John, John Greer, and Erick Thorbecke. "A Class of Decomposable Poverty Measures." *Econometrica* 52, no. 2 (1984): 761–65.

Government of Pakistan. *Household Income and Expenditure Survey.* Karachi: Statistical Division, various issues.

Government of Pakistan. *Income Inequality and Poverty in Pakistan.* Islamabad: Federal Bureau of Statistics, 1994.

Griffin, K., and Azizur Rehman Khan. *Growth and Inequality in Pakistan.* London: Macmillan, 1972.

Harriss, John. "Urban Poverty and Urban Poverty Alleviation." *Cities* (August 1989): 186–94.

Irfan, M., and R. Amjad. "Poverty in Rural Pakistan." In *Poverty in Rural Asia,* ed. A. R. Khan and E. Lee. Bangkok: ILO/ARTEP, 1984.

Krujik, H. De., and Myrna van Leeuwen. "Changes in Poverty and Income Distribution in Pakistan During 1970s." *Pakistan Development Review* 24, nos. 3&4 (autumn & winter 1985): 407–22.

Malik, M. H. "Some New Evidence on the Incidence of Poverty in Pakistan." *Pakistan Development Review* 27, no. 4 (winter 1988): 509–16.

Malik, M. H., and Najam-us-Saqib. "Tax Incidence by Income Classes in Pakistan." *Pakistan Development Review* 28, no. 1 (spring 1989): 13–26.

———. *Poverty in Pakistan: 1984–85, 1987–88, and 1990–91* (mimeographed). Washington, D.C.: International Food Policy Research Institute, 1994.

Moser, Caroline. "The Asset Vulnerability Framework: Reassessing Urban Poverty and Reduction Strategies." *World Development* 26, no. 1 (1998): 1–19.

Mujahid, G. B. S. "A Note on Measurement of Poverty and Income Inequalities in Pakistan: Some Observations on Methodology." *Pakistan Development Review* 17, no. 3 (autumn 1978): 365–77.

Naseem, S. M. "Mass Poverty in Pakistan." *Pakistan Development Review* 12, no. 4 (winter 1973): 317–60.

———. "Rural Poverty As a Constraint on Rural Development in Pakistan." Paper presented to the 16th World Conference of the Society for International Development, Colombo, Sri Lanka, May 1979.

Rakodi, Caroline. "Poverty Lines or Household Strategies." *Habitat International* 19, no. 4 (1995): 407–26.

Sweester, Anne T. "Healing Power and Medical Practice in Pakistani Society." In *Pakistan: 1992,* ed. Charles H. Kennedy. Boulder, Colo.: Westview Press, 1993: 95–108.

United Nations Development Program. *Human Development Report, 1997: Human Development to Eradicate Poverty.* New York: Oxford University Press, 1997.

World Bank. *World Development Report, 1990: Poverty.* New York: Oxford University Press, 1990.

———. *Poverty Reduction and the World Bank: Progress and Challenges in the 1990s.* Washington, D.C.: World Bank, 1996.

Wratten, Ellen. "Conceptualizing Urban Poverty." *Environment and Urbanization* 7, no. 1 (1995): 11–36.

IV. Society

A. General

Ahmed, Akbar S. *Millennium and Charisma Among Pathans.* London: Routledge and Kegan Paul, 1976.

Ahmed, Feroz. "Pakistan: Ethnic Fragmentation or National Integration." *Pakistan Development Review* 35, no. 4 (winter 1996): 631–48.

———. *Ethnicity and Politics in Pakistan.* Karachi: Oxford University Press, 1998.

Barth, F. *Political Leadership Among Swat Pathans.* London: Atholone Press, 1959.

Burton, Richard F. *Falconry in the Valley of the Indus.* Karachi: Oxford University Press, 1997.

Chaudhry, M. I. *Pakistani Society: A Sociological Perspective.* Lahore: Aziz Publishers, 1980.

Hafeez, Sabeeha. *The Changing Pakistani Society.* Karachi: Royal Book, 1991.

Harrison, Selig S. "Ethnicity and the Political Stalemate in Pakistan." In *The State, Religious, and Ethnic Politics: Afghanistan, Iran, and Pakistan,* ed. Myron Weiner and Ali Banuazizi. Syracuse, N.Y.: Syracuse University Press, 1986.

Hastings, Donna, and Pnina Werbner, eds. *Economy and Culture in Pakistan: Migrants and Cities in a Muslim Society.* London: Macmillan, 1991.

Matheson, Sylvia. *The Tigers of Baluchistan.* Karachi: Oxford University Press, 1997.

Moorhouse, Geoffrey. *To the Frontier.* New York: Holt, Rinehart, and Winston, 1985.

Mujtaba, Hassan, and Jamshyd Masood. "Djinn Tonic: The Ritual of Exorcism Brings Hundreds of Devotees to the Shrine of Gaji Shah." *Newsline* (May 1998): 61–67.

Reeves, Richard. *Passage to Peshawar.* New York: Simon and Schuster, 1984.

Schackle, Christopher. "Punjabi in Lahore." *Modern Asian Studies* 4, no. 3 (1970): 239–67.

Tambiah, Stanley J. *Leveling Crowds: Ethnationalist Conflicts and Collective Violence in South Asia.* Berkeley: University of California Press, 1996.

Tandon, Prakesh. *Punjabi Century.* Berkeley: University of California Press, 1968.

Waseem, Mohammad. "Ethnic Conflict in Pakistan: The Case of MQM." *Pakistan Development Review* 35, no. 4 (winter 1996): 617–30.

Weiner, Myron, and Omar Noman. *The Child and the State in India and Pakistan.* New York: Oxford University Press, 1995.

Weiss, Anita M. *Culture, Class, and Development in Pakistan: The Emergence of an Industrial Bourgeoisie in Punjab.* Boulder, Colo.: Westview Press, 1991.

Zia, Shehla, Hina Jilani, and Asma Jahangir. *Muslim Family Laws and the Implementation in Pakistan.* Islamabad: Government of Pakistan, Women's Division, 1982.

B. Education and Health

Afzal, Mohammad. "Some Differentials in Infant–Child Mortality Risks in Pakistan: 1962–1986." *Pakistan Development Review* 27, no. 4 (winter 1988): 876–923.

Behrman, Jere R., and Nancy Birdsall. "The Quality of Schooling. Quantity Alone is Misleading." *American Economic Review* 73, no. 5 (1983): 928–46.

———. "Communication on 'Returns to Education: A Further Update and Implications.'" *Journal of Human Resources* 22, no. 4 (fall 1987): 603–6.

Guisinger, S. E., J. W. Henderson, and G. W. Scully. "Earnings, Rates of Return to Education and the Earnings Distribution in Pakistan." *Economics of Education Review* 3, no. 4 (1984): 34–52.

Haq, Mahbubul. *Human Development in South Asia, 1997.* Karachi: Oxford University Press, 1997.

Haq, Mahbubul, and Khadija Haq. *Human Development in South Asia, 1998: The Education Challenge.* Karachi: Oxford University Press, 1998.

Ismail, Zafar H., Hafiz A. Pasha, and Rauf A. Khan. "Cost Effectiveness of Primary Education: A Case Study of Pakistan." *Pakistan Development Review* 33, no. 4 (winter 1994): 876–913.

Jimenez, Emmanuel, and Jee-Peng Tan. *Educational Development in Pakistan: The Role of User Charges and Private Education.* Washington, D.C.: World Bank, 1985.

Khan, Shahrukh Rafi, and Muhammad Irfan. "Rates of Return to Education and the Determinants of Earnings in Pakistan." *Pakistan Development Review* 24, nos. 3&4 (autumn & winter 1985): 234–56.

Mincer, Jacob. *Schooling, Experience and Earnings.* New York: National Bureau of Economic Research, 1974.

———. "Human Capital and the Labor Market: A Review of Current Research." *Educational Researcher* (May 1989): 27–34.

Myers, Robert. *The Twelve Who Survive: Strengthening Programmes of Early Childhood Development in the Third World.* London: Routledge, 1992.

Shabbir, Tayyeb. "Sheepskin Effects in the Returns to Education in a Developing Country." *Pakistan Development Review* 30, no. 1 (spring 1991): 1–19.

———. "Misspecification Bias in the Rates of Return to Completed Levels of Schooling" (mimeographed). Pakistan Institute of Development Economics, 1993.

———. "Mincerian Earnings Function for Pakistan." *Pakistan Development Review* 33, no. 1 (spring 1994): 1–18.

World Bank. *Priorities and Strategies for Education.* Washington D.C.: World Bank, 1995.

C. Religion

Abbot, Freeland. *Islam and Pakistan.* Ithaca, N.Y.: Cornell University Press, 1968.

———. "Pakistan and the Secular State." In *South Asian Politics and Religion,* ed. Donald E. Smith. Princeton, N.J.: Princeton University Press, 1966: 352–70.

Adams, Charles J. "The Ideology of Mawlana Maududi." In *South Asian Politics and Religion,* ed. Donald E. Smith. Princeton, N.J.: Princeton University Press, 1966: 371–97.

Ahmad, Aziz. *Studies in Islamic Culture in the Indian Environment.* Oxford: Clarendon Press, 1964.

———. *An Intellectual History of Islam in India.* Chicago: Aldine, 1969.

———. *Islamic Modernism in India and Pakistan, 1857–1964.* New York: Oxford University Press, 1969.

Ahmad, Imtiaz. "The Ashraf-Ailaf: Distinction in Muslim Structure in India." *Indian Economic and Social History Review* 7, no. 3 (September 1966): 268–78.

———, ed. *Caste and Social Stratification Among the Muslims.* Delhi: Manohar, 1973.

———. *Family, Marriage and Kinship Among Muslims in India.* Delhi: Manohar, 1976.

———, ed. *Ritual and Religion Among Muslims in India.* Delhi: Manohar, 1981.

———. *Modernization and Social Change Among Muslims in India.* Delhi: Manohar, 1983.

Ahmad, Kurshid, and Zafar Ishaq Ansari. *Islamic Perspectives: Studies in Honour of Mawlana Sayyid Abul Ala Mawdudi.* London: Islamic Foundation, 1979.

Ahmad, Mumtaz. "Pakistan." In *The Politics of Islamic Revivalism,* ed. Shireen T. Hunter. Bloomington: Indiana University Press, 1988.

Ahmad, Parwez Ghulam. *Islam: A Challenge to Religion.* Lahore: Idara-i-Tule-e-Islam, 1968.

Ahmed, Akbar S. *Pakistan Society: Ethnicity and Religious Identity.* Karachi: Oxford University Press, 1986.

———. *Discovering Islam: Making Sense of Muslim History and Society.* London: Routledge and Kegan Paul, 1988.

Asad, Muhammad. *The Principles of State and Government in Islam.* Los Angeles: University of California Press, 1961.

Baxter, Craig, and Charles Kennedy, eds. *Pakistan: 1997.* Boulder, Colo.: Westview Press, 1998: 101–22.

Binder, Leonard. *Religion and Politics in Pakistan.* Berkeley: University of California Press, 1961.

———. "Islam, Ethnicity, and the State in Pakistan: An Overview." In *The State, Religion, and Ethnic Politics: Afghanistan, Iran, and Pakistan,* ed. Myron Weiner and Ali Banuazizi. Syracuse, N.Y.: Syracuse University Press, 1986.

Brown, Daniel. *Rethinking Tradition in Modern Islamic Thought.* London: Cambridge University Press, 1997.

Carrol, Lucy. "Nizam-i-Islam Process and Conflicts in Pakistan's Programme of Islamization with Special Reference to the Position of Women." *Journal of Commonwealth and Comparative Politics* 20, no. 4 (1982): 57–95.

Esposito, John L. "Islam: Ideology and Politics in Pakistan." In *The State, Religion, and Ethnic Politics: Afghanistan, Iran, and Pakistan,* ed. Myron Weiner and Ali Banuazizi. Syracuse, N.Y.: Syracuse University Press, 1986.

Faruki, Kamal A. *Islamic Constitution.* Karachi: Khokrapur Gateway Publication, 1952.

———. "Pakistan: Islamic Government and Society." In *Islam in Asia,* ed. John L. Esposito. New York: Oxford University Press, 1987.

———. *Islam: The Straight Path.* New York: Oxford University Press, 1988.

———. *Islam and Politics.* Syracuse, N.Y.: Syracuse University Press, 1991.

Faruqi, Zia ul-Hasan. *The Deoband School and the Demand for Pakistan.* Bombay: Asia Publishing House, 1963.

Gellner, Ernest. *Muslim Society.* Cambridge: Cambridge University Press, 1983.

Gilmartin, David. *Empire and Islam: Punjab and the Making of Pakistan.* Berkeley: University of California Press, 1988.

Government of Punjab. *Report of the Court of Inquiry Constituted Under Punjab Act II of 1954 to Enquire into the Punjab Disturbances of 1953.* Lahore: Government Printing, 1954.

Hakim, Khalifa Abdul. *Islamic Ideology: The Fundamental Beliefs and Principles of Islam and their Application to Practical Life.* Lahore: Institute of Islamic Culture, 1965.

Hamid, Abdul. *Muslim Separatism in India.* Karachi: Oxford University Press, 1971.

Haq, M. U. *Muslim Politics in Modern India.* Meerut, India: Meenakshi, 1970.

Hardy, Peter. *Partners in Freedom and True Muslims: The Political Thought of Some Muslim Scholars in British India, 1912–1947.* Lund, Sweden: Studentlitteratur, 1971.

———. *The Muslims of British India.* Cambridge: Cambridge University Press, 1972.

Haydar, Afak. "The Politicization of the Shias and the Development of the Tehrik-e-Nifaz-e-Fiqh-e-Jafaria in Pakistan." In *Pakistan: 1992,* ed. Charles H. Kennedy. Boulder, Colo.: Westview Press, 1993: 75–94.

Iqbal, Muhammad. *The Reconstruction of Religious Thought in Islam.* London: Oxford University Press, 1934.

Kennedy, Charles H. "Islamization in Pakistan: Implementation of the Hudood Ordinances." *Asian Survey* 28, no. 3 (March 1988): 307–16.

———. "Islamization and Legal Reform in Pakistan, 1979–1989." *Pacific Affairs* 63, no. 1 (spring 1990): 62–77.

Khuhro, Hamida. "Masjid Manzilgah, 1939–40: Test Case for Hindu–Muslim Relations in Sind." *Modern Asian Studies* 32, no. 1 (1998): 49–89.

Malik, Hafeez. *Moslem Nationalism in India and Pakistan.* Washington, D.C.: Public Affairs Press, 1963.

Marlow, Louise. *Hierarchy and Egalitarianism in Islamic Thought.* London: Cambridge University Press, 1997.

Maududi, Maulana Abdul. *Islamic Law and Constitution.* Karachi: Jamaati Islami Publications, 1955.

———. *First Principles of the Islamic State.* Lahore: Islamic Publications, 1960.

———. *Political Theory of Islam.* Lahore: Islamic Publications, 1960.

Memon, Ali Nawaz. *The Islamic Nation: Status and Future in the New World Order.* Beltsville, Md.: Writers Inc., 1995.

Metcalf, Barbara Daly. *Islamic Revival in British India: Deoband, 1860–1900.* Princeton, N.J.: Princeton University Press, 1982.

Minault, Gail. *The Khilafat Movement: Religious Symbolism and Political Mobilization in India.* New York: Columbia University Press, 1982.

Nasr, Syed Vali Reza. *The Vanguard of the Islamic Revolution: The Jama'at-i-Islami of Pakistan.* Berkeley: University of California Press, 1994.

Nichols, Robert. "Challenging the State: 1990s Religious Movements in the Northwest Frontier Province." In *Pakistan: 1997,* ed. Craig Baxter and Charles H. Kennedy. Boulder, Colo.: Westview Press, 1998: 143–80.

Rahman, Fazlur. *Islam.* Chicago: University of Chicago Press, 1966.

———. *Islam and Modernity: Transformation of an Intellectual Tradition.* Chicago: University of Chicago Press, 1982.

Rahman, Matiur. *From Consultation to Confrontation: A Study of the Muslim League in British Indian Politics, 1906–1912.* London: Luzac, 1970.

Rajput, A. B. *Religion, Politics, and Society.* New York: Oxford University Press, 1987.

Robinson, Francis. "Islam and Muslim Society in South Asia." *Contributions to Indian Sociology* 17, no. 2 (1983): 185–203.

Rodison, M. *Mohammed.* Harmondsworth, England: Penguin, 1983.

Roff, William, ed. *Islam and the Political Economy of Meaning: Comparative Studies of Muslim Discourse.* London: Croom Helm, 1987.

Rosenthal, E. I. J. *Political Thought in Medieval Islam.* Cambridge: Cambridge University Press, 1958.

Rosenthal, Franz. *The Muslim Concept of Freedom.* Leiden: E. J. Brill, 1960.

Schact, Joseph. *An Introduction to Islamic Law.* Oxford: Clarendon Press, 1964.

Smith, Donald E., ed. *South Asian Politics and Religion.* Princeton, N.J.: Princeton University Press, 1966.

Smith, Wilfred Cantwell. *Pakistan as an Islamic State.* Lahore: Ashraf, 1951.

———. *Islam in Modern History.* New York: Mentor Press, 1959.

————. *Modern Islam in India.* Lahore: Ashraf, 1963.

Syed, Anwar. *Pakistan: Islam, Politics and National Solidarity.* Lahore: Vanguard, 1984.

Taylor, David. "The Politics of Islam and Islamization in Pakistan." In *Islam in the Political Process,* ed. J. P. Piscatori. Cambridge: Cambridge University Press, n.d.: 181–98.

Voll, John O. *Islam: Continuity and Change in the Modern World.* Boulder, Colo.: Westview Press, 1982.

Weiss, Anita M., ed. *Islamic Reassertion in Pakistan: The Application of Islamic Laws in a Modern State.* Syracuse, N.Y.: Syracuse University Press, 1986.

Winkel, Eric. *Islam and the Living Law: The Ibn-Al-Arabi Approach.* Karachi: Oxford University Press, 1997.

D. Sports and Culture

Farrukhi, Asif, ed. *Fires in an Autumn Garden: Short Stories from Urdu and Regional Languages of Pakistan.* Karachi: Oxford University Press, 1997.

Friskin, Sydney. *Going for Gold: Pakistan at Hockey.* Karachi: Oxford University Press, 1997.

Gazdar, Mushtaq. *Pakistan Cinema, 1947–1997.* Karachi: Oxford University Press, 1997.

Hussain, Abbas. *Poetry from Pakistan: An Anthology.* Karachi: Oxford University Press, 1997.

Khan, Lutfullah. *Sur Ki Talash* [Urdu: *In Search of Harmony*]. Karachi: Fazelsons, 1998.

Rutnagar, Dicky. *Khans Unlimited: A History of Squash in Pakistan.* Karachi: Oxford University Press, 1997.

Shamsie Muneeza. *A Dragon in the Sun: An Anthology of Pakistani Writing in English.* Karachi: Oxford University Press, 1997.

Siddiqui, Muhammad Ali. *Common Heritage.* Karachi: Oxford University Press, 1997.

E. Women

Agarwal, B. *A Field of One's Own: Gender and Land Rights in South Asia.* Cambridge: Cambridge University Press, 1994.

Ashraf, Javed, and Birjees Ashraf. "An Inter-Temporal Analysis of the Male–Female Earnings Differential in Pakistan." *Pakistan Development Review* 32, no. 4 (winter 1993): 1023–56.

Duncan, Ann. *Women in Pakistan: An Economic and Social Strategy.* Washington, D.C.: World Bank, 1989.

Government of Pakistan. *Report of the Commission on the Status of Women in Pakistan.* Islamabad: Pakistan Commission on the Status of Women, 1986.

International Labour Organisation. *Women at Work.* Geneva: ILO, 1975.

Ismail, Zafar H. "Gender Differentials in the Cost of Primary Education: A Study of Pakistan." *Pakistan Development Review* 35, no. 4 (winter 1996): 835–52.

Jahan, Rounaq. *The Elusive Agenda: Mainstreaming Women in Development.* London: Zed Books. 1995.

Minturn, L. *Sita's Daughters: Coming out of Purdah.* New York: Oxford University Press, 1993.

Moser, Caroline O. N. *Gender Planning and Development: Theory, Practice and Training.* London: Routledge, 1993.

Mumtaz, Khawar, and Farida Shaheed. *Women of Pakistan: Two Steps Forward, One Step Back?* London: Zed Press, 1987.

Sathar, Zeba. "Women's Status and Fertility Change in Pakistan." *Pakistan Development Review* 27, no. 3 (autumn 1988): 415–32.

Shah, Nasra M., ed. *Pakistani Women: A Socioeconomic and Demographic Profile.* Honolulu: East–West Population Institute, 1986.

Shaheed, Farida, and Kanwar Mumtaz. *Women's Economic Participation in Pakistan.* Islamabad: UNICEF, 1992.

Staudt, Kathleen. *Women, Foreign Assistance and Advocacy Administration.* New York: Praeger, 1985.

Weiss, Anita M. "The Consequences of State Policies for Women in Pakistan." In *The Politics of Social Transformation in Afghanistan, Iran and Pakistan,* ed. Myron Weiner and Ali Banuazizi. Syracuse, N.Y.: Syracuse University Press, 1994.

———. *Walls Within Walls: Life Histories of Working Women in the Old City of Lahore.* Boulder, Colo.: Westview Press, 1992.

V. Newspapers and Magazines

A. Newspapers: English-Language Dailies

Business Post, The (Islamabad)
Business Recorder, The (Karachi)
Dawn (Karachi and Lahore)
Frontier Post, The (Peshawar)
Leader, The (Karachi)
Muslim, The (Islamabad)
Nation, The (Lahore and Islamabad)
News, The (Lahore and Islamabad)

B. Newspapers: Urdu-Language Dailies

Jang (Karachi, Lahore, Islamabad, and Multan)
Khabrain (Lahore and Islamabad)
Nawa-i-Waqt (Karachi, Lahore, Islamabad, and Multan)

C. Newsmagazines

Economic and Political Weekly (Karachi)
Economist, The (London)
Far Eastern Economic Review. Weekly (Hong Kong)
Friday Times, The. Weekly (Lahore)
Herald. Monthly (Karachi)
India Today (Delhi)
Newsline. Monthly (Karachi)
Urdu Digest. Monthly (Lahore)
Zindigi. Urdu monthly (Lahore)

Important Personalities

Governors-General

Muhammad Ali Jinnah	August 1947–September 1948
Khawaja Nazimuddin	September 1948–October 1951
Ghulam Muhammad	October 1951–October 1955
Iskander Mirza	October 1955–March 1956

Presidents

Iskander Mirza	March 1956–October 1958
Muhammad Ayub Khan	October 1958–March 1969
Agha Muhammad Yahya Khan	March 1969–December 1971
Zulfikar Ali Bhutto	December 1971–August 1973
Fazal Elahi Chaudhry	August 1973–September 1978
Zia ul-Haq	September 1978–August 1988
Ghulam Ishaq Khan	August 1988–July 1993
Waseem Sajjad	July 1993–December 1993
Sardar Farooq Ahmad Khan Leghari	December 1993–December 1997
Muhammad Rafiq Tarar	January 1998–

Prime Ministers

Liaqat Ali Khan	August 1947–October 1951
Khawaja Nazimuddin	October 1951–April 1953
Muhammad Ali Bogra	April 1953–August 1955
Chaudhri Muhammad Ali	August 1955–September 1956

H. S. Suhrawardhy	September 1956–October 1957
I. I. Chundrigar	October 1957–December 1957
Feroze Khan Noon	December 1957–October 1958

Presidential form of government was in place from October 1958 to August 1973.

Zulfikar Ali Bhutto	August 1973–July 1977

Presidential form of government returned in July 1977 and was in place until March 1985.

Muhammad Khan Junejo	March 1985–May 1988

There was no prime minister from May 1988 to December 1988.

Benazir Bhutto	December 1988–August 1990
Ghulam Mustafa Jatoi	August 1990–November 1990
Mian Nawaz Sharif	November 1990–April 1993
Balkh Sher Mazari	April 1993–June 1993
Mian Nawaz Sharif	June 1993–July 1993
Moeen Qureshi	July 1993–October 1993
Benazir Bhutto	October 1993–November 1996
Meraj Khalid	November 1996–February 1997
Mian Nawaz Sharif	February 1997–

Chiefs of the Army Staff (COAS)

Frank Messervy	August 1947–January 1949
Douglas Gracey	January 1949–January 1951
Muhammad Ayub Khan	January 1951–October 1958
Muhammad Musa	October 1958–September 1966
Agha Muhammad Yahya Khan	September 1966–December 1971
Gul Hassan	December 1971–March 1972
Tikka Khan	March 1972–March 1976
Zia ul-Haq	March 1976–August 1988
Aslam Beg	August 1988–August 1991
Asif Nawaz	August 1991–January 1993
Abdul Waheed Kakar	January 1993–January 1996
Jehangir Karamat	January 1996–October 1998
Pervez Musharaf	October 1998–

About the Author

SHAHID JAVED BURKI has graduate degrees in physics and economics from Punjab, Oxford, and Harvard Universities. He went to Oxford as a Rhodes Scholar and to Harvard as a Mason Fellow.

Burki joined the Civil Service of Pakistan in 1960. His assignments in Pakistan include chief economist of West Pakistan, and economic advisor, Ministry of Commerce, Government of Pakistan. He also worked as a senior research fellow at Harvard's Center for International Affairs and the Harvard Institute for International Development.

Burki joined the World Bank in 1974. Among the positions he has held at the World Bank are director of the China Department and vice president of Latin America and the Caribbean.

Burki has written several books on China, Pakistan, and human development.

954.91   Burki, Shahid Javed.
Bur
         Historical dictionary
         of Pakistan.

DATE			